# CEMETERIES
## of
# UNICOI COUNTY
# TENNESSEE

## including genealogical information

by
**Unicoi County Historical Society**
**Erwin, Tennessee**

REVISED

*The Overmountain Press*
JOHNSON CITY, TENNESSEE

ISBN-0932807-70-4
First printed in 1989
Reprinted with Revisions/Copyright © 1992
by the Unicoi County Historical Society
Printed in the United States of America

1  2  3  4  5  6  7  8  9  0

Dedicated

to

Pat Alderman

and

Vernon Sims

# Unicoi County Cemeteries

## Introduction

This labor of love began as one of the first major projects of the newly formed Unicoi County Historical Society, in the early 1970s. By 1973, about 35 cemeteries, all in the northern part of the county, had been copied by Bill Norris and Mildred Brittain; Mildred had previous experience in copying many of the cemetery records of Washington County, for that publication. However, two other members of our original cemetery committee died, and Bill Norris' eyesight was deteriorating.

Fifteen years went by, then in the winter of 1987-88 the project was begun again. A new committee was formed and plans were made. Our first discovery was that the cost of commercial publication of a book of cemetery records was far beyond our means, as long as our purpose was to keep the selling price as low as possible. We decided to do the entire book ourselves. We would type the data, duplicate it, and bind it. Our first step was to reserve a booth for Apple Festival Days 1989, to sell our book and recover the dollar costs of preparation. Then we began research.

We found that in 1960 Charles Bennett had copied 15 cemeteries, mostly in the southern part of our county, and had published the data in the WAG Bulletin. So we had a total of 50 cemeteries copied earlier, and this was useful, because we discovered that many markers were no longer present or had become illegible, especially when the only identification was the "temporary" metal funeral home marker. This experience confirmed the importance of publishing the county's cemetery records before further deterioration.

Our own copying began in late April 1988 and was completed a little over a year later. Hilda Padgett and Ruth Pieper copied 12 of the largest cemeteries, including Evergreen, and Barbara Ann Dowden copied Jones Cemetery. Bill Cooper and co-workers Harry Erwin, Ned Brown, Bob Harris, and Truman Smith copied 153 cemeteries. The total of 165 includes an update of the 50 cemeteries done earlier.

Locating cemeteries was interesting and challenging, since most were not shown on the quadrangle maps of the county, and many were small private plots, sometimes abandoned. But everywhere we went we found enthusiastic local citizens who would point us in the right direction, and often explain the relationships of the persons we listed. So truly this was a community project.

# Introduction

## (continued)
## (2)

Copying was done with steno pads — we filled about 17 of them, and we soon established a format. We listed the names as we found them, walking down the rows of headstones, so that readers could guide themselves to the same stone. Wives were listed after their husbands, and if we were confident we indicated thus: (w). Likewise with sons (son) and daughters (dau).

A unique source enhanced this entire project: the burial records of the former Boyd-DeArmond Funeral Home, 1926-64, provided by Frank Gentry. This helped us to establish parentage and also provided data on persons buried in unmarked graves. However, not all unmarked grave data could be used, because of the many cemeteries with the same name, where we were not sure which was the site of the burial.

Early on, we learned to contact the owner of the property, if possible — the very first cemetery done (Day) resulted in the police being called. Other research problems were beyond our control, such as heat, cold, insects, thorns, leaf-covered stones, steep hills, and snakes.

"Office" work included: (1) typing, mostly by Mildred Conley, with help from Hilda Padgett; (2) proofing, by Hilda Padgett, Ruth Pieper, Bill Cooper and Virginia Hatcher; (3) indexing, by Hilda, Ruth and Bill; (4) reproduction (120 copies) by Hilda; and (5) sorting and binding, by Hilda, Ruth, Bill and Shane Elliott. An additional 50 copies were reproduced by Bill.

The results of our research include: (1) we found 87 Union Army veterans' stones and 7 Confederate Army veterans' iron crosses; (2) we found 75 persons, in 23 cemeteries, buried here prior to the formation of Unicoi County in January 1876. Their names read like a roll call of the pioneers of this county, and the fact that these same names predominate today shows the deep roots of our families here; (3) the hundreds of babies that we found buried testify to the heartache of a day when the medical knowledge we take for granted was not available; and (4) we discovered a social phenomenon (which led to much soul-searching as to whether to include first names in the index) — a most unique variety of first names, probably resulting from the limited number of common surnames, and probably accounting for the frequent use of initials among the men and boys of the community, and nicknames among the women and girls.

# Introduction

## (continued)
## (3)

This book will be a helpful companion to "Around Home in Unicoi County" and "Marriages in Unicoi County 1876-1907", for genealogical research in the county.  Together with the published cemetery listings of Washington, Carter, Johnson and Sullivan Counties, genealogical research throughout upper East Tennessee will be facilitated by this book.

In addition, we hope that this book will prove to be a catalyst for maintenance of cemeteries, erection of stones where needed, and pride in the heritage of our county.

A question often asked concerns the oldest stones we found. They were:  Christopher McInturff, died 1796, and Edward Wiet, died 1797, both found in Peoples Cemetery.

"The History of Unicoi County", by Judge Walter Garland, is expected to be published soon,   and the Unicoi County Historical Society has additional books planned for the near future.  The search for our roots and the preservation of our heritage will always be the twin goals of the historical society.

Please see additional remarks on page 406.


### Preface to revised edition

Since publication in 1989, several additional cemeteries have been found, and these have been added to the map and incorporated in the listing. The discriptions and contents have been added to the book beginning with page 400.

Also, corrections to errors in the 1989 edition have been made and incorporated into the book. Everything has been re-indexed where appropriate.

No attempt has been made to add names and dates of persons buried after the copy date made on each cemetery.

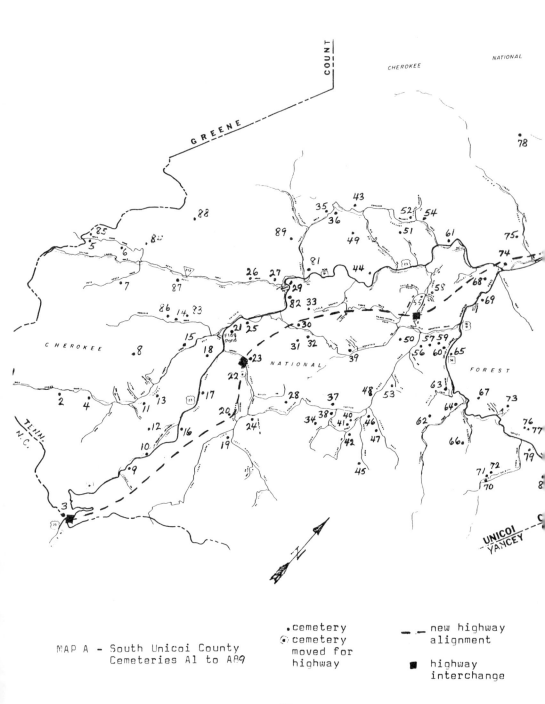

MAP A – South Unicoi County
Cemeteries A1 to A89

• cemetery
◉ cemetery
   moved for
   highway

– – new highway
      alignment

■ highway
   interchange

—viii—

# MAP A CEMETERIES

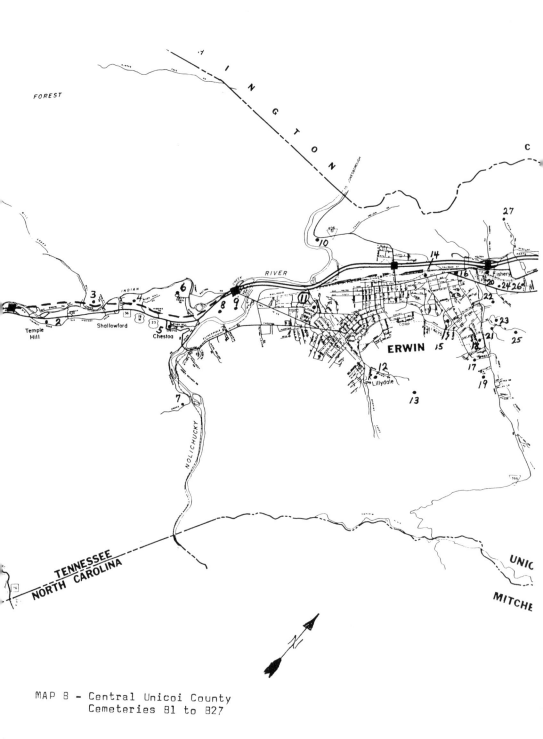

MAP B - Central Unicoi County
Cemeteries B1 to B27

## MAP 3 CEMETERIES

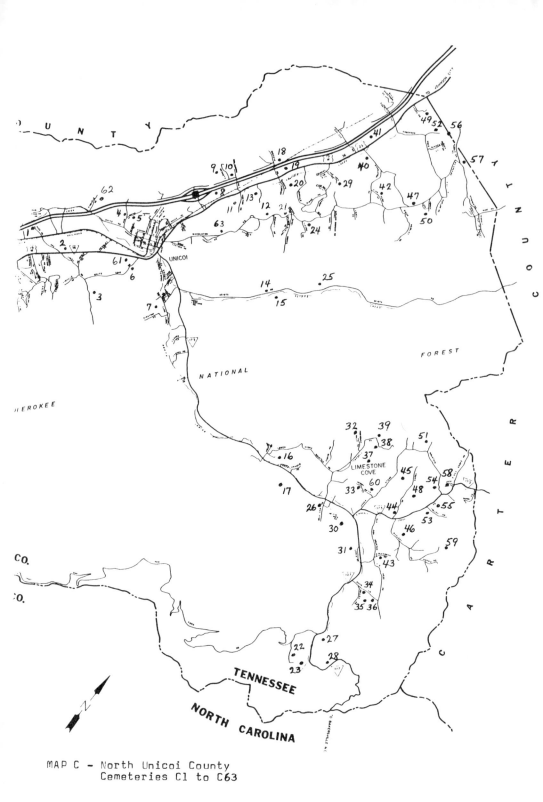

MAP C - North Unicoi County
Cemeteries C1 to C63

## MAP C CEMETERIES

# LOCATION OF CEMETERIES
## (ALPHA ORDER)

Located in the 800 block of North Main Avenue in Erwin

Copied April 27, 1988 and April 29, 1988

RICE, Grant,  May 8, 1890 - July 26, 1971
RICE, Altha (w),  June 10, 1890 - March 23, 1960

HARRIS, Thomas Carl,  1884-1973
HARRIS, Lottie R. (w),  Jan. 4, 1899 - Nov. 17, 1967
HARRIS, Willard (Son),  July 7, 1915 - Jan. 5, 1917
HARRIS, Shaler Lee, b/d 1948
         Child of Lee Roy and Pearl E. Harrington Harris

GREENWELL, Helen,  Nov. 25, 1915 - Dec. 9, 1915
         Dau. of E. H. and Anna Greenwell

YOUNG, Ben,  March 20, 1840 - Feb. 16, 1910

GOUGE, Infant,  b/d 1913
GOUGE, Infant,  b/d 1914
         Sons of B. L. and Effie Gouge

HIGGINS, Holt L.,  Jan. 15, 1912 - July 26, 1978
         PFC, US Army, WWII
HIGGINS, Ricky Lynn,  April 14, 1957 - Aug. 13, 1966

FORD, R. E. L.,  May 31, 1868 - Aug. 3, 1928
FORD, Rosa S. Horton,(w), Dec.26,1869-May 30,1921 (Md. Oct.27,1892)
DUFFY, Betty Ford, Feb.4,1898- Dec.10,1977
BUNDY, Addie G.,  1874-1954
         Dau. of W. B. and Winnie Meade Hartsock
BUNDY, Winifred Mae,  Dec. 30, 1899 - June 4, 1958
BUNDY, Buster B.,  Sept. 24, 1906 - March 6, 1970. US Army WWII

BLEVINS, Will M.,  March 8, 1884 - Jan. 29, 1958
BLEVINS, Lillie Slagle (w), 1886-1937
BLEVINS, Frank,  1905-1984

ERWIN, Thelma,  April 30, 1915 - April 27, 1916
         Dau. of G. C. and M. E. Erwin

BOONE, Grace and Helen,  Feb. 4, 1891 - Sept. 23, 1920
         Wife and Dau. of Paul Boone
BOONE, Zeb,  Oct. 27, 1919 - Oct. 30, 1919
BOONE, Clyde,  d. Oct. 4, 1920
         Sons of Sam B. and Irene Boone

LAMBERT, Warren G.,  Dec. 30, 1893 - July 30, 1920
LAMBERT, Helen Mae,  aged 3 months
         Dau. of W. G. and Pearl M. Lambert

DeVAULT, Georgia Meredith,  1878-1918

CRUMLEY, A. M.,  Oct. 2, 1853 - Sept. 25, 1923

RENFROE, Nancy Phillips,  1877-1933
        Dau. of William and Margaret McCroclin Phillips
CROWE, William E.,  Feb. 8, 1917 - Sept. 22, 1918

LIPE, William F., 1861-1921

TAYLOR, J. W.,  1873-1935
TAYLOR, Lucretia (w),  1876-1958
        Dau. of J. S. and Ruth Radford Angel
TIPTON, Fred E.,  June 14, 1892 - Feb. 7, 1968
TIPTON, Nora T. (w),  June 16, 1897 -

HENSLEY, W. H.,  Oct. 15, 1860 - Dec. 28, 1927
HENSLEY, M. J. (w),  Feb. 22, 1862 - May 20, 1947
        (Mary Jane) Dau. of Noah and Sallie Ayers Letterman
HENSLEY, Nancy,  1902-1981
COIN, Nettie,  1893-1968

MARION, Harry E.,  Dec. 21, 1894 - Jan. 27, 1944
MARION, Cora Price (w),  July 4, 1897 - Nov. 6, 1978
MARION, W. E.,  Dec. 22, 1866 - Oct. 15, 1929
        Son of Jackson Marion
MARION, Laura Simpson (w),  April 15, 1865 - June 22, 1957

WEBB, John R.,  1874-1943
        Son of Frances Newton and Oakley Snodgrass Webb
WEBB, Audrey (w),  1874-1931
        Dau. of George and Josephine Burton Kilmer
WEBB, Pat,  1896-1928. Son of J. R. and Audrey Kilmer Webb
FRYE, Hazel Webb,  1898-1931. Dau. of J.R. & Audrey Kilmer Webb

DAVIS, Cecil T.,  Nov. 1, 1900 - Dec. 26, 1971
        Tenn. PVT., Co. F., 117 Infantry, WWI
DAVIS, Helen Bolton (w),  July 16, 1904 -

WILLIAMS, Robert Lee,  Feb. 12, 1886 - May 7, 1967
WILLIAMS, Anna Myrtle (w),  Feb. 26, 1889 - July 14, 1984
WILLIAMS, Marvin Lee (Son),  June 2, 1914 - July 8, 1944
        PVT., Co M, 314 Inf., 79 Div., Killed In Action,

BAILEY, Martin Luther,  Feb. 11, 1887 - Oct. 4, 1929
        Son of Isaac and Mary Jane Laughrum Bailey
BAILEY, Myrtle Burton (w),  May 25, 1889 - Oct. 1, 1961
        Dau. of Joshua and Melissa Burton

BAUCOM, John F.,  Feb. 17, 1886 - Oct. 31, 1964
        Son of Riley and Betty McNeil Baucom
BAUCOM, Mamie I. (w),  Feb. 2, 1893 - Oct. 2, 1982
BAUCOM, Juanita (Dau.),  June 28, 1933 - Feb. 1, 1942
BAUCOM, James Henry,  May 7, 1916 - May 7, 1982
        PFC, US Army, WWII

JOBE CEMETERY (continued)

DOUGLAS, Mollie,  April 25, 1887 - Dec. 15, 1914
        Wife of Aaron Douglas
DOUGLAS, Archie (Son),  Nov. 27, 1910 - June 23, 1911

McCURRY, Infant
McCURRY, J. C.,  Dec. 12, 1923 - Jan. 23, 192?
McCURRY, Martha,  Oct. 9, 1927 - Feb. 23, 1928

McLAUGHLIN, Isaac,  May 15, 1902 - Nov. 6, 1934

CALHOUN, William Clyde,  Nov. 30, 1901 - Feb. 8, 1968
CALHOUN, Cora Griffith (w),  Feb. 14, 1902 - July 24, 1978
CALHOUN, Jack (Son),  b/d June 17, 1930
CALHOUN, Barbara (Dau.),  April 11, 1939 - Feb. 25, 1941

CALHOUN, Alvin G.,  1919-1972.  PVT. US Army

TIPTON, Bessie,  1885-1971

FOSTER, John Wayne,  Jan. 17, 1951 - Nov. 23, 1969
        PFC, US Army, Vietnam

LUTTRELL, Isaac W.,  d. Oct. 4, 1922
LUTTRELL, Mary E. (w),  Oct. 18, 1872 - July 29, 1931
        Dau. of Samuel and Nannie Ambrose Tittle

AMBROSE, James,  Aug. 22, 1889 - Nov. 22, 1923
AMBROSE, Cora (w),  Dec. 27, 1886 - Aug. 24, 1928

TAPP, Jacob,  1842 - Feb. 4, 1925
        Co. A, 3RD NC Mtd. Inf., Union Army
TAPP, Nancy (w), born Aug. 22, 1864.  Maiden name Miller
TAPP, Fannie,  Oct. 24, 1906 - May 1, 1926

BRYANT, Jim R.,  1900-1922

FULTON, B. F.,  1849-1927

McNABB, Robert Henry,  May 10, 1892 - March 24, 1948
McNABB, Bessie Lee Keever (w),  Oct. 1, 1894 -
McNABB, James Harry,  Feb. 7, 1914 - Oct. 11, 1971
        1st Lt. US Army, WWII, Korea
McNABB, Madge Eloise,  Jan. 2, 1917 - Sept. 3, 1934
        Dau. of Robert Henry and Bessie Lee Keever McNabb

BEAVER, Mack C.,  1891-1963
BEAVER, Savannah G. (w),  1895-1926
BEAVER, Robert E (Son),  March 14, 1924 - Feb. 17, 1974
        PVT., US Army, WWII

McLAUGHLIN, George Edward,  1866-1934
McLAUGHLIN, Minnie L. Treadway (w),  1866-1927
McLAUGHLIN, William Oscar (Son),  1891-1959

SMYRE, Emory E., March 16, 1900 - Dec. 22, 1971
SMYRE, Edith P. (w), Dec. 4, 1897 - Feb. 15, 1970

McINTURFF, David B., 1857-1929
McINTURFF, Achsa Ferguson (w), 1884-1930

KEEVER, Drew N., May 10, 1875 - Jan. 22, 1950
KEEVER, Jennie (w), Born Nov. 15, 1881
KEEVER, D. N., Jan. 22, 1834 - June 12, 1924. Confed. Army
KEEVER, Mary E. (w), Born Oct. 29, 1840
        Dau. of Joe and Sabrey Ducker Erley

TITUS, Bobbie Joan, d. June 21, 1936.
        Infant dau. of H. & R. Titus

WITCHER, Reuben L., Feb. 9, 1892 - Aug. 11, 1939
        Son of Wm. Reuben and Rebecca Caswell Gammon Witcher
WITCHER, Lela Mae (w), May 10, 1899 - Feb. 1, 1957
        Dau. of Wm. J. and Martha Emmaline Guinn Willis
WITCHER, James (Son), Sept. 28, 1922 - Oct. 1, 1922

WING, Charles Edwin, 1879-1958
WING, Susie Wattles (w), 1883-1934
        Dau. of W. S. and Ellen McNabb Wattles

RICH, Bertha E., 1910-1966

GREEN, Elizabeth, April 23, 1933 - March 4, 1935
        Dau. of Tom Green
GREEN, John, Nov. 13, 1900 - Oct. 16, 1918. WWI

MATHES, Harlin, July 26, 1932 - April 17, 1933
        Son of Edward and Alice Green Mathes

BENNETT, Eulalah Tolley, Aug. 15, 1920 - Oct. 11, 1952
        Dau. of J. C. and Golda Miller Tolley. D./in childbirth

WILLS, Bessie Tipton, 1890-1929
WILLS, Leonard Tipton (Son), 1918-1933
TIPTON, Rachel Rebecca McInturff, 1860-1940
        Wife of Charlie C. Tipton
TIPTON, Fred E., June 13, 1882 - May 7, 1953

JACKSON, Lou Creta, July 14, 1881 - March 20, 1946
        (Ester Lucretia) Dau. of Wm. Calvin & Alzy Jane Odom Jackson
JACKSON, Edward A., June 1, 1889 - Feb. 12, 1923
JACKSON, Bertha E. (w), July 22, 1893 - May 14, 1966
JACKSON, Mabel (Dau.), Jan. 4, 1914 - April 4, 1930
JACKSON, Ruby L. (Dau.), Sept. 2, 1911 - May 18, 1938

COOPER, Jessie, died Jan. 11, 1929

WILSON, Polly, died April 23, 1930
        Dau. of Tom and Hannah Ledford Wilson

HUTCHINS, Walter Fredrick,  May 14, 1934 - June 26, 1935
HUTCHINS, Barbara Jean,  June 6, 1940 - June 13, 1940

KERNS, William E.,  April 12, 1869 - May 25, 1946
KERNS, Myrtie J. (w),  March 16, 1875 - Sept. 30, 1927
KERNS, Junior D.,  1895-1922
KERNS, Anna L. McNabb (w),  born 1896

TAYLOR, Samuel P.,  1873-1928. Son of W.K. & Mary Collins Taylor
TAYLOR, Ellen Barnette (w),  1880-1964

WEBB, Mary,  March 12, 1862 - Dec. 31, 1922
WEBB, Dexter,  Oct. 17, 1886 - Sept. 2, 1947
        Son of Garlan Wiley and Mary Collier Webb

JOHNSON, J. O.,  - age 6 mos.

HURD, Virginia C.,  Nov. 5, 1920 - June 8, 1922

McATKINS, Cornelia,  Nov. 16, 1871 - Jan. 28, 1962

SIMMONS, Henry,  Jan. 19, 1883 - June 4, 1940
SIMMONS, Sarah (w),  Nov. 5, 1885 - June 20, 1923
SIMMONS, Reva,  Nov. 24, 1903 - May 3, 1940

MORGAN, John Clayton,  Nov. 25, 1889 - April 23, 1925
MORGAN, Pauline Roberts (w),  June 30, 1898 - Dec. 19, 1987
MORGAN, Sam C.,  April 22, 1851 - April 14, 1923
MORGAN, Laura (w),  April 17, 1856 - April 23, 1926

MILLNER, R. L. "Bob",  1886-1934
MILLNER, Eliza A. (w),  1868-1926

YOUNG, Kathleen A.,  1898-1952
HELTON, W. Fred,  1888-1956
HELTON, Lela A. (w),  1889-1974

PATE, Garrison,  1871-1957
PATE, Dilla (w),  1873-1960

MYERS, Okie,  1893-1949

WILLIAMS, Anna Darlene,  d. Oct. 10, 1932
        Dau. of R. L. & Ann Myrtle Atkins Williams
WILLIAMS, Horace Elmer,  June 12, 1916 - April 29, 1928
        Son of Bob and ----------Atkins Williams
WILLIAMS, Mary Virginia,  d. Aug. 14, 1919

BENNETT, Arch Sr.,  April 1, 1910 - March 20, 1977
BENNETT, Sussana L. (w),  Feb. 28, 1910 - Jan. 29, 1962
        Dau. of Mac Daniel and Lilly Ellen Lewis

NELSON, Joe,  May 1, 1865 - March 11, 1924

JOBE CEMETERY  (continued)

DUNCAN, James Ollie,  Nov. 24, 1910 - Nov. 9, 1980
GRIFFITH, James,  Oct. 3, 1924 -
GRIFFITH, Helen,  Jan. 29, 1922 - April 24, 1977
DUNCAN, Frank,  1885-1947.  Son of Wm. Duncan
DUNCAN, Gertrude (w),  1893-1971
DUNCAN, Pauline (Dau.),  Feb. 9, 1916 - March 12, 1919

HENSLEY, James H. Sr.,  Sept. 1, 1883 - Nov. 27, 1964
HENSLEY, Martha E. (w),  April 4, 1884 - Jan. 26, 1970
HENSLEY, Edna,  1913-1933
HENSLEY, Frank,

BARRY, D. A.,  1891-1957
          Son of L. Kaney and Elizabeth Estep Barry

TILSON, Harold Donnelly,  Aug. 3, 1906 - Aug. 14, 1907
          Son of R. T. and Ethel Tilson
TILSON, Robert T.,  April 5, 1877 - July 15, 1915
TILSON, Ethel B. (w),  June 12, 1880 - Dec. 3, 1932
          Dau. of Wm. W. and Lucy Jones Bailey

RALSTON, Ruth,  d. Sept. 19, 1905
STARNES, Sarah,  Feb. 25, 1843 - July 1, 1907

SHIPLEY, Roy G.,  d. 1950.  Son of Nathan S. & Adeline Curtis Shipley

HENSLEY, Thomas A.,  Oct. 14, 1889 - April 30, 1911
          Son of W. H. and M. J. Hensley

WHITE, Laban W.,  May 25, 1856 - Feb. 18, 1899
WHITE, Emma M. Erwin (w),  Dec. 9, 1859 - June 8, 1920
SCRUGGS, Lewis D. Jr.,  Jan. 21, 1918 - Feb. 26, 1918
          Son of Louis D. and Ada Scruggs

SILL, Thomas R.,  July 31, 1819 - Jan. 12, 1894. b. in Bedford, PA.

KEGLEY, John Wesley,  March 28, 1869 - Nov. 16, 1959
          Son of J. W. and -----Clark Kegley
KEGLEY, Leiudeemia Carter (w),  July 16, 1865 - March 12, 1916
KEGLEY, Edgar L. (Son),  March 4, 1893 - June 10, 1923
          Cpl. US Army, WWI
KEGLEY, Victor D. (Son),  Feb. 4, 1899 - Aug. 16, 1924
          Sgt. US Army, WWI

TILSON, Dr. L. S.,  1854-1926.  Son of Wm. O. Tilson
TILSON, Eliza J. Parks (w),  1860-1936
          Dau. of Wm. E. and Jane Davis Parks
HIGGINBOTHAM, Lora Tilson,  1884-1922

HUNNEYCUTT, Lieut. J. M., Co. B, 13TH Tenn. Cav. Union Army
GARLAND, John W.,  Sept. 5, 1807 - Aug. 5, 1887

RYBURN, Dr. J.P.S., Dec. 24, 1845 - April 3, 1899. Confed. Army
RYBURN, Arabella     , May 17, 1871 - Feb. 8, 1886
CRUMLEY, Caroline Agnes, Jan. 30, 1847 - Aug. 2, 1903
RYBURN, Walter W. J., June 17, 1913 - Oct. 17, 1918
   Son of W. W. and A. L.
RYBURN, Antonie W., May 11, 1910 - Sept. 4, 1910
   Son of W. W. and A. L.
RYBURN, Hattie Agnes, May 30, 1904 - March 25, 1905
   Dau. of J.D.S. and Cora L. Ryburn
RYBURN, Wm., Nov. 11, 1914 - Oct. 17, 1918
   Son of W. M. and Allie Erwin Ryburn

CLARK, Walter B., Jan. 5, 1864 - Feb. 13, 1888
CLARK, James O., May 23, 1866 - March 3, 1886
CLARK, Adah, June 6, 1887 - May 28, 1888

KEVER, Henry L., Nov. 23, 1879 - Feb. 2, 1907
KEVER, Mary E., Dec. 1, 1871 - Nov. 1, 1892
KEVER, J. F., Oct. 18, 1868 - Dec. 31, 1884
   Children of D. N. and M. E. Kever

EMMERT, Nannie Taylor, Feb. 15, 1882 - April 17, 1882
EMMERT, Willie Nora, Aug. 10, 1880 - Sept. 15, 1881
   Daus. of P. W. and Senie Emmert
EMMERT, Edgar F., Feb. 14, 1890 - June 17, 1890
   Son of Mr. and Mrs. R. R. Emmert

McINTURFF, Robert N., Aug. 18, 1865 - Oct. 29, 1951
McINTURFF, Ida L. Timberlake (w) and (dau.)
   Nov. 27, 1871 - Nov. 25, 1903 - d. in childbirth

GALLOWAY, Joseph H., April 17, 1888 - Feb. 28, 1968
   SFC, US Army, WWI
GALLOWAY, Maude McInturff (w), 1895-1921
GALLOWAY, Infant Dau. d. 1921

MILLER, Kate, March 26, 1854 - Jan. 19, 1912. Wife of Geo.L.Miller
McINTURFF, Jesse Marshall, **1889-1960**
   Son of John and Sarah Clark McInturff
McINTURFF, Julia H. Click (w), 1887-1973
McINTURFF, Isable (Dau.), 1918-1938
McINTURFF, Earnest L., July 10, 1912 - March 4, 1914
   Son of J. M. and J. H. McInturff
DAVIS, J. C., May 31, 1859 - Feb. 17, 1916
DAVIS, Mollie E., Jan. 6, 1870 - Aug. 1, 1965
DAVIS, Wesley P., June 20, 1891 - Oct. 25, 1962
   Son of James Cade and Mary Elizabeth Booth Davis
DAVIS, Robert H., June 20, 1891 - July 29, 1960
   Son of James Cade and Mary Elizabeth Booth Davis
DAVIS, Lula R. (w), March 22, 1894 - July 26, 1982
DAVIS, Robert Harry, died 1928
   Son of R. H. and Lula Rice Davis
DAVIS, Faye E., Dec. 22, 1919 - Oct. 3, 1937
   Dau. of R. H. and Lula Davis
DAVIS, Hazel, Sept. 16, 18-- - Nov. 3, ?

COIN, Harry L., June 29, 1898 - Dec. 18, 1918

TIPTON, Infant, b/d March 15, 1915
          Dau. of C. F. and C. C. Tipton

DUNCAN, Pearl Davis, May 3, 1889 - Feb. 21, 1911
          Wife of W. F. Duncan
DUNCAN, Son, b/d Feb. 11, 1911

NUGENT, Jacob, b. 1801 - March 17, 1882

FARNOR, James C., May 3, 1864 - Feb. 23, 1885
FARNOR, Mollie, b/d May 19, 1886
          Children of Rev. J. S. and Rebecca J. Farnor

HULIN, E. S., July 1832 - June 25, 1902
HULIN, Sarah Brown (w), Nov. 9, 1832 - July 4, 1921
HULIN, Greeley, July 4, 1875 - May 5, 1911

BAKER, Charles R., March 4, 1903 - Nov. 19, 1923
BAKER, Mildred Irene, Oct. 6, 1914 - Oct. 7, 1921

BIRCHFIELD, William E., Aug. 17, 1881 - April 23, 1935
          Son of Robert and Mary Garland Birchfield

JOB, J., d. April 22, 1849 - age 78

MARTIN, Alford, Co. K., 8TH Tenn. Cav. Union Army

TIPTON, Jacob, Co. A., 3RD NC Mtd. Inf. Union Army

JONES, Infant, b/d Dec. 13, 1894
JONES, Nellie, d. Nov. 8, 1900 - age 6 weeks
          Children of Rev. and Mrs. O. G. Jones

WOHLFORD, Charles Ross, 1878-1943
          Son of George and Jane Mustard Wohlford
WOHLFORD, Roetta Ryburn (w), 1875-1921
WOHLFORD, Louise Lynde (Dau.), 1902-1934
WOHLFORD, Charlotte (Dau.), b/d 1912

ALBERTSON, "Little Jack", Aug. 26, 1918 - Jan. 10, 1922
ALBERTSON, Infant dau., d. 1917
          Children of Jack and Ethel Albertson

McLAIN, Wade H., 1892-1920
McLAIN, Jeannette (w), 1899-1933
          Dau. of A. D. and Emma Weld Franklin
McLAIN, Wade H. Jr. (Son), Dec. 18, 1917 - Dec. 30, 1941

ABEL, Thomas B., Oct. 27, 1917 - March 18, 1918
          Son of T. F. and Arminta Abel

HILBERT, J. Ralph, Jan. 17, 1893 - Feb. 17, 1916. B.of LF&E
HILBERT, Mae (w), Sept. 26, 1896 - July 10, 1921

FULTON, Annie Deitz, March 28, 1846 - Nov. 29, 1913
        Wife of Benj. F. Fulton, Dau. of John & Polly Deitz
WATSON, Mollie A. Fulton, April 11, 1881 - Nov. 24, 1927
        Wife of Y. N. Watson. Dau. of Benj. & Annie Fulton


O'BRIEN, B. F., Feb. 2, 1846 - April 29, 1919
O'BRIEN, Mollie E. Tucker (w), May 31, 1852 - May 14, 1901
        Married March 26, 1874
O'BRIEN, Katie Lillian (Dau.), d. Jan. 10, 1892. aged 12 days
O'BRIEN, Mabel Fay (Dau.), June 24, 1890 - March 13, 1891


PHILLIPS, W. Emory, July 24, 1897 - July 18, 1960
PHILLIPS, Minnie B. (w), Dec. 12, 1904 - June 20, 1980


McLAUGHLIN, Capt. Nelson, Jan. 26, 1826 - Jan. 19, 1908
        Co. M., 8TH Tenn. Cav. Union Army
McLAUGHLIN, Amanda (w), July 15, 1849 - May 17, 1920
McLAUGHLIN, Mary Etta Ray, Jan. 16, 1881 - Jan. 11, 1930
        Wife of J. H. McLaughlin
DAVIS, T. D., - Co. E, 1st Tenn. Lt. Artill. Union Army
DAVIS, Catherine (w), July 4, 1833 - Nov. 24, 1893
DAVIS, Will D., 1859-1911
DAVIS, Georgie Cleo (Dau.), 1891-1892
DAVIS, Roby M., Oct. 31, 1897 - Oct. 17, 1898


FRANKLIN, Aaron D., 1864-1945
        Son of Lawson A. and Sarah Dellinger Franklin
FRANKLIN, Emma Weld (w), 1876-1925


LYLE, Martha J., March 6, 1847 - May 3, 1917. Wife of Wm.B.Lyle


TUCKER, Joseph H., April 10, 1810 - July 31, 1886
TUCKER, Allie Caroline McGimpsey (w), Feb. 8, 1822 - Sept.5,1913
TUCKER, Wesley S. (Son), 1854-1933
TUCKER, Polly Ann, 1855-1943
        Dau. of Lewis and Sarah Erwin Bailey
JEFFRIES, Rollin E., 1895-1964
JEFFRIES, Totannbaby Tucker, 1897-1969


 CAPPS, Manuel R., May 30, 1879 - Feb. 7, 1953
        Mother's maiden name was Ledford
CAPPS, Annie (w), May 4, 1886 - Sept. 30, 1973
CAPPS, Ruth H. (Dau.), Dec. 9, 1912 - Oct. 28, 1914


LEWIS, C. E., March 4, 1877 - Feb. 9, 1920
LEWIS, Ollie (w), 1882-1958. Dau. of Mack Campbell
LEWIS, Infant Son, d. 1911


BOONE, Zeb V., April 23, 1878 - March 27, 1921
BOONE, Sam, 1885-May 6, 1936. Age 51 yrs., 11 mos., 29 days
        Son of J. S. and Emily Ray Boone
TITTLE, R. C., May 30, 1887 - Oct. 1888
TITTLE, E. W., Dec. 25, 1869 - Oct. 1886
TITTLE, Ida E., May 18, 1890 - Nov. 1891
        Infant dau. of Wm. and A. A. Tittle

LYLE, W. B., - Co. D, 13TH Tenn. Cav. Union Army

JACKSON, N. C., Sept. 20, 1842 - Oct. 25, 1916
JACKSON, C. B., Sept. 19, 1879 - June 14, 1909
      Sgt. 14TH Batt. Field Art. Spanish-American War
JACKSON, Alzy, April 10, 1862 - Jan. 4, 1928

BROYLES, John S., 1840-1916. Confed. Army
BROYLES, Margaret Eldridge (w), 1854-1920
BROYLES, Frank E. (Son), Jan. 7, 1890 - May 24, 1950

TONEY, Rhoda V., May 4, 1838 - Feb. 23, 1893. Wife of S.W.Toney

PRESNELL, W. M., Aug. 21, 1891 - July 10, 1892
      Son of J. and W. M. Presnell

TUCKER, E. S., March 28, 1857 - Oct. 11, 1929
TUCKER, Lou T., April 12, 1875 - Feb. 6, 1936

TONEY, W. C., 1858-1909
TONEY, Mary L. (w), Oct. 12, 1867 - Dec. 28, 1886
TONEY, Claudia R. E. (Dau.), Feb. 6, 1886 - Aug. 1, 1886

TITTLE, Alex G., May 27, 1857 - March 2, 1930
TITTLE, Hannah E. (w), June 8, 1853 - Sept. 13, 1890

COFFEY, Sarah A., Aug. 3, 1844 - March 18, 1910
      Wife of Perry Coffey
COFFIE, Julia, March 15, 1879 - Nov. 5, 1907

EDWARDS, Mary V., March 19, 1874 - May 29, 1958
      Dau. of Stephen and Emmaline Williams Beaver

DICKSON, James A., July 27, 1884 - April 22, 1926
      Son of Wm. Dickson
DICKSON, Nola M. (w), May 16, 1885 - Dec. 25, 1917

FRANKLIN, Thelma Lee, Sept. 25, 1907 - May 15, 1976
PRICE, William J., Jan. 23, 1871 - May 8, 1957
PRICE, Rettie Laws (w), Sept. 14, 1873 - Aug. 4, 1928
PRICE, Infant, d. June 9, 1916

BURLESON, Isaac G., Aug. 17, 1856 - July 25, 1914
BURLESON, Margaret E. (w), Aug. 1, 1863 - Feb. 27, 1948
      Dau. of Wm. and Mary McCallister Casida
BURLESON, Irene, Sept. 4, 1939 - Sept. 7, 1939

SCOTT, Lorenzo, QM Sgt., Co. H. - 13TH Tenn. Cav. Union Army
SCOTT, Naomi, April 18, 1832 - Nov. 1, 1886
CLOYD, Margaret Don Turnbull, March 5, 1855 - July 27, 1927
      Wife of S. K. Cloyd

McNABB, Mollie F., Jan. 26, 1869 - June 19, 1882
      Wife of W. F. McNabb

TONEY, Rachel S.,  Jan. 14, 1840 - Dec. 19, 1910
        Wife of J. J. Toney
TONEY, Grover Dow,  Sept. 19, 1892 - Aug. 23, 1893
TONEY, Cyrus Harrell,  May 8, 1897 - June 10, 1897
        Sons of W. J. and E. B. Toney

BRITT, Frank Hannum,  March 21, 1880 - Sept. 9, 1950
        Son of Elbert C. and Nancy Ann Brummett Britt
BRITT, Dora E. (w),  May 7, 1882 - Oct. 12, 1951
        Dau. of Franklin and Caroline Grimsley Price
BRITT, Fred E. (Son),  Dec. 7, 1901 - May 11, 1930
        US Navy, WWI

BARNETT, Marioha A.,  Sept. 30, 1852 - May 9, 1916
        Wife of Benj. F. Barnett

RUNNION,  Minnie Hurdt,  July 14, 1896 - March 13, 1926

JONES, Joseph Albert,  Dec. 24, 1871 - June 5, 1919

CALLOWAY, Sanders,  1916-1917
CALLOWAY, Jack,       1928-1932
        Son of Daniel and Lizzie Smith Calloway
CALLOWAY, Daniel,  1854-1942. Son of Sanders & Orpha Kelly Calloway
CALLOWAY, Martha E. O'Brien (w),  1858-1907
CALLOWAY, John,  1878-1890
CALLOWAY, David,  1880-1890
CALLOWAY, Charlie,  1883-1896
CALLOWAY, Neal,  1889-1891
CALLOWAY, Infant,  b/d 1891

HARRINGTON, William B.,  Oct. 18, 1844 - Nov. 26, 1918
HARRINGTON, Annie E. Fry (w),  Aug. 24, 1850 - Nov. 12, 1904

JONES, L. Salina,  Oct. 12, 1839 - Dec. 26, 1923

McKAY, Jocie,  March 10, 1850 - Feb. 22, 1921

HARRISON, C. W.,  July 19, 1860 - Nov. 28, 1913

McNABB, William B.,  Nov. 14, 1862 - Sept. 29, 1913
McNABB, Mollie J. (w),  b. April 13, 1868
McNABB, Clifton,  July 6, 1904 - Sept. 13, 1922
        Son of Grover S. and Ella Belle Erwin McNabb
McNABB, Ella B.,  Dec. 16, 1887 - Feb. 8, 1936
        Dau. of Wm. Stuart and Hester Woodward Erwin
McNABB, Annie Elizabeth,  May 7, 1911 - Aug. 9, 1921
        Dau. of Grover S. and Ella Belle Erwin McNabb
McNABB, Infant,  d.Feb. 4, 1920. Son of G. S. & Ella B. McNabb
McNABB, Ralph Deton,  Oct. 30, 1913 - Dec. 20, 1914
        Son of G. S. and Ella B. McNabb
McNABB, George Chownin,  Feb. 10, 1914 - Nov. 2, 1914
        Son of George and Edith
McNABB, Nora Alice,  July 22, 1892 - Dec. 6, 1898
        Dau. of R. G. and Kate McNabb

McNABB, J. A., May 5, 1865 - Sept. 18, 1894
McNABB, Alice (w), June 24, 1870 - Nov. 30, 1890
McNABB, Henry Clay (Son), d. at 18 mos.
McNABB, J. P., July 7, 1843 - Jan. 20, 1902
McNABB, Hannah (w), Aug. 1, 1841 - Oct. 13, 1915

MILLER, Solomon, Co. M., 8TH Tenn. Cav. Union Army

ELLIOTT, John R., April 12, 1870 - Nov. 19, 1907

HUNT, Will H., born Dec. 27, 1868

EMMERT, Lucile, May 30, 1892 - Sept. 13, 1896
          Dau. of Mr. and Mrs. R. R. Emmert

PIPPIN, Griff D., March 20, 1862 - Sept. 21, 1952
PIPPIN, Rebecca D. (w), July 22, 1864 - Oct. 19, 1914
ERWIN, Jesse B., July 25, 1823 - Aug. 12, 1902
HALE, Mary C., Nov. 7, 1851 - Nov. 5, 1916. Wife of Henry Hale
ERWIN, Lydia Harriett Ann, Dec. 13, 1856 - April 13, 1935
          Dau. of Jesse B. & Elizabeth McMahan Erwin. Member O.E.S.
MURRAY, Pearl E., March 29, 1879 - Dec. 13, 1933
          Dau. of W. S. and Julia Ray Erwin
MURRAY, Jessie G., d. March 19, 1925 - age 65 years

BAUMGARDNER, Ruth, Sept. 20, 1921 - May 20, 1923
          Dau. of Mr. and Mrs. T. C. Baumgardner
MORGAN, Infants of C. D. and Bessie Woods Morgan

EMMERT, William C., Dec. 10, 1823 - July 8, 1893
          Lieut., Co. I, 5TH Tenn. Vols. Mexican War
EMMERT, Mary Amanda Renshaw (w), July 4, 1827 - May 28, 1906
EMMERT, Peter Wesley, Oct. 4, 1854 - May 10, 1930
          Son of Wm. C. and Mary Renshaw Emmert
EMMERT, Senie Bogart (w), March 26, 1856 - July 20, 1911
EMMERT, Ola Belle (Dau.), Nov. 17, 1887 - Nov. 2, 1911
LOVE, Mary Etta, May 23, 1856 - Dec. 4, 1902
EMMERT, Ella Demarcus, April 14, 1892 - Nov. 13, 1899
          Dau. of P. W. and Senie Emmert

WILLIAMS, P. J., Oct. 17, 1853 - June 3, 1898

BANNER, Fay, Jan. 1, 1914 - Feb. 12, 1914
          Son of J. C. and Virginia White Banner

BUCKNER, George W., June 5, 1881 - Sept. 7, 1972
BUCKNER, Katherine Chandler (w), 1885 - 1925

PHILLIPS, Thomas W., Aug. 21, 1881 - April 22, 1924
PHILLIPS, Mattie C. (w), March 6, 1890 - July 15, 1965
          Dau. of Madison F. and Augusta Hatcher Booth

MILLER, Cleo, Nov. 4, 1909 - Feb. 8, 1910
          Dau. of J. K. and Nora Miller

JOBE CEMETERY (continued)

PRATER, Joseph, April 1, 1848 - Aug. 8, 1929
        Co. K, 4TH Tenn. Mtd. Inf. Union Army
PRATER, Salinia Gier, April 10, 1841 - July 19, 1923
ADAMS, Callie Prater, Oct. 6, 1891 - May 4, 1932
        Dau. of J. R. and ------Powell Prater

DRYMAN, Carl F., 1894-1928
DRYMAN, Infant of C. F. and Naggie

GARLAND, Roy Sr., 1910-1985. M/Sgt. US Army, Korean War
GARLAND, Lela G. (w), May 22, 1906 - June 14, 1980
GARLAND, Edward Wayne, Oct. 9, 1943 - March 29, 1946
        Son of Roy and Lela Westall Garland

BARE, James Gordon, Nov. 25, 1879 - June 4, 1963
        Son of H. G. and Rebecca Hash Bare
BARE, Etta Phipps (w), Jan. 25, 1878 - 1965
PHIPPS, Larkin, Dec. 26, 1858 - March 13, 1922
PHIPPS, Sarah Ellen (w), Oct. 4, 1858 - Sept. 22, 1934

SORTORE, Frank R., July 9, 1869 - March 31, 1918

WISEMAN, Martha P., 1893-1987
WISEMAN, James W., June 5, 1920 - March 25, 1971
        Capt. US Army, WWII, Korea
HENSLEY, Martha Wiseman (Dau.), Aug. 21, 1922 - Feb. 8, 1958

BROWN, B. F., May 5, 1830 - March 28, 1900. CSA, Civil War
BROWN, Lucretia (w), April 17, 1831 - Sept. 29, 1923

COOPER, H. Jack, April 20, 1915 - Jan. 1, 1987
COOPER, Rose Baxter (w), July 4, 1917 -
COOPER, Earl Wesley (Son), March 1942 - April 1942

MILLER, Peter, April 7, 1849 - April 25, 1897
MILLER, Jamima (w), May 15, 1854 - Feb. 6, 1934
MILLER, Solomon D., April 2, 1871 - Dec. 5, 1937
MILLER, Mary K., Sept. 14, 1876 - Aug. 14, 1952
MILLER, James, b/d 1899. Son of S. D. and M. E.
MILLER, Frank, April 8, 1901 - Sept. 7, 1912
        Son of Mr. and Mrs. S. D.
MILLER, Vestel W. (Son), March 16, 1906 - Feb. 13, 1931

WHITE, J. C., Feb. 6, 1886 - July 26, 1962
ROCHELEAU, Geneva M. White, March 10, 1935 - May 4, 1963

MILLER, Ben, 1882-1914
MILLER, David, Co. M., 8TH Tenn. Cav. Union Army

GARLAND, Wesley, Oct. 30, 1911 - Feb. 20, 1912

DUNKLEBERGER, Mable Leone, Dec. 1, 1919 - June 1, 1920

ANDERSON, Mary, Oct. 16, 1876 - July 9, 1911. Wife of Landon
ANDERSON, Taylor Jones (Son), Oct. 11, 1900 - March 26, 1912
ANDERSON, James (Son), April 8, 1911 - July 23, 1911

WHITE, William N., July 6, 1874 - Jan. 19, 1959
        Son of Chris and Mary Simmons White
WHITE, Saba N. (w), Oct. 17, 1887 - Aug. 4, 1911
WHITE, Opal (Dau.), March 4, 1911 - Sept. 9, 1911

BAKER, William S., April 24, 1892 - Jan. 28, 1916
BAKER, James S., April 18, 1912 - Dec. 12, 1912
        Son of D. W. and L. E. Baker

CAMPBELL, John Wiley, April 3, 1878 - Dec. 21, 1927
CAMPBELL, Infant (Dau.), Nov. 27, 1918 - Nov. 28, 1918
CAMPBELL, Eleanor V., Oct. 26, 1914 - Aug. 19, 1918
        Dau. of J. W. and Agnes E.
CAMPBELL, Infant, d. Nov. 20, 1914
        Infant of W. A. and Josephine Campbell
CAMPBELL, Doris, Jan. 21, 1921 - June 16, 1921
        Infant of W. A. and Sarah Campbell

DUNCAN, Charles F., 1881-
DUNCAN, Ina May Worthen, 1886-1922
DUNCAN, Jerome W., 1886-1965
DUNCAN, Roxie E., 1892-1967

LAWS, James S., Dec. 24, 1923 - Dec. 28, 1923
        Son of Mr. and Mrs. D. M. Laws

WARRICK, Fielden J., June 9, 1885 - Sept. 8, 1927
        Son of George W. and Jane Griffith Warrick
WARRICK, Madeline T., Dec. 7, 1914 - April 12, 1966
WARRICK, Imogene, May 21, 1921 - Nov. 24, 1921
SLAGLE, Emory M., March 19, 1890 - April 6, 1968
SLAGLE, Sudie Edna, June 8, 1892 - May 22, 1976

KILBY, James A., Nov. 24, 1916 - Jan. 30, 1917
        Son of J. H. and M. W. Kilby

BUCHANAN, Mollie Edward, March 17, 1888 - June 6, 1924
        Wife of Avery Buchanan
BUCHANAN, Clarence, Dec. 1, 1912 - Sept. 27, 1920

RANDALL, Alberta, April 3, 1912 - July 20, 1913
        Dau. of Wm. C. and Maggie Randall

COOPER, William, 1871-1963
COOPER, Dora (w), 1874-1962. Married April 29, 1893

ELAM, Rosco M., March 13, 1910 - Nov. 10, 1910
        Son of David and Vesta Elam

JOHNSON, Evelyn, Sept. 10, 1920 - April 7, 1921
        Dau. of J. Lee and Carey T. Johnson

PICKERING, L., no dates

JOBE CEMETERY  -  UNMARKED GRAVES

BENNETT, Infant,  d. Dec. 15, 1949
        Son of Jack and Eulala Tolley Bennett

BENNETT, Infant,  d. Jan. 1, 1951
        Child of Jack and Eulala Tolley Bennett

BIRCHFIELD, Paul Eugene,  d. Oct. 26, 1930.  Age 14
        Son of Robert and Lydia Randolph Birchfield

BLANKENSHIP, Donal Neal,  d. Dec. 14, 1948
        Child of Ralph and Hattie Pate Blankenship

BLANKENSHIP, Infant,  d. Dec. 6, 1939
        Child of Ralph and Hattie Pate Blankenship

BURLESON, Irene,  d. Sept. 7, 1939.  4 days old
        Dau. of David and Polly Peterson Burleson

CROW, Mrs. Maude,  d. Feb. 7, 1930.  Age 38
        Dau. of Robert and Lula Keever Davis

DANIEL, Charles David,  d. Nov. 25, 1934
        Son of Harold Thomas and Iris Jones Daniel

DAVIS, Martha Cassandra,  May 11, 1858 - May 21, 1946
        Dau. of Alexander and Teressa Riley Booth

DICKSON, Martha Jane,  July 14, 1895 - Oct. 15, 1949
        Dau. of Wm. Patton and Nancy M. Holbrook Campbell

DICKSON, Matthew Columbus,  d. Sept. 3, 1935
        Son of Henry and Ann Smalling Dickson

DOBBINS, Christine,  d. April 9, 1930.  1 year 5 mos. 4 das.
        Dau. of Wm. and Victoria Simmons Dobbins

DUNCAN, Nannie,  d. July 19, 1950

FOX, Infant,  d. April 24, 1933
        Child of O. J. and Katherine Bishop Fox

GARLAND, Margaret,  d. Sept. 8, 1930.  22 mos. old
        Dau. of Mack and Celie Garland McNabb

HALL, Infant,  d. Aug. 26, 1932
        Child of R. D. and Grace Dougherty Hall

HAWKINS, Infant,  d. Nov. 12, 1940
        Son of John and Frances Tucker Hawkins

HAWKINS, Melinda,  d. April 5, 1936.  8 days old
        Dau. of J. F. and Frances Ann Tucker Hawkins

HELVEY, Infant,  d. Dec. 2, 1941
          Child of James Christian & Lucille Catherine Lane Helvey

HENSLEY, Mrs. Cornealy,  d. Sept. 19, 1929
          Dau. of Lucindy Hensley

HIGGINBOTHAN, Pearl Tilson,  d. Nov. 8, 1927.  Age 5
          Dau. of Ben Higginbothan

JARVIS, Polly,  Jan. 28, 1871 - Oct. 20, 1957
          Dau. of James A. and Sarah Ann Briggs Buckner

KERR, Infant,  d. Sept. 10, 1945.  Dau. of Ernest Kerr

LYLE, Gracie May,  June 4, 1909 - Jan. 30, 1930
          Dau. of Robert R. and Rebecca Jones Lyle

MASHBURN, Jacob S.,  April 19, 1879 - July 29, 1929
          Son of Calloway and Della Pate Mashburn

MILLER, Soloman Deal,  d. April 27, 1945
          Infant son of Carl Ernest and Dora Lloyd Miller

MILLER, Infant,  d. Feb. 29, 1944
          Child of Carl Ernest and Dora Lloyd Miller

MORLEY, Infant,  d. Nov. 23, 1941
          Child of Andrew Paul and Margaret Tilson Morley

MULLINS, Mrs. Bud,  d. March 1, 1928.  Age 57

McCURRY, Scott,  d. Nov. 16, 1946
          Son of Jackson and Mary Jane Tipton McCurry

McEWEN, James Robert,  d. Oct. 16, 1936
          Son of A. C. and Mary Needam McEwen

McINTURFF, Brenda Kay,  d. Nov. 6, 1954
          Infant dau. of James Milton and June Story McInturff

McINTURFF, Infant,  d. Aug. 22, 1956
          Child of J. M. and June Lucille Story McInturff

McINTURFF, John C.,  d. July 15, 1942.  Age 93
          Son of Emmanuel and Elizabeth Buck McInturff

McINTURFF, Mrs.        ,  d. April 30, 1928.  Age 79

McINTYRE, Mrs. J. K.,  July 6, 1872 - Jan. 1, 1930
          Dau. of Hugh and Cora McIntyre Herrell

McNABB, Mary Jane,  d. June 28, 1945.  Age 77
          Dau. of Thomas and Sarah Laws Davis

NELSON, Sadie Loretta, d. Aug. 25, 1936
      Dau. of Silas and Jane Hughes Stevens

NOWLAND, A. L., Oct. 8, 1870 - Oct. 22, 1927

O'BRINE, Janice Sue, d. June 17, 1935. 2 mos. old
      Dau. of George Clifton and Nancy Peterson O'Brine

PATE, Nettie Joe, d. Dec. 10, 1937. 9 mos.
      Child of Neal and Martha Miller Pate

PHILLIPS, Daughter, d. April 26, 1926
      Dau. of Jack and Horneta Wolfe Phillips

PRATT, Audree Fern, d. June 30, 1936. 1 mo.
      Dau. of Jack and Audree Webb Pratt

QUESENBERRY, Tobias Jackson, d. Dec. 13, 1934. Age 52
      Son of Enos and Rebecca Hewitt Quesenberry

QUESENBERRY, Tempa Virginia, Dec. 2, 1892 - Jan. 21, 1952
      Dau. of Wm. Henry and Addie G. Hartsock Bundy

RAY, Nerva, d. Nov. 17, 1937. Age 56. Dau. of Isaac Luttrell

ROBBINS, James Calvin, d. Nov. 7, 1929. Age 64
      Son of Jackson and Martha Ann Robbins

SCRUGGS, Barry Anthony, d. Dec. 7, 1944
      Infant son of Chas. Richard & Mildred Nave Scruggs

SIMMONS, W. M., d. Nov. 15, 1937. Age 57
      Son of James and Emmaline Mashburn Simmons

SMITH, Dee O'Dell, Sept. 1, 1907 - Aug. 8, 1929
      Son of John and Jude Day Smith

STEPHENS, Thomas J., d. May 19, 1937. Age 53
      Son of Silas and Jane Hughes Stephens

STEWART, J. M., May 29, 1848 - May 8, 1929
      Son of Bob and Roeksie (?) Garland Stewart

TIPTON, Alvin, d. Sept. 27, 1931. 9 mos. 29 das.
      Son of Lattie and Henrietta Anderson Tipton

TIPTON, Mary Jane, d. Oct. 16, 1939. Age 75
      Dau. of ------Lewis and Eliza Riddle Lewis

TITTLE, Howard, d. April 8, 1928. Age 2
      Son of Hobert and Ruby Cash Tittle

TONEY, Bonnie Mae, d. April 24, 1938. Age 35
      Dau. of David S. and Lilly Bryant Toney

TONEY, Infant, d. Oct.31,1934
      Child of Hazen House and Amanna Ruth Emmish Toney

TUCKER, Joseph Lewis, d. April 12,1935. Age 58
      Son of Wesley and Polly Ann Bailey Tucker

VANCE, Virginia Paulette, d. Jan.13,1938. Age 4
      Dau. of Paul McCoris and Mary Ruth Bannister Vance

WATSON, Yancey Nathaniel, d. Dec.5,1942. Age 71
      Son of John Watson

WHITE, David J., d. Dec.26,1936.
      Infant son of J.C. and Bessie Harris White

WHITE, Mrs. N.C., Feb.6,1849 - Nov.31,1927
      Dau. of Alec and Celia Goodwin Smith

WHITE, Robert Edison, d. Feb.13,1946. 4 mos. 9 days
      Son of Joseph Christopher and Bessie Marie Harris White

## MARTINS CREEK CEMETERY

Located on Carolina Extension, Across From
State Fish Hatchery.      Copied May 10, 1988

HARRIS, Terry Lee, June 15, 1946 - Dec. 5, 1949
        Son of Jake and Myrtle Harris
HARRIS, Myrtle Price, March 7, 1923 - Dec. 17, 1971

PUCKETT, Frances,   1937-1949

SHEHAN, Samuel Tilden, May 16, 1884 - June 8, 1949
SHEHAN, Rissie Elizabeth (w), May 29, 1893 -

WELLS, Robert S., May 11, 1898 - Sept. 10, 1958
        TN. Pvt. 307, GR REG Service QMC, WWI

ENGLE, James Willie, Oct. 8, 1907 - Oct. 28, 1963
        TN. Pvt. Co. M, 22 Infantry, WWII
ENGLE, Lousie (w), Aug. 16, 1907 - Sept. 15, 1948

JOHNSON, Hank Sherman, Mar. 14, 1894 -
JOHNSON, Alice Britt (w), Sept. 11, 1899 - Jan. 26, 1987
        Daughter of Frank and Dora Price Britt
JOHNSON, Samuel Lee, 1924-1948
        Son of Harley Sherman and Alice Elizabeth Britt Johnson
GOUGE, Mary K., Dec. 30, 1951 - Sept. 12, 1952
        Dau. of L. A. and Ramona Johnson Gouge and
        Granddaughter of Hank and Alice Johnson

STAMPER, Roger Dale, Sept. 22, 1948 - Jan. 19, 1950

BAILEY, Zebb, 1856-1950
BAILEY, Hannah (w), 1863-1947
        Dau. of Ned and Elizabeth Deaton Wilson
BAILEY, John Calvin, Nov. 15, 1895 - Aug. 2, 1967
        Pvt. US Army, WWI
BAILEY, Leona (w), Dec. 8, 1890 - July 27, 1949
        Dau. of Baxter and Lovie Taylor Hughes
BAILEY, Clyde, July 14, 1927 - Feb. 13, 1972, SI, US Navy, WWII

WILSON, Nathan D., 1889-1946, Son of Zeb & Louvina Bryant Wilson
WILSON, Leona H.(?) (w), 1892-1977

HARRIS, James Edward, May 5, 1923 - March 28, 1950
        Son of Barnett and Cora Lee Horne Harris

BAILEY, Virgie, Jan. 29, 1935 - April 30, 1951

HIGGINS, Claude Smith, April 10, 1893 - June 12, 1952
        Pvt. 166 Inf., WWI
HIGGINS, Bessie E. (w), July 22, 1900 - July 24, 1984

TIPTON, Edward E., Sept. 3, 1924 - March 11, 1961
        T. Sgt., AAF, WWII
TIPTON, Molly, 1900-1976

MARTINS CREEK CEMETERY (continued)

MATHES, George W., May 8, 1889 - July 24, 1966
MATHES, Clyde A., March 17, 1911 - Feb. 1, 1957
        Pvt. 329 FA BN, WWII, Son of Geo. W. & Maggie Tittle Mathes

ANGEL, Mack, 1900-1957 - Son of Theodore & Zettie Anglen Angel

RIDDLE, James M., May 2, 1900 - June 9, 1958

SPARKS, Myrtle Alice, d. March 1941 (child)
BURLESON, Tommy Wayne, d. April 1948

TIPTON, Zeak, Jan. 1, 1908 - Dec. 31, 1933
TIPTON, Jack, July 21, 1930 - May 10, 1969, Sp 4, US Army

McCOURY, Maxine, April 16, 1926 - Sept. 28, 1926

HIGGINS, Shelby, March 6, 1872 - Aug. 3, 1953
HIGGINS, Fronie M. (w), March 9, 1874 - July 11, 1934
HIGGINS, Frank, Jan. 30, 1908 - March 18, 1931
        Son of Shelby and Nora McCurry Higgins
WILLIAMS, Donnie B., Sept. 29, 1909 - Nov. 27, 1944

ROBERTS, Lenys, Feb. 11, 1926 - Jan. 12, 1927
ROBERTS, Lucy , Feb. 11, 1926 - Jan. 30, 1927

BAILEY, Infant, March 20, 1925 - March 21, 1925
        Son of Mr. and Mrs. John C. Bailey
BAILEY, J. C. Jr., Jan. 23, 1929 - June 15, 1930
        Son of Mr. and Mrs. John C. Bailey

BROOKS, James P., Sept. 17, 1859 -
BROOKS, Ann B. (w), Jan. 30, 1859 - Aug. 23, 1919
BROOKS, Roy Roberts, Feb. 28, 1903 - Nov. 27, 1963
        Son of James and Ann Barr Brooks
BROOKS, Maxine Rowe (w), Jan. 11, 1905 -

ROBERTS, Infant, b/d Dec. 30, 1913 - Son of J.H. & Zora Roberts
ROBERTS, Jake H., 1881-1943
ROBERTS, Zora C., 1897-19--
ROBERTS, Daniel C., b. 1920 (?) broken stone

LOVE, J. R., March 31, 1844 - March 28, 1912 - Confederate Veteran

LOVE, Isaac R., d. Oct. 29, 1931 - age 86 years
        Son of Wm. and Nancy Hartsell Love
LOVE, Mary E. (w), d. Feb. 20, 1928 - age 85 years
        Dau. of Daniel Roberts

ROBERTS, Mary B., March 19, 1819 - Feb. 20, 1904
        Wife of D. G. Roberts
ROBERTS, D. G., d. Dec. 19, 1889 (?) - broken stone

HUGHS, Moses, Nov. 9, 1854 - Oct. 17, 1913
HUGHS, Mary Etta (w), b. March 6, 1864
HUGHS, William R. (Son), Jan. 17, 1882 - March 28, 1882
HUGHS, Celila (Dau.), Nov. 16, 1888 - July 14, 1889

HUGHS, Frank E., d. Jan. 12, 1903

HENSLEY, Rachel E., Jan. 24, 1838 - Sept.12, 1891
        Wife of J. A. Hensley

BAILEY, Dovie, Nov. 8, 1896 - Sept. 3, 1907
        Son of B. G. and Mrs. Bailey

ALDRIDGE, Isaac Edmund, Dec. 20, 1870 - Jan. 30, 1940
ALDRIDGE, Elizabeth Harris (w), Dec. 15, 1875 - June 14, 1957
ALDRIDGE, Ruthie (Dau.), Jan. 14, 1906 - March 1, 1906
ALDRIDGE, H. M., d. Sept. 6, 1900 - age 28 das

BAILEY, Hiram, June 15, 1825 - June 14, 1906
        Son of John and Lovada Ray Bailey
BAILEY, Sarah (w), July 3, 1825 - Aug. 14, 1905
        Maiden name Deyton
BAILEY, Hiram B., Aug. 25, 1858 - March 9, 1936
        Son of Hiram and Sarah Deyton Bailey
BAILEY, Delcena B. (w), Oct. 23, 1861 - Feb. 23, 1926
        Dau. of Charlie and Eliza Byrd
BAILEY, James D., 1884-1949 - Son of Alfred and Jane Slagle Bailey
BAILEY, Essie, 1886-1928 - Dau. of Hiram & Delcena Byrd Bailey
BAILEY, Infant, b/d Aug. 30, 1910 - Son of M.A. & Mary L. Bailey
BAILEY, Infant, b/d Sept. 28, 1905 - Son of M.A. & Mary L. Bailey
BAILEY, Infant, b/d June 26, 1913 - Son of M.A. & Mary L. Bailey
BAILEY, Son, July 4, 1923 - Dec. 22, 1923
        Son of Jas. and Essie Bailey
BAILEY, Johnnie Austin, Sept. 28, 1927 - Sept. 23, 1929
        Son of Charles L. and Ethel Bailey

BAILEY, Toby Joe, Aug. 23, 1932 - May 23, 1933
        Son of Mr. and Mrs. C. L. Bailey, Sr.

O'BRIEN, Eugene O., Oct. 29, 1914 - March 13, 1966
        PFC 687 FA, WWII

HOYLE, J. M., 1869-1943 - Son of Hiram and Myra Blankenship Hoyle

CHANDLER, Auther, b/d Jan. 30, 1920

TIPTON, Phoebie, May 30, 1885 - Jan. 7, 1974
HARRIS, Frank, May 27, 1931 - PVT 127 Inf. 32 Div.
HARRIS, Infant, b/d March 27, 1916
        Daughter of J. F. and Jennie Harris

HORNE, Drew F., March 14, 1886 - July 10, 1932 - Son of Frank Horne
HORNE, C. L. (?) (w), July 10, 1874 - Nov. 10, 1945
LAWING, Margaret, May 30, 1856 - June 26, 1937
HORNE, William R., March 7, 1884 - March 31, 1954
HORNE, Eliza J. (w), July 17, 1889 - Jan. 16, 1979

BANNER, Cordie, Dec. 16, 1879-July 18, 1908 - Wife of D.S. Banner
BANNER, Earnest Carter (Son), March 29, 1905 - Sept. 1, 1905
BANNER, Virgie Mae (Dau.), Dec. 17, 1907 - April 7, 1908

TIPTON, Sam L., Co. J., 3RD NC Mtd. Inf. Union Army

CASH, Sarah C., d. April 11, 1912, age 84 yrs

BAILEY, M. B., 1853-1933
BAILEY, Rebecca E. (w), 1862-1938
        Dau. of Ben W. and Lucinda Sams Woodward
WOODWARD, B. W., Dec. 24, 1830 - May 31, 1898
WOODWARD, Lucinda Sams (w), Jan. 17, 1834 - March 17, 1925
WOODWARD, Lockey A. (Dau.), 1872-1939

BENNETT, Anderson, Aug. 15, 1870 - Nov. 24, 1941
BENNETT, Harriet, ----

RENFRO, John, June 25, 1890 - March 18, 1961
RENFRO, Allie Mae, 1895-1980

WOODFIN, David, ----- Son of John B. and Lula Lewis Woodfin
WOODFIN, Margaret (w), ------
WOODFIN, Mary (Dau.), -------
WOODFIN, Arthur (Son), ------
WOODFIN, Fred (Son),   ------
WOODFIN, Baby (Son),   ------


ROBERTS, Sallie L., May 16, 1856 - Sept. 5, 1883 (or 1893)
        Wife of I. E. Roberts

McINTURFF, William, Jan. 14, 1837 - Oct. 25, 1902
        Son of Gabriel and Achsa Nelson McInturff
        (Served Unicoi. Co. as Commissioner, Magistrate,
        Sheriff and Postmaster)
McINTURFF, Rhoda (w), April 11, 1838 - Feb. 8, 1882
        Maiden name Dyer
McINTURFF, Mary E. (Dau.), May 5, 1862 - Nov. 14, 1886

HUSKINS, Sarah L., Feb. 28, 1836 - June 5, 18?8
HUSKINS, S. C., Dec. 17, 1880 - Feb. 20, 1882
HODGE, Mary, Dec. 28, 1889 - Oct. 20, 1890
HUSKINS, John, March 15, 1839 - March 4, 1914
        Co. M, 8TH Tenn. Cav., Union Army
HUSKINS, Elizabeth (w), b. Feb. 22, 1859

HUSKINS, Cinda E., Jan. 18, 1885 - June 5, 1890

CROWDER, Mary Evelyn, June 20, 1935 - Sept. 19, 1935

HANEY, Oscar, March 19, 1938 - July 2, 1938
HANEY, James Garfield (Bro.), March 30, 1941 - June 5, 1941

TAPP, Fannie, Nov. 7, 1877 - Jan. 26, 1931

BOGART, Mattie Lee, March 11, 1885 - May 20, 1906
        Wife of J. C. Bogart
BOGART, Eldrige, b/d May 20, 1906, Son of J. C. & M. L. Bogart

MATHES, Eugene, Oct. 7, 1929 - Sept. 10, 1933
        Son of Clyde and Ada Mathes

ROBERTS, Jacob Russell, April 25, 1897 - July 3, 1897
        Son of W. A. and Lizzie Roberts

LOVE, William, d. June 8, 1876 - aged 58 years
LOVE, Nancy A., July 12, 1823 - Dec. 21, 1918
LOVE, Jacob W., March 5, 1872 - Nov. 5, 1878
LOVE, W. Archia, Oct. 25, 1887 - July 13, 1888
LOVE, Wm. M., b/d Dec. 21, 1888
LOVE, Jacob. D., Nov. 9, 1842 - May 10, 1907 - Confederate Veteran
LOVE, Phoeba Stout (w), April 10, 1840 - Jan. 26, 1923

CROSSWHITE, Jennie, June 16, 1829 - Jan. 10, 1894
CROSSWHITE, I. J., June 10, 1857 - Aug. 12, 1940
        Son of George Crosswhite
CROSSWHITE, Nannie, Aug. 12, 1855 - May 1, 1931
        Daughter of Sam and Syndia Green Love

SHORES, Elva Donnie May, Jan. 14, 1896 - April 1, 1896
        Dau. of W. W. and Ellie V. Shores

SMITH, Thomas M., Sept. 1, 1862 - March 3, 1941
        Son of George and Mary Ann White Smith
SMITH, Clara, May 1, 1861 - Oct. 12, 1936
        Dau. of Robert and Sara McInturff Allen

HARRIS, Isaac, April 9, 1883 - May 19, 1966
HARRIS, Sallie E. (w), June 11, 1885 - Dec. 5, 1961
        Dau. of Thomas M. and Clara Allen Smith
HARRIS, Clyde, Sept. 22, 1905 - July 23, 1906
        Son of I. J. and S. E. Harris
HARRIS, Clarence, Aug. 5, 1915 - Sept. 6, 1943
        Son of I. J. and S. E. Harris

McNALLEY, Henry T., 1882-1952
McNALLEY, Rebecca Ann (w), 1890-1933

GENTRY, Christopher P., 1883-1947
        Son of John Butler and Sarah Moore Gentry
GENTRY, Mary D., 1900 - 19--. Dau. of G.W. & Hester Edwards White

FOSTER, Colonel E., Sept. 29, 1886 - April 12, 1968
        Pvt. US Army, WWI
FOSTER, Lula Mae, July 7, 1891 - July 4, 1982

WHITE, James W., Sept. 2, 1897 - May 22, 1959
        Son of G. W. and Hester Edwards White
WHITE, Phebie E. Hampton (w#1), Aug. 31, 1904 - Jan. 27, 1943
        Dau. of Robert and Mollie White Hampton
WHITE, Julia McInturff (w#2), May 29, 1905 - Jan. 16, 1951

HASKETT, Columbus, 1893-1965 - Son of John & Amanda Keever Haskett
HASKETT, Martha (w), 1895-1954
        Dau. of Geo. Washington & Hester Ann Edwards White
HASKETT, Robert Earl (Son), Sept. 12, 1918 - Dec. 7, 1970
        US Navy, WWII
HASKETT, Cecil David (Son), Oct. 11, 1922 - Feb. 7, 1978
        Seaman, US Coast Guard, WWII

WHITE, G. W., March 3, 1884 - July 15, 1921
WHITE, Hester A. (w), Oct. 2, 1872 - Nov. 13, 1939
        Dau. of Wilson and Martha Gouge Edwards
WHITE, Little Edith L. (Dau.), Oct. 18, 1918 - Feb. 9, 1919

LAWING, Virgie May, d. 1904 - Dau. of ? and J. F. Lawing

SIMMONS, Anna Banner, July 4, 1840 - Aug. 1, 1927
        Dau. of Earl and ------ Banner McIntosh

HARRIS, W. H., Aug. 2, 1846 - Nov. 6, 1922
HARRIS, Judy (w), Aug. 22, 1850 - June 9, 1927
        Dau. of Joe and Lizzie Banner Murry

BANNER, Elizabeth, Sept. 17, 1817 - Oct. 30, 1892
BANNER, Henry C., Aug. 22, 1850 - Aug. 30, 1904
BANNER, Pheoba A., Oct. 28, 1850 - Sept. 3, 1918

EDWARDS, R. Burr, July 12, 1902 - ---- 5, 1911
        Son of J. P. and M. Edwards

BAILEY, Debby Jane Edwards, Aug. 25, 1869 - Dec. 6, 1921
        Wife of S. G. Bailey
DAVIS, Robert, d. age 3 mos., Son of J. C. and Polly Davis
EDWARDS, Feeldon, Oct. 20, 1877 - Feb. 27, 1901
EDWARDS, William, May 7, 1881 - -------- 1903
EDWARDS, Wilson, June 6, 1847 - March 12, 1918
EDWARDS, Martha A. (w), April 17, 1846 - June 5, 1932
        Dau. of Tom Gouge
EDWARDS, Sarah L., April 20, 1864 - July 14, 1936
        Dau. of Wilson and Martha Gouge Edwards

WIDENER, Andrew J., 1860-1942
WIDENER, Mary E. (w), 1889-1980
WIDENER, Infant (Dau.), Sept. 14, 1913 - Sept. 19, 1913
WIDENER, Charles Howard (Son,) Feb. 25, 1910 - June 5, 1913

LOVE, James Robert, 1880-1942
        Son of J. R. and Mary E. Loveless Love
LOVE, Infant, b/d Jan. 13, 1908- Dau. of J.R. and Lola Love
LOVE, Robert J., March 3, 1911 - Aug. 13, 1963
        Sgt. 73 Tank Bn, WWII, Korea

WHITE, Carlton Emmert, Dec. 5, 1937 - Dec. 12, 1937
        Son of James Wilson & Phoebe Elizabeth Hampton White
WHITE, Kathleen, Nov. 21, 1925 - Dec. 23, 1925
WHITE, Carrie Adeline, Aug. 21, 1921 - Sept. 21, 1921

LOVE, William P., 1883-19??
LOVE, Minnie Jane (w), 1882-1943
MASTERS, Larry Joe, Feb. 14, 1944 - May 12, 1944
        Son of Jack and Blanche Kerns Masters

LOVELESS, James R., Lieut., Co. C, 2ND Tenn. Cav. - Union Army
LOVELESS, Mary E. (w), Aug. 10, 1856 - Feb. 2, 1923

ELLIS, Richard, May 28, 1924 - June 2, 1924
        Son of R. T. and Kate Ellis

NORRIS, Thomas M., Sept. 23, 1847 - June 30, 1913
NORRIS, Sarah E. Tinker (w), March 11, 1862 - Oct. 14, 1888
ROBERTS, Ellen, May 12, 186? - April 9, 18??

GILBERT, John L., Jan. 11, 1858 - 1880
GILBERT, Sary E., Sept. 25, 1878 - 1879
GILBERT, Dora B., Jan. 10, 1876 - Aug. 22, 1891

TINKER, J. A., Feb. 22, 1860 - Sept. 3, 1896
TINKER, Maria H., Aug. 6, 1889 - March 3, 1904

HAMPTON, Dan'l, Co. F, 3RD NC Mtd. Inf., Union Army

WHITE, Sue Emma, Jan. 17, 1873 - Dec. 3, 1887

McNABB, Glena Lee, Dec. 4, 1887 - Feb. 8, 1888
        Dau. of R. G. and Kate McNabb

ALLEN, Alfred L., May 8, 1873 - Aug. 31, 1890
ALLEN, Claudia E., March 24, 1884 - April 2, 1891 (?)
        Dau. of G. S. and D. A. Allen

HARRIS, Thomas W., b/d 1904 - Son of J. H. & M. F. Harris

SMITH, Thomas G., b/d 1901 - Son of Mr. & Mrs. T. H. Smith

LOVE, James R., d. March 3, 1902 - age 75 years

HAMPTON, D. P., March 3, 1898 - June 2, 1900
HAMPTON, Jane, March 9, 1900 - Apr. 27, 1900

MURPHY, Winnie, d. Feb. 18, 1908 - age 64 years

HAMPTON, Mr. Ike,          ----------------

ALLEN, Isaac G., Jan. 4, 1866 - Aug. 30, 1940
          Son of Robert A. and Sarah F. McInturff Allen
ALLEN, Emma (w#1), Nov. 18, 1870 - June 18, 1902
ALLEN, Laura B. (w#2), Feb. 25, 1882 - Jan. 6, 1907
ALLEN, Infant (Son), b/d Dec. 9, 1906
BAILEY, Hafford A., March 3, 1915 - June 6, 1983
ALLEN, Robert A., Nov. 15, 1829 - Dec. 14, 1905
ALLEN, Sarah F. McInturff (w), June 11, 1832 - May 10, 1917

HAMPTON, William, April 4, 1917 - Aug. 8, 1918
          Son of A. S. and S. E. Hampton

DAVIS, J. C., d. Oct. 29, 1910 - age 29 years
DAVIS, Pollie (w), March 3, 1879 - Oct. 29, 1914

GILLIS, Joni Marie, b/d 1963 - Dau. of Wm.L. & Betty Jean Engle
          Moved to Evergreen Cem. July 1989                Gillis

ENGLE, John Quillen, June 20, 1902 - May 31, 1946
          Son of Aaron Engle
ENGLE, Clara N. Harris (w), June 19, 1907 -

EDWARDS, Toy, Feb. 17, 1924 - March 22, 1924
          Son of J. J. and Bessie Edwards
EDWARDS, R. B., April 10, 1882 - Oct. 16, 190?

HARRIS, Elizabeth, d. Dec. 5, 1910 - age 84 years
          Wife of Hugh Harris

ALLEN, Isaac G., Feb. 20, 1889 - Dec. 4, 1973
ALLEN, Cassie W. (w), Feb. 4, 1889 - Feb. 18, 1966
ALLEN, James Virgil, Jr., April 7, 1913 - Jan. 15, 1919
ALLEN, Wilma E., Sept. 30, 1931 - Oct. 20, 1931
          Dau. of Isaac and Cassie Whaley Allen

LUTTRELL, James Thomas, b. Jan. 15, 1872
LUTTRELL, Margaret Emiline Coffee, Dec. 7, 1865 - April 17, 1946

HAMPTON, Sherman A., 1867-1934- Son of Dan. & Katherine Masters
HAMPTON, Sarah E.,    1882-1964                     Hampton
          Dau. of Landon and Mollie Tinker Masters

MASTERS, Charlie H., 1880-1963

HAMPTON, Hannah, March 6, 1854 - Oct. 18, 1923

HAMPTON, Grant, 1869-1936 - Son of Daniel & Catherine Masters
HAMPTON, Sarah Ann, 1874-1937                   Hampton

ALLEN, Elva L., April 8, 1901 - Sept. 10, 1902
          Dau. of J. S. and D. A. Allen

MARTINS CREEK CEMETERY (continued)

ANDREWS, Ross, Co. E, 1st Tenn. L.A. - Union Army

MASTERS, Nancy, March 29, 1890 - July 9, 1890
        Dau. of A. L. and Analize (Anna Liza) Masters
MASTERS, Analize, Aug. 8, 1866 - March 23, 1892
        Wife of A. L. Masters
MASTERS, Abraham, April 23, 1823 - Sept. 1, 1865
MASTERS, Henry, Sept. 19, 1865 - June 2, 1885
MASTERS, Nancy Elam, March 11, 1835 - May 2, 1921

WHITLOCK, W. S., broken stone
WHITLOCK, Sara A. (w), Feb. 9, 1818 - Jan. 16, 1904
WHITLOCK, A. G., Dec. 8, 1848 - Feb. 18, 1907
WHITLOCK, Maggie E. Crosswhite (w), Aug. 29, 1860 - Oct. 23, 1923

BANNER, M. L. and wife,

MASTERS, Biga, July 26, 1897 - July 24, 1899
        Son of Mr. and Mrs. A. L. Masters
ALDRIDGE, William A., March 1, 1842 - June 22, 1927
ALDRIDGE, Allie, b. Nov. 6, 1869 - Dau. of Hiram and Elzira
                                Blankenship Hoyle

MASTERS, Mary A., May 29, 1847 - Feb. 3, 1923
        Dau. of James and Nancy A. Tinker
MASTERS, William, Co. D, 39th US Vol. Inf. - Span.-Am. War(?)
TINKER, J. F., Corp'l Co. K, 38th US Vol Inf.

ROBERTS, Infant, b. Dec. 29, 1902
ROBERTS, Pearl Bell, b. April 9, 1907
        Children of F. B. and Liddia A. Roberts

MASTERS, Grant, Oct. 24, 1866 - Aug. 7, 1903
MASTERS, Emma, 1871-1954 - Dau. of Wm. & Sarah Ledford Capps

GARLAND, Celia, June 18, 1868 - Feb. 13, 1919
BYRD, E. M., 1853-1936
BYRD, Marry, 1863-1930

HARRIS, Nola, Jan. 5, 1905 - Aug. 13, 1913

HIGGINS, J. D., Oct. 23, 1925 - March 23, 1926
        Son of E. Q. and Ella Higgins

BAILEY, Hattley, Dec. 17, 1917 - Nov. 11, 1922

HIGGINS, Susie, 1842-1901

WIGGAND, Pansey Peterson, 1905-1943

MATTINGLY, Mrs. Mandy, -
FOSTER, Mary, Dec. 25, 1878 - March 3, 1905
        Wife of Lewis Foster

COPP, Ludy, Dec. 10, 1886 - Oct. 18, 1963
COPP, Edith Foster, March 9, 1901 - Oct. 16, 1942
        Dau. of Louis and Mary McLaughlin Foster

GARLAND, Elisha L., June 6, 1884 - Feb. 23, 1966
       Pvt., Spanish American War
GARLAND, Virgil Butler, Feb. 6, 1913 - April 23, 1944
       Son of E. L. and Cora Garland
GARLAND, Evelyn, March 9, 1922 - March 24, 1935

CARPENTER, J. W., Nov. 26, 1873 - April 4, 1915
CARPENTER, Rosa (w), Dec. 30, 1874 - Jan. 27, 1960
       Dau. of John Wm. and ------- Martin Morison
CARPENTER, John Wesley, Jr. (Son), April 13, 1900 - Feb. 10, 1909
CARPENTER, Guy B. (Son), Aug. 23, 1898 - Dec. 31, 1951

MASTERS, Alexander, March 8, 1895 - Aug. 2, 1961
       Pvt., 57 Pioneer Inf., WWI
MASTERS, Rebecca Lou, April 23, 1900 - Jan. 31, 1982
MASTERS, Alex Z. -

MASTERS, James H. -
MASTERS, Landon C. -

BANNER, Rhoda, May 17, 1879 - Jan. 12, 1895
       Dau. of C.M.E. and M. L. Banner
BANNER, Julia E., Aug. 6, 1883 - Oct. 21, 1914

HILTON, Ernest Ronald, June 13, 1942 - Nov. 16, 1943
       Son of Ernest Patrick & Beatrice Gilbert Hilton
GILBERT, Robert W. H., June 4, 1863 - Dec. 28, 1939
GILBERT, Serene E. (w), Jan. 3, 1856 - Jan. 10, 1926
GILBERT, S. Dora R., July 19, 1894 - Aug. 23, 1895
GILBERT, Grace Eva, Nov. 19, 1884 - March 17, 1886

PIPPIN, William Perry, 1820-1900
PIPPIN, Catherine, Feb. 20, 1830 - Oct. 8, 1886
PIPPIN, Laura I., Oct. 5, 1867 - Oct. 23, 1885

BURCHFIELD, Robert, March 3, 1832 - Feb. 4, 1914
BURCHFIELD, M. A. (w), April 12, 1850 - Feb. 26, 1908

RAY, Infant, b/d 1902 - Infant of Mr. & Mrs. G. B. Ray

HOYLE, Hiram, Oct. 27, 1837 - April 6, 1912
HOYLE, Elzina (w), Aug. 25, 1839 - April 29, 1912
HOYLE, Fleety, Feb. 22, 1925 - June 17, 1945
       Son of Jerry Mack and Susie Roberts Hoyle
       Pvt. 38 Inf., WWII

LEWIS, William S., 1881-1956
LEWIS, Phoebe E., 1887-1950
LEWIS, Cora Lee (Dau.), Sept. 22, 1908 - Nov. 28, 1914
LEWIS, Opha (Dau.), Jan. 24, 1911 - Dec. 23, 1914
LEWIS, Willard (Son), Jan. 27, 1916 - July 11, 1916
LEWIS, Jessee W., Feb. 25, 1923 - June 9, 1941

MARTINS CREEK CEMETERY (continued)

OLLIS, Minnie, June 22, 1921 - Feb. 11, 1978
GRASON, Sara, 1902-1987

TUCKER, Audrey T., Jan. 10, 1912 - Feb. 23, 1912
TUCKER, Infant, Dec. 25, 1910 - Dec. 26, 1910
        Children of N. T. and Nora S. Tucker

KEEVER, Arthur Nelson, June 23, 1898 - Oct. 30, 1938

SHOOK, John A., 1874-1933
SHOOK, Jerry W., June 10, 1889 - June 13, 1909

BROWN, Jasper, Co. C., 2 NC Inf., Union Army
BROWN, Eunice, March 6, 1824 - July 24, 1900 (or 1906)

HARRIS, Roy, June 20, 1903 - Jan. 16, 1971
HARRIS, Bonnie, March 26, 1920 -

COGGINS, Chas., d. June 26, 1921 - age 19 years
COGGINS, William, d. Jan. 6, 1946
COGGINS, Minty, d. Feb. 1, 1940
        (Minty Jane) Dau. of Timothy & Sally Bennett Miller

HARRIS, Walter, 1893-1970
HARRIS, Bessie B. (w), 1894-1974
HARRIS, Henry, May 10, 1869 - Dec. 16, 1942
        Son of Harrison and Jude Banner Harris
HARRIS, Carrie, Dec. 16, 1866 - Feb. 25, 1940
        Dau. of George and Jennie Allen Crosswhite

BANNER, Walter, 1909-1975

YARBROUGH, George W., Oct. 12, 1833 - March 25, 1905

WALKER, Baxter S., Dec. 6, 1880 - Nov. 1, 1975
WALKER, Lillie R. (w), June 6, 1881 - Dec. 31, 1963
WALKER, Baxter, Jr., (Son), March 31, 1921 - Aug. 29, 1938
WALKER, Carrie (Dau.), March 6, 1907 - Feb. 27, 1910

CRAIN, Carl, Aug. 19, 1915 - Oct. 6, 1916
        Son of Joe and Dora Crain
CRAIN, Sam Jr., July 5, 1923 - Jan. 22, 1924
CRAIN, Infant, April 24, 1924 - April 27, 1924
        Son of Joe and Dora Crain

BOONE, Infant, d. Oct. 8, 1918 - Son of Troy & Ollie Boone
BOONE, Infant, d. July 10, 1925 - Son of Troy & Ollie Boone

CHANDLER, Infant, d. Jan. 30, 1920 - Son of Arthur & Annie Chandler

OLLIS, Tilmon, Oct. 14, 1876 - Nov. 30, 1941
        Son of John and Polly Stanley Ollis
OLLIS, Annie, June 19, 1879 - June 22, 1938
OLLIS, Don, April 4, 1912 - May 24, 1976

OLLIS, Arthur, May 8, 1914 - Aug. 11, 1921
OLLIS, Annie, July 24, 1918 - May 16, 1920
OLLIS, Franklin, Oct. 24, 1932 - Dec. 24, 1932

PRICE, Isaiah, Co. G, 3RD NC Mtd. Inf. - Union Army

HOWEL, Dillie, d. Feb. 27, 1893 - Wife of J. W. Howel

HIGGINS, Paul W., -

POORE, Joe, May 11, 1906 -
POORE, Dessie (w), April 7, 1900 - April 8, 1960
POORE, Homer, June 19, 1930 - April 9, 1933
        Son of Joe and Bessie Hughes Poore

SAYLOR, James O., 1895-1896 - Son of J. S. Saylor

BALMON, Mamie E., 1893-1927 - Dau. of J.S. & Bennie Hogan Saylor

IVERSON, Muriel Joy, Jan. 22, 1897 - Feb. 19, 1898
        Dau. of Martin and Maggie Iverson

LEMMON, Ira, June 24, 1919 - July 29, 1919
LEMMON, Irene, June 24, 1919 - March 16, 1920
        Son and dau. of Ira and Edith Lemmon

BANNER, Alvin, Oct. 17, 1919 - June 26, 1923

HENSLEY, Zeb, Sept. 24, 1870 - March 26, 1923
HENSLEY, Dorothy -

SHELL, Walter, April 18, 1893 - June 22, 1931

PEAKE, James W., April 9, 1877 - Nov. 2, 1959
PEAKE, Mary P. (w), Oct. 27, 1872 - March 28, 1939
        Dau. of -------------- and Laura Price
PEAKE, Edith (Dau.), Feb. 7, 1908 - Dec. 4, 1928
PEAKE, Julia V., Aug. 1, 1882 - June 20, 1914 - Wife of W. Peake
PEAKE, James Franklin, Sept. 21, 1944 - Sept. 22, 1944
        Son of James Willis and Hannah Adkins Peake

NEAL, Marion Albert, May 9, 1914 - Feb. 20, 1915

KING, William B., b. June 20, 1865 -
KING, Mary E. (w), July 27, 1867 - Dec. 4, 1941
        Dau. of Abner and Anna Hileman Wright
KING, Gilbert F., 1888-1954
CASH, Charlie A., 1886-1948
        Son of Samuel L. and Margaret Ann Smith Cash
CASH, Charles W., 1921-1964
        Son of Chas. A. and Lillie King Cash

HARRIS, Pinkston, 1854-1920
HARRIS, Lueretia, 1855-1928
HARRIS, Jason, 1880-1941

GUINN, Pattie, 1842-1935

BAILEY, Mary Jane, Aug. 12, 1857 - Aug. 4, 1930
          Dau. of Albert and Susie Riddle
          Wife of Alfred Bailey

BLANKENSHIP, W. G., April 23, 1865 - Nov. 5, 1910

COFFEE, Robert Gillam, 1882-1964
COFFIE, Mary, 1886-1969
O'BRINE, Kenneth Reed, 1941 - 1945
O'BRINE, Janice, 1942-1945
COFFEE, McKenley D., b/d 1939 - Son of Ray & Rosa Harris Coffee
COFFEY, Joe, Jan. 18, 1916 - Oct. 28, 1918
          Son of R. G. and Mary Coffey

HAREN, Zeb Glynn, Feb. 23, 1880 - April 21, 1946
HAREN, Lou Peterson (w), March 14, 1880 - May 13, 1963
HAREN, E. P. (Dau.), March 4, 1917 -

HAMPTON, W. S., 1886-1945
HAMPTON, Gertha T. (w), 1894-1974
HAMPTON, Hazel Frances (Dau.), Aug. 1, 1917 - Oct. 12, 1918
HAMPTON, Lary, April 15, 1919 - Feb. 27, 1921
HAMPTON, Woodard, 1924-1929 - Son of W.S. & Gertha Tipton Hampton
HAMPTON, Parley, March 5, 1921 - Feb. 27, 1926
          Son of W. S. & Gertha Tipton Hampton
HAMPTON, Delia, March 5, 1898 - Aug. 17, 1928
          Dau. of Dan and Hannah Hampton

SCOTT, J. S., Oct. 7, 1863 - Nov. 4, 1939
SCOTT, Mary, Jan. 7, 1870 - Nov. 3, 1947

ALLEN, Jasper C., Aug. 12, 1870 - Jan. 13, 1932
          Son of R. H. and Sarah McInturff Allen
ALLEN, Edna (w), July 11, 1871 - Nov. 30, 1946
          Dau. of Wm. H. and Deanie Harris Edwards
ALLEN, Edna Elizabeth, Nov. 24, 1922 - April 18, 1946

HENSLEY, Mrs. Mary,

BANNER, Lindy Hensley,

HENSLEY, Sallie, April 16, 1841 - March 9, 1925

LETTERMAN, Noah W., March 30, 1877 - March 11, 1916
LETTERMAN, Hannah, May 7, 1874 - Nov. 28, 1958

HUSKINS, W. M., April 28, 1859 - May 19, 1926
          Son of John and Jane Grindstaff Huskins
HUSKINS, Jane G. (w), Sept. 19, 1861 - Dec. 21, 1944
HUSKINS, James H., 1882-1946
HUSKINS, Alice G. (w), 1879-1921
HUSKINS, Ella C., 1906-1955

GRINDSTAFF, Wilson, April 12, 1864 - Feb. 23, 1865
GRINDSTAFF, Mary, Nov. 18, 1828 - Dec. 22, 1915

WILLIAMS, S. Vanus, Nov. 15, 1863 - Jan. 13, 1949
WILLIAMS, Bessie (w), Feb. 14, 1884 - Aug. 2, 1958
        Daughter of George and Lizzie Hampton
WILLIAMS, Jesse (Son), Oct. 10, 1911 - Nov. 26, 1914
WILLIAMS, Dollie (Dau.), Oct. 27, 1913 - Dec. 21, 1918
WILLIAMS, Oliver, Jan. 24, 1907 - Oct. 16, 1926

WALDROP, Martha, June 14, 1872 - April 17, 1938
        Daughter of Henry and --------Riddle Foster

LLOYD, Margaret F., June 6, 1850 - Sept. 2, 1929
        Daughter of Bill and --------Tittle Foster

THOMPKINS, Harriett Foster, June 23, 1864 - April 14, 1940

WELBORN, John R., May 16, 1823 - Sept. 8, 1898
WELBORN, Nancy S. (w), April 27, 1826 - Dec. 2, 1907
FREEMAN, Maggie Welborn, Aug. 12, 1870 - Feb. 19, 1927
        Wife of J. A. Freeman
        (Plus large stone face down in center of plot)

HUGHES, Rachel, Jan. 6, 1862 - June 8, 1922 - Wife of W.M.Hughes
HUGHES, Clifford, May 19, 1909 - July 4, 1910
        Son of T. N. and D. B. Hughes
HUGHES, William Henry, Nov. 2, 1920 - Aug. 20, 1921
        Son of T. N. and D. B. Hughes

WILLIAMS, Archabold F., Feb. 20, 1887 - June 21, 1928
        Son of J. A. and Rachel Williams
WILLIAMS, Nancy E. (w), 1892-1982
WILLIAMS, Leoney, Aug. 14, 1912 - Dec. 19, 1915
        Daughter of Archabold F. and Nancy E. Williams
WILLIAMS, Leatey, Aug. 20, 1914 - Oct. 31, 1915
        Daughter of Archabold F. and Nancy E. Williams

BANNER, I. W., 1874-1930
        (Isaac Wm.) Son of Matt and Mollie Crosswhite Banner

BURGESS, Roy, Aug. 24, 1899 - Oct. 20, 1914
BURGESS, E. Dalton, May 8, 1869 - July 5, 1917

PARR, Rufus Calvin, 1878-1966
PARR, Mary Jane (w), 1888-1941
PARR, George W. (Son), Nov. 24, 1913 - Oct. 6, 1916

FOX, Charles B., 1885-1935
FOX, Mary E., 1886-1974
FOX, Charles S., 1908-1919
FOX, Gwendolyne, 1912-1924
FOX, Earl W., Jan. 30, 1912 - Dec. 1, 1912
        Son of M. A. and C. P. Fox
FOX, Otho E., 1910-1970
FOX, Belle M., 1909-1950
TAYLOR, Louise Fox, April 22, 1915 - March 12, 1939

BAILEY, Theodore, Oct. 21, 1933 - Nov. 21, 1933
BAILEY, Ross, Aug. 13, 1934 - March 18, 1935
        Sons of Bernie C. and Pearl T. Bailey

ALLEN, John Wesley, Aug. 17, 1900 - Sept. 28, 1963
        Son of Isaac G. and Emma Bradshaw Allen
ALLEN, Willie May (w), Sept. 26, 1902 - Sept. 28, 1963
        Daughter of Chas. Edward and Delcenia Salea Johnson

WILLIAMS, A. S., March 23, 1861 - Jan. 13, 1936
WILLIAMS, Hester (w), April 23, 1859 - Dec. 6, 1940

WESTALL, Thomas B., 1880-1918
WESTALL, Mary E. (w), 1879-1952
        Daughter of Henry and Lucretia Boone Butner
WESTALL, Hurman (Son), Aug. 23, 1909 - Nov. 24, 1914

WILLIAMS, Jeff, Oct. 24, 1889 - July 12, 1918

FURCHES, W. T., 1871-1936
FURCHES, Renie J. (w#1), April 19, 1870 - Feb. 4, 1919
FURCHES, Nancie (w#2), b. May 2, 1882
FURCHES, Samuel, b. May 4, 1926
FURCHES, Ruth, July 5, 1920 - May 19, 1927
        Daughter of W. T. and Nancy Engle Furches

TIPTON, George, April 29, 1919 - Jan. 27, 1958 - Cpl. AAF, WWII
TIPTON, Clifton Robert, Nov. 29, 1940 - Dec. 3, 1940
        Son of George and Jessie Lee Gilbert Tipton

HUGHES, Dora, 1892-1956
        Daughter of Henry Bert and Venia Riddle Foster

CLAYTON, Otis P., 1893-1922

PHILLIPS, Pearl, July 15, 1901 - Aug. 10, 1901
        Daughter of Mr. and Mrs. J. H. Phillips

JONES, Kathrine, 1857-1929 - Wife of R. P. Jones

SHEHAN, Elizabeth, June 22, 1870 - June 6, 1910

GARLAND, William, Aug. 6, 1864 - June 10, 1915

McINTOSH, Roy, 1921-1923 - Half brother of Wm. J. Jones, Sr.
JONES, Roda, 1896-1924 - Mother of Wm. J. Jones, Sr.

HAMPTON, Elizabeth, Feb. 6, 1878 - Nov. 10, 1927

YELTON, Mrs. Effie Isabel Bailey, May 12, 1893 - Jan. 22, 1917

TIPTON, Steve, Nov. 22, 1883 - April 18, 1942
TIPTON, Mayrean, Dec. 31, 1916 - June 8, 1924
TIPTON, Rosie Bell, d. Aug. 13, 1923 - age 32 years

TAPP, Mrs. Mary, 1879 - March 27, 1937
        Daughter of Harrison and Jude Banner Harris

HAMMITT, Patricia M., b/d 1947 - Dau. of Albert & George Ann
                                Tapp Hammitt

JONES, Elmer, Dec. 12, 1912 - Dec. 16, 1924
        Son of A. H. and C. M. Jones

CAYSEL, Ernest W., March 25, 1913 - May 1, 1913
        Son of J. W. and M. E. Caysel

PARKER, Handy, June 14, 1881 - Nov. 13, 1958
        Son of Martin Parker
PARKER, Essie S. (w), 1895 - April 1952

LONG, John W., d. July 24, 1939 - Pvt. 37 US Vol. Inf.

McVAY, Silas, 1879-1928
McVAY, Della, 1883-1971

BENNETT, Walter L., April 12, 1923 - Oct. 22, 1925
        Son of Johnnie and Annie Bennett

BAILEY, Elbert L., 1848-1935 - Son of Jessee & Millie Curtiss
BAILEY, Sarrah Vista, 1866-1940                        Bailey
        Daughter of Eliza Street

TAPP, Ollie, April 20, 1905 - Dec. 9, 1930

COOPER, Dave, 1896-1967
COOPER, Joe S., Aug. 14, 1893 - Nov. 1935

LEDFORD, Troy E., July 8, 1900 - May 24, 1917
        Son of Joseph A. and Mary J. Ledford

JOHNSON, Dorthy Evelyn, Sept. 7, 1925 - June 28, 1930
        Daughter of Sherman and Alice Britt Johnson

BRYANT, Lea, May 25, 1914 - May 16, 1932

PARKER, Elijah M., July 25, 1875 - July 27, 1968
PARKER, Daisy J. (w), Jan. 8, 1885 - April 28, 1970
PARKER, Virgie Mae, 1909-1911
PARKER, Dollie, b/d 1911
PARKER, Annie, b/d 1913
PARKER, Mollie, b/d 1919

NOLAND, Valda H., Feb. 16, 1897 - Dec. 11, 1910

BARNETT, Sara, 1896-1925
BARNETT, Infant, b/d 1925
LAWS, Rebecca, 1869-1940

TITTLE, Mary C., April 1, 1851 - March 7, 1912
  Wife of John Tittle - Maiden name "FOSTER"
TITTLE, Gladis Irean, July 1, 1901 - Aug. 14, 1914
  Daughter of Frank and Rose Anna Salts Tittle
TITTLE, Rose Anna, Sept. 30, 1875 - Feb. 27, 1931
  Daughter of Tom and Sarah Williams Salts,
  Wife of George Franklin Tittle
TITTLE, Elmer E., Aug. 16, 1912 - May 9, 1927
  Son of Frank Tittle and Rose Anna Salts Tittle
TITTLE, Bobby Lee, Aug. 23, 1940 - Nov. 21, 1944
  Son of Troy and Dessie Shehan Tittle

SAMS, Woodward, d. 1913 - Son of Bessie Sams

EDWARDS, Jason, 1883-1940
EDWARDS, Bessie, 1890-1973
EDWARDS, Jason M., Aug. 12, 1908 - Aug. 27, 1964- Pvt.35 Inf.,WWII
  Son of Asbury and Cora Lee Pate Edwards
EDWARDS, Walter P. B., June 6, 1912 - July 4, 1960, Pvt., WWII
  Son of Asbury and Cora Lee Pate Edwards

COLEY, Jeffrey L., 1959-1966
ANDERS, Elbert G., 1868-1947 - Son of Rosa & Rachel Hampton Anders
ANDERS, Martha E. (w), 1872-1937
ANDERS, Elsie (Dau.), March 22, 1906 - April 6, 1923

PIERCY, Stanley Virginia, April 20, 1921 - July 29, 1979

LAWING, Stanley, April 22, 1900 - Sept. 6, 1920
LAWING, June, Dec. 22, 1898 - Feb. 6, 1985

WILLIAMS, Dave, June 17, 1896 - April 1, 1971 - Pvt., 56 Inf.,WWI
WILLIAMS, Martha, 1904-1985
WILLIAMS, Tereley, Feb. 6, 1921 - Jan. 23, 1923

THOMAS, W. Clifford, May 21, 1905 - June 30, 1943
THOMAS, Sarah Jane (w), Oct. 5, 1905 -

USIALIS, William, May 6, 1890 - June 7, 1944 - Pvt. 5 Div., WWI

LEWIS, Robert H., April 19, 1855 - Aug. 31, 1945
LEWIS, Ban Hensley, Sept. 13, 1867 - May 22, 1943
  Wife of H. R. Lewis
LEWIS, Elizabeth, Nov. 25, 1837 - Aug. 2, 1922 - Wife of M.A.Lewis

WILLIAMS, J. W., Oct. 16, 1888 - May 11, 1923
WILLIAMS, Dora (w), d. Aug. 30, 1922 - age 24 years
WILLIAMS, William, Son of Willis Williams
WILLIAMS, Willis W., Aug. 11, 1950 - March 14, 1970
   Pvt., 6TNG Bn., Vietnam
WILLIAMS, Cornelia A., b.Sept. 17, 1900 - Wife of Henry Williams
BAILEY, Hudson, Nov. 11, 1931 - May 15, 1933

MATHES, Loda, May 15, 1875 - Aug. 29, 1936
MATHES, Lula Foster (w), April 12, 1887 - Feb. 26, 1922

MARTINS CREEK CEMETERY (continued)

MASTERS, Ramel Howard, Sept. 26, 1914 -
MASTERS, Hazel Lee, Sept. 19, 1923 - May 13, 1977
MASTERS, Estes B., May 24, 1891 - Aug. 16, 1967
MASTERS, Anna Lee, Sept. 1, 1892 - Dec. 5, 1976
MASTERS, Ralph Edgar, Jan. 18, 1919 - Dec. 28, 1973
        Sgt., US Air Force, WWII
MASTERS, Shirley, Aug. 28, 1935 - Feb. 1, 1936

HENSLEY, Mary J., 1908-1934

RUNION, W. T. (Tommy), Oct. 22, 1889 - Dec. 2, 1958
        Son of George and Nan Gillis Runion
RUNION, Lydia M. Coffie (w), July 18, 1890 - May 24, 1974

LANCE, Rube, Feb. 28, 1878 - June 10, 1955
LANCE, Lulie M., Jan. 5, 1888 - April 25, 1966

WALDROP, W. B., Nov. 13, 1863 - Oct. 12, 1934

RIDDLE, Mollie Gouge, Nov. 11, 1889 - Feb. 22, 1923

GARLAND, Augustus, Feb. 24, 1872 - March 13, 1945
GARLAND, Adina Griffith (w), Feb. 4, 1872 - April 28, 1957
GARLAND, Herman D., July 14, 1911 - July 29, 1937
GARLAND, Myrtle, April 21, 1903 - Sept. 6, 1921
RICHARDSON, Ruth Kitty, Oct. 6, 1913 - Feb. 3, 1960
        Daughter of Augustus G. and Adina Griffith Garland
ERWIN, Verna M., Sept. 23, 1894 - Jan. 27, 1923
WILSON, Lowell Gene, Aug. 8, 1934 - Sept. 23, 1934

BARNETT, Leonard J., 1910-1974 - TEC 5, US Army
BARNETT, William Ted (Son), Sept. 23, 1934 - Oct. 9, 1934
BARNETT, Marion, 1868-1947
BARNETT, Ellen M. (w), 1876-1951
BARNETT, Marie (Dau.), May 17, 1917 - April 19, 1921

HONEYCUTT, Dora Lee, Sept. 3, 1873 - Jan. 21, 1968
McCRACKEN, Joe T., March 16, 1912 - Aug. 9, 1968

HIGGINS, Nellie Hughes, Sept. 3, 1902 - Feb. 1, 1981

HOPSON, William C., Co. D, 3NC Mtd. Inf., Union Army
HOPSON, Martha Jane, Dec. 25, 1851 - Oct. 24, 1924
HOPSON(?), Little Jack, June 28, 1919 - Sept. 29, 1921
        No family name on stone

HARRIS, Samuel Isaac, June 6, 1903 - Dec. 6, 1977
HARRIS, Bessie J., -
HARRIS, Willard (Son), March 29, 1927 - May 17, 1927

ADKINS, Samuel H., d. Oct. 19, 1957
        Son of Dennis Hoyt and Macie Imogene Harris Adkins

LEWIS, Theodore, 1883-1962 - Son of Wm. Lewis
LEWIS, Ida B., 1885-1928
FANNING, Heather Marie, b/d 1976
          Plus 3 stones "Infant" within plot

PHILLIPS, James H., 1873-1961
PHILLIPS, Alice (w), 1881-1966

CAPPS, William M., May 9, 1842 - March 11, 1921
          Co. H, 3 NC Mtd. Inf., Union Army
CAPPS, Sarah (w), May 9, 1852 - 1922

GILBERT, Carl R., June 4, 1898 - March 27, 1982
GILBERT, Melda P. (w), Dec. 19, 1898 -
GILBERT, Edward (Son), April 17, 1919 - Feb. 27, 1921

PETERSON, Grover, 1879-1933
PETERSON, Geneva Treaty (w), March 2, 1882 - May 13, 1960
PETERSON, Pearl, 1900-1934 - Dau. of Grover & Treatie Jones Peterson

WHITE, Charlie C., March 30, 1888 - Aug. 19, 1949
          Pvt. 5 Cav., WWI (?)
WHITE, Jennie M. (w), March 22, 1889 - Feb. 11, 1965
WHITE, Chas. Jr. (Son), May 20, 1915 - Sept. 15, 1915

HARRIS, William M., Sept. 9, 1881 - June 4, 1959
          Son of Harrison and Judy Banner Harris
HARRIS, Jossie (w), Jan. 2, 1885 - Jan. 22, 1968
HARRIS, Linda (Dau.), Sept. 25, 1920 - Jan. 23, 1926
HARRIS, George, March 6, 1917 - Jan. 12, 1979
HARRIS, Harry H., Oct. 15, 1910 - June 15, 1951
HARRIS, Ulise, Dec. 18, 1918 - Nov. 17, 1948 - PFC, 393 Inf, WWII
          Son of W. M. and Jane Hampton Harris

STRICKLAND, Ressie L., May 26, 1896 - Aug. 6, 1985
STRICKLAND, Helen, April 26, 1918 -
STRICKLAND, Charles, Sept. 3, 1909 -
STRICKLAND, Mary, March 25, 1908 - Feb. 2, 1981

TILSON, Jesse F., Sept. 26, 1889 - Feb. 9, 1971
TILSON, Mamie Higgins, Nov. 11, 1895 - Sept. 18, 1980
TILSON, Jesse Dwight, April 21, 1920 - March 24, 1946
TILSON, Dellar May, June 27, 1916 - Aug. 19, 1923

STRICKLAND, D. N., July 24, 1867 - Oct. 4, 1948
          Son of Wm. and Lucretia Need Strickland
STRICKLAND, Madge M. (w), Jan. 15, 1877 - May 10, 1935
STRICKLAND, Earl R. (Son), b/d Sept. 6, 1920

TITTLE, Walter A., b. Nov. 7, 1892 -
TITTLE, Lucy M., April 15, 1898 - Jan. 25, 1959
TITTLE, Luther James, Dec. 24, 1920 - Dec. 27, 1946
TITTLE, Lula Mae, Sept. 28, 1927 - Jan. 20, 1947

BAXTER, Lorenzo D., Sept. 12, 1884 - July 23, 1970
BAXTER, Elizabeth (w), Feb. 23, 1886 - Aug. 23, 1970
BAXTER, Gene Edward, March 27, 1927 - Dec. 16, 1969
       PFC, M. P. Co., WWII

POPE, William E., 1878-1931 - Son of Pat Pope
POPE, John R., Co, F, 59 Tenn. Mtd. Inf. - Confederate Army
DUNCAN, Ibbie Pope, March 27, 1888 - Dec. 31, 1981
FOSTER, Sallie Bailey, d. April 18, 1920 - age 61 years
       Wife of H. B. Foster

BAXTER, John Kenneth, March 11, 1914 - Nov. 25, 1958, USNR, WWII
BAXTER, Little Joe, June 21, 1916 - June 24, 1916
       Son of L. D. and E. R. Baxter

RUTHERFORD, Lisa Gay, July 9, 1960 - Oct. 10, 1960

HARRIS, John Henry, Jan. 23, 1885 - Oct. 30, 1969
HARRIS, Mary Frances, Aug. 12, 1888 - May 10, 1946
       Daughter of Thomas Marion and Clara Allen Smith

LAWING, W. A. "Dock", Aug. 6, 1876 - Dec. 4, 1959
LAWING, Parlee Alford (w), July 24, 1887 - Dec. 19, 1975
LAWING, Page (Son), d. March 20, 1923 (Infant)
LAWING, Paul (Son), 1909-1919
LAWING, Lucinda, d. May 19, 1920 - age 77

COOPER, Mose, Feb. 13, 1900 - March 2, 1985
COOPER, Nell (w), May 2, 1910 -
COOPER, Theodore (Son), Sept. 26, 1928 - Aug. 16, 1930
STALLINGS, Edd, 1873-1954

THOMAS, Pearl Lee. Jan. 14, 1901 - July 30, 1917
       Wife of Bill Thomas

SQUIBB, Margaret Lou, April 14, 1861 - Oct. 27, 1939
       Daughter of -----Jamison and Hettie McCracken Jamison
WILLIAMS, G. C., 1866-1920
WILLIAMS, Fannie Hensley, 1870-19--
WILLIAMS, Ruth, Nov. 6, 1903 - Dec. 5, 1926

MILLER, Hyder R., Jan. 8, 1896 - May 13, 1960
MILLER, Cecil, Dec. 29, 1900 - March 10, 1920

JOHNSON, Ivery, April 11, 1890 - Sept. 26, 1918
JOHNSON, Georgia (w), b. Aug. 11, 1891 -
JOHNSON, Robert C. (Son), 1918-1928
JOHNSON, J. Theodore C. (Son), 1914-1928
JOHNSON, Delcenia, 1868-1954
       Daughter of James and Martha Henderson Sales
HOYLE, William E., July 20, 1932 - Aug. 2, 1970 - Cpl, US Army,Korea
SMITH, Cordia J., July 29, 1899 - Oct. 28, 1986

NORRIS, Charlie Thomas, 1890-1952
NORRIS, Addie Johnson, 1897-1943
        Daughter of Edward and Delcenia Sell (Sales?) Johnson
NORRIS, Richard, b/d 1918
NORRIS, Lila Jean, 1927-1928

FOSTER, Bernie C., July 10, 1911 - Oct. 18, 1956
        Son of Arthur and Cordia Johnson Foster
FOSTER, Viola E. (w), March 4, 1914 -
        Daughter of J. K. and Lula Jarvis Erwin

ENGLE, Isaac G., b. Aug. 22, 1880 - Son of A.B. & Sarah Hensley Engle
ENGLE, Lockie Ann (w), Aug. 28, 1883 - Dec. 7, 1945
        Daughter of P. J. and Lucindia Tipton Briggs

WORSHAM, Thelma M., 1902-1919, Dau. of W.J. & Myra M. Worsham
        Plus 2 illegible stones in same plot

FANNING, Ruby Lee, Feb. 3, 1888 - Aug. 15, 1919

GARLAND, John L., 1885-1950
        Son of Wm. N. and Martha Miller Garland
GARLAND, Credy H. (w), 1885-1942
GARLAND, William, Sept. 3, 1909 - Nov. 18, 1949
        Tec 5, US Army, WWII
GARLAND, William, Aug. 6, 1864 - June 10, 1951
GARLAND, Martha Miller (w), April 15, 1867 - Sept. 24, 1948
MATHES, Belle Garland, Sept. 25, 1905 - Sept. 26, 1935
        Daughter of John L. and Crety Honeycutt Garland

GARLAND, Roy Thomas, July 22, 1898 -
GARLAND, Roberta Poore (w), Oct. 7, 1896 - Jan. 15, 1981
DUNCAN, Mae, July 12, 1916 - April 20, 1920
        Daughter of S. D. and Ella Duncan

PRICE, Stward, Oct. 5, 1919 - Oct. 10, 1937
        (Stuart) Son of Sam and Clercie Cooper Price
PRICE, Martin, March 27, 1921 - May 23, 1941

HARRISON, William, "Chief Little Bear", Sioux Indian
          d.Mar.8,1929            Medicine Man
COOPER, Martin,d. April 24, 1921, Pvt. 11 Inf. 5 Div.
COOPER, Sam, d. 1936
COOPER, Naomi, d. 1921

PRICE, Samuel, April 4, 1886 - Feb. 21, 1972
PRICE, Clarsie (w), Dec. 4, 1896 - Feb. 9, 1982

MONFALCONE, Ethel Harrison, Nov. 13, 1896 - Sept. 1, 1986
HARRISON, Alice, April 12, 1904 - June 4, 1905
        Daughter of Mr. and Mrs. E. N. Harrison
HARRISON, Callie Love, 1880-1958
        Daughter of Wm. C. and Cena Emmert Love
LOVE, William C., 1852-1926
LOVE, Delcena E. (w), 1858-19-- , Dau. of W.C. & -----Renshaw
                                          Emmert

MARTINS CREEK CEMETERY (continued)

KERNS, Charles H., Oct. 11, 1899 - Nov. 29, 1963
        Son of Wm. Ellsworth & Myrtie Jane Rogers Kerns
KERNS, Laura Love, March 26, 1902 - Dec. 15, 1942
        Daughter of Wm. Pinkton & Minnie Jane Williams Love

MILLER, Robert N., 1861-1940
MILLER, Lillie B., 1859-1923
MOON, Mary Miller, July 2, 1887 - Nov. 10, 1982

JONES, Bud, 1888-1978
JONES, Eliza Jane (w), 1890-1957
        Daughter of James Madison and Nancy Sams Foster
JONES, Dorothy Sue, 1922-1924
JONES, Douglas, Aug. 30, 1934 - Oct. 28, 1934

BROUGHMAN, Alice, d. Dec. 12, 1950
        Daughter of Joe and Virginia Smith Cash

MATHES, Phillip, 1963-1983

CHURCH, William "Bill", 1882-1942(?)
        Son of Henry and Susie Estep Church
CHURCH, Polly Miller (w), 1875-1942 - Daughter of Timothy Miller
CHURCH, Sara May, 1910-1924

HORTON, David M., 1844-1924

GUINN, Marion Pierce, Aug. 16, 1897 -
GUINN, Florence (w), June 7, 1901 - Nov. 10, 1987
GUINN, Virginia Lee (Dau.), Sept. 15, 1926 - Oct. 23, 1928

MASTERS, Abraham L., Nov. 6, 1861 - Oct. 12, 1941
MASTERS, Delia Hoyle (w), July 2, 1873 - Feb. 6, 1941
MASTERS, Melvina, Oct. 13, 1859 - May 3, 1862
NORRIS, William O., June 30, 1883 - Sept. 1, 1924

MILLER, Ernest, Dec. 5, 1901 - Jan. 2, 1964

WEBB, Landon C., April 10, 1876 - Jan. 29, 1941
WEBB, Hester Lewis (w), b. May 30, 1866 -
WEBB, Oscar, April 10, 1898 - Jan. 9, 1929
BOONE, Earnest P., 1915-1965

KEERL, William L., Co. G, 2 Va. Inf., Confederate Army

BLANKENSHIP, Floyd, May 11, 1895 - Sept. 26, 1974
BLANKENSHIP, Glenna M., May 30, 1900 - May 5, 1952
        Daughter of Grant and Emma Capps Masters

WEBB, Cris, Aug. 3, 1886 - Oct. 29, 1967
WEBB, Snow B. (w), Dec. 25, 1890 - March 11, 1971
WEBB, May, Nov. 9, 1908 - Oct. 5, 1925

ROBERTS, Fielden Beex, Dec. 28, 1874 - April 17, 1949
        Son of Francis and Margaret Kegley Roberts
        Pvt., 38 US Vol. Inf.
ROBERTS, Lydia Ann (w), April 9, 1874 - Feb. 3, 1949
ROBERTS, Child, Aug. 6, 1906 - Sept. 21, 1924

TIPTON, Mark, March 25, 1858 - March 26, 1938
TIPTON, Mary T. (w), Dec. 15, 1886 - Nov. 23, 1962
TIPTON, Dave, June 20, 1905 - Oct. 2, 1984
TIPTON, Zettie (w), April 6, 1910 - Feb. 15, 1978
TIPTON, William F., May 4, 1942 - July 27, 1942

RUNNION, Thomas Cling, June 28, 1855 - June 25, 1930
        Son of Thomas L. and Betty Harris Runnion
RUNNION, Sue Guinn (w), March 28, 1875 - April 23, 1957
        Daughter of Wm. and Mary Jane Woodward Guinn
RUNNION, Frank Toney, May 7, 1891 - Sept. 13, 1925
RUNNION, Dora Sparks (w), Sept. 9, 1892 - Feb. 26, 1932
        Daughter of Henry and Lagentie Harris Sparks

SHELTON, Southwick W., Aug. 10, 1891 - Dec. 27, 1976
        Sgt. US Army, WWI
SHELTON, Deane S. (w), Feb. 3, 1902 -

STRICKLAND, John F., Dec. 13, 1899 - Feb. 12, 1968
STRICKLAND, Kate B. (w), Feb. 1, 1905 -
STRICKLAND, Barbara Anne, Aug. 14, 1936 - April 16, 1940 (Dau.)

POE, James Euel, April 16, 1930 - Sept. 25, 1987, Cpl, US Army
                                                         Korea
CRAIN, Mack D., 1891-1942
        Son of Wm. and Emaline Higgins Crain
CRAIN, Texie, 1894-1980

HIGGINS, W. M., b. April 4, 1856 -
HIGGINS, Susana (w), Feb. 12, 1859 - July 15, 1932
        Daughter of Andy and Polly Wilson Crain

HONEYCUTT, Christopher C., 1886-1965
HONEYCUTT, Lillie Adkins (w), 1891-1947
HONEYCUTT, Arvel Lee (Son), Oct. 25, 1925 - Nov. 25, 1925

CARTER, Robert Daniel, d. Oct. 6, 1951
        Son of Sgt. and Mrs. R. S. Carter

RUNNION, Dana Harmon, Dec. 30, 1898 - Sept. 30, 1961
        Son of Thomas Cling and Sue Guinn Runnion
RUNNION, Mary Ethel, March 5, 1900 - Nov. 10, 1980
RUNNION, William Dana, Sept. 19, 1921 - Oct. 30, 1940
        Son of Dana and Mary P. Runnion

MARTINS CREEK CEMETERY (continued)

McCURRY, Ernest, Sept. 15, 1899 – March 18, 1973
McCURRY, Ethel (w#1), July 16, 1902 – Nov. 12, 1924
McCURRY, Pearl (w#2), May 25, 1908 –
McCURRY, Ruby, April 12, 1924 – Nov. 26, 1924
McCURRY, Beulah, 1928-1930
McCURRY, Gail, b/d 1939
          Daughter of Ernest and Pearl Fender McCurry

LONGMIRE, Rhoda, Dec. 11, 1815 – March 11, 1857
          Consort of Charles Longmire
McENTURFF, Mary, d. Sept. 1, 1857 – Consort of John McEnturff

CRAIN, Joe, Aug. 22, 1878 – May 8, 1927
          Son of Sm. and Emeline Higgins Crane
CRAIN, Dora Higgins, April 17, 1883 – July 16, 1951
CRAIN, Frank, July 18, 1899 – July 9, 1943

PARKER, Susan C., Feb. 15, 1846 – Jan. 27, 1939
PARKER, Child, April 30, 1909 – June 2, 1928
          Daughter of Mr. and Mrs. W. S. Parker

HARVEY, Etta –

LEDFORD, Charley, May 7, 1903 – July 15, 1934
          Son of Alford and M. Tipton Ledford

ROBERTS, W. A., 1874-1938
ROBERTS, Nancy Elizabeth, May 4, 1874 – Oct. 13, 1961
ROBERTS, Isaac R., 1879-1954
ROBERTS, Alcy Lee, 1876-1941

BANNER, William, March 12, 1862 – April 24, 1933
BANNER, James Monroe, Feb. 20, 1891 – Sept. 27, 1972
BANNER, Mary E. Harris (w), July 5, 1897 – Nov. 28, 1924

POORE, James David, Nov. 22, 1857 – Oct. 14, 1935
POORE, Dealie Edwards (w), Jan. 7, 1858 – Sept. 12, 1949
STORY, Hattie, Sept. 8, 1894 – Jan. 27, 1925

ARROWOOD, Arlene, 1938-1939 – Dau. of Bernie & Judie Poore Arrowood

ARRWOOD, Eugene, June 19, 1934 – Dec. 23, 1937
          Child of Bernie and Judy Poore Arrowood

PETERSON, Rebecca Lynn, b/d 1974

KEGLEY, Wade H., Feb. 1, 1891 – Nov. 13, 1976
KEGLEY, Harold W., April 1, 1913 – Oct. 22, 1927
          Son of Wm. Kegley

WHALEY, Virginia Lee, Aug. 12, 1931 – Sept. 24, 1931
          Daughter of Charlie and Rebecca Mashburn Whaley

TIPTON, Meade B., 1904-1975
TIPTON, Opal I., 1908-1977

HAMMITT, Valdean, 1926 - 1927 - Dau. of W.H. & ----Gentry Hamm.

TIPTON, Ada M., Aug. 6, 1914 - April 24, 1984

HIGGINS, Turner, 1870-1954
HIGGINS, Jane (w), 1868-1957

MASHBURN, Clyde, Oct. 8, 1909 - Nov. 4, 1957 - USNR, WWII
MASHBURN, Bertha (w), Nov. 25, 1909 -
MASHBURN, J. L., 1877-1929
MASHBURN, Nancy (w), May 2, 1887 - Sept. 17, 1976
MASHBURN, Helen, (Dau.), b/d 1928

THOMAS, Grady L., d. April 12, 1930 - Pvt. 117 Inf., 30 Div.
        Son of Wm. and Viola Renfro Thomas
THOMAS, Ruby, June 11, 1924 - April 15, 1926
        Daughter of Grady and Mary Ollis Thomas
BOONE, Pollie O., 1900-1986
        Married 1st, Grady Thomas - Married 2nd, Sam Boone

PETERSON, Mosses C., b. June 4, 1861 -
        Son of Reuben and Polly Hampton Peterson
PETERSON, Sarah A. (w), April 10, 1862 - Feb. 2, 1925

EDWARDS, Happy, Oct. 25, 1908 - April 25, 1984

FANNING, Little Alvin, May 3, 1925 - April 10, 1925
        Son of Mr. and Mrs. Fransco Fanning

GILBERT, Ida G., April 26, 1894 - Sept. 4, 1980
GILBERT, W. T., Dec. 3, 1921 - March 30, 1943 - PFC, US Army
GILBERT, Earl A. Jr., March 5, 1925 -
GILBERT, Helen, Nov. 20, 1920 - Nov. 5, 1979
GILBERT, D. B., 1915 -
GILBERT, Hazel, (w), 1917 - 1969

WILLIAMS, William P., Feb. 13, 1883 - April 19, 1974
WILLIAMS, Ethel J., June 6, 1886 - May 23, 1927
WILLIAMS, William L., March 18, 1924 - Jan. 27, 1968
WILLIAMS, Virginia Ethel, May 16, 1927 - Aug. 26, 1927

BOONE, James K., 1908-1973

EDWARDS, Donald Harvey, 1921-1979 - PFC, US Army

JOHNSON, James Earl, June 19, 1903 - Feb. 22, 1983
JOHNSON, Sarah Augusta, March 2, 1904 -

LOVE, James M., 1858-1930 - Son of Wm. & Nancy Hartsell Love
LOVE, Maggie W., 1862-1946

HAMMITT, Etta E., 1900-1978

TITTLE, J. Frank, Feb. 20, 1883 - April 7, 1949
TITTLE, Eletha, May 13, 1916 - Aug. 8, 1932
    (Leitha Lillian), Daughter of Ike & Blanch Loyd Tittle
TITTLE, Sarah Alice, d. May 3, 1927 - age 63 years
    Daughter of Tom and Emma Chandler Foster

EDWARDS, Andrew E., March 13, 1881 - Dec. 13, 1967
EDWARDS, Marion, 1926-1940
CLOUSE, James M. Jr., 1917-1937
    Son of James Madison and Dora Belle Hensley Clouse
CLOUSE, James Madison, Sr., 1867-1927
CLOUSE, Dora B. (w), 1879-1963

GUINN, Ambrose, Dec. 5, 1852 - July 9, 1925
GUINN, Lennie Harris (w), Oct. 12, 1855 - Nov. 10, 1929
    Daughter of Marion and Ruhamie Hensley Harris
GUINN, Retta, April 9, 1881 - Sept. 20, 1957
    Daughter of Ambrose and Lennie Harris Guinn
GUINN, Callie (Sister of Retta), July 20, 1893 - May 8, 1982

FOSTER, Albert John, 1906-1978 - CM2, US Navy, WWII
FOSTER, Lucy B. (w), 1904-1982

BLANKENSHIP, Lewis Taylor, May 16, 1873 - Jan. 28, 1955
    Son of Jasper and Polly Runion Blankenship
BLANKENSHIP, Laura Elizabeth (w), Aug. 8, 1878 - April 28, 1946
    Daughter of W. W. and Lurena Murray Lawing
BLANKENSHIP, Herman Lee (Son), 1902-1930
BLANKENSHIP, Lenace Lillian (Dau.), May 28, 1907 - March 19, 1925

MEEK, Oscar S., June 17, 1886 - May 7, 1926
MEEK, Bessie E. Kilmer (w), June 23, 1893 - May 7, 1926
SCHWEGER, Ida M., May 3, 1916 - Jan. 19, 1973
HART, Lucy Meek, July 17, 1918 - Jan. 15, 1963
    Wife of Harold W. Hart
KILMER, George Henry, Sept. 27, 1898 - Aug. 10, 1966
    S2, US Navy, WWI
KILMER, Ulysses S., 1870-1968
KILMER, Lucy Ada (w), 1874-1950
    Daughter of John H. and Nancy Thompson Moore

WILSON, Marcus W., April 7, 1860 - Dec. 28, 1930
    Son of Samuel Wilson

HATCHER, J. A., 1864-1941
HATCHER, James W., Aug. 10, 1930 - April 4, 1972

RAY, G. C., 1875-1927
RAY, Nannie Belle, 1877-1957

PHILLIPS, Danny Wendell Jr., June 13, 1954 - Aug. 3, 1959

MARTINS CREEK CEMETERY (continued)

BOONE, Troy S., March 4, 1898 - Dec. 27, 1958
BOONE, Ollie C., Dec. 28, 1900 - June 25, 1978
BOONE, Raymond Ernest, Feb. 12, 1932 - June 5, 1955
        Son of Troy Boone - S/Sgt. 30th Air Div., Korea

FRENCH, George H., Feb. 28, 1878 - April 24, 1949
        Son of Preston and Sally Burton French
FRENCH, Roy E., March 19, 1908 - May 17, 1926

STRICKLAND, William C., Oct. 10, 1904 -
STRICKLAND, Florence (w), April 14, 1906 - Aug. 29, 1974
STRICKLAND, Randy (Son), 1957-1977

MARTINS CREEK CEMETERY - UNMARKED GRAVES

ADAMS, Chas. H., Boston, Mass., birthplace, d. Feb. 8, 1931

ADKINS, Janie, age 21, d. March 24, 1934

ANDERS, Isaac Grady, age 18, d. Sept. 21, 1933
        Son of Hazen and Levis Fletcher Anders

ANDERS, Rachel Mahala, age 80, d. June 16, 1930
        Daughter of Wm. and Melina Lisenbure Hampton

ANDERS, Stuart, age 46, d. July 24, 1959

ARROWOOD, Tony Dennie, Infant, d. March 29, 1960
        Son of Mack and Ethel Edith Hunter Arrowood

BAILEY, Anna Liza, b. Sept. 9, 1881, d. Aug. 3, 1950
        Daughter of Mannan and Jane Morris Bailey

BAILEY, Curtis, age 1 mo., d. Nov. 21, 1932
        Son of Burnie and Pearl Tipton Bailey

BAILEY, Sam, b. 1869, d. Jan. 5, 1932
        Son of Ancel and Mary Bailey

BAILEY, Virgie, age 6 mos., d. July 30, 1935
        Daughter of R. C. and Reba Prather Bailey

BAILEY, Virgil A., d. in Ind. on Dec. 22, 1957

BANNER, Infant, d. April 25, 1945
        Child of James Floyd and Mary Elizabeth Wilfong Banner

BANNER, John Frank, age 18, d. April 18, 1944
        Son of Martin L. and Linda Hensley Banner

BANNER, Linda Hensley, age 34, d. March 16, 1936
        Daughter of Zeb and Mary Taylor Hensley

BANNER, Mathison Lewis, age 82, d. Oct. 15, 1935
    Son of Lewis and Viona Whitson Banner

BANNER, Melvin Wesley, age 3, d. March 18, 1945
    Son of Junior E. Banner

BARNETT, T. C., age 82, d. Feb. 22, 1930
    Son of Dave and Hannah Stanley Barnett

BEAVER, Chas. McThaddus, age 72, d. Feb. 25, 1937
    Son of Stephen and Emily Williams Beaver

BEAVER, Georgia Cleo, age 3 mos., d. Oct. 27, 1946
    Daughter of Effie Beaver

BEAVER, Infant, d. Aug. 29, 1947 — Daughter of Effie Pearl Beaver

BENNETT, Lillian Tipton, age 23, d. Feb. 27, 1937
    Daughter of Walter and Bessie Bennett Tipton

BENNETT, Marie, Infant, d. July 8, 1943
    Daughter of Clarence and Inez Riddle Bennett

BENNETT, Rebecca Ann, 2 years, d. Nov. 17, 1950
    Daughter of Wm. and Mabel Ingram Bennett

BENNETT, Ruth, 3 years, d. May 7, 1935
    Daughter of Wm. and Mable Ingram Bennett

BOONE, Samuel, b. Sept. 9, 1879, d. March 31, 1957
    Son of Samuel and ----- Young Boone

BRACKINS, Seley, b. 1841, d. July 14, 1927

BRADY, Jennetta A., age 72, d. March 21, 1936
    Daughter of ------- Vandwater

BRIGGS, Hezekiah Hubert, age 40, d. Dec. 16, 1940
    Son of Wm. Milton and Hester Buckner Briggs

BRIGGS, Infant Daughter, d. Feb. 20, 1937
    Daughter of H. K. and Nellie Harren Briggs

BRIGGS, Norman Eugene, age 3, d. June 5, 1941
    Son of Hezekiah and Nellie Herren Briggs

BRYANT, Thomas Wesley, age 18, d. May 6, 1932
    Son of C. W. and Cordella McCurry Bryant

CAMPBELL, June Carolyn, Infant, d. July 21, 1935
    Dau. of Clarence Albert & Velma Mae Thompson Campbell

CAMPBELL, Elaine, Infant, d. June 2, 1933
    Daughter of Emmett and Julia Renfro Campbell

CASH, Mrs. Margaret Ann, age 78, d. March 6, 1928
      Daughter of John Smith

CLAYTON, John Wesley, age 74, d. April 14, 1937

CLAYTON, Mary, age 80, d. April 12, 1932
      Daughter of Manuel and Marion Wilson Austin

COOPER, John D., age 23, d. May 14, 1936
      Son of Samuel and Oma Tipton Cooper

COPELAND, Infant, d. July 19, 1945
      Child of Harrell Derring & Mildred Irene Parker Copeland

COX, Infant, d. Dec. 6, 1943
      Child of Wm. R. and Grace Parker Cox

CRABTREE, Julia Ann, Infant, d. Jan. 20, 1942
      Daughter of Garland and Virginia Higgins Crabtree

DAVIS, Bettie, d. Sept. 2, 1954

DEES, Infant, d. April 9, 1938
      Daughter of Paul and Nell Randolph Dees

DUGGER, (Not Named), b. Jan. 15, 1931, d. Jan. 16, 1931
      Child of M. M. and Mary Lou Miller Dugger

EDWARDS, Finetta, age 76, d. Sept. 9, 1939

EDWARDS, Mrs. Hester, age 79, d. July 8, 1939

EDWARDS, Infant, d. Nov. 17, 1934
      Child of Happy and Ruth Boone Edwards

EDWARDS, Johnie Kate, age 10 mos. d . Feb. 27, 1943
      Daughter of L. C. and Flossie Higgins Edwards

EDWARDS, Mitchell Paul, age 2 mos., d. Jan. 19, 1946
      Son of Lee Clifton and Flossie Higgins Edwards

EDWARDS, Robert Asbury, age 70, d. Feb. 17, 1951
      Son of Wilson and Finetta Harris Edwards

EDWARDS, Wm. A., age 78, d. July 18, 1946
      Son of Shelt Edwards

EDWARDS, Wilson, age 63, d. Feb. 11, 1932
      Son of Wilson Edwards, Sr.

ENGLE, Tony Michael, age 6 mos., d. Oct. 22, 1963
      Son of I. G. and Wilma Tinker Engle

ERWIN, Lela Pearl, age 46, d. April 27, 1935
      Daughter of W. and Rosa Jervis Callahan

FANNING, Ernestine, age 5, d. May 27, 1940
        Daughter of Wm. McKinley and Ollie Banner Fanning

FOSTER, Arthur, b. 1880, d. Feb. 7, 1929
        Son of Harriett Foster

FOSTER, Carolyn, age 12 days, d. Feb. 28, 1941
        Daughter of Orville and Stella Tipton Foster

FOSTER, H. B., b. 1859, d. Feb. 3, 1932
        Child of Carmen Foster

FRANKLIN, Mrs. Hester, b. June 3, 1861, d. Sept. 10, 1926
        Daughter of Joe and Millie Ray Waldrop

FRENCH, Annie Elizabeth, b. Aug. 1884, d. May 10, 1965
        Daughter of W. H. and Belle Robinson French

FURCHES, Marie May, age 2, d. June 3, 1927

GARDNER, Donna, age 20, d. Oct. 12, 1933
        Daughter of D. and Sally Forbes Gardner

GARLAND, Tom, b. Dec. 1897, d. Oct. 13, 1929
        Son of David and Sarah Jane Tipton Garland

GILLIS, Sue Marie, age 2, d. Oct. 28, 1932
        Daughter of Frank and Lula Sparks Gillis

GREEN, Edna Elizabeth, age 23, d. April 18, 1946
        Daughter of Wm. Henry and Edith Elizabeth Hampton Allen

GUINN, Edward Sherrill, age 3 mos., d. Dec. 12, 1946
        Son of Edward Sherrill and Virgie Lawing Guinn

HAMPTON, Mallie, age 68, d. March 23, 1930
        Child of Ray and Sadie White Click

HAMPTON, Wm. Sink, age 66, d. Aug. 29, 1945
        Son of Robert and Mallie Click Hampton

HARRIS, Mrs. Cora, age 64, d. Nov. 10, 1940
        Daughter of Frank and Ida McCrackin Horn

HARRIS, Dorothy, age 20, d. Jan. 26, 1932
        Daughter of Hays Harris

HARRIS, Ernest, age 6, d. May 17, 1927
        Son of Sam and ------Gillis Harris

HARRIS, Infant Son,  d. Jan. 31, 1938
        Son of Bob and Dixie Harris

HARVEY, Howard, age 6, d. Aug. 19, 1932
        Son of Alfred Harvey and Essie Parker Harvey

HARVEY, Maxine, b. Feb. 1908, d. June 6, 1931
        Daughter of Tom and ------Slagle Harvey

HATCHER, Catherine C., b. May 2, 1851, d. Nov. 2, 1931
        Daughter of Henry and ------Shipley Bullock

HATCHER, Fred D., age 13 days, d. Dec. 28, 1932
        Son of Henry and Sarah Bartie Hatcher

HATCHER, James Henry, b. May 31, 1884 , d. Sept. 2, 1954
        Son of Jonothan Alvin and Catherine Bullock Hatcher

HATCHER, Mildred, b. Sept. 24, 1922, d. April 9, 1927
        Daughter of L. H. and Sarah Ruth Bartee Hatcher

HENSLEY, Baby, age 3, d. Feb. 20, 1928

HENSLEY, George Sampson, age 71, d. March 21, 1943
        Son of Enoch and Margaret Banks Hensley

HENSLEY, Margaret, age 51, d. Dec. 9, 1932
        Daughter of George and Elizabeth Hensley Shelton

HENSLEY, Robert Edward, age 6, d. Dec. 18, 1936
        Son of Wallace and Mary Rogers Hensley

HIGGINS, Infant,  d. Aug. 10, 1929
        Child of Frank and Helen Doan Higgins

HIGGINS, Julia Alberta, b. 1865, age 65, d. Aug. 9, 1930
        Daughter of Jim and Isobel Carmichael Spear

HIGGINS, Nancy Janet,  Infant,  d. Sept. 29, 1940
        Daughter of Claude Smith and Bessie Harris Higgins

HIGGINS, Samuel,  Infant,  d. June 6, 1931
        Son of Ed and Pearl Bailey Higgins

HODGE, Rose Etta, age 29, d. April 3, 1931
        Daughter of Jim and Maggie Bennett Hodge

HOWELL, Joseph Wm., age 89, d. Sept. 5, 1943
        Son of David Wilson

HOWELL, Lester B., age 25, d. Oct. 25, 1939
        Son of Joe Wm. and Polly Bailey Howell

HOYLE, Martha, age 75, d. Feb. 9, 1936
        Daughter of Hiram and Myra Parton Hoyle

HUGHES, Andrew, age 10, d. June 20, 1932
        Son of Thomas Hughes and Dora Foster Hughes

HUGHES, Ernest Casey, age 1, d. May 7, 1935
        Son of Robert H. Hughes and Gladys Whisnant Hughes

HUGHES, Earl Eugene, Infant, d. Feb. 23, 1936
        Son of Robert and Gladys S. Wisnant Hughes

HUGHES, Margaret, b. 1864, age 66, d. Sept. 1, 1930
        Daughter of Robert and Jennie Tapp Love

HUGHES, Robert Hiram, Jr., Infant, d. May 3, 1938
        Son of Robert Hiram and Gladys Whisnant Hughes

HUSKINS, Margaret Elizabeth, b. Feb. 22, 1862, d. March 24, 1948

HUTCHINS, Joseph H., age 70, d. March 14, 1944
        Son of Wright and Polly Stanley Hutchins

INGLE, Fred, b. Nov. 24, 1930, d. Dec. 26, 1930
        Son of Mack and Maude Wilson Ingle

JEWELL, Ellen, age 67, d. Oct. 10, 1938

JONES, Mrs. S. C., age 77, d. May 13, 1946
        Mother of Bud Jones

JONES, Vilma Ann, age 8, d. May 17, 1953
        Daughter of Luther and Isabella Williams Jones

KEEVER, Infant Daughter, d. Feb. 4, 1953
        Daughter of Virgil and Kathleen Harris Keever

KEEVER, Rosa Lee, b. Aug. 28, 1905, d. Feb. 25, 1932
        Daughter of Dan and Etta Tipton Griffith

KIRK, Alice, age 69, d. May 4, 1940
        Daughter of Dan and Rebecca Hampton Kirk

LAWING, Jack, age 2, d. March 27, 1930
        Son of W. M. and Bessie Thomas Lawing

LAWING, James Berry, b. June 28, 1874, d. Sept. 20, 1956
        Son of ----------- and ------------Harris

LEDFORD, Samuel R., b. 1911, age 53, d. Sept. 4, 1964

LONG, Harley D., age 8 mos., d. May 8, 1930
        Son of Dana and Etta Shelton Long

LONG, Infant, d. April 24, 1929
        Child of ------Edwards and Callie Long

LONG, Mozella, age 1, d. Sept. 25, 1934
        Daughter of Wm. Martin and Cora Mae Higgins Long

LONG, Myrtle Alvelia, age 41, d. April 29, 1951
        Daughter of John W. and Mary Blankenship Long

LONG, Pansy May, age 20 days, d. July 7, 1932
        Daughter of --------- and Myrtle Long

LOVE, Gertrude Beatrice, age 68, d. Feb. 28, 1944
        Daughter of James and Delia Wiseman Stewart

LOVE, Helen Rene, Infant, d. Feb. 20, 1941
        Daughter of Joe L. and Lannie Richards Love

MATHES, Amanda, b. 1889, age 38, d. May 26, 1927
        Daughter of Wm. and Tildy Foster Cooper

MATHES, Estelle, b. Sept. 22, 1931, d. Oct. 4, 1932
        Daughter of Ben and Teressa McCann Mathes

MATHES, Ray, age 32, d. April 29, 1957

MATHES, Ruth, age 1, d. Sept. 16, 1929
        Daughter of Ben Mathes

MATHES, Tressa, age 37, d. May 1941 (29th)
        Daughter of Dillard and Lou Higgins McConn

MATHES, Wm. Monroe, age 3, d. Sept. 21, 1943
        Son of Edward and Alice Green Mathes

MILLER, Infant, d. Feb. 6, 1935
        Child of Hobart and Amanda Watts Miller

MILLER, Orville, age 17, d. Sept. 27, 1935
        Son of Wm. Miller

MILLER, Roscoe, Jr., age 3, d. Jan. 22, 1928
        Son of Roscoe Miller

MILLER, Tempa Ann, age 58, d. Nov. 12, 1934
        Daughter of Wm. and Myra Bailey Barnett

MORRIS, Betty, age 95, d. March 4, 1942
        Daughter of Isaac and Liza Green Morris

McCURRY, Mrs. S. A., age 23, d. Jan. 14, 1926
        Daughter of -------Howell

McINTURFF, Wm. S., age 67, d. Jan. 20, 1937
        Son of Wm. and Rhoda Smitley McInturff

O'BREIN, Cena H., age 72, d. April 3, 1952
        Daughter of Harrison and Jude Banner Harris

O'BRIEN, Janice Marie, age 2, d. Nov. 5, 1945
        Daughter of Howard Harry and Daise Deanie Coffee O'Brien

O'BRINE, Kenneth Reed, age 4, d. Nov. 7, 1945
        Son of Howard Harry and Daisy Deanie Coffee O'Brine

OLLIS, Infant Son,   d. Feb. 21, 1947
        Son of Bradley Wm. and Mary Mashburn Ollis

OLLIS, Margaret Anne, age 1 mo., d. Feb. 5, 1941
        Daughter of Bradley Wm. and Mary Mashburn Ollis

PARKER, Baby,  age 5 mos.  d. Dec. 22, 1927
        Child of Handy Parker and -------------

PARKER, Harley, age 2 mos., d. Sept. 16, 1937
        Son of Handy and Elsie Smith Parker

PARKER, Madge, age 16, d. Jan. 11, 1932
        Daughter of Handy and Hessie Smith Parker

PARSLEY, Charlotte, b. March 30, 1861, d. Feb. 11, 1931
        Daughter of Abner and Millie Young Jones

PARSLEY, Thoma J. & Willis D., Infants,  d. Feb. 23, 1931
        Children of Charlie A. and Mable Square Parsley

PETERSON, Infant,  d. May 27, 1935
        Child of W. N. and Edith Cash Peterson

PETERSON, Joshua, age 65, d. June 24, 1930
        Son of John and Ann Radford Peterson

PETERSON, Linda Jane, age 83, d. Feb. 27, 1955
        Daughter of Jake Justice and ------------

PHILLIPS, Infant,  d. April 20, 1931
        Child of Jessee and Mary Lewis Phillips

POORE, Clifton, age 5 mos., d. June 28, 1935
        Son of James and Valeria Bailey Poore

POORE, Raymond,  Infant,  d. March 12, 1943
        Son of Charles and Rassie Edith Chapman Poore

POORE, Valerie Bailey, age 37, d. Dec. 7, 1942
        Daughter of Alfred and Martha Ayers Bailey

PRICE, Infant Son,  d. June 11, 1938
        Son of Albert W. and Mary Holloway Price

PRICE, Ollie Bell, age 8 mos., d. June 5, 1930
        Child of Furman and Susie Broocks Price

PRICE, Simon Lee,  d. Dec. 19, 1954

RAY, Mammie Bell,  b. June 11, 1877, d. Feb. 19, 1957
        Daughter of James and Sally Lane (or Lance) Roberts

RANDOLPH, Mrs. Irene, age 30,  d. Jan. 24, 1948

RENFRO, Thelma, age 6, d. Aug. 12, 1929
    Daughter of Tom and Nettie Hampton Renfro

RICE, Infant, d. Oct. 10, 1931
    Child of --------- and Sarah Phillips Rice

RICH, Phillip Bozell, age 2 mos., d. March 27, 1944
    Son of Clyde E. and Bertha Edwards Rich

RUNNION, Clifford, Infant, d. Jan. 26, 1931
    Son of Dana and Ethel Peterson Runnion

SALTS, Infant, d. Jan. 24, 1937
    Child of Jack F. and Lillian Lewis Salts

SCOTT, Laura Lee, b. Dec. 31, 1917, d. Feb. 11, 1950
    Daughter of Boyd and Rebecca Engle Scott

SHELL, Kenneth, age 5 mos., d. May 12, 1938
    Son of Harley and Pearl Shell Shehan

SHELTON, Infant, d. Dec. 7, 1939
    Child of Herbert and Ethel Tipton Shelton

SIZEMORE, Danny, age 1, d. May 11, 1934
    Son of J. H. and Carrie B. Harrison Sizemore

TAPP, Infant, d. May 18, 1930
    Child of Blaine and ------Fender Tapp

THOMAS, Betty Jane, b. Nov. 3, 1930, d. Jan. 5, 1931
    Daughter of Grady and Polly Ollis Thomas

THOMAS, Viola, age 16, d. Feb. 8, 1943
    Daughter of Grady and Polly Ollis Thomas

THOMPSON, A. L., b. 1869, d. Nov. 29, 1931
    Son of W. E. and Kezie Reynolds Thompson

TILSON, Elsie Salts, age 21, d. May 20, 1930
    Daughter of Felix and Mary Ellen Salts Miller

TINKER, Wayne Franklin, age 2 mos., d. Oct. 31, 1932
    Son of George and Leona Mullins Tinker

TIPTON, Bobby Lee, Infant, d. Oct. 21, 1933
    Son of Bascomb and Lela Pierson Tipton

TIPTON, Mrs. Dona Hughes, b. May 1911, d. Oct. 1, 1930
    Daughter of Baxter and ------Deaton Hughes

TIPTON, Happy, b. Sept. 20, 1926, d. Sept. 30, 1926
    Child of Sam and Bell Bennett Tipton

TIPTON, Infant Daughter, d. Feb. 14, 1953
    Daughter of Edward Edison and Genevive Elaine
                              Silvers Tipton

TIPTON, Lela, age 3, d. April 25, 1934
    Daughter of Zeke and Hassie Hughes Tipton

TIPTON, Mrs. Margaret, age 71, d. Dec. 2, 1929
    Daughter of Tom and Sally Foster

TITTLE, Infant, d. Oct. 23, 1935
    Child of Brady and Ethel Tipton Tittle

TITTLE, John, age 78, d. April 13, 1928
    Son of Ephriam and Kate Pate Tittle

TITTLE, Kathy Ann, Infant, d. June 29, 1957
    Daughter of Arlene Tittle

TITTLE, Teresa Ann, Infant, d. July 22, 1963
    Daughter of Joseph Roscoe and Judy Ann Hodges Tittle

TOMPKINS, Harriett Foster, d. April 14, 1940
    Daughter of Kann and Becky Owens Foster

WATTS, Blake, b. July 22, 1909, d. April 24, 1927
    Son of Wm. and Nancy Jones Watts

WATTS, Wm. Estill, age 30, d. April 2, 1945

WHALEY, James, b. Aug. 30, 1875, d. Aug. 30, 1931
    Son of Jake and Della Tipton Whaley

WHALEY, Mary Edonona, age 55, d. April 19, 1936
    Daughter of Will and Mary Poore Huskins

WHITE, Charles C., (Spanish Amer. War Vet.), d. April 19, 1949

WHITE, Child, d. Dec. 22, 1925 - Child of James W. White

WILLIAMS, Bonnie, age 9, d. May 28, 1962
    Daughter of Mitchell and Velleree Moore Williams

WILLIAMS, Cornelica, b. Sept. 7, 1900, d. April 3, 1964
    Daughter of John Anders

WILLIAMS, Edith Mae, b. Dec. 24, 1925 - d. April 28, 1927
    Daughter of W. T. and Nancy McCurry Williams

WILLIAMS, Fannie Hensley, b. April 25, 1870, d. Nov. 13, 1954
    Daughter of William and Harriett Proffitt Hensley

WILLIAMS, Henry Clay, age 86, d. Dec. 9, 1941
    Son of William Williams

WILLIAMS, Infant,  d. Feb. 25, 1929
          Child of Hiram and Nettie Loveless Williams

WILLIAMS, Sanders, b. March 1, 1904, d. April 18, 1927
          Son of W. T. and Rena McCurry Williams

WILLIAMS, Sylvannus, b. Nov. 15, 1883, d. Jan. 13, 1949
          Son of James and Rachel Williams

WILLIAMSON, Louisa,  b. 1851,  d. Feb. 22, 1933
          Daughter of Sam Estep

WILSON, ----------,  d. May 6, 1929

WILSON, Infant Daughter,  d. Aug. 1943
          Daughter of Paul and Ethel Presnell Wilson

WORSHAM, Mrs. Myra,  age 68,  d. Feb. 9, 1930
          Daughter of Benjamin and Lydia Duncan Birdwell

 COLLINS, Georgia Lee,     d. 1918

 LOVE, James Pickering, d. 1890's

 LOVE, Amanda Hartselle (w)

## FISHERY UNION CHURCH CEMETERY

Located north of Erwin, left off Highway 107,
just beyond U. S. Fish Hatchery - about ¼ mile
on left of road.
Copied July 7, 1988 and July 15, 1988

HUSKINS, Charlie, 1890-1968
HUSKINS, Martha,  1900-1977

DeROCHER, Brian, b/d 1984

HOLLIFIELD, Ronder, Aug. 30, 1916 - June 10, 1969
HOLLIFIELD, Edith Coleman, March 20, 1917  -

FOSTER, Gordon, Aug. 13, 1938 - July 20, 1977

BAILEY, Virgil L., Sept. 7, 1927 - Nov. 19, 1975

TAPP, Geter E., Oct. 2, 1906 - June 18, 1970
TAPP, Olive M., July 8, 1910 -

TITTLE, William C. (Bill), Nov. 26, 1910 - Nov. 7, 1980
TITTLE, Kathleen N., July 27, 1921 -

SMITH, Lizzie Harris, April 28, 1923 - June 29, 1986

McCOURRY, Lattie, Apr. 16, 1909 - June 1, 1983
McCOURRY, Ethel Tapp (w), July 1, 1911 - March 22, 1974
McCOURRY, William Kenneth (son), Aug. 19, 1930 - Sept. 3, 1949

TAPP, Sam, 1881-1954
TAPP, Hattie (w), 1882-1968

PETERSON, R. L., Feb. 14, 1936 - April 4, 1955 - SR, US Navy
PETERSON, Mary Lee, June 3, 1907 - Nov. 1, 1985

NELSON, Ralph B., June 5, 1898 - Jan. 2, 1975
NELSON, Ethel B. (w), Aug. 19, 1902 -
NELSON, Lola Alenia, 1948-1949

BOWMAN, Frankie Gene, d. 1975 - Infant
BOWMAN, Linda, Dec. 7, 1947 - 1948
        Daughter of Mr. and Mrs. Raymond Bowman

HOLLIFIELD, Ed, June 10, 1913 -
HOLLIFIELD, Evlee Rogers (w), May 11, 1918 - March 20, 1951
        Daughter of Sam H. and Pearl Riddle Rogers

HOLLIFIELD, Max, 1910-1984
HOLLIFIELD, Mattie May (w), Aug. 2, 1916 - May 5, 1945

HOLLIFIELD, Jacob Lee, 1869-1945
HOLLIFIELD, Samanthy Pate (w), 1871-1962

HOLLIFIELD, John Rex, July 20, 1909 - July 6, 1947
        Son of Lee and Sarah Pate Hollifield
HOLLIFIELD, Ethel Nelson (w), May 1, 1910 -

GARLAND, Pauline H., March 12, 1937 - Dec. 23, 1981

SMITH, James C., May 22, 1903 - Jan. 26, 1965
SMITH, Pansy W. (w), June 27, 1905 -
SMITH, Dorothy Sue (dau), d. April 12, 1945
SMITH, James C., Jr. (son), Aug. 2, 1924 - Sept. 5, 1966
         PFC, 29 Engr., WWII
SMITH, Sam, 1926-1981, PFC, US Army, WWII
SMITH, "Biddy", -

JONES, Pearl Whitson, April 16, 1908 - June 7, 1978, "Wife"
JONES, Barbara Sue, April 7, 1941 - Feb. 20, 1942
         Dau. of Lester Burton and Pearl Whitson Jones
JONES, Herman, 1921-1978

WHITSON, Mollie McCurry, May 26, 1882 - July 10, 1970, "Mother"

MILLER, Thomas M., 1864-1943
MILLER, Rebecca V (w), 1876-1957

PIPPIN, James W., 1874-1942
         Son of Shepherd and Sarah Fleenor Pippin
PIPPIN, Florence B., 1889-1965
         Daughter of John Scott & Harriett Brown McInturff

AMBROSE, James H., Sept. 3, 1863 - Dec. 23, 1943 - "Father"

McDERMOTT, Thurman O., Dec. 14, 1922 - Nov. 15, 1979
McDERMOTT, Marie A., Dec. 8, 1921 -

AMBROSE, Wade R., March 5, 1894 - Oct. 26, 1984
AMBROSE, Bessie Boone, Aug. 14, 1895 - Aug. 14, 1975

ALLEN, Harley Isaac, Oct. 2, 1918 - July 27, 1987, US Navy, WWII
ALLEN, Louise A., June 18, 1916 -

GILLENWATER, Joe B., 1923-1986

HARRIS, Robert Fay, 1903-1958, "Father"

HARRIS, Sam, -
HARRIS, Mag, -

REED, Robert, 1882-1964
REED, Rachel (w), 1885-1958

JONES, Hiram S., June 19, 1898 - Dec. 26, 1975
JONES, Carrie A. (w#1), Jan. 4, 1902 - Jan. 13, 1957
         Daughter of Wm. and Mallie Miller
JONES, Kathleen Renfro (w#2), July 15, 1919 -
JONES, Phillip S., d. Nov. 20, 1941
         Infant son of H. S. and Carrie Jones

HUSKINS, Marshall E., Oct. 15, 1890 - April 15, 1954
        Son of Napoleon and Mary Smith Huskins
HUSKINS, Nora Tittle (w), Feb. 19, 1897 - Jan. 3, 1971
        Married July 11, 1914

AMBROSE, J. Morris, b/d 1938

NELSON, Rexter, Aug. 29, 1901 - July 23, 1976
NELSON, Naoma (w), March 4, 1900 - April 22, 1982
NELSON, Betty Arlene, Oct. 4, 1929 - July 30, 1940
        Daughter of Rex and Oma Higgins Nelson

HOLIFIELD, Roscoe, June 2, 1901 - Oct. 3, 1983
HOLIFIELD, Myrtle Tittle (w), Sept. 8, 1908 - Jan. 6, 1972
HOLIFIELD, Shirley Jean (dau), June 26, 1940 - Sept. 23, 1940

HINKLE, William F., 1904 - 1956
HINKLE, Nellie M., 1908-1952
HINKLE, Lesley W., d. Jan. 6, 1938

KIRK, Rosa, 1894-1938 - "Mother"
        Daughter of Ebb and Elizabeth Tapp Jones

HIGGINS, Elmer, July 3, 1940 - Dec. 23, 1941
HIGGINS, Billy, b/d Dec. 14, 1942
HIGGINS, Moat, March 20, 1915 - Nov. 8, 1948, PVT, WWII
HIGGINS, Virginia B., Sept. 3, 1914 -
HIGGINS, Ernest R., Dec. 1, 1945 - Jan. 27, 1970

HUGHES, M. D., July 22, 1871 - June 29, 1942
HUGHES, Elizabeth L., 1871-1964

GARLAND, Ralph Daniel (Danny), Dec. 18, 1966 - Dec. 2, 1975

HARRIS, Hurb J., June 18, 1898 - June 26, 1969
HARRIS, Martha E. (w), May 29, 1905 - May 13, 1976
HARRIS, Harry Noble, Aug. 6, 1941 - April 28, 1942

TITTLE, Wm. I. (Boss), 1908-1954
TITTLE, Elizabeth M. (w), 1916-1949

CALLAHAN, Addie M., 1922-1966

DINSMORE, Lilburn, d. 1948
DINSMORE, Lucy Bell, 1874-1966

HIGGINS, Earnest, Sept. 22, 1930 - Nov. 30, 1951
        Son of Gaither and Mae White Higgins

HARRIS, Madge White, 1904-1974

WHITE, Jonathan L., 1879-1962
WHITE, Jason, b/d 1977

HONEYCUTT, Mamie White, 1915-1987

ROGERS, Sam H., Sept. 19, 1885 - Jan. 22, 1951
            Son of Joseph David and Rebecca Huskins Rogers
ROGERS, Ada Pearl, Nov. 17, 1888 - July 14, 1975

MILLER, Bertha, Aug. 6, 1909 - Oct. 15, 1978 "Sister"

LIGHT, Clarence, 1902-1982
LIGHT, Etta (w), 1905 -       married Sept. 19, 1926
LIGHT, Dorothy Gene, Dec. 18, 1937 - June 10, 1939

HILL, Mary Louise, d. May 21, 1939
            Infant daughter of Robert and Belle Hill

CHANDLER, Wolford, Nov. 18, 1895 - April 14, 1969
CHANDLER, Betsy,   Mar. 18, 1903 - Jan. 3, 1950
            Dau. of Dove and Deborah Justice Lewis
SMITH, Sam, Feb. 20, 1882 - April 24, 1960
SMITH, Anna R. (w), May 11, 1889 - May 22, 1950
            Daughter of James and Harriett McInturff Ambrose
SMITH, Willie, Sept. 5, 1919 - June 1, 1966 - "Brother"

MEADOWS, Paul G., Feb. 8, 1937 - July 4, 1977
MEADOWS, Betty J. (w), Aug. 13, 1934 -
            Married Aug. 13, 1960

HIGGINS, Claude, Aug. 6, 1911 - Aug. 21, 1967
            PFC, 738 Fld. Arty., BN, WWII

EDWARDS, Charlie, July 7, 1921 - March 20, 1959
            Son of Rex and Winnie Ledford Edwards
EDWARDS, June Wilson (w), June 20, 1923 -

LYLE, Frank H., June 12, 1913 - June 24, 1971
LYLE, Linnie S. (w), Feb. 9, 1913 -

JONES, William R., 1895-1954
JONES, Martha M., Sept. 16, 1894 - Aug. 15, 1962

LYLE, Jack B., July 11, 1911 -
LYLE, Louise L. (w), Sept. 1, 1913 - Nov. 25, 1984

LYLE, Robert R., March 4, 1884 - June 18, 1957
            Son of Burton and Martha Ambrose Lyle
LYLE, Rebecca J., Oct. 16, 1890 - May 1, 1983

HIGGINS, Hassle, b/d 1953
            Son of Claude E. and Eulala White Higgins

DAY, George William, Nov. 17, 1903 - June 24, 1951
            Son of Dean and Lissie Tittle Day
DAY, Florence Smith, Sept. 11, 1906 - Sept. 16, 1964
            Daughter of Samuel and Annie Ambrose Smith

EDWARDS, J. Stanley, 1921-1968
EDWARDS, Mildred E. (w), 1923 -

BARNETT, James, Oct. 18, 1877 - Oct. 3, 1960 - "Father"
BARNETT, Rosetta, April 9, 1891 - July 24, 1981

HARRIS, Joe, - --------

GRAY, Vickey, 1963-1987

STOCKTON, R. Wesley, Oct. 19, 1887 - April 17, 1979
STOCKTON, Polly Jane, July 9, 1889 - Aug. 21, 1966  "Mother"

WARRICK, John H., d. 1968

EDWARDS, Clyde Verlon, 1933-1987

McCURRY, Sidney A., Oct. 19, 1895 - May 15, 1970 , PVT, US Army

COX, William F., Aug. 23, 1902 - Aug. 22, 1984, PVT, US Army

BARNETT, Cecil, 1926-1970
BARNETT, Mary K. (w), 1936 -

RICE, Jessie, d. Aug. 15, 1919

CONNORS, Bryn Michael, b/d 1983

ROLL, Delmas A., 1907-1974, Tec 5, US Army
ROLL, Hattie B., 1910 -

BANNER, R. W., May 8, 1927 -
BANNER, Thelma C., March 4, 1926 - Nov. 1, 1986

LEWIS, Walter Clifford, 1912-1986, PVT, US Army, WWII
LEWIS, Pansy T. (w), 1920 -

TAPP, Frank C., Jan. 5, 1893 - April 17, 1984
TAPP, Rachel Jones (w), Oct. 11, 1895 - Aug. 12, 1969
TAPP, Anna June (dau), June 23, 1936 - Nov. 11, 1936

JONES, Earl F., June 12, 1905 - Dec. 5, 1965
JONES, Lula H. (w), Feb. 19, 1908 - March 30, 1981
JONES, Woodward Swain Nov. 14, 1926 - May 10, 1934
        Son of Earl Franklin and Lula Annie Higgins Jones
CRAIN, Bertie V., Oct. 10, 1905 - Jan. 13, 1943, "Mother"
        Daughter of Calvin and Emmaline Story Crain

RIDDLE, Sam, 1897-1946
RIDDLE, Sarah, 1899-1987

HIGGINS, James Thor, 1880-1970
HIGGINS, Caldonie, June 3, 1881 - July 5, 1937

TITTLE, Lorettie Higgins, May 10, 1879 - July 22, 1927
        Wife of John Tittle

JACKSON, Jacob A., 1899-1951
        Son of Calvin and Alzy Odum Jackson
JACKSON, Virgie M., 1898-1961
        Daughter of Thomas and Molly McInturff Tapp

HUSKINS, Micheal Eugene, July 29, 1954 - Jan. 29, 1955
        Son of Paul W. and Bessie Paulsen Huskins
HUSKINS, Bessie, 1925-1977

BANNER, Guard E., Nov. 6, 1899 -
BANNER, Clara M. (w), July 23, 1901 - March 14, 1972

McINTURFF, Clarence Brown, Jan. 26, 1894 - Aug. 29, 1987
McINTURFF, Hazel Anderson, Nov. 20, 1903 - April 18, 1951
        Daughter of Landon T. and Mary Simmons Anderson

AMBROSE, Cloyd E., May 6, 1902 - April 26, 1983
AMBROSE, Juanita M. (w), Sept. 14, 1914 -

HOLLIFIELD, Howard M., b/d May 1, 1945
HOLLIFIELD, Francis L., Sept. 15, 1935 - Oct. 9, 1935
HOLLIFIELD, Hubert, b/d 1933

HOLFIELD, Rolley, d. Nov. 1, 1924, NC PVT, 45 Regt, Coast Art.Corps

HIGGINS, Ethel Cooper, March 29, 1908 - Feb. 15, 1925
        Daughter of Mr. and Mrs. (J.orF.) T. Higgins

HASTINGS, Annie Lee, Aug. 9, 1922 - Nov. 19, 1928
HASTINGS, Hazel Helen, March 26, 1925 - Feb. 17, 1932
        Daughters of E. F. and Sallie Hastings

HIGGINS, Woodard G., Aug. 10, 1883 - June 7, 1947
HIGGINS, Vergie Hastings (w), Aug. 14, 1886 - April 16, 1966
HIGGINS, Virginia (dau), Feb. 8, 1924 - Sept. 21, 1929
HIGGINS, Ralph, (son), Dec. 27, 1919 - Jan. 20, 1923


HIGGINS, Mildred, June 17, 1923 - Jan. 7, 1925
        Daughter of Mr. and Mrs. M. B. Higgins

DAWSON, James, Feb. 14, 1915 - May 3, 1947, Cpl.Air Corp, WWII
DAWSON, Florence A., 1942-1943
        Dau. of James and Dorothy Ann Brown Dawson
BROWN, Margaret E., Oct. 20, 1921 - Sept. 28, 1922
        Daughter of W. H. and H. L. Brown

PATE, Samuel F., Co. E., 94 N.Y. Inf., Union Army

TITTLE, Samuel Ernest, Feb. 27, 1902 - July 21, 1926
        Son of James and Elizabeth Tittle

TAPP, Roy, Sr., Jan. 22, 1894 - April 24, 1972
TAPP, Bessie E. (w), June 18, 1892 - Nov. 9, 1967
TAPP, Mafra L., 1917-1987

KEESECKER, Wilbur O., April 28, 1890 - July 15, 1957
   Son of Adrain Garrett and Ella Mae Allbright Keesecker
KEESECKER, Ida Ray (w), Nov. 4, 1891 - July 10, 1972
KEESECKER, Wilbur Jr., April 5, 1918 - April 27, 1927
   Son of W. O. and Ida Ray Tapp Keesecker

AMBROSE, Charles, Aug. 24, 1896 - Dec. 6, 1984
AMBROSE, Ethel (w), Dec. 25, 1898 - Oct. 3, 1967
AMBROSE, Lyle Woodward, Feb. 26, 1926 - Jan. 25, 1988
AMBROSE, Ralph, March 8, 1928 - April 14, 1928 (son)

AMBROSE, Alfred, Jan. 16, 1924 - Nov. 6, 1925 (son)

EDWARDS, Lowes Irine, Aug. 19, 1928 - Aug. 9, 1929 (Lois Irene?)
   Daughter of Frank and Phoebe Jones Edwards

BANNER, W. Henry, Dec. 16, 1865 - Jan. 10, 1944
BANNER, Dora Bell (w), Jan. 19, 1875 - Aug. 17, 1929
   Daughter of Will and Mary Ann Tapp Love

JONES, John, 1850-1919
JONES, Jane, 1866-1940

HIGGINS, Charles B., 1908-1986

McINTURFF, George Edgar, Nov. 28, 1898 - Dec. 18, 1966
McINTURFF, William A., May 30, 1862 - March 29, 1932
   Son of J. S. and Emeline Tinker McInturff
McINTURFF, Alice Tinker (w), Sept. 28, 1861 - Sept. 16, 1916

TAPP, Thomas, Feb. 29, 1868 - Dec. 15, 1937
TAPP, Mollie McInturff (w), March 9, 1870 - Nov. 30, 1941
TAPP, Infant (dau), Oct. 3, 1913 - Oct. 30, 1913
TAPP, Lola M., May 9, 1891 - July 23, 1937
   Daughter of Thomas Marion & Mollie M.A.McInturff Tapp

TITTLE, Samuel, Co.A, 3 NC Mtd. Inf., Union Army
TITTLE, Annie A. (w), Feb. 17, 1846 - Jan. 1, 1925
TITTLE, Dora Evelyn, Oct. 28, 1924 - Sept. 11, 1925
   Daughter of Mr. and Mrs. C. E. Tittle
TITTLE, Infant, b/d Jan. 29, 1931 - Dau. of Mr.& Mrs. C.E.Tittle

LEWIS, Rhoda, April 3, 1883 - July 2, 1970

JONES, Charlie R., Dec. 21, 1892 - Sept. 7, 1928
JONES, Pheby Ambrose, July 12, 1886 - Jan. 29, 1960 "Mother"

HUGHES, Charles, 1849-1932
HUGHES, Amy Brooks (w), b. 1856
   Daughter of David and --------Garrett Brooks
HUGHES, David M., 1876-1946
HUGHES, Cenia, b. 1894

EDWARDS, Walter, April 28, 1915 - Aug. 19, 1916
        Son of J. F. Edwards
EDWARDS, Maggie Jones, April 15, 1881 - Jan. 1, 1920
        Wife of J. F. Edwards

LYLE, Frank H., July 24, 1882 - Jan. 26, 1960
        Son of Bert and Martha Ambrose Lyle
LYLE, Martha (w), May 15, 1876 - Aug. 24, 1949
LYLE, Elmer (son), Jan. 17, 1907 - Oct. 17, 1907

TAPP, George Washington, Jan. 12, 1861 - April 25, 1943
        Son of Wilke Masters and Janette Tapp
TAPP, Jennett, Jan. 11, 1837 - April 2, 1912

TITTLE, Charles B., June 21, 1874 - April 20, 1924
TITTLE, John R., Co.H, 8 Tenn. Cav., Union Army

WHITE, Mattie and Baby, d. Nov. 1, 1912, age 29
        Wife and child of J. L. White

HIGGINS, Burrell, Sept. 15, 1933 - July 20, 1940
        Son of Gaither and Mae White Higgins
HIGGINS(?), 1887-1929, "Mother", In Same Plot

CAPPS, Mark, June 1, 1874 - July 16, 1907

TAPP, William H., Sept. 25, 1890 - Sept. 29, 1923
        Sgt. 54 Inf., 6 Div., WWI
TAPP, Mattison L., 1857-1935, Son of Wilbain Tapp
TAPP, Emma C., 1863-1937
        Daughter of P. H. and Susie Combs Johnson

EDWARDS, Dan W., 1907-1973
EDWARDS, Berta M., 1904-1980
EDWARDS, Mary Evelyn, b/d 1941

OWENS, Alice, April 9, 1895 - March 1, 1926
        Wife of T. B. Owens

BANNER, Hubert, d. Sept. 24, 1935, Sgt. 2 Cav., WWI

TAPP, Bob, 1858-1926

McNABB, Emma L. Smith, Dec. 18, 1862 - July 14, 1916
        Wife of A. W. McNabb

TAPP, Billy, 1813 - 1890
TAPP, Betsy, 1823-1897
TAPP, Sarah, Dec. 11, 1842 - Feb. 19, 1911, "Mother"

HUSKINS, Mary A., April 12, 1853 - April 25, 1916
HUSKINS, Jubal H., Oct. 5, 1829 - Oct. 19, 1905
        Co. A, 3 NC Mtd. Inf., Union Army

BROOKS, John Jr., Co. B, 13 Tenn. Cav., Union Army

BENNETT, Bashana,  d. Nov. 20, 1911, age 86
        Wife of Emry Bennett
BENNETT, Sherman, Aug. 31, 1870 - Jan. 26, 1931, Son of Emry &
                                Bachana Young Bennett
HAMMER, Mary,  --------

BROWN, George W. N., April 2, 1858 - Oct. 29, 1943
        Son of A. W. and Mary -------Brown
BROWN, Margaret McNabb (w), Aug. 12, 1858 - Jan. 11, 1930
        Daughter of David and Corina Cooper McNabb
BROWN, Cecil Fay (son), Sept. 30, 1898 - March 2, 1900

WHITE, Caroline Huskins, Jan. 14, 1880 - March 17, 1903
        Wife of C. C. White, Jr.
WHITE, Criss, d. March 17, 1917 - age 35 years, 6 mos, 14 dys
        Pvt. 27 US Inf., WWI

TAPP, Vincent, Co. A, 3 NC Mtd. Inf., Union Army

BROWN, Winfield Scott, Dec. 22, 1862 - Jan. 21, 1912
BROWN, Louisa (w), Aug. 6, 1866 - Dec. 20, 1951
        Daughter of David and Corina Cooper Brown

PEEBLES, Cyntha Brown, Sept. 9, 1822 - Jan. 26, 1911
        Wife of A. Peebles

GOFORTH, Blanche B., 1896-1964 - "Aunt"

BROWN, William Henry, 1889-1968

DAVIS, Emma L., June 22, 1862 - June 2, 1885

CROW, Edward , d.July 25, 1902
CROW, Rebeca Brown (w), b. Aug. 13, 1819

BROWN, Joseph A., Nov. 19, 1828 - May 17, 1916
BROWN, Lucinda McInturff (w), Dec. 16, 1835 - July 14, 1927
BROWN, Mary, Dec. 23, 1820 - Sept. 24, 1884, Wife of A.W.Brown

McINTURFF, John Scott, 1828-1899
McINTURFF, Harriett E. Brown, 1854-1896

WHITE, C. C., d. March 24, 1917

HARRIS, Dora E., June 30, 1878-May 24, 1911, Wife of S.F.Harris
HARRIS, Ruth, May 23, 1911 - June 15, 1911
HARRIS, Paul, May 23, 1911 - June 23, 1911

WHITE, Lorena, March 31, 1903 - April 20, 1903
WHITE, Willie, Feb. 10, 1908 - Feb. 11, 1908
WHITE, Tom, June 9, 1909 - July 1, 1909
        Children of J. L. and Mattie White

WHITE, Martha, March 1848 - Oct. 30, 1899, Wife of D.J.White

WHITE, Ellen, b. Oct. 5, 1874, Dau. of D.J. and M. White

BROWN, Estella J., March 2, 1873 - June 18, 1891
BROWN, Infant, Nov. 7, 1854 - Nov. 8, 1854
       Daughters of J. A. and L. J. Brown

PHILLIPS, William L., July 23, 1866 - July 21, 1954
       Son of Parnell and Edna Britt Phillips
PHILLIPS, Rachel E., June 20, 1870 - May 18, 1952
       Daughter of Joseph A. and Lucinda McInturff Brown

BROWN, John C. Jr., Jan. 14, 178? - Mar. or May 7, 1830(?)
BROWN, Jane, May 12, 1787 - Dec. 4, 1840
       Consort of John C. Brown, Jr. (?)
BROWN, Martha Jane, April 26, 1849 - Sept. 23, 1849
       Daughter of N. T. (?) and M. Brown

BROWN, Melissa, ----------

AMBROSE, Nealie, Jan. 21, 1889 - Feb. 7, 1907
AMBROSE, Ossie, May 16, 1879 - Dec. 4, 1918
AMBROSE, Harriett, Aug. 19, 1867 - May 22, 1931
       Dau. of Jackie and Marlie Tipton McInturff
CORRELL, Frances "Lizzie", 1888-1925

PHILLIPS, Lucinda, Dec. 31, 1818 - April 16, 1886

NELSON, Rebeckie, 1849-1925, Wife of Isaac Nelson

WOOD, Lizzie, July 7, 1876 - April 4, 1934

COLLINS, Martha, 1894-1962

HUSKINS, William H., Co. M., 8 Tenn. Cav., Union Army


FISHERY UNION CHURCH CEMETERY - UNMARKED GRAVES

AMBROSE, Bernie Sherwood, age 1, d. May 24, 1933
       Son of James and Bessie Coffee Ambrose


AMBROSE, Infant Daughter, d. Jan. 4, 1962
       Daughter of James Adrin and Freda Lou Bailey Ambrose

BAILEY, Infant Daughter, d. May 8, 1963
       Daughter of Virgil Lee and Beatrice Hollifield Bailey

BRYANT, Fred, age 51, d. Dec. 23, 1939

CRAIN, Infant, d. Jan. 3, 1943
      Child of Bascomb Whitt and Bertie Vance Crain


GOUGE, Mrs. Nellie, March 8, 1888 - Feb. 9, 1929
      Daughter of David and Martha Garland White

GREEN, Infant, d. July 17, 1947
      Child of Geo. Washington and Annie Edney Green

GREEN, Joyce Jene, 5 mos., d. Feb. 13, 1949
      Daughter of Geo. Washington and Annie Edney Green

HARRIS, Chester, age 27, d. Oct. 25, 1932
      Son of Harrison and Maggie Nelson Harris

HARRIS, Eva Marie, age 5, d. June 29, 1938
      Daughter of Fay and Madge White Harris

HARRIS, Infant Son, d. Jan. 8, 1947
      Son of Estil Homer and Clarice Hopson Harris

HARRIS, James, age 41, d. Aug. 29, 1927

HARRIS, Naomi, age 71, d. Dec. 5, 1937
      Daughter of --------Lovett and Vina Edwards Lovett


HODGE, Margaret Siltony, Aug. 31, 1871 - June 29, 1947
      Daughter of Emory and Basha Young Bennett

HOLLIFIELD, Chas. Douglas, 5 mos., d. March 29, 1951
      Son of Barbara Jean Hollifield

HOLLIFIELD, Francis, age 4, d. Oct. 9, 1935
      Child of Max and Mattie Rogiso Hollifield

HOLLIFIELD, Infant Daughter, d. Nov. 13, 1961
      Daughter of Mildred H. Hollifield

HOLLIFIELD, Infant Son, d. March 20, 1951
      Son of Ed and Evlee Rogers Hollifield

JONES, Elbert, age 57, d. March 24, 1930
      Son of John and -------Whaley Jones

JONES, Infant, d. June 3, 1930
      Child of Dillard and Nannie Stallard Jones

JONES, Katherine, age 86, d. Nov. 30, 1929

JONES, Lewis David, age 19, d. Dec. 19, 1927
        Son of Henry and ------Tapp Jones

JONES, Lora Dean, age 24, d. Aug. 13, 1935
        Daughter of John and Nancy Jane Tittle Jones

KIRK, Billie Jene, 8 mos., d. Feb. 16, 1936
        Child of Bill and Rosa Jones Kirk

LEDFORD, Frances Louise, Infant, d. Feb. 19, 1940
        Daughter of Dora Ledford

MILLER, Rebecca, Aug. 15, 1872 - June 17, 1947
        Daughter of Allen and -----Renfro McCurry

MORROW, Lee, d. Nov. 6, 1960

McINTURFF, C. B., age 51, d. Sept. 8, 1929
        Son of Jack and Marie Crow McInturff

McINTURFF, Eva Sue, Infant, d. July 16, 1952
        Daughter of James and June L. Story McInturff

NELSON, Infant Daughter, d. Sept. 6, 1956
        Daughter of Earl and Julia Bell White Nelson

NELSON, Raymond Franklin, Sept. 6, 1905 - Dec. 28, 1949
        Son of Thomas and Molly Day Nelson

PATE, Eliza, age 76, d. Jan. 13, 1936

PATE, Samuel F., Nov. 30, 1846 - Jan. 23, 1929
        Son of Tom Pate

PETERSON, Fred Eugene, 2 mos., d. May 7, 1949
        Son of Chas. Nelson and Mary Miller Peterson

RIDDLE, Freddy Guy, 1 mo., d. Feb. 25, 1943
        Son of Sam and Sarah Vance Riddle

RIDDLE, Infant, d. Aug. 23, 1943
        Child of Margaret Riddle

RIDDLE, Susie, age 47, d. Feb. 13, 1937

ROBERTS, Earl, 5 mos., d. Sept. 30, 1950
        Son of Fred and Narnea Virginia Broyles Roberts

SIFERD, Elizabeth, Infant, d. Jan. 31, 1929
        Daughter of L. J. Siferd

SIMMONS, John, age 50, d. Jan. 7, 1930

SMITH, Dorothy Sue, Infant, d. April 12, 1944
      Daughter of James Clinton and Pansy Webb Smith

SMITH, Henry, age 75, d. Aug. 10, 1935
      Son of Alex and Jane Smith

SMITH, Infant Daughter, d. Feb. 22, 1951
      Daughter of R. C. and Irma Jean Gearhart Smith

SMITH, Lora Marlene, 4 mos., d. May 25, 1950
      Daughter of Robt. Clinton and Irma Jean Gearhart Smith

SMITH, Nancy, age 59, d. March 31, 1932
      Daughter of Harrison and Cresa Tapp Huskins

STALLARD, Ella Marie, age 1, d. July 3, 1929
      Daughter of Nannie Stallard

TAPP, Emma, age 84, d. July 29, 1938
      Daughter of John and Polly Clouse Tapp

TAPP, George, age 48, d. Jan. 5, 1929
      Son of John and -----Foster Tapp

TITTLE, James Elbert, age 64, d. Sept. 24, 1938
      Son of Sam and Annie Ambrose Tittle

TITTLE, Mrs. John (Lorettie), May 10, 1879 - July 24, 1927
      Daughter of --------Higgins

WHITE, McDaniel, Infant, d. Sept. 23, 1946
      Son of Walter and Margaret Ellen White

# BEALS CEMETERY
## ALSO CALLED GARLAND CEMETERY

Located on Rt. 107, 1½ miles west of
Erwin, near the Devils' Looking Glass

Copied by Charles Bennett, January 12, 1963 - Updated July 1, 1988

BEALS, Buford Frederick, July 12, 1889 - May 13, 1950

BEALS, Victor Eugene, May 8, 1907 - Sept. 15, 1948

TUCKER, Benjamin Harrison, Dec. 9, 1888 - May 22, 1960
TUCKER, Ethel Elizabeth Beals, March 22, 1904 -

PRESNELL, J. P., Sept. 12, 1883 - April 15, 1955

PRESNELL, Herman, Sept. 17, 1921 - Oct. 9, 1941

HARRIS, Carol Ann, b/d 1962

HIGGINS, James F., 1888-1962

PETERSON, Wm.Finn, May 5, 1904 - April 7, 1947
          Son of James and Nora Belle Peterson

TITTLE, Blanche L., 1896-1961

BAILEY, Grace Lee, Feb. 4, 1906 - Apr. 7, 1956
         (Grace Lloyd Bailey ?) - Wife of Marcus Bailey

SHELL, Mary M., Mar. 5, 1908 - Dec. 14, 1952
         Daughter of Benjamin B. & Blanche Payne Lloyd

LOYD, Paul T., Nov. 14, 1924 - Apr. 5, 1944
        Son of Ben and Blanche Loyd (Lloyd?)

LLOYD, Eliza, Oct. 18, 1886 - Jan. 19, 1955

BAKER, David W., 1876-1941

BAKER, George Samuel, Nov. 25, 1919 - Sept. 23, 1962
        PFC, Btry A, 929th FA BN. WWII

BAKER, Ida Irene, Sep. 23, 1899 - July 26, 1940

BAKER, Tallulah, d. June 3, 1939
        Daughter of Joseph B. and Ida Spray Baker

ROGERS, Finia B., 1883-1939

SHELL, Mary Elizabeth, 1877-1962

PETERSON, Retta Murphy, d. Mar. 15, 1948 at age 48

POORE, Woodward, June 27, 1913 - Sept. 6, 1940 - Son of Frank
                      and Melvina Huskins Poore

POORE, Frank, June 27, 1879-July 15, 1935
        Son of Robert and Sue Starnes Poore
POORE, Melvin H., June 26, 1878 - July 15, 1956
        (Melvina ?)

HERRELL, Marie, May 20, 1930 - Feb. 4, 1934

BRIGGS, Infant, b/d 1958

WATTS, Biddie Sue, 1882-1956

FOSTER, Robert Lemon, Dec. 20, 1935 - Dec. 23, 1935
        Son of Roy and Leora Foster

HUSKINS, William P., Mar. 6, 1855 - Mar. 31, 1941
HUSKINS, Mary, Aug. 19, 1848 - Dec. 4, 1937

WATSON, Juanita Marie, b/d 1929

BENNETT, Maud, Feb. 3, 1927 - Oct. 1, 1929

BENNETT, James, Aug. 6, 1881 - Oct. 9, 1917
        Son of Matt and Cordie Bennett

CORDELL, Nancy,  no dates

BOGART, E. P., Mar. 6, 1853 - July 29, 1917
BOGART, Jane, Apr. 19, 1851 - Feb. 3, 1910
BOGART, E. G., Aug. 26, 1858 - Dec. 26, 1929
        Son of Sam and Mary Erwin Bogart
BOGART, Sarah E. Whaley, Oct. 23, 1870 - Jan. 14, 1910

BOGART, Mary Erwin, Nov. 26, 1820 - Mar. 22, 1902
        Wife of Samuel W. Bogart

BROOKS, Vernie L., June 9, 1891 - Nov. 10, 1891 - (dau)
BROOKS, Oliver J., Nov. 14, 1892 - Mar. 15, 1893 - (son)
BROOKS, Clauda I., May 1, 1896 - Dec. 19, 1901 - (son)
        Children of J. P. and Ann Brooks

WHALEY, Jacob H., Dec. 9, 1847 - June 14, 1916

HUGHES, Sudeth, Apr. 6, 1908 - May 9, 1908
        Son of S. N. and D. B. Hughes

ANDERS, Robert Franklin, Dec. 2, 1898 - Feb. 6, 1900
        Son of E. G. and M. E. Anders

HUGHES, Isaac Henry, Aug. 3, 1892 - June 22, 1893
HUGHES, Jacob Orvel, July 8, 1890 - Jan. 30, 1891
HUGHES, John Russell, Nov. 22, 1887 - Mar. 30, 1888
        Sons of Charles and Amy C. Hughes

WOODFIN, Mamie, Nov. 16, 1896 - Oct. 23, 1919
        Wife of W. T. Woodfin

BEALS (ALSO CALLED GARLAND) CEMETERY - (continued)

WHALEY, Jesse, Oct. 29, 1866 - Sep. 19, 1896

BEALS, Mary Jane, June 10, 1869 - Mar. 30, 1937
BEALS, J. H., Jan. 23, 1868 - Apr. 19, 1915
BEALS, W. N., May 9, 1856 - Oct. 4, 1908

BEALS, William N., Oct. 2, 1821 - Apr. 4, 1896
BEALS, Catherine, Mar. 14, 1826 - July 23, 1852
BEALS, Catherine, Apr. 9, 1852 - Nov. 9, 1863 - (dau)

BEALS, John S., Mar. 30, 1801 - July 22, 1855
BEALS, Elizabeth, June 16, 1798 - Nov. 21, 1875
BEALS, John W., Sep. 25, 1833 - Dec. 22, 1833
BEALS, James, b/d May 20, 1841

TITTLE, I. E., Dec. 18, 1834 - Aug. 2, 1870
TITTLE, Anna, d. July 8, 1861

TINER?, Emily, d. Aug. 3 (?), 1870
        Tinker? Tittle?

HUSKINS, W. G., Mar. 27, 1836 - Oct. 20, 1886

EDWARDS, Lula, Aug. 5, 1921 - Sep. 29, 1923
EDWARDS, Esther A., d. Sep. 17, 1920

POORE, Charlie L., May 2, 1894 - Dec. 30, 1909

POORE, 5 graves - children of Frank Poore

WETHERFORD, Helen, Sep. 3, 1923 - Aug. 21, 1927
        Daughter of Will Weatherford

STORY, Mrs. Annas, Nov. 27, 1873 - Aug. 17, 1954

## ADDITIONS (AND CHANGES)
### Copied July 1, 1988

MATHES, Edith, 1929-1985
MORGAN, James H., Feb. 11, 1952 - July 5, 1980

MORGAN, Johnathan H., Mar. 25, 1913 - Sep. 10, 1968
MORGAN, Della M. (w), May 18, 1929 -

STROUPE, William A., Aug. 12, 1911 - Mar. 3, 1979
        US Army, WWII

WHALEY, --------, 1911-1972

BENNETT, Lucinda, 1876 - 1972

EDWARDS, Anthony Kim, Oct. 26, 1961 - Oct. 6, 1966

PRESNELL, James M., Mar. 23, 1915 - Nov. 23, 1968

BEALS (ALSO CALLED GARLAND) CEMETERY - (continued)

HARGETT, Artha E., Aug. 18, 1919 - Mar. 4, 1971
HARGETT, Wilma D. Presnell, Jan. 23, 1916 - May 23, 1986

LOCKNER, Albert B., 1910-1979

GARLAND, Sam, 1882-1965
GARLAND, Handy, 1884-1966

PRESNELL, J. P., Sept. 12, 1883 - April 15, 1955
PRESNELL, Della B. (w), June 5, 1889 - Oct. 17, 1970

PRESNELL, Elma Jean, b/d July 9, 1948
        Daughter of Thomas Stanley and Margie Ruth Moore Presnell
PRESNELL, Herman, Sept. 17, 1921 - Oct. 9, 1941
PRESNELL, Thomas Stanley, Apr. 28, 1924 - Sept. 10, 1967
        PFC, US Army, WWII

COFFIE, Bernie, 1902-1950 - Son of J. Wesley & Judy Smith Coffie
COFFIE, Dora H. (w), 1900-1961

COFFIE, Vernon, June 28, 1936 - Jan. 5, 1974
COFFIE, Mary R. (w), May 29, 1934 -
COFFIE, Hillard, Sept. 17, 1926 - Jan. 10, 1986

AYERS, Wayne Oscar, May 20, 1977 - May 22, 1986
AYERS, Donald Lynn, Oct. 31, 1971 - May 22, 1986

BEALS, Eva Mae, May 6, 1912 - June 21, 1985
BEALS, Linda,  1964-1983

BEALS, Roscoe, July 28, 1930 - Feb. 22, 1983
        (Roscoe Elonzo Beals - PFC, US Army, Korea)
BEALS, Martha, April 12, 1937 -

BEALS, Darrell, Aug. 27, 1962 - May 22, 1986
BEALS, Wayne H., May 17, 1928 - Mar. 1, 1977
        (Wayne Hawkins Beals, PFC, US Army, Korea)
BEALS, Trula B., July 13, 1932 - May 22, 1986

MORROW, Elizabeth, 1898-1976

BEALS, Alvin Hawkins, Mar. 20, 1901 - Dec. 12, 1966

BEALS, Belinda Ora, Dec. 26, 1897 - Jan. 4, 1974 (Sister)

BEALS, Richard Lee, Jr., 1980-1982

LANE, Clyde Wilson, 1919-1987, PFC, US Army, WWII
LANE, James Edward, May 7, 1950 - July 22, 1972
        SP5, US Army, Vietnam

WOODFIN, Evelyn, 1932-1946

ROGERS, Cecil, 1921-1980, Pvt., US Army, WWII

BEALS (ALSO CALLED GARLAND) CEMETERY - (continued)

TURNER, Richard B., 1938-1971

BRITT, Joe Lee, b/d 1969

BENNETT, Cheves, 1904-1969
BENNETT, Cora C. (w), 1908-19??

CARSON, Essie B. July 27, 1901 - Dec. 7, 1970 (Mother)

PETERSON, Finn, May 5, 1904 - Apr. 7, 1947 (Father)

BAILEY, Marcus, June 2, 1906 - Oct. 20, 1985

TITTLE, Isaac E., Dec. 4, 1889 - Apr. 2, 1967
TITTLE, Blanche B. Lloyd, Nov. 26, 1896 - June 8, 1961

SHELL, Clem B., 1903-1971
SHELL, Mary M. (w), March 5, 1908 - Dec. 14, 1952

POORE, Mary Ann, d. 1973

SHELL, Paul, Sept. 17, 1910 -
SHELL, Roxie (w), Apr. 22, 1911 - July 5, 1982

TITTLE, Della B., Mar. 29, 1890 - Nov. 29, 1967

LOYD, Ben B., Mar. 30, 1879 - Aug. 17, 1968
LOYD, Blanch P. (w), June 2, 1887 - Dec. 10, 1964

BEALS, Warren H., Feb. 7, 1922 - Mar. 19, 1978
BEALS, Madellon C., Feb. 10, 1920 -

BAKER, George Samuel, Nov. 25, 1919 - Sept. 23, 1962
          PFC, Btry A, 929 Field Arty. BN, WWII
BAKER, David W., 1876-1941
BAKER, Laura Y. (w), Apr. 28, 1881 - July 12, 1967
BAKER, Myrtle L., Oct. 18, 1904 - May 31, 1986
BAKER, Clyde Wilson, Feb. 1, 1907 - Aug. 10, 1972

HARRIS, Larry P., 1948-1969
HARRIS, Linda M., 1949-

SHELL, Jerry Lynn, b/d 1966
SHELL, Helen, 1928-1962
SHELL, Angeline, 1869-1938
SHELL, William A., 1867-1938

SLEMONS, David Britt, b/d Jan. 26, 1942
          Infant son of Mr. and Mrs. J. R. Slemons
                (James Raymond & Mary Marie Shell Slemons)

GRINDSTAFF, Hobert, 1898-1988
GRINDSTAFF, Bertha, 1919-1985

PHILLIPS, Doris M., 1945-1988

SHELL, (First name missing),  ----- - 1972
SHELL, Juanita, 1909-1988

SHELL, Alvin Loss, Sept. 7, 1877 - Aug. 25, 1949
SHELL, Elizabeth B. (w), May 26, 1877 - Aug. 9, 1962

TREADWAY, Biddie M., Mar. 24, 1866 - Jan. 11, 1934
TREADWAY, Roxie Mae, Oct. 6, 1892 - Sep. 11, 1968

MATHES, George,  1896  -
MATHES, Mammie,  1903-1968

O'BRIEN, Howard H., Mar. 15, 1910 -
O'BRIEN, Deanie Daisy, Feb. 7, 1909 - June 20, 1987

BAKER, Joseph B., 1899-1940 -
BAKER, Ida Spray (w), 1907 - 1956  (also see p. 69)
BAKER, Tallulah, d. June 3, 1939 (Infant daughter)

ROGERS, Finia B., 1883-1939  (Mother)

THORTON, Jason B., Apr. 11, 1976 - Oct. 23, 1984

HEAD, Sarah Cathern, 1893-1980

HIGGINS, Minnie, 1932-1976

MILLER, Charles G., Mar. 8, 1955 - Mar. 12, 1974, U.S.N.R.

BENNETT, Gaither, 1897-1988
BENNETT, Annie W. (w), 1896-1969, married Oct. 14, 1915

MOSLEY, Backus, 1913-1968

GRINDSTAFF, Otis M., 1900-1964
GRINDSTAFF, Bobby J. Jr.,  d. 1968

OLIVER, Walker E., 1906-1971

BENNETT, Maggie, June 27, 1909 - Nov. 5, 1978
BENNETT, Lloyd Cecil, 1921-1978, PFC, US Army, WWII

PETERSON, Dove W., 1892-1964
PETERSON, Loretta M., 1900-1948

WATSON, Juanita Marie, d. 1929

FURCHES, Emmett L., Jan. 28, 1904 - Jan. 29, 1982
FURCHES, Ella Bogart (w), Feb. 17, 1904 -

BROOKS, William F., (Broken Stone)

WHALEY, Cordelia Tipton, - Wife of Jake Whaley

BEALS (ALSO CALLED GARLAND) CEMETERY - (continued)

HERRELL, William M., May 27, 1895 - May 12, 1978  (Dad)

SAMS, Roy, 1922-1987

LANE, Hobert, Feb. 20, 1898- May 23, 1984  (Father)

HERRELL, Simon E., 1889-1971
HERRELL, Sarah J., 1900-

LANE, Louary Henry, Aug. 19, 1899 - Aug. 5, 1972 (Mother)
LANE, Guy Nelson (son), Nov. 3, 1919 - July 19, 1971

BENNETT, Marion, 1887-1967
BENNETT, Milisia, 1898-1977  (Mom)

POTTER, Daniel Jr., 1929-1985, US Navy, WWII

WATTS, Biddie Sue, 1882-1956

HUSKINS, Marie, May 12, 1928 - Nov. 18, 1929
        Daughter of Joe and Alice Nelson Huskins

ELLIOTT, Eliza Jane, Aug. 5, 1855 - Jan. 5, 1931  (Mother)

BEALS (ALSO CALLED GARLAND) CEMETERY - UNMARKED GRAVES

BENNETT, Ike, age 57, d. Nov. 21, 1927
        Son of Arch and Jane Hensley Bennett

COFFEE, Lester, age 1, d. Sept. 25, 1929
        Son of Burnie and Dora Huskins Coffee

HALL, Infant, d. Nov. 6, 1950
        Child of Wintfred and Maddeline Huskins Hall

HUSKINS, Brenda Gali, Infant, d. Sept. 27, 1946
        Daughter of Earl and Nellie Miller Huskins

IMLER, David E., age 79, d. Oct. 2, 1942

LAUGHRUM, Lula, age 55, d. Aug. 29, 1948

MOORE, James, age 55, d. March 29, 1931

McBRIDE, Frank M., age 55, d. Nov. 16, 1933

ROGERS, Infant Daughter, d. March 6, 1948
        Daughter of Cecil and Irene Lloyd Rogers

SHELL, Doran Lee, Jr., Infant, d. Nov. 2, 1963
        Son of Doran Lee and Patsy Lee Nichols Shell

SHELL, Helen, age 1, d. Aug. 24, 1929
        Daughter of Alvin and L------P----- Shell
RUNION, Infant, d. April 1, 1934
        Child of Huey Thomas and Melba Mae Foster Runion

METCALF, Infant, d. 1948
        (Donald Ray), Son of Hubert & Atlas Beatrice White Metcalf
WHITSON, Infant, d. 1947
        Son of Fate and Ruth Crowder Whitson
CROWDER, Infant, d. 1940

CROWELL, Frank A., 1881-1950
        (Frank Ashton) d. Nov. 22, 1950

HENSLEY, Hobert, Feb. 11, 1897 - June 20, 1940

TIPTON, Mary Gail and Sherry Nell, d. 1956
        Twins of Hubert U. and Elinor Louise Elliott Tipton

JOHNSON, Ed, Jan. 21, 1906 -
JOHNSON, Nora, Feb. 12, 1900 - Oct. 21, 1972

ELLIOTT, Richard S., Oct. 7, 1866 - June 10, 1951
ELLIOTT, Adeline B. (w), May 14, 1873 - June 24, 1935
        Daughter of Willy A. and Clarisa Roark Broswell

MILLER, Paul T., Jan. 14, 1934 - Mar. 11, 1934
        Son of Oscar and Maude Day Miller

MILLER, Oscar H., Sept. 15, 1888 - Mar. 10, 1958
MILLER, Maude Day   (w), Oct. 2, 1897 -

ALLEN, Fred M., Dec. 26, 1938 - Aug. 31, 1979
ALLEN, Sara M. (w), Aug. 31, 1941 -

PATE, Ronnie Lee, July 14, 1949 - Jan. 26, 1952
        Son of Samalee and Louise Pate

MILLER, George W., Mar. 10, 1858 - May 19, 1937
MILLER, Nancy Esther (w), Apr. 29, 1865 - Feb. 14, 1945
        Married Aug. 26, 1883
    FOOTSTONES:  George - son of John Miller and Sarah
                    Mitchell/ married 1849
                    Esther - daughter of J. Henry Ambrose, Sr.
                    and Rachel Tittle/ married 1858

COOPER, Harvey H., 1887-1955
        Son of Louis Eggleston & Susan Catherine Booker Cooper
COOPER, Sarah E., 1886-1964
        Daughter of Geo. W. and Esther Ambrose Miller

MILLER, Infant, b/d 1937 - Son of Mr. and Mrs. Conway Miller

HENSLEY, George S., Nov. 18, 1874 - Mar. 21, 1943
HENSLEY, Maggie Cantrell (w), Oct. 31, 1877 - June 18, 1945
        Daughter of Thomas Cantrell

LUTTRELL, Albert L.,  July 8, 1899 -
LUTTRELL, Gladys H. (w), March 6, 1901 - Nov. 3, 1983

HENSLEY, Wallace C.,  May 1, 1903 - June 12, 1960
        Son of George and Maggie Cantrell Hensley
HENSLEY, Mary M. (w),  Aug. 14, 1905 - Oct. 15, 1974

MILLER, J. Matt,  1881-1948
MILLER, Laura Dean (w),  1884-1952

MILLER, Ernest,  Oct. 1, 1909 - May 6, 1967, USNR, WWII

SEARLES, Rose Miller,  1916-1971

MILLER, Conway C.,  Jan. 8, 1907 - May 14, 1980
MILLER, Ora M.,  Aug. 12, 1908 -

AYERS, Solmon J.,  Sept. 3, 1895 - June 9, 1960
AYERS, Mae V.,  Feb. 18, 1918 - Jan. 17, 1956

SMITH, Tommie Marion,  Sept. 5, 1924 - July 5, 1980
        US Army, WWII

SMITH, Alfred M.,  1902-1979
SMITH, Nora E. (w),  1906-1978

TOLLEY, Hubert,  1897 -
TOLLEY, Ethel, 1900-1953, Dau. of W. B. and Fannie Tapp McNabb

TAPP, William Blaine, Mar. 23, 1903 - June 29, 1957 - US Army, WWII
        Son of Wm. Tapp

HENLEY, David Frank,  1911-1949

EDWARDS, James M.,  July 16, 1894 (or 1896) - Dec. 29, 1953
        Pvt., 11th Inf., WWI
EDWARDS, Pearl T. (w),  1902 -

DAVIS, Ruth Honeycutt, Oct. 31, 1915 - Feb. 23, 1940

HONEYCUTT, D. L.,  1886-1971
HONEYCUTT, Minnie Belle (w),  1886-1962
HONEYCUTT,(Footstone) Belle Gibbs, Jan. 20, 1886 - May 1, 1962
HONEYCUTT, Jack,  1913-1915 (son)

ELLIOTT, William Turner, Sr.,  May 27, 1897-Apr.17,1977, US Army
ELLIOTT, Josie R.,  June 22, 1903 - Oct. 6, 1972          WWI

ELLIOTT, Thomas C., Nov. 10, 1892 - Dec. 25, 1962
        Son of Richard E. and Adeline Buazwell Elliott
ELLIOTT, Nellie Short (w), May 27, 1892 - Mar. 27, 1979

VANOVER, Conley E.,  1910-1979
VANOVER, Mary J. Elliott (w),  1915-1965
VANOVER, Roby A.,  July 15, 1885 - Apr. 6, 1968
VANOVER, Eula Edney (w),  Nov. 9, 1880 (or 1889) - 1987

VANOVER, Liza Tolly, 1868 - Feb. 27, 1942

EDNEY, PFC Boney, Mar. 1842 - 1932
EDNEY, Miltdia (w), Feb. 1852 - 1932

PARSLEY, Earl, May 29, 1919 - 1920
PARSLEY, Victoria, Aug. 2, 1893 - May 30, 1921

PARSLEY, Margaret, Aug. 26, 1924 - Sept. 26, 1924
PARSLEY, Audrey , Aug. 26, 1924 - Nov. 26, 1924

ELLIOTT, Herman, d. 1931, Son of Turner & Josie Riddle Elliott

EDWARDS, Atla Kate, Apr. 5, 1907 - Sept. 6, 1954

ODOM, Nancy, 1840-1925

MILLER, John K., Jan. 29, 1862 - June 20, 1947
        From Kentucky PFC, Hosp. Corp

MILLER, Nora E. Edwards, Aug. 30, 1884 - July 6, 1964
        Daughter of Wm. and Nettie Elliott Edwards

STOCKTON, Lyda Ben, Jan. 31, 1909 - Aug. 12, 1969
STOCKTON, Etta Harris (w), Feb. 17, 1910 - Jan. 18, 1976

COPELAND, James Caroll, Oct. 8, 1957 - Oct. 9, 1957
COPELAND, Vivian Smith, Sept. 18, 1936 - Oct. 11, 1957

SMITH, Lum, Feb. 13, 1901 -
SMITH, Dorothy Peterson, Mar. 8, 1908 -

HAMPTON, Daniel W., 1865-1935   (Father)
HAMPTON, Hannah A., 1867-1947

KEEVER, Baby Boy, b/d 1951

SIMMONS, Wilby, March 26, 1907 - Dec. 5, 1968
SIMMONS, Nora Peterson (w), Dec. 19, 1905 -

MILLER, Robert, Oct. 7, 1894 - Feb. 8, 1952
MILLER, Estella Allen, Dec. 28, 1895 - Mar. 5, 1975

DAVIS, Bob, 1873-1948

TALLEY, William James, July 12, 1912 - Apr. 15, 1984

MILLER, Jacob, Co. A, 3 NC Mtd. Inf., Union Army

McINTURFF, Jim, 1834-1862

WHITE, Edna Parsley, May 8, 1896 - June 19, 1927
        Daughter of Mose and Charlotte Jones Parsley
WHITE, Bruce Jr. (son), Apr. 18, 1926 - Dec. 22, 1926

MARVIN, Lucille Markland, May 30, 1916 - May 5, 1986

WHITE, Baby, -
WHITE, Baby, -
WHITE, Baby, -
WHITE, Baby, -

HICKS, Luther K., 1896-1953

RANDOLPH, John D., Jan. 29, 1907 - July 30, 1966 - USNR, WWII

DOVER, Maggie B., 1883-1967

BUCK, Andy, 1866-1945

DOVER, John Stover, May 5, 1879 - July 15, 1963, PVT, Cavalry

HAMPTON, Wade P., 1900-1947
HAMPTON, Woodford, 1902-1977
          Brothers

RENFRO, Thomas B. Jr., Oct. 14, 1918 - Feb. 28, 1985
RENFRO, Nell V. (w#1), Mar. 29, 1923 - Dec. 29, 1953
RENFRO, Della B. (w#2), June 10, 1935 -

RENFRO, Thomas "Tom", Mar. 15, 1891 - Dec. 4, 1968
RENFRO, Millie H. (w), Aug. 30, 1892 - Apr. 10, 1987

RENFRO, Ray, Feb. 7, 1930 - May 10, 1947

ELLIOTT, Grover B., 1908-1983, PVT, US Army, WWII

WHITE, Troy, 1907-1974, PVT, US Army
WHITE, Julia, 1905-1974

WHITE, Harvey H., 1876-1947
WHITE, Fannie B. (w), 1874-1951

HUSKINS, Henry, Mar. 14, 1885 - June 22, 1940
HUSKINS, Julia White (w), Mar. 26, 1891 - Dec. 20, 1938

EDWARDS, no other marking

WHITE, Chriss, Oct. 22, 1850 - Aug. 22, 1918
WHITE, Mary Simmons (w), Oct. 12, 1852 - June 7, 1919
WHITE, Labe (son), Feb. 3, 1887 - Nov. 3, 1919

SIMMONS, George W., 1850-1927
          Son of Leander Simmons

ANDERSON, Jake L., Oct. 1, 1905 - Sept. 24, 1947
          Son of Landon Taylor and Mary Simmons Anderson
          Tec 4, Co.B, 592 Engr, WWII

WHITE, Katie, July 4, 1911 - Feb. 2, 1914
          Daughter of H. H. and Fannie White

JOHNSON, Elisa E. White, 1862-1884

McINTURFF, William, 1886-1940
McINTURFF, Shelton, 1881-1947

McCURRY, Mack, 1886-1955
McCURRY, Laura A. (w), 1892-1928

FENDER, Jackie, 1936-1958
        Daughter of Mack and Lora Hughes McCurry

BENNETT, Roy, 1910-1931  (Son)

SIMERLY, Lucille, d. 1934

MILLER, Joe Fuller, Mar. 4, 1882 - Dec. 23, 1947
MILLER, Mattie (w), Nov. 3, 1887 - Apr. 30, 1976

HUGHES, Harrison C., July 8, 1892 - Aug. 8, 1977
        PVT, US Army, WWI
HUGHES, Laura L. (w), Mar. 5, 1899 - May 6, 1975

JOHNSON, Linnie R., 1909-1973

LEWIS, Sandra J. Renfro, Apr. 19, 1960 - Mar. 26, 1985 ("Dau")

PETERSON, Alfred, 1920-1964
        Son of Robert W. and Ester Miller Peterson

PETERSON, James T., May 24, 1869 - Aug. 29, 1961 - "Father"

PETERSON, Willard, June 25, 1913 -
PETERSON, Lura V., Oct. 9, 1918 -

BARNETT, Pamela Dawn, 1956-1961

BENNETT, Moses E., Nov. 8, 1894 - Feb. 10, 1967
BENNETT, Ellie H. (w), Feb. 18, 1904 -
BENNETT, Cpl. Albert, Apr. 1, 1923 - Jan. 21, 1945
        Son of Mose and Ellie Bennett.  Husband of Alverta J.
        Bennett.  Killed on Active Duty Jan. 21, 1945 with
        US Army Air Corp

JONES, Henry, b. 1876 -
JONES, Martha Peterson, 1874-1945

PETERSON, John L., Sept. 27, 1898 - Feb. 13, 1983, "(Father)"
PETERSON, Julia, July 18, 1901 - May 4, 1956

JOHNSON, Robert L., July 30, 1888 - Nov. 24, 1954
JOHNSON, Sarah Bennett, May 4, 1892 - Aug. 9, 1963

POLLARD, Darlene, Aug. 3, 1937 - Sept. 13, 1972, "Dau"

HARRIS, Geneva, Feb.28,1910 - May 20,1945
HARRIS, Armetta, July 18,1940 - Jan.17,1945

DUNAWAY, Paul C. 1896-1972

CARPENTER, Exie Ingram, 1911-1954 (Momma)
          Daughter of Dick and Katy Harrell Ingram

HENSLEY, Mrs. Dark -

SIMMONS, Marth Jane Clouse, Oct.13,1885 - Jan.21,1969

RIDDLE, Virginia, 1911-1978

INGRAM, Katy M. 1880-1968
INGRAM, Mr. Dick
INGRAM, Mert - Son of J.D. and Kate Harwelle Ingram

EDWARDS, John Henry, May 3,1893- Sept.25,1968
EDWARDS, Allie White, (w), June 22,1898 - July 30,1936

3 Stones marked "EDWARDS"

HENSLEY, Burnie -
HENSLEY, Infant, - Son Of Mr. and Mrs. Blane Hensley

HONEYCUTT, P.L., Co. B 13 Tenn. Cav. Union Army
HONEYCUTT, Ann Tipton, 1859 - 1927

BARNETT, Spencer -
BARNETT, Nannie, (w) -

COOKE, Alice, 1913 - 1943

BANNER, Lillie, -

LaFOLLETTE, Henry, -

WHITE, D.Landon, May 22,1898 - Sept.12,1971
WHITE, Josephine H. (w), May 22,1902 - Nov.14,1942
WHITE, Paul,-
WHITE, Claralee, -
WHITE, Irene, -
WHITE, Mable, -

SCALF, Emily White, Nov.22,1928 - Jan.2,1962 ("Dau.")

UNMARKED GRAVES

RENFRO, Jack, Jan.16,1930 - Jan.20,1930
RENFRO, Oliff, May 25,1931 - Oct.24,1931
      Sons of Ruben and Frances Honeycutt Renfro
RENFRO, Julia, d. July 17,1932 at 61
      Dau. of Jom and Nancy Renfro
RENFRO, Nathan,
RENFRO, Rube Mack, Jr., b/d Jan.25,1959 (1960?)
      Son of Rube Mack and Gladys Louella Hutchins Renfro
      Grandson of Rube M. Renfro on page 265

## McLAUGHLIN CEMETERY

On McLaughlin Road (1 mile N. of
Unicoi Exit) on W. side of expressway

Copied June 11, 1988

HORTON, Taylor J., 1908-1968

HORTON, Mamie Alice, Mar. 23, 1937 - June 14, 1938
    Daughter of James Taylor and Mary Belle McLaughlin Horton

McLAUGHLIN, George W., Mar. 22, 1880 - Aug. 26, 1952
McLAUGHLIN, Effie B. (w#1), July 26, 1878 - June 9, 1944
McLAUGHLIN, Orpha (w#2), Jan. 14, 1893 - Mar. 8, 1952

McLAUGHLIN, Rosalie, Aug. 22, 1940 - Sep. 4, 1940
    Daughter of S. Eugene "Gene" & Rachel Elizabeth Linville
                           McLaughlin

McLAUGHLIN, Lynn, b/d 1959
    Dau. of Foya and Ruby McLaughlin

McLAUGHLIN, R. C. Jr., May 8, 1934 - June 27, 1934
    Son of R. C. and Lottie Horton McLaughlin

PRESLEY, Robert A., d. 1969

PHILLIPS, Infant, b/d Mar. 26, 1891 - Dau. of W. L. Phillips

BURNETT, Baxter, 1885-1934

BRITT, Louis, d(?) 1875
             Plus Many unmarked stones


## HORTON CEMETERY

Across highway from McLaughlin Cemetery
to right, rear of small white church on
Johnson City Highway on top of hill
Copied June 11, 1988

HORTON, Zeph F., July 29, 1877 - Oct. 18, 1959
HORTON, Betty Ann (w), 1880-1950

HORTON, William Finn, 1852-1940
HORTON, Rosylinn Bennet (w), 1854-1938

HORTON, James Taylor, Mar. 19, 1889 - Oct. 25, 1978 (Mason)
HORTON, Polly Birchfield (w), Aug. 13, 1894 - Feb. 18, 1969
HORTON, Nettie (dau), b/d 1921

SHEPARD, Annie, Apr. 1, 1891 - July 10, 1928

JOHNSON, Ella Horton, 1916-1951 (Eastern Star)

MOORE, Paul Martin Sr., Oct. 15, 1903 - Dec. 20, 1962

BENNETT, Mona,  May 2, 1929 - Oct. 27, 1931

BENNETT, Baxter,  Mar. 14, 1882 - Jan. 20, 1934

BOWMAN, Nettie B.,  July 18, 1886 - Apr. 4, 1935
        Dau. of David & Ella Buchanan Birchfield - d. Apr.21, 1930

HORTON, Helen Marie, d. Aug. 14, 1928 (baby)
        Dau. of Milton and Beulah Horton

BOWMAN, Pamela, d. Oct. 1, 1951 (baby)
        Daughter of Jack and Betty Head

BIRCHFIELD, David B., 1850-1939
BIRCHFIELD, Ella,     1861-1930

                    plus several unmarked stones, including:

FORD, John W., d. Dec. 31, 1945 - age 75
BOWMAN, Ernest,
BOWMAN, Afred (Alfred?),
BOWMAN, Dave, age 25 - died Dec. 23, 1929
        Sons of John H. and Nettie Birchfield Bowman


                    DAVIS - GOUGE CEMETERY

            On Davis Road, off Route 107, Limestone Cove

                    Copied June 29, 1988

PATE, Beryl Grant, June 29, 1927 - Aug. 28, 1978
        PFC, US Army, WWII
PATE, Elaine (w), Sep. 27, 1933 -

McCOURY, Grady,  Oct. 18, 1901 - Dec. 1, 1981
McCOURY, Ethel D. (w),  Aug. 27, 1911 -

DAVIS, Willard,  Sep. 2, 1929 - Apr. 21, 1980
DAVIS, Bernice (w),  Aug. 19, 1929 - married Sep. 2, 1948
DAVIS, Johnnie Ray, b/d 1970
DAVIS, Ronald Lee (son), Dec. 9, 1949 - July 27, 1982

LACEY, Brown, Mar. 16, 1918 - June 11, 1988
LACEY, Mary (w),  Aug. 3, 1917 -

DAVIS, Rev. Frank,  May 21, 1921 - Jan. 15, 1972
        Pvt., Co. H, 351 Inf., WWII
DAVIS, Nina (w),  1913 -

DAVIS, Ralph,  May 13, 1932 - Apr. 12, 1954

DAVIS - GOUGE CEMETERY (continued)

DAVIS, Charles H., Apr. 12, 1885 - Oct. 25, 1961
DAVIS, Rachel Hill (w), July 3, 1890 - Oct. 9, 1942

DAVIS, Earl T., Sep. 24, 1917 - Mar. 12, 1956
          PFC, Co. G, 330 Inf., WWII

DAVIS, John D., 1871-1940
DAVIS, Judy Gouge (w), 1879-1960

WHITSON Rissie C., Feb. 9, 1896 - Aug. 10, 1976

DAVIS, Charles Eugene, 1948-1968

JOHNSON, Eva May, Feb. 4, 1915 - Feb. 10, 1918
          Daughter of S. J. and Luta (?) Johnson

GEOUGE, J. S., June 16, 1853 - June 3, 1925
GOUGE, Mary,   July 15, 1853 - Nov. 30, 1939

MILLER, Dock,  no dates
MILLER, Lizzie (w), no dates

DAVIS, Thomas, d. June 7, 1919

PATE, Infant, d. Mar. 16 (?), 1919
PATE, Infant, d. July 12, 1923 - children of Dewey Pate

MOORE, Edward, 1911-1941

GRINDSTAFF, Sidney R., Nov. 29, 1917 -
GRINDSTAFF, Okie D. (w), Jan. 23, 1923 - Dec. 24, 1975

BYRD, Margaret, Mar. 26, 1888 - Feb. 12, 1912
          Daughter of Blake and Caroline Byrd
DAVIS, Howard, Jan. 24, 1909 - Aug. 28, 1928
DAVIS, Lurla (w), Sep. 7, 1902 - Mar. 20, 1926

DUDLEY, James, May 7, 1928 - July 20, 1928

DAVIS, Infant, d. 1930

                Plus many unmarked stones

# WOODBY CEMETERY

On Simerly Creek Road, near junction
w/ Piney Grove Road , up dirt road at
junction

Copied June 29, 1988

McLAUGHLIN, William J. , July 27, 1916 - Sept. 19, 1983
        S2, US Navy, WWII

SMITH, Scottie C., d. May 18, 1974

MILLER, Roby, 1899-1971

SMITH, Betty Lou, Nov. 17, 1946 - Mar. 18, 1971

WOODBY, Henderson W., June 24, 1884 - June 11, 1977
WOODBY, Maggie H. (w), Apr. 10, 1892 - July 5, 1979

HILL, Kern, 1898-1964
HILL, Nell (w), 1907 -

BENNETT, Nathan W., Feb. 23, 1885 - Apr. 12, 1963
BENNETT, Edith H. (w), June 27, 1894 - Sep. 11, 1968

BENNETT, Neta Hyder, July 24, 1920 - Dec. 15, 1963

CHAMBERS, Janet Michelle, 1969-1977

CAMPBELL, Billy Jr.,   1932-1986
CAMPBELL, Mary A. (w), 1936 -
CAMPBELL, Gary Lynn (son), 1956-1984
CAMPBELL, Allen Dean (son), Dec. 9, 1960 - Mar. 11, 1987

WARD, Woodrow C., 1913-1981

DAVIS, Thomas William, Feb. 18, 1888 - Jan. 6, 1946
        Cpl., 157th Inf., 40th Div., WWI

WOODBY, Toney, 1903-1979

WOODBY, Pefro, 1872-1917

CLARK, Luther M., Oct. 29, 1893 - Oct. 13, 1933
CLARK, Lockey Woodby (w), July 8, 1899 - Mar. 25, 1917
CLARK, Infant Son, d. Feb. 15, 1916

SNEYD, Joe, 1892-1945
SNEYD, Robert W., 1918-1970

SMITH, Bert, 1909-1951

WOODBY, Herbert W., 1908-1983

WOODBY, Floy, 1921-1974
WOODBY, Maxi, d. at 3 mo.

BYRD, Harrison, Aug. 3, 1904 - Sep. 10, 1979

WOODBY, Linda Beth, Aug. 1, 1985 - Jan. 25, 1986
        Daughter of Dan Woodby


HILL, Earl,          1903 -
HILL, Millie Stanley (w),  1913-1953
HILL, Shirley (dau),   b/d 1937
HILL, Mary (dau),    b/d 1947

WOODBY, John,    1878-1952
WOODBY, Lydia (w),  1883-1963
WOODBY, Ida,     d. 1909    "Mother"

BAILEY, Edward,    1888-1965
BAILEY, Polly D. (w),   1892-1969
BAILEY, Ethel (dau?), Jan. 24, 1910 - Jan. 10, 1944
BAILEY, Infant (dau),   Jan. 18, 1931 - Feb. 6, 1931
BAILEY, Reece (son),    Apr. 28, 1927 - July 10, 1927

CAMPBELL, James S., Oct. 15, 1891 - Dec. 12, 1974
CAMPBELL, Bessie M. (w),  1896-1936
        Daughter of John and Jane Stapleton  Markam
CAMPBELL, Lucy, Mar. 5, 1928 - July 27, 1962
CAMPBELL, Ray A., May 30, 1932 - July 10, 1932

WOODBY, William P., Apr. 25, 1863 - Aug. 1, 1944
WOODBY, Margaret Gilbert (w),  Mar. 13, 1870 - July 12, 1937
WOODBY, Mary Elizabeth (dau),  Aug. 10, 1902 - Sept. 11, 1918

WOODBY, Harrison, Oct. 9, 1900 - Aug. 14, 1965
WOODBY, Mae Tolley (w),  Oct. 11, 1913 -

WOODBY, James,  June 15, 1858 - July 7, 1893

CAMPBELL, Baby,  d. Mar. 12, 1964 - son of John Campbell

SNEYD, Lidy,  1832(?) - 1945
SNEYD, J. L., 1888    - 1940
LACEY, Reece, June 20, 1905 -
LACEY, Ethel Byrd (w),  Aug. 21, 1909 - July 27, 1944

BYRD, Blake, July 20, 1853 - May 12, 1932
        Son of George and Jane Phillips Byrd
BYRD, Caroline (w),   Apr. 10, 1855 - July 27, 1937
        Daughter of Wilburn and Sassama Lusk Clark
WOODBY, Hezekiah,  Co. B., 13th Tenn. Cav.,  Union Army

BYRD, Ira J.,  May 8, 1915 -
BYRD, Avanell Smith (w),  Jan. 25, 1922 - Aug. 30, 1964
BYRD, Gail M. (dau),  Jan. 3, 1950 - Apr. 3, 1968
BYRD, Clay J. (son),  Dec. 1, 1948 - Dec. 3, 1948
BYRD, Bradley (son),  b/d May 17, 1960

BYRD, John Sherman,  July 31, 1879 - Dec. 2, 1965
        Son of Blake and Caroline Byrd
BYRD, Emma Woodby (w),  Jan. 22, 1877 - May 18, 1951
BYRD, Sam (son),  July 3, 1907 - June 27, 1931

WOODBY, Alfred, Aug. 1845 - Nov. 1919
WOODBY, Fannie Gilbert (w), 1847 - July 1912

WOODBY, Anna McCarley, Nov. 24, 1873 - May 27, 1910
        Wife of William Woodby

HILL, Harry, Oct. 29, 1894 - Apr. 21, 1964

COMPTON, Neptie Hill, Dec. 26, 1906 - Apr. 25, 1934
        Wife of Walter Compton

HILL, Charles B., Sep. 12, 1864 - June 23, 1947
HILL, Minerva Street (w), June 28, 1873 - Oct. 23, 1938

STREET, Gay Hill, June 22, 1912 - Oct. 19, 1939
        Wife of Finley Street

STREET, Ethel, Sept. 4, 1936 - Nov. 27, 1942

HILL, Sarah, Apr. 16, 1909 - Dec. 23, 1942

BARNETT, Patsy Hill, Apr. 6, 1843 - May 26, 1939

SMITH, Annie, Sep. 13, 1870 - Sep. 4, 1960

SMITH, Charlie A., Mar. 31, 1891 - June 6, 1970 - Pvt. WWI
SMITH, Adline (w), 1900-1985

GREGG, Ruby S., Jan. 25, 1925 - Dec. 26, 1974

HILL, Brenda Louise, 1951-1952

HILL, Lonnie, July 21, 1918 - Apr. 6, 1954

ROBERTS, Isaac H., Aug. 21, 1903 - June 8, 1966
ROBERTS, Reptie H. (w), April 26, 1901 -

SMITH, Barbara Ann, Mar. 18, 1956 - Dec. 28, 1960
        Daughter of Carroll R. and Nora Mae Morrow Smith

                    Plus a few unmarked stones, including:
CAMPBELL, Thomas Batay, age 87 - d. Feb. 24, 1941
        Son of Evans and Betsy Frye Campbell

SNEED, Alfred, age 74, d. Feb. 1, 1937
        Son of Seth and Martha Woodby Sneed

# HAYNES CEMETERY

On Rt. 23 near Marbleton Road,
On west side toward expressway

Copied July 8, 1988

HAYNES, Nathaniel T., Apr. 4, 1838 - Mar. 8, 1931
HAYNES, Elizabeth Luvenia (w), 1846-1908
HAYNES, Rhosavene, 1885-1906
HAYNES, Lesley,    b/d Feb. 6, 1909

HAYNES, David,    1788-1868
HAYNES, Rhoda Ann, (w) 1795 - 1861, Dau. of Matthew Taylor
          Parents of Landon Carter Haynes
HAYNES, James P., 1832-1853

HAYNES, George G., Apr. 11, 1867 - May 3, 1924
HAYNES, Alice V. (w), May 17, 1870 - May 27, 1943

BELL, David Haynes, d. Apr. 21, 1913
       Infant son of David T. Bell


No other unmarked stones

## UNAKA SPRINGS MEM. CEMETERY

On Unaka Springs Road, 1.1 mi. from
Bridge at Chestoa

Copied September 8, 1988

ARWOOD, Luther W. Sr., 1925-1983

HENSLEY, Reges, 1922-1979

TIPTON, Hugh,  1900-1988

BROCKUS, James H., 1899-1958

BROCKUS, William P., June 22, 1873 - May 2, 1953
         Cpl., Co F, 6th US Vol. Inf., Span-Am War
BROCKUS, Dortha (w), June 15, 1883 - June 15, 1951

RAY, Will D.,  1893-1915

FOSTER, Mary L., Apr. 9, 1963 - Apr. 10, 1963
HOWELL, William C.,  1881-1963
HOWELL, Zeania (w),  1883-1947

FOSTER, Bud, d. 1913 (?)

FOSTER, Clinton,  Oct. 15, 1915 - June 17, 1979

FOSTER, Leander J., July 2, 1890 - July 2, 1942
FOSTER, Nancy C. (w), Apr. 3, 1892 - Feb. 16, 1971

DAVIS, Donald W., 1913-1982

TOLLEY, Infant, b/d 1964

FOSTER, Nancy E., May 15, 1966 - Apr. 22, 1967

LOVETTE, John, b. May 23, 1910

TIPTON, Infant, b/d 1940

BANNER, Ralph E., Dec. 26, 1903 - May 18, 1949
        Son of Isaac W. and Julia Tapp Banner
BANNER, Inez (w), Nov. 2, 1910 - Feb. 24, 1962
        Daughter of Leander and Nancy Tipton Foster
BANNER, Gail 1929-1988
BANNER, Infant, d. Mar. 9, 1944
        Son of Ralph Edison and Inez Foster Banner

HENSLEY, Jody J., b/d Aug. 19, 1970

LOVETTE, David, June 8, 1886 - Oct. 7, 1976
LOVETTE, Minnie (w), Oct. 18, 1893 - Dec. 3, 1983

PRICE, Ollie, 1872-1961

PRICE, Fred, 1904-1956

HOWELL, Raymond, Apr. 7, 1907 - Apr. 8, 1982
HOWELL, Jack (son), July 13, 1937 - June 22, 1960

HOWELL, Eliza, 1851-1939

FOSTER, Will "Pap", 1868(?) - 1915
FOSTER, Maggie "Ma", 1870    - 1972
FOSTER, Charlie, no dates
FOSTER, Bud, 1913-1935

SHELTON, Earl, 1944-1978

FOSTER, William, 1896-1967
FOSTER, Marietta Howell (w), Dec. 14, 1905 - Oct. 7, 1930

COOPER, H., 1874-1941

COOPER, Nelce, Aug. 12, 1901 - Mar. 29, 1960
        Son of H. and Omah Cooper

STRANGE, Morgan, Nov. 6, 1928 - Oct. 9, 1959
        Son of Daniell Earl and Kathy Wright Strange
STRANGE, Mary Lou (dau), b/d Nov. 10, 1949

COOPER, Catherine,  1904-1974

COOPER, Willie,  1935-1984

HOWELL, Joe, Apr. 27, 1908 - Feb. 19, 1953

ANDERS, Demmey Howell, Feb. 18, 1893 - July 20, 1950
        Sister of Joe Howell

TIPTON, Callie,  1907-1908

TIPTON, Hester,  1879-1972

PRICE, Ped,  May 23, 1912 - May 2, 1968
PRICE, Nellie H. (w), May 23, 1921 -
        Maiden name Hensley
PRICE, Micheal (son), Nov. 6, 1948 - Nov. 12, 1953
PRICE, Minnie, d. 1953 - age approx. 66, d. June 18, 1953
        Daughter of -------- and Betty Taylor Price
PRICE, Betty,  no dates

                    Plus many unmarked stones

Also buried in this cemetery in unmarked graves:

BANNER, Ralph William, age 14, d. Sept. 5, 1942
        Son of Ralph and Inez Foster Banner

BROTHERTON, Johnie Carol, age 1 year, d. Mar. 28, 1951
        Child of Homer and Matill Banner Brotherton

DAVIS, Infant Son, b/d Aug. 6, 1948
        Son of Wade D. and Nancie Lovette Davis

FOSTER, Betty, age 1 day, d. June 19, 1941
        Daughter of Clarence and Vada Foster

HIGGINS, Demmie, Feb. 11, 1895 - July 20, 1950
        Daughter of Pete and Lizzie Hubbard Howell

HOWELL, Eliza, age 76, d. Mar. 29, 1935
        Daughter of Jake and ------Roberts Justice

HOWELL, Connie Jene, age 1 mo. d. Oct. 24, 1948
        Daughter of Raymond and Hamie Bradford Howell

HOWELL, Lou Zenia, Oct. 29, 1883 - June 22, 1947
        Daughter of Marcus Bennett

TIPTON, Infant, b/d Dec. 28, 1942
        Child of Kenneth and Marie Tinker Tipton

# FAGAN CEMETERY

On Fagan Road, Off Old Rt. 19/23,
near Carter County line (near
Wisemans' Store)

Copied for "Cemeteries of Carter County" 1960
Field Checked September 11, 1988

FAGAN, R. S., 1878-1914
FAGAN, Bess Geisler (w), May 24, 1881 - June 23, 1918

FAGAN, William R. Sr., Nov. 16, 1830 - May 12, 1906
FAGAN, Ella E. (w), Feb. 16, 1836 - Sept. 9, 1921
FAGAN, William R. (son), May 21, 1880 - May 1, 1904

FAGAN, James M., Aug. 19, 1854 - Oct. 7, 1892
FAGAN, Margaret A. (w), Nov. 12, 1858 - Aug. 3, 1903

FISHER, James Andrew, Aug. 16, 1853 - Nov. 29, 1928
FISHER, Margaret J. Sexton (w), Sep. 30, 1857 - Sep. 1, 1927


# ANDERSON CHAPEL CEMETERY

Off Anderson Road, near Anderson Chapel
Near Carter County Line
Copied October 6, 1988

CAMPBELL, Chester, d. 1985
CAMPBELL, Mary Willie Kate, Sep. 9, 1923 - Jan. 8, 1969
CAMPBELL, Virginia T., Dec. 23, 1946 - Aug. 1, 1964

OWENS, Hugh H., 1895-1946
OWENS, Lucy E. (w), 1899-1930

WHITTIMORE, Betty Gene, d. July 7, 1931
        Daughter of R. T. Whittimore

TIPTON, Infant, d. Sep. 15, 1945 - Son of Ross Tipton

SORRELL, Joseph C., May 10, 1882 - Dec. 12, 1960
SORRELL, Mary Etta (w), Apr. 10, 1891 - Sep. 8, 1971
SORRELL, Sarah Christine (dau), 1912-1934

HENSON, Charles David, Mar. 30, 1932 - Nov. 29, 1969
        USAF, Korean War
HENSON, Ida Pearl Casteel (w), June 4, 1910 - July 3, 1987

MEDLEY, Infant, d. Feb. 1946

SALTS, Raymond P., 1930-1988

SALTS, Mack Sr., Feb. 12, 1884 - July 9, 1969
SALTS, Annie (w), Sep. 9, 1885 - Jan. 21, 1929

GADDY, Una H., 1878-1954

GADDY, Herman Jack, Jan. 11, 1927 - May 19, 1972
        S/Sgt. US Army, WWII

HARVELL, Vernon Lane, June 25, 1918 - Nov. 19, 1948
        US Navy, WWII

WOODBY, Cecil, July 28, 1922 - July 8, 1974, US Army, WWII
WOODBY, Daisy M. (w), Jan. 16, 1926 -

WOODBY, Charlie, June 8, 1918 - Dec. 16, 1935
        Son of W. B. and Bessie Gaddy Woodby

WOODBY, Barnett, Dec. 12, 1884 - Jan. 22, 1957
WOODBY, Bessie G. (w), Mar. 10, 1896 - Apr. 24, 1957

JARRETT, George, May 10, 1865 - Feb. 13, 1951
JARRETT, Sarah J. Shepard (w), Feb. 28, 1869 - May 30, 1945

WOODBY, James, July 8, 1920 - Sep. 26, 1971 - US Navy, WWII

GOBBLE, Retta, May 13, 1888 - Dec. 6, 1940 - Wife of M.P. Gobble

JONES, Elbert J., Oct. 29, 1909 - June 3, 1972

JONES, Rev. R. D., 1868-1928
JONES, Alice R. (w), 1871-1955

JONES, David Franklin, 1902-1956
JONES, Agnes P., d. 1986

JONES, David F., Mar. 10, 1933 - Oct. 12, 1938

TRIVETT, Frank L., Oct. 1, 1955 - Dec. 28, 1955

ROWE, Lucy E., Feb. 6, 1878 - Nov. 25, 1949
        Daughter of Nat and Harriett Britt Peoples

ROWE, W. Lawrence, May 3, 1915 - Dec. 26, 1942
        Son of Wm. H. and Lucy Peoples Rowe

CORRELL, W. Andy, Mar. 3, 1876 - June 22, 1926

CORRELL, Frank Anderson, Apr. 8, 1912 - Nov. 30, 1966
        US Army, WWII

WIDENER, Bert Homer, Feb. 21, 1900 - Sep. 25, 1946

HEAD, Andrew J., 1872-1940

MEDLEY, William R., 1917-1971
MEDLEY, Pauline (w), 1918-

CASTEEL, Jack, May 22, 1870 - May 22, 1925

CASTEEL, Mandy,  d. June 19, 1952

CASTEEL, Bill,  1893-1941

CASTEEL, Elmer Frank, Oct. 12, 1902 - May 4, 1978
CASTEEL, Nannie C.,  Aug. 26, 1903 - Aug. 3, 1968

CASTEEL, Bell,  no other data

CASTEEL, Rosie Clark (?), d. 1977 (?)
CASTEEL, Venie,        Oct. 14, 1912 - Jan. 2, 1929
CASTEEL, John,  Feb. 6, 1915 - Nov. 3, 1918
CASTEEL, Linna Rose, d. Jan. 12, 1934
        Infant daughter of Sidney and Effie Casteel

CASTEEL, Jane,  1864 - July 3, 1923

CASTEEL, John,  Dec. 6, 1852 - Nov. 11, 1937

CORRELL, Julia,  Apr. 15, 1886 - Apr. 27, 1954

JONES, Maggie Key,  1866-1941
JONES, Dall W.,  1884-1964

OWENS, Ruth Ann,  d. 1925 - Daughter of Jim & Mattie Owens

FAIR, W. M.,  Mar. 13, 1901 - Apr. 15, 1918

JARRETT, Robert S.,  1897-1968
JARRETT, Rosa Lee (w),  July 7, 1899 - Sep. 13, 1936

WHITE, Mary E.,  1856-1926

CARROLL, Delah,  1837-1916

MILLER, Frances E., July 7, 1880 - Jan. 13, 1926
        Wife of J. C. Miller

GADDY, William,  Dec. 17, 1884 - Jan. 12, 1922 - Son of Tom Gaddy

WOODBY, Brownlow, Nov. 29, 1918 - Feb. 10, 19--?

GADDY, Marine, Mar. 14, 1902 - Oct. 14, 1918
        Son of Tom and Arilla Gaddy

DAVIS, Elizabeth,  1843(?) - 1928(?)

GADDY, Lucy Arilla, Jan. 20, 1922 - July 7, 1923
        Daughter of Andrew Gaddy

TAYLOR, Martin N., Mar. 9, 1853 - June 17, 1910
TAYLOR, Mary S.,  1852-1933

PEOPLES, Walter,  Mar. 4, 1887 - Aug. 18, 1908

JARRETT, R. S., Mar. 30, 1922 - Mar. 24, 1925

JARRETT, Selma Georgie, Mar. 13, 1920 - Nov. 26, 1925

WHITTEMORE, Taylor W., Jan. 20, 1872 - Nov. 1, 1955
WHITTEMORE, Florence M. (w), Jan. 6, 1876 - Dec. 20, 1927
WHITTEMORE, Linda (dau), Mar. 29, 1907 - Mar. 8, 1934
WHITTEMORE, Elbert (son), Dec. 28, 1896 - Jan. 12, 1897
WHITTEMORE, James (son), Feb. 28, 1892 - Aug. 16, 1927

JARRETT, Ethel, Mar. 28, 1921 - Apr. 1, 1921

WOODBY, Lois, July 12, 1929 - Dec. 10, 1930(?)

FRAZIER, Marion C., Feb. 11, 1920 - Feb. 15, 1984
        Pvt., US Army, WWII

McKINLEY, Hobert, Feb. 28, 1908 - July 18, 19--(?)

CORRELL, Dora, no other data

CORRELL, Cleora(?), no other data

BEAVER, Zeb V., May 13, 1868 - Aug. 11, 1907
BEAVER, Infant Daughters, no names or dates

DELLINGER, James P., d. Aug. 19, 1907 - at 62 years

WHITTEMORE, William H., d. June 6, 1935
        Wagonner 45th Inf., 9th Div., WWI (?)

WHITTEMORE, Rhoda Hamett, Mar. 20, 1870 - Nov. 28, 1903
        Wife of Alex Whittemore

CORRELL, Jane, no other data

WHITTEMORE, E. L., Aug. 25, 1868 - July 22, 1933

ELMORE, Amanda "Jackie" Whittemore, Feb. 8, 1885 - Feb. 21, 1970

WHITTEMORE, Samuel, Sep. 24, 1885 - Nov. 15, 1915

WHITTEMORE, Thomas, Sept. 18--(?) - May 3, 1888
WHITTEMORE, Mary E. (w), Dec. 10, 1842 - Mar. 4, 1915
WHITTEMORE, Frances, June 2, 1862 - 1883

WHITTEMORE, Ida, Dec. 3, 1875 - 1897

SMITH, Elem, d. July 16, 1881 - at 36 years

BOWMAN, William, Aug. 1, 1853 - Jan. 27, 1915

BOWMAN, T. M., May 15, 1849 - Dec. 3, 1899

TIPTON, Eva Bowman, d. Dec. 9, 1898 at 82 years
        Wife of G. T. Tipton

ROWE, Lula Bowman, June 23, 1872 - Mar. 17, 1898
        Wife of A. L. Rowe

BOWMAN, Saraphina Johnson, Aug. 13, 1830 - Mar. 6, 1900
        Wife of C. P. Bowman

LINVILLE, Rev. J. H., 1884-1959
LINVILLE, Lucy C. (w), 1880-1963
LINVILLE, Charlie (son), Jan. 21, 1910 - Sep. 22, 1976

ANDERSON, Shepherd M., May 9, 1883 - Feb. 7, 1927
ANDERSON, Willie E., Oct. 16, 1887 - July 18, 1986

BOWMAN, Martha A. Peoples, June 19, 1848 - Jan. 25, 1908
        Wife of J. M. Bowman

PAYNE, A. J., 1882-1954
PAYNE, Ida P. (w), 1896-1971
        Plus 5 "Payne" stones, for children (?)

ANDERSON, Elbert Luther, 1873-1954
ANDERSON, Flora Crouch (w), 1874-1961
ANDERSON, Juanita E. (dau), Sep. 21, 1901 - Sep. 14, 1904
ANDERSON, William Lloyd (son), Oct. 21, 1907 - May 7, 1909
ANDERSON, Naoma Pearl (dau), Oct. 30, 1913 - Dec. 5, 1913

ANDERSON, William G., June 4, 1849 - June 15, 1927
ANDERSON, Lucinda C. Bowman (w), Jan. 21, 1848 - Feb. 23, 1920

ANDERSON, Isaac H., Dec. 16, 1854 - Jan. 27, 1927
ANDERSON, Nanna J. Martin (w#1), Apr. 6, 1857 - July 12, 1880
        Married Feb. 22, 1876
ANDERSON, Eliza A. (w#2?), Jan. 27, 1864 - Dec. 25, 1947

ANDERSON, Thomas Ray, Oct. 19, 1910 - Mar. 14, 1957

ANDERSON, S. M., Nov. 27, 1825 - July 28, 1915
ANDERSON, Elizabeth Greer (w), Mar. 1, 1820 - Feb. 8, 1897
        Married Dec. 31, 1846

RAY. Lowell C., Mar. 12, 1910 - May 20, 1967
RAY, Berta Anderson (w), Sep. 12, 1913 -

WOODBY, Scott, d. 1934(?)

HONEYCUTT, Polly B., 1920-1986

BAILEY, Addie Woodby, Jan. 16, 1895 - May 2, 1956

WOODBY, Mose E., May 9, 1867 - Jan. 11, 1945
WOODBY, Mary J. (w), May 11, 1870 - Aug. 24, 1962

AMRELL(?), Etta W., 1878? - 1929?

McKINNEY, Liddia Y., May 12, 1881 - Feb. 6, 1966

## ANDERSON CHAPEL CEMETERY - UNMARKED GRAVES

CASTELL, William, d. Nov. 12, 1938, age 44
        Son of Jack and Mandy Castell

BLEVINS, Mrs. Malissa, d. Feb. 8, 1940, age 78
        Daughter of John and Delilah Carroll

SHERFEY, Freddie Lee, b/d Sept. 18, 1941
        Child of John Earl and Ruby Frances Hensley Sherfey

## LITTLE CEMETERY

At junction of Paddle Br. Rd. and Whispering
Terr, near Carter County line

Copied October 7, 1988

LITTLE, Walter George, Apr. 2, 1890 - June 22, 1937
LITTLE, Alma (dau), Oct. 4, 1918 - Feb. 8, 1919
LITTLE, Infant Son, b/d Sep. 26, 1916
        Children of W. G. and Abby Little
LITTLE, J. Frank, May 8, 1888 - 1972
LITTLE, Gena Moore (w), Mar. 9, 1893 - Apr. 6, 1944
        Married Feb. 14, 1911
LITTLE, Gracie Pearl (dau), Mar. 14, 1912 - Mar. 17, 1912

LITTLE, John A., Aug. 2, 1863 - July 29, 1939
LITTLE, Vicie Ann Humphreys (w), Oct. 16, 1860 - May 17, 1946

LITTLE, Bishop Simpson, Jan. 1, 1886 - Mar. 22, 1962
LITTLE, Nettie Uzela (w), Apr. 17, 1894 - 1976

LITTLE, William McKinley, Aug. 31, 1899 - Oct. 2, 1919

# LINVILLE CEMETERY

Off Paddle Branch Dr., on hill behind
farm, on Carter County Line

Copied October 7, 1988

LINVILLE, George C.,   Mar. 14, 1883 - June 23, 1956

LINVILLE, W. D.,   d. Sep. 10, 1899 at 26 years

LINVILLE, Rettie M.,   d. Aug. 24, 1899 at 22 years

LINVILLE, Cora A., d. at 3 months - dau. of G.W. & M.J.Linville

BOWMAN, Christopher P.,   1816 - Aug. 13, 1879

KEEN, Rhoda A.,   Aug. 8, 1873 - Sep. 10, 1873

KEEN, Sarah E., Jan. 25, 1877 - Feb. 22, 1879(?)

KEEN, William,   1837-1922

BOWMAN, Martha Ann,   Feb. 28, 1840 - Sep. 26, 1901
        Daughter of W. M. Keen

CAMPBELL,   ?      ,   d. July 4, 1809(?)

SWARTHOUT, Mary E.,   Dec. 7, 1861 - Dec. 26, 1932

McINTURFF, Saraphina Bowman,   May 20, 1829 - Nov. 28, 1904

LINVILLE, G. W., d. Apr. 10, 1905 at 62 years
        Co. M, 8th TN CAV,  Union Army

LINVILLE, Charles M., Apr. 9, 1875 - Dec. 11, 1936
LINVILLE, Cora E. Keene (w), Sep. 4, 1881 - Aug. 21, 1936

        Plus several unmarked stones

        In very poor condition, high brush, and
        most gravestones knocked over by cows

## O'BRIEN CEMETERY

On Davis Lane (Limestone Cove) near J. S. Head Road

Copied October 20, 1988
Update of Bill Norris's 1973 record


MILLER, Rev. John W.,    Feb. 22, 1870 - June 15, 1925
MILLER, Phebie L. (w),   Sep. 16, 1887 - May  13, 1938

MILLER, J. B.,  Sep. 20, 1826 - May 10, 1911
MILLER, Julia (w),   Apr. 11, 1884 - Nov. 5, 1914

MILLER, Julia,   d. July 11, 1890 at 11 mos., 15 days
         Daughter of O. R. and M. E. Miller

LEONARD, Esther S.,   Sep. 27, 1811 - Feb. 5, 1885

HEAD, Jesse,   Nov. 3, 1905 - July 28, 1927
HEAD, Carl ,   May 3, 1922 - June 21, 1926
         Sons of W. J. and Dora Head

BIRCHFIELD, Infant,   no dates,   not visible in 1988
         Child of W. M. and Eliza Birchfield

JONES, T. J.,   Aug. 4, 1852 -  Sep. 28, 1922
JONES, Mary A. (w),   Oct. 19, 1846 - Feb. 24, 1924

O'BRIEN, William H.,   Oct. 25, 1840 - Mar. 14, 1893

O'BRIEN, William D.,   d. Mar. 21, 1891 at 81 years

O'BRIEN, James M.,   d. Mar. 25, 1891 at 47 years
O'BRIEN, Melvina,    d. 1884 at 67 years

CARVER, Jack,   May 19, 1918 -  Oct. 24, 1918
         Son of J. H. and H. A. Carver

SHULTZ, Dr. Daniel D.,   Nov. 18, 1843 - July 20, 1919
SHULTZ, Mary J. "Polly" (w),   Aug. 15, 1849 - June 23, 1913

HEAD, J. S.,   Jan. 17, 1907 -
HEAD, Grace D. (w),   Dec. 15, 1914 -

HEAD, Richard Allen,   Nov. 20, 1933 - Nov. 22, 1933

# MOSLEY CEMETERY

On Route 107 on Iron Mountain, on left
just before last series of curves - not
far beyond Red Fork Cr. Road

Originally copied by Bill Norris in 1973,
Field-checked and Updated March 15, 1989

TIPTON, Charlie F., 1887-1962
TIPTON, Vista W. (w), 1887-1957

HALMAN (HILMAN?), David, June 10, 1886 - Mar. 8, 1963

HILMAN, Mallie, Sep. 6, 1884 - May 20, 1916
        Wife of David H. Hilman
        (New stone says Mallie Hillman  1884-1916)

OGLE, Martha Biggs, 1873-1910
        (Replaced stone that said Nancy M. Ogle, 1874-1910)

OGLE, Nebraksa (son),     1900 - 1989

SLIMP, Mary J. Mosley,  d. Dec. 24, 1922 at 46 yrs.
        Wife of J. A. Slimp

HONEYCUTT, Polly, June 7, 1869 - May 19, 1939

MOSLEY, Nathaniel, May 12, 1822 - Dec. 9, 1905
MOSLEY, Eliza (w), Aug. 5, 1827 - Feb. 1, 1901
        Married Aug. 25, 1845
MOSLEY, Sarrah Amanda (dau), Feb. 12, 1860 - Jan. 30, 1864

WEST, Isaac, Sep. 9, 1861 - Mar. 20, 1918
WEST, Manda, Dec. 25, 1866 - May 23, 1936

HONEYCUTT, Jesse M., May 3, 1889 -
HONEYCUTT, Maude W. (w), Jan. 13, 1891 - Apr. 4, 1959
HONEYCUTT, Ruth, Mar. 6, 1919 - July 13, 1920

HOLT, Glenn Dora, May 16, 1917 - Apr. 6, 1948

CROWDER, Addie McLemore,  Nov. 15, 1904 - May 31, 1955

McLEMORE, Henry, Oct. 10, 1871 - Nov. 4, 1947
McLEMORE, Julia (w), Oct. 18, 1866 - Sep. 26, 1930

DAVIS, Edd,  1905 - 1971
DAVIS, Martha (w),  1917 -

WOODBY, Eli,  May 5, 1899 - Nov. 5, 1948

DAVIS, Josie,  Feb. 25, 1869 - Jan. 24, 1957

DAVIS, Frank,  Sep.  6, 1907 - Apr. 28, 1940

MOSLEY, Herbert,  Mar. 13, ----? - July 7, 1928
        died young, according to epitaph

MOSLEY, Maggie Davis,  1903-1968

HILLMAN, A. G. Howard, Dec. 22, 1921 - Oct. 4, 1952

HILMAN, Floyd,  b/d Feb. 26, 1927

HALMAN (HILMAN?), Jess James, June 10, 1911 - June 7, 1968
        S2, US Navy, WWII

HALMAN (HILMAN?), Roger Lee, Jan. 24, 1952 - Apr. 15, 1966

McLEMORE, Ruben, Feb. 22, 1891 - Apr. 11, 1959
McLEMORE, Hester , June 10, 1891 - Aug. 3, 1936

BRYANT, William G., gov't marker sunk in ground
            name no longer visible in 1988

BRYANT(?), Kenneth,  d. Sep. 11, 1945
BRYANT(?), Norma Jean,  d. Dec. 15, 1942
BRYANT   , Bonnie, Dec. 20, 1914 - Nov. 18, 1951

McLEMORE, Nathan L., June 17, 1896 - July 26, 1964
McLEMORE, Rebecca G. (w), July 5, 1904 - Dec. 5, 1956

PATE, William H.,  Aug. 30, 1871 - July 11, 1950
PATE, Eliza A. (w), June 16, 1873 - Mar. 5, 1933

PATE, Dewey S., Sep. 10, 1898 - May 13, 1977
PATE, Litha M. (w), Jan. 5, 1901 - Apr. 14, 1971

            Plus several unmarked stones

## ADDITIONS - MARCH 15, 1989

WEST, Bill, Feb. 11, 1861 - Oct. 6, 1921
WEST, Nancy Harrol (w), July 25, 1861 - Aug. 21, 1933

ARROWOOD, Levi David,  b/d Apr. 20, 1943

WEST, Bernie, May 27, 1902 (1904?) - July 25, 1987, US Army,WWII
WEST, Martha (w),       1919 -

McLEMORE, Richard,  May 25, 1897 - Sep. 23, 1978
McLEMORE, Julia, Apr. 25, 1906 - Sep. 22, 1938

BUCHANAN, Bryson,  1908-1988

HILMAN, Buster,  Mar. 9, 1928 - Dec. 24, 1983

HILMAN, Sudie E.,  1897-1977

MOSLEY CEMETERY - (continued)

WEST, Mallie,  June 27, 1897 - Dec. 17, 1973

HOWELL, Luther,  d. 1979

McLEMORE, Earnest, July 17, 1907 - Apr. 18, 1987
        buried near Nathan McLemore
WEST, Nelia Pate,  1903 - 1989

## GOUGE CEMETERY #1

        Off Rt. 107, up Red Fork Cr Rd., then first
        left to top of hill, cemetery on left.
        Originally copied by Bill Norris in 1973; field
        checked November 1, 1988.

GOUGE, John Wesley, Dec. 24, 1833 - Jan. 6, 1908
GOUGE, Rachel Forbes (w), Mar. 23, 1834 - Feb. 26, 1913

GOUGE, Robert Castle, Oct. 29, 1859 - Dec. 28, 1931
        Son of John W. and Rachel Gouge
GOUGE, Ollie Woodby (w), Sep. 4, 1869 - 1951
GOUGE, Ezekiel F. (son), Mar. 25, 1892 - Mar. 2, 1915
GOUGE, David (son),   no dates
GOUGE, Martha (dau),   no dates
GOUGE, Mabel (dau),   no dates
GOUGE, Bertie (son?), no dates
GOUGE, Nelson (son),  no dates
GOUGE, Mamie (dau),   no dates
        these children probably died young
GOUGE, Dave,  1865-1951
        probably son of John W. and Rachel Gouge
GOUGE, James Thomas, July 22, 1876 - Mar. 4, 1947
        Son of John W. and Rachel Gouge
GOUGE, Harriett Grindstaff (w), Jan. 5, 1881 - Aug. 11, 1966
GOUGE, Martin Luther (son), Dec. 29, 1899 - Nov. 14, 1900
GOUGE, William Clarence (son), Feb. 21, 1903 - Dec. 9, 1970
        Pvt., US Army, WWII
GOUGE, Bonnie Lee (dau), Apr. 9, 1908 - Sep. 14, 1911

GOUGE, Lareene L., Apr. 9, 1936 - Aug. 23, 1939

GOUGE, Fred H., Feb. 5, 1940 - Apr. 5, 1941

GOUGE, Mary E., May 16, 1934 - June 29, 1936

DAVIS, Jane, Mar. 9, 1859 - Mar. 7, 1906

OVERHOLSER, Martha Adeline, Sep. 22, 1878 - Dec. 24, 1924

GOUGE, William Joel, July 5, 1979 - Jan. 24, 1985

HUNT, Virginia Gouge,  June 10, 1907 - Apr. 6, 1986

GOUGE, Charles B., Mar. 13, 1901 - Feb. 1, 1975
       Son of James and Harriett Gouge
GOUGE, Bonnie Hill (w),  b. June 19, 1915 -

HILL, Infant,  b/d 1910
HILL, Infant,  b/d 1914
       Sons of John and Delia Hill

## BURLESON CEMETERY

> Beyond the Gouge Cemetery on Red Fork Cr.
> Rd., and just across the fence, on gov't.
> land, near Johnny Gouge's mobile home.

> Originally copied by Bill Norris in 1973;
> field-checked in mid-1980's.

BURLESON, Aaron,  NC Infantry - Cherokee Wars

## BUCHANAN CEMETERY

> On old Rt. 107 in Limestone Cove, about
> $\frac{1}{4}$ mile from Simerly Road intersection.
> Take left at dirt road up hill, just
> before fork in road.

> Originally copied by Bill Norris in 1973;
> Updated December 4, 1988.

FRY, William F., July 26, 1873 - Mar. 14, 1943
FRY, Nancy Lewis (w), Sep. 23, 1877 - Dec. 3, 1977
FRY, Jesse W., July 22, 1914 - Feb. 22, 1915
     Son of W. M. and Nancy Fry
BIRDWELL, W. W., Sep. 11, 1902 - Feb. 5, 1933
     Son of Jim and Hester Higgins Birdwell
BIRDWELL, Virginia (w), Nov. 24, 1903 - June 12, 1937
BIRDWELL, Nadine (dau), Jan. 13, 1925 - July 30, 1926

FRY, Henry M., Sep. 26, 1894 - July 10, 1930
FRY, Della (w), June 20, 1895 - Nov. 14, 1925
FRY, Henry M. Jr.,(son), Feb. 13, 1923 - Nov. 15, 1924

GOUGE, Walter, July 28, 1898 - Feb. 12, 1920
      stone broken up in 1988
McKAMEY, Nancy Parker,  1827-1923
      Wife of Newton McKamey

BUCHANAN CEMETERY - (continued)

GOUGE, John Harvey,  July 22, 1871 - May 25, 1945 - son of John Wesley
GOUGE, Joanna McKamey (w),  Jan. 2, 1863 - Aug. 25, 1948)& Rachel Gouc

ROBERTS, Richard W., Oct. 6, 1898 - Mar 31, 1936

BUCHANAN, George Kenneth,  May 10, 1913 - Apr. 7, 1941

MARTIN, Lloyd, Dec. 17, 1899 - May 16, 1937

ELLIOT, Walter B.,  1868-1950
ELLIOT, Mary Elizabeth (w), Jan. 15, 1861 (1870?)- Jan. 26, 1937
ELLIOT, Infant son,  d. Apr. 1, 1904
ELLIOT, Infant dau,  d. Mar. 16, 1907
ELLIOT, Infant son,  d. Oct. 29, 1909

FRY, W. R.,  Dec. 5, 1892 - Aug. 31, 1927

BARNETT, Betty Lou,  Oct. 14, 1929 - Dec. 30, 1929
        Dau. of C. E. and Daisy Barnett

FRY, W. E.,  Oct. 1861 - June 15, 1900

ROBERTS, Infant,  d. Mar. 3, 1931 - Dau. of R.W. & Nola Roberts
ROBERTS, Infant,  d. May 22, 1924 - Son  of R.W. & Nola Roberts

MILLER, James Eugene,  Dec. 11, 1932 - Dec. 22, 1932
        Son of John and Nola Miller
MILLER, Nora Cochran, Feb. 28, 1907 - Dec. 18, 1932
        Wife of John J. Miller, & Dau. of James T. & Sue Cochran

COCHRAN, George C.,  Oct. 21, 1901 - Sep. 2, 1927
        Son of James T. and Sudie Garland Cochran

BIRCHFIELD, David W.,  Apr. 11, 1894 - July 25, 1929
BIRCHFIELD, Millie (w), May 2, 1896 - Nov. 17, 1933
        Dau. of W. W. and Sarah Buchanan

BUCHANAN, Jonathan, Jan. 14, 1827 - Nov. 28, 1902
BUCHANAN, Millie (w), Jan. 19, 1828 - Sep. 14, 1902

HUGHES, Norma B.,  Apr. 24, 1900 - Jan. 19, 1928

HUGHES, Willa Mae,  Oct. 16, 1925 - Aug. 2, 1926

BUCHANAN, W. W.,  1855-1953
BUCHANAN, Sarah (w),  1859 - 1945
BUCHANAN, Robert M. (son), Feb. 12, 1898 - Mar. 7, 1899

GOUGE, Arthur, Oct. 24, 1886 - Oct. 18, 1934
GOUGE, Nora B., Aug. 5, 1890 - Aug. 20, 1939

BARNETT, Jeter,  Jan. 28, 1890 - Nov. 30, 1932

BUCHANAN CEMETERY - (continued)

BUCHANAN, Hazel,  d. Apr. 15, 1913
        Daughter of Arthur and Lucy Buchanan

ROBERTS, John,  1890-1980
ROBERTS, Dora (w),  1901-1951

ROBERTS, Velva,  Aug. 14, 1920 - July 16, 1921

BURCHFIELD, Ezekiel Jr., 1865-1952-Son of Ezekiel & Sarah Gouge Burch-
BURCHFIELD, Cordelia Daniels(w), Nov. 20, 1873 - July 22, 1926) field

BIRCHFIELD, Geneva,  b.(d?) Apr. 30, 1903

BLEVINS, W. Ross,  May 1927 - Oct. 1928

BENNETT, Mary Roberts,  Aug. 27, 1919 - Sep. 24, 1983

COCHRAN, James T.,  1871-1958
COCHRAN, Sue G. (w),  1875 - 19--?

COCHRAN, Frank W., Sep. 23, 1909 - May 9, 1977
COCHRAN, Volena H. (w), Dec. 15, 1915 -

COCHRAN, Frank James,  Nov. 26, 1949 - July 26, 1985
        PFC, US Army, Vietnam

GOUGE, Winfield,  1865-1951
GOUGE, Clarsia (w),  1868-1945  (Clarisa?)

GOUGE, Norma Dean,  Oct. 11, 1934 - June 23, 1971

GOUGE, Clyde,  1899-1986
        Son of John Harvey and Joanna Gouge
COX, Robert, 1886 - Jan. 31, 1931
        Son of Melburn and Elizabeth Fry Cox

GARST, Martha Gouge,  1932-1983

ROBERTS, Olean (mother), Oct. 8, 1932 -
ROBERTS, Jack (son),  Nov. 16, 1962 - July 24, 1985

LAUGHREN, Linda G. (child),  d. June 20, 1969

# GRINDSTAFF CEMETERY #1

On Simerly Creek Road, ½ mile from
Limestone Cove School, First Road
On Left. (Young Road)
Copied by Bill Norris in 1973; and Updated
December 4, 1988.

WOODBY, Robert L., Apr. 18, 1863 - Dec. 29, 1947
WOODBY, Hester Banks, Aug. 5, 1863 - Mar. 6, 1937

WOODBY, Mose, Feb. 25, 1883 - Jan. 8, 1944
WOODBY, Alfred, Feb. 25, 1883 - Dec. 23, 1945
        Twin brothers

YOUNG, William A., June 18, 1877 - no date
YOUNG, Basha F.,(w), Aug. 23, 1876 - Oct. 10, 1946

CAMPBELL, Earnest, May 3, 1911 - Apr. 3, 1912
CAMPBELL, Edith, Aug. 5, 1918 - July 3, 1919
        Children of J. N. and R. Campbell

CAMPBELL, Worley Jack, 1873-1967

CAMPBELL, Zellie P., 1893-1964

JONES, Samuel F., Mar. 20, 1882 - Mar. 3, 1946
JONES, Cindy Woodby (w), Sep. 18, 1881 - Nov. 19, 1973

ROBINSON, Johnnie R., Oct. 10, 1870 - Jan. 21, 1947

JAMISON, Glen West, July 18, 1940 - Nov. 10, 1940

BOYD, Ed, 1878-1957
BOYD, Charlotte Grindstaff (w), 1882-1971

GRINDSTAFF, Amos, Feb. 20, 1851 - Mar. 5, 1938
GRINDSTAFF, Ellia Hyder, Feb. 11, 1856 - Apr. 27, 1930

TOLLEY, Lester C., Dec. 8, 1935 - June 4, 1968
TOLLEY, Eula Mae, June 19, 1935 - Aug. 24, 1976

COCHRAN, George, Co. B, 13th TN CAV - Union Army

PATE, Susan H., May 1, 1876 - July 11, 1879

GARLAND, John G., Feb. 15, 1810 - Feb. 3, 1883

GOUGE, Thomas, no dates
GOUGE, Sarah Blevins (w), no dates
        Parents of John Wesley Gouge
HURT, Claude, Jan. 5, 1925 - Feb. 2, 1947
HURT, Elnore (w), May 8, 1926 - Feb. 2, 1947
HURT, Lee Roy (son), Mar. 15, 1945 - Feb. 2, 1947

HURT, Martin L., Aug. 17, 1879 - Mar. 18, 1965
HURT, Phina M., Nov. 8, 1897 - Sep. 15, 1984

GRINDSTAFF CEMETERY #1  (continued)

DOUGHERTY, Sarah Ann,  Jan. 2, 1864 - Mar. 21, 1947

SNEED, Steve Lynn,  Sept. 9, 1952 - July 18, 1978

BUSBY, John W.,  Feb. 10, 1902 - Mar. 26, 1976

GARLAND, Hugh R.,  Mar. 31, 1936 - Apr. 1, 1936

YOUNG, Jerry,  Mar. 20, 1944 - Mar. 21, 1944

YOUNG, Cecil,  Dec. 5, 1945 - Dec. 6, 1945
          Sons of Wayne and Rosie Mae Williams Young

GRINDSTAFF, Mary J.,  Aug. 11, 1893 - Mar. 20, 1965

BOYD, Elmer, Aug. 3, 1905 - Sep. 3, 1984 - brother of Ed Boyd

BRYANT, James A.,  Nov. 2, 1904 - Jan. 26, 1986
BRYANT, Ida Mae (w), Sep. 26, 1907 - Mar. 14, 1985

JAMISON, John W.,  1903-1983
JAMISON, Grace (w), 1910 -

GRINDSTAFF CEMETERY - UNMARKED GRAVE

GRINDSTAFF, John Martin,  age 85, d. Feb. 1, 1941
          Son of Wm. and Mary Campbell Grindstaff


### GARLAND CEMETERY

In field across from Hills Store in
Limestone Cove, Route 107

Copied by Bill Norris in 1973 & updated Dec. 4, 1988

STEVENS, Brownlow,  1878-1958
STEVENS, Emaline (w),1881-1953

GARLAND, William M., Aug. 11, 1875 - Aug. 11, 1960
GARLAND, Mary Lee S.,  Mar. 7, 1878 - Jan. 31, 1958

GARLAND, Delia,  Dec. 15, 1891 - Mar. 10, 1912

GARLAND, Garfield, July 15, 1885 - Feb. 23, 1901

GARLAND, Carcie,  Feb. 6, 1910 - Nov. 24, 1925

GARLAND, Maud,  May 22, 1901 - June 23, 1901

GARLAND, W. M., Co. B, 12 TN CAV - Union Army
GARLAND, Minerva,  1846 - Apr. 13, 1931

MILLER, James M., 1873-1945
MILLER, Mary "Polly" (w), 1877-1949
MILLER, William Theodore (son), Jan. 11, 1902 - Oct. 29, 1915

McCURRY, Cleo, Jan. 25, 1894 - Feb. 3, 1923
        Son of J. H. and Ann McCurry
McCURRY, Lena, d. Dec. 3, 1918 at 21 yrs.

SMITH, Jane, June 7, 1870 - Apr. 27, 1934

SMITH, Wilder, June 30, 1887 - Mar. 30, 1928
        Pvt., Co. F, 323rd Inf., US Army

SMALLING, Michael Fate, 1957-1983 - US Marine Corps

GARLAND, Howard, May 30, 1905 - May 28, 1970
GARLAND, Elsie M. (w), July 23, 1914 -

GARLAND, Clifford, (infant), d. Apr. 12, 1933

LEDBETTER, Claude L., 1910-
LEDBETTER, Vada G. (w), 1912-1976

GOUGE, Sam L., Jan. 16, 1914 - Mar. 1, 1981 - US Army, WWII

GOUGE, Kenneth D., Oct. 30, 1935 - June 28, 1977

GOUGE, Edna, Oct. 30, 1916 - June 2, 1983

GOUGE, Ethan J., Mar. 10, 1952 - Sep. 16, 1978
GOUGE, Deborah S. (w), Mar. 13, 1957 -

GOUGE, Verne W., Dec. 10, 1920 - May 4, 1979 - SGT, US Army, WWII
GOUGE, Dollie D. (w), June 2, 1921 - Sep. 8, 1987

## BIRCHFIELD #2 CEMETERY

On Upper Stone Mountain Road, $\frac{1}{4}$ mile beyond
Limestone Cove School, on right up hill behind
abandoned brick house.  Built by Nathan Birchfield, below.

    Copied by Bill Norris in 1973 and updated
Dec. 6, 1988


CAMPBELL, Adline Birchfield,  Jan. 23, 1864 - Dec. 2, 1902
        Wife of E. J. Campbell
        Daughter of Ezekiel and Sarah Birchfield

BIRCHFIELD, Ezekiel,  Jan. 15, 1826 - Oct. 25, 1916
BIRCHFIELD, Sarah Gouge (w),  1841 - Jan. 14, 1911
BIRCHFIELD, David S. (son),  May 11, 1883 - Apr. 9, 1885
BIRCHFIELD, Charlie (son),  July 25, 1885 - Sep. 11, 1886
BIRCHFIELD, Samuel (son),  Feb. 17, 1862 - Jan. 20, 1911
BIRCHFIELD, Julia (dau),  June 30, 1871 - May 9, 1911

BIRCHFIELD, Nathan,  Sep. 10, 1855 - Mar. 2, 1941
        Son of Ezekiel and Sarah Birchfield
BIRCHFIELD, Hattie (w),  Mar. 16, 1879 - Apr. 5, 1940

GARLAND, Nerva Birchfield,  July 14, 1879 - Apr. 3, 1906
        Wife of Walter Garland
        Daughter of Ezekiel and Sarah Birchfield

ROGERS, Roy L.,  1929-1933


        plus many unmarked stones

# McINTURFF #1 CEMETERY

On Marbleton Road (Back Road) Beside New Hope Church

Copied by Bill Norris & Mildred B. on November 11, 1973,
Updated September 12, 1988

McINTURFF, Wesley,  Co. B, 12th TN CAV, Civil War
        Son of Thomas and Nancy Scott McInturff
McINTURFF, Rachel, Feb. 14, 1820 - Dec. 9, 1899
        Maiden name Boyd

McINTURFF, D. J.,  Mar. 5, 1856 - May 30, 1918
        (David J.), Son of Wesley and Rachel Boyd McInturff
McINTURFF, Mary A. Toney,  Oct. 15, 1858 - Aug. 10, 1925

McINTURFF, James W.,  July 28, 1874 - Dec. 14, 1967
McINTURFF, Roxie,  June 14, 1885 - Apr. 12, 1902
McINTURFF, Hattie Mae,  Nov. 10, 1909 - Apr. 20, 1930

McINTURFF, Mattie Jo-Anne,  Apr. 12, 1876 - May 19, 1946

McINTURFF, Will J.,  1907-1964

McINTURFF, John W.,  June 26, 1879 - Apr. 10, 1963
McINTURFF, Donie (?) Dillinger,  June 14, 1885 - Apr. 12, 1902
        First Wife of John W. McInturff
McINTURFF, Emma Dillinger, June 13, 1883 - Feb. 22, 1930
        Second Wife of John W. McInturff

GARLAND, Dinnah McInturff,  1886-1934

GARLAND, Dorothy,  Aug. 25, 1922 - Oct. 18, 1931
        Daughter of Bill and Dinah McInturff Garland
GARLAND, Wilson,  May 15, 1914 - Nov. 26, 1937
        Son of John and Eliza Dillinger(?) Dillender Garland

McINTURFF, Walter P.,  June 5, 1896 - Apr. 16, 1920

McINTURFF, J. W.,  July 25, 1923 - Oct. 7, 1924

TIPTON, Millie(?),  Aug. 10, 1922 - Feb. 10, 1924

WHITTEMORE, Emery,  Nov. 26, 1907 - Sept. 17, 1970
        TN Pvt., Hq. Co. 54, QM Base Dep., WWII
WHITTEMORE, Isaac,  Oct. 10, 1903 - Nov. 22, 1925
WHITTEMORE, Oscar,  May 11, 1905 - Nov. 21, 1923
        Sons of T. M. and Maggie Whittemore

GARLAND, John H.,  May 9, 1888 - Oct. 31, 1971
GARLAND, Eliza D., Apr. 19, 1896 - Dec. 3, 1964

DILLINGER, Reble,  Apr. 28, 1914 - May 1, 1914

STREET, Pearl,  1910-1928

GARLAND, Lida (mother),    1931-1956
GARLAND, Janie (dau),      1953-1955

WILLIAMS, Carol Ann,    1968-1969

OSBORNE, Goldie,    1900-1971
OSBORNE, Alonzio M.,    May 19, 1902 -

OSBORNE, Ivan A.,    June 5, 1924 - May 8, 1944
        PFC, 36 Cav. Recon Troops,    WWII

STREET, Landon,    1874-1948
STREET, Mary,      1880-1919

DILLINGER, John W.,    1877-1956
DILLINGER. Hattie M. (w),    1885-1972

STREET, Claude,    Feb. 1, 1915 - Oct. 5, 1955
        TC4, Ord. Co. AVN,    WWII

STREET, Stephen,    1861-1942
STREET, Tishey J.,    1866-1942

HARRELL, Andrew Harrison "Shvety", Feb. 14, 1908 - Oct.31, 1972

DILLINGER, Amandy Bailey,    d. Dec. 5, 1947 at 95
        Wife of J. P. Dillinger

COLEMAN, David J.,    June 15, 1925 - May 6, 1951

HUGHES, Lee,    July 17, 1929 - July 25, 1959

GRINDSTAFF, Star Lynn D.,    b/d 1960

GARLAND, Rix,    1858-1945

CAMPBELL, Rev. John,    Oct. 20, 1850 - May 22, 1925
CAMPBELL, Lucinda,    Mar. 17, 1852 - Aug. 10, 1926

YARBOR, John N.,    July 20, 1876 - Apr. 10, 1932
        Co. K, 4th TN Vol. Inf., - Span-Am. War

YARBOR, Rachel J. (w),    June 18, 1888 - Feb. 22, 1972
        Wife of John N. Yarbor

PUTNAM, A. M.,    Nov. 18, 1864 - Aug. 18, 1941
PUTNAM, Julia W.,    Jan. 22, 1866 - Jan. 24, 1946

RADFORD, Ronald Dean,    Feb. 21, 1949 - Aug. 23, 1950

TABOR, Maffrey,    Feb. 10, 1932 - May 5, 1965

JONES, Etta,    Oct. 20, 1904 - Nov. 25, 1957

McINTURFF #1 CEMETERY - (continued)

HAMMETT, Hannah B., May 7, 1892 - Aug. 20, 1966

FOUSTER, Settie Garland, Apr. 9, 1884 - Apr. 16, 1954

HUGHES, Julia, June 22, 1887 - Nov. 3, 1943
        Wife of Ivin Hughes

TIPTON, Ben, 1894-1949
TIPTON, Sallie, 1898-1973

WALKER, Margaret Ann, b/d 1947

WALKER, Sam T., no dates

WALKER, William Alfred, Aug. 2, 1932 - Oct. 15, 1955
        A 2C, US Air Force

GARLAND, Wilson (dad), 1889-1954
GARLAND, Manilla (mom), 1901-1975

MILLS, Ollie, d. Aug. 7, 1936 at 50

JONES, Charles M., d. 1962

JONES, Mollie Jane, 1872-1953

JONES, LeeRoy, 1883-1955
JONES, Cora B., 1891-1973

AYERS, Joan Lucile, Mar. 12, 1949 - Feb. 12, 1957

GADDY, General Arthur, Mar. 16, ----(?) - ------17, 1936
        Son of G. R. and Bessie Gaddy

BOWMAN, William S., 1839-1933

GARLAND, Thurman E., Apr. 1, 1940 - June 12, 1968

BOWMAN, Ruth G., d. 1925 - dau. of Ed and Rose Bowman

WHITE, Macie E., d. 1929 - dau. of Hobart & Pearl White

GADDY, John C., 1888-1958
GADDY, Dora E., 1900-1943

GADDY, John C., Apr. 4, 1888 - Apr. 5, 1958
GADDY, Sarah Ann Bowman, Dec. 26, 1892 - Sep. 23, 1922
GADDY, Dora E. Hughes, 1900-1943

WHITE, Rosa Edna, d. 1932 (dau)
WHITE, E.D. and G.E., d. 1930 (twins)
        Children of Hobart and Pearl White

BOWMAN, Edward, Jan. 7, 1880 - Mar. 21, 1931

McINTURFF #1 CEMETERY - (continued)

BOWMAN, Lillie,  June 15, 1914 - Aug. 13, 1930

BOWMAN, Dora Garland,  1890-1972
        Believe it to be the same as buried with husband Tine
                                                    (below)
BARNETT, C. S.,  1868-1920

TIPTON, Bill,  Mar. 4, 1907 - Sep. 23, 1928

BOWMAN, Tine,  May 1, 1880 - Oct. 27, 1961
BOWMAN, Dora G.,  May 18, 1890 -  ?

TIPTON, Joe H.,  1879-1961
TIPTON, Nancy B. (w),  1889-1975

COOPER, Nora M.,  1891-1951

COOPER, Ralph L.,  Oct. 6, 1922 - July 10, 1959
        PFC, 8 Trans. Co. TC, WWII - Son of Nora M. Cooper

MOORE, Eugene,  May 28, 1931 - Apr. 21, 1971

MOORE, Clyde A.,  1896-1956
MOORE, Alfred,  Oct. 22, 1928 - Oct. 27, 1928
        Son of C. A. and Alice Moore

MOORE, Grover,  Aug. 31, 1890 - Oct. 5, 1921

MOORE, Bertie May Stone,  July 1, 1901 - Dec. 7, 1941
        Wife of George Moore

WARRICK (WORRIX), June Moore,  1860-1925

MOORE, James P.,  Oct. 18, 1868 - Sep. 6, 1933
MOORE, Mary J. Woodby,  June 28, 1864 - Aug. 2, 1933


## ADDITIONS

WHITTIMORE, Clyde R. (father),  June 15, 1915 - Nov. 1, 1976
TIPTON, Betty Jo,  Infant 1936
TIPTON, Harvy J.,  Infant 1937

TIPTON, Lydia Gaddy,  Jan. 10, 1910 - Aug. 16, 1939
        Wife of Frank Tipton

TIPTON, Carl D.,  1932-1935
TIPTON, Valdine,  Mar. 17, 1942 - Dau. of Mr.&Mrs. Frank Tipton

CLARK, Claude,  1924-1983
CLARK, Gladys,  1920-1983

BOWMAN, James Edgar,  Aug. 28, 1933 - May 5, 1968
        Tenn. Sgt., 4 Air Comd Sq. AF

BOWMAN, Alexander,    1870-1964
BOWMAN, Cora W.,      1892-1973

TIPTON, Nora E.,   Apr. 16, 1909 - Mar. 23, 1980

RODIFER, Wm. G. Tipton,   1915-1977
RODIFER, Martha Jane  ,   1887-1980

HUGHES, Mary Opal,   Mar. 20, 1909 - Nov. 23, 1976

RAMEY, Harry Willis,   May 3, 1897 - May 11, 1973

BENNETT, Gustia Lee,   May 1, 1884 - Aug. 16, 1977

WALKER, Carrie J.,   1895-1976

SNYDER, Ronald L.,   1957

COLEMAN, Horace (father),   Feb. 27, 1903 -

COLEMAN, Nathaniel,   Nov. 25, 1928 - Dec. 29, 1986
COLEMAN, Lettie,   July 26, 1907  -

BUCKNER, Betty,   1910-1988

McINTURFF, Dewey,   Apr. 20, 1904 -
McINTURFF, Myrtle (w),   Aug. 23, 1908 - Oct. 10, 1980

CASIDA, Anna R.,   Aug. 19, 1912 - Sept. 29, 1971

POWELL, George J.,   1908-1943
POWELL, Mollie L.,   Aug. 5, 1876 - June 22, 1956

McINTURFF, Gilmon T.,   Oct. 14, 1909 - Aug. 1, 1982
McINTURFF, Willie M. (w),   Aug. 10, 1917 -

STREET, Edd,   Feb. 1, 1904 - Jan. 8, 1980

WILLIAMS, Charlie,   1940 - 1974

WILLIAMS, Mary M.,   1946 - 1947

GARLAND, Minnie,   Jan. 9, 1912 - Dec. 7, 1916

COXS, ---------,   Headstone,  no other marking

GARLAND, William,   May 12, 1864 - Mar. 27, 1954
GARLAND, Lizzie McInturff (w),   Dec. 22, 1864 - July 13, 1904

SHEHAN, Marcus,   1899-1983

McINTURFF, Louise,   no dates

McINTURFF, Liddie,   Dec. 31, 1918 - Jan. 5, 1919

McINTURFF #1 CEMETERY - (continued)

RUSSELL, Earl,    1901-1986
RUSSELL, Mary Alice,    1901-1980

ENGLE, Caroline Street,  Sept. 22, 1883 - Apr. 29, 1952
        Daughter of Stephen and Tishey Day Street
        Wife of T. C. Engle

WHITTEMORE, Thomas M. (father),  Feb. 11, 1876 - Apr. 15, 1966

WHITTIMORE, Maggie,  Mar. 4, 1874 - Dec. 8, 1948

YARBER, Jack W.,  Jan. 28, 1924 -
YARBER, Beulah K.,  Dec. 12, 1925 - Sept. 4, 1980


## JONES CEMETERY

Located off Highway 19-23 at Dry Creek
Between Erwin and Unicoi
                        Copied July 1988

ADKINS, Clingman David, Jr.,  May 7, 1882 - July 31, 1946

ANDERSON, Infant,    child of John Anderson

BANNER, Charles,  1918-1974  -  PFC, US Army

ADKINS, Baxter (Back),  1907 - 1979

BENFIELD, Everett H.,  Feb. 15, 1890 - Dec. 16, 1924

BLEVINS, Bertha Mathes,  July 14, 1918 -
BLEVINS, Cad,        -
BLEVINS, David Bell,  July 12, 1880 - May 8, 1951
        Son of William and Louise Wheelock Blevins
BLEVINS, Lockie,  d. 1906 - age 18
BLEVINS, Louise,  Dec. 8, 1851 - July 9, 1907
BLEVINS, Paul Henry,  June 25, 1918 - Dec. 5, 1978
        Son of David Bell and Sarah Elizabeth Smith Blevins
BLEVINS, Roy T.,  July 17, 1902 - June 19, 1982
        Son of David Bell and Sarah Elizabeth Smith Blevins

BLEVINS, Sarah Elizabeth,  June 13, 1880 - May 21, 1967
        Daughter of Henry and Sarah Whaley Smith
BLEVINS, William,  Oct. 7, 1845 - May 6, 1915

BOWMAN, Daniel,  b. April 1852
        Son of Joseph and Katherine Cline Bowman
BOWMAN, Everett,  June 25, 1900/1902 - Aug. 26, 1972
        Son of John and Sally Bowman
BOWMAN, Gene,  one date - May 20, 1910
BOWMAN, Hattie E.,  Oct. 5, 1899 - Apr. 25, 1972
        Wife of Everett Bowman

BOWMAN, Hubert Lee, Oct. 4, 1953 - July 2, 1972
BOWMAN, Joseph,        b. July 1823 - Wife - Katherine Cline
BOWMAN, Kathleen, one date - Feb. 14, 1923
        Wife of Gene Bowman
BOWMAN, Robert, Son of John and Sally Bowman
BOWMAN, Sally K., March 1882 - Sept. 5, 1948
        Wife of John Bowman

BRADSHAW, Betty Shelton, July 30, 1909 - April 1, 1986
        Wife of Ralph N. Bradshaw
BRADSHAW, Ralph N., April 6, 1899 - Nov. 8, 1982

BULL, W. Frank, Oct. 13, 1910 -
BULL, Susie Pauline (w), April 30, 1913 -
        Daughter of Henry Franklin & Julia Ann Jones Norris

CHAMBLER, Catherine, Dec. 24, 1929 - July 13, 1988

COFFEE, Jude, d. July 2, 1924 - Wife of Wesley Coffee

COLEMAN, Stanley A., Sept. 9, 1909 - July 22, 1961
        Tenn. PVT - Btry. D. 378, CAB, WWII
COLEMAN, Verna, March 15, 1885 - Jan. 20, 1929
        Daughter of Dave and Nannie Whaley Smith

CONSTABLE, Abbie Rosemond, Jan. 2, 1880 - Nov. 21, 1958
        Daughter of David N. and Matilda Watson Constable
CONSTABLE, David N., Dec. 8, 1849 - Aug. 15, 1925
        Son of Jacob and Celuissa Constable
CONSTABLE, Josie McInturff, April 29, 1878 - June 21, 1967
        Daughter of James Samuel & Sarah Katherine Jones
                                    McInturff
CONSTABLE, Matilda, Oct. 2, 1848 - Nov. 15, 1910
CONSTABLE, Nathaniel Taylor, June 1889 - 1971
        Son of David N. and Matilda Watson Constable
CONSTABLE, Sarah Matilda Cleo, May 17, 1907 - June 14, 1907
        Daughter of William Jacob & Josie McInturff Constable
CONSTABLE, William Jacob, May 25, 1875 - Aug. 31, 1945
        Son of David N. and Matilda Watson Constable

CORRELL, Charles, Dec. 21, 1882 - April 19, 1958
        Son of Alfred and Lucy Morton Correll
CORRELL, Pearl J., b. Sept. 8, 1897

COX, Arthur, Dec. 11, 1898 - Oct. 19, 1918

DAVIS, Anthony, 1977-1977

DOVE, Catherine, Sept. 4, 1844 - Jan. 1, 1917
        Wife of Jonah D. Dove. Dau. of John and Nancy Jane
                                    Whitson Nelson

ENGLE, Vickie Lynn, Dec. 28, 1966 - Dec. 29, 1966
        Daughter of Leslie and Dale Miller Engle

JONES CEMETERY - (continued)

HARRIS, Florence,      1920-1946
HARRIS, George,        1904-19--
HARRIS, Infant,        Son of Harry Harris
HARRIS, Infant,
HARRIS, Infant,
HARRIS, Infant,
HARRIS, Pauline Lena,   1925-1980
HARRIS, Sadie Lou,  1906 - May 6, 1937
        Daughter of John and Maggie Smith Nelson

HENSLEY, Burles F.,   Feb. 22, 1909 - Sept. 9, 1965
        Husband of Venia Bell McInturff Hensley
HENSLEY, Greenberry,  Jan. 25, 1873 - Aug. 9, 1963
HENSLEY, James Roscoe,  1907-1908 - Sgt. US Army, WWII
HENSLEY, Kate,  May 29, 1911 - March 18, 1981
HENSLEY, Leona F.,  March 25, 1910 - Nov. 12, 1978
HENSLEY, Venia Bell,  Aug. 13, 1917 -
HENSLEY, Nellie Ann,  d. Jan. 5, 1940

HICKS, David A.,  b. 1915 - Son of James and Martha W. Hicks
HICKS, James,  June 18, 1868 - Oct. 7, 1950
        Son of John and Martha Combs Hicks
HICKS, Martha W.,  Feb. 22, 1885 - Dec. 1, 1970
HICKS, Virgie C.,  1918 -

HIGGINS, Phebe Ann,  Nov. 30, 1890 - July 13, 1913
        Wife of J. E. Higgins

HUNTER, Julia White,  Jan. 10, 1878 - April 22, 1901
        Wife of McDonnell Hunter. Daughter of John C.
        and Delia Simmons White

HUNTTON, James Lloyd,  Sept. 26, 1899 - March 21, 1956
        Husband of Pauline Tinker. Son of William and
        Myra Butler Huntton

HUSKINS, James A.,  Sept. 15, 1919 - Dec. 13, 1977
        PVT, US Army,  WWII
HUSKINS, Mary Louise, 1920 - Dec. 30, 1983. Wife of Roy
        Edward Huskins. Daughter of Charlie and Mamie
        Peterson McInturff
HUSKINS, Roy Edward,  May 17, 1917 - Dec. 24, 1972
        PFC, Tenn.,  WWII

HUTCHINS, Celia,  1885-1962
HUTCHINS, Daisy,  1911-1979
HUTCHINS, Jess,  July 6, 1887 - July 9, 1955
        Son of Dave Gilley and Letha Hutchins
HUTCHINS, Sendy,  March 7, 1904 - July 20, 1973
HUTCHINS, Thomas,  March 3, 1918 - Oct. 29, 1952
        TN, S.Sgt., Co.E, 21 Inf., BSM, PH, WWII
HUTCHINS, Willard,  Aug. 18, 1931 - Nov. 15, 1983

JOHNSON, Gary Wayne, Feb. 3, 1964 - Feb. 3, 1964
        Son of Joseph Wayne & Connie Ruth McInturff Johnson

JONES, Anna Bell Smith, Dec. 29, 1898 - Jan. 20, 1978
    Wife of George Chester Jones
JONES, Bessie L. Bell, 1910 -
    Wife of James Richard Jones
JONES, Billie, Feb. 8, 1926 - Aug. 30, 1926
    Son of Everette Wilson and Jeanette B. Jones
JONES, Calvin Lee, Dec. 26, 1925 - Jan. 9, 1926
    Son of George Chester and Anna Bell Smith Jones
JONES, Daniel David, June 20, 1874 - Aug. 22, 1898
    Son of Solomon Hendrix and Julia Ann Haun Jones
JONES, Elizabeth Ida, Jan. 20, 1857 - April 25, 1929
    Daughter of Henry and Martha Lyle Ambrose
JONES, Everette A. B., May 22, 1861 - Aug. 29, 1946
    Son of Solomon Hendrix and Julia Ann Haun Jones
JONES, Everette Wilson, 1889-1963
    Son of James Madison and Margaret Ellen Jones Jones
JONES, Frank D., July 25, 1887 - Aug. 24, 1969
    Son of James Madison and Margaret Ellen Jones Jones
JONES, Gennett B., 1905 -
    Wife of Everette Wilson Jones
JONES, George Chester, May 12, 1896 - April 17, 1961
    Son of James Madison and Margaret Ellen Jones Jones
JONES, Infant, b/d 1924
    Child of George Chester and Anna Bell Smith Jones
JONES, Infant, b/d 1923
    Child of George Chester and Anna Bell Smith Jones
JONES, Infant, b/d 1922
    Child of George Chester and Anna Bell Smith Jones
JONES, James Madison, Feb. 28, 1856 - Jan. 15, 1941
    Son of James Henry and Elizabeth Feathers Jones
    Husband of Margaret Ellen Jones
JONES, James M., Dec. 8, 1856 - April 4, 1857
    Son of Solomon Hendrix and Julia Ann Haun Jones
JONES, James Richard, 1905-1957
    Son of James Madison and Margaret Ellen Jones Jones
JONES, Julia Ann, Sept. 16, 1834 - Nov. 1, 1911
    Daughter of Daniel and Susannah Van Huss Haun
    Second wife of Solomon Hendrix Jones
JONES, Louise, June 14, 1855 - Aug. 8, 1855
    Daughter of Solomon Hendrix and Julia Ann Haun Jones
JONES, Margaret Ellen, June 24, 1864 - July 30, 1954
    Daughter of Solomon Hendrix and Julia Ann Haun Jones
JONES, Nola Banks, May 19, 1901 - Nov. 13, 1972
    Daughter of John and Nannie Grindstaff Banks
    Wife of Sam Hendrix Jones, Sr.
JONES, Phoebe, Nov. 1844 - 1909
JONES, Sam Hendrix, Sr., March 18, 1894 - Feb. 20, 1965
    Son of James Madison and Margaret Jones Jones
JONES, Sarah Elizabeth, April 24, 1811 - Mar. 13, 1853
    Maiden name Baker. 1st wife of Solomon Hendrix Jones
    (First person buried in Jones Cemetery)
JONES, Solomon Hendrix, April 16, 1813 - Nov. 11, 1885
    Son of William B. and Nancy A. Kuhn Jones

JONES, Susan Elizabeth,  July 22, 1858 - Jan. 27, 1942
        Daughter of Solomon Hendrix and Julia Ann Haun Jones
JONES, Una Minnie Okie,  Sept. 4, 1871 - July 18, 1946
        Daughter of Solomon Hendrix and Julia Ann Haun Jones

KINSLANE, William Buist,  Sea 2,  US Navy,  WWI

LEWIS, Grady H.,  Dec. 5, 1910 -
        Son of Riley L. and Myrtle M. Lewis
        Husband of Lee Margaret Norris
LEWIS, Lee Margaret,  Nov. 22, 1910 - Oct. 10, 1978
        Daughter of Henry Franklin and Julia Ann Jones Norris
LEWIS, Myrtle M.,   1893-1972
LEWIS, Riley L.,    1882-1962

LINVILLE, Bessie B.,  June 1900 -
        Daughter of Rev. Wm. A. & Nancy E. Nelson Linville
LINVILLE, Bernie,  March 27, 1910 -
        Son of Rev. Wm. A. & Nancy E. Nelson Linville
LINVILLE, Charles,   -
LINVILLE, Elizabeth J.,  Sept. 11, 1893 -
LINVILLE, Howard,   -
LINVILLE, Maggie,   - , Dau. of Rev. Wm. A. & Nancy E. Nelson
LINVILLE, Nancy E.,  May 1871 - 1941          Linville
        Maiden name Nelson
LINVILLE, William A.,  Feb. 1868 - 1952
        Husband of Nancy E. Nelson Linville

LIVINGSTON, Frances Ann,  Aug. 26, 1947 - Oct. 15, 1949
        Daughter of Wayne and Fannie O. Norris Livingston
LIVINGSTON, Gary Wayne,  May 30, 1954 - Oct. 23, 1954
        Son of Wayne and Fannie O. Norris Livingston

LLOYD, John A.,  Aug. 6, 1914 - Nov. 20, 1982
LLOYD, Lena C.,  1917 - 1971

McINTURFF, Agnes,  1924 - ,  Maiden name Huskins
McINTURFF, Anna Lucille,  March 16, 1925 - June 2, 1925
        Daughter of Sarah Ella McInturff
McINTURFF, Basel,  ---
        Son of Noah J. and Myrtle Nelson McInturff
McINTURFF, Bruce K.,   ------
        Son of Noah J. and Myrtle Nelson McInturff
McINTURFF, Cora Alice,  March 1, 1892 - Aug. 22, 1954
        Daughter of James Madison and Margaret Ellen Jones Jones
        Wife of William R. McInturff
McINTURFF, Delia Alice,  March 10, 1909 - May 27, 1987
        Daughter of Solomon H. and Flora Smith White
        Wife of Sam Orville McInturff
McINTURFF, Dora,  July 7, 1870 - Oct. 1, 1959
        Daughter of James Samuel & Sarah Katherine Jones
McINTURFF, Earl,  Mar. 23, 1909-Apr.13, 1933          McInturff
        Son of N. K. and Julia McInturff
McINTURFF, Elizabeth Jane,  Sept. 24, 1868 - Feb. 3, 1918
        Wife of William Hendrick McInturff

McINTURFF, Ernest, Jan. 2, 1923 - April 20, 1987
        Son of Sarah Ella McInturff
McINTURFF, Frankie, Dec. 9, 1895 -
        Daughter of William Hendrick and Elizabeth Jane
                                        Nelson McInturff
McINTURFF, Jenevee/Genasse, Nov. 4, 1929 -
        Daughter of Noah J. and Myrtle Nelson McInturff
McINTURFF, James Samuel, March 4, 1839 - March 4, 1910
        Son of John and Rachel Edna Scott McInturff
        Husband of Sarah Katherine Jones
McINTURFF, Janet Marie, Dec. 1, 1960 - Dec. 1, 1960
        Daughter of Paul Clinton & June Dean Hilton McInturff
McINTURFF, Jannis Earline, March 14, 1935 - March 31, 1935
        Daughter of Willard James & Pansy Inez Miller McInturff
McINTURFF, June Dean, June 26, 1933 -
        Maiden name Hilton - Wife of Paul Clinton McInturff
McINTURFF, Lula, Sept. 1885 - Jan. 30, 1935
        Daughter of Nathaniel K. & Barbarba Ann Coffee/Cobble
                                        McInturff
McINTURFF, Myrtle Nelson, Sept. 23, 1890 - Nov. 27, 1969
        Wife of Noah J. McInturff
McINTURFF, Noah J., Nov. 8, 1883 - March 7, 1966
McINTURFF, Pansy Inez, April 29, 1918 -
        Daughter of James William Madison and
        Lora Dean Miller Miller
McINTURFF, Paul Clinton, Oct. 31, 1931 - Dec. 2, 1985
        Son of Sam Orville and Delia Alice White McInturff
McINTURFF, Peggy Jean, Jan. 22, 1936 - Jan. 25, 1936
        Daughter of Willard James & Pansy Inez Miller McInturff
McINTURFF, Ralph McKinney, Mar. 29, 1953 - Oct. 18, 1954
        Son of Everette Franklin and Ruth Renfro McInturff
McINTURFF, Sam Orville, Aug. 22, 1909 - May 14, 1974
        Son of John Swanner and Susan Eugenia McInturff
McINTURFF, Sarah Ella, June 1, 1897 - April 19, 1925
        Daughter of William Hendrix and Elizabeth Jane
                                        Nelson McInturff
McINTURFF, Sarah Katherine, Nov. 1839 - Aug. 15, 1894
        Daughter of Solomon Hendrix and Sarah Elizabeth
        Baker Jones. Wife of James Samuel McInturff
McINTURFF, Sherrill Lynne, Nov. 28, 1956 - Nov. 28, 1956
        Daughter of Paul Clinton & June Dean Hilton McInturff
McINTURFF, Susan Eugenia, July 17, 1883 - June 18, 1968
        Daughter of James Samuel & Sarah Katherine Jones
                                        McInturff
McINTURFF, Ted Eugene, June 24, 1942 - Dec. 7, 1966
        Son of Willard James & Pansy Inez Miller McInturff
McINTURFF, Thelma, Jan. 30, 1934 - Jan. 30, 1934
        Daughter of Willard James & Pansy Inez Miller McInturff
McINTURFF, Willard James, Oct. 16, 1911 - Aug. 15, 1983
        Son of William R. and Cora Alice Jones McInturff
McINTURFF, William Hendrick, July 4, 1868 - Feb. 6, 1933
        Son of James Samuel & Sarah Katherine Jones McInturff
        Husband of Elizabeth Jane Nelson

McINTURFF, William R., Aug. 6, 1889 - May 29, 1914
     Son of David James McInturff and Lucinda Borders.
     Husband of Cora Alice Jones

McLAUGHLIN, Abraham T., Sept. 24, 1848 - Jan. 24, 1901
     Son of Wm. K. and Lavina Whitson McLaughlin
     Husband of Nancy Caroline Jones
McLAUGHLIN, Alford A. T., Sept. 11, 1889 - Jan. 14, 1976
     Husband of Alice Smith McLaughlin
McLAUGHLIN, Alice Smith, May 3, 1887 - Dec. 24, 1974
     Daughter of Henry and Sarah Whaley Smith
McLAUGHLIN, Alvin, Sept. 1884 -
     Son of Ephrian Bill and Mary Ann Cole McLaughlin
McLAUGHLIN, Bessie Wilcox, June 18, 1884 - April 27, 1951
     Wife of William K. McLaughlin
McLAUGHLIN, Charles W., April 9, 1891 - Nov. 15, 1968
     Son of Ephrian Bill and Mary Ann Cole McLaughlin
McLAUGHLIN, Cornette, 1925-1987
McLAUGHLIN, Ephrian Bill, Mar. 30, 1860 - Dec. 7, 1943
McLAUGHLIN, Frank C., Nov. 30, 1922 - Dec. 25, 1972
     Son of Ephrian Bill and -------McLaughlin
     GA, PFC, US Army, WWII
McLAUGHLIN, Fred, June 21, 1927 - May 14, 1954
     Son of Jess and Stella McLaughlin
McLAUGHLIN, Jack P., Aug. 11, 1920 - Feb. 25, 1966
     Son of Jess and Stella McLaughlin
     Tenn. Pvt. 1473 5 VC Comd. Unit, WWII
McLAUGHLIN, Jess, Sept. 1886 -
     Son of Ephrian Bill & Mary Ann Cole McLaughlin
McLAUGHLIN, Lola, Mar. 26, 1890 - Dec. 14, 1942
     Daughter of Ephrian Bill & Mary Ann Cole McLaughlin
McLAUGHLIN, Manson Willette, Sept. 25, 1920 - April 4, 1926
     Daughter of Wm. K. and Bessie Wilcox McLaughlin
McLAUGHLIN, Mary Ann, July 15, 1857 - April 11, 1913
     1st wife of Ephrian Bill McLaughlin
McLAUGHLIN, Melissa, Dec. 1869 - 1884
     Daughter of Wm. K. and Lavina Whitson McLaughlin
McLAUGHLIN, Nancy Caroline, June 28, 1850 - Mar. 13, 1918
     Daughter of Solomon Hendrix and Sarah Baker Jones
     Wife of Abraham T. McLaughlin
McLAUGHLIN, Nelse, Sept. 24, 1848 - Dec. 29, 1929
     Son of Wm. K. and Lavina Whitson McLaughlin
     Twin to Abraham T. McLaughlin
McLAUGHLIN, Nora Vern, April 28, 1873 - Feb. 4, 1899
     Daughter of Abraham T. & Nancy Caroline Jones McLaughlin
McLAUGHLIN, Robbie, 1914 - April 4, 1932
     Son of Alford A. T. and Alice Smith McLaughlin
McLAUGHLIN, Stella, 1904 - May 20, 1978
     Maiden name McCarter. Wife of Jess McLaughlin
McLAUGHLIN, William K., July 7, 1892 - Feb. 22, 1928
     Son of Ephrian Bill and Mary Ann Cole McLaughlin

McNABB, Vena L., Aug. 2, 1907 - May 26, 1973

MILLER, Anna Lois,  July 8, 1934 - March 25, 1935
        Daughter of Marshall and Dessie Arwood Miller
MILLER, Earl,  b/d June 11, 1933
        Son of Marshall and Dessie Arwood Miller
MILLER, Elizabeth,  June 30, 1880 - Mar. 2, 1960
        Daughter of Melvin Cox. Wife of James Tobe Miller
MILLER, James Tobe,  Mar. 28, 1877 - June 1, 1945
        Son of -------- and Sudie Bell Miller
MILLER, Sudie Bell,  no dates
MILLER, Vernie,  May 4, 1915 - July 24, 1973

NELSON, Barba Ellen,  Feb. 12, 1838 - Aug. 16, 1917
NELSON, Bertha Thelma,  April 15, 1910 - Sept. 3, 1959
        Daughter of Andrew Jackson & Lula Ann Franklin Hite
        Wife of Martin Nelson
NELSON, Hannah L.,  July 3, 1869 - Mar. 7, 1894
        Wife of Joseph Nelson
NELSON, John Newton,  June 16, 1846 - Oct. 11, 1919
        Son of John and Nancy Jane Whitson Nelson
        Husband of Rachel Alice Jones
NELSON, John Wesley,  April 28, 1879 - Dec. 9, 1919
        Husband of Maggie Smith
NELSON, Maggie Smith,  April 3, 1876 - Sept. 8, 1949
        Daughter of David and Jane Whaley Smith
NELSON, Margaret C.,  Oct. 13, 1883 - Sept. 28, 1903
        Daughter of I (or T) and R. Nelson
NELSON, Martin,  1900-1962
NELSON, Nancy Jane,  June 13, 1820 - Mar. 30, 1885
        Maiden name Whitson - Wife of John Nelson
NELSON, Rachel Alice,  Jan. 7, 1843 - Jan. 22, 1929
        Daughter of James Henry and Elizabeth Feathers Jones
        Wife of John Newton Nelson
NELSON, Wordie B.,  Nov. 29, 1908 - Apr. 27, 1970

NORRIS, Arra I.,  July 1, 1927 - Feb. 11, 1973
        Daughter of Henry Franklin and Julia Ann Jones Norris
NORRIS, Henry Franklin,  May 12, 1885 - Jan. 22, 1948
        Son of Thomas and Sarah Tinker Norris
NORRIS, Julia Ann,  June 11, 1885 - May 13, 1966
        Daughter of James Madison & Margaret Ellen Jones Jones

PEAKE, Hannah R.,  1910-1988

PETERSON, Fannice Elizabeth,  1901 - Mar. 25, 1958
        Wife of Todd G. Peterson
PETERSON, Todd G.,  1896 - Jan. 2, 1975

PIERCY, Edna Beatrice,  Oct. 1, 1917 - April 11, 1988
        Daughter of Everette Evans and Maggie L. Jones White
        Wife of Robert Lee Piercy
PIERCY, Patricia Ann,  May 11, 1937 - Dec. 27, 1941
        Daughter of Robert Lee and Edna Beatrice White Piercy
PIERCY, Robert Lee,  Sept. 1, 1913 - May 1, 1988
        Son of Herbert and Hattie Bailey Piercy

POORE, Fred,  Dec. 20, 1924 - Feb. 23, 1968
POORE, Julia Grace,  -  , maiden name Coffee
          Wife of Jim Poore, Jr.

PRESSNELL, Charles M.,  April 4, 1885 - Sept. 24, 1937
          Husband of Duffie L. Bishop
PRESSNELL, Duffie L.,  July 12, 1889 - Oct. 22, 1947

RAY, Annette,  d. 1976
RAY, Harold Lynn,  d. Dec. 1956
          Son of Howard and Barbara Mae Huskins Ray
RAY, Infant,  d. Mar. 13, 1967

RENFRO, Wm. McKinley,  Sept. 26, 1895 - Sept. 22, 1970

RIDDLE, David Lee,  Dec. 21, 1945 - Dec. 24, 1945
          Son of Willie and Thelma Elizabeth Tapp Riddle
RIDDLE, Wayne,  Aug. 12, 1949 - Aug. 8, 1954
          Son of Willie and Thelma Elizabeth Tapp Riddle

ROWE, Mary Elizabeth,  1876 - 1947
          Wife of Rev. Nathaniel K. Rowe
ROWE, Rev. Nathaniel K.,  -

RUNION, Cornelious B.,  May 3, 1892 - July 2, 1964
          Son of John and Nancy Foster Runion
          Husband of Linda Miller
RUNION, Linda,  1895 -
RUNION, Millard Franklin,  April 17, 1917 - Dec. 4, 1953
          Son of Cornelious and Linda Miller Runion

SMITH, Aughet (?),  -
SMITH, David,  May 1855 - , Husband of Mary E. Bowman
SMITH, David Carl,  Feb. 12, 1883 - June 25, 1954
          Son of Henry and Sarah Whaley Smith
          Husband of Lucy Jane Britt
SMITH, Earl J.,  April 9, 1923 - June 3, 1974
          Son of Fred and Oma McInturff/McCellan Smith
SMITH, Frank,  Feb. 26, 1915 - Dec. 1, 1962
SMITH, Fred, Sr.,  Mar. 20, 1894 - Feb. 25, 1968
          Son of David and Julia Hardin Smith
          Husband of Oma McCellan McInturff Smith
SMITH, Garfield,  1909-1912
SMITH, James,  Aug. 4, 1892 - Jan. 26, 1950
SMITH, Lucy Jane,  Dec. 6, 1886 - Feb. 9, 1947
          Daughter of Elbert C. & Esther Benfield Britt
          Wife of David Carl Smith
SMITH, Mannis,  d. 1984
SMITH, Mary E.,  April 1856 -
          Daughter of Joseph and Katherine Cline Bowman
          Wife of Daniel Smith
SMITH, Oma,  July 4, 1896 - Feb. 4, 1966
          Wife of Fred Smith, Jr.
SMITH, Oscar,  1919-1982
          Son of Fred and Oma McCellan/McInturff Smith

TAPP, Beverly Eleanor, 1940 - Mar. 1, 1941
        Daughter of David and Mamie Jones Tapp
TAPP, Charles Robert, Dec. 14, 1933 - July 17, 1962
        Son of David and Mamie Jones Tapp
TAPP, David, Mar. 10, 1905 - Jan. 29, 1980
        Husband of Mamie Jones Tapp
TAPP, Luther Bernard, Apr. 29, 1939 - May 12, 1939
        Son of David and Mamie Jones Tapp
TAPP, Mamie, Dec. 30, 1910 -
TAPP, Thomas, d. Aug. 13, 1941

THOMPSON, Lila Adeline, June 13, 1914 - Oct. 31, 1960
        Daughter of Charles M. and Duffie L. Bishop Pressnell
        Wife of Lewis Thompson

TINKER, Anne Edna Elizabeth, June 1874 - Nov. 28, 1948
        Daughter of James Samuel & Sarah Katherine Jones
        Wife of John Wm. Tinker.          McInturff.
TINKER, Beatrice M., b. 1920 -
TINKER, Cora Bell, b. 1903 - , Wife of Murrell Tinker.
        Daughter of Wm. Hendrick & Elizabeth Jane Nelson
                                        McInturff
TINKER, Earl Woodward, June 5, 1918 - Dec. 2, 1955
        Son of John Wm. and Anne Edna McInturff Tinker
        Husband of Hazel Daugherty
TINKER, Everette Cecil, 1908-1971
        Son of John Wm. and Anne Edna McInturff Tinker
TINKER, Everette H., 1916 - 1978
TINKER, George F., Sept. 1899 - 1970
        Son of Joel and Minnie E. Tinker
        Husband of Leona Mullins
TINKER, George Robert, no dates
TINKER, Hazeline, b/d 1923
TINKER, Joel, May 1876 - 1906
TINKER, John William, Nov. 4, 1869 - Nov. 1, 1927
        Son of Robert F. and Vinace Claiborne Tinker
TINKER, Kathleen, 1926 - April 15, 1927
        Daughter of George F. and Leona Mullins Tinker
TINKER, Leona, Aug. 16, 1902 - July 12, 1950
TINKER, Linda Lou, Oct. 6, 1940 - April 10, 1941
        Daughter of Earl Woodward & Hazel Daugherty Tinker
TINKER, Maggie May, April 4, 1902 - Nov. 21, 1931
        Daughter of John Wm. & Anne Edna McInturff Tinker
TINKER, Mary Emma, Sept. 8, 1877 - July 23, 1898
TINKER, Mary Ellen, d. Feb. 1908. Mother of Joel & Will Tinker
TINKER, Minnie E., Jan. 1878 - 1968 - Wife of Joel Tinker
TINKER, Murrell, April 27, 1905 - Aug. 13, 1954
        Son of John Wm. and Anne Edna McInturff Tinker
TINKER, Sarah Belle, no dates
TINKER, Thelma, March 5, 1931 - March 26, 1931
        Daughter of George F. and Leona Mullins Tinker
TINKER, Wayne, no dates - Son of George F. & Leona Mullins Tinker
TINKER, Richard Jack, Jan. 1, 1956 - Jan. 17, 1956
        Son of George F. and Leona Mullins Tinker

VANCE, Calvin,     d. 1946
VANCE, Emaline,    d. 1948 - Wife of Calvin Vance
VANCE, Golda,      d. 1949
VANCE, Joe,        1904 - 1955
VANCE, John Henry, 1919-1983,  US Army, WWII
VANCE, Judy A.,   1922-1967
VANCE, Thomas F., 1916-1985


WALKER, Andrew Jackson,  April 2, 1937 - June 1, 1956
         Son of James Mason and Dora A. Eastridge Walker
WALKER, Dale Conley,  June 2, 1943 - Oct. 6, 1962
         Son of James Mason and Dora A. Eastridge Walker
WALKER, Dora A.,  June 23, 1908 - Jan. 12, 1986
WALKER, James Mason,  March 4, 1905 - June 27, 1984
WALKER, Sherry A.,  b/d 1968
         Daughter of Frank and Ruth Walker


WHALEY, Catherine,  July 2, 1821 - Aug. 25, 1898

WHEELER, Jennie,  Sept. 23, 1884 - April 14, 1915

WHITE, Alan Eugene,  Jan. 24, 1948 - Nov. 30, 1968
         Tenn. L.Cpl., Btry.1313, Vietnam PH&G
WHITE, Bert,  no dates - Son of Solomon Hendrix and
         Flora Smith White
WHITE, Birtie,  Feb. 5, 1912 -
         Maiden name Barnett - Wife of Floyd "Tom" White
WHITE, Charles H.,  Jan. 29, 1904 -
         Son of Solomon and Flora Smith White
WHITE, Charles H. Jr.,  Jan. 29, 1934 - Jan. 29, 1934
         Son of Charles H. and Minnie B. White
WHITE, Chester Orville,  July 7, 1921 - June 9, 1952
         Son of Labe Wm. and Mary Emmaline Smith White
WHITE, Claude C.,  1908 -
         Son of Everette T. and Maggie L. Jones White
WHITE, Delia,  Jan. 13, 1849 - May 20, 1927
         Maiden name Simmons. Wife of John C. White
WHITE, Dwight Eli,  Jan. 20, 1953 - Oct. 22, 1984
         Son of Eli and Sarah Woodby White
WHITE, Eli,  1916 -
         Son of Solomon Hendrix and Flora Smith Jones White
WHITE, Everette Evans,  Mar. 8, 1898 - Dec. 26, 1983
         Son of Joseph and Mary McInturff White
WHITE, Everette T.,  Dec. 1883 - 1909
         Son of John C. and Delia Simmons White
         Husband of Maggie L. Jones
WHITE, Flora Smith,  April 4, 1883 - Feb. 25, 1968
         Daughter of Henry and Sarah Whaley Smith
         Wife of Solomon Hendrix White
WHITE, Floyd "Tom",  Feb. 23, 1908 - Nov. 7, 1975
         Son of Labe Wm. and Mary Emmaline White
         Husband of Birdie Barnett
WHITE, Infant,  d. May 11, 1947
         Child of Floyd "Tom" and Birdie Barnett White

WHITE, Infant,   no dates
        Child of Floyd "Tom" and Birdie Barnett White
WHITE, John C.,   March 1848 - Co. M. 8 Tenn. Cav.
        Husband of Delia Simmons
WHITE, Labe William,  May 18, 1875 - Sept. 7, 1951
        Son of John C. and Delia Simmons White
        Husband of Mary Emmaline Smith
WHITE, Maggie L.,  April 1882 - 1964
        Daughter of John and Nancy J. Jones
        Wife of Everette T. White
WHITE, Mary,  Jan. 1874 -    , Wife of Joseph White
        Daughter of Nathaniel K. & Barbara Ann Cobble/Coffee
                                    McInturff
WHITE, Mary Emmaline,  Oct. 26, 1880 - Mar. 28, 1951
        Daughter of Thomas and Sally Edwards Smith
        Wife of Labe Wm. White
WHITE, Mrs. Bert,  no dates
WHITE, Minnie B.,  Sept. 14, 1910 - Dec. 27, 1984
        Wife of Charles H. White
WHITE, Opal Carter,  1905 - Dec. 13, 1930
        Son of Labe Wm. and Mary Emmaline Smith White
WHITE, Pearl Irene,  Jan. 19, 1900 - Dec. 29, 1983
        Daughter of Labe Wm. and Mary Emmaline Smith White
WHITE, Sarah,  1924 -
        Wife of Eli White - maiden name Woodby
WHITE, Solomon Hendrix,  Jan. 4, 1881 - Sept. 10, 1966
        Son of John C. and Delia Simmons White
        Husband of Flora Smith
WHITE, Ted Lester,  May 17, 1930 - Oct. 18, 1941
        Son of Charles H. and Minnie B. White
WHITE, Thelma,  no dates  - wife of Claude C. White
WHITE, Walter,  May 16, 1903 - June 12, 1965
        Son of Joseph and Mary McInturff White
WHITE, Wilburn,  Aug. 17, 1932 - Jan. 13, 1956
        Son of Charles H. and Minnie B. White

WILSON, Harrison,   b/d 1889
WILSON, Infant,   no dates
WILSON, Judy Ann,   1863-1889


## JONES CEMETERY - UNMARKED GRAVES

ADKINS, Mrs. Cling,  -
ADKINS, Mrs.        ,  -

BLEVINS, Cad,        -
BLEVINS, Celia Bell, -
BLEVINS, Infant    , -
BLEVINS, Infant    , -
BLEVINS, Lula Bell , -

JONES CEMETERY - UNMARKED GRAVES - (continued)

BOWMAN, K/Catherine, b. Aug. 1830 - Wife of Joseph Bowman
BOWMAN, Infant, Child of Gene and Katherine Bowman
BOWMAN, Infant, d. May 20, 1910 - Child of John & Sally Bowman
BOWMAN, John, Dec. 1869 - Dec. 25, 1956
        Son of Joseph and K/Catherine Cline Bowman

COFFEE, Wesley, d. Nov. 30, 1929
        Son of Terry and Sarah Berry Coffee

COLEMAN, Doris Lola, d. March 31, 1941
        Daughter of James Smith and Etta Coleman
COLEMAN, Jim, d. Jan. 26, 1927
COLEMAN, Mrs. Vernie, March 15, 1885 - Jan. 20, 1929
        Daughter of Dave and Nannie Whaley Smith

HARRIS, Edgar Guy, -
HARRIS, Mrs. Carl, -
HARRIS, Pauline Lena, 1925-1980
HARRIS, Thelma, -
HARRIS, Togo, -

HENSON, Callie, -
HENSON, Mrs. , -

HOWELL, Edna Beatrice, -

HUNTER, Infant, - , Child of McDonnell & Julia White
                                              Hunter

HUSKINS, Infant, d. July 8, 1962
        Son of Phyllis Ann Huskins
HUSKINS, Kieth Allen, Oct. 7, 1957 - Oct. 8, 1957
        Son of Harry Leonard and Florence Johnson Huskins
HUSKINS, Leroy, -
HUSKINS, Thelma, -

HUTCHINS, Mrs. Thomas, -

JONES, Elizabeth Whaley, Jan. 20, 1867 - April 25, 1929
JONES, Infant, - , Child of John and Nancy Jones
JONES, Vickie Henson , -

LINVILLE, Charles, -

McCELLARS, - , -

McINTURFF, David J., May 23, 1897 - July 8, 1929
        Son of Robert J. and Susan Baker McInturff
McINTURFF, Donald, Jan. 23, 1957 - Jan. 23, 1957
        Son of Everette Franklin & Ruth Renfro McInturff
McINTURFF, Infant Son, d. July 11, 1950
        Son of Evans R. and Sarah Jane Herr McInturff
McINTURFF, Infant Son, d. Feb. 24, 1956
        Son of Evans R. and Sarah Jane Herr McInturff
McINTURFF, Infant, d. Sept. 11, 1951
        Daughter of Evans R. & Sarah Jane Herr McInturff

- 126 -

McINTURFF, Infant Daughter,  d. Feb. 1, 1955
        Daughter of Evans R. and Sarah Jane Herr McInturff
McINTURFF, Infant Daughter,  d. July 25, 1958
        Daughter of Evans R. and Sarah Jane Herr McInturff
McINTURFF, Rudy M.,  Dec. 2, 1924 - Jan. 31, 1929
        Son of David J. and Cora Alice Jones McInturff

McLAUGHLIN, Infant,  - Child of Alford T. and Alice Smith
                                          McLaughlin
McLAUGHLIN, George, d. Feb. 24, 1968
        Son of Ephrian Bill and Mary Ann Cole McLaughlin
McLAUGHLIN, Infant,  -
McLAUGHLIN, M. K.,  d. Feb. 25, 1928
McLAUGHLIN, Tish,  Aug. 1897  -
        Daughter of Ephrian Bill and Mary Ann Cole McLaughlin
McLAUGHLIN, W. Kendrick,  -

MILLER, Pearl,  -

NELSON, Ike,  -
NELSON, Laura Kever,  -
NELSON, Lee Roy,  d. Dec. 8, 1941 - Son of Rex & Sadie Nelson
NELSON, Nettie Luttrell,  1903 - Jan. 20, 1939
        Daughter of Isaac and Mollie Tittle Luttrell

PETERSON, Nealie,  -

PRESSNELL, Lila Adaline,  Mar. 10, 1857 - Sept. 7, 1898

RICH, Infant,  Child of Hattie Rich

RIDDLE, Infant,  -

ROWE, Mattie,  -

RUNION, Matalda,  -

SLAGLE, Mrs.,  -

SMITH, Bob,  -

SMITH, Infant,  -
SMITH, Infant,  -
SMITH, Infant,  -
SMITH, Infant,  -
SMITH, Julie Orton,  Dec. 1880 -
        Daughter of David and Mary E. Bowman Smith
SMITH, Mary, d. Jan. 23, 1939 = age 83
        Daughter of Joseph and Katherine Cline Bowman
SMITH, Sarah Whaley,  Wife of Henry Smith

TINKER, Campbell Eugene,  -
TINKER, George W.,  -

VANCE, Mrs.,            -

WHALEY, Margaret,       -

WHEELER, Paul,          -

WHITE, Johnny,          -
WHITE, Lois,            -


    The work of copying Jones Cemetery was done by Barbara Dowden, daughter of Pansy McInturff. The data for unmarked graves was copied by her from a board on the wall of a shed, at the cemetery.

## BIG BRANCH OR EFFLER CEMETERY

Behind church of same name, crest of Big Branch Road
and left short distance, beyond junction with Edwards
Branch Road.

Copied June 25, 1988

LLOYD, M. Presley,    1877-1955
LLOYD, Sarah L. F. (w),   1871-1958
     ("Stepmother")

PRICE, Zear E.,   1901-1963

PRICE, Grace L., 1908-1966

LLOYD, Thomas E.,   May 31, 1898 - Mar. 26, 1971
LLOYD, Nola M. (w),   July 31, 1902 - May 28, 1984

BOONE, Thomas Roscoe,   Jan. 29, 1917 - Sep. 30, 1980
BOONE, Sylvia Lloyd (w),   Nov. 17, 1916 -

EFFLER, Pauline,  Apr. 24, 1921 - Oct. 24, 1934

EFFLER, Charles,  1927-1984

EFFLER, E. Lloyd,  1913 - not marked

EFFLER, C. W.,  Mar. 14, 1841 - May 19, 1896

RICE, Joseph,   1856-1907
RICE, Elizebeth (w),   1867-1924

EFFLER, Mary -     d. Nov. 10, 1860 at 69 years
          Wife of
EFFLER, Lorance, about 1795 - Apr. 6, 1886 , Soldier in War
                                              Of 1812
EFFLER, Samuel T., Apr. 1875-May 1957
EFFLER, Martha S. (w), Mar. 1880-Jan. 1960

EFFLER, John Carmon,  May 22, 1884 - Oct. 27, 1968
EFFLER, Rhodila Ramsey (w),   Jan. 28, 1886 - May 5, 1937
          Daughter   of Robert and Catherine Willis Ramsey
LLOYD, Mrs. Winnie,  Mar. 19, 1863 - June 16, 1952

HENSLEY, Emily H.,   1878-1955

### ENGLISH CEMETERY
On Edwards Branch Road, on rt. behind home of Linnie Edwards
Copied June 25, 1988

ENGLISH, Theodore,  Dec. 5, 1918 - Aug. 21, 1982
ENGLISH, Linnie E. (w),  Mar. 18, 1920 -
ENGLISH, Ted J. (son), June 12, 1951 - June 14, 1951
          Son of Theodore and Lennie Franklin English

# EDWARDS BRANCH CEMETERY

On Edwards Branch Road, on rt.  Copied June 25, 1988

## Upper section:

HENSLEY, John J.,  Mar. 3, 1911 - Oct. 15, 1978
HENSLEY, Bonnie S. (w),  May 12, 1913 -

SLAGLE, Donald R.,  Mar. 22, 1932 - June 29, 1983
        US Navy, Korean War

HAYNES, Bobby Gene,  Feb. 26, 1948 - Sep. 6, 1969
        Sgt. 11 Armd. Cav. Regt., Vietnam War

CORN, Jimmie C.,  May 2, 1941 - Feb. 14, 1959

CHANDLEY, Infant,   b/d Sep. 23, 1962

CORN, Alvin W.,  Oct. 2, 1901 - May 2, 1973
CORN, Sarah R. (w),  July 2, 1910 -
CORN, Gladys M.,  Aug. 5, 1940 -

RAY, Nellie Mae,  1907 - 1949

AYERS, John H.,  1874 - 1962
AYERS, Rosa C. (w),  1890 - 1944

AYERS, Dallas L.,
        CPL 332 FA BM, 86 Inf. Div., WWII

FRANKLIN, Jack,  Mar. 6, 1900 - Dec. 27, 1955

RAMSEY, Oma A.,  1878 - 1930

                Plus several unmarked quartz stones

## Lower section:

POTTER, Brenda J.,  Nov. 4, 1946 - Oct. 25, 1982

WHITEHEAD, James D.,  May 5, 1958 - Aug. 19, 1977

WHITEHEAD, Polly,  Mar. 10, 1912 - Feb. 18, 1975

SHELTON, Ronnie DeWayne,  d. 1966 (infant)

GARLAND, Fonzy,  June 3, 1918 - Dec. 19, 1948
        Pfc., 13th Inf. Div.,  WWII

SHEPARD, Rosa Lee,  Mar. 15, 1920 - Dec. 28, 1956

EDWARDS, Jackson,  July 26, 1820 - Jan. 22, 1903
EDWARDS, Lucretia (w), Jan. 3, 1828 - Apr. 25, 1890

Lower section - (continued)

EDWARDS, George Washington,  Mar. 3, 1862 - Dec. 25, 1913

EDWARDS, J. D.,  Apr. 17, 1932 - Oct. 13, 1958

EDWARDS, Andy Jack,  Nov. 25, 1891 - Apr. 26, 1962
        Pfc, 137th Inf. Div., WWI

EDWARDS, Louanna,  July 29, 1908 - July 14, 1975

EFFLER, Alice E.,  1936 - 1968

EDWARDS, Elroy,  1939 - 1986

WATTS, Maude,  Mar. 24, 1906 - May 15, 1981

CLAUSE (CLUSE?), John,  May 28, 1830 - Nov. 3, 1892
CLAUSE (CLUSE?), Elizabeth (w), Nov. 17, 1827 - Dec. 20, 1907

RAMSEY, Eliza Elizabeth,  July 31, 1884 - Aug. 6, 1972

EDWARD, Oscar Shell,  June 18, 1883 - June 22, 1972 (Edwards?)

EDWARDS, Bessie Watts,  June 26, 1905 - Apr. 14, 1983

EDWARDS, James Dedrick,  June 9, 1889 - Jan. 3, 1968

EDWARDS, Samuel T.,  Apr. 27, 1894 - Sep. 23, 1959

CLOUSE, Belva A.,  1900 - 1907
CLOUSE, Twins,     b/d 1904
CLOUSE, Carbie G., 1892 - 1895
CLOUSE, Vertie L., 1889 - 1890

TILSON, Rachel,  June 11, 1861 - Nov. 24, 1902
TILSON, Jack,    Feb. 6, 1886  - May  18, 1890
TILSON, Ida,     Jan. 7, 1892  - Aug.  7, 1893

# EDWARDS #2 CEMETERY

Just behind Baptist Church in Coffee Ridge,
Copied by Charles Bennett on Dec. 7, 1960, updated July 6, 1988

LEDFORD, James D., May 20, 1888 - Aug. 5, 1950
      Pvt., 11th Inf., 5th Div., WWI

LEDFORD, Sarah Jane, Dec. 5, 1847 - Feb. 28, 1936

LEDFORD, Ida Myrtle, 1918 - 1942, - not visible in 1988

EDWARDS, Samuel Jack, Sep. 7, 1879 - Jan. 9, 1939
EDWARDS, Dollie L. (w), 1881 - 1959

EDWARDS, Bradie, Nov. 7, 1914 - Feb. 23, 1958, US Navy, WWII

EDWARDS, A. C., Mar. 17, 1854 - Oct. 31, 1891

EDWARDS, Floyd, Feb. 26, 1903 - May 25, 1920

EDWARDS, Edwin, d. Jan. 5, 1952 at 70 yrs, 5 mos, 20 days

EDWARDS, Gertha Hazel, Jan. 17, 1902 - Dec. 14, 1945

EDWARDS, William T., Oct. 17, 1920 - Dec. 14, 1945
      Tec 5 Eng., WWII
EDWARDS, Juanita (w), Oct. 20, 1921 - Dec. 14, 1945

McINTOSH, Clyde, Jr., Feb. 24, 1935 - Apr. 15, 1935
      Son of Clyde and Ollie McIntosh

HENSLEY, Roscoe, 1890 - 1956
HENSLEY, Martha J., 1879 - 1947

DUGGAN, Johnny H., 1928 - 1959

## ADDITIONS: July 6, 1988

EDWARDS, Troy C., June 10, 1905 - Feb. 26, 1984
EDWARDS, Bertha P. (w), Mar. 19, 1908 - Mar. 10, 1987

LEDFORD, Aunt Babe, Dec. 6, 1901 - May 2, 1968

EDWARDS, Joe, Apr. 12, 1905 - May 1, 1981
EDWARDS, Bonnie (w), June 3, 1912 -

EDWARDS, Loretta L., May 13, 1869 - May 14, 1966

DUGGAN, Glenn Freeman, Sept. 2, 1918 - Oct. 8, 1973
      Sgt., US Army, WWII

EDWARDS, Bertha D., May 19, 1898 - 1987

Plus many wooden crosses

## EDWARDS #1 CEMETERY

3/4 mi. S.W. of Edwards #2 Cemetery on high knoll on N. side
of road up Coffee Ridge - go to first driveway on right on
Gentry Mt. Rd.
Copied by Charles Bennett on Dec. 7, 1960 - updated Jan. 28, 1989

CLAUSE, Josephine, Jan. 17, 1875 - Nov. 13, 1893
        Wife of J. M. Clause

HENSLEY, Andrew J., June 12, 1835 - July 4, 1907

EDWARDS, Andrew J., 1863 - 1959 (not visible in 1989)
EDWARDS, Amanda (w), June 21, 1867 - Oct. 3, 1919
EDWARDS, Manoda E. (dau), July 9, 1892 - Sep. 5, 1894
HARRIS, Ruhamie, Mar. 4, 1838 - Sep. 5, 1917

CLOUSE, Mirtie M., Apr. 3, 1890 - Feb. 2, 1918
        Wife of T. C. Clouse

EDWARDS, Dorsey D., d. Feb. 25, 1934
        Wagoner, 105th Eng. 30th Div. (WWI)

WILLIS, Van B., Jan. 6, 1893 - Aug. 27, 1893
        Son of D. F. and Martha Willis

WILLIS, Hester Jones, Nov. 10, 1882 - Sep. 23, 1916
WILLIS, Robert C., Jan. 18, 1915 - Mar. 10, 1915
        Wife and son of Jasper Willis

ADDITIONS: - January 28, 1989:

JONES, Margaret E., Sep. 3, 1857 - Aug. 2, 1941

## SAMS #1 CEMETERY

Located .2 mi. N.W. of Coffee Ridge Baptist Church, across
Coffee Ridge Rd., beside house on hill

Copied by Charles Bennett on Dec. 7, 1960 - Updated Apr.9, 1989

HENSLEY, Infant, b/d Jan. 13, 1954 - dau. of W. F. Hensley

MURRAY, J. L., May 4, 1853 - Sep. 18, 1889
MURRAY, Mary E. Harris (w), Feb. 9, 1858 - July 28, 1904
        married June 8, 1876

RIDDLE, John, 1840 - 1889, Co. E, 3rd NC Mtd. Inf. - Union Army
RIDDLE, Sarah M. (w), 1842 - 1936
RIDDLE, Leroy (son), June 1, 1891 - May 5, 1912
RIDDLE, Georgie (son), Sep. 6, 1886 - Sep. 5, 1916

FOSTER, Jim Matt, Feb. 10, 1866 - July 27, 1942
        Grandson of Kan Foster

TILSON, Mary E., Sep. 25, 1887 - July 12, 1969

EDWARDS, Dana F., Jan. 13, 1927 - Feb. 2, 1954
        Son of Floyd and Elva Edwards

TILSON, Mary E., Jan. 16, 1863 - May 2, 1932

TILSON, Troy, 1904 - 1986

        plus many unmarked stones, including:

FOSTER, Nancy Sams, 1870 - 1903/06 - wife of Jim Matt Foster

FOSTER, Enza Mae, Mar. 31, 1910 - Mar. 30, 1913
        Daughter of Larkin & Minta Edwards Foster
        Granddaughter of Jim Matt and Nancy S. Foster

## HIGGINS #1 CEMETERY

Located off Farnor Rd., ¼ mi. past Coffee Ridge Baptist Church
Copied July 6, 1988

BLANKENSHIP, Joseph M., Mar. 1, 1871 - June 22, 1938
BLANKENSHIP, Nancy L. (w), July 31, 1866 - Jan. 19, 1968
BLANKENSHIP, William B. (son), Nov. 4, 1892 - July 30, 1894
BLANKENSHIP, Joe H. (son), Apr. 20, 1897 - Aug. 5, 1898
BLANKENSHIP, Jesse H. (son), Jan. 22, 1901 - Sep. 20, 1907

BLANKENSHIP, Rachel C., Dec. 30, 1833 - Oct. 15, 1900
        Wife of J. T. Blankenship

TIPTON, W. S., Aug. 23, 1850 - Sep. 18, 1894
        Erected by J. M. Tipton

PRICE, Deckie Zetty, 1912 - 1978

BLANKENSHIP, Frank H., Dec. 22, 1901 - Oct. 5, 1938
BLANKENSHIP, Wade H., Apr. 14, 1915 - Dec. 14, 1945
        Pfc., US Mil. Police, WWII

EDWARDS, Clyde F., Feb. 11, 1924 - Aug. 9, 1957
        Sgt., US Army, WWII

HENSLEY, William E., Mar. 17, 1891 - June 8, 1969
HENSLEY, Sarah H. (w), July 19, 1897 - Feb. 25, 1977

COUSINS, Sue Tipton, 1897 - 195-

HIGGINS #1 CEMETERY - (continued)

HIGGINS, Cora,  Mar. 19, 1895 - Apr. 18, 1896
HIGGINS, Murty, Aug. 29, 1903 - Apr. 21, 1905
HIGGINS, Rosa,  Aug. 18, 1910 - Sep.  1, 1910
HIGGINS, Panzy, Apr. 18, 1919 - Apr. 18, 1919
        prob. sisters - (similar stones)

HIGGINS, John W.,  Feb. 12, 1898 - Aug. 7, 1922

HIGGINS, Will E.,  Dec. 7, 1870 - 1956
HIGGINS, Ivyand Tipton (w),  May 22, 1876 - Oct. 15, 1945

HIGGINS, Dorsie Lee,  July 19, 1909 - Mar. 23, 1979
        US Navy Sea Bees,  WWII
HIGGINS, Dicie (w),  d. 1988

HIGGINS, Harley,  1926 - 1987

EDWARDS, William E.,  Nov. 6, 1871 - Oct. 13, 1958
EDWARDS, Minerva "Nervi" E. (w), Nov. 14, 1871 - Apr. 22, 1958

HIGGINS, Arthur J.,  Aug. 24, 1884 - Sep. 7, 1948
HIGGINS, Bertha H. (w),  Dec. 12, 1902 - June 6, 1955
HIGGINS, Pansy (dau),  b/d Mar. 7, 1918

TIPTON, John Henry,  Mar. 25, 1882 - May 1, 1954
TIPTON, Suemer (w),  Aug.  2, 1892 - Dec. 10, 1918

FOSTER, Huel,  Jan. 23, 1937 - Jan. 9, 1943

TIPTON, Valentine T.,
        Co. C., 3NC Mtd. Inf., Union Army
TIPTON, Mary (w),  Apr. 5, 1827 - Dec. 1, 1917

HIGGINS, John H.,  Dec. 7, 1873 - June 14, 1909
HIGGINS, Luke,  Mar. 19, 1908 - July 25, 1909
        Son of J. H. and Eddie Higgins

HIGGINS, Holland, d. Dec. 25, 1910 at 88 yrs.
HIGGINS, Thurse (w), July 26, 1915 at 82 yrs.

HIGGINS, G. W.,  Oct. 13, 1867 - June 28, 1915
HIGGINS, Dulcinia (w?), May 5, 1865 - May 24, 1956
        Daughter of Oliver and Margaret Angel Pate

FOSTER, Clarence,  Mar. 27, 1924 - Apr. 10, 1924

FOSTER, J. Cephas,  May 14, 1891 - Aug. 18, 1968
FOSTER, Flossie A. (H?) (w), May 6, 1897 - Apr. 27, 1975

BRITT, Joyce P.,  Oct. 20, 1942 - Dec. 25, 1964

JONES, Vinie,  Apr. 22, 1866 - July 11, 1923

FOSTER, Infant dau.,  b/d 1965

HIGGINS, Carl D.,  Apr. 1, 1902 - Dec. 7, 1968
HIGGINS, Lela Mae (w),  Apr. 22, 1907 - Dec. 6, 1968
        married Oct. 12, 1923

Plus many concrete crosses

## CRANE CEMETERY  (ALSO CALLED COATES)

On Upper Higgins Creek Road, .8 Mi. from Rt. 23, on knoll.
(This cemetery has been moved due to construction of the new
highway. There were 28 bodies moved, 15 from unmarked graves.
The remains were re-intered at different cemeteries. All the
COATES family members were re-intered at Evergreen Cemetery)

Copied Oct. 16, 1988

EDWARDS, Robert G.,  1867 - 1912
EDWARDS, Sarah J. (w),  1866 - 1945

RICE, Linda Lou,  d. Sep. 30, 1951
        Infant daughter of Parley F. Rice

McGEE, Maria,  June 21, 1891 - Feb. 19, 1924

HARRIS, Lula May,  July 20, 1923 - Feb. 28, 1924
        Daughter of Clay Harris

COATES, J. Gabriel,  1851 - 1929
COATES, Eliza J. (w),  1866 - 1936
        Daughter of Nathan and Lucinda Wheeler Allen

COATES, John N.,  1893 - 1932

COATES, Charlie G.,  Apr. 22, 1894 - Dec. 28, 1939
COATES, Gertie G. (w),  Jan. 18, 1895 - Feb. 24, 1936
COATES, Ethel C. (dau),  Feb. 7, 1932 - Aug. 28, 1964
SHELTON, Ann B. Coates,  Aug. 1, 1925 - Feb. 23, 1985
        Daughter of Charlie and Gertie Coates
TILSON, William Harold,  b/d 1936


## TILSON #1 CEMETERY

Off Upper Higgins Creek Road, at Gentry Hollow
Copied Oct. 16, 1988


TILSON, William Arvil,  Dec. 10, 1894 - Aug. 13, 1971, WWI
TILSON, Grace G. (w) ,    1900 - 1941

TILSON, Henry G.,  Sep. 19, 1860 - Aug. 11, 1949

TILSON, Bassie L.,  Aug. 6, 1890 - Apr. 11, 1969

TILSON, G. T.,  May 24, 1938 - Jan. 20, 1982, Sp5, US Army

TILSON, Thomas V.,  1902 - 1988
TILSON, Zora G (w), 1909 -
TILSON, Freeman (son),  1924 - 1941
TILSON, Gladys Lee (dau),  b/d 1940

WILLIAMS, Peggy Lou, 1952 - 1955

DRISCOLL, Robert Allen, May 9, 1963 - Aug. 19, 1974
       "Love you Johnny" on stone

GENTRY, William R., June 9, 1875 - Jan. 29, 1947
GENTRY, Lula S. (w), Nov. 29, 1875 - Apr. 20, 1961

## HENSLEY #1 CEMETERY

Off Upper Higgins Creek Road, at Gentry Mt. Road

Copied Oct. 16, 1988

HENSLEY, Berry Oliver, Nov. 24, 1913 - Sep. 20, 1974
HENSLEY, Lula Edwards (w), Apr. 20, 1922 -

plus unmarked stones nearby

## HENSLEY #2 CEMETERY

Spivey Mt. Rd., behind old Van Hensley Store, on right

Copied Oct. 24, 1988

HENSLEY, Sylvanus "Van", Feb. 28, 1892 - Oct. 16, 1978, US Army
HENSLEY, Katherine (w), Mar. 8, 1900 -

HENSLEY, Roger E., Nov. 17, 1941 - Sep. 6, 1967

WATTS, Vernon, 1913 - 1961

## FOSTER #1 CEMETERY

Spivey Mt. Rd. on left, just past old Van Hensley Store

Copied Oct. 24, 1988

FOSTER, Ray, b/d Jan. 23, 1917
FOSTER, Oliver, Aug. 1919 - Feb. 1920
       brothers

BROCKUS, Lissie A. Foster, Apr. 3, 1877 - Jan. 21, 1904
       Wife of W. P. Brockus

SIMMONS, Spencer "Spence", Feb. 15, 1875 - Feb. 2, 1956
SIMMONS, Fronia F. (w), Jan. 25, 1875 - June 21, 1976
SIMMONS, Mary M. (dau), Feb. 8, 1912 - July 5, 1955

FOSTER, Andy T., Nov. 18, 1895 - Mar. 29, 1974
FOSTER, Zettie L. (w), Nov. 28, 1895 - Nov. 8, 1976

FOSTER, Arvil H. "Baldy", Nov. 8, 1929 - Aug. 10, 1985
FOSTER, Raymond R., Jan. 13, 1921 -
       brothers

FOSTER CEMETERY - (continued)

FOSTER, William Andy "Junior",   Dec. 27, 1924 -
FOSTER, Flora M. "Boots" (w),  July 31, 1924 -

FOSTER, Merle L.,   Sep. 7, 1904 - Dec. 24, 1908
FOSTER, Mamie,   Feb. 11, 1901 - May 5, 1901
FOSTER, Bertie, Apr.  6, 1897 - Apr. 24, 1897
FOSTER, Freddie,   b/d Dec. 13, 1895
FOSTER, (dau),     b/d Dec. 20, 1894
          Children of J. H. and Melda Foster

FOSTER, Thomas,
          Co. H., 10th Tenn. Cav., Union Army

FOSTER, Naoma,   no dates

FOSTER, Hester,   Apr. 10, 1887 - Nov. 10, 1946

FOSTER, Mary Gladys,   Apr. 17, 1934 - Feb. 14, 1935
          Daughter of Roy and Leora Foster

HENSLEY, Lester,   1886 - 1959

COUSINS, Noah,   d. 1960
COUSINS, Martha (w),   1904 - 1957

HENSLEY, Floyd H.,   d. 1979

HENSLEY, Wayne Oran,   Jan. 25, 1944 - May 20, 1983


## FOSTER #2 CEMETERY

  Off Spivey Mt. Rd., in Willis Cove behind house, on
  hill a short ways
                            Copied Oct. 27, 1988

FOSTER, Dolphus B.,   Mar. 8, 1890 - June 22, 1980
FOSTER, Minta J. Hensley (w), Mar. 13, 1895 - July 30, 1929
FOSTER, Dolphus B. Jr. (son),   1921 - 1977
          Pvt., US Army,  WWII

FOSTER, Infant,   b/d 1959

# TUMBLING HILL CEMETERY

Off Spivey Mt. Rd., up Tumbling Cr. Rd. to steep road
on right, to top of hill
                              Copied Oct. 27, 1988

MARTIN, James Kelly,  Jan. 10, 1947 - Aug. 18, 1947

PEEK, Hadley S.,  Apr. 22, 1884 - Mar. 17, 1932
          Son of Dr. W. A. and Margaret Conley Peek
PEEK, Sarah E. (w),  May 27, 1889 -  no date

KISER,    -      ,  1884 - 1959

MARTIN, Clifton,  Oct. 29, 1921 - Nov. 10, 1924
MARTIN, Wrothy,  Jan. 18, 1926 - Feb. 9, 1926
          Sons of Luther and Lora Martin

FOSTER, Charles,  1857 - 1945
FOSTER, Melissie (w),  1861 - 1945

WILLIS, Ardilla F.,  1887 - 1925

WILLIS, Vergia,  1910 - 1914

LEWIS, Lydia,  Jan. 10, 1910 - June 27, 1912
          Daughter of R. L. and Rebecca Lewis

SEEMAN, Ernest,  Nov. 13, 1886 - Oct. 19, 1979
          US Navy, WWI

JONES, Rufus B.,  May 9, 1895 - June 12, 1968
JONES, Renia J. (w),  May 10, 1898 - May 10, 1981

JONES, James E.,  June 16, 1867 - Dec. 30, 1939
JONES, Elvira (w),  Oct. 10, 1871 - Apr. 23, 1923

WILLIAMS, Lizzie,  Jan. 13, 1899 - Aug. 18, 1940

JONES, Walter H.,  Feb. 24, 1889 - Sep. 6, 1943
          "M/Sgt" - WWI ?

FOSTER, Mart,  1892 - 1955
FOSTER, Ida (w),  1905 -

FOSTER, Shirl,  Aug. 1929 - Aug. 1955

WILLIAMSON, Alvin,  June 22, 1924 -
WILLIAMSON, Lena F. (w),  July 22, 1926 - Mar. 3, 1983

plus several unmarked stones

## WILLIS #3 CEMETERY

Off Spivey Mt. Rd., up Tumbling Creek Road near end, on
right on top of hill

Copied Oct. 27, 1988

WILLIS, Dave E.,   Apr. 10, 1892 - no date
WILLIS, Myrtle (w),  Feb. 20, 1898 - May 3, 1955

WILLIS, John P.,   Nov. 24, 1891 - Aug. 28, 1941
WILLIS, Rhoda,    Dec.  4, 1889 - Feb. 25, 1945
WILLIS, William T.,  Sep. 25, 1860 - Sep. 28, 1942
WILLIS, Elizabeth Heath(?) (w), Mar. 18, 1852 - Aug. 20, 1930

BYRD, Myrtle Marie,  b/d June 20, 1936

WILLIS, Johnny W.,  Aug. 28, 1932 - Apr. 29, 1967

plus several unmarked stones

## TILSON #2 CEMETERY

On Tilson Mt. Rd. 1.3 mi. beyond Willis Store and across
from old Tilson Farm

Copied Nov. 7, 1988

WATTS, Anderson,  Mar. 15, 1885 - Feb. 4, 1961
WATTS, Rhuhamie (w),  Dec. 25, 1894 - July 30, 1965

WATTS, Bert,    1890 - 1971
WATTS, Alpha L. (w),   1886 - 1968

WATTS, Isabella,  Jan. 26, 1920 - Oct. 13, 1973

AULT, Ashley R.,  b/d 1988

WATTS, William R.,    1928 - 1982

WATTS, Texie Pauline,  Oct. 2, 1915 - Aug. 9, 1918

WATTS, Garrison,  Mar. 13, 1887 - Jan. 11, 1946
        (From S.C.) Pvt., US Army, WWI

WATTS, Leroy "Roy" T.,  Apr. 26, 1880 - Sep. 16, 1957
WATTS, Lizzie I. (w),   Nov. 11, 1884 - July  8, 1976
WATTS, Arthur E. (son), Oct. 16, 1905 - Aug. 22, 1911
WATTS, Mary E. (dau),   Mar. 31, 1910 - July 16, 1910

RUNION, Avie E.,  Nov. 8, 1887 - Apr. 8, 1897
        Daughter of T. N. and Rebecca Runion

TILSON, Ertha E.,  Mar. 26, 1887 - Dec. 28, 1888
TILSON, Lula May,  Oct.  7, 1894 - July 31, 1897
        Daughters of Dr. L. S. and Eliza J. Tilson

TILSON, Paul Romare,  Nov. 18, 1906 - Aug. 25, 1986

TILSON, Lula May, Oct. 20, 1868 - Oct. 13, 1893

TILSON, W. E., Apr. 29, 1827 - Apr. 24, 1915 - Confed. Army
TILSON, Katherine Sams (w), Sep. 5, 1831 - Sep. 22, 1911

TILSON, John Quillen, Apr. 5, 1866 - Aug. 14, 1958
        Majority Leader U. S. Congress, 1925 - 1931
TILSON, Marguerite North (w), June 28, 1883 - June 23, 1963

SHAFER, Brice, Oct. 15, 1912 - May 10, 1979
SHAFER, Margaret Tilson (w), Nov. 26, 1912 -
        Daughter of John Quillen & Marguerite North Tilson

TILSON, George W., Dec. 2, 1860 - Sep. 1, 1936
TILSON, Marion (w), Mar. 10, 1858 - Sep. 2, 1936

TILSON, Elizabeth, Dec. 4, 1830 - Dec. 30, 1914
        Wife of James Tilson

TILSON, Rachel E., Feb. 3, 1875 - June 30, 1894

GILLIS, Anna, Sep. 19, 1797 - Feb. 28, 1874

GILLIS, Matilda, May 19, 1865 - Mar. 2, 1888
        Wife of W. T. Gillis

TILSON, John A., May 21, 1824 - Apr. 27, 1906
TILSON, Rebecca (w), Nov. 20, 1827 - June 25, 1914
        Daughter of Jesse Balis and Nancy Balis

TILSON, Margaret, Nov. 4, 1853 - Feb. 19, 1918

TIPTON, Frank A., Apr. 30, 1920 - May 25, 1988
TIPTON, Wanda M. (w), Sep. 27, 1928 -

FOSTER, William,
        Co. M., 8 TN Cav., Union Army

TILSON, Nancy Allen, Apr. 14, 1800 - Jan. 13, 1859

TILSON, George, b. Nov. 18, 1820
TILSON, Katherine Beals (w), no dates

ERWIN, Jesse Frank, Nov. 14, 1874 - June 18, 1875
        Son of J. M. and Eliza E. Erwin

TILSON, John Franklin, June 6, 1883 - Sep. 15, 1886
TILSON, Quillen Ransom, 1888 - 1889
TILSON, Levi Everett, Dec. 17, 1894 - Mar. 28, 1896
TILSON, George W., Jan. 1, 1881 - Dec. 10, 1917
        Sons of A. B. and E. J. Tilson

TILSON, A. B., Jan. 28, 1850 - Mar. 29, 1927
        Son of George Tilson
TILSON, Eliza J. (w), Dec. 27, 1851 - Nov. 26, 1924

TIPTON, Matilda,  d. June 5, 1935 at 49

PRICE, William M.,  Apr. 14, 1881 - (no date)
PRICE, Sarah Tilson (w),  Sep. 28, 1885 - Mar. 25, 1960

ASKEW, James Adrain,  Sep. 28, 1937 - Aug. 18, 1967, US Navy
ASKEW, Doris F. (w),  July 21, 1944 -

WILLIS, Bertha Mae,  June 16, 1909 - Nov. 6, 1977

MONROE, Martie,  b/d 1955
        Child of Ray D. and Hilda Milisie Price Monroe

PRICE, Sherman T.,  Feb. 28, 1920 - Nov. 19, 1963
PRICE, Sarah O. (w),  Jan. 11, 1921 -

TINKER, Rausa,  Apr. 12, 1892 - May 28, 1920
        Wife of Charlie Tinker

TIPTON, Luke B.,  Oct. 5, 1911 - Mar. 18, 1968
TIPTON, Tilda E. (w),  Sep. 27, 1910 -

TIPTON, Ellic,  Jan. 22, 1919 -
TIPTON, Nella Kate (w),  Mar. 29, 1921 - Apr. 6, 1983

HOYLE, Sophia T.,  Aug. 21, 1907 - June 22, 1984

WILLIAMS, Odas,  Jan. 15, 1919 - Apr. 3, 1947

MURRAY, William,  May 23, 1789 - May 3, 1875
MURRAY, Elizabeth (w),  Mar. 11, 1790 - Oct. 18, 1876

TILSON, Elmer J.,  1913 - 1988

BRACKINS, Lelan Jeffrey,  d. Nov. 1, 1958
        Infant son of Lelan and Phyllis Brackins

TIPTON, Teresa Linn,  Nov. 23, 1968 - Nov. 24, 1968

TIPTON, Mary Tilson,  Dec. 20, 1923 - May 4, 1964

TILSON, Dolphus,  Mar. 5, 1883 - Feb. 5, 1962
TILSON, Eliza (w),  Sep. 30, 1888 - Oct. 9, 1977

TIPTON, Walter Grant,  May 24, 1932 - Sep. 5, 1985
        Cpl. US Army, Korea
TIPTON, Hilda Mae (w),  Mar. 11, 1934 -

TIPTON, Henry,  Nov. 16, 1916 - Mar. 16, 1985
TIPTON, Pauline (w),  Dec. 9, 1921 -

INGLE, Aaron,  1848 - 1948

TIPTON, Joseph M.,  Mar. 29, 1886 - June 8, 1952
TIPTON, Daisy (w),  1892 - 1980

TIPTON, Dwight Dale, Oct. 8, 1950 - July 5, 1978
        Sgt., US Army, Vietnam

TIPTON, Albert "Bud", Jan. 2, 1938 - May 29, 1984
TIPTON, Liselotte J. (w), July 6, 1934 -

MASHBURN, William, Jan. 1, 1857 - Mar. 21, 1936
MASHBURN, Catherine Tilson (w), Feb. 21, 1856 - Dec. 5, 1940

TIPTON, Elizabeth, no dates

WILLIS, William F., Nov. 18, 1886 - Mar. 8, 1960
        Pvt., 112 Inf., WWI
WILLIS, Martha J. (w), Apr. 2, 1887 - Sep. 23, 1963
        Daughter of Granison and Mary Foster Chandler

                plus many unmarked stones


## BRADFORD CEMETERY

   On Spivey Mt. Rd., on right near Mountain Dale, just
   beyond church, in field (visible from highway)
                Copied Dec. 2, 1988

BRADFORD, Andy R., Mar. 12, 1907 - Dec. 20, 1974
BRADFORD, Pearl L. (w), July 12, 1913 -

HENSLEY, Howell, Jan. 22, 1875 - Mar. 24, 1962

BRADFORD, Woodroe, May 3, 1912 - Nov. 18, 1973
        US Army, WWII

## EDWARDS #3 CEMETERY

   Spivey Mt. Rd. one mile past Mt. Dale Church, take
   right into hills ¼ mile
                        Copied Dec. 2, 1988

WHITSON, Goffery, Nov. 10, 1885 - Nov. 10, 1961
WHITSON, Etta L. (w), Mar. 16, 1884 - (no date)

MARTIN, W. Cornelius, 1884 - 1964

ADKINS, Martin L., July 29, 1873 - Apr. 21, 1956

EDWARDS, Braskie, June 9, 1903 -
EDWARDS, Lula (w), Jan. 5, 1898 - July 27, 1977

TIPTON, Ova Odell, 1927 - 1972, US Army, WWII

TIPTON, John H., 1885 - 1968
TIPTON, Princie E. (w), 1893 - 1952

WILSON, Irene, Jan. 22, 1938 - June 22, 1940

EDWARDS #3 CEMETERY - (continued)

EDWARDS, Emily H., July 29, 1874 - Apr. 30, 1958

WILSON, Paul, Dec. 10, 1930 - Apr. 2, 1974

EDWARDS, Thomas, 1898 - 1975, US Army, WWI

EDWARDS, Lattie, Feb. 29, 1900 - Aug. 1, 1980

WILSON, Hilyard Isam, June 27, 1902 - Dec. 20, 1979
WILSON, Mary Jane (w), Aug. 22, 1905 -

HONEYCUTT, Tice, Jan. 29, 1928 - Sep. 18, 1941
        ("son")

HILEMON, J. Thore, Aug. 12, 1889 - Dec. 25, 1935
HILEMON, L. Birdie (w), Mar. 31, 1891 - July 15, 1968

HONEYCUTT, Tom "Paw", Jan. 26, 1856 - May 28, 1927
HONEYCUTT,      "Maw"    , July 18, 1879 - Apr. 28, 1951

HONEYCUTT, Aught, June 20, 1864 - Aug. 30, 1930
HONEYCUTT, Ruth    , June 27, 1881 - Dec. 4, 1946

WALKER, Dina (Dian?), Jan. 3, 1901 - Nov. 8, 1955

HARLESS, George C., Dec. 23, 1912 - Oct. 8, 1972
HARLESS, Reatha M. (w), May 3, 1912 -

                plus several cement crosses, unmarked

Nearby to the left is a smaller cemetery, with all Edwards
                                        families:
EDWARDS, Oscar, Jan. 23, 1916 - Apr. 15, 1974
EDWARDS, Hazel, Feb. 10, 1912 - May 16, 1962

EDWARDS, Kimmie K., Dec. 23, 1968 - Feb. 8, 1979

SHEALY, Sheila D., 1957 - 1985

EDWARDS, Onida, Sep. 10, 1896 - Apr. 11, 1972
EDWARDS, Lula H., May 4, 1884 - Jan. 21, 1970

EDWARDS, Luther J., July 18, 1928 - Jan. 11, 1982
EDWARDS, Pauline (w), Dec. 22, 1932 - Sep. 20, 1986

EDWARDS, Luther B., Mar. 21, 1908 - July 25, 1983
EDWARDS, Emma P. (w), June 28, 1908 - Feb. 8, 1985

## GILLIS #1 CEMETERY

On Tilson Mt. Rd., ½ mile up from Willis Store, on
hill on left, above Hoyle house

Copied Jan. 23, 1989

RUNION, Thomas N., Mar. 16, 1870 - Nov. 16, 1902

TIPTON, W. A., May 18, 1880 - Nov. 24, 1904

SAMS, Rev. William A., Dec. 8, 1851 - May 14, 1908
SAMS, Sarah Gillis (w), Apr. 26, 1845 - Mar. 28, 1925

SAMS, Elijah (Elisha) B., Apr. 15, 1881 - Feb. 25, 1943
SAMS, Pearl Gentry (w), Aug. 17, 1886 - Jan. 24, 1967

GILLIS, William Tilson, Oct. 11, 1849 - Apr. 14, 1922

EDWARDS, E. E., no dates (field stone)

GILLIS, John G., Sep. 13, 1819 - Sep. 3, 1901
GILLIS, Ruth (w), Feb. 14, 1822 - Nov. 10, 1899

TIPTON, Charles C., Sep. 9, 1857 - Dec. 18, 1942
TIPTON, Mary Kathrin Gillis (w), July 21, 1858 - Dec. 10, 1928

TIPTON, Dovie Bell (dau), Aug. 3, 1899 - Oct. 28, 1947

TIPTON, Ora, Apr. 26, 1918 - Feb. 1, 1923

LEWIS, Ward B., Nov. 11, 1821 - Dec. 30, 1823

TILSON, Kittie L., May 18, 1909 - July 12, 1913
TILSON, Russle B., Aug. 22, 1911 - May 20, 1913
        Children of W. H. and Ella Tilson

plus several unmarked stones

# RICE CREEK CEMETERY

3 miles S. of Flag Pond, on Rice Creek

Copied by Charles Bennett on Dec. 9, 1960 and
updated July 27, 1988

BRIGGS, Lucille,  May 20, 1940 - Nov. 25, 1954

McINTOSH, Eliza Jane,  Jan. 6, 1875 - May 5, 1944

McINTOSH, I. N.,  Jan. 19, 1850 - June 3, 1910
McINTOSH, Marcine (w),  May 12, 1855 - July 20, 1935

McINTOSH, Elizabeth Shelton,  1837 - 1909
        Wife of Allen Morris McIntosh

McINTOSH, Dolphus Earnest,  Oct. 25, 1866 - Jan. 5, 1905

RICE, Arling,  1904 - 1960

BRIGGS, J. Logan,  Feb. 28, 1848 - Nov. 22, 1934
BRIGGS, Bulo,      Sep. 15, 1854 - Apr. 24, 1941

BRIGGS, Virgie McIntosh,  May 16, 1901 - Apr. 14, 1934

BRIGGS, Douglas K.,  1933 - 1934

BRIGGS, Seth Barnard III,  b/d 1949

McINTOSH, Harry B.,  Dec. 18, 1893 - May 17, 1945

McINTOSH, Samuel C.,  May 10, 1858 - Nov. 6, 1951

BRIGGS, Dora Gregory,  July 7, 1908 - June 29, 1949

BRIGGS, E. E.,  Oct. 21, 1863 - Mar. 29, 1945
BRIGGS, Betty (w),  Sep. 13, 1866 - Dec. 4, 1947

SHELTON, Armstrong,  Nov. 21, 1845 - Mar. 31, 1898

BRIGGS, Lue,  May 20, 1880 - May 13, 1935

RICE, Joe Wilse,  Oct. 27, 1877 - Jan. 21, 1955

BAILEY, Andy,  d. Feb. 14, 1949 at 73 yrs 6 mo 6 da

RICE, Mary,  Aug. 8, 1905 - Oct. 4, 1922

HENSLEY, Delie,  d. Feb. 3, 1924

RICE, Ritta,  Aug. 18, 1888 - Apr. 6, 1939

RICE, Joe A.,  Aug. 4, 1869 - Apr. 9, 1957

RICE, Fred,  Sep. 9, 1906 - Nov. 7, 1944
        Son of E. J. and Bertha Briggs Rice

<u>RICE CREEK CEMETERY</u> - (continued)

RICE, Claude,    1916 - 1941
RICE, Dewey,    Jan. 8, 1900 - Feb. 5, 1942

WEST, Sarah E., 1856 - 1956

RICE, Randy Lynn,  Sep. 30, 1950 - Mar. 25, 1951

RICE, Kay,  Nov. 22, 1934 - July 5, 1935

RICE, Bidey,  Aug. 13, 1837 - Sep. 26, 1883

RICE, John W.,    June 26, 1866 - May 26, 1950
RICE, Mordecia (w),  Mar. 25, 1873 - Apr. 11, 1949
RICE, Lenard,    May 25, 1910 - Aug. 5, 1911

RICE, Jesse S.,,
        Sgt. Co. K, 13th TN. CAV., Union Army
RICE, Margaret L. (w),  Oct. 6, 1865 - June 24, 1905
RICE, Evert,  Nov. 2, 1890 - Aug. 28, 1893
RICE, Chester A.,  Sep. 4, 1898 - Dec. 7, 1901
RICE, Carie,  Sep. 7, 1908 - Nov. 10, 1908
RICE, Infant,  b/d June 7, 1905
RICE, Mary A.,  Oct. 29, 1900 - July 14, 1911
        Children of J. S. and M. L. Rice

RICE, Roy,  Aug. 23, 1892 - Mar. 29, 1958

RICE, Charlie,  1917 - 1952
        Son of James Deadrick and Ethel Briggs Rice

HENSLEY, Claude,  d. (?) May 1941

EDWARDS, John,  1891 - 1957
        Son of Jasper and Nancy Ledford Edwards

LEWIS, Winfred,  Apr. 16, 1935 - Mar. 6, 1954
        Air Force, WWII

BRIGGS, John Lee,  Mar. 27, 1888 - Mar. 27, 1954

RICE, Gill C.,  Aug. 11, 1953 - Sep. 5, 1954
        Son of Chester and Grace Fender Rice


<u>ADDITIONS</u>:  Field-checked July 27, 1988

TIMBERLAKE, Robert B.,  Feb. 26, 1933 - Feb. 24, 1974

BRIGGS, Homer York,  1892 - 1976,  Pvt. US Army, WWI
BRIGGS, Flora P. (w),  1899 -

LLOYD, Horace B.,  Sep. 28, 1901 - Oct. 20, 1972
LLOYD, Verna Rice (w),  June 28, 1907 - Nov. 11, 1963

BRIGGS, Posey Lee, May 12, 1912 - Mar. 30, 1987
    US Army, WWII

BRIGGS, Beatrice Bowman, Dec. 10, 1926 - Nov. 6, 1974

BRIGGS, Seth Bernard, July 9, 1894 - May 31, 1985
    Pvt., US Army, WWI
BRIGGS, Nola R. (w), Mar. 29, 1924 -

McINTOSH, Samuel M., Aug. 15, 1886 - Apr. 25, 1971
    115th F.A., US Army, WWI
McINTOSH, Cora Pack (w), May 16, 1897 - Apr. 4, 1925

McINTOSH, John, b/d Feb. 18, 1925

HENSLEY, Josephine, Apr. 28, 1920 - May 25, 1920

RAY, Infant, b/d Feb. 7, 1919, dau. of W. S. Ray

McINTOSH, Edward P., Sep. 12, 1884 - Sep. 23, 1961

McINTOSH, Will, Aug. 1, 1899 - June 6, 1986
    US Army, WWI

McINTOSH, Walter, June 24, 1895 - Apr. 17, 1975

McINTOSH, Alexander, Sep. 15, 1934 - May 17, 1936

McINTOSH, Richard P., Sep. 28, 1904 - Mar. 19, 1984

BRIGGS, James Barry, prob. 1948-1948, possibly 1848-1948

BRIGGS, Lee Moore, Oct. 27, 1886 - June 13, 1935
BRIGGS, Bessie L. (w), Feb. 22, 1894 - Dec. 29, 1913 or 1918

BAILEY, John, d. Oct. 5, 1926

RICE, Rhonda Jane, b/d 1961

RICE, Grady C., June 14, 1914 - Aug. 30, 1969

RICE, Brandon N., 1982 - 1987

RICE, William R., June 25, 1880 - July 17, 1968
RICE, Lillie A. (w), July 8, 1882 - Oct. 14, 1965

RICE, Elbert J., Feb. 2, 1877 - Nov. 8, 1964
RICE, Bertha Briggs, Oct. 8, 1888 - Aug. 10, 1957

RICE, Baby, Apr. 5, 1908 - May 11, 1908

RICE, Floyd J., May 28, 1910 - June 21, 1911
    Son of J. A. and Rittie Rice

RICE, Randy Lynn,  Sep. 30, 1950 - Mar. 25, 1951

SHELTON, Nellie Rice,   d. 1917,   wife of Stokely Shelton

RICE, Flossie,   1902 - 1917
RICE, Ouillian,   1896 - 1917

RICE, George W.,  Nov. 1, 1861 - May 5, 1944
RICE, Eliza N. (w),  Mar. 16, 1868 - Mar. 19, 1940

RICE, Lonnie,  May 26, 1950 - Jan. 3, 1962

RICE, Cecil Landon,  Oct. 16, 1911 - Mar. 13, 1981
RICE, Elva (w),  Sep. 15, 1917 -

RICE, Robert Wallace,  May 25, 1900 - May 5, 1982

RICE, Dana Harmon,  Aug. 18, 1896 - June 22, 1987

RICE, Manley,  Dec. 12, 1921 - Apr. 21, 1987
RICE, Margaret I. (w),  July 30, 1930 -

RICE, Roscoe,  b. May 19, 1908 -

RICE, Edd L.,  July 5, 1894 - May 5, 1979
RICE, Thelma B. (w),  Feb. 15, 1908 - June 26, 1986

HENSLEY, Harold,  Sep. 8, 1918 - Sep. 26, 1973
HENSLEY, Emeline (w),  Aug. 15, 1912 -

RICE, Dedrick,  Feb. 23, 1896 - Sep. 1, 1940
RICE, Ethel (w),  June 13, 1898 - Oct. 10, 1938

RICE, Charlie,  Mar. 16, 1917 - Mar. 10, 1952

HARDING, Agnes,  Jan. 1, 1939 - Apr. 6, 1939

FENDER, Winfred J.,  Aug. 28, 1904 - Aug. 14, 1981
FENDER, Addie E. (w),  Mar. 3, 1904 -
        married June 27, 1920

BRIGGS, Jason Scotty,  b/d 1975

RICE, Emerson,  Apr. 16, 1924 - Aug. 11, 1968

RIDDLE, Chaple, Mar. 14, 1870 - Oct. 7, 1964


RICE CREEK CEMETERY - UNMARKED GRAVES INCLUDE:

BRIGGS, Jimmy Michael,  b/d Jan. 28, 1957
        Son of Glade and Nattie Louise Tilson Briggs

CLOUSE (CLOUTZ), Feba Jane,  age 29 - Jan. 24, 1929 (d.)
        Daughter of J. W. Rice

RICE CREEK CEMETERY - UNMARKED GRAVES - (continued)

RICE, Claude, June 21, 1941 - June 23, 1941
        Son of E. J. and Bertha Briggs Rice

RICE, Gerald, 5 mos. - died July 7, 1951
        Son of Hestel and Jessie McCurry Rice

RICE, Hestel, age 39 - died Nov. 14, 1951
        Son of Thomas Grant and Altha Briggs Rice

RICE, John Calvin, Nov. 19, 1860 - Sep. 17, 1929
        Son of Jackson and Matilda Briggs Rice


## BLANKENSHIP CEMETERY #1

        About two miles south of Flag Pond, on Rice Creek
Copied by Charles Bennett on Dec. 9, 1960 and updated on
                    July 18, 1988

SHOOK, Berlin, July 29, 1920 - Oct. 7, 1935
        Son of Neal and Sis Blankenship Shook
SHOOK, James, Apr. 19, 1917 - Dec. 17, 1933
        brothers

BLANKENSHIP, J. W., July 25, 1890 - Mar. 31, 1934

BLANKENSHIP, Sarah, Nov. 29, 1869 - July 4, 1936

BLANKENSHIP, John W., Apr. 7, 1844 - Feb. 15, 1943
        Son of Alec Blankenship

BLANKENSHIP, Bobby Lee, b/d 1935
        Son of B. B. and Zora Blankenship

BLANKENSHIP, Jimmie, June 22, 1934 - Mar. 16, 1936

BRIGGS, James Doyle, d. Mar. 30, 1956 (infant)
        Son of John Doyle and Norma Ruth Harris Briggs

HOPE, Julia, b. June 4, 1931 (d.?)

HOPE (?), Aletha, Feb. 9, 1912 - Feb. 25, 1912

McFARLAND, Charles Elbert, Dec. 6, 1916 - Oct. 17, 1938
McFARLAND, Edna C. (w), Feb. 4, 1913 - Apr. 16, 1951

BLANKENSHIP, Jonah O., July 22, 1856 - Apr. 5, 1946
BLANKENSHIP, Ann Eliza (w), Dec. 16, 1856 - Apr. 17, 1928

WILSON, Hiram T., Nov. 4, 1870 - Sep. 8, 1958
WILSON, Sevilla (w), Nov. 10, 1883 - Nov. 9, 1936

McINTOSH, Vira, 1883 - 1954


                    - 150 -

BLANKENSHIP CEMETERY - (continued)

McINTOSH, Andy B.,  Aug. 15, 1869 - July 4, 1943
McINTOSH, Delphia (w),  Oct. 2, 1869 - June 12, 1901

BLANKENSHIP, Jasper,  Aug. 12, 1850 - Feb. 2, 1893
BLANKENSHIP, Polly M. (w),  June 7, 1849 - Apr. 19, 1915

BLANKENSHIP, J. W.,  Dec. 23, 1882 - July 21, 1934
BLANKENSHIP, Dillie "Silivers" (w), Nov. 5, 1886 - March 28,1992
        married Jan. 28, 1902              Age 105

BLANKENSHIP, W. E.,  July 16, 1871 - July 1, 1936
BLANKENSHIP, Betsy Jane (w),  Aug. 22, 1878 - Nov. 22, 1953
        Daughter of Thomas Jefferson & Liza Carter Stockton

BLANKENSHIP, Florence,  Feb. 18, 1896 - Aug. 15, 1897
BLANKENSHIP, Infant,     b/d May 15, 1901
BLANKENSHIP, Fred,       Oct. 7, 1906 - June 24, 1911
BLANKENSHIP, Roy,        June 20, 1917 - Jan. 20, 1918
BLANKENSHIP, Ethie Lee, Apr. 13, 1909 - Feb. 8, 1953
        Daughter of W. E. and Betsy Jane Stockton Blankenship
        Siblings

TIPTON, Hazel Mae,  Mar. 7, 1945 - Nov. 3, 1957

TIPTON, Cal,  Jan. 1, 1873 - Jan. 1, 1957
TIPTON, Cordelia S. (w),  Dec. 10, 1875 - May 11, 1958

McINTOSH, Elsie Mae,  May 8, 1918 - Sep. 3, 1919
        Daughter of C. W. and Annie McIntosh

TIPTON, Thomas,  Feb. 6, 1900 - Mar. 16, 1900

TIPTON, James C.,  1850 - 1929
TIPTON, Mandy J. (w),  1856 - 1889

HENSLEY, Kirt,  Mar. 13, 1886 - no date
HENSLEY, Lizzie (w),  July 7, 1887 - Oct. 2, 1954
        Daughter of Kirk and Maudie Blankenship Tipton

GENTRY, Edith P.,  b. Apr. 3, 1950, d. at age 8

MORROW, Elbert G.,  Cpl.
        Co. A, 1st East Florida Cav.,  Union Army

GENTRY, John B.,  Oct. 7, 1854 - Sep. 2, 1922
GENTRY, Sarah C. (w),  Nov. 14, 1854 - Aug. 31, 1919
GENTRY, S. L.,  Mar. 1, 1877 - May 8, 1896

HENSLEY, Robert B.,  May 26, 1872 - May 21, 1954
HENSLEY, Dollie Silvers (w),  Mar. 15, 1870 - May 22, 1970
HENSLEY, Ida B. (dau),  July 23, 1907 - Aug. 27, 1912

BRIGGS, A. E.,  Aug. 20, 1844 - Nov. 13, 1898

BLANKENSHIP CEMETERY - (continued)

BRIGGS, E. J.,  Mar. 8, 1879 - Mar. 20, 1879
BRIGGS, E. J.,  May 3, 1882 - July 29, 1883
        brothers

BRIGGS, Rufus Franklin,  Mar. 11, 1885 - Nov. 3, 1906

TRAFINESTEAD, Joseph H.,  Sep. 16, 1833 (?) - Jan. 1, 1911

PROFFITT, Melvina,  b/d Sep. 13, 1886

NANNEY, Sarah Alvira,  Aug. 28, 1881 - Nov. 29, 1883
        Daughter of J. A. and M. N. Nanney (sp?)

PROFFITT, E. S.,  June 22, 1856 - Feb. 12, 1935
PROFFITT, Julia A. (w),  May 12, 1860 - Dec. 30, 1952
        Daughter of Presley and Sarah Banks Blankenship

SHELTON, Eli,  Aug. 10, 1905 - Jan. 1, 1924
SHELTON, Pimilton,  Dec. 13, 1909 - Jan. 1, 1943

FENDER, A. F.,  Aug. 20, 1886 - Sep. 6, 1952
FENDER, Bonnie Eloise (w),  Nov. 16, 1881 - May 9, 1927

BLANKENSHIP, Eli,  Jan. 1, 1849 - Jan. 26, 1940
BLANKENSHIP, Mary Ann (w),  Aug. 15, 1847 - Mar. 22, 1932

CODY, Mornin Blankenship,  Mar. 11, 1865 - Oct. 4, 1946

TREADWAY, C. V., Jr.,  Oct. 23, 1924 - Oct. 27, 1924
TREADWAY, Carris Vance,  Oct. 2, 1926 - Apr. 25, 1951

HENSLEY, Cornelia B.,  Mar. 22, 1881 - Mar. 2, 1951

ROBERTS, Henry,  Aug. 22, 1932 - Jan. 17, 1954

HARDING, Samuel,  Apr. 24, 1893 - Feb. 8, 1942

                plus many unmarked stones

BLANKENSHIP CEMETERY - ADDITIONS - July 18, 1988:

BRIGGS, Leslie York,   b/d 1962
BRIGGS, E. E.,         1933 - 1934
BRIGGS, Julia,         b/d 1926
BRIGGS, Vera,          b/d 1925
BRIGGS, Baby,          b/d 1924
BRIGGS, Fairy,         b/d 1922
        - siblings

SHELTON, Winfred,      no dates

HARDIN, Bob,  1900 - 1984

McINTOSH, Luther C.,  Sep. 1, 1897 - May 19, 1972
McINTOSH, Eunice E. (w),  May 18, 1905 -
        married Apr. 19, 1925

                    - 152 -

McINTOSH (?), Nellie,  1911 - 1912

McINTOSH, Ella Mae,  June 22, 1893 - Mar. 18, 1962
        Daughter of Frank and Viena Hensley Shelton

BLANKENSHIP, A. Clyde,  July 15, 1917 - July 5, 1938

BLANKENSHIP, Cecil,     no dates
BLANKENSHIP, Mary (w),  no dates

RICE, Vunard,  Aug. 11, 1920 - Oct. 27, 1922
        Son of N. B. and Leota Rice

BLANKENSHIP, Willie D.,  Mar. 7, 1899 - Apr. 9, 1899

BLANKENSHIP, David E.,  Aug. 27, 1940 - June 27, 1969

BLANKENSHIP, Bernie,  Dec. 30, 1912 - Jan. 21, 1973

TIPTON, John E.,  June 6, 1888 - Nov. 16, 1966
TIPTON, Myra (w),  May 9, 1888 - July 13, 1974

TIPTON, Arlene,  b/d 1976

TIPTON, Floyd,  Apr. 23, 1913 - June 24, 1944

TIPTON, Pearlee,   b/d 1928
TIPTON, Rex,       b/d 1926
        - siblings

TIPTON, Earl,  Feb. 18, 1916 - June 14, 1936

TIPTON, Alda,  July 2, 1933 - June 23, 1935
TIPTON, J. C., Feb. 27, 1927 - Feb. 7, 1928
        - siblings

TIPTON, Lee Roy,  Oct. 18, 1876 - June 18, 1976
TIPTON, Martha Silvers (w),  Apr. 4, 1884 - Mar. 10, 1911

TIPTON, Zeak,  Apr. 3, 1905 - Apr. 10, 1906

HENSLEY, Robert,  Jan. 27, 1936 - Jan. 29, 1936

TIPTON, Wesley,  Nov. 4, 1878 - Mar. 19, 1941
TIPTON, Barbara Jane "Janie" (w), Jan. 1886 - May 29, 1970

SILVERS, Claude,  Aug. 14, 1926 - Feb. 28, 1929
SILVERS, Ola    ,  Aug. 8, 1921 - Mar. 1, 1929

SILVERS, George,  July 20, 1893 - Feb. 22, 1977
SILVERS, Marietta (w),  Apr. 12, 1896 - Sep. 19, 1984

MOORE, Samuel,  Oct. 1, 1827 - June 27, 1912
        Co. H, 3rd NC Regt.,  Union Army
MOORE, Charity Brown (w),  Sep. 10, 1835 - Feb. 4, 1920
        married Jan. 27, 1853

TREADWAY, Ethel,  b/d Apr. 7, 1930
TREADWAY, Bethel,  b/d Apr. 7, 1930   twins
TREADWAY, Glen,   Sep. 12, 1931 - Mar. 19, 1932
        - siblings

ATKINS, Bobby,  1940 - 1975

ROBERTS, George,  Sep. 10, 1896 - Feb. 19, 1963
ROBERTS, Allie F. (w),  Apr. 14, 1894 -  no date

JOHNSON, Elizabeth Shelton,  Oct. 10, 1903 - Mar. 21, 1961

SHELTON, Docia B.,  Mar. 5, 1887 - Oct. 14, 1966

FENDER, Infant,     no dates,   Son of Hobart Fender

BLANKENSHIP, George P.,  Mar. 29, 1900 - Jan. 21, 1950

FENDER, Andrew J.,  Dec. 20, 1921 - Feb. 24, 1973
        Sfc., US Army, Korea, Vietnam

HARDING, Merritt,  1918 - 1961


## BLANKENSHIP CEMETERY (CONTINUED)

Near main cemetery  -  1 stone

BLANKENSHIP, Arthur,  May 14, 1920 - June 24, 1979


## ROSEVILLE CEMETERY

On Hogskin Branch, about 1 mile S.W. of Flag Pond
Copied by Charles Bennett Dec. 9, 1960 & updated July 27, 1988

STOCKTON, Clarence C.,  Jan. 23, 1924 - Jan. 2, 1946
        Cpl. US Air Force, WWII

LEWIS, Lucinda Jane,  Jan. 16, 1904 - Jan. 27, 1904
        Daughter of L. S. and Rachel Lewis

MASHBURN, Harold H.,  Feb. 12, 1915 - Apr. 14, 1947

STOCKTON, James H.,  June 23, 1877 - July 10, 1915
STOCKTON, Sarah C. (w),  Aug. 11, 1881 - Apr. 26, 1926

STOCKTON, Ollie M.,  Mar. 18, 1907 - Aug. 1, 1908
STOCKTON, Maude E.,  Oct. 6, 1905 - Apr. 25, 1907

ROSEVILLE CEMETERY - (continued)

STOCKTON, John W., Sep. 24, 1855 - Apr. 23, 1926
STOCKTON, Rebecca P. (w), Mar. 30, 1851 - May 11, 1906
STOCKTON, Melvina C. (dau), Aug. 10, 1872 - Mar. 7, 1893

CODY, Noah C., Feb. 27, 1863 - June 18, 1932
CODY, Montie M. Briggs (w), Mar. 28, 1862 - June 1, 1895

CARTER, Arminta, d. at 20 years

HIGGINS, Donna L., July 24, 1912 - Aug. 16, 1912
        Daughter of W. G. and V. E. Higgins

STOCKTON, Wm. Henry, Mar. 13, 1881 - no date
STOCKTON, Laura A. Willis (w), June 27, 1879 - Nov. 7, 1958

STOCKTON, Mintie E., Sep. 23, 1907 - Sep. 8, 1911


                plus many unmarked stones

ROSEVILLE CEMETERY - ADDITIONS - July 27, 1988:

STOCKTON, Hubert F., Aug. 20, 1900 -
STOCKTON, Mendia Tipton (w), Sep. 3, 1901 - May 14, 1961

LEWIS, Harce F., Mar. 22, 1905 - Dec. 2, 1906
LEWIS, Mary M., Mar. 24, 1909 - June 20, 1911
        - siblings

STOCKTON, Roscoe B., 1901 - 1987
STOCKTON, Leakie A. (w), 1905 - 1966
STOCKTON, Bobbie, 1948 - 1966
STOCKTON, Mary K., 1938 - 1939
STOCKTON, F. James, b/d 1935
        Children of Roscoe and Leakie Stockton

MASHBURN, James C., Dec. 9, 1885 - May 30, 1969
MASHBURN, Lonie S. Nov. 11, 1892 - Dec. 7, 1975

STOCKTON, Buford H., Sep. 28, 1928 - Sep. 17, 1966
        Pvt., Army Air Corps, WWII

STOCKTON, Earl B., 1946 - 1973
STOCKTON, Brenda (w), 1950 -

EDWARDS, Guy E., Oct. 25, 1912 - Feb. 5, 1978
EDWARDS, Medie J. (w), May 5, 1912 -

EDWARDS, Leca (Lesia?), June 12, 1966 - Nov. 1, 1966
        Daughter of Dillard and Faye Edwards

HENSLEY, Kittie S., Apr. 2, 1899 - Aug. 18, 1976

WALL, Gaston C., Oct. 31, 1913 - May 17, 1968, WWII
WALL, Louise H. (w), Nov. 21, 1930 -

STOCKTON, William Jake,  Feb. 17, 1904 - June 19, 1973

HARDIN, George W.,  Dec. 25, 1841 - Mar. 5, 1917
HARDIN, Jane Briggs Carter (w), Oct. 15, 1832 - Dec. 2, 1905

CRAIN, Andy Jack,  Oct. 13, 1890 - Nov. 2, 1962
CRAIN, Jane Silvers (w),  Jan. 6, 1881 - Oct. 18, 1973
CRAIN, Wash,  (child)

## RICE CEMETERY

.7 mi. SW of Rice Creek Cemetery
on Rice Creek Road
Copied July 27, 1988

RICE, Jasper Slola,  Apr. 5, 1899 - Feb. 7, 1984
RICE, Linda Aldora "Dora" (w),  Oct. 27, 1902 - Jan. 13, 1961

RICE, W. S.,  Dec. 2, 1854 - Aug. 26, 1939
RICE, N. C. (w),  Dec. 25, 1855 - July 17, 1938
RICE, Matilda (dau),  Oct. 23, 1896 - Nov. 1, 1918

RICE, Love,  Aug. 16, 1924 - Aug. 22, 1987
RICE, Dorothy S. (w),  Oct. 14, 1926 -

RICE, Wesley S. "Dorsie",  Dec. 21, 1936 - June 12, 1980

RICE, James W.,  1957 - 1958
RICE, Michael,  b/d 1958
          Sons of Wesley and Shirley Rice

## LEWIS CEMETERY #4

1.5 mile beyond Rice Creek Cemetery on Rice Creek Road
Copied July 27, 1988

LEWIS, Richard,  1907 - 1975
LEWIS, Creasie (w),  1913 -

LEWIS, Buster J.,  Oct. 22, 1942 - Sep. 23, 1946
          Son of Richard Lewis

LEWIS, Leroy Sam,  May 5, 1876 - Mar. 6, 1953
LEWIS, Rachel T. (w),  Oct. 28, 1874 - Feb. 24, 1940

LEWIS, Elzie M.,  Nov. 27, 1913 -
LEWIS, Agnes P. (w),  Oct. 5, 1922 - Nov. 20, 1982

plus many unmarked stones

<u>SAMS #2 CEMETERY</u>

On Rt. 23, about 2 miles S. of Flag Pond on E. side of road
Copied by Charles Bennett in 1963 and updated Aug. 10, 1988

SAMS, Lee Washington,  Oct. 15, 1861 - Nov. 1, 1951
        Son of Josiah B. and Emmaline Murray Sams
SAMS, Ella F. McCarthy (w),
        b. Feb. 5, 1864 - d. June 10, 1964 at 99 yrs
        Daughter of Rev. William McCarthy & Frances Amelie West
SAMS, Frederick Hoy (son), Apr. 23, 1887 - Sep. 25, 1888
SAMS, Florence Esther (dau),  Jan. 25, 1893 - Apr. 10, 1895
SAMS, Infant son,  b/d Dec. 4, 1897

ANDERSON, John F.,  Sep. 4, 1890 - Dec. 8, 1959
        Son of J. S. and Harriett Wilson Anderson
        Sgt. 316 FA, 81 DIV., WWI
        Son-in-law of Lee W. Sams
ANDERSON, Estelle Sams (w),  Jan. 31, 1900 -

CORNETT, William Lundy,  Feb. 16, 1909 - Oct. 21, 1947
        Son of Thomas Crockett and Mattie Lundy Cornett
        82nd Airborne, WWII - Son-in-law of Lee W. Sams
CORNETT, Jessie Sams (w),  Aug. 26, 1906 -

SAMS, Theron E.,  Nov. 12, 1890 - Sep. 22, 1950
        Son of Lee W. and Ellen F. McCarthy Sams
SAMS, Golda Bruce (w),  Aug. 9, 1891 - Aug. 19, 1987
CODY, Harriet Murray,  Oct. 1, 1853 - July 25, 1896
        Wife of Wilburn Cody

MURRAY, Samuel J.,  Dec. 11, 1876 - Jan. 6, 1899

MURRAY, Isaac J.,  Aug. 27, 1869 - July 20, 1898
MURRAY, Joe,        no dates    (brothers)

SAMS, Dr. Harry L.,  Mar. 19, 1879 - Sep. 14, 1905
        Son of J. P. Sams

SAMS, Josiah B.,  Jan. 27, 1828 - Aug. 13, 1908
        (Built home near cemetery) - in Confederate Army
SAMS, Emeline Murray (w),  July 6, 1829 - Jan. 2, 1906

PHILLIPS, E. P.,  May 3, 1846 - Jan. 13, 1922
PHILLIPS, Mary E. (w),  Nov. 20, 1855 - Oct. 16, 1950
        Daughter of Josiah B. and Emmaline Murray Sams
PHILLIPS, Little Jacob,  Mar. 8, 1886 - Sep. 3, 1888
        "Son of F. P. and Mamy E. Phillips"

BRIGGS, Little Dell,  Mar. 25, 1898 - May 28, 1898
        Daughter of N. N. and Jimmy Lee Briggs

SAMS, Jack Gleason,  Dec. 17, 1916 - Jan. 28, 1917
        Baby son of R. M. and Hettie Sams

GUINN, Jimmie Lee,  Jan. 1, 1883 - Jan. 19, 1929

CRAIN, J. W.,
        Cpl., Co. D, 4th Tenn. Inf., - Span-Am. War

CODY, Sallie Murray,      no dates
CODY, Fred,               no dates
CODY, Geneva,             no dates

SAMS, May,    May 18, 1890 - June 27, 1906
SAMS, Clarence,  Feb. 17, 1893 - Oct. 4, 1897
SAMS, Minnie,    Sep. 2, 1897 - Dec. 25, 1897
SAMS, "Little Emma",  Apr. 24, 1899 - June 2, 1902
SAMS, Infant,    Mar. 11, 1912 - Mar. 12, 1912
        Children of John B. and Liza Sams

BAILEY, W. W.,   July 18, 1852 - July 8, 1912
BAILEY, Lucy A. (w),   June 17, 1859 - Mar. 5, 1945
BAILEY, Lucile (dau),   Dec. 1, 1887 - Sep. 20, 1909

EDWARDS, Valeria J. Bailey,  Sep. 24, 1876 - Apr. 28, 1908
        Wife of Dr. C. P. Edwards. Dau. of W.W. & Lucy Bailey

BLANKENSHIP, Thomas L.,  Nov. 13, 1870 - Dec. 19, 1925
BLANKENSHIP, Emma B. (w),  Oct. 18, 1874 - Aug. 12, 1963
        Daughter of Fidel and Mary Elizabeth Sams Phillips
BLANKENSHIP, Roy J. (son),  July 31, 1901 - Oct. 24, 1902
BLANKENSHIP, Infant (son),  July 31, 1903  - Aug. 11, 1903

PHILLIPS, Bernice,  Nov. 26, 1929 - Apr. 16, 1932
        Daughter of Joe and Pearl Basher Phillips

BLANKENSHIP, William Zeb,  d. May 9, 1929
        Son of Tom and Emma Phillips Blankenship
        Pvt. WWI (?)

HENSON, Myrtle I.,  June 24, 1899 - Sep. 21, 1929
        Daughter of Tom and Emma Phillips Blankenship

SAMS #2 CEMETERY - ADDITIONS - Aug. 10, 1988:

ENGLISH, Guy,     1897 - 1944
ENGLISH, Grace Sams (w),  1904 - 1986

SAMS, John B.,   June 14, 1871 - Nov. 11, 1962
SAMS, Eliza Guinn (w),  Jan. 28, 1872 - Apr. 19, 1966

PHILLIPS, William J.,    1878 - 1963
        Son of Fidel Patton and Mary Elizabeth Sams Phillips
PHILLIPS, Pearl P. (w),  1886 - 1973

ENGLISH, George W.,  Oct. 21, 1897 - Dec. 9, 1963
ENGLISH, Lola J. (w),  Jan. 18, 1909 - Feb. 4, 1968
ENGLISH, Gene W.,  Aug. 31, 1927 - Aug. 17, 1984
        Tec4, US Army, WWII

BLANKENSHIP, Cecil,   June 15, 1893 - Feb. 6, 1962
          Son of Thomas L. and Emma Phillips Blankenship

BLANKENSHIP, Guy,   July 22, 1912 - May 1, 1963
          Son of Thomas L. and Emma Phillips Blankenship

BLANKENSHIP, Audrey,   May 4, 1914 - Dec. 28, 1969

BLANKENSHIP, Wade,   July 14, 1903 - Dec. 29, 1970
          Pvt., Co. E, 415th Inf., WWII

          Very nice cemetery - no unmarked stones

## SAMS #3 CEMETERY

     On Rt. 23, on right, 1 mile beyond Sams #2 Cemetery
                  Copied Aug. 10, 1988

SAMS, James,     Jan. 1797   -  Oct. 1841
SAMS, Mary (w), July 6, 1799 - Aug. 6, 1885

     These are the original Sams settlers of Flag Pond.
     They came across Sams Gap in 1830's.

## FLAG POND SCHOOL CEMETERY

     Behind Flag Pond School, take road opposite Crain Store
                  Copied Aug. 10, 1988

HENSLEY, James B.,   June 21, 1875 - May 1, 1966

HENSLEY, S. S.,   Oct. 29, 1834 - Mar. 28, 1915
HENSLEY, Cordelia (w),   Apr. 11, 1853 - Jan. 31, 1904

HENSLEY, Elsie A.,   Mar. 27, 1899 - Dec. 23, 1914
HENSLEY, Lizzie Edna,   Apr. 1, 1895 - Oct. 1, 1895
HENSLEY, Infant,   no other data
          Children of Dr. T. C. and Mary A. Hensley

SHELTON, Eliphus,
          Co. G, 3 NC Mtd. Inf.,   Union Army

SHELTON, David,
          Co. F, 10 TN CAV.,   Union Army

CARTER, Margaret Birley,   Nov. 7, 1880 - Dec. 20, 1965

CARTER, Ned,   1919 - 1985

TREADWAY, Olive Carter,   Mar. 12, 1915 - Apr. 9, 1970

CODY, Mahala "Hail" Harris,   1860 - 1942

HARRIS, Hobert, June 18, 1898 - Oct. 15, 1918
          2nd Lt., 127 Inf., WWI Killed In Action

FLAG POND SCHOOL CEMETERY - (continued)

CHANDLEY, Mormon,  May 15, 1893 - Aug. 6, 1914

HENSLEY, Harry,  Jan. 14, 1912 - Feb. 5, 1913
        Son of Staplin and Harriet Hensley

SHELTON, Bonnie,  June 9, 1910 - Sep. 8, 1912
        Daughter of R. E. and Minnie Shelton
HENSLEY, Caroline,  d. Feb. 12, 1901 at age 46
        Wife of Ellis Hensley
HENSLEY, Birtha (dau),  June 3, 1888 - June 10, 1902
HENSLEY, Walter (son),  Nov. 6, 1900 - June 12, 1901

HARRIS, Laura,  Mar. 10, 1876 - Feb. 3, 1897

HARRIS, Frank,  no dates

CARTER, John E.,  Aug. 23, 1865 - May 15, 1895

CRAIN, Bayless E.,  Jan. 6, 1877 - Apr. 9, 1905

MOORE, Thomas H.,  Dec. 17, 1889 - Dec. 20, 1914
        Son of W. N. and R. J. Moore

RICE, J. T.,  June 25, 1885 - July 27, 1908

RUNNION, Elizabeth,  Nov. 19, 1832 - Mar. 31, 1887
        Wife of B. O. Runnion
RUNNION, Sarah E. (dau),  June 18, 1877 - Dec. 31, 1877
RUNNION, Carrie Atlas,  June 14, 1894 - Aug. 30, 1894
        Daughter of B. O. and S. M. Runnion

RUNNION, Thomas,  June 5, 1813 - Dec. 12, 1890
RUNNION, Elizabeth (w),  Mar. 2, 1817 - July 13, 1903

RUNNION, Robert G.,  Mar. 9, 1866 - Apr. 5, 1892

HIGGINS, Ellis,  Feb. 9, 1812 - Jan. 5, 1909
HIGGINS, Ruth (w),  Oct. 21, 1811 - May 24, 1882

McCRAY, Elmira,  Aug. 4, 1821 - June 26, 1891

VANCE, Alice G.,  1924 - 1939

CRAIN, Luis E.,  June 16, 1883 - Apr. 11, 1887

plus many unmarked stones

Other names - from death certificate (1914 film):

SHELTON, Nathan Garfield,  Jan. 15, 1881 - Mar. 6, 1914
        Son of Levi and Arminda Shelton

## DIVIDE CEMETERY

On Rt. 23 at Sams Gap, about 150 ft. from the NW side
of the road
    Copied by Charles Bennett on Dec. 2, 1962 and up-
    dated Oct. 1, 1988

METCALF, John,   Feb. 17, 1899 - Jan. 8, 1953
METCALF, Willard,  Sep. 6, 1900 - June 18, 1957
METCALF, Joel,   Aug. 1906 - May 1, 1948
        brothers

METCALF, Susan Glendennon,  Feb. 17, 1859 - Nov. 16, 1940
METCALF, Robert R.,  d. Feb. 13, 1939 - Pvt. QM Corps
METCALF, Flona Mae,  Feb. 21, 1938 - May 19, 1939

METCALF, Paul H.,  Apr. 27, 1956 - Apr. 27, 1956

METCALF, Henry,  June 11, 1884 - Oct. 27, 1947

METCALF, Wesley,  May 28, 1854 - June 20, 1931
METCALF, Louise (w),  Jan. 1, 1854 - Apr. 25, 1947

METCALF, Hobert E.,  Jan. 26, 1897 - June 1, 1957
        Pvt. US Army, WWI

METCALF, James H.,  d. Mar. 7, 1953, age 77
        Son of Henry C. and Sarah Ann Crawford Metcalf

METCALF, Backes,  1904 - 1953

METCALF, Howard,  1950 - 1950

METCALF, Johnnie,  Feb. 19, 1930 - Apr. 3, 1930
        Son of Dempsey and Ruby Metcalf

METCALF, G. D. and Wife,   no dates

HENSLEY, Deronie,  Apr. 18, 1919 - Mar. 3, 1940

HENSLEY, Lucindy,   1820 - 1917 (?)

HENSLEY, Sindy,  1825  - Sep. 14, 1909

HENSLEY, W. H.,  Dec. 10, 1876 - Nov. 8, 1955
HENSLEY, Laura Jane,  1880 - 1957

HENSLEY, John W. Sr.,   1869 - 1946

WHEELER, Garry Zane,  d. Jan. 24, 1960 at 4 days

MELTON, Sidney M.,  Aug. 10, 1875 - Dec. 21, 1958
MELTON, Katy W. (w),  Apr. 7, 1875 - Nov. 3, 1958

BARRETT, A. J.,  Oct. 6, 1841 - Oct. 14, 1900
BARRETT, Mary Ann (w),  July 4, 1845 - June 14, 1932

<u>DIVIDE CEMETERY</u> - (continued)

BUCKNER, Janie Barrett,  Mar. 27, 1871 - June 20, 1951

BARRETT, Sue,  May 13, 1876 - July 24, 1940

WHITE, Polly,  1800 - 1894

EDMONDS, Katherine,  Oct. 30, 1836 - Dec. 31, 1930

plus several unmarked stones

<u>DIVIDE CEMETERY - ADDITIONS - Oct. 1, 1988:</u>

CARVER, Rev. Emerson,  May 23, 1906 - Apr. 7, 1973
CARVER, Della M. (w),  Oct. 11, 1905 -

PHILLIPS, Boyd,  Apr. 21, 1918 - Dec. 3, 1986

EDWARDS, Eldridge Sr.,  Oct. 9, 1939 - Sep. 22, 1977

HENSLEY, Pauline P.,  Mar. 17, 1933 - Jan. 23, 1981

TEAGUE, Sidney A.,  Aug. 3, 1956 - Aug. 27, 1965

HENSLEY, Linnie,  Apr. 13, 1884 - Apr. 6, 1966
HENSLEY, Guss M. (     son),  Nov. 9, 1900 -

METCALF, Ulys,  Apr. 29, 1900 - Apr. 14, 1979

SKIPPER, Harriett H.,  May 31, 1907 - Feb. 4, 1980

HARRIS, Geneva Metcalf,  Aug. 29, 1927 - July 16, 1957

METCALF, Dempsey,  Dec. 22, 1904 - Feb. 2, 1975
METCALF, Ruby (w),  Jan. 15, 1913 -
        Married June 20, 1926

METCALF, Lattie,  1907 - 1972

HENSLEY, Talmadge McCall,  Aug. 8, 1917 - June 18, 1975

HENSLEY, Dewey,  Jan. 5, 1909 - Dec. 14, 1987 - US Army, WWII

HENSLEY, Clarence E.,  1915 - 1981

KING, Jenette Metcalf,  Dec. 24, 1936 - Sep. 2, 1966

METCALF, Wayne Wesley,  Apr. 7, 1920 - Mar. 21, 1970
        US Army, WWII

METCALF, Eva Jane,  Mar. 19, 1886 - May 20, 1973

WHEELER, C. Emerson,  July 4, 1895 - Dec. 30, 1975
WHEELER, Essie Metcalf (w),  Apr. 10, 1898 - Feb. 29, 1980

METCALF, Robert Roscoe,  May 20, 1895 - Apr. 22, 1983

- 162 -

## LEDFORD CEMETERY #1

On Coffee Ridge Loop road, E. side, near Willis #2 Cemetery
Copied Nov. 3, 1988

LEDFORD, Hubert C. "Chet",   Sep. 4, 1931 – July 18, 1965
          Pvt., US Air Force
LEDFORD, Ann (w),   1935 –

LEDFORD, Theodore,   1926 – 1937
LEDFORD, Texie,      1917 – 1919

LEDFORD, William Cornelius,   Dec. 28, 1876 – July 7, 1978
LEDFORD, Mariah Fender (w),   Apr. 25, 1892 – June 13, 1981

INGRAM, Willard,   Aug. 3, 1923 – Sep. 2, 1982
          Tec 5, US Army, WWII

## WILLIS #2 CEMETERY

On Coffee Ridge Loop road, E. side, next to Ledford Cemetery
Copied Nov. 3, 1988

EVELY, Garland M.,   Mar. 12, 1924 – July 23, 1972
EVELY, Creola W. (w),   Nov. 11, 1924 – June 27, 1974

RICE, David Lee,   b/d July 6, 1964

WILLIS, J. B.,   Nov. 7, 1922 – June 21, 1949
          Pfc., 84th Div., WWII

WILLIS, Roger Dale,   Feb. 11, 1945 – Feb. 14, 1945
          Son of Wm. Joseph and Thelma Ray Willis

WILLIS, Jasper,   Apr. 4, 1883 – Apr. 25, 1959
WILLIS, Thelma R. (w),   July 10, 1905 – Sep. 11, 1985

WILLIS, Quinton,   1919 – 1988

## WILLIAMS #2 CEMETERY

Off Coffee Ridge Road – take first gravel road on left,
then right at fork to house on hill
Copied Dec. 14, 1988

WILLIAMS, Ronda K.,   1960 – 1970
          Daughter of Frank Williams

          Possibly other graves, but no other
          stones or markers

## WATTS CEMETERY

Off Spivey Mt. Rd., left on John Hensley Rd.
Copied Dec. 29, 1988

WATTS, John M., 1866 - 1947
WATTS, Elizabeth P. (w), 1871 (or 1873) - 1961

SHELTON, Vira, d. Dec. 11, 1922 age 63
        Wife of Armstrong Shelton

WATTS, William,
        Co. K, 13th TN CAV., Union Army

            plus many unmarked stones


## KAN FOSTER CEMETERY

Off Coffee Ridge Rd., 1st left, right at fork, top of
ridge, above Williams Cemetery
Copied Dec. 26, 1988

FOSTER, Kennedy "Kan", ca 1814 - ca 1890

FOSTER, Rebecca Kersawn (w), ca 1818 - 1860s

        One of the original settlers in this area,
        Kan was granted 640 acres in 1839.


            5 graves, field stones only


## WILLIS #1 CEMETERY

Coffee Ridge on left, Foster Road to top of hill on
right, under pine tree
Copied Dec. 26, 1988

LEDFORD, Amos, Sep. 2, 1904 - Sep. 4, 1933

WILLIS, David E., Jan. 30, 1837 - Aug. 25, 1924
        Co. M, 8th TN CAV - Union Army
WILLIS, Mary Liz (w), likely the daughter of Kan Foster
FAGG, Infant dau., d. 1961

WILLIS, Murphy, son of David Willis
WILLIS, Lee , son of Murphy Willis
WILLIS, Ruby ,
        markers rusted away in 1988

            plus 4 or 5 other field stones

## SHERMAN LEWIS CEMETERY

djacent to Hensley #1 Cemetery, on Spivey Mt. Rd.,
eft just before Little Bald Creek Road
Copied Dec. 29, 1988


S, William Sherman,  Mar. 27, 1888 - Dec. 6, 1987
    Pvt., US Army, WWI
S, Cinda Jane (w),  Apr. 12, 1899 - June 11, 1984
    Married Dec. 2, 1917

OLER, Claude H.,  June 1, 1900 - Feb. 8, 1983
OLER, Minnie (w),  Feb. 1, 1906 - Jan. 10, 1975

SON, Cherry Lynn,  b/d July 29, 1959

LEY, Robert B.,  May 27, 1878 - May 12, 1958
LEY, Nellie Catherine Foster, July 29, 1878 - Feb. 17, 1953

LEY, Worley,  Jan. 14, 1904 - Oct. 21, 1973

LEY, Carroll,  Mar. 11, 1938 - Mar. 14, 1986 - US Navy

New cemetery - no unmarked stones


## HOLLOWAY CEMETERY

n Shilow Road, left off Norton Creek Road, off Rock
eek Road, Erwin

Copied Jan. 16, 1989

There is only one grave, unmarked, on hill behind barn

WAY, Tracy,  b/d Aug. 1956
    Daughter of Haru and Lucy (Buchanan) Holloway

## PEOPLES OR PEEBLES CEMETERY

Located near Buffalo Creek, on the right, on Marbleton Road - just off old highway 23, between Unicoi and Johnson City.

Copied October 29, 1988

FORBES, Ralph,    Sept.23,1909 - Dec.28,1936
FORBES, Hobart,    Died March 24,1936 - Pvt. Coast Art. Corp.

McKINNEY, Cart,    March 14,1877 - Jan.9,1942

WHITSON, Emma,    1862 - March 24.1932
    Dau. of Nathan and Eliza Wilson Mosley

McKINNEY, Mrs. Jane,    Dec.23,1858 - Jan. 18,1930

BROWN, Otto A.,    Jan.1,1885 - Sept. 10,1949
    Texas Sgt. 13 Field Art. 4 Div. WW1

WINTERS, George W.,    Oct.12,1866 - April 19,1940
WINTERS, Debbie,    (w), Jan. 14,1878 -    -----

TIPTON, Ruth,    Infant, b/d Aug. 27,1908

TIPTON, M.C.,    Feb.14,1851 - Oct.18,1932
TIPTON, Sarah,    (w), 1853 - 1915

TIPTON, William H.,    (Father) 1873 - 1943

FORBES, Calvin C.,    (Father) Aug.5,1907 - Sept.7,1929

TIPTON, Eva R.,    July 8,1887 - Dec.2,1911

SHEPARD, General,    July 13,1899 - July 25,1914

JARRETT,    Infant of George and Sarah. b/d May 3,1915

SHEPARD, Frankie Carolina,    Aug.18,1913 - March 6,1916
    Dau. of J.A. and Phoebe Shepard
SHEPARD, Eli,    Feb.18,1897 - April 11,1917
    Son of J.A. and Phoebe Shepard

JARRETT, Florria,    Nov.4,1921 - Nov.25,1921
JARRETT, James Roscoe,    April 2,1895 - Nov.11,1926

WHITSON, James,    Died April 2,1897 - Age 71 years

TIPTON, Georgia A.,    Oct.18,1890 - Aug.2,1892

PRICE, Franklin,    1840 - July 2,1892 - Co D 13 Tenn.Cav. Union Army
    Son of Christopher and Mary McInturff Price

BRUMMETT, Laura McInturff,    Died Aug.3,1899 - Age 43 years
    Wife of J.A. Brummett

PEOPLES CEMETERY  (continued)

McINTURFF, S.W.,   Oct.15,1864 - Feb.16,1889

NORRIS, A.C.,   July 26,1879 - Aug.2,1934

BRUMMETT, Thomas M.,   March 26,1856 - June 29,1894
BRUMMETT, Julia A.Norris,   (w), Feb.4,1858 -   ----

BRUMIT, Thomas,   Co. B 12 Tenn. Cav.  Union Army

BRUMMETT, Talitha,   (Mother) Feb.6,1823 - Jan.18,1895
          Dau. of Thomas and Nancy Scott McInturff
          Wife of Thomas Brummett

WHITSON, Mary Price,   Died June 16,1888  - Age 58 years
          Wife of James Whitson

ERWIN, Robert H.,   Nov.10,1888 - Jan.2,1893
          Son of I.L. and M.E.Erwin

PEUGH, Joseph,   Oct. 1861 -  April 1,1878

CLARK, Alexander,   1843 - Sept.4,1886
CLARK, Dicie,   1845 - Nov.2,1899

SUTPHIN, Florence V.,   1881 - 1955
          Dau. of William and Jane Vaughn
SUTPHIN, E.H. Sr.,   1879 - 1964
SUTPHIN, Sarah M.,   (Mother)  May 29,1885 - May 20,1939

McINTURFF, Lucretia,   March 7,1833 - July 19,1870
          Dau. of Thomas and Nancy Scott McInturff

BAKER, Annie Jane,   Jan.28,1840 - Jan.9,1871
          Dau. of Thomas and Nancy Scott McInturff

BRUMMETT, Louise Adline,   April 16,1858 - Nov. 1879

McINTURFF, Thomas,   Aug.2,1792 - March 21,1881
McINTURFF, Nancy,   (w), Dec.23,1796 - April 25,1881

McINTURFF, Mary Adaline,   Jan.19,1831 - Sept.1,1912
          Dau. of Thomas and Nancy Scott McInturff

NORRIS, Rachel E.,   Aug.19,1835 - June 25,1893
          Dau. of Thomas and Nancy Scott McInturff
          Wife of Christopher C.Norris - Union soldier
          buried in Gallatin Tennessee

NORRIS, Lucinda,   Nov.19,1863 - July 17,1936

McINTURFF, Wilson,   Nov.27,1825 - April 19,1909
          Son of Thomas and Nancy Scott McInturff

NORRIS, Minnie Bowman,   (Mother)  Jan.28,1880 - Jan.2,1911
          Wife of A.C. Norris

NORRIS, Bessie Love,   May 15,1884 - Nov. 9,1930
        Wife of A.C.Norris

NORRIS, William P.,   Nov.27,1855 - March 12,1923
NORRIS, Amanda J.McInturff,  (w)  Dec.11,1859 - Oct.10,1924
        Dau. of Thomas and Nancy Scott McInturff

DIETS, Bessie E.,   May 18,1897 - Feb.13,1942

PHILLIPS, Robert,   Aug.5,1902 - April 27,1927

NORRIS, Nancy Ann Brummett,   Nov.26,1851 - April 11,1912

NORRIS, James M.,   March 5,1851 - April 11,1912

NORRIS, Infant Son of G.F. and Cora Norris, b/d Feb.24,1912

NORRIS, Sallie M.,   June 4,1873 - March 15,1894
        Wife of J.M.Norris

NORRIS, Martha E.,   (Mother) Sept.15,1855 - Jan.21,1889
        Wife of J.M.Norris

NORRIS, William O.,   May 3,1882 - July 30,1905

WHITSON, Lula,   1958 (Only date)

HONEYCUTT, Sis,   Aug.4,1860 - April 19,1936

SCOTT, Emeline D.,   March 31,1829 - Dec.6,1902

SCOTT, Elizabeth G.,   July 4,1806 - Feb.2,1868

PRICE, William W.,   Aug.4,1854 - Oct.12,1864

TONEY, Mary,   Died Dec. 1866  -  Age 70 years

McINTURFF, Mary J.,   Died Aug.4,1874   -   Age 19 years

BOGART, Callie Norris,   July 26,1861 - Nov.23,1887
        Wife of E.G.Bogart

NORRIS, Richard N.,   Feb.20,1819 - March 4,1896
NORRIS, Lucinda McInturff,  (w),  May 16,1818 - Feb.19,1904
        Dau. of Thomas and Nancy Scott McInturff

NORRIS, Mary E.,   Dec.2,1843 - Jan.17,1924

NORRIS, Richard N.Jr.,   Jan.16,1884 - May 28,1909

NORRIS, David B.,   April 13,1854 - March 21,1912

NORRIS, Nancy A.,   Sept.12,1845 - Jan.15,1921

NORRIS, John W.,   Feb.28,1856 - March 16,1937
NORRIS, Nancy Whitson,  (w)  Feb.25,1856 - Jan.20,1948

NORRIS, Dana H.,   Nov.2,1894 - Aug.25,1907

PEOPLES, Elizabeth,   June 16,1831 - March 10,1870

PEOPLES, Alfred C.,   April 16,1817 - Dec.31,1862

PHILLIPS, Lewis,   Oct.4,1862 - May 27,1940

HELTON, Bonnie C.,   b/d  Oct.11,1948

NORRIS, Ben,   April 14,1897 - June 10,1956  - Pvt.U.S.Army - WW1

PEEBLES, George W.,   1814 - 1856

PEEBLES, James L.,   1836 - 1855

PEEBLES, J.W.,   1819 - 1839

DUNCAN, David,   Died Sept.14,1845  - Age 11 mos.7 days

DUNCAN, Rev. George W.,   June 14,1819 - April 20,1850

McKINNEY, Billy Mack,   Died Aug.22,1937  - Age 5 years

RIDDLE, Thad C.,   April 19,1889 - June 24,1924
RIDDLE, Bessie E.,  (w)  April 20,1896 - 1984
          Maiden name Winters

OWENS, James,   May 25,1886 - Aug.6,1959
OWENS, Deborah L.,  (w)  Dec.15,1881 - Oct.2,1956

PEOPLES, Madison T.,   1825 - 1913

BUSHONG, M.Bruce,   1867 - 1943

SIMERLY, Pheba Barnett,   March 5,1878 - Sept.30,1958

RAINWATERS, Mary,   1873 - 1953

McINTURFF, Christopher,   March 25, 1772 - April 29,1796
     Here lieth the body of Christopher McInturff, Juner, he wors
boren March 25, 1772 and Dyed April the 29, and buryed the 30,1796,
his age wors 14 year, 1 month, and 4 days.

WIET, Edward,   July 22,1718 - Dec.3,1797
     Here lieth the body of Edward Wiet. He was born the 22 day
of July 1718, and died December the 3 day 1797. His age was 79
years, 4 mo. and 16 days.

A TALL MARBLE SHAFT WITH THE FOLLOWING INSCRIPTIONS

```
PEEBLES, William,    Oct.15,1787 - June 30,1875
PEEBLES, Elizabeth S.,   (w),   Sept. 7, 1794 - Dec.4,1886
PEEBLES,   G.W.   1814- 1856
PEEBLES,   H.C.   1817 - 1863
PEEBLES,   J.W.   1819 - 1839
PEEBLES,   J.L.   1836 - 1855
PEEBLES,   N.S.   1816 - 1894
PEEBLES,   P.P.   1822 - 1895
PEEBLES.   E.C.   1833 - 1912
PEEBLES,   M.T.   1825 - 1913
PEEBLES,   A.J.   1829 - 1918
PEEBLES,   W.J.   1831 - 1919
```

Additional information on this family from the Bible
record of William Peebles, Jr. follows.

PEEBLES, William, born Oct.15,1787 in Washington County, North
Carolina.(Afterwards Carter County Tenn. - now Unicoi County, Tenn.)

SHEETS, Elizabeth, born Sept.7,1794 at Eagle Rock, Botetourt
County, Virginia. Daughter of Jacob and Catherine Sheetz.

William Peebles and Elizabeth Sheetz married at her father's
home in Botetourt County Va. Nov. 16,1813, by Rev. John Helms.

BIRTHS

```
George W.    Sept. 14 1814
Nancy S.     March 20,1816
Harriet C.   Dec. 18,1817
John W.      Dec.19,1819
Phenetta     Sept.8,1822
Madison T.   Jan.2,1825
Andrew J.    Jan.16,1829
William J.   Jan.18,1831
Elizabeth C. Feb.8,1833
James L.     Dec.22,1836
```

MARRIAGES

```
Nancy S. Peebles   -  Jacob D. Akard   -  Sept.10,1839
Harriet C. Peebles  - Samuel Bachman  - Nov.25,1841
Phenetta Peebles   - George W.Duncan  -  Sept.3,1844
Phenetta Peebles Duncan  - Nathaniel T.Brown  -  Dec.1,1853
Andrew J.peebles   - Clarissa H.Ray   - Feb.11,1858
Elizabeth C. Peebles  - William Bushong  - Oct. 7,1862
William J. Peebles  - Mary Jane Lyon   (no date)
```

BUSHONG, Elizabeth Peebles,   1833 - 1912

BRUMMETT, Lindy Curtis,   June 8,1931 - Jan.13,1932
          Child of Henry A. and Martha Phillips Brummett

HENSON, Rachel E. Norris,   Aug.13,1858 - Aug. 9, ???

PETERSON, Pearl,    June 5,1905 - Jan.10,1972

PETERSON, Dr. Earl,    1923 - 1967
PETERSON, Ann Moody, (w),    Died 1976

HILL, Jessie,    Aug.6,1909 - July 5,1971

BABB, Harold A.,    Dec.21,1932 -  ------
BABB, Wanda,    July 15,1936 - Jan.1,1972

NORRIS, Luttie G.,    1908 - 1987

BRUME(TT), John H.,    1852 - 18??

McELYEA, Beulah Price,    1923 - 1971

PRICE, John

PRICE, Banner Lee,    1900 - 1977

PRICE, Benjamin P.,    March 6,1971 - Sept.20,1971

WINTERS, Jess,    Aug.25,1907 - March 2, 1984

GRINDSTAFF, Godphry,    Died 1980
GRINDSTAFF, Pearl,    Died 1983

FEATHERS, George R.,    1898 - 1977
FEATHERS, Flossie V.,    1911 - 1974
FEATHERS, Robert D.,    May 15,1935 -  -----
FEATHERS, Frances D.,    Nov.29,1938 -  -----

MICKELS, Alex J.,    1913 - 1973

McKINNEY, Stanley,    Died 1983


## UNMARKED GRAVE

JACOBS, Estell DeWane, - Died July 16,1933
          Dau. of D.E.and Elsie Chestine Brummett Jacobs

# SWINGLE CEMETERY

Located at Unicoi - on Swingle Road, off Massachusetts Ave.

HOILMAN, Tammie Renee,   June 20,1970 - Aug.21,1970
HOILMAN, Kristie Marie,   March 26,1974 - April 12,1974

HOPSON, Ronnie T.,   April 29,1942 - Jan.23,1944
        Son of Jess and Rebecca Luttrell Hopson

HOPSON, Jess J.,   1894 - 1958
        Son of Nicholas and Phoebe Masters Hopson
HOPSON, Rebecca,   1897 - 1976

McCOURRY, James H.,   1871 - 1958
McCOURRY, Annie L.,   1878 - 1965

LAWS, L.C.Jr.,   Dec.13,1936 - May 3, 1987

McCOURRY, Gladys Jones,   Aug.22,1911 - Dec.10,1945

HIGGINS, Barry,   1897 - 1965
HIGGINS, Mary,   1907 - 1984
        Dau. of Elbert C. and Axie McCurry Britt
HIGGINS, Linda D., May 31,1948 - June 20,1948
HIGGINS, Lincoln E.,   April 14,1926 - July 14,1943
        Children of Barry and Mary Britt Higgins

Jordan, Ira C.,   July 2,1910 - March 6,1946

GARLAND, Dave J.,   1899 - 1942
GARLAND, Minnie S.,   1915 - -----

GARLAND, D.J.,   Aug.17,1935 - Aug.14,1966 - PFC U.S.Army

McINTURFF, James Samuel,   Dec.13,1867 - Aug.11,1944
McINTURFF, Julia Brumett, (w),   Jan.20,1866 - -----

COATS, Walter,   June 10,1887 - Nov.10,1954
        Son of William and Jane Coats

HARRIS, Dallas K.,   May 12,1947 - May 22,1947
        Son of William and Billie R. Harris

MILLER, Mable E.,   May 31,1906 - Sept.18,1962

PATE, Arthur R.,   1884 - 1935
        Son of Nathan and Vina Garland Pate
PATE, Hannah White, (w),   Aug.3,1883 - Nov.22,1955
PATE, Clifford,   April 21,1912 - Sept.7,1983

HOWELL, Sherman,   May 16,1882 - March 6,1935
HOWELL, John F.,   Feb.5,1893 - July 13,1934
HOWELL, ROBERT,   Aug.21,1899 - Dec.27,1937
HOWELL, Bernie,   Sept.19,1902 - Dec.25,1957
        Sons of Samuel Peter and Mary Headrick Howell

SWINGLE CEMETERY   (continued)

HOWELL, Lorna Mae,   June 1,1893 - May 28,1934
         Wife of Frank Howell
HOWELL, Jeff,   Feb.28,1895 - Feb.13,1935
HOWELL, Willard W.,   Aug.3,1925 - Nov.15,1948

MILLER, FRED,   Feb.10,1893 - Nov.1,1972
MILLER, Etta O.,   (w)  May 7,1899 - June 3,1963
         Dau. of James Madison and Margaret Jones
MILLER, Mildred P., (Dau.) July 27,1931 - June 8,1932

McLAUGHLIN, Judea U.A.,   Died May 20,1875
         Wife of H. McLaughlin
McLAUGHLIN, Hazel M., March 19,1911 - Sept.1,1949
         Dau. of Bradley and Nora Williams Meade

TOLLEY, Edna M.,   1917 - 1918
TOLLEY, Mary L.,   Jan.22,1924 - May 6,1924

GARLAND, Susan,   Sept.29,1812 - May 12,1917

PATE, Nathan,   April 3,1846 - April 3,1920
PATE, Luvina Garland,   (w)  June 8, 1848 - Jan.16,1926

HUSKINS, Carie,   1911 - 1918
         Dau. of Alvin and Leah Huskins

STREET, William M.,   Feb.12,1910 - June 25,1976
STREET, Gertha,  (w),    (no dates)

STREET, John H.,   June 5,1877 - Sept.15,1952
STREET, Texas H.,   Nov.23,1884 - Dec.11,1968

MILLER, Bessie,   1891 - 1918

HOWELL, Minnie,   March 22,1879 - Aug.20,1959

STREET, Ulysses C.,   One date - Dec.5,1922 -PVT 307
                              Fire Truck and Hose Co.

HOWELL, Harriett,    (no dates)

HOWELL, Sarah,   Oct.6,1895 - July 25,1938

HOWELL, James,   Jan.15,1844 - Dec.14,1934
         Co F 3 NC Mtd Inf Union Army
         Son of William and ----Honeycutt Howell
HOWELL, Lovada Adkins,  (w),  May 10,1848 - June 23,1922

ADKINS, Herman,   1903 - 1943
ADKINS, Mary H.,   1881 - 1949
ADKINS, Jim,   1898 - 1950

HIGGINS, Bessie H.,   1904 - 1960

MILLER, Mollie,   Aug.19,1868 - Jan.1,1946
         Dau. of Jack Peterson and Susie Sweeney Miller

<u>SWINGLE CEMETERY</u>  (continued)

HOWELL, Alice A.,   Aug.18,1884 - May 12,1907
        Dau. of James and Lovada Howell

HOWELL, John,   Aug.23,1913 - July 31,1949 -   PFC  WW2

MILLER, Cordia S., Dec.10,1898 - Aug.29,1903
        Dau. of J.M. and Vertie Miller

MILLER, Ralph,   1918 - 1918
MILLER, William F.,   1921 - 1922

MILLER, J.O.,   July 30,1892 - Nov.8,1950
MILLER, Bunia Troutman  (w),  March 17,1898 - July 4,1977

BRYANT, Nick,   April 32,1915 - Feb.25,1950  - WW2
BRYANT, Charles Wesley,   1910 - 1966

CULLER, Willis H. (Bill),   Oct.29,1902 - Aug.30,1958

BAKER, W.H.,   1890 - 1951
BAKER, Vina M.,   1892 - -----

McINTURFF, Julia N.Baker, July 4,1878 - Sept.26,1914
McINTURFF, Loyd,   Died 1905
McINTURFF, Edna,   Died 1912
        Son and Dau. of R.N. and Julia N.McInturff

BAKER, Grace,   1893 - 1895
BAKER, Nancy   1884 - 1898

WHALEY, Sgt. J.R.,   Co H 8th Tenn Cav - Govt Marker - no dates

CUTSHALL, Malinda,   Feb.1,1888 - Dec.21,1938
CUTSHALL, Garnel,   Aug.13,1919 - May 4,1943
        Son of B.B. and Malinda Cutshall

MILLER,Carmen,   May24,1913 - May 22,1935
        Son of Robert and Emma Bryant Miller
MILLER, Emma B.,   Jan.15,1889 - July 18,1931
        Dau. of J.W. and Omie Tipton Bryant

RICH, Jess H.,   May 2,1890 - Oct.27,1921

LAWS, Alson,   1906 - 1907

McNABB,  Infant of Mr. and Mrs. V.S. McNabb

BUCHANAN, Elvira,   June 17,1849 - June 9, 1920
BUCHANAN, Robert,   March 10,1872 - Nov.9,1953
BUCHANAN, Lillie,  (w),  April 7,1882 - Sept.12,1971
BUCHANAN, Gertrude,   Aug.2,1909 - Nov.28,1933
        Dau. of Robert and Lillie Buchanan

LEDFORD, John,    May 30,1872 - March 24,1957
LEDFORD, Lyda,    July 15,1884 - May 24,1970

SLAGLE, Hobart,   May 24,1897 - Aug.5,1978
SLAGLE, Gladys Phillips,   May 24,1902 - -----

PHILLIPS, Dwight Afton,    Dec.26,1899 - Feb.10,1970
PHILLIPS, Lucile Lillian,   Aug.19,1902 - March 8, 1968

HOPSON, Angeline,   No dates

HOPSON, Neom L.,    May 30, 1917 - Oct.10,1926
            Dau. of Robert and Nella

JONES, Walter,    April 13,1906 - Nov.15,1918

PHILLIPS, Zeb Vance,    April 16,1873 - June 13,1924
PHILLIPS, Mary E.Byrd,    Feb.15,1880 - July 25,1957
            Dau. of J.C. and Martha Miller McEwen

McEWEN, John C.,    Aug.22,1838 - Feb.12,1916
McEWEN, Martha Jane,   Dec.12,1859 - Sept.7,1931

HUGHS, Roseburg,    March 22,1907 - Aug.25,1909

LEDFORD, Susie,   Died Feb.7,1910   - Age 80 years

STREET, Isaac,   Feb.18,1867 - Nov.13,1949
STREET, Lockie,   Oct.23,1865 - -------

LEDFORD, George W.,    June 23,1894 - Oct.30,1979

POWERS, Walter M.,    Sept.21,1897 - May 19,1948
POWERS, Nettie Derafield,    July 16,1898 - April 28,1965
            Dau. of James and Laura Hall Derafield

DAVENPORT, Sarah,    June 28,1808 - Jan.31,1865
            Wife of A. Davenport

HAUN,  Sarah E.,    Feb.16,1842 - Sept.28,1866
            Wife of George Haun

SWINGLE, Lora Alice,    May 11,1852 - Nov.22,1872
            Dau. of B.F. and Margaret Swingle

WHITSON, Blanch,   Nov.6,1909 - Feb.1,1932
WHITSON, Arnald Lee,   March 31,1903 - Aug.17,1910
WHITSON, Burtha May,   Dec.1,1911 - Dec.2,1911
            Children of J.B. and Mollie Whitson

HOPSON, Nicholas Woodfin,   Died Nov.26,1922  - Age 71 years
HOPSON, Phoeba,   Died Dec.4,1918  - Age 62 years

JONES, Donald R.,    Died May 12,1937
          Infant of Robert Jacob and Elizabeth Moat Jones

BARRY, Everett,   Died 1915

WHITSON, Ruth,   Nov.6,1908 - Oct.30,1909
          Dau. of C.W. and Emma Whitson

SWINGLE, Mellisa M.,   June 9,1854 - May 15,1855
          Dau. of E.F. and M.L. Swingle

LUCAS, James W.,   March 3,1850 - June 23,1916
LUCAS, Julia C. Creech,   Feb.9,1860 - May 17,1914

COLLINS, James Walter,   Oct.4,1869 - July 14,1933
COLLINS, Verna Barry,   June 15,1872 - June 19,1938

BARRY, Mary Elizabeth,   April 6,1850 - March2,1907

HANNUM, F.H.,   1837 -1915

BARRY, Charlie A.,   April 6,1875 - Jan.21,1949
BARRY, Senia J.,   June 15,1888 - Feb.3,1976

BENSON, Kathleen H.Barry,   April 10,1877 - March 21,1952
BENSON, Wyeth,   1909 - 1910

HORTON, Rose Penland,   1872 - 1939
          Dau. of Milton Fredrick and Rachel Williams Penland

STREET, James,   1877 - 1938
          Son of Clingman and Evelyn Troutman Street
STREET, Mary Jane,   1879 - ------

PENLAND, Dr. Milton,   1840 - 1916
PENLAND, Louise,   1842 - 1915

GARLAND, Fred D.,   Aug.27,1939 - Sept.19,1939
GARLAND, Freddie A.,   Aug.27,1939 - Oct.4,1939
GARLAND, Charles,   Dec.5,1940 - Dec.18,1940

BRITT, Jewell J.,   Nov.7,1923 - Feb.3,1924

HICKS, Robert Franklin,   April 2,1904 - Feb.22,1926

HICKS, Robert Franklin,   Jan.15,1936 - Feb.14,1936
          Son of George Dewey and Anna Mae Vest Hicks

INGRAM, Nathan,   1862 - 1922
INGRAM, Charles W.,   Nov.27,1879 - Oct.11,1955

SNIDER, Billie and Bert,   Died 1928
SNIDER, Iris,   1918 - 1938
          Dau. of Isaac Newton and Mary Pauline Erwin Snider

STREET, William Jr.,   b/d  Feb.17,1933

INGRAM, Helen C.,   April 14,1935 - May 30,1935
          Dau. of Harley and Virgie McInturff Ingram
INGRAM, Bobby G.,   Oct.21,1933 - Oct.24,1933

CLARK, Silas Paul,   June 13,1908 - April 4,1981
CLARK, Mary Louise,   Oct.30,1946 - Jan.4,1947
          Dau. of Silas and Elva Clark

BRITT, James Ray,   1915 - 1969
          Son of Walter H. and Maude Sutphin Britt

BARNETT, James,   1925 - 1982
BARNETT, Edith M.,   1924 -   ---

MAPLES, Gladys M.,   1911 - 1958

STREET, Luther M.,   1888 - 1974
STREET, Bert L.,   1890 - 1940

KILLINSWORTH, Bertie, Jan.1,1900 - Jan.6,1970

BRIGGS, Geneva,   1912 - 1983
BRIGGS, Gladys,   1921 - 1983   Sisters

BRIGGS, Roger S. "Doots",   Aug.1,1943 - Sept.23,1962
          Son of Ike and Bessie Briggs

BRIGGS, Leonard C.,   1874 - 1959
BRIGGS, Nancy S.,   1881 -   ----

BANKS, James Brian,   1934 - 1973  - SFC U.S.Army Korea
BANKS, Chester,   Dec.12,1899 - May 11,1959
BANKS Alice,   April 9,1907 -   ----

HORTON, Bernie O.,   1898 - 1955
HORTON, Mollie B.,   1894 - 1972

CLARK, Callie S.,   May 27,1914 - April 4,1957

BRADLEY, Worley O.,   1895 - 1944
          Son of Wm. Harrison and Sarah Elizabeth Stallard Bradley
BRADLEY, Millie A. Robinett,   1897 - 1947
BRADLEY, Arthur Harrison,   1920 - 1985 - F2 U.S.Navy  WW2

SONGER, Thomas E.,   1868 - 1926
          Son of Christian and Virginia Early Songer
SONGER, Lydia B.,   (w)  1885 - 1960
          Dau. of Elbert C. and Easter Benfield Britt

SONGER, Virginia L.,   1930 - 1930
          Dau. of Giles E. Sr. and Ella Ashley Songer

SONGER, Giles E. Sr.,   1904 -   ----
        Son of Thomas and Lydia Britt Songer
SONGER, Ella N.,   1907 - 1982
        Dau. of Benjamin B. and Bertha L. Corum Ashley

ASHLEY, William M.,   1909 - 1975

DAVIS, Jake,   1890 - 1967
DAVIS, Mary,   (w#1), 1891 - 1938
        Dau. of Charles and Nancy Lewis Tolley
DAVIS, Maude,   (w#2),  1888 - 1975

ERWIN, I.L.,   1864 - 1943
ERWIN, Margaret,   1867 - 1953

SNIDER, Isaac N.,   July 30,1891 - Aug. 29,1971
SNIDER, Mary P.,   July 24,1901 - Feb.15,1970

ERWIN, J.L.,   1891 - 1956
ERWIN, William Samuel,   Sept.8,1887 - Aug.11,1941
ERWIN, Martha Pugh,   (w),  Aug.29,1890 -   ----

McLAUGHLIN, Emma Bradley,   Dec.30,1899 - July 4,1981
McLAUGHLIN, Clyde,   Sept.3,1903 - June 6,1986
BRADLEY, Roy Milburn,   Feb.8,1893 - May 10,1935
        Son of W.H. and Sarah Stallard Bradley

ROBINETTE, Alvin L.,   Aug.10,1875 - May 25,1952
ROBINETTE, Mary F.,   Dec.5,1877 - July 31,1968

WILSON, M.A.,   April 29,1892 - May 21,1983
WILSON, Ida Mae,   (w),  Nov.24,1894 - Sept.4,1974

JORDAN, Martha H.,   April 7,1890 - Jan.17,1982

FROST, Eva E.,   July 10,1897 - Oct.12,1985

MOYERS, Charles D.,   May 20,1914 - April 19,1964
        Son of James and Dinah Deaton Moyers
MOYERS, Ruth Lyle,   (w),  Sept.21,1920 -   ----

MOYERS, James W.,   May 2,1876 - Jan.24,1960
MOYERS, Adinah D.,   Sept.12,1888 - Dec.9,1972

HOWELL, Edgar,   1905 - 1981
HOWELL, Pearl t.,   1913 -   ----

HOWELL, Lester F.,   July 18,1910 -   ----
HOWELL, Ethel R.,   Nov.22,1909 - Feb.25,1987

JORDAN, Hurcle J.,   1917 - 1981 - Sgt. U.S.Army   WW2
JORDAN, Ellene,   1922 -   ----

(continued)

HOPSON, John Wesley,   July 19,1980
            Infant son of Jeff and Jennie Hopson

WHITE, Alvin,   Aug.6,1906 - April 20, 1984 -Pvt U.S.Army  WW2
WHITE, Edith L., (w), 1914 - 1975

HOPSON, Jacob A.,   1883 - 1973
HOPSON, Hassie P.,   (w),  1893 - 1980
HOPSON, Charles Eugene,   Feb.3,1918 - May 9,1939
HOPSON, Ross A.,   July 3,1920 - April 51,1963 - PFC 16 Field Hosp
                                                            WW 2
McNABB, Charles S.,   Sept.23,1883 -Nov.8,1955
McNABB, Robert Pierce,   Aug.6,1886 - July 23,1966

McNABB, Virgie,   1884 - 1960
McNABB, Nannie,   1874 - 1945
            Dau. of John B. and Eliza Miller Laws

SEWARD, Frank J.,   Dec.1,1912 - May 14,1958

McINTURFF, Shep,   1883 - 1960
            Son of N.K. and Julia McInturff
McINTURFF, Lelia,   1888 - 1976
            Maiden name McNabb

McINTURFF, Kenneth,   Feb.23,1929 - Jan.30,1988
McINTURFF, Naomi,   March 19,1931 - ----

JONES, Mack H.,   1906 - 1961
JONES, Mabel M.,   1910 - ----

MILLER John D.,   Sept.17,1908 - July 12,1968
MILLER, Pearl H.,   Aug.26,1911 - Aug.29,1965

MILLER, Sam J.,   March 8,1920 - July 18,1955  - S/Sgt

HAWKINS, Sallie,   Dec.30,1884 - Jan.29,1973
HAWKINS, Mabel Kathleen,   Aug.25,1907 - May 22,1945

PERRY, Dillard E.,   1904 - ----
PERRY, Juanita B.,   1912 - ----

DAVIS, Nervie Sneed,   1915 - 1947

BRITT, Walter H.,   1877 - 1945
            Son of Elbert C. and Nancy Ann Brummett Britt
BRITT, A.Maude,   1880 - 1945
            Maiden name Sutphin

MAY, Robert Lee,   July 24,1910 - ----
MAY, Hazel Opal,   March 2,1912 - Aug.13,1976
            Dau. of Walter H. and Maude Sutphin Britt

SWINGLE CEMETERY (continued)

## UNMARKED GRAVES

BAKER, Edna, Jan.9,1847 - June 26,1931
   Dau. of Bert Lyle

BRADLEY, Kenneth Richard, Died March 2,1942
   Infant of Richard Elmo and Gladys Sparks Bradley

CUTSHAW, Malinda Emogene, Died May 28, 1940 - Age 3

GOSNELL, Steven Dale, Died May 6,1952
   Infant of Buster Gosnell

HOWELL, Mary Lavada, March 1,1866 - April 1,1958
   Dau. of Mack and ----Adkins Headrick

HOWELL, Sidney, Died Nov.24,1934 - Age 61
   Son of James and Livitia Atkins Howell

JENKINS, Julia Ann, Died Dec.19,1939 - Age 75
   Dau. of Rick and Rebecca West McInturff

JONES, Guy Elwood, April 15,1919 - Oct.16,1962
   Son of Albert G. and Delia Hopson Jones

MILLER, Richard Roy, Died July 23,1941 - Age 1 year
   Son of John David and Pearl Hankins Miller

MILLER, William Elbert, Died July 25, 1938 - Age 71
   Son of Jack and Susan Sweeney Miller

PETERSON, Bert, Died April 16,1964

WILSON, Betty Sue, Died Nov.22,1937
   Infant of Ernest and Pearl Barnett Wilson

SONGER, Virginia Lydia, Feb.19,1930 - Feb.26,1930

## AYERS CEMETERY

Norton Hollow Road, on right, .6 mi. from Rock Creek Road

Copied May 30, 1988

HARLEY, Mary Ruth,   d. June 16, 1938  (1 year old)

LOVE, James,     1934 - 1939
LOVE, Joyce Lou, 1936 - 1936
LOVE, Penny Jo,  1948 - 1948
LOVE, (Infant),

BOSTON, Lillian,  1899 - 1984

EDWARDS, Andy,    1892 - 1958

AYERS, Seen,   Nov. 15, 1888 - Feb. 15, 1944
        Cpl. 161st Inf., WWI


                    plus several unmarked graves, including:

AYERS, David Floyd,  b/d Dec. 15, 1931
        Son of Sol and Ida Day Ayers


## HAUN CEMETERY

Norton Hollow Road, on right, .3 mi. from Rock Creek Road

Copied May 30, 1988

HAUN, Peter,
        Co. B., 3NC Mtd. Inf., Union Army

WHITE, Julia Reed,  May 9, 1859 - Apr. 3, 1931- widow of Peter
        Wife of W. N. White                              Haun
        Daughter of William and Maggie Miller Reed
KIRK, Jack,   1908 - 1957

GREENE, Bruce Lattie,   Feb. 14, 1931 - Sep. 7, 1981
GREENE, Ruby C.,  Aug. 9, 1934 -

HAUN, Bret Allen,  b/d Oct. 1, 1985

BEZDEK, Albert,    1897 - 1984
BEZDEK, Winnie Haun (w),  1901 - 1975

HAUN, Herman C.,  Mar. 22, 1904 -
HAUN, Sarah E. (w),  Nov. 14, 1903 - Apr. 10, 1981
HAUN, Jimmy Hobart,  Apr. 5, 1933 - July 6, 1934
        Son of Herman and Sarah Miller Haun

HAUN, Samuel George,   Jan. 1, 1940 - May 13, 1970

HAUN, William Earl,    Sep. 25, 1911 - Apr. 9, 1970

HAUN CEMETERY - (continued)

HAUN, Terry Lawrence,    d. Apr. 4, 1945
        Son of Lawrence and Gladys Haun

HARDIN, Clyde,    1907 - 1964
HARDIN, Maude,    1904 - 1982

KLOPFER, Mable Gladys,  1917 - 1986

WHITE, Blaine,    July 11, 1906 -
WHITE, Myrtle,    Jan.  8, 1910 - Apr. 10, 1986

WHITE, Stephen,    Oct. 24, 1956 - Feb. 12, 1975
WHITE, Frank,    b/d Mar. 1, 1940
WHITE, J. B.,    Nov. 7,  1936 - Nov. 21, 1936

WHITE, Glenn Franklin,  Aug. 3, 1954 - Dec. 15, 1976 "son"

POTTER, Dwight W.,    1951 - 1984

POTTER, Stanley W.,    1932 - 1982

EDWARDS, Dave,    Sep. 25, 1899 - May 16, 1931
        Son of John and Hester Poor Edwards
EDWARDS, Francis (w),   July 31, 1904 -

SMITH, Horace L.,    1898 - 1962
SMITH, Addie Lee,    1898 - 1976

HAUN, Effie,    1895 - 1923
HAUN, John Loyd,    1921 - 1922
        Son of Peter L. and Effie Haun

SMITH, D. Richard,  1863 - 1923
SMITH, Molly,    1859 - 1956

HAUN, Arthur,    June 1, 1888 - May 8, 1965
        Pvt. in Air Service, WWI
        Son of George and Loretta Honeycutt Haun

HAUN, Dan'l.,
        Cpl., Co. B, 3rd NC Mtd. Inf.,  Union Army

HAUN, Margaret Perry,  Aug. 20, 1848 - Mar. 12, 1880
        "Our sister"

KIRK, W. C.,
        Co. E, 38th U.S. Vol. Inf.

KIRK, Dan'l.,
        Co. E, 2nd NC Mtd. Inf., Union Army

BENNETT, Archibald,
        Co. F, 3rd NC Mtd. Inf.,  Union Army

HUNNICUTT, Martha C.,  Nov. 10, 1850 - Nov. 9, 1921
        Wife of S. B. Hunnicutt

HAUN, George W.,  1867 - 1922
HAUN, Loretta (w), 1870 - 1951


                plus many unmarked graves, including:

JONES, Shirley,  infant,  d. Apr. 24, 1937
        Daughter of Mitchell and Ollie Simmons Jones

McCURRY, Mack,   July 15, 1886 - Oct. 5, 1955
        Son of Washington and Harriett Tipton McCurry

TAPP, William,   age 67,  d. Dec. 31, 1946
        Son of Vince Tapp


## JOHNSON CEMETERY

North Main and Elm Street, Erwin

Copied May 31, 1988

JOHNSON, James V.,  May 6, 1810 - June 17, 1876
        Son of Noel Johnson
JOHNSON, Mary McInturff (w),  May 20, 1819 - July 20, 1883
        Daughter of John "Crowner" & Rachel Edna Scott McInturff

            plus two unmarked graves:

JOHNSON, Noel,   1798 - 1888
        Son of William Johnson

JOHNSON, Nancy Lucy,
        Daughter of Patrick Henry Johnson


## BOOTH CEMETERY

  Fishery Road, Erwin, just S. of access road for Main
  Street exit to expressway
                        Copied May 31, 1988

BOOTHE, Florence C.,  Nov. 21, 1874 - Jan. 8, 1886

BOOTH, Frank,   May 20, 1909 - Sep. 11, 1910
        Son of W. H. and Margaret Booth

BOOTH, A. H.,   1840 - 1922
BOOTH, M. F.,   1842 - 1920

                also 1 unmarked stone

# DAY CEMETERY
## (Also called Booth Cemetery)

.2 mile SE of Main Street exit of Expressway, in Erwin,
on Roy Day farm
### Copied Apr. 24, 1988

AYERS, Infant,　d. 1961

BOOTH, C. H.,　1887 - 1923

BOOTH, Lora D.,　1869 - 1928

BOOTHE, Hiram,
　　　　Sgt., Co. B, 12th Tenn. Cav., Union Army
　　　　Son of John and Elizabeth Parks Booth
BOOTHE, Elizabeth Reed (w),　May 1, 1851 - Jan. 26, 1923

BROWN, Fred Clifford,　Apr. 21, 1893 - Oct. 12, 1965
　　　　US Army, WWI
BROWN, Ella Day (w),　Jan. 22, 1895 - Apr. 4, 1922
　　　　married Apr. 18, 1917

BROWN, Infant,　d. 1928

DAY, Alex A.,　Feb. 23, 1855 - Nov. 28, 1941
DAY, Sarah E. (w),　Mar. 1, 1872 - Dec. 4, 1959
　　　　married Nov. 12, 1891

DAY, Anna Mae Johnson,　Nov. 4, 1921 - Feb. 11, 1972

DAY, Charles Walter,　Sep. 2, 1892 - July 5, 1974
DAY, Myrtle Hampton,　Apr. 30, 1896 - Nov. 30, 1927

DAY, Charles Woodard (Woodward),　July 19, 1913 - Jan. 17, 1944

DAY, Ernest Lester,　Apr. 15, 1917 - Oct. 8, 1968
　　　　S/Sgt. 678th AC&W Sq. , WWII

DAY, James,　d. Apr. 17, 1939
　　　　Infant son of C. W. and Fannie Day

DAY, Leonard,　Nov. 18, 1914 - Dec. 30, 1916
　　　　Son of Charles Walter and Myrtle Day

DAY, Tommy,　Oct. 26, 1951 - Oct. 23, 1969

HARVEY, Gracia Cornelia Booth, May 29, 1887 - Feb. 26, 1931
　　　　Daughter of Hiram and Elizabeth Reed Booth

KIRK, Robert,　1875 - 1927

McINTURFF, David Andrew (Andy),　1891 - 1951

McINTURFF, Nora E.,　Mar. 13, 1906 - Feb. 3, 1913
　　　　Daughter of David A. and Lona McInturff

MILLER, Henry C., Oct. 10, 1892 - Apr. 10, 1894
    Son of John and Jennie Miller

MILLER, John, 1826 - Mar. 31, 1900
    Co. A, 3rd NC Mtd. Inf., Union Army

MILLER, Willard, b/d Sep. 13, 1914
    Infant son of N. T. and M. M. Miller

NELSON, David, Apr. 10, 1855 - Oct. 30, 1931

NELSON, Isaac, Mar. 7, 1851 - Sep. 18, 1936
    Son of John and Nancy Whitson Nelson
NELSON, Sabra Putnam, Aug. 18, 1861 - Aug. 27, 1928

NELSON, Tom, Feb. 15, 1857 - Jan. 19, 1933

SALTS, Infants, b/d Jan. 26, 1915
    Daughters of W. M. and L. B. Salts

ULRICH, Gus Adolph, d. Oct. 18, 1937
    Engineman 1st Class, US Navy, from Texas

DAY, Henrietta Marie, Aug. 23, 1935 - Oct. 10, 1947
    (located near the barn at the Day Farm)

    ADDITIONS from Charles M. Bennett, Jan. 2, 1961:
            (no longer visible in 1988)

ADKINS, Edythe, d. Apr. 9, 1945 at 21

CANTRELL, Billy Glenn, b/d Oct. 22, 1952

TITTLE, Laura, 1866 - 1953

DAY, Mrs. Mabel, d. June 7, 1948 at 82


            plus many unmarked graves, including:

MILLER, Saraphina, born c. 1829 - d. July 7, 1889
    Daughter of William and Emaline Mitchell Miller

DAY, Infant, Aug. 5, 1937 (d.)
    Child of George William and Florence Smith Day

HARRIS, Grover Carter, d. Mar. 12, 1937
    Son of Harrison and Maggie Nelson Harris

NELSON, Ella Belle, age 53 - d. Mar. 13, 1934
    Daughter of Hiram and Elizabeth Reed Booth

NELSON, Floyd Headrick, age 8 - Aug. 21, 1942
    Son of Joe Henry and Geneva McCurry Nelson

NELSON, Geneva McCurry, age 36, d. Aug. 12, 1937
        Daughter of Wilburn Henry Nelson

NELSON, Joseph Henry, age 45, d. July 21, 1941
        Son of Thomas and Molly Day Nelson


## ERWIN #1 CEMETERY

Sandy Bottom Road to Polly Erwin Road, .5 mi. west of
Route 19/23 at foot of River Hill

Copied May 31, 1988

GRIFFITH, Joe, 1870 - 1941

BENNETT, Mrs. Fannie H., 1902 - 1941
BENNETT, unk.,
BENNETT, unk.,

HIGGINS, Jackie C. (baby), d. Jan. 28, 1973

SANDERS, Seth (baby), d. 1982

TIPTON, Charles, 1875 - 1947
TIPTON, Ibbey, 1885 - 1982

TIPTON, Ancil T., Oct. 16, 1917 - July 19, 1968
TIPTON, Ethel W., Sep. 29, 1916 -

LAWING, William M., 1889 - 1958
LAWING, Bessie, 1892 - 1939

LAWING, Rickey Dean, (baby), d. 1962
LAWING, Douglas Taylor, 1914 - 1957

HARRIS, Lula, May 28, 1900 - May 20, 1976

HARRIS, Glen, Feb. 11, 1928 - Feb. 26, 1986, US Army

HYATT, Isaac Jacob, May 18, 1875 - Mar. 14, 1958

TIPTON, Bonnie, (baby), d. 1943

TIPTON, Madgeline, 1929 - 1936

FROST, Magdalene, Aug. 9, 1957 - Apr. 3, 1962
        Daughter of Aaron and Ruby Frost

ERWIN, Gaither C., Nov. 4, 1893 - July 4, 1973
        Pvt., US Army, WWI
ERWIN, Vida Nanettie, Sep. 28, 1899 -

INGLE, William G., Jan. 10, 1855 - June 27, 1938
        Son of Isaac and Sally Penix Ingle
INGLE, Elizabeth C., May 1,1852 - Feb.23,1924

INGLE (ENGLE), Thomas Clingman,  May 17, 1876 - Jan. 11, 1961
        Son of Wm. Gaither and Elizabeth Chapman Engle
INGLE, Elizabeth (w#1),  Dec. 25, 1876 - July 10, 1908
INGLE, Maggie B. Hughes (w#2),  Jan. 31, 1884 - Feb. 25, 1940

INGLE, Tracy,  Dec. 5, 1902 - Sep. 13, 1903
        Daughter of T. C. and E. J. Ingle
INGLE, Willie Viola,  Feb. 6, 1914 - Feb. 13, 1917
        Daughter of T. C. and M. B. Ingle

HARRIS, Farris,  Mar. 2, 1904 - Oct. 2, 1966
HARRIS, Blanch,  June 6, 1914 -

HARRIS, Katherine Jean,  1950 - 1952

PRICE, Furman,  1903 - 1973

COGGINS, Arthur,  1913 - 1971
COGGINS, Florence,  1920 -

COGGINS, Henry,  1937 - 1987

HARRIS, Charlie Lee,  Nov. 28, 1895 - Sep. 25, 1980
HARRIS, Pansy C. (w),  Apr. 4, 1915 -
        married May 8, 1931

HARRIS, Wilma A.,  June 18, 1934 - Jan. 12, 1943

RUNION, Cecile Yvonne,  Feb. 4, 1922 - Jan. 2, 1973

ERWIN, Eugene,  1931 - 1932
        Son of Arthur and Bertha Erwin

ERWIN, George K.,  Apr. 26, 1868 - Dec. 16, 1930
        Son of Samuel Erwin
ERWIN, Mary Jane D.,  Feb. 10, 1869 - Oct. 22, 1966
        Maiden name Duncan
ERWIN, Jesse,  1892 - 1926

CALLAHAN, Ora Lee,  June 11, 1903 - Dec. 7, 1903
        Daughter of J. W. and R. M. Callahan

RUNION, Glena Erwin,  Aug. 7, 1898 - Feb. 1, 1933
        Wife of B. L. Runion

BENNETT, Ada M.,  1898 - 1964

HENSLEY, Rosie,  Mar. 9, 1907 - June 9, 1972

HENSLEY, Joe,  Mar. 8, 1879 - Nov. 16, 1948
HENSLEY, Mary (w),  Apr. 13, 1882 - Dec. 25, 1950
HENSLEY, Mack (son),  May 4, 1918 - Sep. 15, 1935
        Son of J.C. and Mary Louise Shehan Hensley

HENSLEY, Tom,   Aug. 3, 1922 - Feb. 24, 1957
          Pvt., Co. I, 423rd Inf., 106 Inf. Div., WWII

DUNCAN, James Lawson,   1858 - 1938 - Son of Frank and Katherine
DUNCAN, Alice (w#1),   Apr. 19, 1869 - Apr. 29, 1902      \Dugger
DUNCAN, Creola Bean (w#2),   1878 - 1962      \Duncan
          Daughter of C. R. and Margaret Brown Bean

FRITTZ, Andy H.,   Sep. 20, 1876 - Aug. 21, 1947
FRITTZ, Lula Pearl Duncan (w),   May 2, 1884 - Apr. 22, 1918
FRITTZ, Robert Earl (son),   Apr. 15, 1915 - Sep. 26, 1935
FRITTZ, Willie (son),   Nov. 24, 1908 - Oct. 21, 1910
FRITTZ, Rollie (son),   Aug. 22, 1910 - Sep. 16, 1910

DEATON, Fitzhugh R.,   1898 - Mar.17,1988
DEATON, Cansadia M.,   1903 - 1980

DEATON, Howard,   1939 - 1940
DEATON, Virginia, 1929 - 1942
          siblings

DUNCAN, Walter L.,   Feb. 1, 1883 - Oct. 29, 1966

ERWIN, Bessie E.,   1898 - 1903
          Daughter of J. K. and Lula Erwin

CORBY, Anna Mae,   Mar. 22, 1905 - Apr. 7, 1923
          Daughter of L. H. Griffith

GRIFFITH, Lemuel H.,   1880 - 1962
GRIFFITH, Lodemmac,   1882 - 1960

FORBES, Elijah,   1850 - 1939- Son of Simon and Rachel
FORBES, Jacester, 1857 - 1938      \Early Forbes

LEDFORD, Mary Josephine Forbs,   1894 - 1948
          Dau. of Elijah and Sister Stewart Forbes
HENSLEY, Alice H.,   1888 - 1975

TIPTON, Maggie,   Mar. 18, 1903 - Aug. 9, 1943

BENNETT, Julia,   1871 - 1943

BENNETT, Isaac,   June 8, 1911 - Aug. 7, 1939

BENNETT, Elva,   d -

LOVETT, Anna,   1875 - 1958

LOVETT, Owen S. (Stewart),   d. July 11, 1936
          Son of John Henry and Annie Higgins Lovette
          Pvt. 138th Engineers, Tenn.

FORBES, Robert,   1885 - 1937

FORBES, Jesse,   1891 - 1930
     Son of E.H. and Serba Stuart Forbes
FORBES, R.,       d. -

BEAM, W. R.,   June 7, 1873 - June 29, 1904

EDWARDS, Norman,   1880 - 1959
EDWARDS, Rosie,   1892 - 1935

TIPTON, Ferrell E.,   Sep. 27, 1912 - Feb. 6, 1946

TIPTON, Jimmy A.,   b/d 1966

TIPTON, Sam H.,   May 10, 1886 - Sep. 15, 1968
TIPTON, Sarah Beam,   June 15, 1892 - Apr. 6, 1946

TIPTON, George W.,   Mar. 3, 1907 - Dec. 10, 1955
     Son of Sam Harrison and Sarah Bean Tipton
HUGHES, James,   b. June 17, 1881
HUGHES, Etta B.,   Oct. 6, 1885 - Mar. 27, 1962

SHEHAN, Lattie,   Apr. 29, 1907 - Nov. 10, 1963
     Son of Jack and Sarah Ann Hensley Shehan

SULLINS, Matthew,   b/d 1963

HARRIS, Jim D.,   1866 - 1940

HARRIS, Buell,   1872 (1869?) - 1942
HARRIS, Tildie,   1884 - 1940 - Dau.of Will R. and Jennie Guinn
HARRIS, Earnie,   d. 1928                                    Tilson

STANLEY, Billie,   Dec. 5, 1934 - Nov. 4, 1939
     Son of Jim and Pauline Stanley

BENNETT, Tony,   Apr. 6, 1949 - Apr. 8, 1949

ERWIN, W. Lewis,   1884 - 1941
MERRILL, Bertha Erwin,   1892 - 1971   (Widow of Lewis Erwin)
MERRILL, Alex,   1886 - 1981 - (Bertha's 2nd husband)

TIPTON, Helen Elizabeth,   Apr. 9, 1938 - Oct. 8, 1938
     Dau. of Brady and Ola Calloway Tipton
HUGHES, Claudette,   Oct. 8, 1937 - Sep. 3, 1938
HUGHES, Mildred,   Apr. 8, 1931 - Apr. 8, 1931
HUGHES, Burnie,   Jan. 11, 1935 - Jan. 28, 1935
HUGHES, Baby,   Mar. 14, 1936 - Mar. 14, 1936
HUGHES, Brenda Sue,   Sep. 19, 1943 - May 15, 1944
HUGHES, C. J.,   Aug. 30, 1942 - Jan. 31, 1944
     Children of Dolphus and Bertie Taylor Hughes (?)
DUNCAN, Joseph E.,   Oct. 10, 1871 - Sep. 15, 1945
DUNCAN, Ethel Erwin (w),   Mar. 17, 1882 - Sep. 19, 1911
DUNCAN, Baby,   d. Sep. 30, 1910

ERWIN #1 CEMETERY - (continued)

ERWIN, Phillip P.,    Apr. 9, 1841 - Feb. 3, 1927

CALLAHAN, William,    1830 - Nov. 30, 1907

FOSTER, Alice,    1883 - 1962

FOSTER, Clarence, 1912 - 1965
        Son of Avery and Alice Jones Foster

HENSON, Mable F.,    1920 - 1970

FORD, Joshua,    Oct. 31, 1879 - Sep. 6, 1954
FORD, Florence,    1886 - 1963

HENSLEY, Howell,    1909 - 1959
HENSLEY, Amanda J. (w),    1908 -
        married Nov. 7, 1931

HENSLEY, Baby,    Dec. 22, 1945 - Dec. 24, 1945
        Daughter of John H. and Ettalee Hensley

EDWARDS, Lenvil,    1897 - 1975
EDWARDS, Joanna M.,    1908 -

DUNCAN, Luther,    Nov. 17, 1884 - Dec. 16, 1968
DUNCAN, Etta B.,    Oct. 8, 1890 - Aug.  2, 1974

DUNCAN, Baby,    d. Sep. 30, 1919
        Daughter of N. C. and Fannie Duncan

DUNCAN, Frank M.,    Dec. 10, 1830 - July 16, 1915
DUNCAN, Cathern,    Jan. 23, 1839 - Mar. 17, 1916

DUNCAN, Andy J.,    1874 - 1941

DUNCAN, David F.,    May 8, 1880 - Jan. 7, 1965

EDWARDS, Allen,    Feb. 28, 1871 - May 12, 1946
EDWARDS, Sarah,    b. Sep. 8, 1873


            plus many unmarked graves, including:

FRANKS, Garrett Murray,    age 86 - Aug. 4, 1935
        Son of Garrett and Dixie Callahan Franks
FRANKS, Harriett Keever (w),    age 88 - d. May 29, 1936
        Daughter of Safrona Ledford

HARRIS, Herman,    age 1 - d. Jan. 6, 1933
        Son of Conda and Lula Thomas Harris

LOVETTE, Mrs. Bertha,    age 24 - d. Oct. 13, 1932
        Daughter of David and Sarah Tipton Garland

RUNION, Berry Lee,    age 47 - d. Nov. 1, 1940
        Son of George Samuel and Nan Jenkins Runion

SHEHAN, Sarah Ann,   Mar. 15, 1882 - July 28, 1964
          Maiden name Hensley
 FRITTZ, Sarah Ann, Infant

## TINKER #1 CEMETERY

.1 mile from Rt. 23, behind Ernestville Freewill Baptist
Church.

Copied June 1, 1988

McINTURFF, Sarah E. Tinker,   Oct. 4, 1835 - May 23, 1885
          Wife of John Scott McInturff

McINTURFF, Laura E. Brumet,   Nov. 16, 1863 - July 16, 1893
          Wife of William A. McInturff (Son of J.S.McInturff)
          Married May 18, 1888

McINTURFF, Bennie H.,   Apr. 25, 1889 - July 4, 1893
McINTURFF, Julia,       Mar. 12, 1892 - June 29, 1893

RUNION, G. S.,   Feb. 11, 1868 - Feb. 10, 1897

TINKER, Samuel,   Dec. 11, 1818 - Aug. 28, 1910

TINKER, R. L.,   Mar. 1, 1829 - Aug. 12, 1879
          2nd Lt., Co. M, 8th Tenn. Cav., Union Army

CLOUSE, Robert,   Apr. 25, 1856 - Nov. 5, 1931
CLOUSE, M. L. (w),   Sep. 3, 1857 - July 22, 1930

TINKER, James P.,   Feb. 18, 1863 - Jan. 4, 1928
TINKER, Maggie Masters,   Jan. 27, 1871 - Jan. 25, 1946

TINKER, Robert L. Jr.,   Dec. 9, 1862 - Mar. 21, 1926
TINKER, Percilla (Priscilla?), Mar. 8, 1872 - Dec. 14, 1959
          Maiden name Taylor

TINKER, William C.,   1903 - 1957

TINKER, George W.,   1901 - 1969

TINKER, William Guy,   1916 - 1957

TINKER, Roy,   d. Apr. 11, 1938 at 27 yrs
          Son of J. P. and Maggie Masters Tinker

McKINNEY, Rex T.,   1903 - 1934

TINKER, Charley B.,   Oct. 25, 1892 - Apr. 8, 1949
          Pvt., 45th Inf., 9th Div., WWI

TINKER, James R.,   1903 - 1971

TINKER #1 CEMETERY - (continued)

TINKER, Eli,   Dec. 26, 1906 - Mar. 2, 1963
          Son of James P. and Maggie Masters Tinker

TINKER, Jesse,  Feb. 5, 1896 - July 22, 1950
          Cpl., 306th Eng. 81st Div., WWI

PEAKE, Richard W.,  Sep. 6, 1934 - June 24, 1935
          Son of Oscar B. and Ida T. Peake

WHITE, Roxie Lillian Tinker, - Sep. 12, 1918 - Oct. 13, 1958

TIPTON, Barbara Ann,  Aug. 5, 1944 - Aug. 10, 1944

TINKER, William Samuel,  Mar. 31, 1894 - Oct. 2, 1950

McCURRY, Mae Bell Tinker,  July 11, 1898 - June 16, 1984
          Wife of Wm. S. Tinker, and wife of ------- McCurry

TINKER, Rosa Lee,  1915 - 1984


                plus many unmarked graves

ADDITIONS: from Charles M. Bennett, Dec. 7, 1960:
              (no longer visible in 1988)

WHITE, Infant,   d. Apr. 28, 1954

CUMBIE, Russell Charles Jr.,  d. Mar. 2, 1949


                TINKER #2 CEMETERY

    Lower Higgins Creek Road, Off Rt. 23/19 .4 mile to
    wooden bridge on left
                    Copied June 2, 1988

SAMS, Clifford,  Jan. 18, 1959 - Oct. 1, 1983
SAMS, Linda Lou,  1960 - 1961
        Daughter of Clarence and Dolly Britt Sams
SAMS,  (no name or date)

SAMS, Ruby,   b/d 1922

HIGGINS,  (no name or date)

SAMS, Walter T.,  Oct. 15, 1886 - June 16, 1944
SAMS, Lovada R.,  Jan. 19, 1894 - Feb. 1, 1976

HOLCOMBE, Allie,  1916 - 1961
HOLCOMBE, Mary Lou,  d. in infancy


                    - 192 -

TINKER #2 CEMETERY - (continued)

SAMS, Will L.,    Oct. 17, 1883 - Feb. 18, 1948
SAMS, Cora L. (w),  Aug. 26, 1900 - June 18, 1929
SAMS, Katherine,    d. in infancy
SAMS, Clyde,        d. in infancy
SAMS, Etta,         d. in infancy
SAMS, Robert,       d. in infancy

SAMS, Fred,    Aug. 16, 1923 - Jan. 28, 1986
         Son of W. L. and Cora Sams

ROBERTS, John Hicks,  d. June 16, 1934 (baby)

WARDRUPE, Mona L.,  1959 - 1986

TINKER, John,    1876 - 1961
TINKER, Dorothy (w),  1877 - 1906
TINKER, Sam (son),   1900 - 1917
TINKER, Cling (son),  1903 - 1987
TINKER, John Jr. (son),  1905 - 1937

WARDRUPE, Joe L.,  Jan. 15, 1891 - Nov. 4, 1978
WARDRUPE, Minnie A.,  Feb. 12, 1894 - May 3, 1986
WARDRUPE, Howard,  d. June 2, 1935, at 18 yrs

SAMS, Cling,  1916 - 1976,  Tec5, US Army, WWII

SAMS, Cleng,  d. 1917

EVANS, George,  1860 - 1933

EVANS (EVENS?), Sada S.,  1892 - 1918

SAMS, Rebecia Foster,  Aug. 5, 1856 - June 5, 1932

SAMS, Mary Lou,  d. 1923

SAMS, Conway,  1898 - 1924

SAMS, Arthur,  1882 - 1942

SAMS, John Henry,  1889 - 1953

SAMS, Fannie Hodge,  1883 - 1960

SAMS, Robert,  1894 - 1982

SAMS, (no name or date)

SAMS, Floyd Lee,  Dec. 3, 1920 - May 17, 1983
SAMS, Bonnie M.,  May 11, 1941 -

             plus many unmarked graves

# CLEAR BRANCH B. C. CEMETERY

Clear Branch Road, behind church, .7 mi. from Rt. 23

Copied June 2, 1988

TILSON, Lattie Estil, Sep. 26, 1917 - May 20, 1979
     Sgt., USA, WWII
TILSON, Adell, Nov. 28, 1923 -

TILSON, Ottie W., Aug. 16, 1907 - Sep. 13, 1976
TILSON, Pauline D., Apr. 12, 1925 -

TILSON, George Franklin, 1883 - 1969
TILSON, Matilda E. (w), 1888 - 1958
     Married Nov. 11, 1906

TILSON, Alvin E., May 7, 1915 -
TILSON, Gladys W., Sep. 17, 1916 - Sep. 18, 1986

FOSTER, Larkin J., July 2, 1887 - Feb. 6, 1942
FOSTER, Minta L. Edwards, Dec. 6, 1891 - Feb. 12, 1973

GUINN, Deadrick R., Feb. 8, 1913 - June 8, 1969
GUINN, Gertrude, June 17, 1916 -

GUINN, Krista Dianne, Feb. 11, 1971 - Feb. 13, 1971

GUINN, Baby, b/d Mar. 8, 1921
     Daughter of O. F. and Maud Guinn

WILLIS, Thomas F., Aug. 29, 1882 - Jan. 12, 1964
     Son of Wm. J. and Martha Guinn Willis
WILLIS, Loretta C., Mar. 28, 1885 - July 2, 1956

HENSLEY, Burgess G., May 6, 1877 - Dec. 1, 1962
HENSLEY, Tilda Jane, May 5, 1880 - Jan. 19, 1959
     Daughter of Frank and Lenna Hensley Foster

HENSLEY, Eva Mae, July 26, 1906 - May 24, 1941

TILSON, Elmer, Feb. 5, 1912 -
TILSON, Zilpha, Feb. 18, 1910 -

TILSON, William J., Feb. 6, 1865 (1868?) - June 15, 1951
TILSON, Barbara, Oct. 27, 1880 - June 26, 1970

WATSON, William G., Oct. 22, 1887 - Mar. 19, 1943
WATSON, Rebecca M., 1890 - 1966
WATSON, Fannie M., d. 1920
WATSON, Edith C., d. 1917

POORE, Burnie, Apr. 16, 1898 - Dec. 16, 1955
POORE, Eliza, Oct. 11, 1892 - Jan. 5, 1978

TILSON, Susie Etta, (baby?) - no date

LANE, Infant,   b/d Jan. 28, 1954
        Son of Hubert Lane

TILSON, Brenda Ellen,   Aug. 27, 1948 - Nov. 24, 1948
        Daughter of Reuben Clyde & Kylene Ellen Richards Tilson

TILSON, Reuben C.,   June 8, 1928 - Jan. 21, 1986
TILSON, Kylene Ellen,   Sep. 15, 1931 - July 15, 1970

TILSON, Mandy,   1900 - 1981

TILSON, Joe Enry (Henry?),   1894 - 1983

GILBERT, Rev. H. W.,   Nov. 5, 1811 - Nov. 16, 1894
GILBERT, Berzilla,   Aug. 27, 1817 - July 19, 1889

EDWARDS, Sarah C.,   Oct. 8, 1866 - Oct. 5, 1912
        Wife of A. Edwards
EDWARDS, Son of A. & S. Edwards, d. 1892

EDWARDS, Son of E. & V. Edwards, d. 1932
EDWARDS, Son of E. & V. Edwards, d. 1940

GILLIS, Infant,   June 1884 - June 1884
        Child of W. J. and Mary Gillis

FARNOR, Rev. Jacob S.,   Aug. 16, 1854 - Feb. 3, 1934
FARNOR, Rebecca Jane Hardon,   Jan. 23, 1852 - Feb. 16, 1939
FARNOR, Horace H.,   Jan. 15, 1894 - Dec. 14, 1897

FARNOR, Jacob H.,   Nov. 8, 1873 - Mar. 29, 1917

BAILEY, Clara Farnor,   Mar. 9, 1891 - Sep. 7, 1976

FARNOR, Edith Lloyd,   1917 - 1952

LLOYD, W. Frank,   1890 - 1977
LLOYD, Bertha S.,   1892 - 1980   (1893 - 1979?)

FARNOR, John B.,   May 24, 1878 - Mar. 30, 1936
        Son of Jacob S. and Rebecca Jane Hardin Farnor
FARNOR, Nancy Melvina,   July 13, 1878 - Dec. 24, 1964

FARNOR, Carl Floyd,   Sep. 27, 1916 - Sep. 30, 1984
        US Navy, WWII
FARNOR, Sarah Geneva Sams,   Aug. 25, 1919 -

HENSLEY, Allison W.,   1873 - Jan. 23, 1938
        Son of Silas and Sally Hensley
HENSLEY, Cordelia,   1876 - 1970

HENSLEY, Walter,   Apr. 29, 1898 - Jan. 3, 1967
HENSLEY, Loretta,   Jan. 18, 1896 - Jan. 16, 1982

CHAIT, Adam Jonas,   June 25, 1964 - June 26, 1964
        Son of Neil and Patsy Chait

CLEAR BRANCH CEMETERY - (continued)

FRYE, Carolyn Sue,   Dec. 13, 1934 - Mar. 21, 1935
          Daughter of Dewey Frye

HENSLEY, Glenn,   July 22, 1918 - Sep. 15, 1985

CHANDLER, Clyde T.,   June 3, 1909 - Oct. 11, 1910
          Son of J. H. and Sallie Chandler

EDWARDS, Nancy,   Apr. 1, 1852 - Mar. 14, 1914
          (Erected by her only son, Allison Edwards)

WILLIS, Robert,   Apr. 14, 1889 - Mar. 25, 1980
WILLIS, Kate L.,   Apr.  7, 1896 - Sep.  6, 1968

EDWARDS, Lee Clifton,   1905 - 1950
EDWARDS, Creola Chandler (w#1),   Jan. 8, 1902 - Jan. 16, 1924
EDWARDS, Carrie Riddle (w#2), 1906 -

BAXTER, Jacob F.,   Feb. 16, 1897 - May 16, 1920

WOOLF, Philip,   June 5, 1915 - Jan. 19, 1919

BAXTER, Byrd D.,   Feb. 10, 1848 - Apr. 10, 1917
BAXTER, Nancy F.,   Mar. 16, 1860 - Nov. 12, 1946

CLOUSE, Oscar Carlyle "Lyle", May 28, 1893 - Dec. 3, 1978
          Pvt., US Army, WWI
CLOUSE, Thelma Lee B.,   Mar. 20, 1909 -

BAXTER, Napoleon Lambert,   Dec. 21, 1885 - Sep. 2, 1947
BAXTER, Ethel Willis,   Oct. 24, 1891 - Juḻ 11, 1978

CHANDLER,   Joe Henry,   Aug. 13, 1866 - Feb. 12, 1962
CHANDLER, Sallie Lucretia Tilson,   June 23, 1882 - Aug. 5, 1978

GUINN, Carl Frank,   1892 - 1975
GUINN, Dora Alice,   1895 - 1964

GOUGE, Aaron Keith,   1968 - 1968
          Son of Roy and Janette Gouge

BROWN, Samuel D.,   1882 - 1961

BLANKENSHIP, Roy,   June 6, 1915 - Apr. 5, 1982
          Pfc., USA, WWII
BLANKENSHIP, Una,   Sep. 9, 1920 -
BLANKENSHIP, Clouse,   1965 - 1965

STEPHENSON, Michael,   Dec. 10, 1952 - June 30, 1972

HOYLE, Robert S.,   Dec. 17, 1893 - Mar. 25, 1968
HOYLE, Ethel C.,   Nov.  5, 1893 -

TILSON, William F.,   Mar. 6, 1884 - Sep. 22, 1969
TILSON, Hattie H.,   Nov. 19, 1889 - Mar. 8, 1985

SAMS, Oscar,   Nov. 10, 1916 - Oct. 19, 1965
SAMS, Belle,   May  3, 1892 - Apr. 27, 1971

TILSON, Lizzie,   May 2, 1895 - (new grave - no date yet)

HENSLEY, Hoy C.,   Dec. 28, 1914 - July 2, 1955

BAXTER, Bill D.,   Sep. 17, 1917 - Dec. 11, 1964
        US Navy WWII, Son of Napoleon L. & Ethel Willis Baxter

TILSON, Ebb,   Mar. 31, 1887 - July 21, 1957
TILSON, Nora (w),   Mar. 28, 1891 - Apr. 6, 1945
TILSON, Carroll B. (son),   Aug. 19, 1925 - Sep. 16, 1944

GUINN, Arthur Blaine,   Feb. 19, 1885 - Mar. 17, 1971
GUINN, Zora Tilson,   Dec. 28, 1896 -

GUINN, Dwight L.,   July 6, 1918 - Sep. 29, 1944
        Pfc., Med. Corps, USA, Killed in Italy in WWII

GUINN, Clyde O.,   July 27, 1916 - Sep. 6, 1916
GUINN, Nettie Geneva,   May 25, 1917 - June 21, 1917

HARRIS, Leroy,   Sep. 5, 1884 - Aug. 6, 1910

HIGGINS, Rachel J. Guinn,   Feb. 26, 1899 - Apr. 14, 1975
HIGGINS, Jimmie Winston (son),   1925 - 1980
        Sgt., US Army, WWII

TILSON, Ernest E.,   May 18, 1888 - July 2, 1979
TILSON, Gracie G.,   Apr. 7, 1888 - June 23, 1966

OZMER, Robert Roy,   Jan. 21, 1899 - Oct. 21, 1969
OZMER, Mamie Emily Willis,   Aug. 24, 1901 - Nov. 17, 1980

WILLIS, William Jasper,   Aug. 15, 1860 - July 4, 1959
        Son of John A. and Edna Martin Willis
WILLIS, Martha E.,   Aug. 4, 1862 - Jan. 3, 1954
        Daughter of Alfred Jackson and LaVina Haun Guinn

TIPTON, Jeff,   Apr. 13, 1909 -
TIPTON, Lockie M. (w),   Nov. 11, 1918 - Jan. 4, 1978
        Married July 28, 1935

HENSLEY, Infant,   d. July 27, 1940 - Dau. of H. C. Hensley

TILSON, Laura Ellen,   1853 - 1933
        Erected by Matilda Tilson

TILSON, Samuel E.,   May 31, 1893 - Feb. 26, 1910
        Son of W. J. and Ellen Tilson

CLEAR BRANCH CEMETERY - (continued)

TILSON, Martha Evelyn,  Feb. 16, 1922 - Mar. 12, 1922
        Daughter of W. J. and Barbra Tilson

CLOUSE, Walter N.,  Aug. 4, 1889 - Feb. 27, 1946
CLOUSE, Sue Emma Hensley,  Mar. 24, 1895 - Mar. 21, 1932
        Daughter of A. W. and Delia Foster Hensley

CLOUSE, Guy,  Apr. 17, 1918 - Oct. 17, 1964

FARNOR, David Powell,  Jan. 10, 1876 - Sep. 6, 1951
FARNOR, Martha J. Tilson,  Aug. 13, 1863 - June 27, 1969

FARNOR, Robert E.,  Apr. 19, 1887 - Nov. 24, 1948
FARNOR, Bertha A.,  Mar. 24, 1892 - Mar. 11, 1981

FOSTER, Arvie E.,  1902 -
FOSTER, Iva G.,  1906 - 1981

PRICE, Linda Lewis,  1946 - 1987

LEWIS, Levi,  b/d June 10, 1936
        Son of J. H. Lewis

LEWIS, James Harvey,  Apr. 27, 1912 - Mar. 5, 1972

TIPTON, Stephen C.,  Apr. 13, 1867 - June 26, 1953
TIPTON, Henry G.,  Apr. 13, 1867 - May 12, 1954
        Twin sons of Valentine and Polly Edwards Tipton

TILSON, Mrs. Martha J. Brown,  Mar. 14, 1855 - Aug. 12, 1949

BROWN, Catherine,  May 9, 1847 - Jan. 11, 1926

BROWN, William,  Mar. 30, 1817 - Sep. 21, 1906

BROWN, Rachel,  d. Jan. 7, 1906 about 85 yrs

TILSON, Margaret M.,  June 24, 1849 - May 7, 1916
TILSON, John S.,  June 23, 1848 - Dec. 11, 1934

PROFFITT, D. W.,  1882 - 1964
PROFFITT, Lockie (w#1),  1886 - 1918
PROFFITT, Lucy  (w#2),  1896 - 1977

TIPTON, Lula B.,  Mar. 31, 1881 - Jan. 28, 1973

CHANDLER, John Frank,  Sep. 11, 1884 - Oct. 22, 1948
CHANDLER, Vina Willis,  Oct. 18, 1886 - Dec. 5, 1980

TILSON, William A.,  1871 - 1962
TILSON, Mary Elizabeth (w),  1869 - 1960
        Married 1893
TILSON, Viola (dau),  Nov. 12, 1894 - Nov. 3, 1921

TOMPKINS, Rev. J. N.,   Aug. 20, 1871 - May 11, 1903

TOMPKINS, Martha,   Mar. 27, 1830 - June 5, 1916
        Wife of John B. Tompkins

TOMPKINS, George W.,   Sep. 15, 1850 - July 20, 1934
TOMPKINS, Ruphina Jane,   Jan. 25, 1870 - May 21, 1930
        Daughter of J. M. and Nancy Loggins Taylor

PETERS, James Lige,   July 13, 1913 - Jan. 29, 1973
PETERS, Annie Mack,   Feb. 8, 1926 -

CHANDLER, Fred A.,   Dec. 3, 1886 - June 29, 1984
CHANDLER, Bessie J.(?) Gilbert (w#1), Oct. 1894 - Jan. 1919
CHANDLER, Elizabeth P. (w#2), Dec. 1, 1911 -

CHANDLER, Richard,   Apr. 16, 1916 - Nov. 20, 1930
        Son of Fred A. and Bessie Gilbert Chandler

GILBERT, Stephen C.,   Jan. 17, 1855 - July 29, 1916

TAYLOR, James M.,   Mar. 29, 1830 - Feb. 27, 1907
        Co. A, 2nd NC Mtd. Inf., Union Army
TAYLOR, Nancy J.,   June 15, 1842 - May 28, 1925

SUTHARD, Clarence F.,   July 26, 1923 - Oct. 8, 1925
        Son of W. F. and Beatrice Suthard

GILBERT, Guy F.,   Jan. 17, 1927 - Feb. 7, 1927
        Son of D. C. and Birdie Gilbert

GUINN, John Wesley,   Sep. 3, 1874 - May 28, 1947
GUINN, Zipporah Taylor,   Apr. 26, 1876 - Feb. 20, 1971

GUINN, James D.,   June 7, 1877 - Sep. 19, 1963
GUINN, Rachel J.,   Mar. 10, 1876 - Dec. 25, 1964

GUINN, Henry S.,   Mar. 31, 1891 - Nov. 5, 1975
GUINN, Aletha M. (w).  Feb. 9, 1888 - Dec. 28, 1981
        Married Nov. 27, 1913

GUINN, Linda A.,   1888 - 1981

CHANDLER, Homer,   1906 - 1969
CHANDLER, Vergie T. (A?),   1909 - 1988

GILBERT, Troy M.,   Nov. 21, 1902 - July 15, 1955
        Son of Stephen and Mary E. Taylor Gilbert
GILBERT, Mary N.,   Apr. 3, 1903 -

GILBERT, Mary Etta,   Mar. 16, 1874 - Feb. 28, 1957

GILBERT, Dorsa C.,   Sep. 28, 1896 - June 23, 1973
GILBERT, Birdie M.,   Oct. 22, 1902 - Oct. 10, 1978

RAMSEY, Zeb,   Mar. 6, 1880 - Apr. 15, 1954

<u>CLEAR BRANCH CEMETERY</u> - (continued)

RAMSEY, Howard,   Mar. 16, 1936 - Nov. 6, 1939

HAYNES, Rev. Nat T.,   Aug. 4, 1860 - July 23, 1934
HAYNES, Betsy Jane (w),   1873 - 1958
HAYNES, Mattie Lee (dau),   Mar. 8, 1901 - Oct. 24, 1902
HAYNES, Maggie May (dau),   Sep. 4, 1904 - Mar.  5, 1916

GILBERT, James H.,   Apr. 6, 1907 - May 25, 1932
          Son of S. C. and Mary E. Gilbert

CLOUSE, Earl F.,   Mar. 23, 1879 - Dec. 3, 1901

GUINN, Bertie L.,   Sep. 2, 1903 - Jan. 5, 1904
          Son of G. F. and E. Guinn

GUINN, G(?). Frank,   1880 - 1961
GUINN, Eunice,   1882 - 1966

BOONE, Callie F.,   1905 - 1988

FARNOR, Lelan C.,   Jan. 21, 1912 - Sep. 20, 1957

FARNOR, Paul Sr.,   1917 - 1968
FARNOR, Clella,   1920 - (no date, but appears to be new grave)

FARNOR, Clella,   d. 1967
FARNOR, Ethel,   d. 1967
          Baby daughters of Paul, Jr. and Anna Farnor

CHANDLER, Martha Riddle,   Dec. 4, 1877 - Feb. 13, 1958
          Daughter of James and Nancy Thompkins Riddle

CHANDLER, George V.,   Feb. 1, 1912 - Aug. 15, 1983, Pvt.US Army
CHANDLER, Vivian Vine,   Apr. 18, 1921 -

CHANDLER, Lark,   Oct. 20, 1879 - Jan. 13, 1961
CHANDLER, Hester,   Oct. 7, 1888 - July 23, 1982

TIPTON, Addie,   May 12, 1903 - Oct. 7, 1975

BENNETT, Walter,   Nov. 9, 1907 - May 28, 1984, US Army, WWII
BENNETT, Nora R.,   Oct. 1, 1910 - May 28, 1977

SILVERS, Harley,   Sep. 3, 1909 - Sep. 19, 1980
SILVERS, Kate,   May 15, 1916 -

JONES, Mary E.,   1881 - 1972

CLEAR BRANCH CEMETERY - (continued)

Additions from Charles Bennett, Dec. 5, 1960:
        (no longer visible in 1988)

EDWARDS, Creola Chandler, Jan. 8, 1902 - Jan. 16, 1924
        Wife of L. C. Edwards

GUINN, Claudine, Mar. 21, 1924 - Aug. 18, 1924

PROFFITT, Lockie, Dec. 28, 1887 - Nov. 13, 1919
        Wife of D. W. Proffitt / dau. of J. S. Tilson


                Also, unmarked graves, including:

FOSTER, Minta Jane Hensley, age 34, d. July 30, 1929
        Daughter of W. G. and Cindia Hensley

GUINN, Infant, d. Mar. 10, 1939
        Child of George W. and Minta Foster Guinn

LANE, Infant Son, d. Jan. 28, 1954
        Son of Hobert L. and Blanche Virginia Poore Lane

TIPTON, J. B., May 1, 1877 - June 21, 1932
        Son of Charles and Axie Cooper Tipton

WILLIS, Mrs. T. Frank, d. July 5, 1956

---------(?), a Civil War veteran, illegible
CHANDLER, Mary Drucilla, 1st wife of Wm. G. Chandler

## MOUNT PLEASANT/HOWELL CEMETERY

Old Ridge Rd., on hill opposite Clear Branch Cemetery

Copied June 2, 1988

BAILEY, Simon W., Jan. 26, 1908 - Feb. 6, 1980

CHANDLER, Lucious, Mar. 2, 1887 - July 1, 1983, US Army, WWI
CHANDLER, Emma, Mar. 12, 1899 - Sep. 9, 1985

CHANDLER, John Wesley, Mar. 22, 1854 - Oct. 23, 1949
        Father of Lucious Chandler

HOWELL, James Royce Sr., Dec. 6, 1927 - July 17, 1982
HOWELL, Willie Mae, May 17, 1936 -

HOWELL, Charles, 1902 - 1968

HOWELL, Martha, 1866 - 1948

HOWELL, Adolphus, Mar. 13, 1893 - Jan. 25, 1908
        Son of W. F. and M. J. Howell

HOWELL, Elizabeth G.,  1895 - 1937

FARNOR, J. Cloyd,  Nov. 23, 1905 - May 28, 1913

SHEHAN, Aaron,
        Co. M, 8th Tenn. Cav., Union Army

CHANDLER, Vestal,  Apr. 12, 1910 - July 26, 1911
        Son of J. M. and L. B. Chandler

CHANDLER, Dessie,  Apr. 28, 1908 - June 19, 1908
CHANDLER, Jesse,   July 25, 1913 - July 25, 1913
        Daughter and son of G. B. and L. V. Chandler

RATHBUN, Vira Eulala,  May 20, 1927 - Sep. 21, 1927

TINKER, Wm. Tilden,  Apr. 4, 1899 - Dec. 1, 1905

TINKER, Lawrence,  Feb. 6, 1868 - June 9, 1947
TINKER, Mary L.,   Mar. 4, 1874 - Nov. 1, 1937
TINKER, Margaret,  no date (baby?)
TINKER, Mae,       no date (baby?)

CORN, Frank,  May 8, 1899 - June 13, 1899
CORN, Eliza,  Feb. 8, 1897 - Feb. 28, 1897
        Son and daughter of James and Winnie Corn

WATTS, Kyle,  June 29, 1918 - June 8, 1920
        Son of Isaac and Julia Watts

WYATT, Maggie A.,  Feb. 10, 1891 - Feb. 16, 1920
        Wife of John W. Wyatt
WYATT, Charles (son),  July 5, 1916 - Feb. 25, 1920

GRINESTAFF, Charles,  Jan. 23, 1868 - Sep. 2, 1953
GRINESTAFF, Mollie Tinker,  Feb. 11, 1863 - Dec. 3, 1944

CHANDLER, Vanus,  1908 - 1986

CHANDLER, Jim M.,  May 29, 1881 - Aug. 16, 1974
CHANDLER, Lila B.,  Jan. 4, 1885 - June 16, 1952

MARTIN, Robert Earnest,  Dec. 21, 1921 - Jan. 25, 1945
        Pvt. Inf. US Army, Killed in Belgium in WWII

CHANDLER, Jehu L.,  July 2, 1866 - June 4, 1951
CHANDLER, Sarah C.,  Dec. 28, 1874 - Nov. 13, 1946
        Daughter of John Squibb and Margaret Brown Tilson

CHANDLER, Lawrence O.,  Apr. 25, 1921 - Jan. 19, 1948

WOODBY, Magdeline,  Apr. 14, 1915 - July 1, 1917
WOODBY, Ailine,    b/d Apr. 14, 1915

TINKER, Margaret, Apr. 11, 1832 - Mar. 6, 1890
    Wife of Samuel Tinker - maiden name Effler
FOSTER, Jonathan,  Feb. 28, 1855 - Oct. 23, 1923
FOSTER, Jeauil,   Feb. 7, 1863 - Aug. 3, 1915

FOSTER, Fred,   Dec. 15, 1900 - Nov. 27, 1924

TINKER, Jeanetta L., Feb. 23, 1922 - Dec. 25, 1925
TINKER, Richard,  (no dates)

TIPTON, Arizona E., May 26, 1863 - Nov. 19, 1959

TIPTON, Martha C.,  Oct. 27, 1868 - Aug. 22, 1895
   Wife of S. C. Tipton
TIPTON, Infant (dau), b/d Mar. 20, 1892

TIPTON, Infant,   b/d Oct. 7, 1888
   Daughter of H. C. and A. E. Tipton

CHANDLER, Horace E., Mar. 1, 1903 - Jan. 8, 1904
CHANDLER, Glyn S.,  Sep. 5, 1910 - Sep. 25, 1911
CHANDLER, Infant,  d. Feb. 9, 1896

TINKER, Lora C., Mar. 24, 1909 - Dec. 15, 1958

McINTOSH, William Jackson,  1848 - 1935
McINTOSH, Rosa Moore,  1847 - 1923

McINTOSH, Emily,  1880 - 1896

TITTLE, Eph'm. (Ephraim),
   Co. M., 8th Tenn. Cav., Union Army

WOLFE, Eliza Jane,  1847 - 1879, Wife of J. D. Wolfe

HAYNES, W. H., Apr. 15, 1873 - Sep. 5, 1902
HAYNES, Martha A., Jan. 6, 1879 - Nov. 24, 1931
   Daughter of Wm. and Jennie Guinn Tilson

SHEHAN, Alvir Lelon, Mar. 26, 1908 - Nov. 23, 1910
   Son of T. E. and R. E. Shehan

CHANDLER, Dora, Mar. 24, 1909 - June 21, 1909
CHANDLER, Infant, Jan. 17, 1899 - Jan. 18, 1899
   Daughter and son of J. L. and S. C. Chandler

CHANDLER, Silas L., Mar. 7, 1832 - Aug. 7, 1917
CHANDLER, Janie M., Mar. 9, 1839 - June 28, 1924

STOCKTON, Juice, May 5, 1930 - May 5, 1930

HENSLEY, A. C.,  May 5, 1868 - May 23, 1937
HENSLEY, Sarah,  b. Jan. 4, 1876
HENSLEY, Goldman (son), July 29, 1910 - July 24, 1911
HENSLEY, Rome (son), July 5, 1906 - July 30, 1924

<u>MOUNT PLEASANT/HOWELL CEMETERY</u> - (continued)

CHANDLER, George Birt,  Apr. 12, 1871 - Mar. 26, 1956
CHANDLER, Elvira "Vira" Jones, June 28, 1873 - Dec. 6, 1957 (w)
CHANDLER, Ida (dau),  Dec. 12, 1901 - Jan. 10, 1939

CHANDLER, Infant,  June 27, 1942 - June 27, 1942
        Son of Everett Chandler

CHANDLER, Robert E.,  Mar. 16, 1896 - May 28, 1955, WWI
CHANDLER, Martha C.,  Mar. 25, 1897 -

CHANDLER, Lila Belle,  1885 - 1952
        Daughter of John and Sarah Moore Gentry

CLOUSE, George Clifton,  July 17, 1894 - Sep. 26, 1972
CLOUSE, Laura Chander,  Sep. 19, 1899 - (no date, but
        (Chandler)               recent grave)

EDWARDS, James,
        Co. H, 10th Tenn. Cav., Union Army

            no unmarked graves observed


                    <u>HORN CEMETERY</u>

    In Rocky Fork - On Devil Fork Road, at top of grade, take
    right at house, and go past barn to top of hill

                  Copied June 14, 1988

HORN, F. M.,    June 5, 1855 - Jan. 14, 1915
HORN, Ida,      Nov. 9, 1861 - Feb. 15, 1911

HARRIS, Lou,  Nov. 5, 1881 - Mar. 25, 1905
        Wife of Buel Harris

HARRIS, Carl,  Dec. 9, 1902 - July 13, 1911
HARRIS, Worley,  Nov. 14, 1904 - Dec. 19, 1904
HARRIS, Lary (girl),  May 31, 1901 - Feb. 22, 1902
HARRIS, Frank,  Jan. 31, 1899 - Mar. 21, 1900
        Children of B. and Lou Harris

HENSLEY, Margaret,  d. July 9, 1903 at 42 yrs
        Wife of John Hensley

HENSLEY, Luther R.,  July 30, 1899 - 1983
HENSLEY, Hazel Loyd, July 16, 1903 - Nov. 13, 1962

HENSLEY, Armp,  Nov. 9, 1823 - Nov. 2, 1911
HENSLEY, Barbrey,  d. Jan. 2, 1911 at 90 yrs

HENSLEY, Andy,  June 15, 1876 - Feb. 8, 1947
HENSLEY, Lattie,  Mar. 3, 1912 - Feb. 18, 1986

WRODROUP, Martha A.,   d. Apr. 15, 1914 at 47 yrs

HENSLEY, Mandy,   1861 - Nov. 1917

GILLIS, Auston,    June 6, 1897 - Jan. 1, 1963
GILLIS, Martha H.,   Apr. 27, 1894 - Mar. 3, 1970

SPARKS, Frank,    Mar. 26, 1896 - July 30, 1917

SPARKS, John M.,   Aug. 7, 1866 - June 12, 1933
SPARKS, Elizabeth C.,   July 7, 1876 - Jan. 1, 1958

SPARKS, Laddie,    Feb. 21, 1917 - June 24, 1935

SPARKS, Robert,    Feb. 14, 1910 - Jan. 9, 1971

SHELTON, Soley,    Jan. 15, 1882 - Sep. 18, 1965
SHELTON, Rutha,    June  6, 1884 - June 28, 1976

SHELTON, Odie,    Mar. 21, 1913 -

WALDRUP, J. L.,   Oct. 14, 1884 - Sep. 24, 1968
WALDRUP, Hannah S. (w),   June 26, 1887 - Oct. 16, 1959
        Married July 19, 1906

WALDRUP, Labe N.,   Oct. 29, 1916 - Feb. 4, 1983

WALDRUP, Disa,    Feb. 29, 1911 - Mar. 22, 1917

SAMS, Carold,   b/d Oct. 26, 1934

SPARKS, Henry A.,   June 22, 1868 - July 20, 1937
        Son of Sidney and Sinda Waldrup Sparks
SPARKS, Loretta H.,   Nov. 15, 1874 - Sep. 2, 1942

SPARKS, H. Tom,   1915 - 1942

RENFRO, Glenia Mae,   b/d Feb. 21, 1938

INGLE, W. A.,   Dec. 7, 1886 - Jan. 2, 1906

plus many unmarked graves

# HARRIS CEMETERY

In Rocky Fork, Devil Fork Road, just past Horn Cemetery, take right at old barn, to top of hill

Copied June 14, 1988

SHELTON, Roscoe C., Oct. 12, 1904 - Jan. 16, 1978
SHELTON, Emily C. (w), Oct. 31, 1902 - Jan. 11, 1979

BROWN, Darden Shelton, Mar. 23, 1925 - Feb. 15, 1964
        Daughter of R. C. and Emily Shelton

SPARKS, Jim, Mar. 17, 1910 - Oct. 7, 1971
SPARKS, Nola C., Jan. 23, 1915 -

SPARKS, Michael Grady, d. Mar. 22, 1960
        Infant son of G. S. and Glenna Sparks

HARDIN, Jessie, 1874 - 1961
HARDIN, Nora, 1878 - 1960
HARDIN, Freddie Lee, Nov. 5, 1941 - Mar. 4, 1943

CUTSHAW, N. D., Oct. 15, 1865 - May 18, 1940

SPARKS, Judy Ann, d. 1943, infant

HARDIN, Vernon C., June 21, 1930 - Oct. 11, 1950
        Pvt. in Engineers, WWII

WALKER, Jim Frank, 1874 - 1949
WALKER, Sue Eller, 1883 - 1908

HARRIS, Barnett, Feb. 20, 1864 - May 26, 1905

SHELTON, James A., Dec. 5, 1879 - Feb. 21, 1957
SHELTON, Muncie (w), Oct. 15, 1879 - Aug. 3, 1963
SHELTON, Lauring (son), Dec. 1, 1905 - Mar. 27, 1963

SHELTON, Carl, Oct. 4, 1939 - Oct. 16, 1985
SHELTON, Muncie F. (w), Apr. 4, 1939 -      married Oct. 15, 1961
SHELTON, Carl Jr., Mar. 24, 1967 - Aug. 29, 1967

SHELTON, Horace, Feb. 16, 1915 - Oct. 11, 1979
SHELTON, Bruce, Sep. 5, 1911 - Apr. 6, 1986 - brothers

SHELTON, Ollen, Feb. 13, 1908 - Apr. 6, 1982
SHELTON, Florence W., Sep. 7, 1907 -

SHELTON, Bobby James, May 7, 1944 - Sep. 29, 1967
        Sp4, US Army, Vietnam and Philippines

SHELTON, Fletcher Dale Jr., Sep. 13, 1962 - Jan. 25, 1981

plus several unmarked graves, including:

TILSON, Ralph,  3 years old - Dec. 17, 1929
        Son of Walter and Nancy Harris Tilson

SELBY, Harry Duanne,  infant, Feb. 18, 1944
        Son of Harry Elder and Iva Tilson Selby

## HIGGINS #2 CEMETERY

On Rt. 19/23, about 5 miles S. of Erwin, about 50' from
Rd., on E. side, just before Granny Lewis Creek

Copied from Dec. 7, 1960 trip by C. W. Bennett

HIGGINS, Holland Sr.,  d. Nov. 30, 1824, Killed by David Greer

LEWIS, Joseph W.,  d. Dec. 27, 1932
        Pvt. 2nd Cav., from Penn. WWI(?)

WALKER, Johnnie,   1863 - 1938
WALKER, Cordelia,  1863 - 1939

Note: Higgins and Lewis stones still visible Mar. 5, 1989

## EDWARDS #4 CEMETERY

On Rock Creek Road, behind Sunnycrest Apts. in Erwin

Copied Aug. 9, 1988

EDWARDS, T. P.,  Co. C, 2nd Tenn. Cav., Union Army

plus 2 unmarked graves

## JEWELL CEMETERY

On Jewell Creek Road, off Odom Branch Road in Lillydale, Erwin

Copied Aug. 19, 1988

JEWELL, Charles Cecil,  Apr. 16, 1895 - July 16, 1944
        Pvt. 163rd Inf., 41st Div. WWI(?)
        Son of Joe Richards and Hester Jewell
JEWELL, Lola May (w),  1898 - 1953

JEWELL, M. D.,  1877 - 1960

JEWELL, Lilly Ellen,  1878 - 1952

JEWELL, John B.,  1879 - 1957   (beside Lilly)

<u>JEWELL CEMETERY</u> - (continued)

BAILEY, John Wesley,  d. 1960/61 at 85/86 yrs
        Son of Mannon and Jane Morris Bailey


                plus unmarked graves, including:

HARRIS, Connie Lee,  infant,  d. Feb. 1, 1950
        Daughter of Dolly Hoyle Harris

JEWELL, Robert,  Oct. 1898 - Feb. 2, 1947
        Son of Ellen Jewell

JEWELL, Ruth Neoma,  6 mos. old, d. Feb. 2, 1943
        Daughter of Homer Banner and Rosa Mae Jewell

LEWIS, John Baxter,  age 77, d. Nov. 15, 1957
        Son of Silas and Mary Ann Hensley Lewis

LEWIS, Lilly Eller,  age 74,  d. Apr. 22, 1952
        Daughter of Manion and Cindy Lewis

RICH, Infant,  d. June 29, 1948
        Child of Clyde and Bertha Edwards Rich

RICH, Michael Wayne,  3 mos. old - d. Dec. 31, 1955
        Son of Jessie H. and Madeline Honeycutt Rich


                    <u>BANNER CEMETERY</u>

   On Graveyard Road in Lillydale, Erwin, off Odom Branch Rd.

                    Copied Aug. 19, 1988

WILLIAMS, Jessie "Bud",  1923 -
WILLIAMS, Jessie H. (w), 1933 - 1988

BANNER, Robert,   1900 - 1986

BANNER, Max Richard,  July 26, 1940 - June 7, 1982

BANNER, Velva K.,  1925 - 1936

BANNER, William F.,  1930 - 1931
        Son of Bob and Julia Bailey Banner

BANNER, Gerald S.,  b/d 1942

BANNER, Sandra Kay,  b/d 1966

BANNER, William W.,  1934 - 1987

HAMPTON, William,  1905 - 1956
HAMPTON, Mary J.,  d. 1966

JEWELL, Ella May,   1906 - 1975

ROBERTS, William E.,   1925 - 1986

ROBERTS, Baby Ronnie,   d. 1958
ROBERTS, Infant,        d. 1960

## HIGGINS CHAPEL CEMETERY

On left Higgins Creek Road, just past fork, beyond church

Copied Aug. 25, 1988

MASHBURN, Infant dau.,   d. Jan. 5, 1892
MASHBURN, Infant son ,   d. Jan. 10, 1890
MASHBURN, Infant son ,   d. Nov. 20, 1887
MASHBURN, Infant son ,   d. Sep. 18, 1885
MASHBURN, Infant son ,   d. Oct. 20, 1881
MASHBURN, Infant son ,   d. Jan. 4, 1875
        Children of John and Malinda Mashburn

MURRAY, Henry E.,   Sep. 28, 1883 - Feb. 21, 1944

MURRAY, Infant son,   d. Oct. 15, 1942

HARRIS, Infant,   d. Nov. 21, 1940 - dau. of Clay Harris

HARRIS, David Glenn,   Oct. 8, 1942 - Oct. 4, 1944
        Son of Tommie Samuel and Ada Maria Boone Harris

HARRIS, Infant,  b/d Mar. 22, 1938 - dau. of S. T. Harris

HARRIS, Tonnie S.,   Dec. 31, 1915 - Feb. 9, 1974
        Pfc., US Army, WWII

HARRIS, Jessivee,   Feb. 23, 1938 - Sep. 28, 1938
        Daughter of Ernest and Hazel Hensley Harris

HARRIS, N. D.,   Sep. 22, 1864 - Oct. 19, 1937
HARRIS, Sarah (w),   Dec. 22, 1866 - Oct. 4, 1934

HARRIS, Armstrong,   Co. E, 2NC Mtd. Inf., Union Army
HARRIS, Polly L. Craine, Jan. 14, 1855 - Dec. 2, 1931
        "Wife of A. Harris"

HARRIS, Joseph,   Nov. 21, 1840 - Aug. 28, 1918
HARRIS, Rachel,   Oct. 27, 1838 - Dec. 17, 1933

BRIGGS, Robert,   Mar. 28, 1912 - Jan. 1, 1981
BRIGGS, Thelma (w),   Apr. 30, 1916 -

HARRIS, J. C.,   1924-1978 - Pfc., US Army, WWII

HIGGINS, Clyde Russell,   Feb. 14, 1911 - Mar. 18, 1978
        US Army, WWII

HARRIS, Clay C.,   July 6, 1894 - Jan. 19, 1978
HARRIS, Jennie R. (w),   Dec. 14, 1896 - Apr. 25, 1967

HARRIS, R. Kenneth,   July 27, 1935 - Dec. 16, 1958

HARRIS, Ralph A.,   Sep. 19, 1919 - May 5, 1961
        Tec4, Sig. Co., WWII
HARRIS, Johnny Mack,   Aug. 5, 1952 - Jan. 9, 1954
        Son of Ralph and Nellie Tipton Harris

McINTOSH, Mary H.,   Sep. 23, 1877 - Dec. 9, 1955

HARRIS, James Frank,   July 18, 1875 - May 11, 1952
HARRIS, Mary E. Shelton (w),   Nov. 20, 1881 - Dec. 4, 1970

HARRIS, Virginia Adele,   July 31, 1949 - Dec. 26, 1949

HARRIS, Hillard Wayne,   Aug. 27, 1923 - Oct. 16, 1979
        Pfc., US Army, WWII
HARRIS, Edith Bejettie (w),   Oct. 11, 1919 -

HARRIS, J. W.,   Aug. 16, 1932 - Jan. 21, 1956
        Son of Joe W. and Rebecca Shook Harris

CORN, Walter H.,   Nov. 8, 1883 - Apr. 13, 1953
CORN, Diana Murray (w),   May 12, 1895 - Oct. 19, 1985

CORN, Jennifer Leigh,   July 2, 1973 - Oct. 8, 1980

HARRIS, Rev. Wade Estil,   Aug. 8, 1914 - June 23, 1982
        S/Sgt., US Army, WWII
HARRIS, Luecreta Crain (w),   Nov. 2, 1919 -

WOODWARD, Otis Robert,   Sep. 19, 1908 - Nov. 15, 1974

NORTON, Tom,   Sep. 29, 1907 -
NORTON, Sally (w),   May 10, 1910 - July 24, 1974

GUICE, Charles R.,   1936 - 1963

CRAIN, Janie,   May 21, 1890 - Oct. 4, 1970

HOPSON, Floyd,   1918 - 1987
HOPSON, Mary Lou (w),   1935 -

BAILEY, Guy,   1916 -
BAILEY, Clara Marie (w),   1923 - 1979

RICKER, Starling M.,   1886 - 1944
RICKER, Marion S.,   1886 - 1962

HOYLE, Oscar P.,    Mar. 15, 1903 -
HOYLE, Narcissus T. (w),  Aug. 31, 1903 - June 9, 1944

EDWARDS, Theora,   Nov. 22, 1914 - Dec. 24, 1914
        Daughter of M. G. and Rosa Briggs Edwards

HIGGINS, William T.,   Dec. 16, 1844 - Mar. 10, 1919
        Sgt., Co. M, 8TN CAV., Union Army

HOYLE, Howard,   1908 - 1966

HOYLE, Infant,   d. 1967

HOYLE, Andrew J.,   1857 - 1922
HOYLE, Cordelia A. (w),  1851 - 1914

HARRIS, Lyda L.,  Sep. 18, 1915 - Oct. 12, 1915

CRAIN, M.,    d. 1937
CRAIN, H.,    d. 1915
CRAIN, B.,    d. 1915

CRAIN, Lewis B.,   June 30, 1879 - Dec. 22, 1948

CRAIN, J. Troy,  Aug. 29, 1909 - July 3, 1968

RAY, W. Shelt,    1885 - 1961
RAY, Laura Mc (w), 1893 - 1965

RAY, N. W.,   d. 1938 at 83

CRAIN, John H.,   no dates - son of A. J. Crain

CRAIN, A. J.,   Mar. 18, 1850 - Feb. 10, 1935

MASHBURN, T. Melvin,  Nov. 14, 1880 - Dec. 30, 1969
MASHBURN, Bessie (w#1), Dec. 14, 1882 - May 3, 1911
MASHBURN, Martha M. (dau),  Sep. 24, 1908 - Apr. 6, 1909
MASHBURN, Lester L. (son),  June 11, 1901 - Oct. 14, 1911
MASHBURN, Esteller C. (w#2),  b. Nov. 4, 1888
MASHBURN, Infant (dau),  b/d Dec. 28, 1913

MASHBURN, China,  Apr. 23, 1930 - June 4, 1972

RYAN, William Filmore,  Apr. 14, 1917 - Feb. 4, 1981

SHELTON, Gertha W.,  Feb. 10, 1942 - Oct. 9, 1960

SHELTON, Willie D.,  June 12, 1902 - Feb. 23, 1984
SHELTON, Mamie B. (w),  Aug. 17, 1906 - Mar. 22, 1965

ENGLISH, Ralph Keith,  b/d Jan. 19, 1965
        Son of Ralph and Linda English

LYNCH, Lisa LuJeana,  Sep. 23, 1968 - Apr. 30, 1969

WALDROP, Marsha Ann,  d. Oct. 10, 1965
         Infant daughter of Richard and Mary Waldrop

EDWARDS, Roscoe R.,  Jan. 5, 1900 - Dec. 11, 1985
EDWARDS, Dullie (w),  May 25, 1908 -

EDWARDS, Brenda Kay,  d. Nov. 23, 1962
         Infant daughter of Jerry and Bertha Edwards

HARRIS, Guy,  Feb. 8, 1903 - July 29, 1967

HARRIS, Nelse H.,  1881 - 1973
HARRIS, Matilda M. (w),  1885 - 1956
HARRIS, J. M. (son),  July 26, 1920 - May 11, 1928

MASHBURN, John,  Aug. 8, 1852 - Apr. 26, 1938
         Son of Calloway and Relia Pate Mashburn
MASHBURN, B. Malinda (w),  Mar. 7, 1850 - Jan. 10, 1921
MASHBURN, Calloway (son),  Mar. 30, 1883 - July 16, 1905
MASHBURN, Franklin (son),  Nov. 8, 1875 - Jan. 31, 1904

HIGGINS, Samuel,  May 13, 1819 - Feb. 1, 1902
HIGGINS, Elizabeth M. (w),  Aug. 12, 1823 - Sep. 22, 1909

HIGGINS, Barbara,  Dec. 27, 1792 - June 14, 1882
         Wife of Holland Higgins (who was killed by Dave
                            "Hog" Greer)

HIGGINS, William Ellis,  Apr. 9, 1856 - Nov. 6, 1934
HIGGINS, Marietta C. (w),  Oct. 17, 1863 - June 9, 1941

HIGGINS, Della M.,  July 29, 1898 - July 1, 1909
HIGGINS, Roy,  Oct. 5, 1900 - July 2, 1906
HIGGINS, Arthur,  May 17, 1904 - July 11, 1904
HIGGINS, Infant son,  b/d Mar. 8, 1894
HIGGINS, Ogle (son), May 27, 1892 - Aug. 24, 1892
         "Children of W. E. and M. E. Higgins"

HIGGINS, Infant,  b/d June 16, 1960, son of Ed Higgins, Jr.

HIGGINS, Harry,  Oct. 22, 1925 -
HIGGINS, Ethelyne (w),  Aug. 28, 1911 - Feb. 16, 1977

HIGGINS, Walter J.,  Aug. 19, 1905 - July 11, 1906
HIGGINS, Infant dau.,  b/d Apr. 20, 1910
         Children of J. L. and R. H. Higgins

CRAIN, Von,  Feb. 29, 1911 - Mar. 23, 1911
         Son of Lattie and Martha Crain

CRAIN, Larence,  Jan. 29, 1915 - Feb. 23, 1915
         Son of Mack and Texie Crain

WALKER, Allisey,  Mar. 23, 1849 - Oct. 18, 1897
        Wife of W. A. Walker

HENSLEY, Austin,   (no dates)

CRAIN, Emeline,  Mar. 17, 1854 - Mar. 17, 1913

EDWARDS, Rufus,  July 22, 1893 - May 16, 1979
EDWARDS, Eliza (w),  Apr. 3, 1897 - Apr. 19, 1948

EDWARDS. Steve,  Sep. 1, 1914 - Nov. 12, 1985
        Pvt., US Army, WWII

STOCKTON, Dewey,  Apr. 21, 1915 - Dec. 22, 1917
STOCKTON, Nellie,  Dec. 10, 1918 - May 26, 1919
STOCKTON, Infant dau.,  b/d Feb. 22, 1924
STOCKTON, Alta (dau),  July 27, 1925 - Apr. 17, 1926
        Children of L. H. and Dora Stockton

EDWARDS, Buckner "Dusky(?)",  d. Mar. 1936

BAILEY, Willis,  Feb. 14, 1862 - Dec. 17, 1949
        Son of Zeke and Mary Phillips Bailey
BAILEY, Elizabeth (w),  Nov. 12, 1864 - Dec. 13, 1946

EDWARDS, William G.,  Dec. 14, 1872 - June 7, 1950
EDWARDS, Lillie H. (w),  Feb. 14, 1876 - May 11, 1971

EDWARD, Floyd J.,  Apr. 16, 1907 - Jan. 20, 1967

EDWARDS, Ronald B.,  1942 - 1980

EDWARDS, Dana,  1929 - 1984
EDWARDS, Thelma (w),  1932 -

EDWARDS, Roy,  1911 - 1988

BAILEY, Timothy D.,  b/d Sep. 7, 1986
        Son of Tim and Deana Bailey

SLAGLE, Mary Ruth Harris,  Dec. 16, 1918 - Aug. 20, 1975

CRAIN, Genevieve Harris,  1927 - 1973

HARRIS, Walter B.,  Nov. 27, 1888 - Dec. 28, 1964
HARRIS, Radie Crain (w),  Dec. 16, 1896 - July 17, 1970

HARRIS, Hughey,  Dec. 25, 1916 - July 1, 1963, S2, USNR, WWII
HARRIS, Marie H. (w),  no dates (?),  married Apr. 30, 1938

WOODY, Henry H.,  July 8, 1930 - Dec. 19, 1966
        Sp5, 6th Medical Lab., US Army

WOODY, Samuel T., Feb. 23, 1902 - Apr. 11, 1958
WOODY, Thelma H. (w), Apr. 2, 1912 - July 24, 1973

HOYLE, William T., Jan. 24, 1891 - Jan. 5, 1976
HOYLE, Lennie B. (w), Sep. 18, 1887 - May 29, 1967

HIGGINS, Love Joy, 1881 - 1951
HIGGINS, Rheuhamie (w), 1885 - 1970

WATTS, Mary L., May 6, 1884 - Mar. 5, 1963

SHELTON, Edna, b/d May 1946 - daughter of Willie Shelton

CORN, Patricia Ann, June 6, 1949 - June 7, 1949
          Daughter of Thomas and Rosie Harris Corn

SLAGLE, Kelsie, 1911 - 1932

HENSLEY, Sarah R., Apr. 14, 1860 - Dec. 11, 1926

CRAIN, Lattie, Jan. 3, 1886 - Feb. 18, 1972
CRAIN, Martha (w), July 29, 1886 - Feb. 10, 1955
CRAIN, Elva (dau), b/d Mar. 27, 1930
CRAIN, Margaret (dau), b/d Jan. 15, 1922

EDWARDS, Infant, d. 1927 - son of Rufus & Eliza Edwards

HARRIS, Opal, Dec. 22, 1900 - Jan. 27, 1901
          Daughter of N. H. and Matilda Harris

HENSLEY, Sylvanus, (no dates)
HENSLEY, Frank, (no dates)

HENSLEY, Zena Crain, (no dates)

CRAIN, Gladys Ann, Dec. 25, 1907 - Jan. 23, 1908

HIGGINS, Vence, Nov. 20, 1910 - Dec. 5, 1910
          Son of Wiley and Iva Higgins

HIGGINS, Della L., May 2, 1909 - Aug. 9, 1967
HIGGINS, Julia V. Mays (w), Mar. 19, 1905 -

HIGGINS, James Edgar, May 19, 1889 - Oct. 10, 1965
HIGGINS, Pearl (w), Jan. 10, 1900 - Aug. 16, 1981

EDWARDS, Ricky Dean, Oct. 6, 1962 - May 18, 1979

EDWARDS, Joy, b/d 1961 - daughter of Albert & Ruth Edwards

HIGGINS, Banner, Oct. 2, 1880 - Feb. 4, 1951
HIGGINS, Margaret (w), Oct. 13, 1881 - Dec. 9, 1943

WALKER, W. A., Jan. 3, 1852 - Jan. 24, 1918

CALLAHAN, "Ammie", 1828 - 1920

BLANKENSHIP, Grace, Feb. 16, 1921 - Jan. 22, 1922

BLANKENSHIP, Presley, May 26, 1860 - Mar. 22, 1929
        Son of David and ------- Moore Blankenship
BLANKENSHIP, Lydia E. (w), Feb. 19, 1861 - Jan. 24, 1939

BLANKENSHIP, Elva M., June 6, 1923 - Feb. 1, 1941

BLANKENSHIP, Fate, June 19, 1902 -
BLANKENSHIP, Eugenia (w), Mar. 26, 1902 - Nov. 13, 1984

HIGGINS, Gary Frank, d. Dec. 30, 1947
        Infant son of Dorsey and Eula Higgins

RUNNION, John R., 1847 - 1936
RUNNION, Nancy K. (w), 1855 - 1944
        Daughter of Thomas and Sally Mashburn Foster

HENSLEY, Hazel Lee, Mar. 6, 1942 - Mar. 26, 1942
        Daughter of Berry and Lula Hensley

FOSTER, Parley, 1908 -
FOSTER, Hattie (w), 1911 - 1982 - married Oct. 17, 1931

OLIVER, William H., Jan. 18, 1931 -
OLIVER, Martha May (w), May 5, 1938 - Oct. 30, 1987

WILLIAM, Golden L., Feb. 27, 1911 - Aug. 23, 1972
WILLIAM, Roberta E. (w), Nov. 2, 1917 -

HARRIS, Estil J., Oct. 9, 1898 - Sep. 16, 1985
HARRIS, Maggie D. (w), Nov. 30, 1906 - July 11, 1986

HARRIS, Raymond M., July 4, 1934 - July 15, 1984
HARRIS, Billie Marie (w), Mar. 27, 1933 -

SAMS, F. Keith, Jan. 8, 1916 - May 13, 1979
SAMS, Myrtle Crain (w), June 20, 1917 -

WOODWARD, Della Marie, July 17, 1915 - Oct. 10, 1972

HIGGINS, Roscoe C., 1907 - 1977
HIGGINS, Annis C. (w), 1909 - 1963

EDWARD, Maynard B., Aug. 20, 1924 - Dec. 26, 1981

EDWARDS, Martha J., 1880 - 1955
        Daughter of John R. and Katherine Foster Runion

RUNION, Dolphus C., 1888 - 1959

CODY, Infant, d. Apr. 9, 1948 - Son of Ernest and Glena Mae
                      Crain Cody

CRAIN, Samuel E., Feb. 5, 1880 - Apr. 13, 1954
CRAIN, Mary Ella Hensley (w), Oct. 27, 1885 - Jan. 6, 1977

CRAIN, William Melvin, May 18, 1856 - Dec. 26, 1944
        Son of Lewis and Elizabeth King Crain
CRAIN, Sallie Higgins (w), Sep. 17, 1892 - Jan. 30, 1986

CRAIN, Norma Sue, d. Sep. 7, 1942 (infant)
        Daughter of Lester and Genevivee Crain

CRAIN, Rubin, d. July 6, 1927 (infant)
        Son of W. N. and Sallie Crain

CRAIN, Wesley Oakey, Feb. 4, 1936 - Mar. 23, 1936
        Son of J. W. and Diana Crain

SHOOK, Pauline, (no dates)
        Infant daughter of Charley and Julia Shook

BAILEY, Thomas Jr., d. June 28, 1945
        Infant son of Thomas and Nancy Bailey

HENSLEY, Ronnie Darrell, July 5, 1947 - July 30, 1951
        Son of Zeak and Vista Hensley

HENSLEY, Vaughn Thomas, July 2, 1921 - July 13, 1977
        Cpl., US Army, WWII

HENSLEY, Ragan, June 28, 1893 - Jan. 19, 1966
HENSLEY, Ida J. (w), b. Dec. 9, 1891

HIGGINS, Holt, Apr. 2, 1911 - Sep. 27, 1974, CM3, US Navy

HENSLEY, Kirt, Mar. 13, 1887 - Mar. 29, 1970
HENSLEY, Callie (w), Nov. 13, 1903 -

HARRIS, Clarence W., Oct. 20, 1913 -
HARRIS, Clesta E. (w), Mar. 5, 1913 - Mar. 2, 1961
        Daughter of Luther H. and Dora Mashburn Stockton

STOCKTON, Luther H., 1883 - 1972
STOCKTON, Dora Mashburn (w), 1888 - 1968

STOCKTON, Ulysess, Oct. 10, 1885 - Feb. 10, 1969
STOCKTON, Byrd (w), Oct. 20, 1894 - Nov. 22, 1976
        Married Feb. 2, 1908

STOCKTON, Vernon, Feb. 6, 1909 - Mar. 27, 1969
STOCKTON, Edith (w), Aug. 14, 1912 -
        Married Jan. 2, 1937

plus many unmarked stones and many steel crosses (not CSA)

ADDITION: noted Apr. 1, 1989:

MASHBURN, Pansy C., 1910 - 1989

### Unmarked graves probably include:

SAMS, James Arthur, age 60, d. July 4, 1943
        Son of Cling and Rebecca Foster Sams


## SHELTON #1 CEMETERY

On Devils Fork Road, 3/4 mile from NC border on south
side of road
                Copied July 9, 1988

SHELTON, Boney Z., June 14, 1894 - Oct. 14, 1966
SHELTON, Carrie L. (w), May 29, 1901 - Apr. 8, 1983

SHELTON, F. Carrie, d. Sep. 8, 1964

SHELTON, Oscar M., 1896 - 1987

           no other stones


## WILLIAMS #1 CEMETERY

On Devils Fork Road, .2 mi. from NC border on south side
of road

           Copied July 9, 1988

WILLIAMS, Bud, d. 1986

WILLIAMS, Judy Ann, May 28,1952 - Jan.21,1990
       Wife of Broyate Williams
       Dau. of Clifford and Pauline Blankenship Willis

# SHELTON #2 CEMETERY

Pete Creek Road, .5 mi. from Jct. with Devils Fork Road

Copied July 9, 1988

SHELTON, Jake,  Jan. 13, 1906 -
SHELTON, Mattie L. K. (w),  Nov. 19, 1903 - Oct. 16, 1976
        Married July 6, 1930

BRIGGS, Bert,  May 19, 1917 - Dec. 19, 1977
BRIGGS, Zella Haire (w),  Mar. 30, 1926 -
        Married May 3, 1943

SHELTON, Robert,  Sep. 5, 1918 -
SHELTON, Gladys (w),  Nov. 13, 1921 - Dec. 15, 1974

ENGLISH, Geneva S.,  Feb. 17, 1924 - Apr. 18, 1973

SHELTON, Charles Ujean,  June 4, 1940 - Apr. 7, 1963
        Pvt., USMC Res.

HENSLEY, Eloise,  d. May 29, 1961  (child)

SHELTON, Jessie,  Jan. 6, 1880 - Feb. 23, 1972

SHELTON, Elminer,  June 6, 1884 - Dec. 11, 1955

SHELTON, Ervin,  Oct. 9, 1900 - Dec. 20, 1968

HENSLEY, G. W.,  1869 - Jan. 30, 1941
HENSLEY, Angeline (w),  1871 - June 1928

SHELTON, Pete,  1851 - 1943
SHELTON, Nancy (w),  1848 - 1903

SHELTON, Reilly,  1850 - 1942

SHELTON, Kenneth,  1939 - 1941

SHELTON, Blake Edward,  b/d 1943

RIDDLE, Darlene,  June 4, 1958 - Mar. 10, 1959
RIDDLE, Karlene,  June 4, 1958 - Mar. 10, 1959  (twins)
        Children of Homer E. and Colena Shelton Riddle

LAMB, Iva Mae,  1916 - 1946

HENSLEY, Waco,  1906 - Apr. 30, 1934
HENSLEY, Sophronia "Phronie",  1891 - Feb. 1940
HENSLEY, Zilphia,  Mar. 23, 1929 - Apr. 4, 1929

HAIR, Camline H.,  1862 - Mar. 26, 1947

CUTSHALL, Amos,  Oct. 19, 1903 - Apr. 5, 1922

SHELTON #2 CEMETERY - (continued)

CUTSHAW, Franklin D., June 3, 1937 - Apr. 5, 1941
        Son of Ora and Gerth Cutshaw

HENSLEY, Berlson, May 21, 1929 - Jan. 4, 1964

HENSLEY, Malissie, d. Feb. 8, 1940

HENSLEY, Matt, 1865 - 1940

HENSLEY, Henry C., July 5, 1895 - Jan. 19, 1958

SHELTON, George N., 1904 - 1987

HENRY, Edward A., July 3, 1941 - Dec. 25, 1971

HENSLEY, Mennie, July 29, 1904 - Nov. 8, 1942
HENSLEY, Matilda H. King (w), Nov. 3, 1911 - Oct. 14, 1948

HENSLEY, Walter W., 1900 - 1955

HENSLEY, George W., June 2, 1939 - July 9, 1957

SILVERS, Lee Hermon, June 27, 1955 - Oct. 30, 1957

SHELTON, Timothy, b/d Jan. 5, 1967

SILVERS, Gerald, Apr. 24, 1952 - Aug. 6, 1970

SHELTON, Naomi H., Aug. 1, 1937 - Dec. 15, 1965

HENSLEY, Raymond, Oct. 4, 1945 - Apr. 8, 1964

HENSLEY, Elezer O., June 3, 1902 - Jan. 29, 1972


                plus many unmarked stones


                GENTRY   CEMETERY

        Behind Jennie Moore Church, Rocky Fork

                Copied July 9, 1988

DEWEESE, William Jack, 1931 - 1933
        Son of Roy and Gertrude Deweese

HARRIS, John Quillen, Feb. 19, 1886 - Nov. 22, 1966
HARRIS, Flossie Lawing (w), Feb. 26, 1895 -
HARRIS, Annis (dau), July 30, 1920 - Jan. 12, 1921
HARRIS, Infant (son), b/d June 20, 1922

GENTRY, John Lewis, d. Nov. 11, 1926
        Son of W. L. and Bonnie Gentry

## GENTRY #1 CEMETERY - (continued)

GENTRY, Sarah K.,    1872 - 1954
GENTRY, Lewis G.,    1860 - 1929
        Son of John and Elizabeth Edwards Gentry
GENTRY, Elizabeth,  1841 - 1911
GENTRY, Newton J.,  1872 - 1929
GENTRY, Laura Alice,  Oct. 5, 1877 - Dec. 17, 1932

BARNES, James B.,  Aug. 5, 1864 - Mar. 9, 1937
        Son of William and Ellen Mays Barnes
BARNES, Mary R. (w),  Dec. 12, 1874 - Sep. 7, 1957
        Daughter of James and Nancy Tipton Randolph
BARNES, Earl (son),  May 9, 1909 - Nov. 4, 1911

WATTS, Mary Elizabeth,  Aug. 25, 1933 - Jan. 19, 1935
        Daughter of Fred and Ethel (Edith?) Barnes Watts

GILLIS, Orville,   Jan. 12, 1919 - Oct. 17, 1920
GILLIS, Leonard E.,  June 11, 1914 - Aug. 1, 1915
GILLIS, David,     Oct. 7, 1922 - Jan. 19, 1923
GILLIS, James,     Oct. 7, 1922 - Nov. 20, 1929
        Children of W. L. and Vivian Gillis

VROMAN, David William,  Sep. 7, 1920 - Sep. 11, 1920
        Son of William A. and Elsie C. Vroman

## HIGGINS #3 CEMETERY

At crest on Rocky Fork Road, on right

Copied July 9, 1988

HIGGINS, Leonard Jack Sr.,  June 14, 1917 - Feb. 2, 1977

HIGGINS, Everette Q.,  Mar. 26, 1893 - Dec. 20, 1972
HIGGINS, Ella S. (w),  Mar. 14, 1895 -

SHELTON, Mildred Higgins,  Mar. 19, 1926 - Feb. 16, 1948
        Wife of Walter Shelton

HIGGINS, Timothy Allen,  Sep. 12, 1963 - Aug. 22, 1964
        Son of Ernest C. and Winnie Higgins

HIGGINS, Ernest C.,  Dec. 9, 1921 - Nov. 4, 1968
        S 1st Cl., US Navy,  WWII

HIGGINS, John L.,  Sep. 23, 1940 - May 24, 1972
HIGGINS, Barbara R. (w),  Jan. 21, 1950 -
HIGGINS, John L. Jr. (son),  b/d 1965

HIGGINS, Everett J.,  1950 - 1971

HIGGINS, Everett Jr.,  Feb. 17, 1927 - Aug. 30, 1967
        Pvt., 96th Inf.,  WWII

HIGGINS, Tony,  1952 - 1980

# TINKER #3 CEMETERY

On Mill Creek Road, left after bridge, then rt. at 3rd House

Copied Oct. 5, 1988

LLOYD, Carlie J.,  June 30, 1919 - Dec. 25, 1949
        Pfc., USA, WWII

McCURRY, Clarence H.,  Dec. 23, 1916 - Jan. 18, 1973
        S2, USN, WWII

TINKER, Parmer,  Jan. 10, 1893 - Feb. 25, 1983
TINKER, Savannah E. (w),  July 10, 1897 - Dec. 16, 1974

RUNION, William Harold,  Sep. 23, 1912 - May 31, 1963
        US Army, WWII
RUNION, Effie May,  Feb. 10, 1910 - Mar. 6, 1984

RUNION, James Samuel,  Jan. 24, 1884 - Oct. 2, 1948
RUNION, Velva Metcalf (w),  Jan. 28, 1890 - Aug. 26, 1962

RUNION, Wilma Ilene,  July 8, 1920 - Oct. 14, 1923
RUNION, Raymond Horace,  Jan. 6, 1923 - Jan. 14, 1923
        siblings

FOSTER, Ennis Metcalf,  May 3, 1898 - Mar. 5, 1929
        Wife of S. A. Foster

METCALF, Amanda C.,  May 10, 1868 - Oct. 3, 1942

PHILLIPS, Melvin,  Dec. 17, 1928 - Oct. 16, 1934
PHILLIPS, Ruby,   Oct. 29, 1932 - Mar. 7, 1933
        Children of Grant and Carrie Garland Phillips

GARLAND, Pauline,  Apr. 12, 1914 - Sep. 3, 1921
GARLAND, Bertha,   Aug. 24, 1912 - July 20, 1928
        -sisters

GARLAND, Stokes S.,   May 10, 1888 - June 1, 1976
GARLAND, Lottie Brown (w),  Nov. 8, 1890 - July 2, 1951

RUNION, Harry,  1918 -
RUNION, Irene (w),  1921 - 1981

RUNION, William S.,  Mar. 5, 1857 - June 30, 1931
RUNION, Lydia E. (w),  June 23, 1852 - May 10, 1929
        Daughter of William and Nancy Erwin Parks

RUNION, Arlee,  Mar. 24, 1887 - Sep. 4, 1974
RUNION, Edyth (w),  Apr. 2, 1895 - May 16, 1972

ERWIN, Guy C.,  Sep. 30, 1916 -
ERWIN, Mae Clouse (w),  Aug. 27, 1915 -
ERWIN, Shirley (dau) ,  June 4, 1937 - July 25, 1952

CLAY, Norman C., 1910 - 1986
CLAY, Edith E. (w), 1913 -

HOWELL, Mary J., Oct. 15, 1854 - June 22, 1940

EDWARDS, Oscar, Feb. 1, 1936 - Aug. 29, 1973
EDWARDS, Shirley T. (w), Oct. 31, 1940 -

TINKER, Hamby P., May 23, 1903 - Dec. 31, 1980
TINKER, Kitty A. (w), Jan. 8, 1910 - Feb. 9, 1975

MOUNTS, John, May 23, 1907 - Dec. 13, 1979, Pfc., USA, WWII
MOUNTS, Arlene (w), May 12, 1926 -

RUNION, William K., 1885 - 1969
RUNION, Della Z. (w), 1891 - 1950

RUNION, Elmer E., Dec. 4, 1908 - Aug. 31, 1964, "husband"

TIPTON, Floyd, May 7, 1915 - Mar. 21, 1981
TIPTON, Frances (w), Apr. 20, 1919 -

COPELAND, George Alvin, May 17, 1857 - Jan. 19, 1936

WILLIAMSON, Richard D., Aug. 21, 1917 - May 17, 1982
WILLIAMSON, Velma B. (w), July 25, 1923 - June 29, 1979

WILLIAMSON, William J., Oct. 3, 1866 - Nov. 18, 1958
        Son of Isaac Williamson
WILLIAMSON, Mary A. (w), Jan. 10, 1867 - Feb. 25, 1963
        Daughter of Samuel Q. and Sarah Banner Cash

WILLIAMSON, Oliver S., Mar. 16, 1916 - Jan. 19, 1951
WILLIAMSON, Evelyn Louise, Feb. 9, 1920 - June 6, 1946
        Children of George A. and Dora Bell Callahan Williamson

RUMPF, Jean E. Tilson, Sep. 11, 1939 - Feb. 19, 1988, "mom"

WILLIAMSON, Beryl, d. Mar. 30, 1926
WILLIAMSON, Margaret, d. Jan. 6, 1923
        - infant siblings

WILLIAMSON, George A., Aug. 19, 1891 - July 11, 1950
WILLIAMSON, Dora B. (w), July 11, 1895 - Jan. 10, 1923

WILLIAMSON, Mary Jane, 1900 - 1980 , "mother"

CHRISTY, James Cooper, 1898 - 1980

TINKER, Jessie A., Aug. 15, 1897 - Aug. 15, 1971

TINKER, Nelson, 1870 - Jan. 29, 1949, Son of Jesse R. Tinker
TINKER, Safronia J. (w), 1870 - 1971

BROWN, Emery,  June 14, 1901 - Feb. 7, 1903
        Son of W. F. and Mary Brown

WHITE, Jerry Mack,   July 11, 1947 - July 16, 1947
WHITE, Richard Jr.,  Oct. 14, 1949 - Oct. 17, 1949
        Sons of Richard Daniel and Mollie Edna Mattingly White

PRESSNELL, Harrison H.,   July 14, 1845 - July 3, 1919

DUNCAN, Phoebe P.,   Apr. 9, 1889 - Sep. 4, 1969

BLANKENSHIP, Mary,   1876 - 1925

CALLAHAN, Jesse W.,   Nov. 6, 1858 - Nov. 5, 1937
CALLAHAN, Rhoda Jarvis (w),  Aug. 19, 1864 - Apr. 20, 1928

CALLAHAN, J. Albert,  Jan. 6, 1893 - Dec. 13, 1962
        Son of Jessee W. and Rhoda M. Jarvis Callahan
CALLAHAN, Clara B. (w),  Apr. 9, 1897 - Nov. 20, 1962
        Daughter of Wm. M. and Virginia Lee Harwood Crouch

CALLAHAN, William Bert,  Aug. 22, 1864 - Dec. 17, 1956
CALLAHAN, Eliza Lenora (w),  Oct. 3, 1880 - Jan. 5, 1955

CALLAHAN, William E. Sr.,   June 14, 1900 - Oct. 21, 1938

HUGHES, Edward Dale,  b/d Apr. 22, 1951
        Son of Daniel and Thelma Hughes

RILEY, Infant,  June 17, 1944 - Dec. 1, 1945
        Son of Norman and Dorothy Riley

HUGHES, Daniel Whitfield Jr.,   July 12, 1926 - Sep. 22, 1973
        M/Sgt., USAF, Vietnam
HUGHES, Thelma C. (w),  Sep. 12, 1929 -

CALLAHAN, James T.,  May 25, 1903 - Dec. 18, 1982
CALLAHAN, Nannie A. (w),  Apr. 13, 1910 -

CALLAHAN, Roy S.,  Feb. 5, 1912 - Nov. 8, 1964

ADKINS, James D.,  Apr. 5, 1870 - Apr. 23, 1954
ADKINS, Nancy E. (w),  Apr. 10, 1872 - July 21, 1940

BRACKINS, John,  Jan. 13, 1856 - June 22, 1927

BRACKINS, Melvin Fuller,  1892 - 1969

LEDFORD, Nancy Elizabeth,  Apr. 20, 1850 - Nov. 15, 1917

CORN, Hezikiah, 1832 - 1864, Killed by Confederate Army
CORN, Ellen Tinker (w), Jan. 25, 1834 - Nov. 25, 1923
        Mother of 3 boys and 2 girls

EDWARDS, Sarah E. "Sallie",  Jan. 3, 1859 - July 4, 1927

CALLAHAN, Alice L.,  Feb. 28, 1929 - May 28, 1930
        Daughter of Fred and Lula Ray Callahan

LEDFORD, Grady Sr.,  Aug. 2, 1900 - Aug. 16, 1959
        Son of Stanford and Amonda Adkins Ledford

MILLER, Andy,  Feb. 22, 1927 - Sep. 29, 1983
MILLER, Ethel (w),  Mar. 31, 1928 -
MILLER, Lonnie Andrew (son),  d. Jan. 22, 1947 at 3 weeks

BOWMAN, Loris Clouse,  Dec. 7, 1913 - Nov. 21, 1953
        Daughter of William P. and Maggie W. Clouse (below)

CLOUSE, William Parks,  Feb. 19, 1888 - Dec. 10, 1980
CLOUSE, Maggie Willis (w),  Jan. 8, 1894 - June 19, 1957
        Daughter of Wm. J. and Martha Guinn Willis

MASTERS, Shell E.,  Dec. 26, 1898 - Dec. 6, 1971
MASTERS, Creta Miller (w),  Sep. 23, 1910 -

MASTERS, Oliver E.,  Dec. 26, 1898 - Jan. 27, 1981
        US Army, WWII, Shell's brother
MASTERS, Roxie Ann,  1903 - 1982, Oliver's sister - never married

WILSON, S. M.,  Apr. 28, 1892 - Dec. 15, 1980
WILSON, Vancy (w),  Apr. 2, 1896 - Oct. 23, 1961

MASTERS, Donald Ray,  b/d 1962

TINKER, Bessie Callahan,  July 1, 1906 - Dec. 5, 1979, "mother"

CALLAHAN, Francis Ingle,  1921 - 1967

CALLAHAN, Arthur P.,  Oct. 6, 1919 - May 5, 1967, US Navy, WWII

CALLAHAN, William Elbert,  June 23, 1923 - Oct. 17, 1972
        From S.C., US Navy, WWII

SMITH, Charles,  Oct. 30, 1934 -
SMITH, Kathleen (Delorese?) (w),  Apr. 20, 1934 - Nov. 20, 1982

RAY, James E.,  Dec. 31, 1861 - Mar. 30, 1947
RAY, Flora Bean (w),  May 17, 1862 - Jan. 14, 1945
        Daughter of Charles Russell and Margaret Brown Bean

MASTERS, Phillip S.,  Nov. 9, 1872 - May 13, 1944
        Co. F, 6th Vol. Infantry, Span-Am. War(?)
        Son of Wilke and Rachel Tinker Masters
MASTERS, Elizabeth Tinker (w),  Oct. 9, 1869 - Aug. 11, 1961

MASTERS, T. R. "Sid",  July 26, 1901 - Mar. 26, 1962 "husband"

BOWMAN, W. S.,   July 28, 1879 - Jan. 20, 1944
BOWMAN, Hannah Howell (w),   Feb. 9, 1876 - July 23, 1954

EDWARDS, Grover C.,   Nov. 28, 1894 - Sep. 21, 1979
EDWARDS, Lina M. (w),   Oct. 10, 1904 -

TIPTON, Zeke,   Sep. 22, 1901 - July 30, 1972
TIPTON, Lucy Miller (w),   Nov. 18, 1908 - Apr. 11, 1974

CALLAHAN, Fred Braxton,   July 23, 1908 - June 27, 1967
CALLAHAN, Lula Ray (w),   Sep. 19, 1910 - Dec. 6, 1984

MASTERS, Ada,   May 15, 1908 - Aug. 16, 1908
MASTERS, Son,   b.d Feb. 14, 1898
          Children of P. S. Masters

FOSTER, William Regeby, 1758 - 1840,   new stone

MASTERS, Son,   b/d July 21, 1928,   son of S. E. Masters

MASTERS, Ada Leigh,   May 15, 1908 - Aug. 16, 1908

MASTERS, Son,   b/d Feb. 14, 1898
          Son of Phillip and Elizabeth Masters

EDWARDS, Clyde Cleveland,   Feb. 11, 1956 - Dec. 28, 1987

HIGGINS, Janie M.,   Apr. 4, 1913 - Dec. 9, 1962
          Daughter John and Sally Presnell Miller (below)

MILLER, John,   July 23, 1846 - June 24, 1922
          Co. M, 8th TN CAV.,   Union Army
MILLER, Sally Presnell (w),   Oct. 31, 1881 - Nov. 29, 1955

FRANKLIN, Mary M.,   1901 - 1978

FRANKLIN, Fred,   1875 - 1963

                plus many unmarked stones

   NOTE:  The new highway will be slightly bent, to avoid
          this cemetery.


                     ERWIN #2 CEMETERY

   South end of former Burrell farm, at Red Bank, near radio
   towers, south of Erwin on Rt. 19/23

                    Copied Mar. 5, 1989

DUNCAN, Mary E.,   Oct. 7, 1860 - July 14, 1895
          Wife of J. L. Duncan

WHITE, Nancy C.,   Jan. 7, 1861 - Nov. 29, 1891
          Wife of G. W. White

ERWIN #2 CEMETERY - (continued)

TINKER, Sara J., 1867 - 1899

BROCKUS, W. K., Co. B, 13th TN CAV., Union Army
BROCKUS, Sara (w), Sep. 22, 1848 - Sep. 21, 1890

BAYLESS, N., Dec. 31, 1796 - Jan. 2, 1879

BAYLESS, W. E., Jan. 19, 1844 - July 18, 18--

PARKS, W. M., Oct. 23, 1813 - Dec. 20, 1885
PARKS, Nancy (w), Feb. 12, 1816 - Jan. 15, 1889
        Married June 13, 1835

BOGART, Samuel W., Oct. 15, 1822 - May 1, 1863
BOGART, Mary Erwin (w), no dates

ERWIN, William C., Dec. 12, 1860 - Jan. 29, 1867
        (dates uncertain)

ERWIN, Elizabeth D., Apr. 27, 1821 - Nov. 8, 1879
        Wife of Jesse B. Erwin (first county clerk)
        Daughter of James B. McMahan

ERWIN, James Madison, July 30, 1846 - Mar. 1, 1896
        Co. C, 3rd NC Mtd. Inf., Union Army

ERWIN, Julia A. Ray, Apr. 8, 1854 - Oct. 28, 1880
        Wife of W. S. Erwin

ERWIN, Iva Mae, Mar. 27, 1897 - July 24, 1898
ERWIN, Elizabeth, Mar. 14, 1894 - Aug. 22, 1895
        Daughters of W. S. and Hester E. Woodward Erwin

WHITE, Jennie L., Apr. 15, 1885 - Aug. 8, 1885
        Daughter of L. W. and E. M. White

PIPPIN, Arthur Toney, July 31, 1886 - June 5, 1887

MORRIS, William C., July 30, 1831 - Feb. 2, 1897
        (not visible by Mar. 5, 1989)

HOWELL, J. A., Feb. 13, 1852 - Apr. 29, 1897

PARKS, William E., May 17, 1838 - Feb. 28, 1887
PARKS, Jane Davis (w), Sep. 16, 1834 - Aug. 23, 1903

BALEY, Lewis E., Oct. 31, 1828 - Mar. 4, 1874
BALEY, Sarah Erwin (w), Jan. 31, 1826 - Aug. 12, 1913

ERWIN, Mary V., Jan. 21, 1853 (1855?) - Feb. 28, 1856

added in 1988:
RUNNION, Robert, July 4, 1893 - Apr. 29, 1894
        Son of W. S. and L. E. Runnion

    many unmarked stones. 2 enclosed areas (wood posts & pipe),
    2 graves each, with field stones

## RAY CEMETERY #1

Near the former Burrell home in Riverview, south of Erwin

Previously recorded; checked Oct. 22, 1988

RAY, E. P.,    Mar. 23, 1851 - Mar. 10, 1912
RAY, Harriett C. (w),   June 22, 1854 - June 4, 1892
RAY, Bertha May (dau),   Aug. 6, 1887 - June 4, 1892
RAY, Samuel T. (son),   1876 - 1879
RAY, Infant (dau),   b/d 1879
RAY, Infant (son),   b/d 1881

PRICE, Effie Bell Ray,   Apr. 24, 1883 - Feb. 19, 1904
        Wife of S. L. Price

RAY, Barnett,   Oct. 29, 1826 - June 12, 1893 (1899?)

RAY, Freddie,   Jan. 8, 1890 - May 24, 1905

RAY, Hannah,   Mar. 17, 1829 - June 13, 1903


## HENSLEY #3 CEMETERY

Off Spivey Mt. Rd., left just before Mt. Dale Church
and Little Bald Creek Road

Copied Jan. 25, 1989

EDWARDS, Vines,   Feb. 1, 1911 - May 10, 1966
EDWARDS, Ebbie F. (w),   June 22, 1916 -
        Married Dec. 6, 1933
EDWARDS, Infant (son),   d. Mar. 18, 1939
EDWARDS, Infant (son),   d. Sep. 29, 1946

FOSTER, James H.,   Feb. 14, 1880 - June 9, 1951
FOSTER, Eliza E. (w),   May 22, 1890 - July 22, 1971

WILLIAMS, Millie R.,   1870 - 1950

WILLIAMS, Joe,    1832 - 1941

EDWARDS, Edna O.,   Apr. 16, 1932 - July 23, 1937
EDWARDS, Nina K.,   Nov. 17, 1937 - Dec. 8, 1938,  sisters

WILLIAMS, Eliza Hensley,   Sep. 8, 1885 - Oct. 2, 1951

WILLIAMS, C. P.,   Oct. 14, 1873 - July 1, 1940

WILLIAMS, Silas,   Co. H, 3rd NC Mtd. Inf., Union Army

WILLIAMS, Axie,   Sep. 14, 1842 - Mar. 18, 1910

- 227 -

WILLIAMS, Mack,    1882 - 1963
WILLIAMS, Texie Honeycutt (w), Mar. 12, 1893 - July 23, 1971

EDWARDS, Joseph B.,   May 17, 1860 - Sep. 15, 1920
EDWARDS, Sina (w),   Nov. 22, 1866 - Apr. 13, 1902

EDWARDS, Louisa J.,   July 4, 1836 - Oct. 2, 1900

HIGGINS, George W.,   Mar. 14, 1824 - July 28, 1863
HIGGINS, Mary (w),   Oct. 24, 1826 - July 21, 1903

HUSKINS, Mary Celeste,  Aug. 18, 1863 - Sep. 20, 1939

JONES, Gaither B.,  d. July 24, 1922,  Cpt., 329th Inf.

HENSLEY, William Kinnsey,  Co. M, 8th TN CAV., Union Army
          Son of William A. and Lucinda Hensley
HENSLEY, Elmira Chandler (w),  Sep. 28, 1827 - Aug. 27, 1910
          Dau. of Joe & Holly Chandler (Chandler #2 Cem.)
HENSLEY, Hiriam Cornelius,  July 4, 1862 - Mar. 12, 1933
HENSLEY, Polly Ann (w),  June 11, 1870 - Jan. 25, 1948

HENSLEY, B. L.,  June 28, 1832 - Nov. 19, 1916

HENSLEY, Lucinda,  Jan. 18, 1837 - Jan. 18, 1898

HENSLEY, Eligah B.,   no dates
HENSLEY, Ida G.,   Nov. 26, 1901 - Aug. 31, 1902
          Children of W. H. and M. J. Hensley

HENSLEY, Thomas Watsel,   Sep. 21, 1876 - June 15, 1953
HENSLEY, Amanda Jane (w), Aug. 19, 1876 - Feb.  6, 1965

HENSLEY, John,   Mar. 19, 1840 - Mar. 29, 1927

HENSLEY, Mary G.,   Mar. 20, 1844 - Sep. 19, 1900
          (Mother of 6 children)

HENSLEY, Vernie E.,  Mar. 19, 1911 - June 19, 1965

HENSLEY, Vanda Bell,  Aug. 18, 1900 - Jan. 16, 1901
HENSLEY, Vernon,   May 11, 1909 - Oct. 23, 1910
HENSLEY, Robert W.,   Aug. 27, 1894 - Nov. 19, 1910
          Children of H. C. and P. A. Hensley

LEWIS, Mallie L.,   Sep. 19, 1891 - Nov. 4, 1946
LEWIS, Mary C. (w), Jan. 22, 1898 - May 16, 1955
LEWIS, Ross (son),  May 14, 1915 - Nov. 11, 1934
LEWIS, Audie (dau), Oct. 20, 1917 - July 7, 1921

HIGGINS, Dora E.,   Mar. 25, 1886 - Feb. 17, 1904

HENSLEY, William A.,    Sep. 18, 1798 - Nov. 5, 1889
HENSLEY, Lucinda (w),   July 8, 1803 - May 24, 1898
          - The first settlers on Spivey Mountain
          - Parents of William Kinnsey Hensley

HENSLEY, Silas,   Nov. 2, 1845 - Nov. 4, 1935
          Son of Wm. A. Hensley
HENSLEY, Sarah E. (w),   Jan. 7, 1846 - Aug. 16, 1936
HENSLEY, Mariah Cordelia (dau),   June 25, 1870 - Apr. 12, 1875

HENSLEY, Hester B.,   Mar. 20, 1881 - Oct. 20, 1930

HENSLEY, Loften M.,   Nov. 26, 1897 - Jan. 25, 1916

HONEYCUT, Cora L.,   Apr. 11, 1879 - May 21, 1904
          Mother of 3 children

HENSLEY, Rebecca Jane,   Nov. 21, 1855 - May 10, 1944

HENSLEY, Cornelius E.,   July 14, 1855 - June 21, 1947

HENSLEY, R. B.,   Mar. 2, 1833 - Feb. 25, 1905
HENSLEY, Chatherine (w),   Mar. 24, 1832 - Apr. 25, 1914

HENSLEY, John B.,   Aug. 4, 1860 - Jan. 14, 1921

HENSLEY, Martha A.,   May 5, 1862 - Mar. 28, 1939

FOSTER, Claude,   1904 - 1960, Son of Joseph H. and Matilda
                                Higgins Foster

ATKINS, David M.,   Aug. 10, 1884 - Aug. 19, 1959
ATKINS, Tokie H. (w),   June 5, 1890 - Dec. 25, 1979

ATKINS, Bruce,   Aug. 7, 1915 - Aug. 20, 1969

FOSTER, Joseph H.,   Jan. 3, 1874 - Apr. 28, 1953
          Son of Bert Hensley and Hannah Foster
FOSTER, Matilda J. (w),   Aug. 8, 1883 - Oct. 8, 1959
          Daughter of Elizabeth Higgins

FOSTER, Clay,   May 18, 1918 - July 16, 1962
          Pfc., 198th AAA Bm, WWII

HENSLEY, William G.,   June 25, 1868 - May 25, 1957
HENSLEY, Cinda E. (w),   Aug. 20, 1875 - Dec. 11, 1963
HENSLEY, Virgie Iola (dau),   Dec. 25, 1902 - July 4, 1906

HENSLEY, Bonnie Kate,   Apr. 29, 1908 - July 19, 1921

HENSLEY, Earnest F.,   Mar. 19, 1896 - May 12, 1905
          Son of E. B. and Celia A. Hensley

HENSLEY #3 CEMETERY - (continued)

HENSLEY, Arthur,  Sep. 19, 1893 - Aug. 25, 1964
HENSLEY, Amanda E. (w),  May 20, 1892 - June 28, 1964
HENSLEY, Orville F. (son),  July 7, 1919 - June 13, 1943
        Pfc., US Army, Killed in North Africa, WWII

WILSON, W. Thomas,  Nov. 7, 1879 - Dec. 26, 1955
WILSON, Cora Etta (w),  Apr. 18, 1884 - Apr. 10, 1950

EDWARDS, Baby,   d. 1948

MARTIN, Preston,   July 2, 1897 -
MARTIN, Martha Lucinda (w),  Jan. 22, 1898 - Apr. 1, 1952
        Daughter of Cornelius and Polly Ann Hensley

        plus many unmarked concrete crosses


                    HEAD CEMETERY

Located on Marbleton Road, on left, opposite the north junction
of County Road
                Copied Nov.13,1990

HEAD, J.L.,  Oct.14,1870 - Aug.29,1928

HEAD, Amanda (w), Dec.16,1884 - Oct.24,1927

HEAD, Lucy, (dau)  d. Dec. 6,1926 (infant)

        plus several unmarked children's graves


                    PRICE CEMETERY

    Coffee Ridge up Price Road to green house, then go rt. up
    rough road to top, then left through field

                Copied Jan. 25, 1989

PRICE, Buster Osko,  June 24, 1904 - Aug. 11, 1978
PRICE, Amanda J. (w),  July 14, 1915 -

EDWARDS, Lina E.,   Feb. 14, 1907 - Nov. 16, 1911
        Daughter of Edeil and Maerkie Edwards

PRICE, McKinley Kelley,  Mar. 1, 1933 - Oct. 8, 1961
        A2C, US Air Force

PRICE, Grady,   Oct. 31, 1931 - Dec. 4, 1931

EDWARDS, Eliza,  Apr. 19, 1861 - May 19, 1902
        Married May 19, 1880  (husband not noted)


                    - 230 -

PRICE, John W.,   Mar. 22, 1882 - Aug. 6, 1965
PRICE, Clara B. (w),  June 14, 1886 - Aug. 16, 1970

HUERTA, Jesus,   1898 - 1988

## WILLIS #4 CEMETERY

West side of Coffee Ridge Loop, up draw beside Willis apple
farm to top of ridge, at left

Copied Jan. 25, 1989

WILLIS, Dave Frank,  Apr. 13, 1863 - Dec. 1, 1945
        Son of Daniel E. and Mary E. Foster Willis
WILLIS, Martha (w),  Nov. 29, 1861 - May 3, 1943
        Daughter of John and Ruth Tilson Gillis

## LEDFORD #2 CEMETERY

On west side of Coffee Ridge Loop, on top of hill, with
"house" visible (best approach is from Gentry Mt. Rd. side)

Copied Jan. 25, 1989

LEDFORD, Amos P.,  Feb. 10, 1849 - Nov. 9, 1933
        Son of Alfred and Artie Christine Sams Ledford
        This tombstone is enclosed by a sort of house,
        visible from the road.

## LEDFORD #3 CEMETERY

SE corner of Coffee Ridge Loop, across ravine

Copied Jan. 28, 1989

LEDFORD, Adah Ruth,   June 11, 1913 - Jan. 10, 1943

LEDFORD, Mabel,   Dec. 20, 1936 - Feb. 10, 1944

LEDFORD, Debra Renee,  Dec. 29, 1956 - Dec. 30, 1956
        Daughter of Lawrence Ledford

## MASHBURN CEMETERY

Off Upper Higgins Creek Road, on Roscoe Edwards Road, left
up to top of bluff
                    Copied Jan. 28, 1989

MASHBURN, Eller,  Oct. 20, 1884 - Mar. 29, 1903
        Wife of T. M. Mashburn

plus 6 unmarked graves

## FOSTER #3 CEMETERY

At end of Coy Williams Road, off Rt. 19 (left)

Copied Feb. 1, 1989

HENSLEY, W. Kim,   Mar. 23, 1869 - Jan. 14, 1944
        Son of William Kimmsey Hensley

SHEHAN, W. G.,   Aug. 25, 1885 - Sep. 4, 1908

FOSTER, Fred,   Aug. 15, 1897 - Oct. 16, 1964
FOSTER, William B.,   Apr. 6, 1874 - Apr. 16, 1930
        Sons of David Frank and Leanna Hensley Foster (below)

FOSTER, David Frank,   Dec. 22, 1843 - Jan. 8, 1922
        In TN unit in Union Army
FOSTER, Leanner (w),   Jan. 8, 1858 - July 3, 1949
        Daughter of Bert and Catherine Edwards Hensley

FOSTER, John A.,   Apr. 12, 1882 - July 5, 1906

HENSLEY, Maggie I.,   June 30, 1884 - July 5, 1919
        Wife of Howell Hensley

FOSTER, Kyle F.,   July 19, 1927 - Nov. 5, 1930
        Son of Harrison and Della Lawing Foster

    plus many unmarked stones, including -
FOSTER, Nellie, b. 1816. Buried above her son, David F. Foster

## HOWELL   CEMETERY

At end of Granny Lewis Creek Road, 3.5 mi. in from Rt. 19

Copied Feb. 1, 1989

Only 3 graves with unmarked field stones, but with "Howell
Cemetery" sign by road.

## WOODWARD CEMETERY

Off Upper Higgins Creek Road, on Gentry Mt. Rd., last house
on left before big hill. Take farm road past barn, keep
straight on. Turn left at culvert. Cemetery is on hill on
right.

Copied March 4, 1989

WOODWARD, James B.,   Apr. 27, 1872 - May 11, 1960
WOODWARD, Elizaem B. (w),   May 1, 1875 - Nov. 13, 1950

TILSON, John,   Aug. 18, 1788 - Dec. 24, 1855

TILSON, John S.,   Apr. 24, 1828 - Nov. 3, 1853

TILSON, J. E.,   Co. H, 8 TN CAV.,   Union Army

HIGGINS, F. Bethel,  Feb. 29, 1888 - Jan. 23, 1916
        Wife of A. J. Higgins

MURRAY, Thomas L.,  July 27, 1907 - Aug. 20, 1908
MURRAY, Finnettie,  b/d Jan. 30, 1909
        Son and daughter of W. A. and M. J. Murray

            plus several unmarked stones


## BEAN CEMETERY

  On Rt. 19/23, S. of Erwin.  Take right just before Engles
  Restaurant, to Davis farm

              Copied Mar. 5, 1989

BEAN, *Charles Russell Jr.,  Aug. 13, 1835 - Jan. 10, 1919
BEAN, Margaret Brown (w),  Apr. 25, 1839 - Mar. 12, 1894
        Probably granddaughter of orig. Jacob Brown

    plus enough fieldstones for about 12 graves, including
    a Jacob Brown, a grandson (?) of the original Jacob
    Brown who settled on Nolichuckey in 1770.

    This cemetery is on Dorothy Davis' farm, and the
    modern marker was put up in 1940's by Bean Family
    Association.

    *Charles was the last to make the famous Bean rifle.
    He was a Sgt. in Confederate Army.  He was descended
    from the Washington County Bean family, the great
    grandson of William Bean, who settled there in 1769.


## RIVER HILL CEMETERY

    Off Rt. 19/23 a few yards, on Chestoa Road, in
    River Hill area
              Copied Mar. 10, 1989

FOSTER, Carl,  Dec. 29, 1907 - Jan. 11, 1982
FOSTER, Bessie L. (w),  Oct. 3, 1915 -
FOSTER, Infant,  b/d 1964

PHILLIPS, Roscoe,  June 12, 1903 - June 20, 1973
PHILLIPS, Mima (w),  Nov. 19, 1906 - Jan. 1, 1979

HIGGINS, Nora Foster,  July 11, 1902 - Jan. 3, 1966
HIGGINS, R. H. "Jim" (son),  1927 - 1983

PETERSON, Ethel,  1877 - 1961

TRUE, Mollie S.,  1909 - 1968

RIVER HILL CEMETERY - (continued)

FOSTER, Muriel Denise, May 27,1966 - Aug. 27,1966
        Dau. of Ted and Doris Foster

SHEHAN, A., June 28,1888 - Dec. 9,1957
SHEHAN, Alta, May 17,1894 - Jan.16,1972
SHEHAN, Ned, d. Dec.8,1923 at age 86
SHEHAN, Nancy Elizabeth, 1868-1938
        Dau. of Samuel and Mary Malissa Shehan Higgins
SHELTON, Burgess H., Aug.10,1889 - May 23,1955
SHELTON, Rose Anna (w), July 10,1890 - Nov.19,1974
SHEHAN, Harley, May 4,1917 - June 11,1940

            plus several unmarked stones

            TILSON #3 CEMETERY

Off Rt. 23 on Little Branch Road. Go straight at first
reverse curve, past steel gate, then right up to top of hill
(fenced)        Copied Mar.10,1989

TILSON, Infant, d. Feb.4,1923
        Son of Grace and Ernest Tilson
TILSON, Hazel Lee, Mar.19,1931 - April 2,1932
TILSON, Billy Richard, b/d June 25,1933
TILSON, Barbrie, Oct.30,1912 - Sept.27,1913
        Dau. of W.J. and N.A. Tilson
HARRIS, Mary K., 1863 - 1949
        plus several unmarked graves, including -
GUINN, David, d. c1900
GUINN, Anna (w), d. c1914
        Parents of John B. Guinn (P-236)
GUINN, Infants (2) Children of J.W. Guinn
SAMS, Dovie                 SELBY, Infant
HARRIS, J.C.                TILSON, W.R.
TILSON, Jennie              TILSON, Elsie
TILSON, Atlas               TILSON, Ralph


            MOORE CEMETERY

On Rice Creek Road, 8/10 mile, on right, from Flag Pond,
up short road
            Copied March 10,1989

PHILLIPS, William Alfred, June 9,1882 - Aug.29,1961
PHILLIPS, Nora Belle Howell (w), Nov.8,1883 - Nov.22,1972
PHILLIPS, Lake F., 1905 - 1988


                    -234-

STOCKTON, Edward F., b. July 25, 1875
STOCKTON, Cora E. (w), Nov. 6, 1880 - Nov. 22, 1952
STOCKTON, Ella Kate (dau), Apr. 14, 1910 - July 17, 1964

STOCKTON, Ottis E., July 25, 1899 - Feb. 3, 1920

PHILLIPS, Elroy Harvy, Sep. 8, 1894 - Jan. 21, 1946

PHILLIPS, Katie C., Feb. 24, 1859 - May 5, 1919

PHILLIPS, N. B., Nov. 1, 1852 - Oct. 11, 1935

PHILLIPS, Robert, b/d Nov. 30, 1932

MOORE, William N., Oct. 1, 1856 - Jan. 22, 1916

MOORE, Rebecca J., July 26, 1857 - Apr. 30, 1927

PHILLIPS, Hiram L., May 7, 1884 - July 10, 1976
PHILLIPS, Bertha S. (w), Aug. 18, 1890 - Sep. 25, 1975

MOORE, Charles Edwin, Sep. 2, 1917 - July 1, 1919
        Son of R. E. and Belle Moore

MOORE, Robert F., Apr. 17, 1886 - Jan. 30, 1922

CRAWFORD, Max Robert, May 21, 1940 - Jan. 2, 1981

CRAWFORD, Infant, b/d Aug. 27, 1953
        Daughter of Bill and Claudine Crawford

CRAWFORD, James A., Mar. 16, 1893 - Jan. 30, 1942
        Son of Nathan and Ruth Crawford

BROOMER, William B., June 25, 1879 - Mar. 21, 1959
BROOMER, Margret J., Oct. 1, 1869 - 1962

## CLOUSE CEMETERY

On Rt. 23, 1/2 mile south of Big Branch Road,
up dirt road, near trailers

Copied Mar. 11, 1989

COX, Charles, Aug. 13, 1902 - Aug. 19, 1922

COX, Milburn, Apr. 2, 1908 - Mar. 22, 1934
        Sons of W. Jason and Elizabeth Gillis Cox

CLOUSE, Dallas Roy, Sep. 7, 1930 - Sep. 25, 1930
        Son of G. C. and Laura Clouse

CLOUSE, W. H., July 9, 1861 - Sep. 1, 1905

CLOUSE CEMETERY - (continued)

EDWARDS, Lydia Clouse, Sept.25,1866 - Nov.9,1915
       Former wife of W.H. Clouse. Their 3 infants buried here
TILSON, Iva,  June 22,1899 - Oct.4,1902
       Dau. of W.L. and M.E. Tilson
GUINN, John B., Aug.21,1860 - Jan.8,1935
GUINN, Sarah B., (w), Mar.23,1863 - May 13,1950
       Dau. of George and Cassie Clouse

## UNMARKED GRAVES

GUINN, David, Nathan and Mary Ellen. Children of John and Sarah.
CLOUSE,  3 infants of W.H. and Lydia Clouse

| | |
|---|---|
| TILSON, John M. | CLOUSE, Jacob |
| TILSON, Mary Ann (w) | CLOUSE, Sarah (w) |
| TILSON, Andy (son) | CLOUSE, Will (son) |
| TILSON, Harrison (son) | CLOUSE, Dusky (son) |
| WILLIAMS, Howard | CLOUSE, George |
| WILLIAMS, Glenna (w) | CLOUSE, Cassie (w) |
| CLOUSE, Peter | CLOUSE, Nancy (dau) |
| CLOUSE, 2 infants of Peter's | GUINN,  2 infants of Jas.D. Guinn |

## TREADWAY CEMETERY

On Rt. 23, just beyond Upper Higgins Creek Road, across
Hwy. behind bar and up hill, then bear left at top

Copied Mar.11,1989

TREADWAY, James Frank, Mar.4,1883 - 1970
TREADWAY, Emma Cody, (w), July 21,1886 - Feb.24,1962
TREADWAY, Montie Bennie, Sept.28,1948 - Sept.29,1967
TREADWAY, Leroy, Apr.14,1855 - Dec.30,1943
TREADWAY, Hannah W. (w), Aug.1,1863 - Oct.12,1954
TREADWAY, Jane Ray,  July 30,1890 - Jan.25,1922
       Wife of Carver Treadway
TREADWAY, Infant Son, b/d April 16,1918
TREADWAY, Albert J., Nov.4,1936 - Nov.23,1936
       Son of Lewis and Kate Treadway
WILLIS, S.C., July 5,1882 - Apr.5,1931

HENSLEY, Elizabeth, April 10,1844 - Feb.25,1917

WILLIS, Macy, Feb.18,1898 - Sept. ??

METCALF, Charlotte A., May 10,1859 - Mar.12,1879

HARRIS, Elizabeth, July 8,1852 - April 1880

HENSLEY, Catherine, Nov.17,1849 - June 10,1886 (?)

WILLIS, J.A., Co H 3NC Mtd. Inf. Union Army
WILLIS, Edney (w), Feb.2,1829 June 9,1887

DENNEY, Callie Oder, Jan.12,1911 - Dec.19,1914
DENNEY, George Frank, May 9, 1902 - Dec.1,1902
DENNEY, Ray Ambers, Oct.2,1913 - Dec.2,1914
DENNEY, Infant Son, b/d Oct.8,1903

       plus many unmarked stones

## SILVERS CEMETERY #1

At upper end of Tipton Branch, on Curt Hensley Road,
off Rice Creek Road, south of Flag Pond

Copied Mar. 14, 1989

SILVERS, Walter B.,  Aug. 23, 1896 - Mar. 13, 1978
        Pvt., US Army, WWI

SILVERS, Helen R.,  May 21, 1915 - Mar. 6, 1942

SILVERS, John,      1850 - July 30, 1934
SILVERS, Narcissa (w),  July 7, 1867 - Dec. 31, 1954

SILVERS, Edward,    June 28, 1927 - June 12, 1936
SILVERS, Elmer,     Jan. 27, 1946 - Apr. 27, 1948
SILVERS, Daniel,    b/d Dec. 21, 1948
SILVERS, Baby,      b/d Apr. 15, 1949
SILVERS, Olive,     b/d Aug. 15, 1950
        - siblings

SILVERS, Thore,    July 17, 1900 - July 14, 1986
SILVERS, Florence (w),  Oct. 19, 1908 - Aug. 29, 1979

SILVERS, Jake,    Feb. 15, 1929 - Apr. 30, 1982
SILVERS, Alena (w),  Nov. 3, 1936 -

HENSLEY, Silas Wesley,  Oct. 27, 1895 - Aug. 13, 1977
        Pvt. US Army, WWI
HENSLEY, Martha B. (w),  Apr. 15, 1903 -

HENSLEY, Clara,  Sep. 21, 1936 - July 6, 1938

BRIGGS, Emery Lee,  May 5, 1916 - Dec. 28, 1984
        Pfc., US Army, WWII

BRIGGS, Nola C.,  1930 - 1983


## CARTER CEMETERY

On Carter Branch section of Tilson Mt. Road, left at white
2 story house, on level portion of road

Copied Mar. 14, 1989

CARTER, Robert Swain,  Feb. 3, 1875 - Apr. 4, 1937
        Son of Sheeve and Sara Katheryn Runion Carter

CARTER, Robert G.,  1940 - 1949

plus several unmarked graves

- 237 -

## GUINN #1 CEMETERY

On hill, on Rt. 23 at beginning of Tilson Mt. Road

Copied Mar. 14, 1989

Cemetery overrun by cattle

GUINN, W. F., Apr. 12, 1848 - Jan. 11, 1917

GUINN, Mary J. (w), 1855 - 1939

GUINN, Luther F., July 20, 1880 - Feb. 6, 1929
        Son of William and Mary Jane Woodward Guinn (above)

GUINN, Little Charlie, Oct. 16, 1904 - Mar. 11, 1908
        Son of Lattie and Gertie Guinn

SHELTON, Guy Lee, June 27, 1930 - Oct. 7, 1935
        Son of Claude and Viola Ford Shelton

SHELTON, C. L., Jan. 14, 1918 - Oct. 26, 1918
        Son of M. M. and Pearl Shelton

SHELTON, N. G., Jan. 15, 1882 - Mar. 6, 1914

SHELTON, Levi, Apr. 24, 1852 - Mar. 12, 1901

SHELTON, Arminda, 1857 - May 25, 1941
        Daughter of Riley Shelton; Wife of David Shelton

plus several unmarked stones


## LLOYD CEMETERY

At highest point on Rocky Fork Road, across road from
Higgins Cemetery, on side road

Copied Mar. 17, 1989

LOYD, David M., 1865 - 1911

LLOYD, Joe, Mar. 17, 1892 - Nov. 9, 1933
        Son of David (above) and Wennie Effler Lloyd

LLOYD, Lattie R., May 26, 1885 - Feb. 16, 1965
LLOYD, Kittie Lee (w), Oct. 5, 1887 - Dec. 5, 1967

LLOYD, Gleason, June 25, 1917 - Apr. 8, 1919
LLOYD, Fred T., Mar. 3, 1915 - Sep. 15, 1926
LLOYD, George, d. July 29, 1926 (infant)

plus several unmarked stones

- 238 -

## LEWIS #1 CEMETERY

On Little Bald Creek Road, .9 mile from Spivey Mt. Road,
on right after culvert, on hill

Updated Mar. 17, 1989

LEWIS, Deborah Vasta Justice,  June 30, 1873 - July 8, 1964
        Wife of David Lewis (unmarked grave)
        Mother of David Lewis, Jr., (unmarked grave)

JOHNSON, Walter Burton Sr.,  Jan. 3, 1902 - Dec. 29, 1951
        Son of Connor and Phoebe Markland Johnson
        Husband of Lucy Jane Lewis
        Father of Jackie & Cleo Johnson (unmarked graves)

LEWIS, Toka May,  July 8, 1901 - Aug. 30, 1912

LEWIS, Freeman,  June 21, 1931 - May 24, 1981
LEWIS, Genevieve (w),  July 20, 1938 -


plus several additional unmarked graves, including:

LEWIS, Harriet,
LEWIS, Shasta,
LEWIS, William,

>       Note:  Lewis cemeteries #1, 2, and 3 were originally
>               researched in March 1988 by Barbara Ann Dowden


## LEWIS #2 CEMETERY

On Little Bald Creek Road, just south of Lewis #1 Cemetery,
on next hill

Updated Mar. 17, 1989

LEWIS, Garrett N.,  Jan. 1, 1893 - July 25, 1970
LEWIS, Mary E. (w),  May 11, 1901 - Aug. 15, 1969


## LEWIS #3 CEMETERY

On Little Bald Creek Road, just south of Lewis #2 Cemetery,
on next hill

Updated Mar. 17, 1989

LEWIS, James Willard,  Jan. 1, 1893 - Sep. 27, 1974
        Son of David and Deborah V. Lewis
LEWIS, Anna Lee Tipton (w),  June 26, 1898 - Sep. 28, 1966
        Daughter of Joe Berry and Biddy Cooper Tipton
        The children of James W. and Anna L. Lewis have
        concrete crosses, with their initials only:
        J.W. Lewis: James Willard Jr., d. age 2. L. Lewis:
        Leonard, d. age 19.  I. Lewis - Ivan, d. age 16.
        S. Lewis - Servinia (dau).

TIPTON, Dock Witt, July 31, 1905 - July 24, 1955
        Son of Joe Berry and Biddy Cooper Tipton and
        brother of Anna Lee Tipton Lewis

LEWIS, Elbert, Sep. 25, 1866 - Sep. 16, 1951
LEWIS, Nancy Jane Byrd (w), Aug. 5, 1866 - Aug. 27, 1949
LEWIS, Addie Lee (dau), July 26, 1896 - May 18, 1981

ENGLISH, Glenn, Jan. 26, 1917 - Nov. 15, 1954
        Son of Fate and Lula Shook English

ENGLISH, Gary Dean Jr., b/d 1968

EDWARDS, Robert Witt, d. Feb. 26, 1952 at 1 mo.

NORDEEN, Gerald C. Sr., Dec. 25, 1917 - July 29, 1979
NORDEEN, Gladys M. (w), July 11, 1915 -

CARPENTER, William A., Sep. 4, 1933 - Apr. 21, 1976
        US Army, Korea

        plus several additional concrete crosses:

M. Lewis: Mae, dau. of Garrett and Mary Lewis (buried
        nearby in Lewis #2 Cem.). W. F. English,
        W. K. English, H. C. Hensley, M. Hensley,
        J. Gouge, and D. W. Edwards.


## HOLCOMB CEMETERY

Spivey Mt. Rd., turn left at trailers just before first
bridge over Spivey Creek. Turn left again at small ford

Copied Apr. 6, 1989

- upper level -
HOLCOMB, Ulysses S., 1880 - 1954
HOLCOMB, Florence (w), 1883 - 1943
HOLCOMB, Enied (dau), Mar. 8, 1908 - Feb. 2, 1915
HOLCOMB, "Geoffey" (son?), 1912 - 1951

- lower level -
HOLCOMB, William P., Apr. 22, 1872 - Oct. 15, 1947
      Son of Wm. and Elizabeth Scoggins Holcomb
HOLCOMB, Linda Belle Lewis (w), Apr. 22, 1884 - Aug. 9, 1967
HOLCOMB, Elzie (dau), - no dates
HOLCOMB, Earl (son?), - no dates

HOLCOMBE, Robert A., 1906 - 1977

WILLIS, Junior, b/d 1958

HOLCOMB, Birdie, 1924 - 1967

FOSTER, Charles David, June 22, 1887 - Sep. 5, 1965
        Pvt., US Army, WWI

FOSTER, Cornelia, 1910 - 1965
        probably wife of Charles D. Foster

FOSTER, Clarence Lawrence, Mar. 30, 1926 - Nov. 21, 1946
        Son of Charles and Cornelia Holcomb Foster

HARRIS, Gurney Lee, 1915 - 1975, US Navy, WWII

HOLCOMB, William, Nov. 25, 1846 - Mar. 4, 1914
        Co. H, 10 TN CAV., Union Army
HOLCOMB, Catherine Elizabeth (w), 1839 - 1908

EDWARDS, Clella Nora, 1927 - 1955
        Daughter of Lee Roy and Amanda Foster Holcomb (below)

HOLCOMB, Leroy, Aug. 4, 1899 - Apr. 17, 1968
HOLCOMB, Amanda (w), June 9, 1903 -


        plus several unmarked stones

## HILL CEMETERY

  At head of Mill Creek, 1.5 miles beyond end of Mill
  Creek Road, on top of mountain

            Copied Apr. 4, 1989


HILL, -----------

        Two brothers, about 16 years old, are reportedly
        buried here, according to two sources. Unmarked stones

# McINTURFF #3 CEMETERY

Dry Creek Road, .6 mile E. of Johnson City Highway

Copied July 24, 1988

McINTURFF, John, d. Feb. 5, 1884
McINTURFF, Rachel Edna Scott (w), Feb. 1798 - Oct. 6, 1894
      Parents of David and Nat.

McINTURFF, David James, Co. B, 8th Tenn. Cav., Union Army
McINTURFF, Cindy Bower (w), d. before 1910 (unmarked grave)

McINTURFF, Nathaniel K., Jan. 29, 1837 - Apr. 30, 1935
      13th Tenn. Cav., Union Army
      Son of John and Rachel Edna Scott McInturff
McINTURFF, Barbara Ann (w), Mar. 10, 1845 - Oct. 29, 1892

McINTURFF, Julia, June 6, 1863 - Feb. 11, 1946
      Daughter of Nathaniel and Ann Cobble (?) McInturff

McINTURFF, Malisey, d. at 6 yrs.


plus several unmarked stones


## BRUMMETT CEMETERY

On Scioto Rd., 2.3 mi. from Rt. 107, on left side of road
behind house.

Copied by Bill Norris and Mildred B. Nov. 25, 1973
Updated by Bill Cooper Aug. 22, 1988 and Oct. 22, 1988

BOWMAN, Molley, 1873 - 1936, Dau. of Lee and Nancy B. Bowman

COLEMAN, William M., Sep. 18, 1887 - May 3, 1969
COLEMAN, Lizzie M. Coleman (w), Apr. 6, 1893 - July 1, 1957

HOILMAN, Denney Ray, b/d 1973

WHITE, A. L., d. 1969

WHITE, Lem, 1902 - 1952

BRUMMETT, Ethel W., Jan. 11, 1895 - Nov. 5, 1931
      Maiden name White. Wife of Sam Brummett

WHITE, G. L., Sep. 1872 - Nov. 1934
      (not visible in 1988)

TAYLOR, Polley Brummett, Oct. 20, 1881 - Oct. 3, 1932
      Former wife of W. F. Brummett

TAYLOR, Frank W., Apr. 2, 1881 - Apr. 12, 1965
      (no longer visible in 1988)

TAYLOR, Robert L.,  Dec. 20, 1925 - Mar. 9, 1926

TAYLOR, Mary E.,  Sep. 8, 1917 - Dec. 29, 1923

TAYLOR, Nieta M.,  Jan. 10, 1909 - Apr. 1, 1912

TAYLOR, Gracie B.,  Jan. 31, 1902 - Feb. 23, 1912
TAYLOR, Lela C.,  Aug. 24, 1911 - Feb. 24, 1912
       - sisters

TAYLOR, Mary Lee,  Dec. 30, 1932 - May 11, 1937
       Daughter of C. A. Taylor

BRUMMETT, Thomas Y.,  Dec. 9, 1889 - Oct. 6, 1931

BRUMMETT, W. Roscoe,  June 3, 1896 - July 25, 1921

BRUMMETT, Thomas J.,  July 16, 1859 - Oct. 6, 1917
       Son of Wm. P. and Malinda Britt Brummett
BRUMMETT, Annie Buck (w),  1860 - 1945

BRITT, Elbert C.,  Aug. 16, 1856 - June 5, 1934
       Son of James J. and Nancy Sink Britt
BRITT, Annie Brummett (w#1),  Nov. 3, 1849 - Mar. 27, 1884
       Daughter of Wm. P. and Malinda Britt Brummett
BRITT, Esther Benfield (w#2),  Feb. 14, 1857 - Feb. 12, 1904
       Daughter of Adolphus L. and Lydia Barlick Benfield
BRITT, James D. (son),  Dec. 13, 1892 - Jan. 4, 1910

BRUMMETT, Rev. Wm. P.,  May 20, 1818 - Nov. 6, 1906
BRUMMETT, Malinda G. Britt (w),  Jan. 22, 1818 - Jan. 14, 1892

BRUMMETT, Rev. W. H.,  Aug. 11, 1853 - May 19, 1903
       Son of Wm. P. and Malinda Britt Brummett
BRUMMETT, Susan C. Branch (w),  May 14, 1856 - Dec. 20, 1919
BRUMMETT, Mary B. (dau),  Mar. 2, 1891 - May 18, 1932

BRUMMETT, Hattie Carver,  Oct. 1905 - Feb. 1936

COLEMAN, Chrisley C.,  Oct. 20, 1919 - Jan. 19, 1977

WHITE, Bertha Isaacs,  1909 - 1975

WHITE, John S.,  Mar. 11, 1905 - Feb. 10, 1986
WHITE, Marie B. (w),  Sep. 6, 1927 - Feb. 23, 1979
WHITE, Jack (son),  Nov. 3, 1947 - Apr. 30, 1948

TAYLOR, Willie,  1909 - 1981

TAYLOR, Frank W.,  Apr. 2, 1881 - Apr. 12, 1965

CARROLL, Sarah Ann,  Sep. 1887 - Oct. 24, 1926
CARROLL, Norma Edna (dau),  Oct. 24, 1926 - Oct. 25, 1927

plus many unmarked stones

## BRITT CEMETERY

On Scioto Road, 1.5 mi. from Rt. 107, on left side,
visible from road

Copied by Bill Norris and Mildred B. Nov. 25, 1973
Updated by Bill Cooper Aug. 22, 1988

BRITT, David Edmond, Aug. 26, 1872 - June 22, 1956
        Son of Isaac Landon and Evaline Whitson Britt
BRITT, Rebecca Price (w), May 19, 1879 - Nov. 27, 1957
        Daughter of Charlie and Susan ------ Price
BRITT, Charlie (son), d. Mar. 25, 1962 (?)
        (not visible in 1988) 61 yrs old
BRITT, Landon (son), Jan. 21, 1905 - Nov. 16, 1932
        Landon was 1st husband of Gladys Isaacs

EDMOND, Ernest (?), Aug. 26, 1929 - July 17, 1970
        US Navy, WWII (?)

HEAD, Martha Britt (dau), June 4, 1899 - Nov. 26, 1942
        Wife of Hunter Head. Dau. of David E. & Rebecca P.
                                                        Britt

POWERS, Hubert John, b/d 1963

POWERS, Truman Lee, b/d 1964

BRITT, Jesse, Apr. 28, 1912 - Feb. 22, 1979
        Son of David Edmond and Rebecca Price Britt
        2nd husband of Gladys Isaacs
BRITT, Gladys Isaacs (w), June 6, 1912 -
        Daughter of Elisha and Margaret Norman Isaacs

STANLEY, William Pierce, June 9, 1919 - Aug. 11, 1987

            probably unmarked stones exist

## BRITT/GRINDSTAFF CEMETERY

On Scioto Road, about 1.5 mi. on rt., through path, near
triple poplar tree at rt. edge of field

Copied by Hilda Padgett Mar. 11, 1977; checked Oct. 22, 1988

GRINDSTAFF, Alfred (Alford?), 1845 (1848?) - 1928
GRINDSTAFF, Eliza (w), 1850 - 1927
        Daughter of James J. and Nancy Sink Britt
GRINDSTAFF, Billie, 1876 - 1904
GRINDSTAFF, Charlie, 1877 - 1896
GRINDSTAFF, Monroe, 1887 - 1889
GRINDSTAFF, David, 1867 - 1925
GRINDSTAFF, Ellen, b/d 1916
GRINDSTAFF, Matty, no dates
GRINDSTAFF, Jessie, b/d 1916
GRINDSTAFF, Earl, b/d 1921

BRITT, James J.,     (b. ca. 1825)
BRITT, Nancy Sink (w),   (b. Apr. 1832)

BRITT, Henderson,  Co. H, 13th TN CAV., Union Army
        Son of David and Anna Harmon Britt

CAMPBELL, Johnny,      no dates

BRITT, Brownlow,      no dates
        Son of Isaac Landon and Alice Pate Britt
BRITT, John,       no dates
        Son of Isaac Landon and Alice Pate Britt
BRITT, Ike,       no dates
        (Isaac Landon),  Son of James J. and Nancy Sink Britt
BRITT, Alice,      no dates
        (Alice Pate) (Wife #2 of Isaac Landon Britt)
BRITT, Evie,      no dates
        (Evaline Whitson) (Wife #1 of Isaac Landon Britt)


            plus several unmarked stones


                BAKER #2 CEMETERY

    On Airstrip Road, on Bradley property, Unicoi, above
    Scotts outlet on Rt. 107

                Copied Oct. 23, 1988


BAKER, James,    June 21, 1886 - Sep. 8, 1908

BAKER, Thomas M.,    Jan. 19, 1869 - Apr. 9, 1898

BARRY, J. H.,  Sgt. Co. E, 13th TN. CAV., Union Army

BAKER, Andrew J.,    Mar. 13, 1883 - May 8, 1888

McCURRY (McCOURY?), Oliver,
        Co. B, 1st US Vol. Inf. - Span.-Am. War
McCURRY (McCOURY?), Polly (w),   Apr. 23, 1848 - Mar. 31, 1906

BRITT, Axie McCourry,  Mar. 26, 1872 - Feb. 6, 1933
        Daughter of Oliver McCurry
        Wife #3 of Elbert C. Britt

HIGGINS, Harold Ray,  b/d Jan. 28, 1932
        Son of Barry and Mary Britt Higgins


BAKER, Ezekiel,  July 9, 1840 - Mar. 17, 1926
BAKER, Martha Charlottie (w),  Sep. 8, 1844 - July 1, 1931


                - 245 -

## McCURRY CEMETERY

Off McLaughlin Road from old Rt. 23, west under new highway, then left to Bill McCurry's farm

Copied Dec. 6, 1988

McCURRY, Will,   Mar. 18, 1867 - June 2, 1938
          Son of Mack and Cinda Hampton McCurry
McCURRY, Ina Mae (w),   1878 - 1957
McCURRY, David E. (son),   1907 - 1964

PHILLIPS, Mary J.,   Sep. 29, 1897 - Feb. 2, 1901

McCURRY, Valeda K.,   Jan. 6, 1930 - June 18, 1930
          Daughter of Britton (Breton?) and Ruby Ingle McCurry

McCURRY, J. B.,   Nov. 27, 1911 - Oct. 23, 1913

McCURRY, Teresa (?),   b. Apr. 29, 1915   (d. young)

McCURRY, Bret,   d. 1910?

## HIGGINS/BOWMAN CEMETERY

Beside old RR bed, off Buckeye Road, near Golf Course in Buffalo Valley

Copied by Bill Norris in 1973, and updated Dec. 6, 1988

AKARD, Lydia,   Jan. 21, 1795 - Mar. 27, 1882, wife of J.A.Akard
AKARD, Infant son,   no dates

BOGART, Jerimiah,   Nov. 1799 - Jan. 28, 1837
BOGART, Elizabeth H. (w),   Oct. 23, 1800 - Aug. 28, 1860
BOGART, L. B. (?),   b. Feb. 25, 1833
BOGART, A. W. (?),   b. Feb. 23, 1833
          1833 stones not visible in 1988

HIGGINS, William Ellis,   Apr. 9, 1859 - Dec. 3, 1939

BOWMAN, George C. (Jr.?),   Feb. 3, 1870 - Dec. 5, 1938

BOWMAN, George C.,   Apr. 19, 1835 - Mar. 27, 1882
BOWMAN, Emily McNabb,   Sep. 19, 1836 - Feb. 22, 1909

HAMMER, Orpah,   d. May 13, 1853 at 44 yrs.

plus several unmarked stones

Unkept cemetery, but good prospect for fencing and cleanup of bushes.

## CARROLL CEMETERY

At edge of Buffalo Valley Golf Course — go to left up hill, overlooking upper pond, and opposite main building

Copied by Bill Norris in 1977, and updated Dec. 6, 1988

CARROLL, Henry Edmond,   Apr. 24, 1881 — Dec. 15, 1943
CARROLL, Martha Brummett (w),   Jan. 25, 1882 — Mar. 9, 1956

CARROLL, W. M.,   1881 — 1958

CARROLL, Edmond,   Mar. 25, 1857 — Mar. 5, 1942
CARROLL, Emma Whitson,   June 25, 1864 — Dec. 20, 1947

CARROLL, W. M.,   Mar. 29, 1857 — Dec. 20, 1910

CARROLL, Emma,   b. Sep. 5, 1861

CARROLL, William Arthur,   July 6, 1892 — Feb. 14, 1909

JONES, John P.,   Feb. 11, 1908 — Feb. 21, 1956
JONES, Jack R. (son?),   1930 — 1931
JONES, James L. (son?),   b/d(?) 1939

BUTLER, John B.,   b. 1898

BUTLER, Anna Kerrigan,   b. 1913   (wife of John B.?)

BUTLER, Lester A.,   1899 — 1943

BUTLER, William T.,   1892 — 1939

BUTLER, Joseph B.,   1859 — 1936
        Son of Caroline Grimsley
BUTLER, Caroline Carroll (w),   1862 — 1940
CAMPBELL, Emma Butler (dau),   1894 — 1941

CARROLL, Cynthia,   no dates

CARROLL, Alexander,   no dates

BUTLER, Alexander M.,   1889 — 1891

BUTLER, Samuel J.,   1890 — 1894

### UNMARKED GRAVES

CARROLL, Bertie Jones
CARROLL, Rosie Brummett
CARROLL, Martha Bowman
CARROLL, Sallie Brummett
CARROLL, Dee

About 20 unmarked concrete blocks

## COOPER CEMETERY

On the Back Rd. (Marbleton Rd.) on w. side of road, just
before McInturff Cemetery, in Unicoi area

Copied by Bill Norris in 1973, and updated Dec. 6, 1988

COOPER, Emma, Mar. 24, 1863 - Mar. 14, 1947
        probably wife of Landon N. Cooper (informant for
        death certificate)
COOPER, Orville Minton, Oct. 4, 1892 - June 27, 1936

COOPER, Landon Nathaniel, Jan. 4, 1867 - Feb. 22, 1914
        Son of James T. and Margaret K. McNabb Cooper
COOPER, James F., Feb. 24, 1873 - Jan. 1, 1908

COOPER, Andrew M., Mar. 14, 1865 - June 4, 1915
COOPER, Lydia L. (w), Aug. 6, 1866 - Nov. 14, 1957

COOPER, James Taylor, Dec. 22, 1833 - Apr. 30, 1916
COOPER, Margaret Katherine McNabb (w), Jan.6, 1834 - May 30,
        Married Sep. 13, 1857                          1907

COOPER, William Isaac, May 11, 1860 - Nov. 22, 1944
        Husband of Dicie Buchanan Cooper

COOPER, Hobart G., 1898 - 1978
COOPER, Ella E. (w), June 10, 1898 - Aug. 27, 1928

COOPER, Infant, no dates, child of Hobart & Ellie Cooper
COOPER, Terry Allen, no dates
        Infant son of Hobart and Faye Cooper

COOPER, Neta F., Feb. 5, 1894 - May 5, 1983

HUNTER, Troy, d. 1980
HUNTER, Margaret (w), d. 1967

COOPER, Kay Ella, Feb. 20, 1946 - Jan. 31, 1985

ST.CLAIR, George L., no dates
ST.CLAIR, Georgia Mae (w), 1907 - 1977

EDWARDS, Roy Lee, 1935 - 1988

HENSLEY, Vaughn, Nov. 1, 1910 -
HENSLEY, Louise C. (w), Dec. 6, 1918 - May 22, 1980
        Married Mar. 19, 1938

                plus unmarked grave:

COOPER, Cecil Verlie, May 26, 1918 - Mar. 27, 1961

## BAKER #1 CEMETERY

On Lower Stone Mt. Rd. (west end) at Hoy Shelton farm
(1st farm on rt.), not far from Rt. 107 in Limestone Cove

Copied by Bill Norris in 1973, and updated Dec. 8, 1988

TEAGUE, Nathan A.,    Feb. 16, 1834 - Apr. 7, 1907
            Co. K, "t Regh", US Vols. Inf.  Could mean 1st Regt,
            or Tenn. Regulars.  U.S. could mean Federal, or Union,
                                                            Army

TOWNSEND, Bell,  Mar. 15, 1916 - Aug. 11, 1919

WHITE, Frank,  June 21, 1895 - June 24, 1939
WHITE, Clara Belle (w),  June 24, 1907 - July 19, 1944

CAMPBELL, Arthur,  b/d 1966

GOODYEAR, Karen,  b/d 1966

CAMPBELL, Robert,  1916 - 1987


                plus many unmarked stones

## DAVIS/GRINDSTAFF CEMETERY

On Lewis Road, up on hill, about 1 mile E. of Hill Store
in Limestone Cove, off Rt. 107 on right

Copied by Bill Norris in 1973, and updated Dec. 8, 1988

DAVIS, John,   Mar. 25, 1883 - Mar. 14, 1980
DAVIS, Mary C. (w),  Jan. 17, 1894 - Sep. 12, 1965

JOHNSON, Jane D.,  1883 - 1947

DAVIS, Arch,  Sep. 21, 1893 - Dec. 7, 1937
        Husband of Lydia Francis

GRINDSTAFF, Ezekiel,  Sep. 13, 1815 - Aug. 28, 1897
GRINDSTAFF, Ann Davis (w),  Dec. 22, 1818 - Oct. 15, 1894

SHELL, Jane Grindstaff,  Aug. 24, 1846 - Oct. 15, 1883
        Wife of Leonard Shell

SMITH, Samuel,  Co. B, 12th Tenn. Cav.,  Union Army

GRINDSTAFF, John,       d. Sep. 18, 1897
GRINDSTAFF, Dave,       no dates
GRINDSTAFF, Charlie,    no dates
GRINDSTAFF, Sherman,    no dates
            probably siblings

<u>DAVIS/GRINDSTAFF CEMETERY</u> - (continued)

plus new section nearby:

YELTON, Floyd,   June 7, 1912 - Mar. 24, 1987
YELTON, Sara (w),   Nov. 2, 1921 -

JERSEY, Wayne D.,   Dec. 8, 1930 -
JERSEY, Mary L. (w),   June 12, 1928 -

HONEYCUTT, Clayton J.,   July 8, 1908 -
HONEYCUTT, Mary J. (w),   Oct. 31, 1913 -


<u>ROWE CEMETERY</u>

Off Johnson City Highway just N. of Unicoi exit, by way of
farm road - visible from expressway

Copied by Bill Norris in 1973, and updated Dec. 8, 1988

ROWE, Albert G.,   Mar. 11, 1842 - Nov. 22, 1906
          Co. B, 3rd NC Mtd. Inf.,   Union Army
ROWE, Gerfina Baker (w),   Aug. 12, 1849 - Apr. 17, 1923

McINTURFF, John W.,   Apr. 3, 1841 - Jan. 5, 1915
          Co. B, 12 Tenn. CAV., Union Army
          Son of Mary McInturff, who married James Van Johnson
McINTURFF, Julia A. Rowe (w#1),   Feb. 26, 1844 - Sep. 7, 1887
          His second wife was Maggie M. Welborn

NORRIS, Alexander,   Aug. 20, 1849 - Dec. 6, 1924
          Son of Richard N. and Lucinda McInturff Norris
NORRIS, Sarah Rowe (w),   Feb. 14, 1851 - Sep. 6, 1911

BAILEY, Sam B.,   1862 - 1940
BAILEY, Harriett (w),   1862 - 1942

McINTURFF, Wilkinson S.,   Dec. 28, 1880 - July 19, 1903
          d. of typhoid
McINTURFF, Alex A.,   Dec. 28, 1880 - Sep. 15, 1903
          Twin sons of John W. McInturff and Julia

HENSON, Emma J.,   1812 - 1903

HERRELL, Samuel,   Oct. 28, 1879 (Oct. 23, 1882?)(on death cert.)
                 - Nov. 11, 1914
          Son of William and Celia Garland Herrell
BRITT, Jacob L.,   1862 - 1924, Son of James J. & Nancy Sink
                                                   Britt
SLAGLE, Floie,   b/d 1904
          Daughter of Solomon and Kate Slagle

plus several unmarked stones

- 250 -

AYERS #2 CEMETERY (Also called NELSON CEMETERY)

On Johnson City Highway, near Fishery, opposite Holiness
Church and mobile home park

Copied Dec. 15, 1988

AYERS, Julia Margery Booth,     Aug. 15, 1874 - Oct. 16, 1934
          wife of Dave Ayers

                    plus two or three sunken graves
                         no other stones


PATE/WOODBY CEMETERY

On upper Stone Mt. Rd., on hill on farm, at east end, near
Simerly Creek Road

Copied Dec. 15, 1988

PATE, Reuben B.,    Nov. 3, 1855 - Aug. 2, 1945
PATE, Sarah Grindstaff,   May 17, 1881 - May 26, 1975

MORTON, J. L.,    no dates
MORTON, W. E.,    no dates

WOODBY, William,   Cpl., Co. B, 13th Tenn. Cav., Union Army

PATE, Nathan,    1883 - 1977

WOODBY, Henry Carl,   1903 - 1982
WOODBY, Kate S. (w), 1904 - 1984

PATE, Mary,    d. Apr. 20, 1896

               one other marker says 1860 - 1941,
               but the name is lost


TOLLEY #1 CEMETERY

On Simerly Creek Road, on rt. (Tolley Road) just before
Upper Stone Mt. Road
                    Copied Dec. 15, 1988

TOLLEY, Robert,    Jan. 15, 1919 -    (lives on farm)
TOLLEY, Birdie Mae Grindstaff (w#1), Sep. 21, 1924 - June 19,1969
TOLLEY, Irene Mast (w#2),  1924 - Oct. 23, 1988

LEWIS, Wendell Scott,   Feb. 19, 1942 - Aug. 23, 1987
LEWIS, Katherine June Tolley (w),  Feb. 7, 1949 -
          Daughter of Robert and Birdie Tolley

# BANKS CEMETERY

Off Simerly Creek Road, on Young Road, past Grindstaff
Cemetery, take right at sharp fork, and up hill, bearing
right

Copied by Bill Norris in 1970, and updated Dec. 15, 1988

BANKS, Jesse,   July 21, 1903 - Sep. 3, 1905

BANKS, John T.,   Nov. 7, 1848 - Jan. 25, 1925
BANKS, Eliza Ann (w#1),   Oct. 12, 1854 - Apr. 26, 1896
        Married Dec. 17, 1872
BANKS, Nannie M. Grindstaff (w#2),   June 9, 1875 - Nov. 17,1943
        Married Mar. 18, 1898
BANKS, Ruth (dau),   Aug. 30, 1913 - Mar. 14, 1930

BANKS, William M.,   Oct. 4, 1854 - Jan. 27, 1894
        Married Emma Moore Jan. 30, 1882 -
        She is buried in Gouge Cemetery, Carter County

BANKS, Robert L.,   June 6, 1907 - Oct. 26, 1934

BANKS, Moses,   1820 - 1904 or 1907
BANKS, Malinda Honeycutt (w#2),   no dates

BANKS, Alfred,   Dec. 13, 1919 - Dec. 2, 1944
        Pvt., 100th Inf. Div.  WWII

BANKS, Walter,   Jan. 21, 1899 - Feb. 21, 1962
BANKS, May (or Mae) (w#1), Apr. 10, 1905 - Aug. 11, 1926
        Married July 31, 1924
BANKS, Helen (dau),   no dates

YOUNG, Helen,   no dates

BANKS, Mary,   no dates

MABE, Effie,   no dates

WOODBY, Infant,   no dates

MOORE, John,   no dates

HURT, Clifford,   1921 - 1988

DAVIS, Isaac H.,   Feb. 10, 1905 - Jan. 26, 1985
DAVIS, Vada H. (w),   May 3, 1919 -
DAVIS, Rhuel E. (son),   Aug. 4, 1943 - Jan. 11, 1978

# BIRCHFIELD #1 CEMETERY

On Tinker Road, near mouth of Dry Creek, next to expressway, at Bill Norris' mobile home

Copied by Bill Norris in 1973, and updated Dec. 27, 1988

JONES, Henry,      Mar. 4, 1804 - Feb. 12, 1877
JONES, Elizabeth Feathers (w),  Feb. 12, 1818 - Nov. 18, 1869

NELSON, Charles "Charley",  d. Mar. 19, 1866, age 25 yrs,6 mo's,
                                                  18 days
          Son-in-law of Henry and Elizabeth Jones
          In Co. B, 12th TN CAV., Union Army

NELSON, John ?,  (field stone only)
          Father of Charley Nelson (hearsay)

BURCHFIELD, Ezekiah,  Oct. 13, 1804 - June 22, 1883
          Son of Nathaniel Birchfield
BURCHFIELD, May (Mary) Baker (w),  June 12, 1807 - May 1, 1874

CONSTABLE, Hannah,  d. Mar. 12, 1843,  age 67 yrs

CORRELL, James D.,  Sep. 9, 1813 - Sep. 13, 1813

TIPTON, Wiley,  Co. B, 13th TN. CAV.,  Union Army
          Killed during Civil War.  Father of Mark Tipton
SMITH, Charles A.,  Co. G, 4th TN. INF.,  Union Army

BURCHFIELD & ERVIN SLAVES

RAMSEY, J. W.,  Cpl. Co. A, 3rd NC Mtd. Inf., Union Army

TIPTON, M. L.,  one of two Tipton boys
          Killed by Confederate soldiers (in same grave). Large
          stone destroyed.  Footstone says M L T and other
          initials unreadable.

WHITSON?, S.,  May 2, 1837 - 1838,  SW on stone
WHITSON?, S.,  1877 - 1888,  SW on stone

K-------, A.,  1745 - 1811,  A.K. on stone

WARD, M. B.,  Feb. 26, 1769 - Oct. 29, 18--?
          no longer seen in 1988

JONES ?, M.,  d. 1819,  age 84,  MJ on stone

WHITSON, Levina,  Mar. 17, 1827 - Nov. 7, 1882
          Wife of Kendrick McLaughlin,  married in 1847
          Hearsay evidence only; this is a field stone

WARD, John B.,

WHITSON ?, S.,  b/d 1844,  SW on stone

## COUNTY FARM CEMETERY

On the Back Road, SW of Jones Circle, near the old
County Farm, near road

Copied Jan. 19, 1989

HELBERT, John Jackson,  Mar. 10, 1888 - June 6, 1959

GAMBLE, Leonous,  1888 - 1957

> Originally there were 7 graves, but most
> of the markers are gone.


## TIPTON CEMETERY

On King Farm Road, N. side, off Marbleton Road, about
1 mile from Rt. 23, in field.

Copied Jan. 19, 1989

TIPTON, A. B.,  Oct. 26, 1851 - July 7, 1925
TIPTON, Hester (w),  b. Sep. 4, 1861

TIPTON, Ethel L.,  Dec. 1, 1911 - Dec. 22, 1911

TIPTON, Robert M.,  Aug. 17, 1906 - May 19, 1928

TIPTON, Nat.,  Feb. 23, 1880 - Mar. 27, 1951

plus 2 unmarked stones


## MORRELL CEMETERY

In woods on hill near Jones Circle, off the Back Road,
near old County Farm

Copied by Bill Norris in 1973, and checked Jan. 19, 1989.
Only 5 stones still visible (*)

*McINTURFF, Alex,  May 15, 1821 - Apr. 1, 1905 (1906?)
*McINTURFF, Saraphina Anderson (w),  May 13, 1822 - May 6, 1904

*MORRELL, Emma A.,  Feb. 12, 1858 - June 2, 1861

*MORRELL, Joseph,  Oct. 16, 1862 - Oct. 12, 1881

*ANDERSON, INTA,  May 1, 1850 - Oct. 13, 1867
        (Isaac N.T.?)

MORRELL, Robert H.,  Oct. 28, 1871 - Jan. 24, 1901

MORRELL, Susannah,  May 20, 1877 - Aug. 31, 1899

MORRELL, Samuel E.,  Oct. 16, 1874 - June 5, 1896

MORRELL, J. O.,   Feb. 4, 1833 - Oct. 22, 1908
MORRELL, Rhoda E. (w),  May 26, 1836 - Oct. 26, 1891

ANDERSON, John,   d. Nov. 22, 1817

ANDERSON, Isaac,   Dec. 27, 1800 - Dec. 1873
ANDERSON, M. E. Mary (w),  June 12, 1797 - Aug. 4, 1874


                plus several unmarked field stones


## FREY CEMETERY

  Near new house, at end of dirt road, left off Upper
Stone Mt. Rd., 1 mile from 2 churches at Limestone Cove

                Copied Jan. 23, 1989


SNEYD, Mary Elizabeth,   Nov. 24, 1865 - Apr. 13, 1903

                plus several unmarked stones, probably
                including Betty Davis Frey.

## CAMPBELL CEMETERY

  At end of road left off Campbell Rd., off Lower
Stone Mt. Rd.
                Copied Jan. 23, 1989

GRINDSTAFF, Milt,   Feb. 14, 1908 - Apr. 15, 1937

CAMPBELL, Avery,  Nov. 20, 1928 - May 26, 1929
          Son of Harvey Campbell

CAMPBELL, James,    1865 - May 20, 1935
          Son of Billie and Mary Fry Campbell
CAMPBELL, Alice (w),  1876 - 1917

CAMPBELL, David C.,   d. Nov. 5, 1948 at age 86
CAMPBELL, Betty (w),  Dec. 10, 1875 - Apr. 30, 1945
CAMPBELL, Joe (son),  Apr. 23, 1898 - May 30, 1929

CAMPBELL, Elisha,   Mar. 9, 1871 - Dec. 13, 1927
          Brother of David C. Campbell
CAMPBELL, Lula (w),  June 14, 1881 - Dec. 29, 1949
CAMPBELL, Piercie (son),  Mar. 13, 1916 - Aug. 2, 1938
CAMPBELL, Ellis B. (son),  Oct. 12, 1918 - May 30, 1952
          Pfc., 149th Inf., WWII
CAMPBELL, Luther (son),   Jan. 21, 1921 - Apr. 25, 1951

McNABB, Sabie Elen,   May 2, 1903 - June 30, 1926

                plus several unmarked stones

## SNEYD CEMETERY

On hill across Cordwood Branch from Campbell Rd., on rt.,
about ½ mile up from jct. with Lower Stone Mt. Rd.

Copied Jan. 23, 1989

SNEYD, Bill,  1882 - 1964, Son of Joe and Susie Sneed

plus several unmarked stones, including:

SNEYD, Semanta, (twin of Bill Sneyd, above)

SNEYD, Seth, and son Wheeler,

SNEYD, Joe, and wife Susie,  parents of Bill, Semanta, & Seth

NOTE:  Ordie Sneyd (1930-33) and her siblings have
been transferred from this cemetery to Bell
Cemetery.

## DAVIS CEMETERY

Simerly Creek Road, on right. Driveway just before Tolley
Road, go to top of hill, near lumbering area

Copied Jan. 26, 1989

DAVIS, Allen,  Aug. 17, 1891 - July 4, 1897
Son of Henry and Lydia Davis

plus 1 unmarked stone
Further up the hill are 7 more graves, mostly Davis,
but with unmarked stones

## McNABB CEMETERY

Marbleton Road, out of Unicoi, on left just before
Duckett Road.

Copied Feb. 4, 1989

DUCKETT, Benjamin W.,  Aug. 18, 1888 - May 16, 1965
Pvt., WWI

McNABB, David T.,   1871 - 1945
McNABB, Rebecca E. (w),  1873 - 1950

McNABB, Donna Lynn,   Jan. 3, 1947 - July 7, 1947
Dau. of D. C. and Kathleen McNabb

McNABB, A. W.,  June 29, 1860 - Sep. 11, 1926
McNABB, Lizzie Hicks (w),  b. Mar. 10, 1868

McNABB CEMETERY - (continued)

PAUL, Will A., Oct. 6, 1889 - Jan. 13, 1947
PAUL, Stella* (w), Nov. 2, 1899 - Apr. 21, 1973
PAUL, Florence (dau), Nov. 6, 1920 - Jan. 18, 1923
          *Estella L.

McNABB, Kenneth, July 6, 1924 - Sep. 13, 1929
McNABB, June, May 2, 1927 - Nov. 21, 1927
          - siblings

HAMTON, Hattie B., Feb. 12, 1883 - Feb. 25, 1884
          Daughter of T. G. and S. M. Hamton

GREGG, Glenn, May 16, 1914 - May 14, 1968
GREGG, Leta McNabb (w), May 29, 1912 -

               plus 1 unmarked grave


## WRIGHT CEMETERY

Off Rt. 107, about 1/4 mile w. of Davis Springs, on
s. side of road*

Copied by Bill Norris in 1973, and updated Mar. 7, 1989

WRIGHT, Thomas J., Oct. 11, 1820 - Sep. 7, 1910
WRIGHT, Susan (w), Jan. 28, 1824 - Nov. 25, 1897

SMITHIMAN, Maria, Feb. 1814 - Nov. 24, 1884

               plus many unmarked field stones
          Cemetery recently cleared, but hard to find

          Also known as Sam Wright Cemetery

* Opposite France Road, at culvert. Follow the right bank
of small creek to escarpment, then follow it to cemetery,
deep in woods.


## MILLER CEMETERY

Off Rt. 107 above Limestone Cove, on hill, across highway
from Red Fork Creek Rd. exit

               Copied Feb. 11, 1989

MILLER, C. R., Aug.25,1849 - April 22,1911
               unmarked grave
BANKS, Ruth Davis, d. c1860, 1st wife of Moses Banks

## BIRCHFIELD #3 CEMETERY

In front of Ham Smith's house, on Hammy Smith Road, off
Upper Stone Mt. Rd. in Limestone Cove

Copied Mar. 3, 1989

BIRCHFIELD, Nathaniel, 1756 - 1863:
        Field stone, with a pipe, which used to have a bronze
        marker, according to Ham Smith, who bought the farm
        in 1942. The bronze marker was installed in 1930 by
        the DAR for Nathaniel Birchfield, reportedly a Rev.
        War soldier for the NC Line. One of Nat's sons,
        Ezekiah, 1804 - 1883, is buried at Birchfield #1
        Cemetery on Dry Creek.

        plus 7 or 8 other graves, with field stones only

## McKINNEY CEMETERY

Off Rock Creek Road, at end of dirt road just past Rock Creek
Presbyterian Church in Erwin

Copied Mar. 11, 1989

McKINNEY, J. W.,  June 27, 1843 - Mar. 18, 1922

        plus 1 or 2 unmarked stones

## HENSON CEMETERY

Off Simerly Creek Road, at end of McCurry Road; turn left at
fork, then past barns on farm track to left on knoll

Copied Mar. 7, 1989

HENSON, Mollie A.,  July 6, 1867 - Sep. 15, 1902
        "my wife"

## HERRELL CEMETERY

Off Old Rt. 19/23 north of Omega Baptist Church, turn east
at Mac's Used Cars, up hill and to the right

Copied Mar. 19, 1989

BENNETT, T. D.,  Feb. 11, 1861 - Apr. 3, 1940
BENNETT, Milissa (w),  May 9, 1860 - Aug. 1, 1944

FORD, W. J.,  -

MOSLEY, Dave,  Dec. 21, 1887 - May 12, 1935
MOSLEY, Nora (w),  b. Apr. 25, 1883

HERRELL CEMETERY - (continued)

MOSLEY, John,    1863 - 1935
MOSLEY, Rebecca (w),   1862 - 1936

SMITH, Bessie Marie,   May 13, 1927 - June 6, 1937
SMITH, Hazel,   Mar. 28, 1931 - Nov. 20, 1933

HERRELL, George Davey,   d. Nov. 24, 1936
          Pvt., 46 Inf., 9 Div., WWI

HERRELL, D. C.,    Apr. 16, 1870 - Apr. 23, 1936
HERRELL, Millie (w),   May 7, 1872 - Oct. 31, 1930
HERRELL, Lobrite (son),   Feb. 20, 1902 - May 4, 1923
HERRELL, Sallie (dau),   Mar. 20, 1891 - Dec. 26, 1924
          Sallie was mother of Georgia and D. C. Sampson

HERRELL, Georgia R.,   1932 - 1933,  d. at 10 mo's.

STANLEY, James,   May 27, 1874 - Jan. 30, 1952   "Father"

McKENNEY, Mrs. Sallie,   Feb. 18, 1845 - Nov. 20, 1929

POTTER, Randolph M.,   Jan. 24, 1951 - Jan. 26, 1951

HARRELL, Audrey Foster,   July 29, 1928 - Aug. 22, 1986


            plus 1 or 2 unmarked stones


## BOWMAN CEMETERY

   Off old Rt. 19/23, take Buckeye Extension east, then left
to edge of Buffalo Valley Golf Course, near 18th hole

                Copied Mar. 20, 1989

BOWMAN, V. S.,    Apr. 20, 1861 - Oct. 22, 1945
BOWMAN, Jennie Hannum (w),   June 3, 1870 - Mar. 27, 1955
          Daughter of Frank Hannum and Sarah Baker

BOWMAN, George H. (son),    May 7, 1894 - Aug. 27, 1958
                no other stones

## HONEYCUTT CEMETERY

   Buckeye Road off old Rt. 19/23 near Golf Course.  Just west
after going under new expressway, turn right into small farm.
Cemetery is fenced and visible.

                Copied Apr. 21, 1989

HONEYCUTT, Nathan,  Feb. 2, 1890 - Mar. 8, 1965
          Pvt. 114th Inf. WWI

HONEYCUTT, Louzina,  1900 - 1975

HONEYCUTT, Worley,  1921 - 1980

HONEYCUTT CEMETERY - (continued)

HONEYCUTT, David Lynn,   1962 - 1983

HONEYCUTT, Stevie,   1954 - 1968


## GRINDSTAFF #2 CEMETERY

Upper Stone Mtn. Rd., 1 mile above twin churches at Limestone Cove, then left to end of dirt road, then through woods on hill

Copied Apr. 25, 1989

GRINDSTAFF, A. J.,   1855 - 1905
GRINDSTAFF, Louisa Morley Bowers (w),   1834 - 1884


NOTE:   Louisa's first husband was --------Bowers. They were
        parents of Elizabeth Bowers, who married William
        Birchfield, and grandparents of Rosa Birchfield,
        who married Dayton Morrell.


plus several unmarked stones

EVERGREEN CEMETERY

Located in East Erwin - bordered on the southeast by
Jersey Extention - on the north by 7th Street.

Copied  November 2-14,1988


LAMBERT, Lola Dangerfield,   Oct.18,1886 - May 19,1962

MILLER, George Bernard,   July 28,1898 - July 3,1977 -E3 USN WW1
MILLER, Clemence E.,   Nov.30,1905 - ----
MILLER, Charles Douglas,   Dec.15,1943 - Jan.1,1976 -Lt. USN Vietnam

RHODES, Lou Gentry,   Oct.1,1871 - Dec.24,1962

MASTERS, Fain C.,   March 29,1906 - Sept.27,1971
MASTERS, Beulah M.,   Jan.17,1914 - ----
KOTIS, Nancy M.,   1940 - 1988
KOTIS, Fain,   July 17,1972 - Feb.18,1979

HAYNES, Russell Lee,   Sept.19,1901 - Feb.8,1972

MOORMAN James J.,   Feb.27,1936 - June 15,1981
            M/Sgt US Marine Corp Korea Vietnam

MASTERS, William Ralph,   May 15,1908 - Dec.11,1986

BOLTON, Robert L.,   July 16,1910 - Jan.4,1988
BOLTON, Beatrice A.,   June 13,1918 - ----

HENSLEY, Albert Ralph,   June 9,1930 - April 13,1983
            Sgt. US Army  Korea
HENSLEY, Rosezell,   Aug.19,1934 - ----

SPARKS, Buynum,   1918 - 1984
SPARKS, Geneva,   ---- - ----

HARVEY, Homer Henry,   Aug.7,1905 - Oct.17,1974

BOGART, Bill L.,   Sept.16,1932 - April 18,1988
            Cpl. US Army Korea
BOGART, Jo Ann,   Feb.9,1939 - ----

POWERS, Teresa Renee,   1956 - 1961
CASH, Eleanor Powers,   1932 - 1959
            Daus. of Glavis and Chloe Bailey Powers

WOODRUFF, Evan E.,   April 8,1904 - Feb.6,1981

KYLE, Robert C.,   1893 - 1975

GREENE, Robert,   July 4,1903 - Sept.21,1974
GREENE, Frances,   May 12,1906 - Nov.6,1974


- 261 -

EVERGREEN CEMETERY (continued)

GRIMES, William M.,   July 12,1900 - Mar.23,1977
GRIMES, Lola C.,   June 27,1908 - Feb.6,1981

JONES, Richard E., "Dick",   Dec.16,1924 - Dec.6,1979

JONES, Robert G., "Pete",   Nov.29,1930 - June 26,1979

LAWSON, W. Branch,   Oct.14,1914 - Aug.30,1977
          PFC  US Army  WW2

GUINN, Leslie Shannon,   Sept.6,1975 - Mar.15,1977

HARVEY, Carl T.,   Nov.15,1907 - June 18,1971
          PFC US Army  WW2

SCHAUB, Bernard C.,   Dec.20,1904 - Sept.17,1967
SCHAUB, Viola R.,   April 13,1908 - April 16,1985

ROBERTSON, John J.,   Mar.31,1894 - Oct.16,1979
          PFC  US Army  WW1
ROBERTSON, Jessie T.,   Dec.30,1899 -  -----

TITTLE, Roscoe L.,   May 25,1916 - Mar.20,1987
TITTLE, Margaret P.,   Feb.27,1921 - May 21,1980

TURNER, James M.,   Apr.23,1891 - Dec.12,1967
TURNER, Nellie B.,   Jan.15,1898 - May 22,1987

TURNER, James M., Jr.,   June 14,1925 - July 14,1982
TURNER, Georgia B.,   Feb.17,1927 -  -----

HUGHES, Fin H.,   Apr.22,1893 - Nov.30,1977
HUGHES, Maude,   June 5,1895 - Feb.27,1985

BANNISTER, Benjamin D.,   June 2,1885 - Sept.19,1957
          Son of J.A. and Siberia Mitchell Bannister
BANNISTER, Pearl K.,   Sept.26,1886 - Apr.18,1974

WILSON, Sam E.,   June 18,1905 - Feb.14,1977

COOKE, Donald R.,   Aug.19,1946 - Oct.26,1970
          CWO 67 Med Group Vietnam

COOKE, Ralph,   Aug.24,1924 -  -----
COOKE, Bonnie H.,   Feb.12,1925 - June 30,1987

PETERSON, Jess Patrick,   Oct.29,1962 - Jan.9,1981

STEPP, Gladys H.,   1926 - 1987
STEPP, Terry Douglas,   Aug.12,1950 - July 9,1970
          PFC US Marine Corp Vietnam

GRUBB, Virginia Pauline,   Sept.12,1925 - July 24,1981
GRUBB, Michael,   May 12,1952 - Nov.17,1969

DOOLEY, Brandon,   1986 - 1986

GRUBB, Donald Lee,   Apr.21,1948 - July 8,1969
          PFC Vietnam

PHILLIPS, W.E.,    Aug.28,1895 -  ----
PHILLIPS, Julia Hensley,    March 23,1901 - May 17,1988

TITTLE, James W.,    May 24,1904 - March 2,1980
         Son of George Franklin and Rosa Anna Salts Tittle
TITTLE, Edith E.,    Dec.27,1908 -  ----
         Dau. of Frank H. and Dora E. Price Britt

ALLRED, Linville H.,    June 14,1876 - Nov.25,1965
ALLRED, Myrtle May,    April 11,1888 - May 2,1928

JONES, Douglas L.,    Nov.4,1941 - Oct.12,1966
         1st Lt. 173 Airborne Vietnam

BANNISTER, Richard W.,    July 27,1948 - Dec.27,1967
         PFC US Marines Vietnam

JONES, Dallas Ray, Sr.,    1914 - 1985
         F1 US Navy WW2
JONES, Beatrice J.,    1915 -  ----

BRITT, James Jay,    June 14,1948 - Dec.31,1968
         Cpl US Marines Vietnam
         Son of John Howard and Hope Buck Britt

BOOTH, Ruth Lillian,    Jan.17,1916 - Feb.20,1972

SHELTON, James Paul,    March 31,1949 - July 12,1984
         L Cpl US Marines Vietnam

RICE, Herman,    Sept.29,1925 - April 27,1987
         Cpl US Army WW2
RICE, Irene Whitson,    March 3,1931 -  ----

ELY, Robert Gilman (Bob),    Dec.26,1901 -  ----
ELY, Sarah Ellen Moss Phetteplace,    Jan.6,1904 - April 2,1986

MANUEL, Eldridge Lee,    1919 - 1986

HUGHES, Frank L.,    Oct.19,1905 - Nov.17,1983

WEAVER, Sam S., Jr.,    Jan. 7,1918 - Feb.23,1988
         US Navy WW2
WEAVER, Vivian A.,    May 2,1928 -  ----

HOYLE, Susie,    Sept.13,1885 - Feb.3,1965
HOYLE, Chester,    Nov.22,1916 - Aug.16,1984

SIMMONS, James Earl,    Nov.4,1931 - Aug.20,1980

HARRISON, Carl R.,    March 26,1906 -  ----
HARRISON, Alma P.,    Sept.2,1907 - May 7,1986

EVERGREEN CEMETERY   (continued)

FOSTER, Avery,   Dec.10,1912 - Sept.18,1984
FOSTER, Elsie D.,   June 13,1919 -   ----

TUCKER, Mr.W.Dove,   March 3,1880 - April 10,1959
          Son of Lucius and Linda Bales Tucker
TUCKER, Mrs. W. Dove,   April 29,1995 -   ----

McCURRY, W.Frank,   March 17,1902 - May 15,1959
McCURRY, Lona,   1901 - 1977

SHELTON, Olsen,   1906 -   ----

HIGGINS, Budd,   1873 - 1969

PERRY, Betty Joe,   Jan.26,1931 - July 6,1986

COLBAUGH, Tom C.,   Oct.28,1936 -   ----
COLBAUGH, Lynn H.,   April 10,1942 -   ----

SHELTON, Herbert K.,   1909 - 1965
SHELTON, Ethel T.,   1909 -   ----

RHODES, Samuel Hawes Jr.,   Dec.5,1925 -   ----
RHODES, Jessima Russell, (w), June 24,1926 -   ----
RHODES, Luanne, (dau), Sept.21,1952 - May 3,1986

WEAVER, Frank,   Jan,7,1918 -   ----
WEAVER, Charlotte A.,   Dec.12,1926 -   ----

HENSLEY, Chester,   Jan.21,1905 - Dec.29,1979

WILSON,Bacchus E.,   Dec.9,1886 - Aug.10,1981
WILSON, Effie M.,   Feb.22,1900 - Aug.5,1978

VANCE, Paul M.,   July 6,1907 - Feb.8,1984

ROBINSON, Lewis E.,   1927 - Oct.23,1988

PHILLIPS, Seth,   Aug.14,1981 - Aug.15,1981

JONES James F.,   1938 -   ----
JONES, Dorris H., (w), 1937 -   ----
JONES, Mandy L.,   Jan.12,1980 - March 14,1981

FOX, James S.,   Jan.9,1913 - April 24,1979
FOX, Edna Mae,   June 1,1932 - Aug.21,1967
FOX, Opal,   June 29,1919 - Jan.9,1971

BRYANT, Dewey A.,   Oct.8,1900 - Sept.17,1963

BENNETT, Roy J.Sr.,   1906 - 1974
BENNETT, Anna D.,   Oct.17,1902 - Jan.18,1988

STOCKTON, Rev. Arcemus,(R.C.),  June 5,1919 - March 6,1976
STOCKTON, Georgie Hopson,  Nov.10,1923
SIMMONS,  Infant son of Bobby J. and Joyce S. Simmons
          Grandson of George H.Stockton

WILLIAMS, Cornelius R.,  Oct.27,1880 - March 18,1937
WILLIAMS, Daisy,  Oct.8,1895 -  ----
WILLIAMS, Brown,  Sept.11,1917 -  ----

WEBB, F.A.,  Aug.24,1899 -  ----
WEBB, Eva Mae,  April 20,1900 - Feb.13,1977
WEBB, Leslie Gordon,  Jan.31,1925 -Sept.16,1965
          PFC Army Air Force WW2
WEBB, Donald Ray,  1941 - 1981

MATHES, Jack,  May 14,1920 - April 6,1968
          S/Sgt  WW2

DOVER, Donald Wayne,  b/d  Nov.16,1973
DOVER, Walter Lee,  b/d  Nov.16,1973

RENFRO, Rube M.,  Dec.14,1892 - Jan.10,1965
RENFRO, Frances H.,  Sept.10,1899 - Jan.2,1988

BAILEY, Floyd,  July 28,1922 - Aug.10,1973
          US Navy WW2
BAILEY, Myma Ramsey,  Sept.29,1928 -  ----

BIBLE, Selma P.,  1915 - 1988
          Wife of L.B. Bible

ALFORD, Paul C. Jr.,  1912 - 1984

GUINN, Orvill F.,  June 22,1897 - Dec.23,1979
GUINN, Maude F., (w),  March 11,1902 -  ----
GUINN, Raymond W.,  July 8,1922 - March 15,1979
          S/Sgt US Army  WW2  Korea
GUINN, Jane Logan,  Feb.17,1930 -  ----

HENSLEY, Gilbert Lowell,  Dec.15,1941 - Dec.17,1980

TILSON, Ralph F.,  July 24,1918 -  ----
TILSON, Beulah M.,  Aug.9,1921 - ----

EDWARDS, Walter J.,  Sept.5,1907 - Oct.7, 1987

FOSTER, Rev. Dana A.,  April 13,1925 - Dec.1,1984
FOSTER, Goldie P.,  Sept.11,1933 -  ----

TOLLEY, Floyd,  March 28,1914 -  ----
TOLLEY, Naomi F.,  Oct.21,1922 -  ----

HENSLEY, John H., April 1,1910 - June 18,1981

WALKER, Fayette, June 29,1899 - Feb.14,1980
        Sea 2 US Navy WW1

PIPPIN, Mary Ellen, March 4,1893 - June 11,1980
STALLARD, LeRoy "Frog", April 13,1909 - Jan.20,1976
        Son of Samuel Covey and Mary Elizabeth Mead Stallard
STALLARD, Pauline Griffith, (w), ---- - ----
STALLARD, Mary Ellen, (dau), July 27,1936 - April 23, 1970

SHELTON, Claude, 1927 - 1975
        Pvt. US Army WW2

LOVE, Kenneth Eugene, Nov.3,1925 - June 1,1986
        US Army

DANENBERG, Ola Tipton, 1911 - 1973

MOORE, Mary Louise Treadway, Nov.23,1916 - March 10,1985

MOORE, Russell O., 1922 - 1975
        PFC US Army WW2

SLAGLE, Roy L., 1924 - 1986 - S/Sgt US Army WW2

RENFRO, Leon, Oct.30,1935 - Nov.16,1959

CLARK, Edward Bowie, Sr., 1897 - 1981
        2nd Lt. US Army WW1

TINKER, Clyde D., Sept.22,1910 - Jan.5,1966
        T Sgt US Air Force WW2
TINKER, Sue S., March 23,1911 - ----

SUTTON, Mary S., Jan.29,1923 - ----

CHANDLER, Erma, April 11,1900 - Dec,19,1972

MATTHEWS, Gordon, Nov.17,1898 - Sept.18,1981
MATTHEWS, Alva, May 11,1910 - ----

HAMPTON, Timothy Oliver, May 2,1951 - April 8,1961
        Son of Ralph L. and Ann Street Hampton

BOONE, James Ernest, Jan.18,1905 - ----
BOONE, Hazel Hampton, March 26,1908 - ----

HAMPTON, Oliver Merritt, March 10,1895 - July 2,1967
        Son of Cornelius Price and Susan M. Higgins Hampton
HAMPTON, Fushia Hensley, June 7,1897 - ----
        Dau. of Thomas A. and Ann Eliza Hall Hensley

HARDIN, Vance Glen, Sept.30,1932 - Aug.19,1966
HARDIN, Carrie E., 1935 - ----

EVERGREEN CEMETERY   (continued)

HARDIN, James Arthur,   May 12,1896 - Sept.10,1968
HARDIN, Omia Lee Edwards,   Oct.2,1905 - Oct.6,1986

METCALF, John H.,   Aug.3,1928 - Jan.1,1971
METCALF, Atlas H.,   Sept.19,1927 - ----

BRUMMETT, Alphonzo L.,   June 14,1918 - Feb.13,1970
          Sgt US Army WW2

GORMAN, Clyde W.,   1900 - 1971

GREGORY, Lonnie B.,   July 16,1915 - Feb.8,1960
          US Navy   WW2

GARLAND, Jack W.,   Nov.18,1905 - Jan.4,1974

CRADIC, Claude H.,   Nov.4,1913 - Jan.11,1987
CRADIC, Thelma H.,   May 7,1921 - Sept. 1988

DAY, Roy J.,   June 4,1907 - Dec.15,1981
DAY, Geneva J., (w),   Dec.14,1914 - ----
DAY, Henrietta Marie,   Aug.23,1935 - Oct.10,1947
DAY, Ella Mae,   May 28,1940 - ----

WHITE, Fletcher B.,   March 10,1893 - June 2,1978
          PFC  US Army  WW1
WHITE, Lottie Tapp,   Feb.2,1897 - Aug.23,1976

RIDDLE, Walter W.,   March 2,1905 - ----
RIDDLE, Myrtle,   Sept.22,1904 - ----
RIDDLE, Herman F.,   Sept.3,1938 - Oct.3,1985

LEWIS, James W.,   Feb.3,1908 - Aug.14,1963
          Son of T.J. and Ada Mae Briggs Lewis
LEWIS, Mildred Huskins,   Jan.11,1918 - ----

TOWNSEND, Agnes G.,   1901 - 1987

BROYLES, Trapier Kieth,   1886 - 1961
          Son of Anderson Robert and Ella Wilkinson Kieth Broyles
BROYLES, Dora Love,   1889 - 1970
OWEN, Roberta Broyles, 1881 - 1960

JONES, Ethel M.,   Nov.2,1919 - April 4,1985

HIGGINS, Johnnie H. Jr.,   Oct.24,1948 - Aug.17,1973

WEBB, John Wyatt,   Jan.12,1891 - April 3,1962
          Son of Wiley and Mary Collier Webb

FOSTER, Harry Roland,   Dec.26,1913 - July 13,1970
FOSTER, Nancy Bradshaw,   Dec.16,1915 - May 11,1981

WYNNE, Lamar A.,    1894 - 1975
WYNNE, Dora D.,    1982 - ----

COFFIE, Ernest,    May 9,1924 - May 22,1982
            Sgt US Army  WW2
COFFIE, Loraine,    Aug.25,1927 -  ----

DEATON, C.H.,    Nov.8,1901 -  ----
DEATON, Pansy,    Jan.27,1901 - April 20,1977

GUINN, Sue B.,    1888 - 1966
GUINN, Leonard T.,    Sept.1,1915 - Aug.5,1978

BLEVINS, Carl C.,    Nov.21,1908 - July 7,1986
BLEVINS, Charles Douglas "Doug",    Sept.6,1933 - Nov.16,1957
            Son of Carl C. and Lillian Davis Blevins

COOK, George Robert,    Feb.17,1886 - Dec.30,1966
COOK, Kate Fagan,    Aug.30,1889 - March 19,1958
COOK, Sallie Virginia,    July 4,1891 - July 30,1970

HOLSCLAW, Clyde A.,    April 21,1895 - Oct.12,1956
            Cpl  WW1
HOLSCLAW, Ethel,    April 27,1926 - Jan.18,1962
HOLSCLAW, Darrell Glenn ,    1926 - 1986  -  Pvt  US Army

ROBERTS, Cas,    1899 - 1965
ROBERTS, Linda E.,    March 20,1903 - Feb.20,1976

ORREN, Carl A.,    Nov.25,1895 - Feb.15,1957  - US Army  WW1
            Son of Jacob L. and Kathleen O'Flaherty Orren

LOZIER, Roy E. "Ed",    Oct.22,1918 -  ----
LOZIER, Ruby W.,    May 23,1919 - Aug.27,1980

LOVE, Lola O'Brien,    April 1881 - Dec.1957
            Dau. of B.F. and Mollie Tucker O'Brien
            Wife of James Robert Love
LOVE, Jack C.,    Dec.14,1923 - March 15,1983  -  US Army WW2
LOVE, Eula M.,    July 15,1925 -  ----

ALTMAIRE, Peter,    1879 - 1924

BRYANT, Walter,    1917 -  ----
BRYANT, Billie M.,    1929 - 1958

EDWARDS, James F.,    May 11,1880 - Aug.7,1970
            Pvt  Spanish American War
EDWARDS, Pheba Ann,    Nov.5,1904 - Sept.10,1984

BOGART, Charles R.,    Nov.29,1911 - Oct.16,1978

BOGART, Anne Clinton,    Sept.7,1946 - Aug.8,1953
            Dau. of Frank and Mary Hattan Bogart

HATTAN, William Cary,    1875 - 1929
            Son of Mark and Jennie Silas Hattan
HATTAN, Sara Stein,    1879 - 1966

DUNCAN,Damon C.,    1900 - 1985   - US Navy   WW1
DUNCAN, Eula E.,    1904 - 1985

GRIFFITH, Matthew,    Jan.16,1896 - Sept.23,1966
GRIFFITH, Nettie,    Feb.16,1897 - April 9,1985

GOUGE, James M.,    March 29,1900 -Oct.25,1980
GOUGE, Abbie W.,    March 18,1901 - Nov.28,1982

ANDERS, Hazen C.,    May 18,1889 - June 6,1954
ANDERS, Lenice,    Aug.22,1893 - Feb.25,1973

ROBBINS, John Carl,    Nov.5,1902 - Sept.18,1971

GRIFFITH, Emmaline L.,    Sept.30,1918 - Oct.17,1973

EDWARDS, Thurman F.,    1928 - Aug.4,1953
            Son of Burt and Minnie Hensley Edwards

ADKINS, William D. "Will",    1887 - 1956
ADKINS, Rosa,    1895 - 1975

DUNCAN, Molt,    Aug.3,1890 - May 15,1968
DUNCAN, Betty Ann,    Jan.9,1932 - April 12,1953

VAUGHN, Howard,    July 9,1913 - Aug.2,1983   US Army   WW2

CHANDLER, Jesse F.,    Aug.30,1895 - Sept.23,1970
            Cpl US Army   WW1
CHANDLER, Louella K.,    Feb.18,1904 - March 25,1969
CHANDLER, Marie,    Jan.11,1922 - Nov.20,1966

BRADSHAW, Robert Henry,    April 11,1876 - Oct.1,1968
BRADSHAW, Ethel Love,    Nov.1,1882 - Aug.5,1969

CROCKETT, Robert Graham,    Oct.31,1914 - Jan.17,1974

LAUGHREN, Rev.D.M.,    Nov.26,1872 - Nov.18,1960
LAUGHREN, Tannie,    June 10,1872 - Aug.3,1964

LOTT, Curtis L.,    Dec.9,1877 - Jan.23,1955
            Son of John and Nancy Roberts Lott
LOTT, Mary Pauline Batey,    Jan.20,1890 - Feb.10,1980
PRINCE, Patricia Allison,    July 20,1950 - Sept.17,1974

OAKLEY, Leslie D.,    Feb.4,1900 - Oct.31,1971
OAKLEY, Lucille B.,    April 2,1908 -  ----

EVERGREEN CEMETERY (continued)

LUCAS, Hal White, Nov.18,1914 - June 1,1957
          Son of C.K. Sr. and Mae White Lucas
LUCAS, Charles "Kib", March 13,1885 - Sept.21,1965
LUCAS, Anna Mae, Feb.11,1889 - Jan.27,1982

HIGH, Joseph Maxwell, Jan.17,1899 - July 16,1974
HIGH, Pauline T., July 18,1913 - May 6,1975
HIGH, Addie R., May 12,1904 - March 30,1955
          Dau. of S.Kennedy and Jannie Riddle
KELLEY, Virginia Sue High, Feb.26,1928 - Dec.23,1965

RICHARDSON, W.E., Jan.15,1879 - July 9,1960
          Son of W.L. and Katherine Lawson Richardson

GARLAND, William E., Sept.16,1872 - Dec.17,1954
          Son of Wm. and Sarah Jane Turbyfield Garland
GARLAND, Florence B., Sept.4,1882 - July 15,1970

TIPTON, Nora, Oct.20,1911 - April 6,1955
          Dau. of Monroe and Bessie Moore Pennington

DAVIS, Jefferson Lee, April 9,1894 - April 11,1953
          Son of David K. and Anna White Davis
          Sgt US Army WW1
GOFORTH, Ivah Baker Davis, Nov.25,1899 - Sept.18,1984

ROBERSON, Ervin, June 22,1870 - Oct.11,1953
ROBERSON, Stella, Oct.14,1883 - Dec.26,1964

HAMPTON, Matt, May 4,1894 - May 13,1965
HAMPTON, Grace, Nov.19,1896 - Feb.19,1970

BENNETT, Rotha, 1904 - 1955
BENNETT, Eva J., 1910 - 1982

BAILEY, C.A. "Bill", 1922 - 1959
BAILEY, Kyle Dennis "Denny", 1943 - 1983

FOSTER, Carl, Sept.12,1907 - Feb.29,1968 PFC US Army
FOSTER, Carrie Lee Whitson, May 27,1920 - Sept.17,1974
WHITSON, Claude L., Sept.1,1907 - March 11,1960
          Son of John C. and Julia Peterson Whitson
RUNION, Robert O., April 18,1922 - May 2,1958 - PFC US Army WW2
          Son of W.T. and Lydia Margaret Coffee Runion

METCALF, Lula, June 15,1901 - July 16,1982
METCALF, Hubert N., March 19,1912 - Sept.4,1965
WHITSON, Julia P., Sept.24,1880 - July 31,1963
          Dau. of Samuel and Tilda Warrick Peterson
WHITSON, Marcus M., 1903 - 1976
WHITSON, Carroll, Aug.19,1909 - March 8,1965 - PFC US Army WW2
          Son of John C. and Julia Peterson Whitson

BAILEY, Milton A.,    March 29,1883 - Dec.5,1947
BAILEY Mary L.,    Sept.23,1887 - Jan.26,1975
BAILEY, Robert,    Jan. 11, 1907 - Jan.24,1941
            Son of Milton Adam and Mary Peterson Bailey

METCALF, Ervin "Buddie",    Feb.29,1897 - April 2,1958
METCALF, Flora Mc.,    Sept.6,1868 - Oct.19,1950

STANCEL, Sim F.,    1886 - 1949
STANCEL, Sarah E.,    1890 - 1956
STANCEL, Arbara,  (one date)  1976

STANCEL, Bessie,    1936 - 1960
STANCEL, Clinvie Haze,    Feb.24,1907 - April 10,1987
STANCEL, Infants of Mr.and Mrs. Haze Stancel 1940 and 1942
            Children of Haze and Mae Woodby Stancel

PARDUE, S.B.Jr.,    Nov.3,1920 - Oct.12,1975 - US Navy WW2
PARDUE, Juanita Norris,    1888 - 1974

BROOKSHIRE, Infant Daughter,    July 25, 1948
            Dau. of Doran and Vivian Brookshire

PETERSON, Allen,    1886 - 1950
PETERSON, Hannah,    1874 - 1954

COFFEE, Margaret Jane,    1856 - 1946
            Mother of J.Z. Roberts
COFFEE, James J.,    1867 - 1935
            Son of Perry and Sarah Ann Berry Coffee

CATON, Robert N.,    1871 - 1932
            Son of Stephen and Matilda Harrison Caton
CATON, Walter R.,    April 21,1907 - June 22,1944 - Pvt USAF WW2
CATON, Rufus M.,    Aug.9,1926  (only date - Govt. marker)

GRIFFITH, Roy,    Feb.22,1900 - July 1,1961
            Son of Don A. and Joanna Bailey Griffith
GRIFFITH, Duane Rodney,    1932 - 1933

ROBINETTE, Ford B.,    May 20,1887 - Aug.11,1936
            Son of James Sullivan and Elinor Rebecca Hoge Robbinette
ROBINETTE, Clara A.,  (w), Aug.8,1887 - Dec.8,1959
            Dau. of John Calvin Morrow
ROBINETTE, Blaine W.,    1918 - 1986  - US Navy WW2

SPARKS, Carrie Bell,    1899 - 1938
            Dau. of Leb and Gidia Guinn Waldrop
SPARKS, Ralph M.,    1915 - 1958

KEPLINGER, Everette Ray,    Feb.18,1891 - Feb.21,1963
            Son of William C. and Anne Scott Keplinger
KEPLINGER, Mary Magdeline Gallian, (w) 1895 - 1937
            Dau. of J.F. and Emma Fleming Gallian
KEPLINGER, Lida Treadway,    March 4,1909 - Oct. 14,1964

McINTOSH, Pierce,    July 8,1878 - Dec.14,1942
McINTOSH, Laura,   Nov.19,1881 - Sept.19,1967

SCHISM, William Oscar,   1897 - 1963
SCHISM, Georgia Lillian Stokes, (w), 1900 - 1926
SCHISM, Lucille Ann,   1907 - 1988
SCHISM, Mary Sue, Infant - 1937
            Child of Mr. and Mrs. W.O. Schism

BULLINGTON, David Ellet,   April 22,1878 - June 17,1944
            Son of Wm. Calvin and Isabel Guthrie Bullington
BULLINGTON, Etha May,   June 16,1881 - Feb. 18,1957
            Dau. of M.Y. And Louise Miller Campbell
BULLINGTON, Vivian S.,   Nov.9,1900 - Dec.27,1938
            Son of D.E. Bullington
BULLINGTON, David Calvin,   April 29,1937 - Sept.6,1954
            Son of Vivian S. and Ruth Duncan Bullington
BULLINGTON, Alice,   May 9, 1936 (one date)
            Dau. of Vivian S. and Ruth Duncan Bullington

GRAYSON, David J.,   1872 - 1958
            Son of Samuel and Mary Alice Furguson Grayson
GRAYSON, Rachel E.,   1870 - 1938
            Dau. of Wm. and Deborah Ingram Clayton
GRAYSON, Stanley,   1904 - 1987
SPARKS, Ernest,   1904 - 1946
            Son of John B. and Minnie Green Sparks

McINTURFF, Carl C.,   Oct.29,1898 - Jan.12,1970
McINTURFF, Ada Conley,   Nov.10,1903 -  ----

SIFFERD, John H.,   1888 - 1940
            Son of Joseph and Molly Dowland Sifferd
SIFFERD, Ina C.,   June 27,1894 - Feb.27,1976

SHIPLEY, James Arthur,   1878 - 1944
            Son of Nathan Shipley
SHIPLEY, Elizabeth,   1884 - 1971

JESSEE, James J.,   April 13,1884 - Sept.10,1942
            Son of George Lee and Elizabeth Campbell Jessee
JESSEE, Ruth R.,   July 31, 1895 - March 25,1987

ROBBINS, James Calvin,   Feb.27,1867 - Nov.7,1929
ROBBINS, Sonora Corvin,   July 15,1861 - July 12,1918
ROBBINS, Edgar Guy,   Sept.23,1897 - Nov.13,1982
ROBBINS, Maude Williams, (w),   Oct.31,1898 - Aug.13, 1982

YELTON, Horace L., "DDS", Jan.24,1886 - Sept.11,1966
YELTON, Georgia, (w), Feb.27,1892 - Nov.29,1974
YELTON, Leland J., "DDS", June 2,1910 - Jan.28,1952
YELTON, Mary R., (w), Sept.12,1911 - April 23,1972
YELTON, Carroll Reese, April 19,1922 - June 10,1922

NANNEY, Harrison Reed, Oct.5,1891 - Dec.23,1961
      Son of Asbury H. and Margaret Reed Nanney
NANNEY, Clara Dalton, Feb.2,1895 - Aug.14,1945
      Dau. of W.M. and Parmelia Elizabeth Jones Dalton
NANNEY, Texie Briggs, Dec.15,1892 - Nov.5,1959
      Dau. of Wm. and Hester Buckner Briggs
NANNEY, Maude B., Dec.28,1918 - Feb.19,1986

TIPTON, Iseec M., Oct.29,1887 - Dec.6,1947
TIPTON, Margie, May 8,1895 - ----

HENSLEY, Hubert, Feb.23,1925 - Nov.19,1974
HENSLEY, Birtha, Sept.3,1944 - ----

GOSSETT, George Dewey, June 1,1898 - July 13, 1977
GOSSETT, Ota Taylor, Sept.25,1905 - June 16,1972
GOSSETT, Jack, (son), Nov.27,1925 - July 20,1946 - US Navy WW2
GOSSETT, George Dewey, Jr."Nick", Nov.28,1935 - May 22,1984

GOUGE, Farnum L., Dec.28,1887 - April 23,1950
GOUGE, Nellie G., May 27,1887 - ----

BYRD, J.B., 1885 - 1971
BYRD, Ollie (w), 1888 - 1948
BYRD, Perry, May 4,1913 - March 16,1987
BYRD, Laura E., March 18,1914 - April 23,1978

BANNER, Buck, April 14,1907 - March 14,1983
BANNER, Terry E., Dec.25,1950 - Dec.30,1950
      Son of Buck and Carrie Tapp Banner

SHELTON, James M., 1876 - 1953
SHELTON, Polly A., 1880 - 1944

SLAGLE, Clayton C., Oct.15,1898 - May 27,1962
      Son of W.Clayton and Martha Parker Slagle
SLAGLE, Bessie C., Dec.1,1899 - July 18,1978
SLAGLE, W.C., March 22,1873 - June 22,1946

McINTOSH, Ferman, Aug.16,1907 - June 1,1956
McINTOSH, Orpha Callaway, July 12,1914 - Nov.22,1973
McINTOSH, Ferman, Jr., Aug.21,1943 - June 25,1945

LOVE, Clarence, Sept.5,1907 - July 28,1985 - US Navy WW2 Korea
LOVE, Myrtle B., March 31,1930 - ----

RAMSEY, Jobe M.,    Sept.2,1888 - April 9,1969
RAMSEY, Lyda,  (w),  Oct.29,1890 - March 29,1975

McCURRY, Ralph,   Dec.20,1923 - Aug.25,1960   - US Army   WW2

GARLAND, Howard T.,    1908 - 1986
GARLAND, Margarete,    1913 - 1968

WILSON, W.A.,    1900 - ----
WILSON, Bessie,   1900 - 1958

ROLLER, Horace J.,    Dec.25,1923 - Oct.5,1966 - Sgt WW2
ROLLER, Madeline W.,    April 4,1924 -  ----

BARNETT, Geder F.Sr.,    June 20,1891 - May 13,1973

SMITH, Nannie Mae,    Aug.9,1890 - Jan.23,1972

GOUGE, Claude E.,    June 10,1891 - April 20,1952

BAILEY, Elbert Lee,    1910 - 1967
BAILEY, Mary Agnes,    1918 - 1988

TIPTON, Sherry B.,    Sept.30,1947 - May 8,1974

TIPTON, Jackie Carl,    June 21,1969
          Infant son of Mr. and Mrs. David Jack Tipton

ENGLE, Guy,    Aug.1,1912 - Sept.5,1963
          Son of Isaac and Lockie Ann Briggs Engle
ENGLE, Louise Elizabeth,    June 4,1913 - June 29,1963
          Dau. of Sam and Cornelia Booth Harvey

MOORE, Harold,    1911 -  ----

SALTS, William M.,    Sept.6,1888 - Jan.31,1968
SALTS, Lula Nelson,  (w), Aug.9,1893 - March 4,1986
SALTS, Kathleen L.Keesecker, (1st wife of Ray) 1929 - 1956
          Dau. of Wm.O. and Ida Tapp Keesecker
SALTS, Dores June Ambrose, (2nd wife of Ray) June 1,1927 - Nov.11,196
          Dau. of Wade Rambo and Bessie Mae Boone Ambrose
SALTS, Phillip Ray, (son of Ray), Dec.17,1951 - Nov.11,1962

PETERSON, Edward Duane "Eddie",  Nov.15,1963 - Jan.25,1981

SCOTT, James Boyd,    Feb.1,1887 - Sept.21,1961
SCOTT, Rebecca Louise,    Dec.23,1888 - May 7,1977
FOSTER, Brian K.,    Oct.26,1965 - Jan.12,1972

JONES, Edward E.,    April 14,1912 - Oct.16,1961   - PFC WW2

NELSON, Roy W.,    July 2,1923 - Aug.11,1967  - PFC US Army WW2
NELSON, Mary Lee,    April 24,1948 - March 6,1966

HENSLEY, Johnny B.,    July 10,1925 - April 23,1986 - US Navy WW2

ROBERTS, Eliza,    1895 - 1956
          Dau. of Jake and Jane Rogers Phillips
ROBERTS, Bessie,    1927 - 1957
          Dau. of Charles and Eliza Phillips Roberts
ROBERTS, Lester,    1921 - 1987

BAILEY, J.R.,    1879 - 1950
          Son of Jimmie and Christine Evans Bailey
BAILEY, Mary M.,    1883 - 1964
BAILEY, Bernie F.,    1906 - 1979

BLEVINS, William M.,    March 29,1892 - Feb.3,1971 - Pvt US Army WW1
BLEVINS, Jennie Rogers,    (w), April 17,1903 - Oct.25,1981

WILLIAMS, Rev. Fulton,    1905 - 1964
WILLIAMS, Glenie D.,    1911 - ----

DEATON, Rev. James,    Nov.5,1878 - Sept.10,1947
          Son of Wm. and Susan Roberts Deaton
DEATON, Cora H.,    1877 - 1958

HOPSON, Baby Larrie,    b/d 1952
          Child of Clifford and Nora Deaton Hopson

CHRISTY, Anna Mae,    1908 - 1977
CHRISTY, Dale Frank,    (one date) May 18,1942
          Son of Frank Curry and Anna Mae Phillips Christy

McINTURFF, Joseph W.,    1875 - 1948
McINTURFF, Louise K.,    1873 - 1953
          Dau. of D.N. and Mary Emily Irby Keener

HONEYCUTT, Fred G.,    Sept.24,1921 - Dec.25,1967 -PFC US Army WW2
HONEYCUTT, Ethel Ingram,    Aug.8,1919 - July 9,1967
HONEYCUTT, Freddy Gene,    Jan.18,1959 - July 30,1978

FOSTER, Richard I.,    1932 - 1982 - Cpl US Army Korea
FOSTER, Steven K.,    Oct.15,1958 (One Date)

DAVIS, Fred E.,    1926 - ----
DAVIS, Ruby M.,    1926 - ----

BEHELER, Gladys Watts,    March 1,1909 - June 25,1976
BEHELER, C.B.,    June 1,1910 - Jan.16,1972 - Military Police WW2

CALHOUN, David A.,    1868 - 1965
CALHOUN, Lottie Riddle,    1889 - 1962
          Dau. of John and Marjorie Bowman Riddle

GERHART, Emma Mae, 1905 - 1973

MILLER, John Henry, March 20,1886 - March 27,1976

McKINNEY, Ella Jane, Oct.1867 - Feb.1947
FOSTER, Alma McKinney, Oct.8,1894 - May 20,1985

PETERSON, Winkler M., Feb.20,1890 - July 28,1963 - PFC WW1
        Son of Josh and Addie Jones Peterson

CALDWELL, Charles A., June 4,1862 - Dec.25,1949
CALDWELL, Mettie A., March 20,1872 - April 27,1958
CALDWELL, Raymond J., March 12,1901 - Oct.15,1977
CALDWELL, Pearl W., Sept.4,1892 - Dec.8,1985

CLARK, Infant, Died March 30,1946
        Dau. of Gorman M. and Ruby Luttrell Clark

KESSL, Frank, 1906 - 1970

METCALF, Wassen Carl, June 3,1893 - June 29,1937
        Son of Dedrick Harris and Amanda Metcalf
METCALF, Aleatha Furchess, July 12,1896 - July 8,1974
METCALF, Jack, 1981 (one date)

HIGGINS, Sam A., Jan.26,1922 - May 5,1945

ANDERS, James H., 1909 - ----
ANDERS, Madge P., 1918 - 1964

WILLIAMS, John H., June 5,1894 - April 4,1960
WILLIAMS, Nora, Dec.14,1894 - ----

WATTS, Teresa Ann, b/d May 6,1970

LAMBERT E.H., 1867 - 1945
        Son of James and Mary Maxwell Lambert

DAVIDSON, Charles, March 2,1880 - March 22,1945 - PFC Cavalry
DAVIDSON, Lillie B., 1878 - 1960
        Dau. of James and Sarah Smith Davidson

GARLAND, Earl, 1895 - 1973
GARLAND, Cleo E.Weeks, (w), 1896 - 1939
GARLAND, Valdine, Nov.23,1919 - Feb.7,1926
GARLAND, Calvin, 1867 - 1941
        Son of Gibbs and Celia Gouge Garland
GARLAND, Lorina D., 1871 - 1941
        Dau. of James and Sarah Smith Davidson

GARLAND, Willie Neas, 1894 - 1981

TITTLE, James Frank, July 11,1900 - Jan.7,1945
        Son of Charles Bean and Mary Elizabeth Simmons Tittle

GRIFFITH, Don A.,    1873 - 1956
          Son of James Madison and Jennie Bradshaw Griffith
GRIFFITH, Anna E.,    1870 - 1959
          Dau. of Elbert and Linda Bailey
GRIFFITH, Sidney H.,    Sept.19,1904 - Nov.27,1978
WRIGHT, Cassie Griffith, July 19,1894 - Oct.3 1942
          Dau. of Don and Joanne Bailey Griffith


BONDURANT, Samuel,    1870 - 1944
          Son of Marrientine Bondurant
BONDURANT, Cornelia Porter, 1877 - 1961
          Dau. of Wm. E. and Fannie Addington Porter
BONDURANT, Buford Douglas,    1902 - 1937
          Son of Sam W. and Cornelia Porter Bondurant
PORTER, Fannie D.,    1858 - 1946
          Dau. of John and Margaret Doty Addington


BARKER, Marietta,    April 21,1923 - Jan.7,1950


WILLIAMSON, Robert L.,    Feb.10,1888 - Dec.26,1958
          Son of Wm. Joseph and Mary Cash Williamson
WILLIAMSON, Pauline E.,    Dec.20,1894 - March 15,1959
          Dau. of Paul P. and Lila Martin Wigand


JUSTICE, G.F.,    April 16,1870 - May 10,1928
JUSTICE, Rachel,    May 8, 1885 -   ----


FOSTER, Isabel W.,    1907 - 1982
FOSTER, Infant Son,    Died Oct.31,1928


WIGAND, Paul P.,    March 7,1870 - May 7,1927
WIGAND, Lila G., (w),  Aug.10,1880 - April 24,1934


RUNION, David S.,    Oct.25, 1880 - Jan.5,1964
RUNION, Lorence W.,    May 15,1900 - Jan.29,1971


PRITCHARD, Lawrence,    Died March 6,1934 - Age 29
          Son of L.N. Pritchard


LAMBERT, Samuel P.,    1874 - 1960
LAMBERT, Mary E., (w),  1884 - 1954
LAMBERT, Aubra L.,    Oct.29,1905 - Jan.11,1952
LAMBERT, Helen M.,    1918 - 1943
          Dau. of Samuel Patton and Mary Elizabeth Lazenby Lambert
LAMBERT, Eugene,    1927 -   ----
          Son of Samuel Patton and Mary Elizabeth Lazenby Lambert


WHITEHEAD, F.L., "DDS",  Nov.17,1892 - April 30,1945
          Son of Alexander Lee and Annie Thacker Whitehead
WHITEHEAD, Ruth P.,    Aug.4,1893 - March 2,1972
WHITEHEAD, A.L.,    Sept.22,1869 - Dec.26,1925

EVERGREEN CEMETERY (continued)

LAWSON, Robert Wesley,   Oct.19,1885 - Aug.4,1958
              Son of Thomas T. and Anna Branch Lawson
LAWSON, Lettie Brown,  (w),  Nov.14,1887 - Dec.4,1967
LAWSON, Robert W.,(son),  Feb.19,1917 - May 22,1959 -USN WW2
LAWSON, Herbert M.,   May 12,1930 - April 13,1981
LAWSON, James W.,   July 14,1923 - Oct.31,1924
LAWSON, Herbert W.,   Jan.23,1927 - Jan.28,1927
LAWSON, Jonathan Branch,   Dec.26,1968 - May 29,1975
              Son of Robert and Martha Alice Hartsell Lawson
WHITLOW, Fred H.,   Dec.2,1909 -  ----
WHITLOW, Anna Brown,  Dec.14,1912 - Dec.21,1981
FULLER, Frank,   Dec.9,1870 - June 24,1923
MASSEY, Mary Lawson,"Aunt Mary",  Dec.27,1875 - Nov.4,1954
              Dau. of Thomas T. and Anna Branch Lawson

BROWN, Albert R.,   July 7,1863 - May 29,1937
BROWN, Tuppie Burleson,   June 24,1873 - Dec.23,1959
              Dau. of C.W. and Olive English Burleson
BROWN, Paul Judson,   Dec.3,1896 - May 22,1898
              Son of Albert and Tuppie Brown

BROWN, William M.,   June 8,1916 - Aug.11,1967 -US Army WW2
BROWN, William H.,   1861 - 1934 - Major 3rd Tenn Inf
              Son of William L. and Nancy Calvin Brown
BROWN, Annie M.,   March 10,1881 - Dec.12,1954
              Dau. of Malcom and Nancy Elizabeth Cauthorn McPherson

MITCHELL, James Henderson,Jr.,  Nov.2,1904 - Oct.3,1929
MITCHELL, Rosa Florence,   Dec.26,1874 - May 20,1927
              Dau. of John and Frances Turner Mitchell
MITCHELL, Lady B.,  Jan.20,1910 - Jan.16,1970
MITCHELL, Mary Atkinson,   Sept.5,1904 - Sept.29,1944

KEEVER, Jack W.,   Dec.19,1919 - June 25,1946
              Son of Guy Keever

MASON, Jeannette B.,   1885 - 1932
              Dau. of Wm.T. and Anna E. Payne Love

KEEVER, R.Guy,   May 1,1898 - Nov.27,1951
KEEVER, Venia H.,   Feb.24,1902 - Dec.18,1986
KEEVER, Betty A.,   Feb.8,1936 - Oct.1,1974
KEEVER, Dwight L.,   Jan.24,1925 - Jan.8,1944
              US Army WW2 - Buried in Liege Belgium

MAY, Albert Charles,   Nov.20,1920 - April 29,1952
              Sgt 21st AF Troop Carr Sqdn WW2 Korea.
MAY, Laura E.,   June 7,1918 - April 25,1982

BROWN, Jesse Burleson,   April 29,1899 - July 13,1964
              Son of A.R. and Tuppie Burleson Brown
BROWN, Anna Sales,   June 6,1896 - April 30,1955
              Dau. of Thomas M. and Emma Caroline Lance Sales

EVERGREEN CEMETERY (continued)

BLAIR, Ida L.,  May 14.1919 - March 28,1980
BLAIR, Justin Lee,  Died 1982 - Son of Marvin and Yvonne Blair

EDWARDS, Andreah Michelle,  b/d Sept.30,1984

LONG, Kelly N.,  Jan.18,1985 - May 21,1985

RAY, Jeffery,  b/d 1985

PETERSON, Baby Boy,  b/d 1979

THOMPSON, Louis P.,  1912 - 1982

BANNER, Orville C.,  Dec.18,1905 - Aug.17,1985
BANNER, Ida J.,  Sept.14,1905 -  ----

RILEY, Ruth,  1894 -  ----

BOLLING, Eva June,  May 18,1917 - Feb.13,1972

HONEYCUTT, Stella,  1917 - 1984

WOODBY, Don F.,  1885 - 1965
WOODBY, Sinda,  1884 - 1970

LAUGHREN, J.B.,  Oct.7,1928 - June 15,1963
LAUGHREN, James B.Jr.,  March 2,1963 - Sept.5,1978
LAUGHREN, R.C.,  Nov.27,1894 -  ----
LAUGHREN, Allie,  Oct.18,1896 - Jan.29,1965
LAUGHREN, Emma,  May 26,1900 -  ----

McCURRY, William Frank,  Dec.26,1885 - Oct.28,1957
McCURRY, Ibbie J.,  May 15,1892 - May 18,1960

WOODBY, William H.,  Aug.12,1883 - May 10,1952
WOODBY, Ollie A.,  April 3,1897 - April 27,1987

BANNER, Eugene,  Feb.13,1928 - July 26,1952
          Son of Orville and Ida J. Hensley Banner

PHILLIPS, Grant,  May 8,1904 - Nov.11,1955
          Son of Cornelius and Nettie Higgins Phillips

HARMON, Olworth T.,  July 26,1904 - June 8,1963
HARMON, Mae Lilly,  (w), Sept.13,1903 -  ----

PETERSON, Clarence,  May,23,1908 - Aug.10,1954 -PFC US Army WW2
PETERSON, Grove,  Feb.25,1879 - March 9,1963
PETERSON, Maud J., (w),  Feb.20,1883 - May 7,1953
PETERSON, John D.,  1915 - 1976  - US Army WW2

FOX, Jodie L.,  May 12,1959 - Feb.8,1972

EVERGREEN CEMETERY    (continued

FOWLER, George W.,    May 8,1891 - July 10,1952
FOWLER, Jack C.,    Aug.11,1889 - July 25,1954 - USNR WW 1
FOWLER, Andrew Jack,    May 16,1935 - May 10,1969 -PFC USMC Korea

BENNETT, Elizabeth,    April 29,1907 - Jan.1,1953

KEGLEY, Thero,    April 12,1917 - Jan.8,1985

McCURRY, James Charles,    July 21,1897 - Jan.23,1957
McCURRY, Bertha Mae,    May 15,1898 - Oct.1,1949
          Dau. of J.H. and Martha Jane Wilson Phillips

WILLIAMS, Hiram,    May 4,1885 - Aug.18,1974
WILLIAMS, Juanita L.,    June 28,1892 - April 15,1977
WILLIAMS, Arthur,    1910 - 1971
WILLIAMS, Harley,    July 29,1931 - Aug.10,1951  - PFC USAF

KEGLEY, Ella,    1877 - 1938

HIGGINS, Malissa,    Aug.9,1888 - Nov.3,1960
          Dau.of Chuck and Sarah Ann McCurry Ramsey

DOUGHTIE, Miss Mollie,    Sept.6,1867 - Dec.21,1953

BARRON, Lee Andrew Hartman,    1858 - 1937
          Son of Daniel and ---- Stout Barron

PETERS, Thomas H.,    March 15,1876 - Oct.19,1964
          Son of John F. Peters
PETERS, Minnie B., (w),    Aug.9,1880 - March 11,1955
          Maiden name Brinkley
PETERS, Shirley Silvers, (dau), May 3,1905 - June 14,1968
PETERS, Hugh Meredith, (son), Feb.23,1910 - Oct.30,1914
PETERS, Lon Frances, (dau), Died Nov.20,1917
PETERS, Vreeland,(son), 1901 -1936

BOYD, Joseph A.,    Aug.10,1880 - June 30,1955
          Son of Elijah and Octavia Hunt Boyd
BOYD, Elizabeth B.,    Nov.15,1885 - April 25,1980
BOYD, Dan McCorkle,    Oct.7,1923 - Oct.9,1923

HINES, Thomas William,    Aug.31,1872 - July 30,1939
          Son of Thomas and Mary Catsell Hines

NORTON, David C.,    April 1,1939 - April 2,1939
          Son of David L. and Thelma Lilly Norton

BOOTH, Alice Virginia,    1872 - 1939
          Dau. of Madison and Augusta Hatcher Booth

PETERSON, Hannah Luevennie,    Dec.23,1897 - Sept.15,1925
PETERSON, Infant Son of Mr.and Mrs.Neil Peterson - Died 1936
PETERSON, James,  Feb.2,1870 - Sept.3,1941
PETERSON, Nora Belle, (w), March 11,1876 - Jan.29,1939

SIMERLY, Henry C.,    May 22,1900 - Feb.12,1945
SIMERLY, Ida May,    Nov.10,1900 - March 17,1982

PAINTER, George K.,    March 17,1895 - May 30,1942
PAINTER, Minnie L.,    June 25,1896 - Sept.26,1978

WOODWARD, Roberta S.,    1886 - 1942
        Dau. of Thomas Martin and Emma Caroline Lance Sales

LANE, John Calvin,"Daddy",  Nov.16,1882 - Jan.6,1940
        Son of Albert D. and Bettie Bell Lane
LANE, Fannie Lane Rouse Ferguson, Feb.1,1898 - Jan.28,1979
NORRIS, Audrey, April 23,1918 - Oct.29,1961
        Son of Clayton and Venie Lou Norris
NORRIS, Emily Lane,    Jan.27,1917 - May 22,1985

REYNOLDS, J.Lee,    Nov.4,1885 - Feb.21,1926

CARTER, Frank,    June 15,1892 - Dec.21,1942
        Son of David and Jennie Starnes Carter
CARTER, Bessie,    April 28,1889 - March 20, 1960

FERGUSON, Walter F.,"Granddaddy", Oct.6,1868 - Nov.4,1945
FERGUSON, Sarah A., "Grandmama", Nov.22,1870 - May 7,1952
FERGUSON, Arthur D.,   Dec.2,1893 - Feb.8,1952 - USN WW1 WW2
FERGUSON, Lillian B.,    Sept.4,1907 - July 20,1930

SCRUGGS, Louis D.,    Sept.16,1871 - Sept.18,1935
        Son of T.V. and Temperance Simmons Scruggs
SCRUGGS, Ada White,    Sept.24,1890 - April 28,1949
        Dau. of Laban and Emma Erwin White

KEESECKER, Adrian Garrett,    1867 - 1936
        Son of Jacob and Elizabeth Jordan Keesecker
KEESECKER, Etta May,  (w), 1868 - 1935
KEESECKER, Infant Daughter,  Jan.13,1909 - Jan.16,1909
        Dau. of A.G. and Etta M. Keesecker

KEESECKER, Parran M.,    Oct.13,1910 - April 23,1982
        Son of A.G. and Etta May Keesecker
KEESECKER, Pauline,  Nov.29,1909 -  ----
        Dau. of C.E. and Rachel Brummett
KEESECKER, Rachel Mae,    Died May 29,1934
        Dau of Paran and Pauline Keesecker

WILSON, John Henry,    July 15,1871 - May 25,1925
WILSON, Martha Ann,    July 6,1872 - June 6,1944

LOVE, Marion Hope,    April 2,1924 - April 14,1932
        Child of Earl and Harriett Wilson Love

KEESECKER, Kyle Ray,    Feb.9,1927 - Sept.7,1973 - USN WW2
KEESECKER, Vinton W.,    Jan.10,1897 - Sept.8,1942 - USN WW1
        Son of A.G. and Etta Mae Allbright Keesecker

HARVEY, Harriett E.,    Aug.22,1859 - July 7,1943
            Dau. of Sam and Mary Catherine Howard Swanner

BANNISTER, Jannie Louise,    1909 - 1936

BANNER, Lula,    1870 - 1964
            Wife of W.M. Banner

WHITT, Paris H.,    July 6, 1885 - March 11,1941
WHITT, Nana H.,    Sept.4,1892 - March 27,1968
WHITT, Thurman Haywood, Oct.6,1913 - Jan.28,1977 -PFC US Army WW2

HUSKINS, William Henry,    1886 - 1955
            Son of William and Mary Poore Huskins
HUSKINS, Anna,    1891 - 1942

MATHES, Edward,    1899 - 1941
            Son of David A. and Ruth Penley Mathes

EVANS, Alfred Francis,    June 5,1884 - Nov.23,1942

KYTE, Chevis Chitwood,    Dec.9,1894 - Nov.15,1942
            Dau. of Wm. and Martha Cassindra Booth Davis

LOWE, Henry Allen,    1930 -1975 - US Army  Korea

FETTY, William L.Jr.,    July 22,1926 - March 23,1943
            Son of Wm. Lonzo and Marie C. St.Aubin Fetty

HARDYMAN, Lassie Hullett,    June 4,1893 - Dec.19,1977

UMHOLTZ, Joseph Vincent,    1876 - 1951
UMHOLTZ, Lula Tittle,    1877 - 1945

PHILLIPS, Samuel C.,    Dec.25,1873 - Feb.22,1941
PHILLIPS, Nellie Higgins, (w), Nov.20,1876 - May 30,1943

WATTS, Jimmie Farrell,    Aug.9,1941 - Feb.6,1942

WILLIAMS, Rushie L.,    Nov.30,1941 - July 15,1982

SHELTON, Viola,    1909 - 1941
            Dau. of Josh and Janie Tipton Ford

PETERSON, Jesse W.,    Aug.20,1897 - Jan.26,1948
PETERSON, Calvin Dwight,    Sept.23,1925 - Nov.29,1941

GUINN, Fred T.,    July 5,1884 - Feb.7,1939
GUINN, Kittie P., (w), March 23,1888 - Feb.23,1969
GUINN, Arthur N.,    Jan.17,1904 - July 13,1969
GUINN, Edward W.,    Jan.6,1909 - Dec.27,1956 - Sgt US Army WW2
            Son of Fred Taylor and Kitty Phillips Guinn
BRUMMETT, Ola B.,    Oct.24,1907 -  ----
BRUMMETT, Betty Jean,    March 2,1928 - Oct.22,1977
BRUMMETT, Baby Thompson,    ----  -  ----

EVERGREEN CEMETERY (continued)

NORTON,Dana Harmon, 1901 - 1935
NORTON, Elmer Lavern, March 14,1924 - Oct.24,1940
        Son of Dana Harmon and Alice Irene Thompson Norton

GRIFFITH, Hulda, 1902 - 1959
GRIFFITH, Madeline, Died 1939
GRIFFITH, Edna, Died 1943
GRIFFITH, Mildred, Died 1944

BANKS, Roy D., 1903 - ----
BANKS, Bessie D., 1918 - ----
BANKS, Nolia Edwards, Feb.18,1907 - March 12,1937
        Wife of Roy - Dau. of Wm. and Loretta Ledford Edwards

WARRICK, Hester, June 16,1879 - Aug.19,1940

WILLIAMS, J.Bliss, May 3,1903 - Dec.6,1968
WILLIAMS, Judy Kay, Died Aug.6,1941
        Dau. of Mr. and Mrs. J.B. Williams

TOLLEY, Golda Miller, June 19,1900 - Nov.16,1964
BARNETT, Mary Miller, June 20,1861 - April 26,1942
PETERSON, Esther, Aug.30,1891 - Dec.12,1979

ENGLE, Brenda Sue, Died Dec.29,1953

BANKS, Wesley, 1880 - 1943
BANKS, Lillie, 1883 - 1965
BANKS, Dewey, 1902 - 1983
BANKS, Edna, (w), 1906 - ----

NORRIS, Lewis A., 1903 - 1961
NORRIS, Julia C., 1903 - 1945
        Dau. of James and Cora Hampton Deaton

LINVILLE, Robert, 1892 - 1988
LINVILLE, Delia, 1898 - 1971

LUTTRELL, Rennie A., April 24,1915 - April 4,1945

KEEVER, Fred H., May 15,1907 - May 11,1944
        Son of Joseph Washington and Mandy Roberts Keever
KEEVER, Claude Henry, Aug.28,1903 - Nov.6,1965

MILLER, Nat T., 1891 - 1971
MILLER, Mary Magdalene, 1896 - 1959
        Dau. of Pete and Lizzie McInturff Honeycutt

WILLIAMS, James Douglas, b/d Nov.28,1942
        Son of Arnold and Marjorie Barnett Williams

JONES, John W., May 19,1872 - June 11,1962
JONES, Vashti T., (w), May 1,1888 - March 18,1987

WILSON, Ida H., March 17,1897 - ----

LEDFORD, W.Amos,    1891 - 1943
LEDFORD, Helen M.,    1894 - 1967

CLOUSE, John B.,    May 19,1863 - Sept.26,1945
CLOUSE,Berzila,    Oct.23,1869 - Oct.14,1941
CLOUSE, Vernia Mae,    July 1,1902 - Jan.18,1939
            Dau. of John B. and Berzila Jarrett Clouse
CLOUSE, Iva Geneva,    Oct.8,1904 -  ----

DALTON, John C.,    1881 - 1938
            Son of John and Belle Stalnacker Dalton
DALTON, Mary R.,    1888 - 1972

PHILLIPS, Neal D.,    1875 - 1956
            Son of Powell and Eddy Britt Phillips
PHILLIPS, Mollie L.,    1878 - 1939
            Dau. of James and ----Whitson Norris

GOUGE, Ronald Patrick "Butch", March 17,1941 - June 14,1947

WILSON, Dave,    March 3,1889 - Sept.6,1951 - PVT US Army WW1
            Son of Sam and Retta Bradshaw Wilson

MURPHY, James T.,    March 26,1882 - April 12,1959
MURPHY, Mary Jane,    March 31,1892 - Jan.2,1980
MURPHY, Margaret Jane,    June 11,1874 - April 8,1928
            Maiden name Cupp

SHELL, Warner,    Dec.23,1891 - Dec.5,1964
SHELL, Mary Katherine Heaton,    Sept.23,1894 - Feb.22,1988
SHELL, Warner,Jr.,    May 18,1924 - July 13,1925

BURGNER, Birdie Moore,    June 11,1890 - April 23,1966

NORRIS, Clayton L.,    1875 - 1965
NORRIS, Venie Lou,    Sept.22,1882 - Nov.17,1977
SHOUN, Eugene Norris,    Sept.17,1922 - Jan.22,1973
WHITE, Mallissa Caroline, Feb.6,1849 - Nov.29,1927

EDENS, Homer R.,    April 15,1911 - April 23,1982
EDENS, Mamie G.,    Jan.4,1904 - Dec.22,1986

CECIL, Etta May,    1869 - 1940
            Dau. of Thomas J. and Martha E. Fulwider Farmer
FARMER, Mrs. Martha E.,    1846 - 1926

CHANDLER, John B.,    Sept.14,1873 - April 10,1965
CHANDLER, Mollie Story,    Aug.12,1873 - Jan.17,1948
            Dau. of Jessee and Margaret Hoffman Story

SHERWOOD, Arthur C.,    June 6,1877 - June 2,1946
            Son of James Justice LaFayette and Sarah Young Sherwood
SHERWOOD, Edith Allen,    July 22,1892 - July 28,1965

HATCHER, George L., 1886 - 1964
     Son of Jonathan A. and Katherine Bullock Hatcher
HATCHER, Fannie L., 1897 - 1966
HATCHER, Lois Celesta, (dau.), Jan.29,1919 - Aug.4,1929
HATCHER, Thomas Edward, (son), 1917 - 1979 - PFC US Army WW2

BOGART Orville Eugene, 1885 - 1965
BOGART, Kate Tilson, 1891 - 1950
     Dau. of LeRoy Sams and Eliza Jane Parks Tilson

GENTRY, A.A., April 25,1878 - May 17,1945
GENTRY, Ruby Pearl, Oct.28,1896 - ----

RIMEL, Robert A., Sept.22,1884 - June 22,1948
     Son of Joseph Rimel
RIMEL, Hattie B., May 22,1887 - Aug.4,1951
     Dau of John W. and Catherine Heffner Eckenroth

EVANS, Samuel Roy, Feb.27,1895 - Jan.31,1949
     Son of George and Sallie Billups Evans
EVANS, Eva, Nov.3,1896 - May 4,1985
EVANS, Infant, Died Aug.7,1929
     Child of Roy and Eva Hickman Evans
EVANS, Clyde H., Feb.11,1922 - March 6,1967 - USN WW 2

HEAD, Blake W., 1899 - 1942
     Son of William J. and Dora Byrd Head

WHITE, Earl D., 1895 - 1977 - Cpl US Army WW1
WHITE, Pearl Mae, 1903 - 1983

LOVE, Ernest Burson, May 29,1878 - April 16,1954
LOVE, Clara White, June 5,1887 - Oct.29,1945
LOVE, Edna Ruth, Dec.12,1912 - June 16,1986

GENTRY, Frank Taylor, 1893 - 1949
     Son of Lewis and Sarah Katherine Guinn Gentry
GENTRY, Love M., 1904 - 1977
GENTRY, Katherine Ann, 1932 - 1938
     Dau. of Frank T. and Love Mooney Gentry

TONEY, James Frank, Jr., Jan.28,1895 - Dec.31,1960 - Sgt Inf WW1
TONEY, Sue Emmerson, Jan.28,1896 - July 17,1980

GARLAND, Byrd Thomas, Nov.19,1915 - Sept.30,1972
GARLAND, Pauline Love, Dec.14,1914 - July 28,1974

MILLER, John C., 1863 - 1933 - Sgt Co G 3rd Tenn Inf
MILLER, Maud Holder, 1871 - 1946
     Dau. of Mark and Martha Burke Holder
MILLER, Fred L., Nov.12,1904 - Feb.20,1961 - Sgt US Armt WW2
     Son of John Clifton and Lillie Maude Holder Miller
MILLER, Kyle Deadrick,Sr., 1906 -1981 - US Army WW1
MILLER, J.Clifton, Jr., 1913 - 1968
FERGUSON, Cecil Miller, 1900 - 1979
FERGUSON, Anita June, 1921 - 1951
     Dau. of A.D. and Cecil Miller Ferguson

LEWIS, Harvey David,    March 25, 1946 (one date)
          Infant of Sam K. and Olive Dobbins Lewis

LOWE, John J.,    1883 - 1946
LOWE, Laura E.,    1883 - 1964
          Dau. of Phillip David and Lou Kinder Howard Street
SPARKS, Ruth Lowe,    1908 -  ----

TONEY, W.C. "Buck",    May 27,1882 - Jan.27,1935
          Son of J.Frank and Fannie Bell Miller Toney
TONEY, Christine Everett, (w),    March 15,1883 - Aug.13,1972

TONEY, Col. J.F.,    1859 - 1940
          Son of Wm. Christopher and Evaline Price Toney
TONEY, Fannie B., (w),    1861 - 1903
TONEY, Evaline,    March 3,1835 - June 28,1913
          Dau. of Christopher and Mary McInturff Price
TONEY, George Lynn,    Nov.30,1892 - July 9,1931 - Co L 39 Inf 4 Div
TONEY, Julia Alice,    Dec.17,1894 - Jan.11,1968
TONEY, Rhoda, March 15,1864 - June 20,1912
WOOD, Helen Toney,    July 1,1910 - Feb.20,1988

BARRY, Richard M.,Sr.,    1879 - 1959
BARRY, Gertrude Eloise,    1884 - 1949
          Dau. of Wesley S. and Polly Ann Bailey Tucker
BARRY, Richard M.,Jr.,    1911 - 1984 - USA   WW2

STAMPLER, Garrett,    1910 - 1983 .
STAMPLER, Donna T.,    1921 -  ----
STAMPLER, Walter D.,    July 14,1947 - July 17,1967   - US Army

TUCKER, Joe L.,    1876 - 1935
TUCKER, Mamie T., (w), 1880 - 1969
TUCKER, Paul L., (son),    1903 - 1920
TUCKER, Joe L.,Jr., (son),    1915 - 1918
HAYNES, Infant Son,    Died 1932
          Child of W.D. and Doris Haynes

TOLLEY, John M.,    June 5,1872 - Oct.26,1946
TOLLEY, Jane S.,    Dec.12,1873 - April 6,1953
          Dau. of James and Lovada Adkins Howell
TOLLEY, Roscoe M.,    Dec.2, 1899 -April 21,1948
TOLLEY, Joseph Melvin,    June 6,1914 - July 27,1975
TOLLEY, Lillian Salts,    Sept.1,1911 -  ----
BYRD, Douglas Kelly,   Died June 8,1955
          Infant of D.C. and Janice Byrd

HOPSON, Infant Daughter,   June 2,1958 - June 3,1958
          Dau. of Mr. and Mrs. Millard H. Hopson

JOHNSON, Alice,   Oct.26,1908 - Feb.26,1948
          Dau. of William and Virginia Angel Riddle
JOHNSON, Bernie Weldon,    March 14,1911 - May 28,1985

EVERGREEN CEMETERY (continued)

HIGGINS, Fred,    Aug.31,1902 - Aug.13,1971

TOLLEY, Junior,    June 12,1952 - Nov.30,1986

MORGAN, Gordon,    Feb.27,1901 - July 29,1971
MORGAN, Ruth,    Nov.1,1917 - Feb.5,1980

EDWARDS, Vennie,    Dec.9,1909 - Jan.4,1977
            Wife of Rev. Fred B. Edwards

ARROWOOD, Dorothy Hughes,    Oct.17,1924 - Sept.20,1957
            Dau. of John L. and Bessie Genett Banner Hughes
ARROWOOD, Charlotte Dorothy, April 23,1945 - Dec.25,1965
            Dau. of Mack and Dorothy Hughes Arrowood

PETERSON, Novella L.,    Jan.30,1930 - Nov.24,1969

BEAM, Rev.W.M.,    April 15,1901 - Jan.4,1975
BEAM, Essie,    April 14,1902 - May 30,1954

EDWARDS, W.D.,    June 15,1893 - March 4,1960
            Son of John and Esther Poore Edwards

HOLLIFIELD, Clyde David,    Dec.20,1894 - Aug.27,1972
HOLLIFIELD, Lillie Quinn,    May 21,1892 - Nov.27,1975
HOLLIFIELD, Mike Charles,    1916 - 1975 - Pvt US Army WW2

HUGHES, Joe Douglas,    May 29,1930 - April 21,1958
HUGHES, John L.,    1893 - 1977

VOGEL, Johnnie Love,    1918 - 1982

HARRIS, Oscar Clinton,    1925 - 1983 - PFC USMC WW2
HARRIS, Stephanie Robin,    Died Feb.3,1959
            Dau. of Mr. and Mrs. O.C. Harris

HARRIS, John H.,Sr.,    1892 - 1969
HARRIS, Dollie W.,    1901 - 1978

MONK, J.Charlie, Sr.,    Dec.13,1887 - Feb.18,1978
MONK, Fannie B.,    Feb.22,1897 -    ----
MONK, Edward Lee,    Jan.22,1914 - June 20,1917

SMITH, Culver S.,    Nov.17,1906 - March 21,1959
            Son of William Smith
SMITH, Charles Doug,    1944 - 1975

WHITT, Charles Laverne,    March 7,1942 - Dec.7,1959
            Son of Alvin Wayne and Agnes Jaynes Whitt

JOHNSON, James C.,    April 12,1922 - April 18,1960 - Sgt USA WW2

WILLIAMS, W.T.,    May 16,1881 - Dec.19,1960
WILLIAMS, Rena,    Jan.19,1886 - Feb.1,1972

<u>EVERGREEN CEMETERY</u> (continued)

GIVENS, Roger W.,    Sept.20,1897 -  ----
GIVENS, Nell C.,    July 4,1899 - Jan.1,1968

GILLIS, Walter G.,    1886 - 1960
GILLIS, Polly L., (w),    1887 - 1982
GILLIS, William Earl,    Sept.28,1914 - Dec.6,1981

BLANKENSHIP, Bob,    Jan.29,1909 - March 17,1985
BLANKENSHIP, Zora O.,    Jan.29,1912 -  ----
RIDDLE, Hazel Blankenship,    June 10,1954 - Jan.15,1975

SHOOK, Elsie L.,    Oct.5,1923 -  ----
SHOOK, Emaline "Sis",    March 20,1892 - March 12,1982
BLANKENSHIP, Texana,    Jan.3,1901 -  ----

HELTON, Ernest P.,    March 14,1918 - Jan.12,1985

BENNETT, Ethel T.,    May 12,1910 - June 5,1979

DOBBS, Alton Amos,"DDS",    June 8,1904 - Aug.30,1987

ERVIN, Thomas Marion,    1917 - 1988

ARROWOOD, Ernest,    Dec.12,1925 - March 26,1988 - US Army Korea

POORE, Adam,    Dec.11,1962 - July 24,1981

HARRIS, Ralph,    Sept.27,1914 -  ----
HARRIS, Bertie B.,    May 25,1917 -  ----
HARRIS Carl,    Dec.27,1932 - April 11,1981

BENNETT, Nancy Corinne,    Sept.12,1978 - Jan.14,1981

HARRIS, Bill,    June 5,1934 -  ----
HARRIS, Beatrice,    Aug.7,1936

HARRIS, Virgil H.,    1909 - 1977

BAILEY, Edna Marie,    June 5,1919 - March 2,1982

STARKEY, Walter,    Oct.17,1912 -  ----
STARKEY, Nina,    May 9,1916 -  ----

MILLER, Herbert C.,    Aug.31,1910 -  ----
MILLER, Evelyn T.,    Feb.28,1913 -  ----

MASTERS, Stewart W.,    Dec.27,1899 - Sept.29,1986
MASTERS, Ethel W.,    Nov.23,1906 - Aug.6,1987
MASTERS, Bruce Stuart, 1930 - 1981 - Sgt USAF Korea

MILLER, Hilda J.,    March 5,1943 - April 20,1982

BAILEY, Chester,    Sept.20,1903 -  ----
BAILEY, Carrie,    Feb.24,1905 -  ----

LEDFORD, Robert F.,Sr.,   Sept.2,1923 - Feb.24,1982 - US Army WW2
LEDFORD, Betty E.,   Dec.18,1937 - ----

CARROLL, William J.,   Dec.18,1910 - Aug.10,1985 - PFC US Army
CARROLL, Mary B.,   Feb.16,1911 - ----

WINTERS, Grace Tipton, 1906 - 1987

SUTHERLAND, Lissie T.,   May 19,1887 - Sept.11,1975

ALLEN, Dennis D.,   March 18,1934 - March 30,1967
ALLEN, Willard,   Nov.23,1907 - June 10,1983
ALLEN, Kate M.,   April 11,1916 - Dec.1,1973
ALLEN Artie Clyde,   1911 - 1982  - PFC USA WW2
ALLEN Hubert Clyde,   May 11,1944 - July 9,1980

HENLEY, Ernest William,   June 27,1927 - June 22,1978 - USN WW2
HENLEY, Novella McKinney, 1922 - ----
HENLEY, Howard,   June 6,1934 - Feb.5,1976  - PFC USA
ROBERTS, Gertrude,   March 30,1884 - Dec.4,1974

DAVIS, Marcella M.,   Feb.5,1922 - Aug.11,1973

HICKS, David S.,   July 27,1959 - April 11,1972

MORGAN, John H.,   Sept.14,1912 - Feb.25,1973
MORGAN, Naomi B.,   Feb.23,1917 - ----

BAILEY, Timmie D.,   1968 - 1970
BAILEY, Judi N.,   1967 - 1967

BRADFORD, John Emory,   1899 - 1975

HENSLEY, Rose Ann,   1913 - 1987

PHILLIPS, John Floyd,   1905 - 1980
PHILLIPS, Benny,   Jan.13,1936 - May 11,1973
PHILLIPS, Shirley Jean, May 2,1937 -  ----

STANCIL, James Freeman,   Feb.7,1921 - May 18,1985 - USA WW2
STANCIL, Ruth R.,   April 4,1943 -  ----

PRESNELL, W. Howard,   Jan.14,1910 - March 7,1986
PRESNELL, Leva H.,   June 2,1918 -  ----

LAWS, Roger L.,   Dec.5,1935 - April 20,1985
LAWS, Janie S.,   Oct.11,1934 -  ----

LAWS, Robert,   April 1,1896 - Dec.17,1968 - PFC WW1

TAPP, William "Buster",   Aug.3,1932 -  ----
TAPP, Isabell,   March 15,1927 - Dec.14,1987

GRUBB, Paul C.,   1927 - 1966

WHITTEMORE, Will,   1900 - 1941
WHITTEMORE, Rena C.,   (w),   1899 - 1966

LEWIS, R.L.,   Nov.7,1919 - Dec.5,1976 - PFC USA WW2

HENSLEY, Jessie M.,   Dec.31,1913 - Sept.28,1964
          Dau. of Thomas and Lydia Harris Honeycutt

HUSKINS, J.Marshall, Jr.,   1926 - 1967
HUSKINS, Jaqueline P.,   ---- - ----

WEEKLEY, William E.,   1894 - 1965
          Son of John Weekley
WEEKLEY, John Ervin,   June 4,1924 - Aug.14,1979 - USA WW2

PETERSON, Frank E.,   Feb.14,1927 - March 9,1961 - USN WW2

WHITSON, John D.,   1892 - 1987
WHITSON, Gertie Bell,   Nov.30,1894 - Feb.7,1972
WHITSON, Andrew J.,   May 13,1922 - Nov.3,1962 - USN WW2

THORNBERRY, Lewis S.,   March 13,1895 - July 28,1966 - USA WW1
THORNBERRY, Flonia Kegley,   Jan.27,1903 - ----

KEGLEY, Flossie A.,   July 23,1900 - Nov.12,1983

BANNER, Donald C.,   July 1,1930 - Oct.23,1966 - Cpl USA Korea

McINTURFF, John Albert,   Feb.9,1919 - May 21,1974

McCURRY, Lela E.,   Aug.23,1923 - June 7,1967

GARLAND, J.W.,   Sept.30,1891 - Feb.11,1977
GARLAND, Mary Saphfrona,   Oct.17,1889 - March 26,1967
GARLAND, G.D.,   May 3,1916 - July 21,1967
GARLAND, Earl C.,   Sept.6,1925 - April 4,1973 - PFC USA WW2

OLLIS, Julia,   May 5,1901 - June 22,1978

LEWIS, Raymond,   Feb.15,1901 - Dec.23,1974
LEWIS, Cora,  (w),  May 26,1903 - ----

PHILLIPS, Jettie,   Feb.22,1896 - Oct.9,1983

BAILEY, Charles Leonard,   1945 - 1981 - US Army

CORRELL, Benjamin H.,   Sept.10,1902 - ----
CORRELL, Ruth B.,   June 20,1909 - Dec.23,1965

EDWARDS, Carmon W.,   May 12,1902 - March 3,1986
EDWARDS, Hattie Hughes,   Sept.24,1886 - Dec.12,1965

<u>EVERGREEN CEMETERY</u> (continued)

TILSON, Grover C.,    Feb.5,1897 - Feb.20,1971 -Pvt USA WW1
TILSON, Lockie,    Jan.16,1898 - June 24,1980
TILSON, George S.,    1927 - 1928
TILSON, Dorothy L.,    1929 - 1930

FRITTZ, Clifford G.,    Oct.30,1911 - Dec.11,1965
FRITTZ, Mildred L.,    Oct.3,1911 - April 24,1978

RUNNION, Ralph T.,    April 6,1913 - Jan.18,1982 - USMC WW2
RUNNION, Anna L.,    Feb.6,1917 -  ----

FAIN, Lydia Haskett,    Aug.3,1889 - July 4,1969

BYRD, Charles W.,    Feb.25,1886 - March 6,1975
BYRD, Emma P.,    April 9,1890 - July 16,1978

ANDERSON, Renzo,    Sept.30,1893 - Nov.29,1968
ANDERSON, Margaret L.,    Oct.13,1907 - Aug.21,1978

BAILEY, Samuel S.,    1885 - 1968
BAILEY, Clyde Buckner,    1889 - 1985

ALLEN, Gurnie E.,    June 22,1916 - Oct.25,1970 - PFC USA WW2
ALLEN, Allie H.,    March 13,1908 - April 5,1981

GAMBRELL, Marsha S.,    1958 - 1969

HARRIS, Mark Herbert,    April 6,1962 - Jan.11,1971

WALLACE, Charlie,    Dec.20,1901 - Nov.10,1981
WALLACE, Douglas Lee,    Sept.11,1942 - Dec.5,1966

JOHNSON, J.Lee,    June 4,1891 - Nov.12,1972
JOHNSON, Carey Taylor,    Nov.6,1891 - March 19,1970

PETERSON, Grady,    1892 - 1966
PETERSON, Rosa T.,    1892 - 1977

McNABB, Charlie C.,    June 7,1898 - March 11,1982
McNABB, Gertrude S.,    May 13,1896 - Jan.27,1986

McINTURFF, Fred E.,    March 30,1912 - June 6, 1969

ENGLE, Millard A.,    Aug.19,1914 - April 5,1968 - Pvt USA WW2
ENGLE, Eliza L.,    March 31,1913 - April 7,1984

JONES, Michael Jason,    b/d 1979

DUNCAN, Nathaniel C.,    Aug.2,1877 - June 15,1960
          Son of Franklin Madison and Catherine Duggar Duncan
DUNCAN, Fannie H.,    April 22,1881 - Aug.5,1964
          Dau. of John W. and Amanda Keener Haskett

EMMERT, Eugene F.,    July 2,1878 - April 17,1958
EMMERT, Finnetta H.,   April 27,1891 - April 19,1964
EMMERT, James Love,Sr.,  1917 - 1979  - Cpl USA WW2

DUGAN, Sharon Kay,   April 7,1953 - Nov.5,1957
            Dau. of John H. and Zeta McIntosh Dugan

WHITSON, Handy H.,   June 22,1909 - Jan.16,1957

WILSON, Savanah Whitson,   Aug.13,1914 - Oct.2,1982

CANIPE, Wallace A.,   Sept.25,1883 - Sept.7,1958

HAUN, Pete L.,   1886 - 1963
HAUN, Ada, (w),  1902 - 1956
HAUN, Gus,  Feb.27,1926 - May 31,1967  - USN WW2

MILLER, Mallie P.,   1894 - 1956
            Son of Jerry and Martha Jane Randolph Miller
MILLER, Birdie,   1894 - 1957
            Dau. of Wesley and Elmena Maer Phillips

JACKSON, William Albert,   1919 - 1983  - Sgt USA WW2
JACKSON, Teresa Lynn,   b/d  1956
            Dau of William A. and Willie Mae Dugger Jackson

CLOUSE, Date,   1913 - 1977  -  USN WW2
CLOUSE, Bonnie W.,   1912 - 1964

KEPLINGER, Dorothy Virginia,   Aug.27,1916 - Feb.14,1985

POORE, Isaac,   June 8,1875 - Dec.29,1963
            Son of Robert and Sue Starnes Poore
POORE, Lillie Miller,   June 4, 1887 - Aug.12,1971

McNABB, Jackie Clyde,   Aug.22,1951 - March 3,1968
McNABB, James Patrick,   Feb.9,1949 - May 14,1960
McNABB, Infant Son,   Dec.20,1954
            Sons of James Polk and Bettie Ruth Davis McNabb

NELSON, Clyde,   Nov.15,1895 - Jan.21,1964
NELSON, Nettie,   June 17,1897 - April 18,1961
NELSON, Effie Louella,   May 14,1927 - July 17,1954

HOLLIFIELD, Roy,   Dec.27,1914 - Oct.22,1966
HOLLIFIELD, Jennie L.,   1914 - 1977

BARNETT, William M.,   1873 - 1950
            Son of Benjamin and Myriah Sneed Barnett
BARNETT, Nellie Smith,   1877 - 1967

BENNETT, Roy Jack, Jr.,   Dec.24,1926 - Aug.6,1957 - Army Air CorpWW2
BENNETT, Avenelle K.,   1923 - 1948
            Dau. of Jonothan and Stella Reynolds Keene
BENNETT, Peggy Oneal,   1931 -1975
BENNETT, Rev. Stephen D.,   June 16,1948 - Feb.1,1967

EVERGREEN CEMETERY (continued)

COX, William R.,    1888 - 1948
        Son of William Taylor and Margaret Jones Cox
COX, Grace C., (w),  1905 - 1977
COX, Wesley T.,    1931 - 1950
        Son of W.R. and Grace Parker Cox

TIPTON, Mose,    Oct.1,1881 - Jan.18,1967
TIPTON, Celia B.,    March 4, 1883 - May 24,1956
        Dau. of Joe and Jane Hicks Buchanon

FORD, Charles,    1869 - 1956
        Son of James and Suzanna Bray Ford
FORD, Anna Jane,    1873 - 1938
        Dau. of George W. and -----Watkins Shaver

EDENS, Ernest Lee,    Feb.25,1893 - April 30,1965 - Pvt USA WW1

HENDRIX, James H.,    Jan.15,1934 - ----
HENDRIX, Velda Lloyd,    Jan.26,1937 - Oct.28,1959

EVANS, Ella M.,    1885 - 1951
        Dau. of Wm.C.E. and Mary Ida Bennett Stanley

DOBBINS, Harry,    July 30,1886 - Oct.3,1955
        Son of Harry and Debra O'Donall Dobbins
DOBBINS, Dora Ferne,    Feb.18,1889 - Oct.20,1973

BOGART, Leora,    Jan.12,1910 - Nov.12,1949

RUNNION, William G.,    Dec.14,1923 - Oct.13,1962
        Son of Tony and Dora Sparks Runnion

PARKER, Wesley S.,    1873 - 1961
PARKER, Lucinda E.,    1882 - 1957
        Dau. of Richard and Mary Barber Frazier
PARKER, Guy,    1912 - 1973
PARKER, Jerry M.,    1939 - 1959

PADGETT, Mack J.,    Nov.22,1895 - April 26,1955
        Son of Charley and Emily Stanton Padgett
PADGETT, A.Belle,    July 22,1902 - Jan.19,1983

BAILEY, Lawrence M.,    May 27,1923 - Jan.10,1949  - PFC USA WW2
BAILEY, Geter, Jr.,    July 4,1927 - Aug.21,1973   - USN WW2

WALKER, Suel McKinley,    Aug.29,1896 - Feb.19,1955 - PFC USA WW1
WALKER, Emma Hazel Duvall,  Oct.2,1907 - Feb.26,1987
DUVALL, Mary Horne,    Oct.13,1882 - Dec.8,1969

NELSON, Hilbert H.,    May 12,1919 - Feb.11,1971 - PFC USA WW2
NELSON, Ruby,    March 27,1922 - ----

RUNNION, Roy J.,    Dec.8,1893 - Nov.7,1955

<u>EVERGREEN CEMETERY</u> (continued)

WILSON, Russell Jack,    1930 - 1985  - USAF  Vietnam
WILSON, Ruby P.,    1929 - ----

SIZEMORE, J.H.,    Nov.18,1893 - Aug.6,1956
            Son of Thomas Newton and Stella Farnsworth Sizemore
SIZEMORE, Carrie,    Mar.19,1899 - ------
COX, James Elias,    July 26,1872 - May 21,1957
            Son of Enoch B. Cox
COX, Martha Curtis,    July 22,1871 - Dec.18,1956
            Dau. of John Curtis

ROBINSON, Fate,    1922 - 1980  - USA WW2

WILLIAMS, Roy V.,    1909 - 1960
            Son of Will Turner and Rena McCurry Williams

STAMPER, John L.,    1883 - 1966
STAMPER, Maggie B.,    1890 - 1985

McINTOSH, Earl,    1906 - 1965
            Son of Thomas J. and Nola Foster McIntosh
McINTOSH, Thomas J.,    1884 - 1970
McINTOSH, Nola Foster,    1888 - 1973

EMMERT, Nellie A.,    1912 - 1988
EMMERT, William C.,    Oct. 23,1921 - June 29, 1980 - USA WW2

WATTS, Frank,    Jan.26,1908 - July 8,1964
            Son of Silas and Jane McIntosh Watts

HIGGINBOTHAM, Harold,    July 13,1933 - April 25,1983
HIGGINBOTHAM, Kenneth A.,    Jan.3,1929 - June 30,1984
HIGGINBOTHAM, Wilma J.,    Nov.27,1926 -  ----

McNABB, Donald A.,    Sept.4,1933 - Sept.18,1987
McNABB, Helen J.,    Dec.10, 1933 -  ----

TUCKER, Dana H.,    1895 - 1974
TUCKER, Mildred G.,    (w),    1897 - 1976

RICE, Sally,    1898 - 1975

BAILEY, Pierce B.,    1925 - 1977
BAILEY, Ronald Rodney,    Sept.22,1947 - Feb. 9,1972 - USN  Vietnam

RUTTER, Bonnie E.,    Nov.19,1909 - March 13, 1986

ALLEN, Juanita Foster,    Aug.24,1952 - March 15,1969

PARKER, Alfred Russell,    Feb.20,1915 - Jan.17,1979
PARKER, Elizabeth "Betty",    March 30. 1919 -  ----

EVERGREEN CEMETERY (continued)

TREADWAY, Braskey,    July 20,1893 - Oct.1,1984
TREADWAY, Viola Pate,  (w),  March 8,1900 - Sept.15,1987
TREADWAY, Fate,   1926 - 1984  - USA WW2

BAILEY, Elmer W.,   1914 - 1975    - USN WW2
BAILEY, Vergie Watts,   1905 - 1981

CLOUSE, Harry B.,   1913 - 1985  - USA WW2

SPARKS, Everett W.,   April 6,1916 - Sept.11,1985
SPARKS, Elizabeth A.,   June 18,1920 - ----

SCHLENK, Grace Edwards,   July 4,1925 - Jan.16,1974

SNEAD, Grace Atkins,   Aug.31,1889 - Feb.13,1983
ATKINS, Jerry F.,   1920 - 1988

TREADWAY, Carver Y.,   1886 - 1971
TREADWAY, Matilda H.,   1904 - 1973

PRICE, Ethel,   1915 - 1986
          Dau. of Carrie Riddle

WATTS, Arthur,   Aug. 23,1899 - July 8,1974
WATTS, Mildred,   Nov.4,1904 - Sept.8,1968

PETERSON, Francis C.,   1906 - 1976  - Pvt USMC WW2

LANTER, Virginia H.,   1920 - 1976

ANDERS, Bill,   June 12,1910 -Dec.8,1981

BAILEY, Fannie A.,   May 30,1881 - Feb.7 1973

WILLIAMS, Willis Mitchell,   March 10,1919 - Jan.24,1972

CRAIN, Stephen,   1889 - 1963
          Son of William and Emmaline Higgins Crain
CRAIN, Rena C.,  (w),  1895 - 1974

BRYANT, Jane,   Jan.6,1894 - Aug.1,1972

GILLENWATER, Tolby,   Oct.15,1919 - May 24,1988
GILLENWATER, Mary L.,   June 14,1925 -  ----

GRIFFITH, Minnie Boundurant,   1898 - 1966
          Dau. of Samuel W. and Cornelia Porter Boundurant

JENNINGS, Oscar Mann,   Dec.28,1893 - Dec.12,1986
JENNINGS, Willie Tiara Spurgeon,  Sept.18,1892 - April 2,1986

KERNS, Louis Charles,   Nov.22,1919 -  ----
KERNS, Peggy Beckelhimer,  Aug.27,1922 - Dec.25,1980

COUK, Frederick G.,    Dec.25,1905 - Feb.27,1970 - USA WW2
COUK, Effie Farnor,    June 27,1914 - June 10,1977

DUNBAR, Jacob Ross, Jr.,    June 7,1927 - Aug.6,1971 - USN WW2
DUNBAR, Jacob Ross, Sr.,    March 19,1896 - Dec.2,1968
DUNBAR, Sallie Broyles,    March 24,1899 - Dec.19,1985

SAMS, James Carl,    April 1,1895 - Aug.4,1981  -  Pvt USA WW1
SAMS, Elizabeth D.,    Aug.28,1894 - Nov.3,1981

MONROE, Harmon L.,    Sept.10,1909 - April 15,1970  -  Capt USA WW2
HUNTZINGER, Bessie Bandy,    Nov.27,1881 - March 9,1966

FRATER, Henry, 1902 - 1980
FRATER, Elsie Baxter,    1911 -  ---

HASTY, Edith M.,    Aug.23,1908 - March 11,1974
HASTY, Kimberly May,    Dec.26,1963 - Dec.28,1963
        Dau. of Jerry and Anne Marie Robbins Hasty

SENTER, William Bryan,    April 17,1896 - Nov.21,1977 - PFC USA WW2
SENTER, Gertrude Hale,    June 16,1900 - May 11,1983

HENDREN, Earl Leon,    May 19,1904 - June 14,1962
        Son of Joseph E. and Maggie Boring Hendren
HENDREN, Maude Card, (w),    Feb.11,1906 - Dec.22,1982

EDWARDS, James Solomon,    Sept.29,1897 - Dec.4,1978
EDWARDS, Mae Peterson,    Feb.19, 1899 - Jan.20,1953
        Dau. of Samuel and Darliska Bryant Peterson

ERWIN, William M.,    1884 - 1967
ERWIN, Allice Ryburn,    1883 - 1972
ERWIN, H. Dennis,    1908 - 1975

DAVIS, William F.,    Sept.3,1872 - July 21,1948

MOORE, Ralph Doyle,    June 18,1914 - Dec.3,1969  -USN WW2

HONEYCUTT, David R.,    Oct.15,1943 - July 14,1971

WOODWARD, Jacob E.,    May 27,1867 - Oct.15,1955
        Son of Benjamin and Lucinda Sams Woodward
WOODWARD, Malla E.,    Aug.18,1873 - Dec.2,1958
        Dau. of James and Eva Taylor Anderson
WOODWARD, George A.,    Sept.5,1897 - May 3,1968

KINSLAND, Dillon L.,    May 9,1895 - June 16,1970  - USA WW1
KINSLAND, Etta Davis,    Aug.22,1899 - April 3,1984

WRIGHT, William H.,    Jan.2,1885 - April 25,1966
WRIGHT, Mary L.,    Feb.18,1886 - Jan.29,1968

FFIN, Vann,   July 25,1880 - July 25,1950
        Son of W.P. and Suzanne Ellen Hamilton Griffin
FFIN, Katherine S.,   May 28,1897 - May 20,1984

EY, K.L.,Sr.,   March 18,1894 - Jan.26,1988
EY, Hattie Taylor,   Feb.1,1894 - Sept.14,1950
        Dau. of John Martin and Mary Jane Odine Taylor
EY, Kelly L., Jr., (son), Nov.14,1923 - Feb.28,1944
        US Army Air Corp. WW2

ELER, William O.,   1886 - 1951
        Son of John H. and Sarah Matilda Duncan Wheeler
ELER, Orla Watts,   1889 - 1967

B, M.B.,   April 22,1898 - Sept.1,1960
        Son of Wm. Clingman and Johann Garland Webb
B, Ola B.,   July 26,1907 - Dec.28,1968
B, Clingman W.,   1858 - 1946

S, James Erwin,   Aug.14,1866 - April 22,1957
        Son of Josiah B. and Emmaline Murray Sams
S, Lucitta English,   Oct.1,1875 - Sept.2,1960
        Dau. of W.M. and Julia Holcomb English
S, Paul E.,   May 23,1900 - Jan.29,1982
S, Inez Wing,   Feb.12,1906 - Oct.7,1961
        Dau. of Charles Edwin and Susie Wattles Wing
S, Alda,   Feb.23,1898 - July 28,1972

TH, Charles A.,   May 23,1880 - March 14,1959
        Son of William Henry and Nancy Mize Smith
TH, Myrtie B.,   Sept.26,1881 - Dec.2,1970

FRO, Robert H.,   Feb.1,1891 - March 13,1979
FRO, Carrie D.,   Jan.10,1892 - Sept.30,1978

IN, David J.N.,   Oct.16,1845 - Sept.22,1914   - Civil War
        Son of William and Annie Baker Ervin
IN, Sue C.Jones,   Feb.19,1860 - May 22,1951
        Dau. of Monterell and Isabel Young Jones

ANLESS, Della Deaver,   July 1,1869 - Nov.5,1922
ANLESS, Clarence A.,   June 10,1900 - March 7,1972

CAID, William Bennett,   March 13,1873 - Jan.23,1940
        Son of Robert N. and Margaret Stanley Kincaid
CAID, Jennie Deaver,   Dec.28,1871 - Aug.18,1943
        Dau. of Reuben Keith and Myra Jane Phillips Deaver
CAID, William Bennett, Jr.,   May 23,1903 - April 25,1980

DER, Myra Howze,   Sept.14,1906 - Aug.16,1938

GHMAN, C.J.,   1884 - 1940
GHMAN, Fred,   1907 - 1939

BOWER, Hiram A.,    1879 - 1940
            Son of Joseph H. and Margaret Firestone Bower
BOWER, Loula P.,    1882 - 1963
            Dau. of William and Mary Bower Brown

CALLAHAN, Walter Hayden,    1895 - 1960
            Son of Edward and Ella Daniels Callahan
CALLAHAN, Della Rule,    Died 1971

STACK, Robert E.,    May 15,1885 - Jan.27,1947
STACK, Etta B., (w), Oct.18,1891 - Sept.5,1974
STACK, Evelyn L.,    1914 - 1937
            Dau. of R.E. and Ella Bradshaw Stack

RAY, Thomas Lafayette,    March 1,1885 - Dec.29,1935
RAY, Mae Burleson,    Oct.25,1900 - Dec.29,1967
RAY, Thomas L., "Dr.",    April 8,1924 - July 7 1987

PARSONS, Richard C.,    Dec.3,1890 - May 13,1923

PHETTEPLACE, L.H.,    April 30, 1871 - March 20,1950
PHETTEPLACE, Mary B.,    March 7,1876 - Jan.20,1946
PHETTEPLACE, Charles M.,    May 25,1908 - Dec.5,1963
            Son of Louis Henry and Mary Walker Burns Phetteplace

BULLINGTON, Harvey C.,    Dec.19,1904 - March 25,1950
            Son of David and Etha Mae Campbell Bullington
BULLINGTON, Mary P.,    Sept.11,1902 - March 21,1950

BRADSHAW, Robert Henry, Sr.,    Aug.31,1859 - Dec.10,1948
            Son of James and Susan Gibbs Bradshaw
BRADSHAW, Rebecca Garland,    Sept.20,1863 - Dec.20,1932

ALLRED, B.M.,    June 26,1875 - May 6,1927
            Son of Joseph and Lurana Allred
ALLRED, Nola S. Wattenbarger,    June 4,1876 - May 10,1951
ALLRED, Anne L.,    May 20,1900 - Sept.18,1982

ROWE, Herman Jasper,    Jan.29,1897 - Aug.8,1935 - USN WW1
            Son of N.K. and Anne Rowe

PRICE, Samuel L.,    Oct.24,1878 - Jan.27,1932
            Son of James L. and Annie E. Feathers Price
PRICE, Blanche P.,    Feb.21,1890 - May 16,1966

LINDSLEY, Rowena A.,    1874 - 1956
            Dau. of John Daniel Sharp and Caroline Crumley Ryburn
LINDSLEY, Infant Son, Died March 13, 1899
            Son of F.E. and Rowena Lindsley
LINDSLEY, Enolia M.,    1902 - 1926

PRICE, Wayne F.,    June 19,1910 - July 6,1927
            Son of J.W. and ----- Ryburn Price
PRICE, John Wheeler, Jr.,    April 27,1914 - Dec.19,1979
PRICE, Marie Love,    Sept.27,1925 - May 23,1988

BROWN, John Quincey,    Aug.10,1895 - Aug.24,1981

JONES, Robert Samuel, April 23,1869 - Aug.1,1930
          Son of Thomas and Annie Johnson Jones
JONES, Laura Young,    Feb.19,1876 - Dec.3,1959

BROWN, W.M.,    Sept.3,1849 - Dec.2,1937
BROWN, Mary V.,    Jan.15,1855 - June 27,1938
          Dau. of John and Lucy Richardson Bower

ROBERTS, James C.,    1848 - 1932
          Son of David Roberts
ROBERTS, Anna,    1872 - 1927
          Dau. of Harrison and Jude Banner Harris

McADAMS, Kate Roberts,    March 5,1901 - Sept.23,1983

SUMMEROW, David F.,    1875 - 1943
          Son of Henry Michael and Sarah Ellen Richards Summerow
SUMMEROW, Ella Howell Newell,  1872 - 1956
          Dau. of Wm. Albert and Margaret Elizabeth White Howell

ERWIN, William S.,    April 9,1854 - March 25,1932
          Son of Jessee B. and Elizabeth McMahon Erwin
ERWIN, Hester E.,    March 28,1870 - July 20,1928
ERWIN, James,    1900 - 1982

MARKLAND, Clyde B.,    1909 - 1937
          Son of James Garfield and Halle Overby Markland
MARKLAND, Jessie Erwin,    April 2,1907 - March 9,1975

YOUNG, Marjorie Lee,    Jan.17,1916 - April 16,1931
          Dau. of W.E. and Bertha Young
THOMPSON, Rebecca Susan,    April 11,1960 - Jan.27,1965
          Dau. of Edward C. and Patricia Barton Young Thompson

MEREDITH, J. Floyd,    May 8,1880 - April 14,1958
          Son of Charles McComas and Amanda Williams Meredith
MEREDITH, Mary R.,    July 20,1878 - July 22,1975

LONG, James Austin,    1897 - 1934
          Son of Jessee L. and Mary Emma Folkner Long
CHAVICOURT, Al L.,    1897 - 1956
          Son of Alfred and Esther Sumbourgh Chavicourt

BURTON, Edward Lee,    Jan.26,1886 - Aug.3,1947
          Son of Benjamin Howard and Maggie Emma Reynolds Burton

WINGFIELD, Pearl Stickley,    Jan.7,1898 - Oct.13,1970

STICKLEY, Nannie L.,    Sept.23,1877 - April 26,1945
          Dau. of Elkana and Mary Elizabeth Dickenson Large

COWARD, John Etsell,    Sept.21,1892 - June 25,1956
    Son of John W. and Amanda Arnett Coward
COWARD, Rowe Smith,    Nov.1,1893 - Oct.20,1983
COWARD, John Etsell, Jr.,    May 7,1916 - May 13,1937

BOOTH, William H.,    Nov.24,1867 - July 28,1962
    Son of Mattison and Augusta Hatcher Booth
BOOTH, Margaret Louisa,    Aug.1,1872 - Dec.3,1952
    Dau. of John Wesley and Sarah Rowe McInturff

SAYLOR, Joseph S.,    1865 - 1958
SAYLOR, Tennie H.,    1867 - 1954
    Dau. of Peter Hogan

FOWLER, Harry A.,    Feb.12,1886 - Dec.18,1953
    Son of George W. and Mary R. Ramsey Fowler
FOWLER, Stella M. Pierce, (w), 1888 - 1935
    Dau. of Dayton and Magdolen Cruis Pierce
FOWLER, Pearl L.,    Nov.11,1905 - June 9,1980
BAILEY, Mary Helen,    Died May 14,1936
    Dau. of Walter and Thelma Fowler Bailey

SAYLOR, Gladys Merie,    April 22,1940 - May 6,1943
SAYLOR, Harry E.,    Aug.7,1902 - Oct.16,1971 - Sgt Coast Art

DAY, Fannie,    March 9,1907 - Nov.19,1960
    Dau. of James and Elizabeth Campbell Davis

DAVIS, William T.,    July 22,1841 - May 7,1928
DAVIS, Sophronia C.,    July 19,1851 - July 2,1938
DAVIS, Robert B.,    June 16,1876 - Oct 17,1932
    Son of Wm.T. and Sophia Seaton Davis - 3 Tenn USV 1898

TUCKER, Wendell I.,    Nov.30,1881 - June 15,1955
    Son of W.S. and Polly Ann Baley Tucker
TUCKER, Glennie Davis,    Nov.24,1881 - Aug.23,1972

WHALEY, Frank,    Jan.5,1891 - June 16,1969
WHALEY, Ora,    May 29,1920 - March 29,1949
    Dau. of Frank and Annie Masters Whaley

BOGART, Jeremiah,    1847 - 1895
BOGART, Florence,    1850 - 1933

HEAD, William J.,    Jan.5,1874 - March 1,1959
HEAD, Dora,    Jan.26,1881 - April 12,1973

DOYLE, George P.,    Oct.5,1915 - April 29, 1928

FANNING, Clarence William,    1927 - 1981 - PFC USA WW2

WHALEY, James C.,    1896 - 1967  - US Army

KEPLINGER, Cyrus S.,    Feb.29,1880 - Jan.11,1948 - Pvt Spanish
KEPLINGER, Sallie Davis, (w), 1878 - 1967            American War

DAVIS, Fred,   1880 - 1940   - Cpl US Inf
DAVIS, Clemmie McCammon (w), 1876 - 1940

BELCHER, Joseph H.,    1860 - 1928
BELCHER, Sarah Ellen,   1863 - 1936
          Dau. of James and Nancy Owens Robinson

SPARKS, Floyd David,   Oct.27,1920 - June 12,1960 - USN WW2
          Son of Thomas S. and Alice Canipe Sparks

FORD, Ethel Mae,   1897 - 1958
          Dau. of William H. and Margaret McInturff Booth
FORD, Thelma Inez,   1925 - 1928
          Dau. of J.H. and E.M. Ford
BRYANT, Rosa L.,   1918 - 1947

COWARD, George Edmond,   Aug.7,1925 - Nov.16,1985 - USN WW2

HALL, Ronald D.,Sr.,   Aug.17,1893 - Jan.2,1964
          Son of Robert Yancey and Clara Atkinson Hall
HALL, Grace Dougherty,   Oct.6,1898 - Oct.3,1945
          Dau of John Carson and Nancy Rebecca Frazier

LONG, James,   1867 - 1939
          Son of William Green and Sarah Ellen Austin Long
LONG, Mary Faulkner,   1873 - 1953
          Dau. of John K. and Victoria Chandler Faulkner

CULTON, Tessie Ann,   1876 - 1956
          Dau. of John B. and Kate Bauman Huskins
JONES, Anna Kate,   1900 - 1983

YOUNG, W.E.,   June 20,1895 - Oct.23,1976
YOUNG, Bertha Hill, (w), Aug.10,1896 - May 17,1968

HALE, George Guy,   Jan.23,1893 - May 22,1941
          Son of J.T. and Helen Burke Hale
HALE, Areller Farris,   Nov.22,1889 - Aug.26,1962
          Dau. of W.O. and June Whitehead Farris
HALE, Garland,   Aug.3,1910 - Feb.3,1931
          Son of Guy and Arlla Farris Hale
HALE, Lee O.,   Oct.20,1915 - Nov.10,1975 - Pvt USA
HALE, James Guy,   April 22,1949 - April 26,1949
          Son of L.O. and Opal Cook Miller Hale

NEWELL, Samuel H.,   1894 - 1947
          Son of Samuel Barnett and Ella Juanita Howell Newell

NOREN, K.E.,   March 26,1881 - April 11,1944

HUSKINS, James Walter,   April 19,1858 - April 26,1944
HUSKINS, Nancy Elizabeth, (w),  Feb.19,1863 - Jan.25,1951
            Dau. of Straley and Caroline Tucker
STROUPE, Nora Lee,   March 6,1878 - Feb.19,1945

CAMPBELL, W.A.,   1869 - 1944
            Son of Ethelbert B. and Mary Payne Campbell
CAMPBELL, Sarah L.,   1880 - 1964
            Dau. of Willis and Samanthy Page Letterford
CAMPBELL, Lillian M.,   1890 - 1965

PATTON, Sidney,   March 15,1883 - May 9,1944

PRICE, John W.,   Nov.16,1876 - July 12,1949
            Son of James L. and Ann Feathers Price
PRICE, Annie R.,   Oct.28,1880 - Dec.28,1954
            Dau. of J.D.S. and Caroline Crumley Ryburn
PRICE, Ann E. Feathers,   Oct.11,1849 - Sept.26,1943
            Dau. of Samuel E. and  ---Watson Feathers
            Wife of James L. Price

SCHAUB, Burton C.,   Feb.2,1883 - Nov.23,1939
            Son of Charles L. and Emily Richardson Schaub

SHOUN, Ora N.,   April 13,1893 - Sept.22,1923
SHOUN, Ellen W.,   June 7,1864 - Jan.13,1945
DOUGHERTY, Nelta H.,   Aug.9,1898 - Feb.15,1973

McINTURFF, Rev. Robert, "DD", 1875 - 1949
            Son of William and Rhoda Smithy McInturff
McINTURFF, Lula Broyles,   1873 - 1951

CARPENTER, A.R.,   June 3,1894 - March 1,1960
            Son of John Wesley and Rosa Morrison Carpenter
CARPENTER, Colleen,   Feb.4,1898 - Sept.7,1985
CARPENTER, Allred W.,   Feb.16,1919 - March 21,1982

WILSON, Rittie,   1856 - 1935
WILSON, D.W.,   May 19, 1893 - July 22,1978
WILSON, Venetta B.,   Aug.13,1899 - Feb.5,1975
WILSON, Ralph,   March 26,1922 - Nov.8,1942 - Sgt USA WW2

YOUNG, Claude M.,   Oct.24,1925 - Nov.6,1962
            Son of Claude and Dorothy Phetteplace Young

PHETTEPLACE, L.H., Jr.,   March 23,1900 - March 20,1950

JOHNSON, Charles Stuart,   Sept.14,1930 - Sept.15,1971
JOHNSON, Bess Phetteplace,   Feb.2,1897 - Dec.23,1939
            Dau. of L.H. Phetteplace

JONES, Theodore Wayne,   Oct.13,1942 - Jan.23,1944
            Son of James Harry and Frances Smyer Jones

DANIEL, William T.,    1874 - 1942
DANIEL, Nancy P.,    1875 - 1939
          Dau. of Jack and Elizabeth Treadway Parris

BOWER, J. Raymond,    1903 - 1971
BOWER, Florence D.,    1902 - 1961
          Dau. of James Walter and Ann Lee Porter Dutton

BAUGHMAN, Harry L.,    1906 - 1986
BAUGHMAN, H.H.,    1859 - 1932
BAUGHMAN, Mary E.,    1862 - 1961
          Dau. of John and Susan Carnell Hawman

HOWZE, Melvin Chappel,    1878 - 1945
          Son of Everette Coke and Frances Kelly Howze
HOWZE, Katherine Deaver,    1881 - 1947
          Dau. of Ruben and Myra Phillips Deaver
HOWZE, Everette D.,    Dec.2,1908 - Feb.25,1978

PEDIGO, P.W.,    1883 - 1945
          Son of Louis L. and Lelia Bennett Pedigo
PEDIGO, Margaret Bonham,    1888 - 1969

GILLIS, John B.,    Nov.30,1907 - April 19,1977
GILLIS, Patsy,    Oct.10,1914 -    ----

SMYER, Lonnie T.,    March 6,1890 - July 2,1953
          Son of John and Agenda Heffner Smyer
SMYER, Earl,    April 23,1915 - July 28,1921
          Son of Mr.and Mrs. L.T. Smyer
WILSON, Addie Smyer,    Aug.5,1897 - Dec.25,1969

RHYMER, Ottis C.,    March 10,1888 - Oct.12,1942
          Son of James Vaughn and Florida Runion Rhymer

HOLT, Nannie L.,    Feb.29,1872 - Aug.29,1949
          Dau. of John and Edna Reid Willis

ERVIN, Thomas J.,    1885 - 1940
ERVIN, Juanita,    March 11,1883 - Oct.11,1969
FERENZ, Blanche Ervin,    Jan.4,1897 - Oct.19,1958
          Dau. of D.J.N. and Sue Catherine Jones Ervin

RENFRO, Mack w.,    1869 - 1946
RENFRO, Nancy P.,    1869 - 1943

DAVIS, Harvey Gordon,    Oct.3,1946 - Oct.4,1946

WOHLFORD, William Thomas,    Oct.27,1875 - June 28, 1955
          Son of George and Jane Mustard Wohlford
WOHLFORD, Ethel Burkholder,    Dec.3,1882 - Feb.25,1954
          Dau. of Judson M. and Virginia M.Johnson Burkholder

TAYLOR, Clifton L.,Sr.,    Dec.23,1894 - April 1,1982 - USA WW1
TAYLOR, Maude Sams,    July 16,1902 - Oct.14,1985

WEBB, Ulis,    Dec.25,1888 - Aug.30,1964

ROSE, Ruby Wheeler,    1908 - 1985

ANNIS, Douglas A.,    Aug.21,1884 - Sept.25,1963
            Son of G.M. and Mary Lou Powell Annis
ANNIS, Donnie M., (w), June 1,1886 - July 9,1971
ANNIS, Brodie W.,    Oct.7,1902 - Nov.7,1970

WRIGHT, Howard L.,    June 16,1907 - Dec.17,1949
            Son Of William H. and Mary Elizabeth Miller Wright
WRIGHT, William Albert,    1913 - 1987
WRIGHT, Julia Beck,    1915 - ----

BOYER, Albert L.,    Feb.2,1883 - Sept.9,1960
            Son of Anthony Louis Boyer
BOYER, Nannie R.,    March 4,1888 - June 12,1949
            Dau. of Fred M. and Margaret Bateman Duchwall

WOODWARD, Aretus S.,    March 9,1879 - May 25,1957
            Son of J.H. and Ollie Carter Woodward
WOODWARD, Margaret M.,    Aug.3,1891 - Sept.9,1977

MOORE, Ralph E.,    July 1, 1894 - Jan.13,1952
            Son of William and Rebecca Runion Moore
MOORE, Melinda Belle,    Nov.2,1894 - May 14,1979
SHELTON, Kitty Moore,    Jan.18,1883 - Nov.29,1969

DAVIS, Nolan,    March 5,1901 - Jan.27,1987
DAVIS, Doris B., (w),  Aug.29,1907 - ----
DAVIS, John Edward, June 30,1931 - Oct.30,1951 - Sgt Air Force
            Son of Nolan and Dorothy Burchfield Davis

SPAINHOUR, Richard E.,    June 7,1904 - March 25,1981

HENDREN, Carol Ann,    Died Sept.23 1958
            Dau of Joe Card and Barbara Jan Young Hendren

SAMS, Mary Mullens,    July 22,1909 - June 27,1981
SAMS, Dr. Charles C.,    Nov.23,1933 - July 4,1983
SAMS, Thomas Charles,    July 26,1963 - April 20,1988 - USAF

DUNBAR, Walter C.,    Oct.15,1920 - Feb.10,1969 - USA WW2

HUSKINS, Rufus O.,    Nov.1,1899 - July 23,1981
HUSKINS, Julia Farnor,    March 11,1904 - ----
HENSLEY, Creede Celeste,    March 18,1908 - Sept.13, 1974

NORRIS, Anna McNabb Kerns,    March 30,1896 - March 21,1982
NORRIS, Robert Clinton,    April 13,1908 - ----

BAILEY, Willard Allen,    Sept.5,1917 - ----
BAILEY, Mildred Kerns,    April 15,1917 - Oct 27, 1976

BISHOP, David Jesse,    Oct.22,1889 - Dec.26,1966
BISHOP, Lillie Jane,    Feb.3,1895 - June 2,1969
BISHOP, E. Wayne,    June 30,1921 - Jan.15,1976
BISHOP, Ruby Mae,    Dec.24,1919 -  ----

WILFONG, R. Earl,    1892 - 1953
            Son of W.H. and Elizabeth Klutz Wilfong
WILFONG, Eula Lee,    1897 - 1968

BRADSHAW, James I.,    March 19,1914 - **Nov.26,1988** - USA  WW2
BRADSHAW, Elizabeth Pope,    July 14, 1916 -  ----

WATTS, L. Jane,    Aug.10,1874 - March 18,1954
            Dau. of Baxter and Cordia Wilson McIntosh
WATTS,    Molt,    1904 - 1982
WATTS, Virgie R.,    1908 -  ----

FOSTER, William Dale,    Aug.30,1954 - May 17,1955
            Son of Edmond Wm. and Joan Smith Foster

EMMERT, Benjamin H.,Sr.,    Aug.28,1889 - Jan.18,1973
EMMERT, Effie Allen, (w),    Sept.8,1897 - Aug.17,1972

STULTZ, Joe M.,    April 22,1906 - Dec.20,1956
STULTZ, Frederick James,    1924 - 1983    - PFC USA WW2
PARSLEY, Benjamin H.,    April 11,1912 - June 8,1957
            Son of Benjamin and Elizabeth Sutphin Parsley

KYLE, John,    April 26,1887 - Nov.16,1962

RIDDLE, Carrie,    Nov.8,1897 - Sept.5,1960
            Dau. of Jason and Adeline Mary Harris
BENNETT, Inise,    April 15,1920 - Dec.23,1964
BENNETT, Clarence O.,    1915 - 1987

LIGHT, Baby,    b/d  1962

WHITSON, Fate,    1914 - 1981  - USMC WW2

WILSON, George W.,    March 29,1887 -  ----
WILSON, Belle Lewis, (w),    Sept.13,1892 - Jan.29,1962
WILSON, Jack,  Nov.9,1919 - Oct.24,1944  - USA  WW2

LOVE, Nathan Douglas,    June 6,1915 - Aug.22,1983 -  WW2
LOVE, Lucille Kelsey, July 24, 1917 -  ----

McCURRY, Charles I.,    July 11,1915 - March 10,1964 - Sgt WW2
McCURRY, Lena Estell,    May 31,1918 -  ----
McCURRY, Amy Brinkley,    Aug.2,1894 - Nov.11,1971

BRIGGS, Riley James,    March 19,1894 - Nov.15,1965
BRIGGS, Theodora Witcher,    Jan.9,1896 - Feb.11,1960
            Dau. of Wm. Reuben and Rebecca Caswell Gammon Witcher
BRIGGS, William Riley,    Oct.15,1926 - Sept.2,1985

<u>EVERGREEN CEMETERY</u>  (continued)

BAILEY, Charles L.,    Aug.9,1896 - Nov.21,1962
          Son of Hiram and Delcena Byrd Bailey
BAILEY, Ethel Norris,   Sept.17,1895 - Feb.16,1973
BAILEY, Harley Richard,    April 21,1924 - July 29,1973   - USA WW2

TITTLE, Diana Lou, Died April 9,1959 - Dau. of Leonard T. and Lockie
SLUDER, Brandon Dwayne,   Died Feb.12,1983            Ledford Tittle

NELSON, William F.,    Sept.14,1877 - Aug.28,1969
NELSON, Ella Bell Booth, (w), March 22,1879 - March 13,1934

HARRIS, Flora L.,    1901 - 1962

TIPTON, John D.,    1880 - 1963
TIPTON, Margaret C.,    1890 - 1972

COLE, John,    March 4,1904 - May 8,1986

GREENE, William Bascom,    1880 - 1958
          Son of J.M. and Polly McKinney Greene
GREENE, Mamie J.,    1887 - 1976

BOOHER, Paul E.,    1894 - 1964
          Son of Wm. R. and Elizabeth Foster Booher
BOOHER, Winnie R.,    1901 - 1978
HOLLAR, Robert B.,    March 29,1901 - Jan.9,1969
HOLLAR, Katherine Meade,   Jan.3,1907 - April 4,1986

TUCKER, Dewitt,   Oct.25,1897 - Nov.28,1984
TUCKER, Katharyn,    April 17,1907 - May 4,1985

SPARKS, E. Wayne,   Dec.6,1903 - June 13,1966

HONEYCUTT, Albert,   Feb.23,1923 - April 28,1981
HONEYCUTT, Mildred,   Sept.24,1926 - ----

AMBROSE, Bessie P.,   May 28,1892 - April 12,1984

HONEYCUTT, Patricia,   b/d  1946
          Dau. of Albert and Mildred Elizabeth Harris Honeycutt

LEWIS, David H.,    Feb.1,1886 - June 20,1960
          Son of Christopher and Virginia Barker Lewis
LEWIS, Margie G.,    March 24,1889 - June 6,1972

HUTCHINS, Paul J.,    Jan.28,1925 - ----
HUTCHINS, Bernice H.,    Dec.25,1926 - ----

RAY, Harold,   Sept.1,1926 - May 15,1955
RAY, Zettie S.,    Sept.7,1907 - June 23, 1968

PETERSON, Glenn,   March 4,1907 - Dec.19,1967
PETERSON, Bonnie W.,    Oct.10,1908 - March 11,1982

ROBERTS, Birtha,    1888 - 1952
HAMPTON, Ann,    1849 - 1958

HELTON, W. Clint,    Aug.7,1895 - Aug.12,1963
          Son of Jerry and Sarah Owens Helton
HELTON, Olga B.,    Jan.14,1901 - Dec.21,1983
HELTON, Roy,    Dec.10,1919 - Oct.12,1986 - USA WW2

CHANDLER, W. Roscoe,    June 21,1907 - May 14,1955
CHANDLER, Loretta,    April 7,1909 - March 11,1978

EDWARDS, George W.,    May 18, 1878 - Feb.12,1959 - Spanish Amer.War

MASTERS, Walter L.,    Jan.3,1887 - July 9,1974
MASTERS, Mary M., (w),    May 28,1890 - March 17,1956
          Dau. of W.H. and Dorothowly Hensley Fanning

WILSON, Greely C.,    Nov.25,1894 - March 11,1983
WILSON, Norman C.,    Oct.31,1935 - July 7,1975  - USAF

HARRIS, Jessie E.,    March 3,1925 - Oct.16,1962 - PFC USAF WW2

MOONEY, Charlie J.,    1901 - 1951

BOGART, Ben F.,    1878 - 1954
          Son of Jere and Florence Couch Bogart
BOGART, Jessie T.,    1886 - 1971
BOGART, Lillian,    1909 - 1967
BOGART, Lucille, 1913 -  ----

ANDERS, Charles B.,    Nov.22,1889 - May 22,1949
ANDERS, Mary F.,    Oct.8,1890 - Aug.2,1972

PADGETT, Herbert,    1903 - 1966
PADGETT, Hubert,    1903 - 1964
          Sons of Charlie and Emily Stanton Padgett

TIPTON, Walter,    1887 - 1947
TIPTON,    (no first name - no date)
TIPTON,    (no first name - no date)

HIGGINS, Gaither,    1901 - 1976   - USN WW1

PADGETT, Henry C.,    Aug.10,1905 - July 13,1956
          Son of Charlie and Emily Stanton Padgett'

BARNETT, Sam,    March 22,1888 - July 8,1944
BARNETT, Harriett M.,    Sept.6,1889 - Jan.6,1982
BARNETT, William M.,    Feb.14,1869 - June 21,1949
BARNETT, Elizabeth G.,    Sept.15,1871 - Feb.12,1948
BARNETT, Bertie Miller,    Aug.8,1880 - Dec.19,1976

SPARKS, Pansy Barnett,    1908 - 1937
          Wife of Clarence Sparks
          Dau. of Sam and Harriett Bailey Barnett

BOGART, Mary L.,    Nov.16,1889 - Dec.26,1937
        Dau. of Samuel and Lizzie Smith Johnson
BOGART, William E.,    May 5,1896 -    ----
BOGART, Anna B.,    1898 - 1988

TIPTON, Charles F.,    Jan.12,1917 - Feb.19,1946
        Son of John and Edith Bright Tipton
TIPTON, Crate,    Jan.2,1879 - Nov.13,1945

PRICE, Shirley Faye,    Nov.13,1938 - Dec.6,1945
        Dau. of Earl and Dennie Anders Price

HENSLEY, Walter,    Sept.21,1899 - May 13,1952    - USA WW1
        Son of Amos and Naomi Estep Hensley
HENSLEY, Willburn M.,    1928 - 1930
        Son of W.A. and Belle Hensley

SNAPP, Samuel James,    1886 - 1957
        Son of John and Laura Henderson Snapp
SNAPP, Nannie Dunn, (w), 1887 - 1937
        Dau. of James R. and Mary Ann Hank Dunn

STEWART, Robert L.,    Oct.31,1879 - May 24,1948 - Spanish Amer. War
        Son of Jasper Milton and Emily Louise Baker Stewart
STEWART, Hassie G.,    May 15,1893 - May 1,1974
STEWART, Joseph M.,    Jan.28,1914 - Nov.9,1973

McNABB, Robert Gilmore,    July 9,1868 - May 21,1937
McNABB, Katherine C.,    Aug.3,1866 - Aug.4,1956
        Dau. of Lee A. and Mary Wolfe White

SANDERS, Francis James,    May 7,1888 - Aug.19,1949
        Son of Harry and Sarah Sherlock Sanders
SANDERS, Donna Lewis,    May 28,1893 - Aug.19,1971

STALLARD, Samuel Covey,    Oct.5,1878 - April 21,1946
        Son of William B. and Elizabeth Holbrook Stallard
STALLARD, Mary Elizabeth, (w), 1880 - 1934
        Dau. of Clayton and Cosby Richardson Mead

PADGETT, Algie Arnold,    July 5,1889 - March 15,1952
        Son of Charlie and Emily Stanton Padgett
PADGETT, Blanche Mae, (w), May 5,1901 - Dec.4,1966
        Dau. of Elihue and Fannie White Hensley
PADGETT, Charles E.,    June 5,1921 - March 15,1946 - Sgt USA WW2
        Son of Algie and Mae Hensley Padgett

ADKINS, Margaret Fender,    April 5,1870 - April 16,1956

HARVEY, Ollie L.,    Sept.28,1882 - Aug.23,1956
        Son of Winfield and Catherine Ferguson Harvey
HARVEY, Eva Lewis Garland, (w),    1885 - 1936
HARVEY, Donald C.,    March 12,1930 - Nov.25,1951
        Son of Carl and Pearl Harvey

SHELTON, Ira Addison,    Feb.8,1945 - Sept.6,1945
        Child of Macon and Neva Mathis Shelton

HICKS, Rebecca Mooney,    June 8,1875 - Dec.1,1957
        Dau. of Jacob and Margaret Klepper Isenberg

SIMMONS, Theo S.,    1888 - 1950
        Son of Jacob and Almira Harrelson Simmons
SIMMONS, Minnie S.,    1888 - 1972

CHAMBERS, Anie Stephens,    Nov.11,1869 - Oct.4,1951
        Dau. of Louis Wm. and Elizabeth Bowman Stephens

SMITH, Reece C.,Sr.,   March 24,1893 - Oct.8,1968
SMITH, Bessie D.,    Dec.3,1894 - March 16,1966
SMITH, Reece Cross, Jr.,    Sept.2,1915 - Nov.25,1950 - USAF WW2
        Son of Reece C. and Bessie Lee Deal Smith

BARTLEY, William E.,    Dec.7,1893 - July 3,1956
        Son of E.E. and Prudence Robinette Bartley
BARTLEY, Carrow Elizabeth, (w), Oct.3,1898 - Dec.27,1980
BARTLEY, Frank E.,   (son), April 14,1918 - Oct.2,1955

HELTON, Dennis Lee,    Died June 18,1951

HIGGINBOTHAN, Jefferson B.,    June 23,1887 - Dec.16,1951 - USA WW1
HIGGINBOTHAN, Ethel L.,    1900 - 1970

BUCHANAN, Burnesie,    Aug.29,1891 - Oct.15,1974
BUCHANAN, Chester, Sr.,   March 20,1915 -  ----
BUCHANAN, Virgie E., (w), March 10,1916 -  ----
BUCHANAN, Alfred Jesse,    June 28,1952 - July 14,1952
        Son of Chester and Virgie Peregon Buchanan

HUTCHINS, Grady D.,    May 15,1895 - Dec.31,1952
        Son of James M. and Cenia Hughes Hutchins
HUTCHINS, Nellie K.,    June 3,1897 - Oct.16,1957
        Dau. of W.E. and Nettie Rogers Kerns
GUICE, Pearl Hutchins,    April 3,1938 - Nov.5,1958
        Dau. of Grady and Nellie Kerns Hutchins

WILKINSON, James M.,    Jan.26,1884 - Feb.20,1959
        Son of Geo. Washington and Mandy Condrsy Wilkinson
WILKINSON, Elsie Frank,    March 18,1889 - Dec.8,1964
        Dau. of Brewer McKeehan
CROWLEY, Albert C.,    May 18,1922 - March 28,1969 - M Sgt WW2 Korea

JONES, Ernest Polk,    April 2,1891 - June 5, 1963

SUGG, John C. Sr.,    1891 - 1974   - US Army
SUGG, Allie T.,    1891 - 1976

BAILEY, David Freeman,    Feb.9,1883 - May 21,1961
        Son of J.M. and Christina Evans Bailey
HYDER, Elsie Bailey,    Feb.2,1896 - July 31,1976

EVERGREEN CEMETERY (continued)

SMITH, Luanne E.,    1963 - 1963

FANNING, Starling S.,    June 12,1898 - June 7,1953
            Son of William Henry and Dorothy Hensley Fanning
FANNING, Rhona M.,    April 29,1898 - March 9,1976

BALLARD, Robert Hughes, 1874 - 1966
BALLARD, Ruth Mason,   1889 - 1979

RAMSEY, Jobie,   Nov.18,1889 - Oct.14,1975
RAMSEY, Virgie A. Cutshaw, (w), Jan.19,1890 - Feb.16,1968
RAMSEY, Rev. Sankey,   Oct.18,1911 - Jan.2,1985
RAMSEY, Audrey Bennett, (w), Jan.29,1912 - April 23,1976

VANCE, Stanley Lonnie,   March 17,1889 - June 29,1953
VANCE, Faye Matney,   Nov.3,1895 - Sept.1,1977

LOVE, William Arthur,   March 2,1874 - Jan.26,1952
            Son of Thomas Love
LOVE, Oma Peterson,   May 24,1878 - March 20,1966

CROWDER, Cecil Edward,   Sept.15,1913 - Sept.17,1952
            Son of Milton Orlando and Estella Crowder
CROWDER, Irene Arrowood,   July 18,1917 -   ----
CROWDER, Robert F.,   1911 -   ----
CROWDER, Gladys M.,   1918 - 1956
            Dau. of John H. and Dellia Morrow Bennett

SPARKS, Tom,   June 12,1882 - Jan.30,1956
            Son of John Sparks
SPARKS, Alice,   Sept.11,1882 - June 3,1972
SPARKS, Ersell,   June 17,1905 - May 22,1979

HARTSELL, David P., "Hoopty",   June 30,1888 - Oct.12,1952
            Son of Jacob Brown and Mary O'Brien Hartsell
HARTSELL, Pauline S.,   May 24,1900 - Dec.10,1960
            Dau. of Leburn Berry and Lydia Burleson Stewart
HARTSELL, Jacob B.,   June 27,1921 - Oct.25,1970 - Cpl USA WW2

HARRISON, Cyrus Lee,   Dec.6,1883 - March 30,1952
            Son of Charles Wesley and Sarah McKay Harrison
HARRISON, Ethel Woodward,   May 15,1896 - Nov.27,1973
HARRISON, William C.,   April 15,1921 - May 26,1983

HARVEY, Raymond L.,   May 10,1898 - Feb.19,1952
            Son of D.H. and Harriett Howard Harvey
HARVEY, Mrs. R.L.,   March 8,1900 -   ----
HOLSHOUSER, Walter A.,   Nov.21,1890 - Nov.30,1960
            Son of ----- and Ornah Moreland Holshouser
HOLSHOUSER, Myrtle E.,   Dec.11,1890 - Dec.12,1967

GOLDSMITH, David Arthur,   Feb.22,1954 - Jan.22,1955
            Son of Harvey and Kylene Dennis Goldsmith

EVERGREEN CEMETERY (continued)

STULTZ, Ben P.,    Jan.25,1881 - Jan.23,1959
            Son of Joe and Letita Philpot Stultz
STULTZ, Rose C.,   Oct.15,1885 - May 19,1969
EUTSLER, Joseph P.,   Dec.20,1903 - Nov.9,1959
            Son of Charles R. and Margaret Boring Eutsler
EUTSLER, Mamie S.,   March 13,1908 - Feb.5,1987

BRUMMETT, Karen,   Died Sept.25,1951

GORTNEY, Bill,   Sept.16,1895 - July 2,1969

SMITH, William,   April 16,1902 - May 20,1972
SMITH, Harriett W., (w), April 2,1906 -  ----
SMITH, William Freddy,   Feb.28,1942 - Dec.29,1982

LITTLE, Ernest W.,   Oct.11,1900 - Oct.23,1980
LITTLE, Texie W.,   April 21,1898 - Jan.3,1988
LITTLE, Barbara Jean,   April 30,1952 - May 1,1952
            Dau. of William E. and Margaret Elizabeth Bishop Little

POPE, Henry C.,Sr.,   Aug.1894 - Jan.1967
POPE, Verna M.,   Sept.29,1894 - March 20,1978
POPE, R.W. "Rod",   Nov.26,1926 - Nov.14,1951  - USN WW2
            Son of H. Clay Pope
GANTT, Irene Pope,   March 29,1921 -  ----

HIGGINS, Daryl Wayne,   Died May 2,1958

HONEYCUTT, Nancy,   1915 - 1986

BRUMMETT, John H.,   April 20,1876 - Nov.30,1948
BRUMMETT, Hattie Norris,   Aug.6,1879 - Dec.7,1962
            Dau. of John and Nancy Whitson Norris
BRUMMETT, Harley C. "Coot",   June 18,1907 -
BRUMMETT, Pearle Buchannon,   Nov.14,1916 - Sept.25,1961
            Dau. of Alfred and Burnice McCurry Buchanan

DUNCAN, Nancy C.,   1897 - 1950
            Dau. of John and Rebecca Bayless Tilson
DUNCAN, D.D.,   1903 - 1956
            Son of William Abner and Nancy Tilson Duncan
DUNCAN, Mae Willis,   1906 -  ----
DUNCAN, Betty Mae,   1931 - 1949
            Dau. of David D. and Mae Willis Duncan

ATKINS, James R.,   April 14,1897 - June 16,1974
ATKINS, Tilda W.,   May 27,1911 -  ----
WILLIS, David Walter,   April 25,1885 - Sept.18,1961
            Son of Dave Frank and Martha Willis
WILLIS, Hester Elizabeth,   April 7,1889 - March 4,1958
            Dau. of Robert Lewis and Rebecca Higgins Taylor

JAYNES, Arthur Kenneth,    1893 - 1985
JAYNES, Inez Hoffman,    1898 - 1950
        Dau. of G.H. and Louvernia Bell Grant Hoffman
JAYNES, Betty Lou,    Oct.30,1930 - Nov.5,1968

MORLEY, Henry Paul,    1884 - 1968
MORLEY, Mary Eliza Entsminger,    1879 - 1950
        Dau. of John A. and Mary Nick Entsminger
MORLEY, Andrew Paul,    Sept.10,1909 - July 15,1974

GOOD, Arthur C.,    July 11,1892 - July 2,1984
GOOD, Kate Propst, (w),    Dec.28,1896 - Jan.15,1984
GOOD, Infant,    Died 1918  - Child of A.C. and Kate Good

BRUCE, Louis Roy,    March 28,1929 - Feb.7,1951  - PFC 2 AMPH
BRUCE, William Wayne,    Nov.14,1934 - Sept.23,1964 - 1st Lt. USAF
        Sons of Henry Bruce

CROWDER, Milton O.,    1873 - 1959
        Son of Henry and Letitia Moore Crowder
CROWDER, Estella R.,    Aug.30,1873 - March 20,1949

STILLMAN, George I.,    1893 - 1954
        Son of George Hunter and Corrie Rachel Neff Stillman
STILLMAN, Florence M.,    1905 - 1951
        Dau. of J.R. and Anna Mae Camp McGranahan

DAVIDSON, Lillie E.,    1902 - 1951

BOOTH, Ernest E.,    1914 - 1978  - Lt.Col.USAF WW2

MORGAN, Clarence Decatur,    Aug.17,1892 - March 31,1986
MORGAN, Bessie Lou Woods,    Oct.26,1892 - April 15,1983
MORGAN, Lee R.,    April 4,1925 - Dec.24,1944 - Pvt Inf WW2
MORGAN, Elva Woods,    Died June 16,1921  (Infant)
MORGAN, Jackey,    Died Dec.18,1929 (Infant)

CAMPBELL, J.H.,    1875 - 1945
        Son of John R. and Ora Lowe Campbell
CAMPBELL, Mary,    May 6,1878 - May 7, 1952
        Dau. of ---- and Nancy Markland Archer

HICKS, John N.,    Aug.1866 - Aug.18,1945
HICKS, Julia Ann,    Feb.20,1883 - Nov.18,1950

SPARKS, Handy,    ----- - -----
SPARKS, Myrtle,    ----- - -----

LAWS, Mack C.,    1898 - 1946
        Son of John and Rebecca Laws

SUMNER, Vada Strickland,    June 8,1900 - May 20,1952

BRUMMETT, Charles E.,    April 27,1879 - Feb.27,1959
            Son of William H. and Susan Branch Brummett
BRUMMETT, Rachel C.Norris, (w),  Aug.28,1884 - June 5,1965
            Dau. of John and Nancy J. Whitson Norris
OAKS, Bernice Brummett,   March 20,1925 - Oct.22,1971

WILLIAMS, W. Bachus,    June 26,1905 - April 2,1974
WILLIAMS, Harold R.,    March 12,1930 - May 8,1972 - USAF - Korea

WALLACE, Robert Young,   Aug.9,1892 - April 7,1961
            Son of William and Laura Ann Smith Wallace
WALLACE, Gwendolyn,    Died 1948
            Infant of Robert Charles and Katherine Crawford Wallace

DOAN, Charles Mack,    Aug.19,1887 - Aug.29,1963
            Son of David and Mandy Waldrop Doan
DOAN, Minnie Eleanor,    March 4,1895 - June 15,1984
DOAN, Infant Daughter,   Died March 19,1947
DOAN, Infant Daughter,   Died April 11,1950
            Infants of Jay David and Ruby Sevier Fanning Doan

LAMB, John Thomas,    1915 - 1979   - 1st Lt USA WW2

BAILEY, Ralph Burns,    Nov.1,1898 - April 19,1974
BAILEY, Mary Gladys,    March 8,1898 - Aug.15,1946
            Dau. of J.M. and Sally Tranbarger Loudy

DEES, Mary Nell,   June 25,1918 - April 19,1946
            Dau. of Adolphus Meriman and Lilly Peake Randolph

CAMPBELL, Elizabeth,    1882 - 1971

COX, Clyde O.,    1903 - 1985
COX. Mildred J.,    1906 - 1984
COX, David Tresco, (son), March 31,1938 - May 14,1945

WOODWARD, William T., "Md.",   1883 -1966
WOODWARD, Mayme E.,    1887 - 1959
            Dau. of Edward J. and Sarah Alice Sawers Vandergrift

TIPTON, Joe V.,    July 27,1918 - July 25, 1950 - USA WW2
            Son of Robert Henty and Nancy Metcalf Tipton
TIPTON, Brenda Faye,    Aug.22,1944 - June 23,1945
            Dau. of Joe Vance and Gladys Marie Masters Tipton

HARRIS, Baby,   b/d/ 1948

DAVIS, Patrick,    June 13,1923 - June 12,1948   - USA WW2
            Son of Dock Davis
STREET, Edna D.,   Dec.14,1924 - May 31,1972

ELMORE, Harold E.,    1897 - 1947
            Son of Frederick Grant and Carrie Bennett Colona Elmore
ELMORE, Arkie A.,    1915 - 1952

WILSON, Richmon C.,    Oct.19,1894 - Nov.26,1956
          Son of John H. and Martha Ann White Wilson
WILSON, Julia T.,    March 18,1901 - April 5,1984
WILSON, Harold R.,    1923 - 1975   -  USN WW2
WILSON, Fred D.,    1927 - 1946  - USN WW2
          Son of R.C. Wilson

HUSKINS, Fred A.,    May 21,1911 - Nov.29,1984
HUSKINS, Mildred B.,    ----- - -----

HICE, Ralph,    1906 -  ----
HICE, Evelyn Mae,    1916 - 1965

GARLAND, C.W.,    Jan.13,1887 - Feb.10,1983
GARLAND, Nancy Elizabeth,    June 6,1887 - June 23,1981

LAWSON, Glenn,    1918 - 1982

DANIEL, Harold Thomas,    Nov.21,1901 - June 14,1960 - USN WW1
DANIEL, Iris B.,    Sept.29,1904 - Jan.22,1986

BAILEY, Robert O.,    1877 - 1964
          Son of Ballard P. and Sarah Casper Bailey
BAILEY, Mary M.,    1893 - 1956
          Dau.of Willard Henderson and Isobel Shufflebarger French
BAILEY, Ethel G.,    1911 - 1978
          Dau. of R.O. and Mary French Bailey

HENSLEY, Ebb, 1904 - 1944
          Son of Marion and Cordelia Cody Rice Hensley
HENSLEY, Paul C.,    1926 - 1936
          Son of Ebb and Florence Harris Hensley
McKEE, Florence Hensley,    Feb.6,1906 - Feb.11,1985

HARRIS, Fuller G.,    July 25,1980 - June 11,1949
          Son of Armstrong and Mary Louise Crain Harris
HARRIS, Lydia M. Guinn,    April 16,1879 - April 9,1938
          Dau. of David Taylor and Melinda Runnion Guinn
HARRIS, Zetta c.,    April 2,1903 -  ----

EARLY, William Guy,    Dec.10,1906 - March 18,1954
          Son of Samuel Ernest and Bertha Emma Walsh Early
EARLY, Elizabeth A.,    July 25,1907 - May 13,1976
EARLY, Richard Carroll,    June 24,1933 - June 25,1933
EARLY, Robert Eugene,    June 24,1933 - June 25,1933
          Twin sons of Wm. Guy and Mary Elizabeth Alford Early

ALFORD, Paul C.,    April 25,1883 - March 22,1967
ALFORD, Bessie Moore,    March 23,1885 - Jan.25,1962
          Dau. of William B. and Martha Bryant Moore
MOORE, Martha B.,    June 24,1859 - April 17,1956
          Dau. of Sidney J. and Amanda Morton Bryant

EVERGREEN CEMETERY (continued)

LARIMER, Samuel M.,   March 23,1885 - April 2,1963
            Son of Edward W. and Mary Shell Larimer
LARIMER, Ethel Brown,   Nov.21,1895 - Aug.2,1975

HOWELL, Z.N.,   1878 - 1935
            Son of Robert Howell
HOWELL, Fannie E., (w),   1883 - 1937
            Dau. of William and Myra Bailey Bennett
HOWELL, Edgar C., (son),   1910 - 1945
HOWELL, Fred Brady, (son), Nov.28,1912 - July 6,1943
            In memory - USN WW2

LILLY, Charles H.,   1862 - 1937
            Son of Warren Henderson and Martha Jones Lilly
LILLY, Mattie S., (w), 1869 - 1947
            Dau. of Noah D. Saylor
LILLY, Thelma G.,   1905 - 1985
LILLY, Robert P.,   1910 - 1969

RIDDLE, Hobart,   April 21,1904 - June 26,1977
RIDDLE, Bonnie Tittle,   April 29,1911 - Jan.23,1984

PALMER, Nelson P.,   June 20,1887 - Feb.7,1932

DAVIDSON, Frederick,   Aug.26,1882 - Dec.2,1932
DAVIDSON, Elizabeth Heath,   Jan.29,1881 - Sept.27,1948
DAVIDSON, Florence K.,   Aug.26,1909 - Oct.8,1972 - USN  - WW2

MITCHELL, Ernest Ray,   1898 - 1970  -  USN WW1
MITCHELL, Elizabeth D.,   July 31,1906 -  ----

CHAPMAN, R.M.,   1896 - 1946
CHAPMAN, Marie C.,   1897 - 1966
CHAPMAN, Bernard C.,   Jan.17,1925 - Jan.21,1945
            In memory

BROWN, Andrew J.,   May 4,1858 - Jan.4,1935
            Son of Benjamin F. and Lucretia Davis Brown
BROWN, Mary J.Tilson, (w), Oct.18,1862 - Aug.11,1944
            Dau. of William Erwin and Mary Hickman Sams Tilson

EDWARDS, Lloyd Marion,   July 4,1926 -  -----
EDWARDS, Minnie Ella Riddle,   July 7,1927 -  ----

FOX, Herchel A.,   June 22,1891 - Sept.28,1934
FOX, Henry G.,   Jan.4,1890 - Sept.3,1944
            Son of Robert Fulton and Hammaleketh Roberta Fox
FOX, Fannie W.,   July 8,1896 - Sept.22,1961
            Dau. of Laban and Emma Erwin White

INGRAM, George Hubble, Aug.23,1883 - March 5,1979
INGRAM, Florence Kelley, (w), April 21,1880 - May 8,1961
        Dau. of Ryburn and Ellen Byars Kelley
INGRAM, William Frank, Sept.12,1911 - May 14,1922
INGRAM, Jacob William, April 26,1886 - July 26,1969
INGRAM, Anna Kelley, (w), Feb.26,1884 - Jan.15,1962
        Dau of Ryburn and Ellen Byars Kelley
SNIDER, Bryan S., Aug.5,1896 - Sept.29,1956
SNIDER, Clarice Ingram, May 11,1909 - June 27,1966

TAYLOR, Jesse Lee, Feb.26,1887 - June 18,1960
        Son of R.M. and Amanda Fagin Taylor
TAYLOR, Florence Ann, Oct.1,1932 - ----

WOMACK, Edmund L., Dec.4,1878 - Oct.22,1937
        Son of Jessee and Elizabeth Pedigo Womack
WOMACK, Leta Vernon Jennings, March 5,1884 - Oct.15,1958
WOMACK, Elizabeth, Feb.2,1911 - Feb.21,1915
WOMACK, Charles V., April 13,1913 - April 3,1968

SLYMAN, Richard, Jan.28,1898 - May 13,1947
        Son of Ollie and Mary Akel Slyman

BENNETT, Lula Duncan, 1885 - 1976
DUNCAN, Samuel Thomas, 1876 - 1935
        Son of John and Myra Hankins Duncan
DUNCAN, Casey Hyland, Sept.2,1906 - July 13,1966 - USMCR WW2
DUNCAN, Mary Vickie, Oct.4,1945 - May 7,1977

GENTRY, Mary Marie, May 12,1932 - June 3,1939
GENTRY, Donald E., Died May 3,1941
        Children of Everett L. and Eva Bailey Gentry

GILLIAM, Lawrence, 1914 - 1964
GILLIAM, Cleo, 1918 - ----

ANDERS, Richard H., Dec.16,1932 - March 24,1970 - Cpl Korea

HUSKINS, James R., 1874 - 1941
        Son of J.H. and Elizabeth Tapp Huskins
HUSKINS, Sarah M., 1877 - 1965
HUSKINS, A. Chester, 1908 - 1941
        Son of James Robert and Sarah Rebecca McInturff Huskins

TAYLOR, R.M., 1896 - 1967
TAYLOR, Pearl, (w), 1900 - ----
TAYLOR, Leonard W., (son), April 30,1922 - Sept.25,1944 - Sgt WW2

DAVIS, Dock, Jr., 1926 - 1978 - USA WW2

FANNING, Birdie E., July 4,1895 - Aug.1,1946 - Cpl USA WW1
        Son of William and Dorothy Hensley Fanning
FANNING, Mattie M., (w), Sept.21,1899 - Dec.21,1974

JOHNSON, Eddie E.,   Feb.11,1873 - Oct.7,1952
          Son of Isaac and Martha Morrison Johnson
JOHNSON, Leonora,   May 3,1875 - Oct.20,1953
          Dau. of John F. and Corinna Lloyd Sugg

RANDOLPH, A.M.,   1876 - 1930
RANDOLPH, Lillie Peak,   1878 - 1961
RANDOLPH, Verna Mae,   April 16,1902 - ----
RANDOLPH, Ruby,   Sept.3,1905 - ----

ALLEN, William D.,   March 4,1896 - April 26,1961 - PFC WW1

DEAN, Harry O.,   1886 - 1970
DEAN, Carrie Jo, (w), 1893 - 1951
          Dau. of David and Bertie Lambright Switzer
DEAN, Harry O.,Jr.,   July 12,1914 - Oct.29,1968

DOAN, Lee Roy,   1913 - 1947
          Son of Charles Mack and Minnie Hollifield Doan
DOAN, Donald Preston,   1935 - 1988
DOAN, Ronnie George Douglas,   Sept.5,1937 - Sept.24,1946
          Son of Lee Roy and Rachel Naomi Doyle Doan

HONEYCUTT, Roscoe C.,   July 12,1884 - June 13,1952
HONEYCUTT, Howard W.,   1918 - 1974 -   USN

WILLIAMS, Bascomb,   1882 - 1948
          Son of Joe Putnam and Adelaide Wilson Williams
WILLIAMS, Sarah Jane,   1877 - 1976

BRUMMETT, Cecil A.,   Feb.25,1912 - Dec.16,1961
BRUMMETT, Infant Son,   Died Oct.27,1947
          Son of Cecil and Pauline Brummett

WALDROP, Zeb,   1875 - 1948
WALDROP, Lydia, (w), Aug.28,1880 - March 17,1971
          Maiden name Guinn

PRINCE, Walter E.,   April 4,1883 - May 4,1961
          Son of Colin Murchison and Ellen Garrison Prince
PRINCE, Mary Hunter,   June 10,1886 - Oct.4,1962
          Dau. of Henry Clark and Nancy Harriett Hyde Palmer
PRINCE, H.Palmer,   Nov.26,1918 - April 6,1945
          Killed in action near Okinawa - buried at sea
PALMER, Meta,   1881 - 1951
          Dau. of Henry Clark and Nancy Harriett Hyde Palmer

TITTLE, Stella M.,   1923 - 1973
McLAUGHLIN, Clara L.,   Aug.9,1902 - June 18,1972
McLAUGHLIN, Joseph P.,   May 2,1925 - July 17,1944 - USA WW2
          Son of Isaac and Clara Williams McLaughlin

JOHNSON, Stewart M.,   April 6,1923 - Aug.24,1977
JOHNSON, Virginia Mauk,   May 1,1923 - June 16,1966
JOHNSON, Claudette Powers,   Aug.27,1938 - ----

WHITLOCK, Neida Faye,   July 19,1938 - May 5,1971

CAMPBELL, Carl A.,   Jan.29,1914 - Aug.13,1978

MORGAN, Charles Samuel,   Aug.8,1882 - Aug.16,1948
          Son of Samuel Calvin and Laura Cordelia Patton Morgan
MORGAN, Belle Sparks,   Sept.6,1888 - May 23,1986

WHITSON, Zachary Taylor,   April 27,1890 - Aug.3,1952
          Son of Charles C. and Millie Webb Whitson
WHITSON, Myrtle Erwin,   Aug.22,1893 - Oct.20,1984

DUNCAN, Jacob,"Nat",   March 15,1897 - March 8,1969
DUNCAN, Charlotte Ann,   Died Oct. 13,1948
          Dau. of Jacob and Ollie Luberto Scarbrough Duncan

CARR, Walter B.,   Oct.1,1882 - March 22,1951
          Son of W.C. and Joana Culbert Carr
CARR, Minnie W.,   Sept.29,1882 - Oct.7,1967
KING, Leonard E.,   Dec.29,1911 - Oct.1,1966
KING, Elizabeth Carr,   Sept.19,1909 - Feb.5,1970

BRUCE, Henry Lancaster,   Feb.2,1907 - Sept.24,1969
BRUCE, Mary Ellen Troxel,   Oct.9,1908 - July 14,1969
BRUCE, Mary Joyce,   July 14,1936 - June 13,1987

LUNDY, John Alvin,   Nov.12,1919 - July 30,1984
LUNDY, Orene Good,   Feb.17,1921 -  ----

MORLEY, Ira M.,   1915 - 1978  -  USAF WW2
MORLEY, Imogene Walser,   May 13,1923 -  ----

JAYNES, Arthur K., Jr.,   Dec.24,1919 - Jan.21,1962 - USAF WW2
JAYNES, Harold E.,   Sept.11,1921 - March 8,1975 - USA WW2

ATKINS, Manassah M.,   March 29,1892 - May 28,1978

DUNCAN, David H.,   July 25,1920 - Aug.9,1969 - USA WW2
DUNCAN, Barbara H.,(w), 1933 - 1972
DUNCAN, Deanna Ruth,   1959 - 1972
DUNCAN, Danny Joe,   b/d 1960
          Son of David Hugh and Barbara Lee Haire Duncan

BRUMMETT, Henry A.,   1900 - 1961
BRUMMETT, Martha,   1899 -  ----

GILBERT, E.A.,   1893 -  ----
GILBERT, Ethel Honeycutt,   1906 - 1951
          Dau. of David Baxter and Sallie Lou Deaton Honeycutt

CLARK, Billie,   1929 - 1931
          Child of Dewey and Sarah Rice Clark
CLARK, Ina Lou,   1947 - 1948
          Child of Wayne Price and Janie Street Clark
CLARK, Dewey,   1899 - 1977

TAPP, Harvey C.,    1909 - 1961
          Son of Thomas Marion and Mary McInturff Tapp
TAPP, Harvey C., Jr.,    1933 - 1934
          Son of Harvey and Lela Hobbs Tapp

HART, John S.,    March 4,1903 - March 5,1982
TANNER, Frank J.,    1871 - 1952
TANNER, Cornelia B., (w),   1873 - 1946
          Dau. of Martin Vandervleet

SIBERT, Ellsworth Herman,    1882 - 1938
          Son of J.C. and Violet Welter Sibert
SIBERT, Mary Maude, (w#1), 1886 - 1934
          Dau. of William W. and Hannah J. Merecle Chamberlain
SIBERT, Rose Lee, (w#2),   1912 - 1941
          Maiden name Simmons

GILLENTINE, James C.,    April 10,1893 - Jan.23,1969
GILLENTINE, Clara Gibbs, (w), Oct.31,1894 - Jan.4,1974
GILLENTINE, Hazel,   July 29,1915 - Jan.21,1937
          Dau. of James Corbett and Clara B. Gibbs Gillentine
CRENSHAW, Mozelle G.,    Sept.15,1917 - April 12,1983

TIPTON, James Wesley,    Died May 22,1964
          Infant of J.W. and Edna M. Tipton

GILLILAND, G.A.,    July 31,1895 - Oct.2,1935
          Son of J.B. and Alice Greenwell Gilliland
GILLILAND, Bessie Diggs,   Nov.10,1894 - Jan.8,1973

AKEL, William Mahmoud,   1886 - 1941
          Son of Mohmoud and Ammeny Alwan Akel
RAFFIH, Harrison M.,   Oct.16,1892 - Feb.25,1962   -   USA WW1

FISHER, L.C.,   Feb.23,1879 - Dec.12,1936
          Son of Henry and Manda Jones Dukes Fisher
FISHER, Virgie M., (w), Aug.5,1882 - Feb.4,1968
          Maiden name Moyers

HUTCHINS, J.M.,   June 26,1871 - Jan.6,1936
          Son of Wright and Polly Stanley Hutchins
HUTCHINS, Frances B., (w), June 4,1888 - Dec.2,1969
ADKINS, Hubert W.,   1915 - ----
ADKINS, Ethel H.,   1915 - ----

TITTLE, Russell,   May 7,1907 - ----
TITTLE, Edna B., (w), Oct.11,1907 - March 8,1978
TITTLE, Ira Kenneth,   July 12,1933 - Dec.3,1938
          Son of Roscoe and Edna Bennett Tittle
BENNETT, Drew Ray,   Oct.24,1913 - July 16,1972
TITTLE, Mary E.,   Feb.19,1880 - Feb.25,1936
          Dau. of James and Emmaline Mashburn Simmons
          Wife of Charles B. Tittle
THRASHER, Mrs. Maude Mae Collier, 1893 -1939

FOSTER, John H.,    1875 - 1936
          Son of Thomas and Naomi Chandler Foster
FOSTER, Amelda Anne, (w), 1876 - 1954
GUINN, George Washington, Sr.,   Aug.5,1884 - Feb.5,1954
          Son of John Bell and Sarah Clouse Guinn
GUINN, Minta Foster, (w), 1898 - 1939 (And Infant Daughter)
          Dau. of J.H. and Melda Sams Foster

MURRAY, Harvey C.,    March 4,1904 - March 2,1984
TILSON, Betsey J.,    1852 - 1939                .
          Dau. of Tommy and Betsy Buckner Runion
          Wife of Joshua E. Tilson

EDWARDS, John Allison,    1873 - 1940
EDWARDS, Vernie Rice,    1889 - 1968

PUTNAM, Milo Lee,    1867 - 1936
          Son of Drewery Alston and Cornelia Irby Putnam
PUTNAM, Louisa Gray,    Oct.31,1878 - Dec.4,1957

LYNCH, John H.,    March 11,1872 - Jan.1,1949
          Son of John Henry and Aran Rebecca Chafin Lynch
LYNCH, Maxie C.,    July 28,1889 - Sept.4,1974

NORRIS, Clifford L.,    1909 - 1985

McKINNEY, Mary,    June 1,1867 - March 28,1938
BAILEY, Carlos Wesley,    Aug.27,1894 - June 24,1959   -WW1
BAILEY, Venia,    1898 - 1973
BAILEY, Nora A.,    Sept.27,1874 - March 23, 1951

ALLEN, Robert H.,    1877 - 1944
          Son of Will and Molly McCurry Allen
ALLEN, Mary Etta,    1890 - 1961
          Dau. of Ben and Sarah Howell Banner

PETERS, Basel D.,    1882 - 1946
          Son of C.B. and Rebecca Peters

PENNEY, Henry Hammond,    Aug.1875 - June 1946
          Son of William Henry and Sarah Hammond Penney
PENNEY, Helen, (w),   Oct. 1880 - June 1954
PENNEY, Sara Mae,    Oct.12,1900 - March 29,1984

LAMIE, James Buchanan, Oct.10,1894 - Dec.23,1950
          Son of William H. and Mattie Buchanan Lamie

WILLIAMS, Ervin Maurice,    Aug.16,1899 - Oct.14,1986

TUCKER, Roy,    Aug.18,1891 - Jan.26,1973
TUCKER, Pansy B.,    Feb.12,1895 - May 31,1980

BRADSHAW, Jas.I.,    Feb.23,1868 - Oct.30,1942
BRADSHAW, Mary Etta, (w), April 23,1871 - May 18,1947
                Dau. of David and Vasheta Piercy Horton

PARSLEY, Frank T.,    Sept.22,1920 - Nov.12,1975
PARSLEY, James Bradshaw,   Nov.26,1915 - Oct.26,1986
PARSLEY, Marie C.,    Sept.7,1917 - Sept.25,1985
PARSLEY, Moses,   1860 - 1940
PARSLEY, Charlotte,   1861 - 1931
HENSLEY, Susan Parsley,   Feb.25,1882 - April 17,1945

ERWIN, Ruby A.,   June 10,1910 - July 13,1979

WALDROP, Pvt. Hugh L.,   Nov.6,1913 - Oct.18,1944 - WW2

OLLIS, Walter N.,   May 16,1908 - Aug.6,1984
OLLIS, Virgie V., (w), May 10,1913 -   ----

HILEMON, Sondra Jean,   Died July 29,1964
HILEMON, Annette,   Died April 12,1962
HILEMON,   Michael Alan,   Died 1968
                Infants of Grady and Nancy Hilemon
SAMS, L. Hayes,   1878 - 1961
SAMS, Nancy B.,   1878 - 1956

TITTLE, Roberta,   April 24,1908 - March 15,1987
TITTLE, Albert F.,   Aug.5,1904 - Feb.3,1956   - USA WW2
TITTLE, Ruth Sams,   1905 - 1948
                Dau. of Lee Roy and Nancy Brezella Clouse Sams
                Wife of Albert Tittle
TITTLE, Infant Son,   March 26,1950 - March 28,1950
                Son of  Albert D. and Marie Whitson Tittle
SMITH, Bertha Tittle,   April 19,1890 - July 19,1944
                Dau. of Alex and Hannah Thornberg Tittle

RYBURN, Frank Lindsey,   1902 - 1975 - USN WW1
RYBURN, Anna B.,   1902 - 1981
RYBURN, Mary E.,   1914 - 1980

ROBERTS, Nelia,   Dec.21,1912 - Dec.16,1983
ROBERTS, Ruth, (w),  June 10,1910 - Nov.10,1946
                Dau. of William Cornelius and Zenia Bennett Howell
TAPP, Richard B.,   Oct.24,1946 - July 2,1982

BRAUNECKER, Mary,   1900 - 1947
MOODY, Pritchard M.,   Feb.14,1878- March 16,1948
                Son of Eli Thomas and Elizabeth McCutchean Moody
MOODY, Johanna,   May 12,1894 - July 21,1978

BLACKBURN, John I.,   March 11,1883 - Feb.13,1949
BLACKBURN, Ina W.,   1890 - 1982

CAMPBELL, Bonnie,   1899 - 1948
        Dau. of Thomas Marion and Clara Allen Smith
LEDFORD, Noble n.,   Nov.22,1922 - March 1,1979
STEVENS, Lloyd B.,   1863 -1949
        Son of Bannister and Louisa Lance Stevens
WHEELER, Elizabeth,   1870 - 1949

HUSKINS, Daniel P.,   Sept.7,1875 - Jan.22,1951
HUSKINS, Berdie W.,   May 3,1881 - March 25,1948
TIPTON, Dock,   Feb.22,1867 - Nov.25,1951
TIPTON, Uslie,   Sept.6,1879 - March 6,1963

PHILLIPS, Floyd D.,   1915 - 1988
PHILLIPS, Delia M.,   1913 -  ----

LETTERMAN, John S.,   Dec.19,1873 - June 29,1960
LETTERMAN, Cora,   Nov.18,1884 - Nov.6,1975

PHILLIPS, Rex L.,   1915 - 1948
        Son of Zebulon Vance and Mary Elizabeth McEwen Phillips

DUNCAN, W.E. "Bill",   1959 - 1977
        Son of Bruce and Lillian Clark Duncan

PETERSON, Patricia Ann,   Oct.18,1939 - May 24,1959
        Dau. of Bert and Elizabeth Bradford Peterson

STALLARD, Arvil T.,   Jan.26,1906 - Feb.5,1975
STALLARD, Inez G.,   Dec.21,1905 - May 8,1988

DUNCAN, William F.,   1881 - 1959
        Son of J.L. and Ellen Ray Duncan
DUNCAN, Bess Buckner,   May 16,1901 - Aug.31,1982
DUNCAN, Elizabeth Woodward,   Sept.22,1912 - March 2,1985

TONEY, Herbert,   1890 - 1977

HUSKINS, Carl,   May 18,1910 - Nov.10,1966   -   PFC WW2
HUSKINS, Lena F.,   Nov.7,1911 - Dec.9,1959

BECKELHIMER, Ida Lee Wintermeyer,   Oct.25,1916 - Dec.25,1948
        Dau. of Fred Adolphus and Ida Lee Lanter Wintermeyer

McNABB, Grover S.,   1884 - 1948
McNABB, Grace P.,   1905 -  ----

RYBURN, Walter W.,   1888 - 1948
        Son of John D.S. and Caroline Crumley Ryburn
RYBURN, Antionette,   April 1,1887 - May 22,1975
        Maiden name Wintzer

EVERGREEN CEMETERY (continued)

BEAM, PFC Bob,    1910 - 1944
TIPTON, Lawson,    Jan.14,1895 - May 31,1947 - USA WW1
TIPTON, Loretta B.,    1898 - 1964
        Dau. of John and Hattie Renfro Beam

ROBERTS, J.Z.,    Aug.10,1883 - May 28,1965
        Son of Francis and Margaret Kegley Roberts
ROBERTS, Cennia B.,    Jan.27,1883 - March 20,1964
        Dau. of W.M. and Myra Bailey Bennett

TAPP, Isaac R.,    July 6,1895 - Dec.2,1984
TAPP, Lina R.,    1905 - ----

RYBURN, John D.S.,    1876 - 1951
        Son of John D.S. and Caroline Crumley Ryburn
RYBURN, Cora Ray, (w),    1879 - 1968
RYBURN, Earl D.,    1909 - 1942
        Son of John D. and Cora Lee Ray Ryburn
RYBURN, Ray,    Feb.19,1906 - Sept.19,1982

MAUK, Samuel L., "Sam",    1891 - 1944
        Son of William E. and Mollie Henley Mauk
MAUK, Leona G.,    1891 - 1972

HENSLEY, John W.,    Sept.4,1875 - March 10,1948
HENSLEY, Margaret A.,    Nov.12,1883 - Aug.7,1978
HENSLEY, Pearl,    Dec.23,1901 - Feb.1,1945
COLE, Anna Mae,    Died 1976

OLLIS, Lola Mae,    July 31,1929 - June 12,1945
OLLIS, Nancy Lou,    March 14,1942 - March 14,1942
        Daus. of Walter Newton and Virgie Viola Smith Ollis
OLLIS, Betsy J.,    b/d 1976

ADKINS, Rice,    1885 - 1965
ADKINS, Anna G. Peoples, (w), 1889 - 1943

PARSLEY, Millard F.,    May 13,1880 - Aug.8,1943
        Son of Mose and Charlotte James Parsley
PARSLEY, Daisy Garland, (w),  Aug.2,1894 - April 18,1961
PARSLEY, Millard F.,Jr.,    April 6,1914 - May 29,1943 - USAF WW2
PARSLEY, Wayne Edward, March 23,1948 - May 2,1960
        Son of Wayne M. and Fanny Mae Parsley

NOLEN, Choice C.,    Nov.3,1884 - June 2,1971
NOLEN, Annie Jones, (w), Feb.15,1885 - Aug.30,1969
NOLEN, Jessie Mae,    May 8,1923 - Sept.18,1956
        Dau. of C.C. and Annie Jones Wood Nolen

BURRELL, Ada M.,    1878 - 1943
BURRELL, Earl L.,    Jan.5,1901 - Sept.7,1969
BURRELL, Pauline F.,    June 23,1899 - Nov.25,1979

LAMIE, Ronnie Stephen,    Aug.23,1942 - Feb.23,1944

PETERSON, Philmore,    March 3,1906 - ----
PETERSON, Elizabeth G., (w), Dec.27,1909 - May 29,1976
PETERSON, Betty Joe, (dau.), June 23,1930 - Feb.2,1939

ADAMS, James,    1893 - 1945
            Son of Frank and Anna Hillman Adams
ADAMS, Mary E.,    1901 - 1961
            Dau. of George Stanley and Nancy Caroline Hood Haun
CRAWFORD, Frank E.,    1890 - 1946
            Son of Jerry Crawford

GOUGE, Charlie H.,    Aug.28,1893 - Jan.6,1941
GOUGE, Hassie,    Nov.11,1896 - July 17,1965
GOUGE, Carrie,    Sept.5,1917 - Oct.2,1937
GOUGE, Ray,    Oct.17,1931 - Aug.28,1932

LUNDY, Cloyd V.,    Sept.19,1886 - Jan.5,1933
            Son of Wiley M. and Rachel E. Lemon Lundy
LUNDY, Elizabeth E., (w), Aug.9,1989 - Sept.22,1979

UPDYKE, Audron Douglas,    1886 - 1938
            Son of William Jordan and Nannie C. Wilkes Updyke
UPDYKE, Flossie,    No dates
UPDYKE, Infant Son,    b/d 1913
            Son of A.D. and F.M. Updyke

BOONE, Hiram K.,    Jan.23,1875 - April 11,1947
            Son of J.S. and Emily Ray Boone
BOONE, Hannah Edge, (w), April 26,1875 - Sept.23,1946
            Dau. of Jason and Mary Boone Edge
BOONE, Burnie J.,    June 7,1896 - July 3,1964 - Co F - 117 Inf.
            Son of H.K. and Hannah Edge Boone
BOONE, Bonnie J.,    May 23,1894 - Nov.24,1981

MURRAY, Joseph F.,    March 17,1881 - Dec.15,1944
            Son of Joseph Lafayette and Elizabeth Harris Murray
MURRAY, Landon C.,    May 2,1877 - Aug.26,1949
MURRAY, Judy,    Aug.18,1883 - May 19,1961

COADY, Ruben C.,    1886 - 1936
            Son of Noah and Mort Briggs Coady
COADY, Verna B.,    1891 - 1970

CODY, Phillip,    Jan.7,1868 - May 27,1952
CODY, Dora M.,    Oct.3,1871 - March 31,1943
DAVIS, H.M.,    Sept.5,1883 - Dec.17,1935
DAVIS, Vertie M.,    (w), March 23,1890 - April 3,1966
DAVIS, Winfred G.,    April 2,1913 - Jan.9,1943
DAVIS, Void Bernard,    March 9,1915 - March 20,1967 - Pvt WW2
DAVIS, Raleigh,    Jan.9,1920 - Aug.6,1931
            Son of H.M. and Vertie Metcalf Davis
HARRIS, Jessie Davis,    Apr.9,1917 - July 20,1939

CLOUSE, Joanna,   Oct.6,1894 - Sept.2,1966
CLOUSE, Phyllis Leota,   Oct.31,1921 - March 2,1933
            Dau. of E.E. and Johanna Adkins Clouse
MOORE, Vera Clouse,   May 4,1910 - Feb.19,1983

HALE, Otis Cleveland, Sr.,   April 10,1885 - March 15,1981
HALE, Effie May, (w),   1887 - 1965
            Dau. of Karl A. and Kate Crandall Smith
SMITH, K.A.,   1850 - 1933 - Father of Mrs. O.C. Hale
            Son of John Smith

MOORE, Wallace,   Feb.22,1876 - Aug.21,1952
            Son of Mose and Sarah Good Moore
MOORE, Lummie Davis,   Aug.22,1886 - July 9,1962
            Dau. of Will and Casendra Booth Davis
MARTIN, Horace L.,   July 20,1883 - Sept.1,1959
MARTIN, Mable Jean,   Aug.16,1888 - Sept.1,1984

HONEYCUTT, Jon Wallace,   b/d  Oct. 9,1943
            Son of John Fred and Marian Beverly Wallace Honeycutt

VANCE, Abner,   1866 - 1944
VANCE, Elzora,   1888 - ----
VANCE, Homer C.,   Feb.3,1912 - Sept.12,1985

GILLILAND, Ira Carl,   March 31,1916 - Dec.26,1976

MORGAN, Helen C.,   June 12,1904 - Aug.18,1960
            Dau. of James H. and Ida McGee Cox
MORGAN, Mary Ida,   Died  June 9,1937
            Infant of David Gordon and Helen J. Cox Morgan

ERWIN, Charlie Ray,   Jan.13,1886 - April 5,1948
            Son of Phillip Parks and Callie Ray Erwin
ERWIN, Lela Pearl,   May 13,1888 - April 27, 1935

ERWIN, John F.,   May 5,1888 - Dec.26,1959
            Son of Phillip P. and Caldonia Ray Erwin
ERWIN, Maggie,   Aug.1,1894 - Jan.1,1965
            Dau. of Marcus and Mary Randolph Wilson

EDNEY, Robert A.,   Feb.24,1884 - ----
EDNEY, Nancy A.,   July 15,1888 - May 13,1969

STREET, James C.,   Feb.29,1888 - Aug.4,1955
STREET, Jennie M.,   Jan.9,1904 - Oct.2,1946

HOBBS, S.L.,   1869 - 1932
HOBBS, Mamie Wilkins,   1883 - 1930
            Dau. of J.A.R. and Teletha Webster Perkins

EVERGREEN CEMETERY (continued)

JOHNSON, Michael William,   Died Dec.27,1956
          Son of Harold B. and Alice Denison Johnson

TUCKER, Isabell Beck,   1904 - 1970

GUINN, Freeman,   Aug.27,1915 - Dec.8,1961   -   USA WW2

HENSLEY, Holt, Sr.,   May 24,1901 - Oct.29,1968
HENSLEY, Estelle B.,   July 15,1901 - June 30,1955
          Dau. of J.O. and Anna Liza Chandler Blankenship

SALTS, Fitz H.,   Sept.15,1895 - May 9,1983
SALTS, C. Maude,   July 28,1896 - Sept.27,1983

LILLY, Mont F.,   May 24,1900 - Sept.4,1976

HENSLEY, Pearl K.,   Sept.13,1911 - Oct.28,1968

GUINN, Lattie,   Oct.19,1882 - March 16,1963
GUINN, Gertrude Hensley,   July 19,1888 - July 10,1959

BUCKNER, Fred William,   June 6,1903 - July 17,1973
BUCKNER, Lela Tilson,   Nov.11,1897 -   ----
BUCKNER, Lillian Goforth,   -----  -  -----
RAY, Fred,   Sept.22,1904 - May 22,1975

SHULL, Ernest Dean,   Nov.29,1870 - April 1,1944
          Son of William Harrison and Frances Dean Shull
SHULL, Fannie Price, (w), April 21,1867 - Feb.14,1956
SHULL, Frank Price, Sr.,   March 22,1899 - Jan.9,1984

HICKEY, Roy Hubert, Jr.,   1909 - 1954

DAVIS, Charles G.,   1897 - 1939
          Son of J.C. and Mollie E. Booth Davis

FRANKLIN, Everette B.,   June 3,1897 - March 11,1969 - Pvt USA WW1
FRANKLIN, Catherine C.,   Jan.10,1901 - Feb.23,1970
BOLTON, Claude C.,   April 1,1906 - April 21,1954 - USA WW2
WHITEHEAD, Lelia S.,   July 20,1880 - Nov.17,1972

PETERSON, Doss,   May 2,1880 - Jan.19,1947
PETERSON, Parliskey,   Dec.2,1888 - Feb.10,1964
          Dau of Dave Bryant
RAY, Francis E.,   1907 - 1982   -   USA WW2

STULTZ, John B.,   Nov.1,1915 - Nov.1,1984
STULTZ, Alonza Arnold,   May 22,1912 - Aug.23,1971
RICHMOND, Jewel Stultz,   July 25,1908 - Oct.14,1984
AUSTIN, Robert H.,   Sept.24,1885 - March 27,1947
          Son of George W. and Maggie V. Dudley Austin

MILLER, George W.,    June 24,1895 - April 24,1952
MILLER, Myrtle A.,    Feb.17,1899 - July 26,1985
GEISLER, Ralph T.,    Oct.1,1911 - Oct.23,1981
GEISLER, Alleene M.,    March 19,1922 - ----

YOUNG, Millard G.,    May 1,1893 - June 28,1965   -   WW1
      Son of Charles and Emma Mulberry Young
YOUNG, Phyllis Ann,    Sept.19,1925 - Aug.4,1940
      Dau. of M.G. and Rose O'Brien Young

BUCHANAN, Alice A.,    1902 - 1985
TATE, Thomas Holt,    1891 - 1975

McINTYRE, Harry W.,    March 30,1906 - Dec.18,1967 - WW2
McINTYRE, Arch K.,    Oct.10,1913 - May 19,1970 - USN WW2

WEAVER, Samuel Shepherd,    Aug.25,1882 - Jan.3,1943
      Son of Thomas Franklin and Malinda Shepherd Weaver
BENTLEY, George A.,    March 2,1890 - Aug.2,1971
BENTLEY, Minnie Weaver,    Aug.9,1891 - March 7,1976

BROCE, Harvey Keith,    Aug.22,1915 - Oct.4,1970 - USA WW2

SURFACE, Fletcher Edward,    Nov.25,1895 - July 30,1948
      Son of George Daniel and Julia Akers Surface
SURFACE, Nora Shull,    Nov.25,1905 - Oct.13,1977

YOUNG, Glenn T.,    Oct.8,1905 - Aug.5,1965
YOUNG, Nell Buckner,    Aug.26,1910 - April 18,1974

RICE, Robert Edward,    1918 - 1978   - Lt USN WW2

BLANKENSHIP, Kate R.,    Dec.5,1898 - April 12,1985

ERWIN, Raymond T.,    Jan.13,1898 - Feb.5,1975
ERWIN, Lucy Gage,    Sept.9,1898 - May 9,1965

TIPTON, John W.,    1879 - 1947   - Spanish American War
      Son of Sebern and Nannie Lewis Tipton
TIPTON, Sue M.,    1884 - 1976

SIMPSON, William P.,    Sept.21,1869 - Feb.11,1950
      Son of Loderick K. and Jemima Harvey Simpson
SIMPSON, Susan W.,    Aug.13,1871 - March 20,1968
WORSHAM, Sallie Ann,    July 30,1873 - Oct.22,1957
      Dau. of William C. and Parthenia Payne Worsham

MERCER, Robert W.,    June 6,1881 - Dec.13,1951
MERCER, Jane M.,    March 1,1890 - Feb.17,1979
MERCER, Robert Markland,    May 4,1908 - Nov.4,1980
MERCER, Frederick Hayes,    Nov.30,1917 - Aug.4,1987 - USN WW2

ERWIN, Thomas Raymond,   Oct.28,1947 - Oct.30,1947
    Son of Isaac Eugene and Marjorie Ann Thomas Erwin


RICE, Walter L.,   May 29,1890 - Oct.25,1966
RICE, Bertha E.,   May 27,1894 - Feb.17,1978
RICE, Walter L.,Jr.   Dec.17,1921 - Mar.2,1945 - Sgt USAF WW2
RICE, Robert E.,   Aug.5,1896 - July 9,1957   - Sgt USAF WW1-WW2


CASH, Samuel Leroy,   Sep.26,1886 - Apr.19,1974
CASH, Vestal Duncan,   Aug.3,1889 - May 25,1978


McEWEN, James R.,   Aug.10,1862 - Oct.16,1936
McEWEN, Samuel A.,   May 7,1888 - May 30,1967 - Cpl WW1
McEWEN, Alice B.,   July 10,1890 - Oct.25,1971
McEWEN, Mildred R.,   Jan.16,1923 - Aug.16,1923


BOYD, Robert Ferrell "Squiz",   Dec.25,1904 - Jan.26,1984
BOYD, Margaret Martin,   Oct.17,1904 - Jan.8,1986
BOYD, Rebecca Lee "Becky", (dau.) Aug.1,1928 - July 7,1942


SHULL, George Francis,   Apr.19,1876 - Sep.8,1953
    Son of Wm. H. and Frances Dean Shull
SHULL, Florence Perlette,   May 3,1878 - Mar.16,1947
    Dau. of Frederick and Sarah Stumbaugh Perlette
SHULL, Frank Perlette,   May 5,1904 - June 7,1972


JONES, William H.,   Aug.18,1875 - May 11,1942
JONES, Lilly Jane, (w), July 29,1878 - Nov.8,1950
CLIVE, Orra,   Jan.29,1903 - July 11,1919


MILLER, John J.,   June 3,1886 - Mar.20,1942
    Son of Peter and Harriett Angeline Miller
MILLER, Mayme K.,   Oct.3,1894 - Sep.13,1976


McINTYRE, Leon Leslie,   1874 - 1944
    Son of Archibald K. and Liza Jane Fletcher McIntyre
McINTYRE, Margaret Walker,   1878 - 1950
    Dau. of George H. and Sarah Bracken McClaugherty Walker
McINTYRE, Leon Leslie, Jr.,   1909 - 1965


BUCHANAN, Dosser W.,   1868 - 1954
BUCHANAN, Martha Anne,   1872 - 1947
    Dau. of Clingman and Evelyn Troutman Street
BUCHANAN, John H., "MD", (son) 1905 - 1939


O'BRIEN, Joseph S.,   Aug.4,1869 - Mar.3,1952
    Son of Joel and Ann Birchfield O'Brien
O'BRIEN, Etta L.,   Feb.5,1873 - Nov.29,1942
    Dau. of Taylor Moore
O'BRIEN, Carrie Augusta,   Aug.31,1903 - Nov.6,1922


MILLER, C.O.,   May 4,1893 - May 3,1969
MILLER, Mae,   Nov.30,1893 - July 31,1981
MILLER, Wayne B.,   Nov.24,1921 - Sep.16,1924

ROYSTON, Charles Clyde,   Oct.27,1892 - July 19,1976
ROYSTON, Mildred Campbell,   April 16,1905 -   -----

STULTZ, Joe J.,   Oct.18,1882 - Aug.7,1962
          Son of Joe and Letita Philpot Stultz
STULTZ, Mamie A.,   April 14,1881 - Feb.10,1969
STULTZ, Alonza W.,   1878 - 1938
          Son of Joe and Letita Philpot Stultz
STULTZ, Sarah M., (w),   1882 - 1957
          Dau. of John W. and Corena Cox Miles

O'BRIEN, Clifton,   Sep.18,1904 - Sep.26,1935
          Son of John and Cenia Harris O'Brien

BOLTON, B.U.,   1875 - 1938
          Son of James Haws and Mary Jane Browning Bolton
BOLTON, Lura S.,   1878 - 1965
          Dau. of Calvin S. and Margaret Sheets

PUGH, Charles Richard,   1894 - 1937
PUGH, Verna L., (w),   1900 - 1932
          Dau. of J.W. and Kate Wilson West
PUGH, Betty Lou, (dau.),   1930 - 1932

WARDRUP, Nelia Jo Tucker,   Nov.12,1899 - April 4,1931
          Wife of Roy G. Wardrup
TUCKER, Maude,   July 16,1893 - July 18, 1984
TUCKER, Nathaniel Taylor,   1861 - 1937
          Son of Joseph S. and Alice McGimpsey Tucker
TUCKER, Nora O'Brien,   1869 - 1950
          Dau. of David O'Brien

SHULL, William Ernest,   Dec.5,1901 - Jan.21,1937
          Son of Ernest Dean and Fannie Bell Price Shell
SHULL, Cora Virginia,   Jan.5,1903 - Oct.8,1973

BUCKNER, William M.,   Sept.8,1866 - Sept.16,1937
BUCKNER, Liza,   Mar.5,1869 - July 19,1931
          Dau. of Clayton and Mary Dillinger Ray

GUINN, William Edwin,   Jan.19,1930 - Sept.23,1934
          Son of Glenn and Wilsie Guinn
HENSLEY, Thena Cody,   Aug.23,1869 - Oct.14,1957

HENSLEY, Thomas C. "Dr.",   May 16,1873 - Aug.4,1931
          Son of S.S. and Cordelia Smith Hensley
HENSLEY, Mary Ann, (w),   Apr.27,1873 - Sept.1,1961
HENSLEY, Mary Lee, (dau.),   June 23,1906 - June 6,1944

FOX, Orville Henry,   1877 - 1935
          Son of Orville Edgar and Lyda Meyers Fox
FOX, Julia Anna,   1879 - 1942
          Dau. of Wm. Ferinand and Mary Voelker Suckuary

SUBLETT, James Walter,   Mar.5,1873 - Feb.15,1932

<u>EVERGREEN CEMETERY</u>  (Continued)

BECK, James Oliver,   1872 - 1937
          Son of Jamison R. and Mary Andrew Beck
BECK, Harriett Jane,   1879 - 1956
          Dau. of Gerald and Sarah Wood Mitchell

JOHNSON, Harold Vivien,   1908 - 1932

CONGDON, Ronald P.,   1890 - 1937
CONGDON, Lessie,   1893 - 1984

JOHNSTON, John Thomas,   Aug.3,1885 - Oct.3,1934
          Son of Ephriam and Catherine Butler Johnston
JOHNSTON, Ethel E.,   July 2,1886 - Apr.19,1963

CUNNINGHAM, W. Fred,   Jan.23,1914 - May 19,1953
          Son of Willis S. Cunningham

BARTON, John S.,   Oct.7,1893 - June 8,1940

CALLAWAY, Dee,   1910 - 1986
CALLAWAY, Bessie,   1914 - 1967

ANDERS, Stewart,   July 28,1912 - July 23,1959
ANDERS, Delcina C.,   May 16,1912 -   -----

VANCE, Robert S. Sr.,  1900 -   -----     US Navy
VANCE, Parthenia C.,   1912 - 1987

CALLAWAY, Elizabeth,   Apr.18,1900 - Dec.14,1969
CALLAWAY, Hazel,   Aug.21,1921 - Aug.2,1985

BANNER, Martin L.,   1896 - 1968
BANNER, Lillian R.,   1913 - 1970

TILSON, Robert E.,   1909 - 1967
TILSON, Della H.,   1915 -   -----
TILSON, David,   1948 - 1968

FOSTER, James C.,   Nov.12,1898 - July 21,1977
FOSTER, Lura Mae,   Sept.5,1895 - Sept.8,1968

TIPTON, Gary D.,   Nov.5,1945 - Feb.1,1967

KING, Alan Earl,   Infant son of Buddy and Kathy King, d.1971

BAILEY, William M. "Bud",   1882 - 1966
BAILEY, Ban Rona,   1903 - 1977

WHALEY, Charles G.,   1906 - 1981
WHALEY, Rebecca M.,   1906 -   -----

WHITSON, Brad Alan, Son of Brad and Barbara Whitson, b/d 1968

MILLER, Charles,   b/d 1967

WILLIAMS, Steve,   1899 - 1966
WILLIAMS, Ollie,   1907 - 1986

EVERGREEN CEMETERY (continued)

CHEEK, Henry D., 1883 - 1966
CHEEK, Carrie Harper, Mar.29,1886 - Jan.4,1974

BENNETT, Rev. George H., Jan.20,1891 - Jan.21,1982
BENNETT, Mary E., Feb.5,1898 - May 6,1966

YATES, Glen E., Apr.27,1908 - Mar.29,1966
YATES, Maude W., (w), May 10,1914 - Nov.5,1966

MOORE, Elmer R., May 27,1889 - Apr.19,1951
            Son of C.G. and Mary Moore
MOORE, Alpha Barlow, Jan.16,1890 - Nov.9,1975

TIPTON, Dove W., 1875 - 1951
TIPTON, Julia, 1873 - 1971

ENGLE, James Blaine, Apr.12,1886 - Nov.12,1957
ENGLE, Anna Mae Horn, June 22,1893 - Jan.14,1953

CLARK, Alice E., Sept.8,1881 - July 4,1953
            Dau. of Crockett and Rebecca Day Varner

EVANS, Albert E., June 29,1885 - Apr.28,1957
            Son of James and Dinah Moore Evans
EVANS, Sarah H., May 28,1890 - June 28,1960
            Dau. of Wm. and Martha Tipton Guinn

RIDDLE, David P., 1888 - 1967
RIDDLE, Eddie S.F., 1881 - 1967

WALLINDER, Eric G., Oct.4,1899 - Dec.15,1968 - PFC USA WW1

SMITH, Oscar Peak, Nov.6,1887 - July 5,1963
SMITH, Dovey, Dec.28,1876 - Jan.28,1963

FULENWIDER, Edward H., 1900 - 1981 - USA WW2

McINTURFF, Jack A., Sept.21,1922 - Dec.5,1986 - USA WW2

BURRELL, Arthur James, June 20,1903 - Apr.21,1971
BURRELL, Pauline Justice, Oct.12,1906 - Oct.6,1974

BLANKENSHIP, Mitchell P., May 15,1889 - Mar.2,1967 - USA WW1

BELCHER, Carlos S., May 7,1907 - Jan.10,1968
BELCHER, Mildred W., Sept.16,1907 - -----

BUCHANAN, Louis John, June 10,1915 - June 12,1967 - USN WW2

BLANKENSHIP, Pearl M., 1902 - 1974

COOPER, Marcus, Dec.13,1892 - Aug.24,1967
COOPER, Vira, May 15,1892 - Feb.21,1972

COMBS, Clint, Sept.15,1903 - Mar.6,1966

<u>EVERGREEN CEMETERY</u>  (continued)

HARRISON, Paul B.,    July 27,1923 - Mar.4,1968

INGRAM, Claude,    1904 - 1971

HARRIS, Clabey,    Aug.8,1917 - Mar.29,1972  - USA WW2

PETERSON, Buford,    May 20,1916 - July 27,1986

LAUGHREN, Willie,    1917 - 1968
LAUGHREN, Mary Lynn,    1927 - -----

McVAY, James,    Mar.22,1916 - June 23,1964  -  USA  WW2

MASHBURN, J.L.,    Aug.29,1925 - Sept.27,1968  - USMC WW2

TITTLE, Brady M.,    Mar.30,1903 - Mar.11,1972

CAMPBELL, William J.,    Dec.5,1902 - Sept.23,1977
CAMPBELL, Juanita W.,    June 24,1908 - Dec.30,1963
          Dau. of Charles C. and Jennie Lilly White

CAMPBELL, Alice Hicks,    Sept.7,1948 - Feb.11,1967

TITTLE, Jack,    March 19,1927 - Jan.23,1964  - USNR  WW2

ERVIN, Charles H.,    1881 - 1927
ERVIN, Lorena R.,    1887 - 1970

HICKS, Haleyda,    1914 - 1969

MASHBURN, Kathy Denise,    Mar.4,1959 - Mar.10,1963
          Dau. of Bobby J. and Peggy Jo Bradley Mashburn

PETERSON, Wayne B.,    1924 - 1969
PETERSON, Mary L.,    1924 - -----

BENNETT, Coy J.,    1904 - 1971
BENNETT, Robbie G.,    1913 - -----

BEAVER, Floyd,    May 6,1902 - Feb.1,1974
BEAVER, Grace,    Aug.8,1901 - June 18,1968

SMITH, Jerry Lynn,    Apr.24,1957 - Feb.3,1971

HALL, Earl J.,    May 10,1898 - Feb.15,1966

CAMPBELL, J.R. "Bob",    1909 - 1964
          Son of Charles and Sally McIntosh Campbell
CAMPBELL, Enolia V.,    1912 - 1978
          Dau. of Samuel Covey and Mary Elizabeth Mead Stallard

NOLEN, James Walter,    1908 - 1961
NOLEN, Pearl,    1900 - 1973

DUGGAN, Rev. J.R.,    1888 - 1986
DUGGAN, Minta J.,    1890 - 1979

ADKINS, Charlie,    Aug.22,1896 - Sept.20,1971  - USA  WW1

ENGLE, James Clifford,    Nov.14,1916 - June 19,1961  - USA  WW2

PIERCY, John C.,    Oct.19,1889 - May 5,1963
            Son of Lycurgres and Mary Moore Piercy
PIERCY, Belle E.,    Mar.4,1900 -  -----
PIERCY, Howard,    1918 - 1980
PIERCY, Selma,    1920 -  -----

RAY, Basil,    Oct.25,1901 - Nov.21,1949

WHITSON, Anna Mae,    Mar.24,1920 - Nov.27,1980

RENFRO, Granville,    1872 - 1957
            Son of Marcus and Harriett McCurry Renfro
RENFRO, Gertrude R.,    1873 - 1950
            Dau. of Columbus and Sally Moore Ray

STALLARD, Fred W.,    Dec.17,1906 - Apr.21,1971
            Son of Samuel Covey and Mary Elizabeth Mead Stallard
STALLARD, Bertha E.,    Dec.31,1908 -  -----
            Dau. of M.M. and Pearl Guinn Shelton

GODSEY, James W. Jr.,    July 14,1906 - Mar.12,1982
GODSEY, Mae S.,    Oct.23,1906 -  -----
            Dau. of M.M. and Pearl Guinn Shelton

HURD, Luther C.,    1889 - 1965
HURD, Flossie Atkins,    1987 - 1974

ALLEN, Oliver L.,    1907 - 1966
ALLEN, Ethel L.,    1912 -  -----

BURGNER, Daniel H.,    1901 - 1968
BURGNER, Mary E.,    1908 -  -----

BROWN, Hoke A.,    June 22,1891 - June 5,1971
BROWN, Cora Ann,    May 16,1892 - Nov.14,1976

HARVEY, James M.,    1883 - 1964
            Son of George L. and Adelaide Marshall Harvey

MOSS, Charles Drayton,    1884 - 1950
            Son of Robert E. and Araminta Hardin Moss
MOSS, Elisabeth Reynolds,    1887 - 1985

NORRIS, Richard Elmer,    June 6,1893 - Sept.20,1978  - USA WW1

BAILEY, Lula(Lola?) J.,    1910 - 1988

PETERSON, Commodore D.,    1900 - 1976  - USN  WW1- WW2
PETERSON, Nell C.,    1913 - 1983

TINKER, Frances Mae,    Sept.1,1898 - May 10,1968

(continued)

DAYTON, Floyd F.,   1897 - 1979
DAYTON, Gladys H.,   1907 - -----

ANDERS, Bertha,   July 10,1918  -  ------

LILLY, Earl D.,   1902 - -----
LILLY, Willie R.,   1902 - 1977

CHANDLEY, Vance,   1914 - 1973
CHANDLEY, Mary,   1921 - -----

ELLIOTT, E. Crawford,   Nov.22,1918 - Aug.1,1977
ELLIOTT, Elizabeth F.,   Dec.20,1920 - -----
ELLIOTT, R.R.,   Sept.12,1894 - July 24,1964
          Son of Dan and Evelyn Bartee Elliott
ELLIOTT, Zola,   June 1,1894 - July 19,1969

BURRELL, Eugene V.,   1912 - 1965
BURRELL, Velma F.,   1914 - -----

RICE, Isaac M.,   Sept.8,1891 - Oct.4,1964

BRADFORD, Lyde,   May 7,1904 - Nov.19,1963

BAILEY, David D.,   May 12,1877 - Jan.25,1952
          Son of Wm. Riley and Rebecca Deyton Bailey
BAILEY, Elizabeth B.,   Jan.27,1887 - Jan.14,1977

HARDIN, Ollie B.,   Mar.9,1905 - Dec.11,1966
HARDIN, Malissea Ray,   Jan.22,1884 - June 19,1961

BEST, Glenn Edward,   May 28,1896 - May 4,1962   - USN WW1   WW2
          Son of Edward E. and Ella Wray Best

HALE, James O.,   Mar.16,1881 - June 17,1947
          Son of William Chamberlin Hale
HALE, Ida Martin,   Sept.28,1881 - Nov.28,1960
          Dau. of John C. and Sarah Bacon Martin

BAILEY, W.Walter,   Nov.1,1907 - Nov. 15,1986
BAILEY, Thelma F.,   Apr.11,1913 - Apr.27,1967

BERNDT, Lucille K.,   Jan.2,1922 - Feb.2,1972

GENTRY, William Labe,   Mar.20,1896 - Mar.3,1962   - PFC WW1
          Son of Lewis and Sarah Guinn Gentry
GENTRY, Bonnie E.,   Aug.19,1905 - Dec.18,1982

METCALF, Thomas,   Mar.20,1894 - June 2,1965   - USA  WW1
METCALF, Hattie M.,   June 21,1901 - -----

BOWMAN, J.R.,   1927 - -----
BOWMAN, Julia B.,   1929 - 1965
          Dau. of James and Rosetta Miller Barnett

WILLIAMS, John Claude,  Sept.11,1889 - Oct.9,1960
WILLIAMS, Callie Pearl,  Jan.21,1898 - Mar.23,1975

BOWMAN, Ray W.,  1908 - 1980
BOWMAN, Prude T.,  1908 -  -----

HARRIS, Julia H.,  Aug.26,1897 - Nov.17,1968

GUINN, James H.,  Nov.25,1881 - Mar.18,1971
GUINN, Hattie M.,  May 14,1884 - Feb.16,1968
GUINN, Glenna,  1906 -  -----

KLINE, Gertrude V.,  Apr.11,1892 - Nov.28,1967

BLANKENSHIP, Stacy,  1921 - 1982

JONES, Ross,  June 19,1885 - Sept.21,1961
          Son of Manfield J. and Margaret Phillips Jones
JONES, Frank A.,  May 29,1894 - Feb.7,1976

SHELTON, Florence J.,  Mar.9,1917 -  -----

DAVIS, Jack Evins,  Feb.17,1892 - Aug.22,1976

FOX, Ed,  1906 - 1972
FOX, Annie M.,  1909 - 1985

FOX, Earl J.,  1927 - 1980
FOX, Lloyd V.,  May 31,1938 - Oct. 18,1982

TITTLE, Troy,  1906 - 1972

LEWIS, H.L.,  June 24,1906 - Aug.21,1978
LEWIS, Della,  Apr.11,1909 -  -----

PHILLIPS, Floyd,  Apr.10,1924 - Aug.26,1970
PHILLIPS, Carrie Mae,  Oct.12,1933 - Apr.3,1981

HICKS, Charles R.,  1886 - 1970
HICKS, Lola N.,  1892 - 1973

BAILEY, James W.,  Sept.28,1912 - June 5,1971
BAILEY, Pansy,  Nov.25,1918 - May 9,1988

GRUBBS, Dexter P.,  1920 - 1988
GRUBBS, Gladys M.,  Oct.25,1924 - Nov.8,1969

JOHNSON, J.Quincey,  Sept.21,1897 - Jan.19,1971
JOHNSON, Lavara G.,  Nov.24,1903 - May 23,1969

TITTLE, C.E.,  May 21,1886 - Oct.14,1971
TITTLE, Minnie,  Oct.27,1888 - July 25,1969

EVERGREEN CEMETERY (continued)

TUCKER, Ralph D., 1894 - 1959
          Son of Wesley Sevier and Polly Ann Bailey Tucker
TUCKER, Lillian A., 1896 - 1980
TUCKER, Ralph Dana Jr., 1917 - 1982 - USN WW2
TUCKER, Ann H., June 7,1921 - Apr.9,1984

PETERSON, Robert C., July 23,1882 - Oct.28,1955
          Son of John and Ann Radford Peterson

LUNDY, Terry H., Sept.1,1884 - Apr.27,1958
          Son of Wiley Martin and Rachel Lemons Lundy
LUNDY, Virginia M., Aug.2,1890 - Mar.20,1975

BRYANT, Frank M., May 17,1898 - Oct.15,1980

HIGGINS, Elmer C., Sept.27,1895 - Apr.23,1983
HIGGINS, Waleska Hoyle, Oct.27,1895 - Oct.15,1957

BRITT, Homer M., 1902 - 1964
          Son of Walter and Maude Sutphin Britt
BRITT, Pansy L., 1900 - 1971
BRITT, Hermon R., 1922 - 1984

INGRAM Jesse Jacob, 1892 - 1976
INGRAM, Ocie S., 1896 - -----

LEDFORD, Brownlow, Apr.8,1895 - Oct.22,1951 - USA WW1
          Son of Joseph and Vicie Street Ledford

PARKER, Hobert, 1914 - 1962
PARKER, Mary Mae, 1909 - -----

WEBB, Jessie Elmer, 1900 - 1953
          Dau. of George Beverly and Virginia Bell Cacy

BLANKENSHIP, Paul, Nov.8,1905 - Nov.29,1975
BLANKENSHIP, Lena, (w), Mar.29,1913 - -----

WEBB, Jake Buck, Sr., 1893 - 1979 - USA WW1

ROWLAND, Shelby R., May 1,1887 - May 15,1955
          Son of Jefferson D. and Rose Farmer Rowland
ROWLAND, Edythe M., May 7,1896 - -----

SMITH, Wayne Burris, July 3,1905 - Oct.3,1960 - USMC

SMITH Anna E., 1906 - 1984

HUFF, Oliver L., Dec.24,1888 - Mar.5,1956
HUFF, W.C. "Clark", Mar.5,1883 - June 13,1959
          Sons of Thomas B. and Eliza Spencer Huff

LOVE, Daniel Whitfield, Mar.28,1869 - Dec.18,1961
LOVE, Mamie Ethel, Dec.29,1877 - Nov.17,1957

EVERGREEN CEMETERY  (continued)

McINTURFF, Charles A.,    Sept.7,1887 - Sept.14,1957
            Son of J.W. and Julia Rowe McInturff
McINTURFF, Annabelle,    Apr.29,1896 - Nov.3,1979
McINTURFF, Jack,    Nov.11,1929 - Oct.17,1965  - USMC  Korea

BAUMGARDNER, Thomas C.,    1891 - 1956
            Son of John Calvin and Emline Costner Baumgardner
BAUMGARDNER, Lutishia H.,    1887 - 1968

RAMSEY, Mager Belo,    June 16,1883 - Apr.28,1954
            Son of Daniel and Evelyn Johnson Ramsey
RAMSEY, Clara Morris,    Sept.28,1891 - July 21,1983

BOWMAN, John E.,    1882 - 1959

CLARK, Albert Jr.,    Oct.10,1932 - Aug.4,1957  -  USAF

BENNETT, A.N.,    July 27,1872 - Aug.30,1966
BENNETT, Rena H.,    Aug.12,1873 - Jan.8,1949
            Dau. of Joel and Nettie Radford Hensley

FORTUNE, Joseph E.,    1895 - 1959
            Son of Earl and Zula Pentoff Fortune

ROBINSON, Thomas E.,    Jan.2,1897 - Mar.24,1955
            Son of John and Nancy Angel Robinson
ROBINSON, Nora R.,    Sept.1,1895 - Dec.10,1974

HARRISON, Charlie Asbury,    July 28,1888 - July 19,1951
HARRISON, Sena McKinney,    Mar.12,1888 - Oct.21,1954
            Dau. of Thomas C. and Vanda Young McKinney

RICE, George E.,    Nov.12,1892 - Nov.6,1960  -  USA  WW1
RICE, Laura Cox,    Nov.22,1905 - May 1,1980

JOHNSON, Eugene P.,    1905 - 1951
            Son of Wayne J. and Cora Jane Francis Johnson

LEDFORD, Martha J.,    Mar.1,1891 - Feb.8,1961
LEDFORD, Deckie Mae,    Mar.21,1920 - May 24,1979

GARLAND, Edgar C.,    Aug.31,1891 - Dec.10,1928

FOSTER, Emory,    July 10,1874 - Dec.29,1963

HUPP, Infant sons of Gordon and Mary Lou Dettrick Hupp b/d Feb.1952

MARTIN, Bell,    1863 - 1957

PETERSON, Jess D.,    1867 - 1952

McNABB, John Robert,    Apr.28,1926 - Jan.11,1988 - USN  WW2

HANEY, Ivory,    1924 - 1967

EVERGREEN CEMETERY (continued)

WHITLOCK, Francis M.,     1888 - 1957
WHITLOCK, May L.,     1895 - 1963
          Dau. of Channa and Sally McDaniel Stevens

CAPPS, Dana H.,     Aug.23,1910 - Aug. 24,1952
          Son of Manuel Rankin and Annie Mae Laws Capps

TONEY, Judy L.,     Jan.7,1957 - Jan.8,1957
          Infant of Reid and Evone McIntosh Toney

MILLER, Rose,     1902 - 1952
          Dau. of Zeb and Mary Moore McCurry

HENSLEY, John B., "Pop",     1888 - 1979
HENSLEY, Nettie F.,     1891 - 1965

ALLGOOD, Timmy,     1969 - 1969

HOILMAN, Myrtle,     1898 - 1986

BAILEY, J. Willard,     1881 - 1952
BAILEY, Naomi Byrd,     1885 - 1972

YELTON, Grover C.,     July 1,1911 - May 28,1964

GROSS, Mary Loretta,     Mar.20,1893 - June 9, 1959

TIPTON, Mark,     Oct.10,1879 - Feb.12,1959
TIPTON, Vista,     Apr.4,1889 - Apr.8,1953

HOLLOWAY, Rev. Moss,     Dec.9,1890 - Dec.14,1987
HOLLOWAY, Lora, (w),     Mar.2,1895 - Mar.24, 1956
          Dau. of Silas and Lina Howell Tolley

PHILLIPS, Noah,     Mar.1,1897 - Apr.16,1959
          Son of Samuel Cornelius and Nellie Higgins Phillips
PHILLIPS, Betty,     Dec.17,1935 - Nov.18,1967

PETERSON, Phoebe C.,     June 3,1903 - June 24,1961

HUGHES, Walter A. Jr.,     Apr.16,1938 - July 23,1961
HUGHES, Nancy Brown,     Feb.3,1938 - July 22,1961

EDMONDS, Myrtle H.,     Sept.26,1896 - Aug.23,1975
EDMONDS, Sandra,     Nov.6,1956 - Nov.7,1956
          Dau. of Douglas and Pauline Puckett Edmonds

LAVERNE, John L.,     Jan.31,1912 - Apr.3,1956  - USA  WW2

EDWARDS, Anna Ray,     June 14,1902 - Jan.5,1955

HARRIS, Clinton "Duck",     1925 - 1987

HASKETT, Robert Lee,     May 31,1896 - June 19,1969

EVERGREEN CEMETERY (continued)

FERGUSON, Clarence Evonia,   1892 - 1952
              Son of Walter T. and Alice Harlowe Ferguson

TAYLOR, J. Lincoln,   Apr.4,1899 - Aug.12,1986
TAYLOR, Mary L.,   Feb.20,1903 - July 3,1970
MARTIN, Kathryn T.,   1929 - 1982

LEWIS, Hiram B.,   Mar.16,1864 - Mar.20,1954
              Son of Elex and Elizabeth Tipton Lewis
LEWIS, Kitty Guinn,   July 20,1878 - Oct.27,1961
              Dau. of Wm.E. and Mary Jane Woodward Guinn

TOWNSEND, Wilton J.,   Oct.17,1895 - Mar.15,1962
              Son of John Andy and Mittie Mobley Townsend
TOWNSEND, Lillian D., (w), Sept.13,1898 - Feb.19,1973
              Maiden name Duncan
TOWNSEND, Wilbur Eugene, (son),   June 26,1928 - Nov.4,1951

KEYS, Thomas Robinson,   Jan.25,1898 - Apr.24,1966
KEYS, Anne Vogle,   Jan.23,1898 - Nov.17,1987

DUFF, Charlotte Robinson,   Sept.30,1923 - Dec.16,1955
              Dau. of Tom Robinson

HARMON, Marion Isaac,   Oct.28,1897 - Sept.19,1953
              Son of C.L. Harmon
HARMON, Hazel E.,   Aug.10,1904 - Aug.7,1968

MITCHELL, William H.,   Mar.10,1898 - June 4,1959
              Son of George Victor and Margaret Musselwhite Mitchell
MITCHELL, Mildred,   Dec.20,1899 - Jan.16,1967

ADAMS, Charles W.,   Mar.7,1876 - Sept.17,1965 - Spanish American War
ADAMS, Mayme Helm,   July 26,1895 - Apr.8,1982

LEWIS, Otto Edward,   Dec.22,1912 - July 27,1965 -   USA   WW2

MOORE, William H.,   Dec.18,1886 - Apr.26,1961
              Son of James Edgar and Harriett Johnson Moore

BANKS, Cecil H.,   1905 - 1975   - USN   WW2
BANKS, Elsie M.,   Apr.19,1905 - May 9,1961
              Dau. of Jessee and Rhoda Margaret Jarvis Callahan

SHERER, Thomas Girard,   Oct.3,1878 - Oct.28,1963
              Son of William Davis and Mattie Moore Sherer
SHERER, Cora Bumgardner,   Aug.27,1884 - Jan.31,1981

ERWIN, Herman,   Jan.5,1892 - Oct.18,1967
ERWIN, Josie B.,   Aug.10,1887 - Feb.13,1980

HIXON, Lonnie L.,   Aug.26,1894 - Sept.23,1961
              Son of Andrew J. and Lora Holt Hixon
HIXON, Pearl Bible,   Aug.3,1894 - Dec.12,1969

HARRIS, Charles Gather,   Dec.28,1907 - Oct.9,1961

EVERGREEN CEMETERY  (continued)

BARNES, Arthur H.,    1901 - 1985
BARNES, Florence,    1900 -  -----
BARNES, James Vance,   Aug.28,1915 - May 11,1959
            Son of James Berry and Mary Randolph Barnes

MILLER, William B.,    1892 - 1964
            Son of James Patton and Candy Plemmons Miller

THORESEN, Carl T.,    May 13.1910 - Apr.24,1959

QUESENBERRY, Lida Moye,    1892 - 1964
            Dau. of Henry and America Ann World Moye
QUESENBERRY, Pauline,    1913 - 1987
QUESENBERRY, Nelsene,    Jan.4,1915 - Feb.15,1974

JONES, Donald Howard,    Mar.11,1912 - Dec.19,1961
JONES, Virginia Lee,    Jan.6,1916 - Mar.28,1983

EVERETT, Linda Sue,    d. Sept.28, 1961
            Dau. of William Ray and Shirley Ann Shields Everett

LANE, John A.,    1894 - 1969
LANE, Lula C.,    1897 - 1975

WYATT, Bill William,    Nov.10,1916 - Apr.2,1962   - USA   WW2

CAPPS, Delia E.,    1902 - 1988

SHIPLEY, Edward B.,    1884 - 1959
            Son of Nathan and Adeline Curtis Shipley
SHIPLEY, Mary L.,    1900 - 1980
            Maiden name Smith

HONEYCUTT, Lovada,    July 18,1884 - Jan.22,1961

JUSTICE, Thomas J.,    Mar.14,1898 - Apr.26,1960

REYNOLDS, John W.,    May 17,1891 - Feb.16,1970
REYNOLDS, Helen Marie,    Apr.13,1899 - Apr.28,1960
            Dau. of Theodore and Alma Marie Bronstop Brigel

BUNDY, Earl W.,    Apr.27,1896 - July 25,1957
            Son of William H. and Addie Hartsock Bundy

FENDER, Mary Jane,    1889 - 1983

WOHLFORD, Mary G.,    Mar.15,1913 - Feb.26,1986 - Capt. USMC   WW2

McKEITHAN, Glenn Richard,    1908 - 1982   - USA   WW2
McKEITHAN, Mary W.,    1912 -  -----

KIZER, Viola W.,    Jan.15,1911 - Oct.21,1987

YEAROUT, Fred H.,    Sept.8,1907 -  -----
YEAROUT, Ethel D.,    Sept.12,1904 -  -----

DeARMOND, James G.,    Dec.10,1870 - Oct.7,1940
DeARMOND, Nannie L.,    Nov.22,1884 - May 17,1971
DeARMOND, J.T. "Jack",   Aug.1,1905 - Nov.27,1966
DeARMOND, Mildred B.,(w), Aug.27,1906 - Apr.23,1980
DeARMOND, Rebecca,  (dau.),  b/d 1928

McNABB, Otto Harry,    Apr.11,1903 - June 26,1955
              Son of Robert G. and Katherine White McNabb
McNABB, Viola Lee,   Sept.9,1903 -  -----

BOOTH, Fred D.,    1891- 1956
              Son of W.H. and Margaret McInturff Booth
BOOTH, Jessie M.,    1894 - 1985

McNABB, Jack,   Mar.18,1906 - Oct.27,1969

MOORE, Margaret S.,    Aug.6,1918 - Feb.15,1975

SPARKS, Verge R.,    May 8,1897 - Aug.13,1979
SPARKS, Ruth C.,    July 10,1895 - Jan.15,1961
              Dau. of Robert and Nora Stewart Fleming

SAMS, Rufus M.,    July 13,1883 - Jan.11,1959
              Son of William A. and Sarah Gillis Sams
SAMS, Hettie P.,    July 4,1893 - Aug.30,1976
SAMS, Beulah,   Nov.25,1913 -  -----

WILSON, Della M.,   Sept.1,1887 - Aug.3,1961

BLANKENSHIP, William P.,    1875 - 1967
BLANKENSHIP, Ellen T., (w),  1885 - 1970

DYER, Mary Ann G.,    Jan.4,1933 - Dec.22,1960
              Dau. of Frank and Virginia Wade Crawford

McINTURFF, Robert J.,    Apr.9,1910 - Jan.13,1972  - USA

MOODY, John Roy, "MD",   Apr.17,1895 - Feb.28,1956
              Son of Joseph H. and Virginia Bula Wolfe Moody
MOODY, Mary Kathleen,  Aug.26,1903 - Dec.8,1982

DUNCAN, William M.,    July 25,1877 - July 23,1960
              Son of Thomas and Mary Shelton Duncan
DUNCAN, Mary,   Nov.30,1875 - Sept.19,1959
              Dau. of Abraham and Dempy Ann Bailey Bennett

ADKINS, G.D.,   Dec.13,1898 - Jan.1,1968

JONES, Claude,   1889 - 1973  - USA  WW1
JONES, Pearl C.,   1896 - 1986

DAVIS, Charles Dolton,   Apr.29,1872 - June 17,1962  - Capt.  WW1
DAVIS, Justine Daphne,   Sept.19,1894 - Feb.20,1987

HEADRICK, Joe Straley,   Feb.15,1888 - June 29,1956
    Son of Orville H. and Molly Brigsley Headrick
HEADRICK, Letha M.,   July 6,1887 - Dec.15,1972

BRYANT, Charlie W.,   Sept.2,1874 - Jan.25,1961
BRYANT, Cordelia M.,   Mar.28,1873 - June 26,1960

RICE, Creasy Higgins,   1906 - 1976

BLANKENSHIP, Horace F.,   Feb.7,1897 - Jan.22,1985
BLANKENSHIP, Mary F.,   Oct.16,1897 - Feb.20,1958
    Dau. of Lee W. and Ella F. McCarthy Sams

McINTOSH, Clifford M.,   Oct.13,1895 - Aug.26,1959
    Son of Andy and Delphin Blankenship McIntosh
McINTOSH, Annie T.,   Dec.30,1896 - Oct.23,1983

ADKINS, Stokes,   Sept.19,1883 - Mar.13,1953
    Son of W.H. and Amanda Hopson Adkins
ADKINS, Sallie,   June 28,1883 - Oct.20,1955
    Dau. of Wm. Bailey

VESTAL, James W.,   May 30,1885 - Aug.23,1953
    Son of Jess I. and Miranda Roe Vestal
VESTAL, Etta Florence,   Dec.3,1887 - Nov.11,1982

FOSTER, Walter,   1892 - 1978
FOSTER,   Sallie L.,   1885 - 1959

REAVIS, Lonnie H.,   Feb.10,1892 - Feb.26,1962
REAVIS, Elfrieda M.,   Nov.9,1897 - Feb.4,1984

SHELTON, Melvin M.,   May 19,1878 - July 17,1962
SHELTON, Pearl Guinn,   June 5,1885 - Aug.16,1979

BUCKLES, C.Harold,   1901 - 1987
BUCKLES, Myrtle S.,   1902 - 1978
    Dau. of M.M. and ˄earl Guinn Shelton

NORTON, Alfred H.,   Aug.17,1873 - Feb.16,1959
NORTON, Mary E.,   Aug.12,1878 - Oct.14,1972
NORTON, David L.,   1897 - 1988
NORTON, Harry Banner,   Apr.5,1905 - Nov.25,1966   - USA   WW2

BAILEY, Lowell Edwin,   1936 - 1967

BERGENDAHL, Oscar E.,   Jan.2,1891 - Oct.5,1960
    Son of Jacob Edward and Mary Sophia Hager Bergendahl
BERGENDAHL, Cora E.C.,   June 10,1895 - Jan.2,1987
    Maiden name Cuddy

DEATON, Joe,   Mar.1,1883 - Mar.4,1961

SILVER, Hugh James,   Dec.26,1916 - Oct.17,1961   - USA   WW2

BENNETT, Eliza W.,    1884 - 1961

HUGHES, Rex Allen,    died Nov.8,1961
            Infant son of Bill and Sheilah Hughes

PROCTER, Henry A.,    May 19,1908 - Aug.5,1964
PROCTER, Ora E.,    Nov.8,1902 - June 14,1961
            Dau. of James Norman

GRUBBS, Clara Maude,    Dec.2,1885 - Nov.2,1962

HUGHES, Daniel Whitt,    Jan.17,1902 - Sept.25,1962
HUGHES, Robert,    Apr.1,1917 - Oct.26,1966  - USA   WW2

HONEYCUTT, John D.,    Jan.17,1908 - Jan.28,1968
HONEYCUTT, Georgia,    Oct.25,1906 -  -----

VANCE, William C.,    Apr.30,1911 - May 26, 1982   USA   WW2
VANCE, Evelyn N., (w),  1912 - 1977

BAILEY, Addie H.,    Oct.16,1883 - Aug.25,1958
            Dau. of Pinkston and Lueretta Hensley Harris

MULKEY, E. Stanley,    Sept.9,1890 - Mar.26,1961

CARPENTER, M.L.,    Apr.17,1875 - May 5,1966
CARPENTER, Laura J.,    Mar.18,1877 - Apr.16,1962

BENNETT, Hannah H.,    1878 - 1962
            Dau. of Gaston Higgins

ANGEL, Gladys C.,    Feb.5,1927 - Apr.20,1958
            Dau. of Rudy and Janie Foster Chandler

LEWIS, Toney J.,    Oct.16,1926 - Jan.3,1969

SMITH Pearl H.,    1923 - 1971

HAMPTON, Clay,    Oct.29,1889 - July 14,1957  - USA   WW1

SHELTON, Anna M.,    1926 - 1962

LINGERFELT, Audie,    1908 -  -----
LINGERFELT, Addie M.,    1910 - 1972
LINGERFELT, David,    1886 - 1968
LINGERFELT, Lydia,    1877 - 1957

HARRIS, Grant,    1889 - 1972
HARRIS, Bertha,    1889 - 1956
HARRIS, David,    June 1,1891 - May 26,1961
            Son of William and Oma Edwards Harris
HARRIS, Isabell,    Mar.18,1897 - Mar.16,1987

TILSON, Lee Roy,    Dec.10,1880 - May 6,1956
TILSON, Emma,    Apr.13,1882 - May 17,1965

McNABB, Hubert,   Mar.20,1894 - Nov.30,1958   USA   WW1
          Son of Isaac and Elizabeth Starnes McNabb
McNABB, Betty G.,   Aug.19,1902 - Sept.25,1979
          Maiden name Adams

RAY, Thomas E.,   Sept.19,1901 - July 24,1971
RAY, Kate Sparks,   Aug.14,1905 - Apr.3,1956
          Dau. of Henry and Loretta Harris Sparks

HUSKINS, Joseph M.,   1890 - 1953
HUSKINS, Alice,   Nov.4,1890 - Mar.18,1973

NORRIS, Linda Darnell,   Oct.25,1942 - Aug.8,1958
          Dau. of Jerry and Pauline Slagle Norris

SLAGLE, W.D. "Bill",   Dec.21,1898 - Sept.16,1962

GARLAND, Donald,   June 27,1898 - Oct.23,1966  - USA   PFC
GARLAND, Chlora D.,   Nov.11,1905 - Dec.5,1953
          Dau. of Joe and Dolly Renfro Deaton

TIPTON, Cleviland,   May 12,1894 - Apr.1,1961   USA   WW1
TIPTON, Essie,   Feb.17,1902 - June 1,1985

MOORE, Rhu Hammie,   Apr.18,1892 - Nov.16,1982

CARTER, James M. "Dutch",   Sept.25,1884 - May 1,1957
          Son of Jerome and Eva Pardue Carter

WAY, D. Newman,   July 25,1892 - May 2,1975
WAY, Laura Randolph,   Jan.14,1904 - Apr.17,1984

LINFERFELT, Louella B.,   Jan.25,1911 - Jan.23,1963

SHELL, David C.,   Jan.16,1897 - Feb.19,1957
SHELL, Martha M.,   Aug.2,1892 - Sept.27,1961

BOWMAN, James E.,   1904 - -----
BOWMAN, Sally G.,   1912 - -----

BOONE, Roy A.,   Mar.19,1906 - Jan.30,1960
          Son of Hiram Kelse and Hannah Edge Boone

BECKELHIMER, Arch F.,   Apr.29,1887 - Jan.30,1957
          Son of W.D. and H.E. Vance Beckelhimer

SAMS, Frank L.,   Mar.31,1901 - July 18,1956
          Son of John B. and Eliza Emeline Guinn Sams

MASHBURN, Alvin,   Nov.10,1904 - Mar.1,1959
          Son of Jake and Nancy Sams Mashburn

McINTURFF, Alfred F.,   1886 - 1964
          Son of John Wesley and Julia Ann Rowe McInturff
McINTURFF, Amner R.,   1885 - 1967

EVERGREEN CEMETERY (continued)

OLLIS, James,   1899 - 1966
OLLIS, Pearl T.,   1906 - 1984

RICE, Newberry,   July 2,1887 - Oct.9,1972
RICE, Leota B.,   May 24,1889 - July 4,1956
          Dau. of Joseph and Polly Melinda Runion Blankenship

WALKER, William B.,   1891 - 1977
WALKER, Maggie D.,   1890 - -----

GOFORTH, Joseph Orr,   Feb.19,1892 - Aug.19,1969
GOFORTH, Bessie A.,   Feb.28,1889 - Mar.27,1956
          Dau. of William and Jerome Mosteller

ROSS, Cora Lee,   May 25,1903 - Feb.12,1986

GENTRY, Kathryn E.,   June 27,1895 - Dec.12,1963
          Dau. of Robert L. and Frances Cross Ross

WIGGAND, Oscar,   1897 - 1955
          Son of Peter Paul and ----- Martin Wiggand

LOUDY, Chessie White,   1887 - 1955
          Dau. of Daniel and Elizabeth Rose White
LOUDY, Myrtle Mae,   1888 - 1955
          Dau. of Daniel and Elizabeth Rose White

SPARKS, Fred J.,   Mar.31,1916 - Jan.15,1964
          Son of Virgil and Ruth Flemming Sparks

PARDUE, Paul Hilbert,   Aug.1,1909 - Oct.12,1959   - USN   WW2
          Son of S.B. and Flora Hilbert Pardue

HARRIS, Billy Joe,   Aug.8,1932 - Sept.16,1987
HARRIS, Mildred White,   Feb.16,1932 - -----
HARRIS, Johnny Gene,   Dec.5,1941 - Oct.30,1966   - USMC

HARRIS, Willie,   Sept.14,1906 - Apr.14,1982
HARRIS, Stella,   (w),   Dec.4,1909 - Dec.3,1963
          Dau. of John Anderson and Cora Johnson Duncan

WITCHER, William A.,   Apr.14,1894 - Feb.21,1963
          Son of W.R. and Rebecca Sammon Witcher
WITCHER, Mae Buckner,   Aug.13,1901 - -----

WITCHER, Sam E.,   Aug.30,1902 - Feb.27,1971
WITCHER, Effie W.,   Aug.18,1907 - Nov.24,1987

WITCHER, John,   Aug.9,1898 - Aug.9,1977
WITCHER, Emma,   July 16,1900 - June 19,1981

SARTAIN, Henry G.,   Feb.22,1893 - Jan.25,1978   - USA   WW1

RIDDLE, Jim,   1894 - 1962

<u>EVERGREEN CEMETERY</u>  (continued)

LINGERFELT, Edward, "Edd",   May 18,1901 - Jan.21,1970

HAMPTON, Annie Mae,   Sept.16,1907 - Feb.27,1963
            Wife of W.A. Hampton

BLANKENSHIP, Oscar R.,   Dec.21,1887 - Apr.12,1963
BLANKENSHIP, Bertha Phillips, (w),   Feb.18,1891 - Apr.28,1969

HENSLEY, Artie Jane,   May 8,1903 - Nov.41,1970

BENNETT, Mable Ingram,   1911 - 1962
            Dau. of Sam and Lilly Phillips Ingram

HENSLEY, Dock,   1906 - 1974
HENSLEY, Easie V.,  (w),   1909 - 1963

BAILEY, Theron,   June 4,1911 - Apr.10,1976

SAMS, David,   1961 -1976

LINGERFELT, Roger Lee,   Feb.5,1953 - Feb.7,1972

BAILEY, Jesse,   1912 - 1986

SHELTON, Robert C.,   Jan.7,1947 - Dec.26,1986

CAMPBELL, Zack,   Mar.1,1906 - Sept.23,1984
CAMPBELL, Grace P.,   Sept.29,1915 -  -----

BRITTON, Tommy J.,   1929 - 1988
BRITTON, Joann L.,   1932 - 1988

WHITSON, Ralph,   1913 -  -----
WHITSON, June,   1924 - 1988

HUGHES, Howard W.,   1915 -  -----
HUGHES, Mae F.,   1917 -  -----
HUGHES, Pamela G.,   1956 -  -----

THOMPSON, Gary Joe,   Aug.31,1938 - June 1,1984

BRITTINGHAM, Vernon C. Jr.,   May 9,1965 - Aug.23,1986

WILLIAMS, Michael Wayne,   May 26,1954 - Aug.22,1986 - USN Vietnam
WILLIAMS, Nicholas Lee,   (no dates)
WILLIAMS, Samantha Marie,   (no dates)

SPARKS, Herman,   1908 - 1988
SPARKS, Bethel,   1905 -  -----

CORLEW, Harry,   1914 - 1982

MASHBURN, William Vance,   1918 -  -----
MASHBURN, Thelma M.,  (w),   1923 - 1986

EVERGREEN CEMETERY (continued)

RENFRO, Walton Lockett, 1901 - 1981 - USA WW2
RENFRO, Beulah, June 20,1928 - -----

McHENRY, Mary C., 1903 - -----

JOHNSON, Emma V., 1900 - 1988

WILSON, Florence M., 1917 - -----

CARPENTER, Harry, 1906 - 1981
CARPENTER, Edith, (w), 1912 - 1985
          Dau. of Charles and Sally McIntosh Campbell

LOVETTE, Billy Gene, Mar.28,1958 - Nov.3,1984 - USA
LOVETTE, Patricia Lynn, Aug.8,1956 - -----

BRITTON, Callie C., Dec.4,1888 - Oct.11,1981

HARVEY, Robert H., 1911 - -----
HARVEY, Dorothy R., (w), 1913 - -----

DEATON, Geter, 1895 - 1988
DEATON, Martha, 1904 - -----
DEATON, Glen, Nov.18,1926 - Oct.22,1986 - USA Korea

COLEMAN, Lloyd M., May 25,1917 - June 26,1985 - USA WW2
COLEMAN, Elva A., 1920 - -----

LEWIS, L. Bernie, 1906 - -----
LEWIS, Lillian C., (w), 1907 - -----

INGRAM, Elizabeth Katy, Sept.5,1929 - Jan.4,1986

HAMPTON, Annie, 1917 - 1984

TAPP, Cecil F., Oct.2,1921 - June 27,1988 - USA WW2

JOHNSON, Hazel Dean, 1908 - 1987

HARRELL, Kathleen, 1925 - 1984

DEATON, Briscoe, Dec.27,1907 - -----
DEATON, Elizabeth F., (w), Sept.24,1912 - June 22,1979

TOLLEY, Claude, 1907 - 1985

WILLIS, Harold Vestal, 1928 - 1976 - USA Korea

MILLER, Eleanor Leana, 1952 - 1979

SAMS, Minervia, 1898 - 1980

PARKER, Roy Edward, May 16,1913 - Sept.19,1983
PARKER, Ola Margie L., Dec.16,1918 - -----

MATHES, Luther David, June 8,1925 - Sept.27,1981

WRIGHT, Janie Gentry,    Feb.14,1934 - Dec.11,1977

HENSLEY, Willard E.,    1912 - -----
HENSLEY, Evie H., (w),   1915 - -----

JONES, Ralph H.,   1912 - 1981
JONES, Harriett W.,    1921 - -----

HENSLEY, Henry,    1882 - 1979

HARRIS, Jake F.,    1893 - 1979
HARRIS, Cora Lee,  (w),  1892 - 1979

HARRIS, Alfred E.,    1906 - 1983
HARRIS, Ruby K.,  (w),  1913 - -----

HENLEY, Vance J.,    1902 - 1975
HENLEY, Hazel M.,    1907 - -----

SALMON, J. McClure Jr.,   1903 - 1986
SALMON, Marguerite T.,    1896 - 1981

LEWIS, Harold D.,    1931 - 1977  - USAF Korea
LEWIS, Yoshie I.,    1932 - -----

DAVIS, Rev. Verno H.,    1915 - -----
DAVIS, Gaynell,   1922 - -----

DAVIS, Gerald Lynn,    1951 - 1974   -   USA

MILLER, Texie G.,    1901 - 1988

TOLLEY, Ada Lucy,    1935 - 1979

HUTCHINS, James W.,   Mar.16,1916 - May 3,1980
HUTCHINS, Hubert,   1918 - 1982  - USA WW2

LANE, Robert Flem,   1923 - 1981  - USA  WW2

BEAVER, Delzie F.,    Aug.3,1905 - Mar.25,1984

TONEY, Jimmy,   Aug.9,1971 - Jan.3,1984

FOSTER, Cordelia,   1895 - 1984

LEWIS, Ford,   1911 - 1981

RUSSO, Dorothy L.,    1931 - 1980

TILSON, Ross,   1916 - 1978   -  USMC  WW2

WILLIAMS, Roger T.,   Apr.11,1956 - Nov.7,1977

HARRIS, Homer,    1924 - 1975   -USA  WW2

EVERGREEN CEMETERY (continued)

ASPIN, A. Wayne, July 26,1899 - Mar.28,1980
ASPIN, Alice E., May 20,1906 - -----

TIPTON, Gertha Pearl, 1898 - 1975

TONEY, Reid, 1904 - 1972

NORRIS, Hallie Parkey, Aug.16,1897 - Nov.19,1972

DODSON, Randall Eugene, July 6,1957 - Oct.16,1973

RAMSEY, Will, July 4.1902 - Mar.25,1975

TIPTON, Josiephine, 1912 - -----
TIPTON, Samuel H., "Sambo", 1925 - 1986
TIPTON, Willard R.C., Apr.27,1931 - Feb.21,1976 - USA Korea Vietnam

HARRIS, Zade, 1914 - 1977 - USA WW2

SILVER, Ruby Blanche, Oct.5,1924 - Aug.27,1979

WILLIS, Kyle Franklin, 1925 - 1979 - USCG WW2

BLAIR, Hazel Nelson, Dec.15,1914 - Apr.21,1974

HUGHES, Dolphus, 1896 - 1988

LONG, William M., Dec.31,1905 - Aug.15,1973
LONG, Cora M., (w), Dec.25,1910 - -----

HARDING, Sarah Ann, May 27,1893 - June 7,1981

CALLAWAY, James Luther, 1923 - 1975 - USA

BLANKENSHIP, Barry, 1912 - 1988
BLANKENSHIP, Mildred S., (w), 1909 - -----

ADKINS, Eugene, June 15,1914 - -----

FOSTER, Lee Roy, 1902 - 1973
FOSTER, Leora, 1904 - -----

SHELTON, Bob, Apr.25,1907 - Feb.7,1973

HUGHES, Walter A. Sr., Aug.16,1905 - May 9,1972
HUGHES, Dollie M., (w), May 11,1909 - -----

KANE, Charles Eugene, died June 8,1973 - Infant

MOORE, Gary E., Jan.30,1946 - June 27,1972

HARVELL, George W., 1901 - 1983
HARVELL, Mary Beatrice, (w), 1923 - 1987

BENNETT, Earnest, Jan.24,1901 - June 22,1972 - USA WW2

MASHBURN, Porter C., 1912 - 1972
MASHBURN, Hachita H., (w), 1915 - -----

MOSS, Frank H. Sr., Sept.12,1892 - Apr.24,1972 - USA WW1
MOSS, Gladys R., Jan.14,1897 - -----

FOSTER, Virginia Cook, Feb.15,1915 - June 23,1987

LEWIS, Ralph, 1920 - 1974 - USN
LEWIS, Edna S., July 27,1923 - -----
LEWIS, Rex, June 8,1894 - Apr.4,1984
LEWIS, Lena T., Feb.14,1913 - -----

RENFRO, Ernest Homer, Apr.30,1907 - Nov.30,1980

SNAPP, Ivan Shields, May 1,1903 - Oct.23,1983

SWINGLE, James Vincent, May 31,1889 - Nov.13,1971
SWINGLE, George D., Nov.15,1922 - May 19,1973 - USAF WW2

TAPP, Lloyd, Dec.12,1918 - -----
TAPP, Ennis, Nov.10,1920 - -----

BROWN, Bennie B., Aug.30,1900 - Dec.10,1985
BROWN, Bertie S., Apr.15,1909 - -----

RICE, Jesse A., May 28,1912 - Nov.2,1975
RICE, Eunice P., ----- - -----

BARNES, William Carl, June 27,1904 - Mar.1,1982
BARNES, Olive P., Oct.2,1913 - -----

HENDRIX, Harold H., Feb.17,1910 - Aug.14,1986

PRATT, Jess Lindsey, Sept.11,1895 - May 24,1978

CHAPMAN, William Blake, Feb.29,1920 - May 25,1981
CHAPMAN, Billie Price, June 2,1922 - -----

JAMISON, Terry R., 1942 - 1987

McCURRY, L.E., June 21,1912 - -----
McCURRY, Mary E., (w), Nov.3,1908 - Jan.30,1983

GUINN, Foy Webb, June 18,1909 - May 18,1978

OAKLEY, Turley Milton, Jan.20,1913 - -----
OAKLEY, Elsie Price, Feb.5,1913 - -----

BLANKENSHIP, Troy, June 20,1917 - May 27,1984 - USA WW2
BLANKENSHIP, Carrie, July 29,1911 - -----

MIXON, Nevin Luke, Oct.16,1910 - Aug.6,1986
MIXON, Ethel Jo, Sept.22,1915 - Nov.3,1974

EVERGREEN CEMETERY (continued)

HUMPHREYS, Loomis,   May 10,1925 -  -----
HUMPHREYS, Zoe,   Aug.20,1922 -  -----

BISE, Cora R.,   Apr.20,1905 - Apr.7,1984

McDANIEL, Kitty Sue,   1947 -  -----

CLOUTIER, Arthur J.,   1920 -1984
CLOUTIER, Betty A.,   1934 -  -----

GILLIS, W. Lattie,   Nov.18,1888 -May 5,1982
GILLIS, Vivian B.,   Mar.25,1896 - Jan.2,1967

TIPTON, Isaac D.,   Nov.17,1902 -  -----
TIPTON, Ruth R.,   (w),   July 20,1918 - July 9,1984

LIGHT, Willard,   Sept.18,1940 -  -----
LIGHT, Dorothy Sue,   Oct.25,1940 - Mar.22,1976
LIGHT, Linda Kay,   July 23.1950 -  -----

SLEMONS, J.R.,   1922 -  -----
SLEMONS, Mary,   1918 - 1977

McCURRY, Fred,   Apr.15,1910 -  -----
McCURRY, Cindy, (w),   Mar.6,1910 -  -----

GRAYBEAL, John W. Sr.,   Aug.10,1927 -  -----
GRAYBEAL, Gladys E.,   Oct.17,1926 - Dec.14,1985

SAWYER, Odell,   -----  -  -----
SAWYER, Kathryn,   -----  -  -----

EDWARDS, Dan,   Apr.30,1903 - July 31,1981
EDWARDS, Grace,   Feb.5,1911 -  -----

WILSON, Willard Tommy,   Dec.12,1941 - June 4,1984

PETERSON, Robert W.,   Jan.16,1891 - July 2,1987

SMITH, Betty Chandley,   Feb.19,1930 - Feb.4,1970

CROWDER, James Henry,   Aug.21,1909 - June 1,1978 -  USA
CROWDER, Edna L.,   Aug.28,1914 - May 9,1973

HONEYCUTT, Fred D.,   1933 - 1983
HONEYCUTT, Anna L.,   1931 -  -----

TIPTON, Britt,   1904 - 1973
TIPTON, Kittie E.,   (w),   1910 -  -----

THOMPSON, Tiney B.,   1884 - 1981

TIPTON, Roger Earl,   1931 - 1974

CHANDLER, Fred S.,   Jan.9,1905 -  -----
CHANDLER, Daisy,   July 18,1920 -  -----

MILLER, Phil,   May 22,1918 -  -----
MILLER, Ira B.,  (w),  June 2,1922 -  -----

WHITSON, Russell,   July 7,1916 -  -----
WHITSON, Cordella B.,  (w),  Nov.22,1926 -  -----

COOPER, David,   Feb.10,1924 -  -----
COOPER, Edith, (w),  Jan.1,1920 - Aug.20,1977

SMITH, Charles P.,   Apr.27,1886 - May 2,1978
SMITH, Irene A.,   Jan.5,1922 -  -----

COOPER, Ida Bell Castell,   Aug.23,1942 - Oct.3,1980

McNABB, David Wintzer,   1908 - 1988
McNABB, Ruth Turner,   1909 - 1980

HARRIS, Clark G.,   May 24,1913 - July 12,1975

TIPTON, Chris,   Feb.5,1911 - Feb.1,1976

McKNIGHT, Charles Ross,   1895 - 1976  - USA   WW1
McKNIGHT, Bessie S.,   1893 - 1983

RAMSEY, Dennis,   1911 - 1982
RAMSEY, Viola,   1914 -  -----

BRADFORD, Arthur,   Jan.30,1902 - Apr.4,1983
BRADFORD, Miliam,   Mar.30,1917 -  -----

LEDFORD, Foster,   Oct.12,1922 -  -----
LEDFORD, Faye,   Aug.7,1932 -  -----

TIPTON, Jasper,   1902 - 1973
TIPTON, Bonnie,   1908 -  -----

STARNES, Jack Martin,   1957 - 1974

ADKINS, Hubert H.,   July 8,1918 - Oct.3,1975
ADKINS, Lula H.,   Jan.31,1922 -  -----

BARNETT, Earl Sr.,   Dec.25,1913 -  -----
BARNETT, Helen Pauline,   Nov.4,1921 - Apr.30,1980

RAMSEY, Luther,   Nov.12,1906 - Feb.20,1984
RAMSEY, Amanda,   Apr.4,1907 -  -----

JONES, Billy Gene,   July 21,1934 - Sept.11,1984

WATSON, D. Ralph,   Nov.4,1906 - May 15,1978
WATSON, Florence H., (w),  Nov.10,1907 -  -----

ADKINS, Craig,   Sept.14,1963 - July 1,1985

EDWARDS, Harley,   Dec.18,1912 -  -----
EDWARDS, Bertha,   May 5,1914 - May 21,1984
HUGHES, R.B.,   Feb.2,1917 - July 18,1980

SHOOK, Buford, Apr.28,1940 -  -----
SHOOK, Erlene, (w),  July 12,1944 - Apr.18,1980
SHOOK, Buford Carrol,   1971 - 1974

SHOOK, Camery,   July 24,1907 - Dec.3,1984
SHOOK, Hattie M., (w),  Feb.26,1910 - Aug.9,1988

McINTOSH, Gerald R.,   Mar.19, 1938 -  -----
McINTOSH, Eula J., (w),  Jan.30,1938 -  -----

McINTOSH, Carl S.,   Nov.24,1901 - Sept.11,1972
McINTOSH, Viola R., (w),  Mar.9,1902 -  -----

GRINDSTAFF, Oscar,   Sept,21,1916 -  -----
GRINDSTAFF, Evelyn,   May 2,1922 -  -----

MOORE, Rufus S.,   Jan.12,1892 - Sept.1,1970

WATTS, Fred,   Mar.3,1908 - Apr.30,1983
          Son of Roy and Lizzie Ingle Watts
WATTS, Ethel,   Apr.20,1911 -  -----
          Dau. of Jim and Mary Randolph Barnes

EDWARDS, John H.,   Sept.11,1903 - June 28,1972

JONES, John Robert,   Dec.1,1914 - Jan.4,1974  - USA   WW2

LYLE, William, "Bill",   1912 - 1972

KIRK, James Ralph,   1905 - 1974
KIRK, Mable Davis, (w),  1908 -  -----

CUMMING, James, E.,   Mar.31,1897 - Mar.16,1975
CUMMING, Margaret M.,   May 9,1904 - Aug.26,1976

COGGINS, John R.,   1901 - 1976
COGGINS, Lona D.,   1904 - 1987

BURLESON, David C.,   Apr.7,1898 - Mar.23,1981
BURLESON, Pollie M., (w),  June 16,1908 -  -----

MARTIN, Betsy Morley, Jan.14,1953 - Mar.29,1977

DUNCAN, Clarence,   Apr.11,1909 - Feb.24,1983
DUNCAN, Hassie, (w),  Nov.9,1906 - June 15,1977

EDWARDS, Gurnie J.,   Sept.23,1944 - Mar.23,1979
EDWARDS, Shelia K., (w),  Sept.10,1948 -  -----

EDWARDS, Jess,   Apr.1,1903 - May 25,1984
EDWARDS, Pearl,   Mar.30,1904 - Oct.25,1982

EVERGREEN CEMETERY (continued)

NIDIFFER, John,    May 13,1912 - Nov.26,1986
NIDIFFER, Lela,    Sept.27,1915 - May 18,1980

RENFRO, Debbie,    May 17, 1957 - Oct.25,1978

MILLER, Carl E.,    Sept.23,1904 - July 25,1986
MILLER, Dora K., (w),  Jan.31,1908 -  -----

ANDERSON, John Alf,    Oct.22,1888 - June 25,1977
ANDERSON, Margaret M.,  (w),  Jan.6,1889 - Mar.21,1985

BUCHANAN, Stokes Milton,    Dec.20,1897 - May 22,1977
BUCHANAN, Fern McGuire, (w),  Oct.12,1905 -  -----

JOHNSON, Edwin Lee,    Sept.22,1927 - Dec.12,1976
JOHNSON, Martha M.,    Apr.17,1925 - Sept.22,1974
JOHNSON, Evelyn L.,    Nov.9,1932 -  -----

WHITE, Fieldon,    Apr.16,1908 -  -----
WHITE, Minnie, (w),    May 9,1910 - Aug.1,1977
WHITE, Hilda, (dau.), Aug.20,1939 -  -----

HARRIS, Eugene B.,    1935 - 1988

AKERS, Robert E.,    Sept.15,1890 - Feb.24,1978
AKERS, Lena M.,    Jan.6,1892 - Nov.10,1976
AKERS, Hugh David, Sept.8,1923 - Jan.1,1974  - USA   WW2

WILLIS, Homer,    Dec.12,1907 - Oct.9,1973
WILLIS, Marie, (w), July 15,1918 - Mar.21,1987

HENSLEY, William F.,    Nov.14,1895 - May 18,1973  - USA   WW1
HENSLEY, Bertha L.,    July 10,1898 -  -----

HAMPTON, John F.,    July 17,1904 -  -----
HAMPTON, Rosetta, (w),  May 26,1907

MILLER, Hobart G.,    Jan.16,1909 -  -----
MILLER, Amanda W.,    Nov.27,1909 -  -----

WILSON, Isaac,    1898 - 1972
WILSON, Etta B.,    1898 - 1979

LOVE. Earl Raymond,    May 28,1901 - Sept.13,1977

MILLER, Roscoe,    Oct.2,1898 - Sept.3,1971
MILLER, Ruby,    Apr.21,1900 -  -----

HARRIS, Buddy Eugene,    Dec.20,1929 - Feb.5,1975
HARRIS, Texie A.,    Jan.2,1904 - Dec.10,1986

HELTON, William Carson,    Apr.3,1909 - Sept.30,1974
HELTON, Stella,    June 26,1916 - Mar.25,1974

SIMS, Vernon W.,    Apr.2,1908 - Aug.28,1985
SIMS, Mary Cochran,    Sept.23,1910 - June 8,1975

EVERGREEN CEMETERY (continued)

MASTERS, Frederick C.,    1941 - 1987

STREET, Darrell R.,    Mar.12,1951 - June 9,1975
STREET, Lola M.,    Feb.16,1951 -  -----

WAGNER, Jack,    July 18,1917 - Dec.2,1983  - USA   WW2
WAGNER, Nelle,    Aug.15,1925 -  -----

COLLIS, Steve,    Apr.8,1927 - Oct.8,1986
COLLIS, Florine J.,    Aug.20,1932 -  -----
COLLIS, Angela Jill,    Jan.18,1963 - Nov.18,1974

TRUE, James E., Sr.,    Nov.25,1903 - Feb.11,1977

ZENTMEYER, D.T.,    Sept.6,1898 - May 17,1985
ZENTMEYER, F.N.,    Aug.25,1903 -  -----

TIPTON, ___,    1929 - 1980

WILLIS, Charles Sidney,    June 24,1931 - Oct.15,1980 - USA Korea
WILLIS, Amolee, Edwards,    Feb.19,1935 -  -----                Vietnam

FOSTER, Garney M.,    June 6,1910 - July 8,1979
FOSTER, Evelyn R.,    Dec.17,1927 -  -----

FOSTER, Ernest J.,    Apr.27,1938 - Jan.14,1982  - PFC USA

SHELL, April Ann,    Mar.18,1985 - July 24,1988

MARTIN, Bernard,    Aug.15,1930 -  -----
MARTIN, Hettie, (w),    Feb.9,1917 - June 12,1981

GORDON, Henry W., Jr.,    Aug.22,1929 - Apr.16,1982 - USN Korea

WHITSON, Zack,    May 22,1906 - Dec.20,1981
WHITSON, Marcella C.,    May 8, 1911 -  -----

TIPTON, Bessie Pauline,    Aug.13,1927 - Mar.15,1979

YATES, Ralph Lee,    May 18,1937 - Sept.12,1977
YATES, Jeannette Elaine,    July 28,1941 -  -----

McINTOSH, John Dallas,    Sept.10,1923 - Apr.25,1977 - USA   WW2
McINTOSH, Mary Grace,    Aug.12,1927 - May 13,1987

MORRIS, Raymond,    -----   -   -----
MORRIS, Beulah Wampler,    -----   -   -----

RICE, Frank,    1919 - 1975  - Pvt  USA

HUSKINS, Mary Ann,    1941 - 1988

HUSKINS, Robert H.,    Dec.12,1903 - July 13,1982
HUSKINS, Bessie T.,    Apr.26,1905 - 1988

EVERGREEN CEMETERY (continued)

ARROWOOD, Cora,   July 18,1897 - Sept.12,1976

ARROWOOD, Landon,   Aug.2,1921 -  -----
ARROWOOD, Pauline W., (w),   Oct.8,1922 - June 24,1983

ARROWOOD, Douglas A.,   July 14,1946 - Mar.23,1974

MALLETT, Robert, Sr.,   1892 - 1972
MALLETT, Edna,   1892 - 1975

THOMAS, Jennie I.,   Aug.20,1902 - Oct.28,1970

NELSON, Ottis V.,   May 3,1915 - May 22,1982
NELSON, Ruth E.,   June 5,1919 -  -----

WAYNICK, Robert William,   Feb.24,1893 - Oct.3,1982
WAYNICK, Hattie Shoun,   1895 - 1982

KEESECKER, Preston B.,   July 15,1905 - Sept.6,1977
KEESECKER, Beulah,   May 29,1917 -  -----

BURNETT, John R.,   1932 - 1974

FOSTER, Clarence D.,   Aug.26,1924 - Dec.12,1973   -PFC USMC
FOSTER, Virginia Belle,   ----- - -----

WILSON, Martin, Sr.,   1888 - 1984
WILSON, Rosie,   ----- - -----

WEXLER, Madeline M.,   1917 - 1988

PIPPIN, J.H. "Jack",   1910 - 1986
PIPPIN, M.Hazel Mauk,   1912 -  -----

PEEK, Harry Smith,   1914 - 1980  - USA  WW2

HIGGINS, Carmon E.,   1903 - 1980
HIGGINS, Carrie R.,   1905 - 1984

O'BRIEN, Albert T.,   Dec.25,1901 - Sept.1,1964

GRIFFITH, Guy,   Mar.13,1927 - Sept.14,1979
GRIFFITH, Willia,   Apr.12,1934 -  -----

JONES, Oscar H.,   Aug.30,1916 -  -----
JONES, Geneva,   June 25,1918 - Mar.23,1983

RENFRO, Thomas J.,   Feb.6,1921 - July 6,1983 - PFC USA  WW2
RENFRO, Kathleen,   Jan.23,1939 -  -----

YELTON, George,   Jan.29,1926 -  -----
YELYON, Mamie,   June15,1928 - July 7,1986

LEDFORD, Dorsie,   Jan.15,1918 - Nov.12,1983  - USA
LEDFORD, Ruby L.,   Mar.12,1923 -  -----

EVERGREEN CEMETERY  (continued)

HOYLE, J.B.,    Sept.30,1927 - Aug.20,1985
HOYLE, Flornia M.,    Apr.24,1932 -  -----

RICE, Alfred A. "Be",    June 2,1923 - Aug.22,1983 -   USN   WW2
RICE, Gertrude Shell,    -----   -   -----

TIPTON, Bascom,    Sept.23,1906 - Oct.10,1984
TIPTON, Lela,    Dec.14,1914 -  -----

EDWARDS, Loyd G.,    Nov.25,1917 - Apr.18,1982  - USA   WW2

HAGER, Viola R.,    Nov.17,1922 - Oct.19,1981

HONEYCUTT, Ernest,    Jan.22,1915 - Sept.15,1986
HONEYCUTT, Nervia B.,    Feb.10,1915 -  -----

SUMLIN, Robert Jay,    Oct.10,1915 - Jan.22,1981
SUMLIN, Cleo T.,    Apr.2,1920 -  -----

HELTON, Kenneth J.,    Oct.26,1928 -  -----
HELTON, Vearl B.,    Sept.12,1925 - Feb.6,1979

HIGGINS, Rev. Horace,    Feb.6,1914 -  -----
HIGGINS, Gladys,    Aug.9,1925 -  -----

HENSLEY, Jerry Lee,    Mar.9,1959 - June 4,1978

STREET, Martha,    Feb.16,1900 - Sept.10,1964

WILLIAMSON, Rev.Robert S.,    Dec.30,1921 - May 14,1975

HENSLEY, Forrest C.,    June 29,1921 - May 15,1974
HENSLEY, Reva M.,    Feb.16,1927 -  -----

MILLER, Charlie,    Jan.17,1887 - May 23,1979
MILLER, Dollie, (w),    Apr.10,1891 - June 10,1982

BURNETT, Finley Reed,    1908 - 1984
BURNETT, Lola Hensley,    Oct.14,1909 - June 17,1976

WILSON, Ray,    Aug.13,1920 - Mar.8,1983   - USA   WW2
WILSON, Phyllis May,    July 1,1917 -  -----

MARTIN, Grant M.,    Sept.30,1892 - June 3,1976   - USA   WW1
MARTIN, Mamie L.,    July 9,1899 - July 30,1977

STREET, Charlie P.,    June 18,1918 - Oct.8,1977   -  USA   WW2
STREET, Hazel T.,    Oct.22,1917 - Nov.14,1983

MOORE, Arnold B.,    Oct.28,1916 -  -----
BRACKINS, Bertha,    June 1,1897 - Aug.25,1978

MATHES, Oscar,    1911 - 1971
MATHES, Thelma H.,    1917 -  -----

LUSK, Frank,    July 17,1909 - Mar.24,1984
LUSK, Essie E.,    Apr.19,1913 - Jan.9,1985

BAKER, John E.,    Feb.25,1910 - May 6,1977

EMERY, William P.,    1948 - 1984

TIPTON, Fred G.,    Dec.17,1906 - July 19,1974   - USMC

HEDRICK, Deckard,    Nov.23,1908 - Mar.17,1981   - PFC USA   WW2

BOWLING, Henry F.,    Nov.6,1922 -  -----
BOWLING, L. Geraldine,    Dec.18,1933 - Apr.1,1975

LEWIS, Dock,    June 28,1931 -  -----
LEWIS, June,    Dec.4,1935 -  -----

RICKER, Ruble,    Nov.25,1909 - Jan.22,1978
RICKER, Maude, (w),    May 7,1915 -  -----

CHANDLER, Kenneth E.,    Feb.25,1908 -  -----
CHANDLER, Elsie Hensley,    Oct.25,1913 -  -----

THOMAS, Virgil F.,    Jan.25,1917 -  -----
THOMAS Laura L.,    Mar.15,1923 -  -----

HENSLEY, Patsy Strickler,    Apr.25,1941 - Sept.9,1986

PEAKE, William C.,    Jan.6,1926 - Dec.13,1981   - USA   WW2

ROBERTS, Jesse L.,    May 29,1936 -  -----
ROBERTS, Daisy,    Apr.15,1920 - June 12,1982

PETERSON, Sarah Christina,    July 9,1983 - Apr.30,1984
            Dau. of Robert K. and Patricia Peterson

AMBROSE, Richard,    May 12,1947 - Mar.25,1984

AMBROSE, J.L.,    June 18,1916 -  -----
AMBROSE, Helen R.,    June 17,1916 -  -----

TEAGUE, Paul A.,    Sept.9,1937 - Jan.30,1985
TEAGUE, Mary E.,    Nov.22,1938 -  -----

BLANKENSHIP, Ernest,    Mar.17,1915 - Nov.28,1986   - WW2
BLANKENSHIP, Myrtie,    May 15,1901 - June 22,1987

FANNING, Everett F.,    -----  -  -----
FANNING, Eunice L.,    Mar.20,1921 - May 9,1984

ADKINS, Will,    Oct.24,1908 - Mar.2,1985
ADKINS, Ina,  (w),    Oct.13,1914 -  -----

WAMPLER, Kay Waterbury,    1924 - 1982

EVERGREEN CEMETERY  (continued)

WILSON, Bruce B.,    July 4,1931 - Feb.2,1988
WILSON, Patricia A.,    Jan.23,1936 - Feb.2,1984

BOWMAN, Charles J.,    Mar.29,1915 - Apr.21,1981
BOWMAN, Clara L.,    Aug.10,1915 -  -----

SHEHAN, Dallas,    May 26,1928 - July 8,1981   - USA Korea
SHEHAN, Betty Jo,    Feb.23,1936 -  -----

COOPER, William Ray,    June 6,1922 - Apr.14,1988   - USA   WW2
COOPER, Eva Mae,    Feb.18,1925 - July 16,1979

TAYLOR, Arnold E.,    1911 - 1986
TAYLOR, Mattie Rose,    1915 - 1978

HOPSON, Roosevelt,    1899 -1988
HOPSON, Lizzie,    1902 -  -----

HARRIS, David,    Feb.25,1946 -  -----
HARRIS, Violet, (w),  May 7,1949 - Sept.17,1977

EDWARDS, Virginia, "Jenny",    Sept.4,1933 - Sept.11,1986

BARNETT, Samuel M.,    May 1,1916 -  -----
BARNETT, N. Gertrude,    Jan.2,1919 - Oct.4,1975

PRICE, Ike,    Aug.1,1922 -  -----
PRICE, Sarah L.,    July 29,1911 - Aug.15,1976

ADAMS, James H.,    May 26,1909 - Sept.12,1987
ADAMS, Amilee N.,    July 21,1909 -  -----
EARLY, Willa Dean A.,    Aug.18,1930 -  -----

WALDROP, Troy,    June 21,1914 -  -----
WALDROP, Nellie, (w),  Jan.2,1913 -  -----
WALDROP, Johnny, (son), May 3,1952 - Apr.19,1978

ROSS, Ebbert,    Jan.13,1922 - Apr.11,1985   - USN  WW2

MILLER, Robert Frederick,    1909 - 1979   - Capt. USA  WW2

PRICE, Elna Harrell,    Sept.28,1903 - May 4,1981

MOONEY, James I.,    1906 - 1979   - USN  WW2

BAILEY, Glenn Isaac,    Oct.17,1919 - Apr.6,1981   - USA  WW2
BAILEY, Gladys F., (w),  Jan.15,1928 -  -----

WYATT, John Wesley,    Oct.8,1885 - May 10,1971
WYATT, Sarah Inez,    May 7,1906 -  -----

WESTALL, Gillon John, 1913 - 1979 -  USA  WW2

MILLER, Albert N.,    Aug.31,1915 - July 27,1981

EVERGREEN CEMETERY   (continued)

RENFRO, Glen M.,   Apr.10,1912 - -----
RENFRO, Eliza S.,   Mar.17,1915 - June 10,1983

LEWIS, Lloyd Burton,   Mar.18,1923 - June 9,1981 -  USA   WW2
LEWIS, Ruby T.,   Sept.16,1927 - -----

SAMS, Harry W.,   Aug.5,1908 - Nov.14,1985  - USA
SAMS, Glenna L.,   Dec.22,1909 - May 30,1987
SAMS, Harold,   Oct.26,1934 - Dec.12,1980
SAMS, Harry William, Jr.,   Nov.18,1931 - Dec.28,1981 - USAF Korea
                                                        Vietnam

HOWZE, William Heath, Aug.18,1914 - Oct.13,1980 - USA   WW2

FOSTER, C.H.,   Mar.14,1921 - -----
FOSTER, Pauline,   April 1,1916 - Nov.24,1981

WATSON, Everet C.,   May 13,1922 - Dec.16,1979
WATSON, Bessie R.,   June 20,1922 - -----

SHELTON, Willard W.,   Sept.16,1926 - June 22,1978
SHELTON, Marie K.,   June 27,1928 - -----

TITTLE, William F.,   July 4,1927 - -----
TITTLE, Freddie D.,   Sept.21,1930 - -----

CLARK, Roby,  Feb.14,1911 - Apr.6,1983
CLARK, Etta F.,   Aug.17,1913 - June 7,1988

RICE, Parley F.,   Mar.27,1913 - -----
RICE, Edith,   Feb.14,1916 - Sept.4,1981

BENNETT, Nancy Delia,   Jan.24,1896 - Apr.8,1981

WEEMS, Fred C.,   Mar.7,1908 - Jan.1,1986
WEEMS, Judy M.,   Sept.5,1922 - -----

VIEDAKA, Joseph William,   Aug.19,1922 - Apr.13,1987 - USN WW2
VIEDAKA, Ernestine M.,   Nov.8,1922 - -----

McINTOSH, Lum,   Oct.6,1908 - -----
McINTOSH, Birdia,   Jan.10,1906 - Dec.29,1986

RICE, Ray Charles,   1945 - 1988

FAULKNER, ----- ,   ----- - -----
FAULKNER, Bonnie G.,   Feb.26,1922 - Jan.21,1988

HAMPTON, Roy L.,   1918 - 1988

STARNES, Troy Cecil,   1927 - 1980  - USA   WW2

CLARK, Horace Y.,   ----- - -----
CLARK, Maude E.,   ----- - -----

BUCHANAN, Ernest,   Feb.16,1905 - Nov.3,1987
BUCHANAN, Cora,   Aug.25,1915 -   -----

PETERSON, Carlis Ralph,   Aug.22,1930 - Mar.11,1985 - USA Korea

WILSON, Brooks J.,   Dec.1,1931 - Nov.3,1987
WILSON, Patsy E.,   July 13,1935 -   -----

CLARK, Theodore H.,   Sept.21,1928 - Aug.27,1983 - USAF WW2 Korea
Clark, Jean,   -----  -  -----                                    Vietnam

BRYANT, Walter,   Sept.14,1917 - Feb.5,1983 - USA   WW2
BRYANT, Laura Belle,   Aug.6,1930 - Nov.11,1983

McCALL, Sherman H.,   July 29,1910 - Mar.9,1984 - USA   WW2
McCALL, Edythe H.,   Aug.1,1918 -   -----

KEEVER, Anita Engle,   May 22,1965 - Sept.15,1987

WILLIS, Regis W.,   Oct.27,1916 - Jan.11,1986
WILLIS, Irene J.,   Aug.16,1914 - June 25,1985

MOORE, Kenneth James,   1930 - 1988

DALY, Christopher B.,   1908 - 1988

ROBERTS, Danie H.,   Aug.14,1919 - Aug.12,1987
ROBERTS, Maude M.,   Oct.5,1920 -   -----

DAVIS, William E.,   June 1,1912 -   -----
DAVIS, Ruth E.,   Sept.20,1905 - Apr.12,1985

LEDFORD, Mae,   Feb.19,1924 -   -----
JOHNSON, Eddie,   Jan.22,1906 -   -----

WHITAKER, Ralph L.,   Sept.6,1923 - Aug.9,1986

LAWS, Hobart,   1915 - 1983
LAWS, Kate,   1916 -   -----

TIPTON, Bill,   May 21,1904 - May 17,1987
TIPTON, Myrtle,   Dec.16,1909 -   -----

TIPTONS, Joel W.,   June 23,1893 - Oct.23,1981   - USA   WW1
TIPTONS, Elva B.,   May 30,1906 -   -----

TIPTION,(TIPTON?), L.V.,   1935 - 1988

THOMPSON, Ivan James,   Apr.14,1917 - Sept.22,1981
THOMPSON, Laura Jean,   Feb.17,1924 -   -----

HARDING, William Guy,   July 19,1917 - July 8,1981
HARDING, Mollie,   Nov.11,1919 -   -----

EVERGREEN CEMETERY   (continued)

RICE, Wade,   Mar.7,1922 - Mar.17,1987
RICE, James P.,   Aug.16,1930 - -----

RICE, Claude "Buck",  Nov.21,1914 - -----
RICE, Maxine B.,   Apr.22,1935 - -----

HORN, Curtis C.,   Nov.28,1918 - June 19,1984
HORN, Bertha W.,   July 20,1918 - ----

McCOURRY, Rev. Loss,   Dec.12,1912 - June 11,1985
McCOURRY, Ethel,   Jan.26,1912 - -----

EVERGREEN CEMETERY  -  GARDEN OF GETHSEMANE SECTION

BUCHANAN, Roy G.,   June 27,1914 - Dec.4,1986

COLE, Anon F.,   July 26,1910 - June 8,1986

WILSON, Ward Paul,   1926 - 1985  - USA  WW2

BRACKINS, James T.,   1913 - 1988

FRANKLIN, Roscoe,   1912 - 1985
FRANKLIN, Mary,   1918 - -----

FRANKLIN, Edward E.,   Aug.27,1936 - Jan.6,1978 - USN

CHANDLER, Viola V.,   1913 - -----

EDWARDS, Arvel,  Jan.5,1925 - Nov.16,1982 -  USN  WW2
EDWARDS, Zula S.,   Apr.19,1926 - -----

CHANDLER, W. Everette,   1897 - 1982
CHANDLER, Marcena,   1909 - 1979

HARRIS, Ricky Gene,   Apr.24,1955 - Mar.4,1978

WILLIS, Crockett Russell,   Dec.22,1908 - Oct.13,1986
WILLIS, Greta Christina,   June 7,1914. - Apr.28,1988

RICE, Hobert C.,   1898 - 1977
RICE, Esther B.,   1905 - -----

FAIN, Dixon Shipe,   Feb.24,1919 - Nov.19,1987
FAIN, Violet P.,   1921 - -----

McNABB, Max Damon,   1922 - 1975  - USA WW2

BUCHANAN, Raymond,   1900 - 1984

EDWARDS, Ralph,   1924 - 1988

LANPHER, Clarence E.,   1919 - 1988

SMITH, Jim J., "Jim Dog",  1961 - 1987

FLANARY, Carl E.,   1915 - 1983

BRYANT, Elmer Jack,   1932 -  -----
BRYANT, Clara Lee,   1930 - 1986

KING, Paul,   1918 - 1984  - USA  WW2

EDWARDS, Orville,   July 12,1898 - July 4,1985
EDWARDS, Pansy,   Jan.19,1913 -  -----

BRIGGS, Glade,   1922 -  -----
BRIGGS, Nettie, 1930 - 1986

HONEYCUTT, Dora Tipton,   Oct.6,1899 - July 28,1972

LOYD, R.D.   1915 -  -----
LOYD, Edna,   1918  -----

SNEED, Aaron,   1917 - 1985  - USA  WW2  Korea
SNEED, Vivian,   1920  -----

BAINES, Earl,   June 21,1924 - Nov.7,1986  - USA  WW2

TAYLOR, Pearl,   1918 -  -----

BARNETT, Martin,   1912 - 1986  - USA

GILBERT, Jesse Meade,   1913 - 1984  - USAF  WW2  Korea
GILBERT, Hazel McCarthy,   July 10,1918 - Nov.22,1970

CRAFT, Velma P.,   1885 - 1978

SCOTT, Gentry M.,   1905 -  -----
SCOTT, Roxie J.,   1907 - 1979

BURKE, Norman Lee,   Sept.16,1932 - Nov.4,1978 - USA  Korea

CALLAWAY, Elsie M.,   1926 - 1985

JONES, Shawn,   June 12,1964 - June 18,1982

LANE, Jack D.,   1921 - 1985  - USAC  WW2
LANE, Beulah H.,   June 20,1930 -  -----

TIPTON, Samuel S.,   July 19,1961 - Apr.26,1986

TIPTON, Taft,   Mar.17,1910 - Dec.12,1976

BARNETT, Willie J.,   1931 - 1983
BARNETT, Irma J.,   1936 -  -----

HARRIS, Mack D.,   Feb.18,1893 - Feb.9,1987  - USA  WW2

ALDERMAN, John Biggs, "Pat",   1901 - 1984
ALDERMAN, Verna Blow,   1898 - 1985

BOOTH, Clyde Calvin, Sr.,   Nov.25,1894 - Sept.27,1977 - USA WW1
BOOTH, Nellie Wilson,   June 28,1898 - Jan.8,1980

WILLIAMS, Gertie M.,   July 22,1907 - Nov.7,1974

EDWARDS, Walter B.,   1885 - 1979
EDWARDS, Lula H.,   1895 - 1985

TILSON, Walter J.,   May 4,1889 - Apr.7,1970
TILSON, Nancy A.,   May 9,1887 - Aug.13,1971

SHOOK, Gus J.,   1916 - -----
SHOOK, Edith,   1919 - -----

HARRIS, Floyd,   July 16,1921 - June 24,1976
HARRIS, Elva,   Nov.29,1929 - -----

HUBBARD, Benjamin Robert,   May 21,1952 - Aug.10,1986

ROBBINS, Lewis R.,   1906 - -----
ROBBINS, Bessie,   1914 - 1970

BOWMAN, Noah C.,   1922 - 1983
BOWMAN, Betty Jane,   1931 - -----

McFADDEN, John H.,   1920 - -----
McFADDEN, Martha W.,   1918 -----

HARRIS, Ernest P.,   1912 - 1983
HARRIS, Birdie B.,   1914 - -----

BYRD, George,   1906 -1987
BYRD, Julia P.,   1907 - -----

WHITSON, Zane C., Sr.,   1913 -1988
WHITSON, Carrie J.,   1914 - -----
WHITSON, Jim R.,   1946 - -----

McNUTT, Charles Earl,   Nov.9,1912 - Oct.16,1985 - USA   WW2

PHILLIPS, James C.,   1903 - 1987
PHILLIPS, Doris C.,   1930 - 1986

JONES, Mildred G.,   1912 - 1986

HOPKINS, Lizzie,   1894 - 1984

JONES, Nannie R.,   1895 - 1986

SENTER, William Marvin,   1909 - 1985
SENTER, Eleanor F.,   1914 - -----

EVERGREEN CEMETERY (continued)    GARDEN OF GETHSEMANE

BLACK, Margaret Ford,    June 1,1908 - June 18,1985

PRICE. Albert W.,    1901 - 1973
PRICE, Mary H.,    1904 - -----

WILSON, Dave M.,    1909 - 1978
WILSON, Nova T.,    1912 - 1979

TOLLEY, James Clearance,    May 20,1893 - Mar.22,1970

LOVE, Lewis L.,    Feb.1,1912 - Jan.24,1985    - USA    WW2
LOVE, Gloria P.,    Oct.17,1927 - May 5,1985

HENSLEY, Herman,    Aug.3,1922 - Dec.22,1969    - USA    WW2

THOMPSON, Roy,    1895 - 1974
THOMPSON, Phoebe T.,    1895 - 1970

GARLAND, Wayne Guy,    Nov.4,1933 - Sept.24,1986 - USN    Korea
GARLAND, Fannie E.,    Sept.29,1931 - -----

RAY, Quetsel C.,    1899 - 1977
RAY, Mary H.,    1902 - 1975

BUCHANAN, Claude,    Nov.4,1917 - Apr.25,1988    - USA    WW2

BANNER, Melvin,    1933 - 1986
BANNER, Louise,    1932 - -----

BURRELL, Roy R.,    1909 - 1987
BURRELL, Virginia W.,    1916 - 1985

SHOOK, Charles S.,    Aug.14,1921 - Apr.25,1978    - USA    WW2
SHOOK, Fannie M.,    1929 - -----

YATES, Roy S.,    1902 - 1978
YATES, Blanche H.,    1909 - -----

FLANARY, Julie Effie,    Apr.7,1929 - Apr.4,1986

DAVIS, Ethel May,    Jan.1,1888 - Jan.24,1975

SALTS, Jay Patrick,    b/d 1976

RANDOLPH, Herman S.,    May 17,1909 - Oct.26,1967    - USA    WW2

WILLIAMS, Dillard E.,    1895 - 1972
WILLIAMS, Nancy L.Mc.,    1896 - 1967

NELSON, Cecil Walter,    1921 - 1984    - USA    WW2

REESE, Willard Copelan,    1910 - 1983
REESE, Betty McPhail,    1914 - -----

McNABB, James Bennett,   1896 - 1984   -   USN   WW1
McNABB, Thelma R.,   1907 -   -----

FOSTER, Garse W.,   1894 - 1979
FOSTER, Myrtle M.,   1906 -   -----

STREET, Jason B.,Sr.,   Jan.14,1904 - June 13,1971   -   USA
STREET, Blanche E.,   Oct.27,1909 - Sept.8,1978

JONES, Jack Q.,   1920 - 1984   -   USN   WW2
JONES, Mamie Tucker,   July 1921 -   -----

MALLETT, Robert A.,Jr.,   1913 - 1986

BURNETTE, Arthur H.,   May 25,1928 - June 23,1984
BURNETTE, Della Margaret,   July 14,1929 -   -----

SEAGROVES, William H.,   Oct.14,1903 - Feb.4,1966

CHITWOOD, H.M. "Pete",   1915 -   -----
CHITWOOD, Margaret, (w),   1919 -   -----
CHITWOOD, Gary S., (son),   1945 - 1967

GRIFFITH, Eugene,   1917 - 1982
GRIFFITH, Alma W.,   1923 -   -----

GARLAND, Darius A.,   1900 -   -----
GARLAND, Mary Ann,   1901 - 1979

RANDOLPH, Norma V.,   Dec.10,1923 - Nov.20,1969

DAVIS, Bob,   1888 - 1968
DAVIS, Alice J.,   1886 - 1964

GRIFFITH, J.Fred, "Todd",   1902 -   -----
GRIFFITH, Bess Gillis,   1903 - 1983

GRIFFITH, Ray M.,   1908 - 1987
GRIFFITH, Flossie M.,   1909 -   -----

WHALEY, Arnold,   Sept.19,1922 - June 11,1988
WHALEY, Artielea,   Aug.20,1926 -   -----

SHELTON, Dwight E.,   1910 - 1972
SHELTON, Eva M.,   1926 -   -----

WILSON, Anna Jo L.,   July 8,1934 - Dec.15,1969

MILLER, Howard Lee,   1917 - 1970

FORD, Thomas J.,   1905 - 1974
FORD, Bonnie M.,   1911 - 1971

HARTMAN, Ella Jo,   1929 - 1970

EVERGREEN CEMETERY (continued)   GARDEN OF GETHSEMANE

MILLER, Alton Terry,   Sept.2,1942 - Dec.25,1969  -  USA

POTTER, Lula Trivette,   Mar.20,1885 - June 26,1971

GARLAND, Madeline Ledford,   June 27,1923 - May 30,1975
LEDFORD, David Jonathan,   died July 12,1977

BUCHANAN, John,   1887 - 1968
BUCHANAN, Minnie J.,   1889 - 1977

BUCHANAN, James L.,   1921 -  -----
BUCHANAN, Betty Jo,   1928 -  -----

McNICHOLS, Arthur W.,   1913 - 1986  -  USA
McNICHOLS, Gorgia E.,   1914 -  -----

INGRAM, William H.,   1935 - 1985  - USAF

HAUN, William B.,   1925 - 1983  - USA  WW2
HAUN, Glossie E.,   Aug.11,1924 - Jan.26,1976

BENNETT, Flora T.,   Dec.1,1919 - Sept.16,1987

WHITE, Clyde W.,   Nov.28,1904 - Dec.26,1985
WHITE, Dorothy B.,   Apr.22,1905

CALHOUN, Charles M.,   1917 - 1974   -  USA

CALHOUN, Ernest C.,   1912 - 1972   USA  WW2
CALHOUN, Beulah M.,   1913 - 1980

FRYE, Dewey,   1900 - 1984

ERWIN, Arthur James, Jr.,   Oct.3,1927 - Oct.30,1986  _  USA  WW2
ERWIN, Martha Shull,   May 16,1932 -  -----

SWOFFORD, Earl J.,   1899 - 1982
SWOFFORD, Bessie L.,   1897 - 1979

RANDOLPH, Josie,   Sept.6,1894 - Mar.12,1972

CARTER, Luther Jerome,   1923 - 1984  -  USA  WW2
CARTER, Edith Rose,   1922 -  -----

DeBUSK, Harold H.,   July 8,1917 - Nov.24,1982

WHITSON, Brown,   Jan.22,1926 - May 3,1988  - USA  WW2

TIPTON, Kenneth,   1922 - 1987
TIPTON, Marie T.,   1925 -  -----

BENNETT, Mack,   Jan.23,1909 -  -----
BENNETT, Lizzie B.,   May 22,1911 - July 25,1986

ROBINSON, Ted,   1946 - 1988

EVERGREEN CEMETERY  (continued)  GARDEN OF GETHSEMANE

JACKSON, Thomas P.,    1926 - 1988
JACKSON, Leona E.,    1928 - -----

HILLIARD, Virgie,    1914 - 1988

BENNETT, Willie,    Oct.22,1909 - Jan.22,1984

HOLLOWAY, Harry Travis, Jr.,    died  Nov.17,1975

TIPTON, Herman J.,    1906 - -----
TIPTON, Belle P.,    1909 - -----

CASH, Larry S.,    Aug.6,1954 - Dec.22,1970

CASH, Raymond Clyde,    Nov.24,1934 - June 20,1984   -   USA

HORTON, Leisa Faye,    1955 - 1970

JOHNSON, Chester W.,    1898 - 1976

BROWN, Arnold A.,    1904 - 1969
BROWN, Joyce E.,    1907 - 1971

EDWARDS, Ted,    1918 - 1974

WILLIAMS, Edgar,    1915 - 1988

BAILEY, Harley L.,    1909 - 1986
BAILEY, Mamel,    1911 - -----

ARWOOD, Wilzia E.,    1900 - 1972
ARWOOD, Mae A.,    1906 - 1972

WILLIAMS, E. Eugene,    Sept.18,1937 - Dec.17,1968

BROTHERTON, Howard F.,    1914 - 1985
BROTHERTON, Pheba A.,    1913 - -----
BROTHERTON, Thomas W.,    May 1,1937 - June 27,1975

CARTER, Luther J.,    1887 - 1977
CARTER, Rachel K.,    1895 - -----

ANDERS, Henry T.,    1917 - 1979
ANDERS, O'Nell S.,    1920 - -----

JONES, Ernest H.,    1910 - -----
JONES, Elizabeth B.,    1915 - -----

KOENIG, Edward W.,    1906 - 1970
KOENIG, Beth Suzanne,    1963 - 1968

HALE, Otis C., Jr.,    1910 - 1974
HALE, Olga C.,    1925 - 1971

McNALLY, Larry D.,    1906 - 1979
McNALLY, Polly C.,    1911 - -----

ADKINS, Dewey, Apr.22,1926 - Feb.14,1968 - USN

PHILLIPS, Suil, 1914 - 1967
PHILLIPS, Julia, ----- - -----

HENSLEY, Roby L., Apr.30,1932 - Sept.8,1971 - USA Korea Vietnam

McNABB, Raymond Holt, July 29,1920 - Oct.14,1971 - USAF WW2 Korea

GREEN, Tracy Lynne, Sept.8,1967 - Apr.2,1982

CHANDLER, Menta W., Feb.21,1922 - June 24,1986

GILBERT, Rosetta H., Apr.22,1907 - Feb.5,1983

GOODIN, Thomas E., Jr., 1903 - 1976
GOODIN, Carolyn Harris, 1902 - -----

KERNS, Howard D., Dec.10,1922 - Aug.14,1987
KERNS, Olivia H., Jan.12,1920 - -----

GARLAND, George, 1917 - -----
GARLAND, Amalee M., 1918 - -----

TIPTON, McKinley, 1912 - 1985 - USA WW2

MEADE, R.C., "Pete", Aug.9,1920 - Feb.11,1981
MEADE, Thelma H., Oct.9,1922 - Feb.10,1987

McCOURRY, Angela Jane, died Sept.23,1968

McCOURRY, Ann Rogers, 1941 - 1974

HANN, Joseph Otto, Jan.3,1919 - May 8,1972 - USN WW2

HIGGINS, Becky Hann, July 29,1953 - Oct.2,1971

LOVE, Frances B., 1911 - 1982

FRANKLIN, Margaret Ann, Sept. 26,1939 - Aug.16,1968

GENTRY, Webb B., 1905 - -----
GENTRY, Florence S., 1908 - -----

STALLARD, B. Ernest, 1901 - 1964
        Son of Samuel Covey and Mary Elizabeth Mead Stallard
STALLARD, Florence E., 1904 - 1968
        Dau. of Aaron and Emma Weld Franklin

BENNETT, John H., 1884 - 1965

RICE, Jackie Lynn, Jan.27,1958 - Jan.13,1982

HARRIS, Orville,   1913 -1979
HARRIS, Bonnie M.,   1917 -  -----

EDWARDS, Richard G.,   Aug.3,1897 - Nov.11,1969 - USA   WW1
EDWARDS. Lillian G.,   Sept.1,1894 - June 11,1979

FRANKLIN, Harry W.,   Dec.14,1901 - Jan.10,1972
FRANKLIN, Annie Beth,   Aug.1,1904 - Aug.25,1982
FRANKLIN, Harry Lawson,   1934 - 1980  -  USN  Korea

McKINNEY, Hayden,   1910 - 1987
McKINNEY, Belle,   1910 -  -----

McKINNEY, Wade H.,   1918 - 1971
McKINNEY, Veralee,   1920 -  -----

RICE, Jean Rogers,   Mar.11,1931 - May 26,1985

ROGERS, William H.,   Sept.3,1925 - Aug.1,1969  - USA   WW2

ROGERS, Gregory T.,   1952 - 1978

HARDIN, Myra,   1959 - 1980

GARLAND, Monroe,   1915 - 1969
GARLAND, Dezzy G.,   June 17,1894 - Dec.25,1968

BAILEY, Michael L.,   May 5,1953 - May 4,1969

INGLE, Clarence,   Sept.2,1892 - Jan.29,1964  -  USA  WW1
         Son of Gaither and Elizabeth Chapman Ingle
INGLE, Dora M.,   Feb.12,1900 - Mar.24,1977

ARROWOOD, Elizabeth M.,   May 8,1880 - Apr.11,1980

BECKER, Susan Franklin,   Nov.5,1958 - Sept.7,1986  - USN

HUGHES, Hazel P.,   1918 -  -----

HOWELL, Kenneth Lynn,   May 13,1945 - Dec.8,1984  - USAF  Vietnam

KAHLER, Mildred E.,   Oct.25,1918 - Sept.12,1980

HOWELL, Harvey L., Sr.,   1923 - 1974  - USA
HOWELL, Sallie E.,   Oct.24,1924 -  -----
HOWELL, Penny Sue,   1957 - 1973

PEOPLES, Ruth P.,   Apr.10,1923 - Apr.8,1970

McBRIDE, Thorne F.,   1909 - 1987
McBRIDE, Ella J.,   1917 -  -----

McINTURFF, William D.,   1886 - 1975
McINTURFF, Mary Leota,   1893 - 1986

EVERGREEN CEMETERY  (continued) GARDEN OF GETHSEMANE

CHURCH, Charles W.,    Sept.20,1904 - -----
CHURCH, Marie L.,   Dec.14,1919 - Mar.4,1972
CHURCH, Keith,   1952 - 1980

TONEY, Horace Borden,   1899 - 1986  - USN  WW1
TONEY, Juanita A.,   1901 - -----

ENGLE, James D.,   1937 - 1977
ENGLE, Betty J.,   1941 -  -----

HOLLIFIELD, William R.,   1908,- 1984  -  USA  WW2  Korea
HOLLIFIELD, Rebecca S.,   Mar.2,1910 - Jan.8,1980

REED, Ella Erwin,   June 3,1922 - June 3,1977

ERWIN, Sammie R.,   1917 - 1978  -  USA
ERWIN, Mildred J.,   June 3,1911 - Sept.16,1976

STITT, Everett Verle,   1915 - 1983 -  USA  WW2

RAMEY, John Daniel,   1924 - 1988

BENNETT, Curtis,   1911 - 1976
BENNETT, Georgia,   1909 -  -----

ENGLE, M. Larry,   1943 - 1982
ENGLE, JoAnne,   1948 -  -----

TIPTON, Johnny E.,   Aug.22,1939 - Mar.15,1983  -  USN

DeHAVEN, Donald E.,   1928 -  -----
DeHAVEN, Marie,   1931 - 1984

TAPP, Harold T.,   1925 - 1985
TAPP, Virgie B.,   1929 -  -----

WHITE, Richard D.,   1917 - 1986  -  USA  WW2
WHITE, Mollie E.,   1918 -  -----

SALYER, Jessie,   1891 - 1973
SALYER, Simelda R.,   1889 - 1966

CASH, George O.,   1900 - 1981
CASH, Edna Earle,   1903 -  -----

HARRIS, Freeman,   1918 - 1979  (son)
HARRIS, Louella,   1901 - 1977  (mother)

SIMMONS, Woodrow S.,   1914 - 1980
SIMMONS, Ira Zell,   1925 - 1977

FURCHESS, Larry,   1948 - 1982
FURCHESS, Linda,   1949 -  -----

POORE, Jim,   1902 - 1976
POORE, Helen,   1928 -  -----

TIPTON, John C.,   1909 - 1981
TIPTON, Dorothy M.,   1920 -  -----

AMBROSE, Pamela L.,   Feb.18,1958 - Dec.14,1973

MILLER, Pearl,   1938 - 1985
MILLER, Garfa,   June 8, 1904 - Oct.9,1972

LEDFORD, Ralph J.,   1925 - 1984
LEDFORD, Olene M.,   1934 -  -----

BYRON, George W.,   1920 -  -----
BYRON, Pauline M.,   1921 - 1976

BENNETT, Thomas M.,   1907 - 1980
BENNETT, Lockie L.,   1904 - 1974

IVEY, John F.,   Feb.1,1889 - Dec.31,1972
IVEY, Mattie P.,   Feb.14,1893 - May 8,1976

HARRIS, Kathryn Ann,   Dec.1,1952 - June 13,1972

WILFONG, Charles Randall,   1946 -  -----
WILFONG, Mary Jane Routh,   1953 - 1971

CROWDER, Robert W.,   June 11,1927 - Oct.8,1984  - USA   Korea

CRABTREE, James W.,   1903 - 1971
CRABTREE, Edith K.,   1905 - 1976

TIPTON, Timothy,   1965 - 1984
TIPTON, David J.,   1952 - 1988

TIPTON, Orville, 1913 -  -----
TIPTON, Ethel,   1918 - 1985

AMBROSE, Belle B.,   June 28,1905 - Jan.25,1971

CHANDLER, Edwin Gale,   1930 -  -----
CHANDLER, Ada Mable,   1928 - 1979

BAILEY, Bathilda,   1895 -  -----

TINKER, Jack,   May 31,1931 - Feb.4,1988  - USAF
TINKER, Jack, Jr.,   Feb.25,1955 - Jan.9,1980

RADER, W. Spears,   1911 - 1975
RADER, Mary Jo,   1906 -  -----

LLOYD, Melvin E.,   1911 - 1981

ARROWOOD, Eddie L.,   June 12, 1942 - May 1,1982

CLAYTON, Creasey,   1887 - 1977
CLAYTON, Joe W.,   1915 - 1975  -  USA   WW2
CLAYTON, Rickey Joe,   Apr.26,1961 - May 26,1971

BYRD, David M., 1898 - 1971
BYRD, Maude H., 1904 - 1985

SPARKS, J.C., 1935 - 1981
SPARKS, Elizabeth O., 1934 - -----

PETERSON, David, 1892 - 1976 - USA WW1

LIGON, Cora Lee, Apr.12,1894 - Nov.22,1977

SURRETTE, Sue Edwards, May 14,1941 - Mar.11,1973

STALLARD, A.F., "Gus", 1897 - -----
STALLARD, M. Ethel Powers, 1898 - 1976
STALLARD, Rachel, 1941 - -----

FENDER, Levi, 1901 - -----
FENDER, Ila Cooper, 1906 - 1987

HARRIS, Robert Ivery, 1912 - 1975 - USA WW2
HARRIS, Dixie, 1917 - 1984

McINTURFF, Roy Edward, June 26,1951 - July 8,1987
McINTURFF, James, Jr., Apr.8,1950 - June 19,1973

HARRIS, Paul H., Oct.28,1905 - Mar.28,1970 - Pvt. Med Dep
HARRIS, Eugene, Jan.5,1933 - Oct.12,1974 - USAF

HARRIS Arthur F., 1907 - -----
HARRIS, Ida S.B., 1907 - -----

SAMS, Cecil Herman, 1927 - 1982 - USA Korea
SAMS, Bathilda, Mar.4,1892 - Sept.1,1971

KEGLEY, Ray M., 1894 - 1972
KEGLEY, Clara E., 1913 - 1976

VANOVER, Gary D., Apr.29,1950 - Nov.23,1969

CROWDER, Jack L., 1908 - 1965
CROWDER, Loretta B., 1920 - 1978

CROWDER, Hubert E., "Bud", 1920 - 1976
CROWDER, Essie P., 1920 - 1983

RENFRO, Hugh G., 1897 - 1973
RENFRO, Clara B., 1906 - -----

McINTURFF, Atlas S., 1934 - 1987

HIGGINS, Fred H., Dec.23,1911 - Apr.19,1971
HIGGINS, Mark, Mar.10,1903 - Apr.26,1974

LUTTRELL, Samuel A.,   1900 - 1981
LUTTRELL, Lexie Ann,   1901 - -----

ERWIN, James A.,   1895 - 1971
ERWIN, Bertha M.,   1898 - 1970

ARROWOOD, Quinter,   1894 - 1972
ARROWOOD, May P.,   1891 - 1976
ARROWOOD, Lawrence,   1926 - 1973

ARROWOOD, Rev. Mack Burnie,   1902 - 1971
ARROWOOD, Judie P.,   1900 - -----

ADKINS, Rev. Rex,   1914 - -----
ADKINS, Mary T.,   1918 - 1977

HENSLEY, Charles B.,   1899 - 1980
HENSLEY, Ellen R.,   1898 - -----

AYERS, Scott B.,   1960 - 1985

DILLOW, David,   1916 - -----
DILLOW, Ella Jay,   1921 - 1985

FOSTER, Stuart M.,   Aug.25,1918 - July 25,1986   - USA   WW2
FOSTER, Ova Lou,   Nov.27,1926 - -----

ARROWOOD. Park,   1920 - -----
ARROWOOD, Mabel Nila,   1925 - 1976

WHITSON, Buster, July 2,1929 - Feb.18,1980   -   USN

McCURRY, Samuel Geter,   1895 - 1975

WHITSON, Angela M.,   1966 - 1979

ROBERTS, Otto,   1915 - 1969
ROBERTS, Pansy B.,   1915 - -----

ROBERTS, Millard,   1914 - 1987
ROBERTS, Zelda,   1931 - -----

HIGGINS, Gregory,   Nov.6,1960 - July 30,1978

DOUGHERTY, John F.,   1885 - 1968
DOUGHERTY, Kate,   1893 - 1978

PHILLIPS, Saundra Jean, Oct.9,1948 - Mar.20,1968
PHILLIPS, Sharon K.,   July 27,1952 - Sept.6,1969
MUHN, Tammy Ilene Phillips,   Sept.14,1961 - Mar.20,1981
           Daughters of F.P. and Bonnie Phillips

<u>EVERGREEN CEMETERY</u> (continued)   <u>GARDEN OF GETHSEMANE</u>

STANCIL, Robert E.,    Aug.11,1953 - Aug.10,1970

DOMIANUS, Bruce L.,    June 30,1948 - Aug.10,1970  -  USA Vietnam

LLOYD, Nellie,    1911 - 1988

MATHES, Lester,    1912 - 1984
MATHES, Mary L.,    1914 -  -----

MILLER, Alvin,    Sept.4,1906 - Dec.3,1965

JACKSON, Robert Fry,    Aug.7,1896 - Nov.15,1971  - USA   WW1
JACKSON, Elza,    1902 - 1974

WHITSON, Richard, Sr.,    May 22,1901 - June 17,1970
WHITSON, Annie,    May 10,1905 - Aug.3,1981

HEFNER, Grover C.,    1909 - 1987
HEFNER, Alma W.,    1908 -  -----

GILLIS, Dennis,  June 7,1962  - July 21,1989

AMBROSE, Infant Son,  Died July 8, 1948
        Son of J.H. and Naomi Ruth Webb Ambrose

ATKINS, Cornelia,  Nov. 16, 1871 - Jan. 28, 1962
        Dau. of Mack and Lucinda Hampton McCurry

BAILEY, Lester Milledge,  May 27, 1923 - Jan. 10,1949
        Son of Geter Pritchard and Hattie Cooper Bailey

BAILEY, Morgan,  Oct. 21, 1883 - Jan. 3, 1961
        Son of Mannon and Jane Morris Bailey

BANNER, Benjamin Franklin,  Age 91 - Died Jan. 21, 1946
        Son of Lewis and Viena Whitson Banner

BAUCOM, Dortha Juanita,  Age 9 - Died Feb. 1, 1942
        Dau. of John and Minnie Ingram Baucom

BAUGHMAN, Eloise,  Feb. 28, 1882 - Oct. 18, 1959
        Dau. of Earl and Nannie Hammersley Pollard

BAUGHMAN, Selma Frances,  Jan. 22, 1903 - April 15. 1965
        Maiden name Luntsford

BOGART, Wm. Albert, July 28, 1894 - Aug. 12, 1962
        Son of Jeremiah and Florence Crouch Bogart

BOONE, Troy Sherman,  March 4, 1898 - Dec. 27, 1958
        Son of James G. and Devonia Phillips Boone

BOWMAN, Clyde E. Jr.  Age 27 - Died April 8, 1930
        Son of Clyde E. Sr. and Cora Price Bowman

BROCE, Harvey Payne,  Age 54- Died Oct. 27, 1942
        Son of Harvey Howard and Ida Sheelor Broce

BROWN, Infant,  b/d Nov. 14, 1927
        Child of E.A. Brown

BRYANT, Rosa Louise,  July 9, 1918 - Dec. 25, 1947
        Dau. of James Hiram and Ethel Booth Ford

CALDWELL, Raymond J. Jr.,  b/d. Feb. 19, 1932
        Son of Raymond J. Sr. and Pearl Wilson Caldwell

CARUTHERS, Jonathan Lafayette Winfield, Nov. 30,1857-June 27,1947
        Son of Wm. Caruthers

CARUTHERS, Infant - b/d April 13, 1931
        Child of James and Myrtle Honeycutt Caruthers

CARUTHERS, Infant - b/d Dec. 10, 1934
        Child of James and Myrtle Honeycutt Caruthers

CARUTHERS, Myrtle May,  Age 38 - Died Mar.22, 1937
        Dau. of Pete and Elizabeth McInturff Honeycutt

CHAPMAN, David,  Age 97  - Died Oct. 7, 1934
        Son of James Chapman

CHAPMAN, Elizabeth,  Age 89 - Died March 3, 1937
        Dau. of Wm. Todd

COLLINS, Robert Sheridan, Aug. 5, 1900 - Sept. 12, 1955
        Son of Lee C. and Minnie Lane Collins

DANIELS, Infant,  - Died Aug. 10, 1942
        Child of Harold T. and Iris Blanch Jones Daniels

DAVIS, Dock,  Jan. 30, 1884 - Dec. 26, 1956
       Son of James and Margaret Butler Davis

DENNIS, J. Kyle,  April 26, 1886 - Nov. 16, 1962
       Son of Chas. Wm. and Lillian Warren Dennis

DILLOW, Infant Son,  Died April 6, 1950
       Son of Samuel David and Ella Jay Cooper Dillow

EDWARDS, Deanna Gail,  Age 7 mos. - Died Jan 25, 1957
       Dau. of Alfred L. and Joyce Caruthers Edwards

EDWARDS, Infant,  Died July 10, 1956
       Child of Harry D. and Hilda Faye Witcher Edwards

EDWARDS, Thurman E. Jr.,  Infant - Died Nov. 13, 1953
       Child of Thurman E. Sr. and Katherine Adkins Edwards

FANNING, Clark Dennis,  Age 1 mo. 16 days - Died July 6,1950
       Child of Clarence W. and Leona Griffith Fanning

FOSTER, Infant,b/d  Nov. 23. 1955
       Child of Winfred Lee and Hazel Lee Higgins Foster

GUINN, Glenn Hensley,  Age 33 - Died Feb. 26,1940
       Son of Lattie and Gertrude Hensley Guinn


HARVEY, Samuel Swanner,  Age 55 - Died Jan 26, 1938
       Drury and Harriett Howard Harvey

HAYNES, Major Lee, Dec. 28, 1866 - Feb. 1, 1959
       Son of Drewery Haynes

HENSLEY, Thomas Richard,  Age 45 - Died May 28, 1953
       Son of Lester Carson and Maggie Eldridge Hensley

HILTON, Infant,  Died Jan 15. 1946
       Child of Luther Corbett and Bertie Ollis Hilton

HOLLIFIELD, Ruby Louise,  Aug. 20, 1916 - Feb. 25, 1950
       Dau. of Walter L. and Lizzie Leasure Hopkins

HOWMAN, Fannie,  - Age 70 - Died Jan 11, 1943

JOHNSON, Edward Elmore,  Age 54 - Died Feb. 22, 1957
       Son of E.E. and Lenora Suggs Johnson

LARIMER, Nancy Brown, Age 2 days - Died Dec. 27, 1932
       Dau. of Sam and Ethel Brown Larimer

LILLY, Infant,  Died Feb. 28, 1940

LYNCH, Infant,  b/d  Feb. 1, 1933
       Child of J.H. and Moxie Coulder Lynch

LYNCH, Phyllis Marie,  Age 3 days - Died Dec. 15,1940
       Dau. of T.T. and Texie Hensley Lynch

MARTIN, Ernest Lee,  b/d/  June 28, 1942
       Son of Ernest Lee and Edith Ruth Fetty Martin

Melton, Samuel,  March 28, 1894 - July 2, 1946
       Son of Wheeler and Maggie Wilson Melton

MILLER, Ada,  May 26. 1929 - March 19, 1948
       Dau. of John and Hulda Webb Miller

MILLER, Wm. Kenneth,  Died Jan 16, 1944
       Infant of Wiley Kenneth and Mattie Lee Parker Miller

McCABE, Denice Allen, Died Jan. 9, 1948
    Child of Albert E. and Pauline Whitson McCabe

McCURRY, Claudette, Infant - 5 mos. - Died Aug. 17, 1950
    Dau. of Charles and Willie Mae Beaver McCurry

McINTOSH, Eliza, - Aug. 9, 1884 - Oct. 28, 1961
    Dau. of Severe and Frankie Bennett Whitson

McNABB, Sue Emma, b/d/ Dec. 5, 1933
    Dau. of J.R. and Rotha Styles McNabb

NELSON, Kenneth Powell, July 16, 1925 - April 13, 1960
    Son of Clyde and Nettie McCurry Nelson

OLLIS, Donald Marion, Age 10 mos. Died Nov. 20, 1942
    Son of Don and Robbie Lawing Ollis

OLLIS, Robbie, Age 22 - Died April 25, 1944
    Dau. of Wm.and Bessie Thomas Lawing

PADGETT, Ruth Marie, Oct. 27, 1923 - Aug. 24, 1950
    Dau. of Walter Hubert and Phoebe Keever Padgett

PETERSON, Grover, Age 55 - Died Aug. 2, 1934
    Son of Joshua and Martha Warrick Peterson

PETERSON, Scotty Dewian, Age 3 mos. - Died June 22, 1960
    Son of Malone and Marzella Gouge Peterson

PHILLIPS, Martin Luther (Dock) - Age 49 - Died April 24, 1952
    Son of Cornelius and Nellie Higgins Phillips

ROBERTS, Charles Donald, - Mar. 17, 1937 - Sept.30, 1950
    Son of Nealie and Ruth Howell Roberts

ROBERTS, Emmaline H., Age 85 - Died April 19, 1942
    Dau. of Peter and -----Anderson Hogan

RULE, Mrs. J.C., Nov. 8, 1873 - Aug 21, 1929
    Dau. of J.M. and Mary Lee Lindsay

RUNION, Roy J., - Died Nov. 7, 1955

SCRUGGS, Chas. Richard, Dec. 20, 1915 - Mat 17, 1964
    Son of Louis Davis and Ada White Scruggs

SCRUGGS, Mildred Hazel, Age 23 - Died Feb. 25, 1940
    Dau. of Floyd Edgar and Nita Henson Laws

SHEHAN, Arkie, Age 37 - Died July 10, 1952
    Dau. of E.L. and Millie Trent Anderson

SMITH, Mary Elizabeth, Sept 20, 1892 - Feb. 4, 1960
    Dau. of George H. and Luvena Knowles Sutphin

SNAPP. Edward, Age 29 - Died March 17. 1944
    Son of S.J. Snapp

SNIDER, Brian Suel, Aug. 5, 1896 - Sept. 29, 1956
    Son of Benjamin and Nannie Snider

STALLARD, Betty Joyce, Nov. 16, 1935 - Nov. 17, 1935
    Dau. of Dalton and Janice Stubblefield Stallard

STALLARD, Marcus Dalton Jr., Age 2 years - Died March 8, 1934
    Son of Marcus Dalton Sr. and Janice Stubblefield Stallard

STAMPER, Roger Dale, Age 1 year 3 mos. - Died Jan. 19, 1950
    Son of Garrett and Donna Tipton Stamper

TEMPLETON, Louise Bannister, Age 26 - Died July 5, 1936
    Dau. of B.D. Bannister

THOMPSON, Infant, b/d Feb. 21, 1936
Child of Sam E. and Fay Blankenship Thompson

THOMPSON, Infant, b/d/ Sept. 24, 1940
Child of S.E. and Faye Robbie Blankenship Thompson

THOMPSON, William Edward, July 2, 1879 - June 5, 1949

TIPTON, Herman, 1904 - Jan. 2, 1958
Son of Collis and Martha AnnTipton

TONEY, Hazen House, Oct. 10, 1888 - April 20, 1964
Son of J.F. and Fannie Miller Toney

WALKER, Infant, b/d Aug. 14, 1956
Child of Vance W. and -----Wilson Walker

WILLIAMS, Ferrell, Infant - Died Feb. 25, 1942
Child of Rushia Lee and Mable Foster Williams

WILLIAMS, Wayne, Age 8 days - Died Feb. 20, 1941
Child of Rushia and Mable Foster Williams

WILSON, Infant, b/d - March 27, 1951

WINTERMEYER, Fredrick Adolphus, Nov. 1, 1893- Aug. 29, 1961
Son of F.A. and Rosa Bell Wilkinson Wintermeyer

WOODSON, John Russell, age 4 - Died Jan 24, 1958
Son of John R. and Vivian Kay Frances Schaub Woodson

WOODWARD, Garrett Ulmont, Jr. Age 2 days - Died May 30, 1943
Son of Garrett U. and Florence Lee Coward Woodward

WOODWARD, Julie Ann, b/d March 29, 1953
Dau. of Jack Woodward

# PETERSON CEMETERY

Located south of Unicoi, about 3/4 of a mile, on White Cove Road. Copied by Bill Norris and Mildred Britton in 1973. Updated on Jan.7,1989.

RAY, Walter H.,    1909 - 1967
RAY, Elizabeth H., (w),  1915 -  -----

TAPP, Hubert Alvin,  May 10,1924 - June 12,1969
TAPP, Beatrice Linville,  Apr.13,1924 -  -----

HUSKINS, Elbert F.,  1920 - 1965
HUSKINS, Bertie M.,  1923 - 1959

LINVILLE, Samuel M.,  Aug.23,1895 - May 4,1976 - USA  WW1
LINVILLE, Bertha G., (w), Apr.23,1907 - Feb.9,1973
LINVILLE, Harold G., (son),  Nov.15,1927 - Nov.29,1943

LINVILLE, Dana H.,  Sept.6,1901 - Jan.20,1959
        Son of W.A. and Nancy Nelson Linville
LINVILLE, Martha L., (w),  Mar.12,1901 -  -----

LINVILLE, Norman E.,  Mar.14,1922 - Mar.11,1940
        Son of Dana Harman and Martha Peterson Linville

HONEYCUTT, Clayton,  Jan.18,1895 - Mar.26,1968

HONEYCUTT, Lobrite,  Feb.26,1921 - Nov.17,1957

WHITSON, John B.,  April 8,1875 - July 27,1943
WHITSON, Mollie E.,  Oct.20,1882 - June 5,1968

BYRD, R.V.,  1863 - 19??
BYRD, Dovie,  1866 -  -----

HONEYCUTT, Lucy,  Oct.25,1918 - Oct.8,1926
        Dau. of C.H. and Allie Honeycutt

HONEYCUTT, Clayton,  Aug.12,1946 - Oct.1,1947
        Son of Lobrite and Dorothy Honeycutt

HONEYCUTT, E.D.,  Mar.5,1923 - July 17,1939
        Son of Clayton and Allie Peterson Honeycutt

PETERSON, Lawson,  June 4,1840 - July 29,1923 - Union Army Civil War
PETERSON, Camelia Tipton,  (w), May 15,1846 - Nov.25,1927

PETERSON, Noah,  Apr.22,1879 - Mar.29,1933
PETERSON, Tiney,  Feb.14,1876 - Aug.18,1953
PETERSON, Walter Noah,  Oct.16,1934 - Oct.29,1934

PETERSON, Robert S.,  May 17,1899 - Feb.23,1959

MONDAY, Augusta Peterson,  Aug.1,1894 - Apr.27,1977
MONDAY, James Ernest,  age 45  - died Nov.30,1937

HOWELL, Vienna Jane,  Dec.5,1907 - Feb.3,1912
        Dau of D.L. and Mattie N. Howell

PETERSON CEMETERY (continued)

HOWELL, Orla,    died  Mar.16,1916

HOWELL, Imogene,    Apr.12,1882 - July 11,1911

BYRD, Bill,    Sept.11,1923 - Oct.21,1923
            Son of Arthur and Mollie Byrd

BIRCHFIELD, Helen,    June 22,1913 - July 13,1913
BIRCHFIELD, Rosa Lee,    June 9,1923 - July 25,1924
            Daus. of Isaac and Mary Birchfield

McVAY, Anderson,    died Feb.2,1931 - age 64
            Son of Jordan and Sabra Miller McVay

McCOURY, Sarah,    Dec.8,1893 - Feb.8,1920
McCOURY, Infant,    b/d 1920
            Wife and Dau. of Luther McCoury

BOOTH, Charles E.,    1897 - 1914
BOOTH, Sarah Amanda,    1874 - 1938

McLAUGHLIN, Malinda,    Mar.4,1875 - July 22,1911
            Wife of W.M. McLaughlin

GRINDSTAFF, Lavada,    May 29,1920 - June 20,1922
GRINDSTAFF, Edman,    Jan.20,1929 - Dec.18,1929
            Children of Mr.and Mrs. W.Sherman Grindstaff

McLAUGHLIN, W.M.,    Nov.1875 - June 1933
McLAUGHLIN, Pearl Smith, (w),    June 1894 - Feb.1967

WYATT, Penley,    Aug.9,1882 - Aug.8,1911

HOPSON, Arthur,    Jan.11,1892 - Mar.13,1913

PETERSON, Charles Berdett,    June 5,1912 - Nov.3,1918
            Son of C.J. and Hannah Peterson

WHITSON, J.W.,    Oct.28,1837 - Apr.22,1911
WHITSON, Elzira, (w),    Aug.28,1842 - Nov.29,1918

BENNETT, Ida J. Whitson,    July 23,1879 - Jan.11,1914
            Wife of W.B. Bennett

DUNCAN, Dovie,    Sept.13,1908 - Oct.13,1918

JONES, Martha Whitson,    Jan.23,1872 - May 1,1937

PETERSON, Charles J.,    Feb.4,1865 - May 9,1945
PETERSON, Hannah E. Laughrum,    June 27,1870 - Dec.9,1947

HOWELL, Dillard D.,    Aug.21,1900 - July 20,1956
HOWELL, Katherine B.,    June 17,1917 - -----

HOWELL, Rev. W.M.,    Mar.22,1873 - Apr.15,1959
HOWELL, Bettie Peterson, (w),    April 24,1873 - Feb.28,1946

JONES, Ralph Glenn,   Oct.4,1932 - Apr.23,1951 -   Korea

JONES, Lenoir Jackson,   Feb.1,1894 - May 18,1937

KEENE, George F.,   1869 - 1952
KEENE, Louise W.,   1885 - 1963

BAILEY, Handy C.,   1887 - 1967
BAILEY, Lillie Whitson,   1889 - 1942

WILSON, Maloie,   Sept.11,1918 - Oct.15,1918
WILSON, Ada,   Sept.17,1919 - Mar.17,1920
          Son and Dau. of M.A. and Mae Wilson

WHITSON, Robert A.,   1882 - 1940

McCURRY, Levi J.,   Oct.26,1885 - Apr.1,1940
McCURRY, Mary Jane, (w),   July 25,1891 - July 9,1986
McCURRY, Bill, Jr.,   1929 - 1955
          Son of Levi and Mary Butner McCurry
McCURRY, Sam R.,   June 9,1918 - Mar.8,1968

HARRELL, Sophia M.,   Sept.15,1923 - June 20,1963

HOWELL, Jeter P.,   Nov.2,1894 - May 7,1985
HOWELL, Cora Lee, (w),   May 22,1899 - July 31,1951

BENNETT, Willie M.,   Died Nov.9,1918 - Pvt 8th Tenn Cav. Union Army

WILSON, Lenora B.,   1898 - 1930
          Dau. of David and Ellen Buchanan Birchfield
WILSON, Infant Daughter  of J.B. and Lenora Wilson

MOORE, William H.,   May 30,1882 - Oct.14,1961 - Spanish Amer. War
          Son of Henry Moore
MOORE, Hassie E.,   1883 - 1959
          Dau. of William Harvell

CARVER, Dock,   Dec.4,1884 - Oct.7,1963
CARVER, Birdie H., (w),   Feb.16,1893 - -----

CARVER, Polley, March 5,1849 - Jan.5,1921

McLAUGHLIN, Hattie Carver,   1900 - 1933
          Dau. of William and ---- Butler Carver

WILSON, Infant Son of Burnie and Jeanette Wilson

BRYANT, Frankie Jane Tipton,   Sept.5,1881 - May 12,1918
          Wife of P.M. Bryant

BLEVINS, William B.,   Sept.3,1903 - July 1,1922

BLEVINS, David,   Oct.8,1849 - June 9,1931

BLEVINS, Sarah E.,    Feb.18,1872 - Dec.1,1951

CONLEY, Charles W.,    May 28,1875 - Dec.22,1956 - Spanish Amer.War
CONLEY, Louisa Garland, (w), Apr.19,1861 - Nov.19,1930
        Dau. of Mack and ---- McKinney Garland

CONLEY, Sarah Woodby,    Aug.14,1900 - Aug.30,1970

PIERCEY, Herbert H., Sr.,    Dec.23,1877 - Feb.4,1937
PIERCEY, Hattie L., (w),  Apr.13,1877 - June 3,1920
PIERCEY, Charles C.,    1903 - 1946
        Son of Herbert Hayes and Hattie Lavine Bailey Piercey
PIERCEY, Lillian Campbell,  (w), Feb.10,1909 - June 25,1943
        Dau. of James Hamilton and Mary Evelyn Archer Campbell

CARVER, W.M.,    Apr.20,1858 - July 29,1913

CARVER, Joe C.,    Feb.6,1893 - Oct.29,1969
CARVER, Pearl H.,    Mar.16,1894 - Dec.25,1971

CARVER, John William,    Oct.25,1919 - Mar.26,1921
CARVER, Hattie Etta,    Jan.31,1917 - Jan.23,1919

HAIRE, George,    Sept.24,1864 - Aug.9,1921

GREEN, Herbert H.,    Sept.30,1928 - Jan.22,1971
GREEN, Mae,    Oct.6,1929 -  -----

GREEN, Alvin,    1966 - 1966

MOORE, Pattie,    1965 - 1965

BRIGGS, Ella Carver,    1887 - 1964

CARVER, Earl,    Sept.29,1918 - May 15,1960

CARVER, Cas J.,    Apr.18,1882 - Jan.26,1954
CARVER, Lillie, (w),  Jan.15,1882 - July 10,1965

BUTLER, William M.,    1896 - 1983
BUTLER, Mary Ellen C.,    1908 - 1971

JONES, Barbara Lynn,    Mar.14,1963 - July 6,1964

BARNETT, Dora Mae,    1907 - 1972

BARNETT, Smith,    Jan.3,1882 - Jan.18,1949

McLAUGHLIN, Steven E.,    July 4,1870 - Dec.8,1964 -Spanish Amer.War
McLAUGHLIN, Bessie, (w),  Sept.22,1906 - Mar.8,1963

HOPSON, Bessie McLaughlin,    Jan.27,1896 - Nov.5,1933
        Wife of Jason C. Hopson

PETERSON CEMETERY (continued)

CARVER, Warren G., June 28,1935 - Nov.14,1973

LAWS, James, Jan.10,1855 - Sept.9,1928

LAWS, Margaret Hughes, 1872 - 1957

HUGHES, Florah, Jan.27,1846 - Dec.25,1938

INGRAM, Manassa, Mar.19,1899 - Aug.4,1966
INGRAM, Rosa, June 3,1902 - Mar.10,1968

HELMICK, Hobert F., Dec.11,1897 - July 3,1972
HELMICK, Emeline, (w), Sept.17,1901 - Oct.6,1970
HELMICK, Raymond, (son), b/d Sept.23,1923
HELMICK, Bobby J., (son), Aug.25,1942 - Sept.29,1942

STANLEY, Mary Jane, July 11,1886 - May 25,1967

McLAUGHLIN, W.B., 1885 - 1940
McLAUGHLIN, Mrs. Hiley Jane, 1865 - 1941
McLAUGHLIN, George Edward, 1901 - 1931

HONEYCUTT, Mary Nell Hopson, June 7,1911 - Apr.22,1935
          Wife of Frank Honeycutt

GRACE, Eulis G., Sept.6,1928 - Dec.12,1950 - WW2 Korea

COZAD, Jimmy, Died 1955

SLAGLE, Celia H., 1890 - 1971

WEBB, Frank, Aug.7,1881 - July 6,1960

CARVER, James C., Nov.4,1891 - Nov.5,1980
CARVER, Nannie B., (w), May 14,1899 - Oct.10,1984
CARVER, Earl James, (son), Sept.10,1933 - Oct.3,1935

RIDDLE, William, Dec.25,1865 - Apr.16,1946
RIDDLE, Jane Woodby, (w), Apr.12,1881 - Nov.21,1941

WOODBY, Mrs. Jane Cox, 1876 - 1941

WOODBY, Joe Bill, June 22,1877 - Apr.21,1966

BAKER, David C., Nov.13,1867 - Aug.10,1944
BAKER, Sarah E. Harvell, (w), Sept.20,1870 - 1976

WHITSON, Thomas D., Jan.16,1945 - June 8,1973

McVAY, Cindy, May 28,1868 - May 2,1952

BIRCHFIELD, Isaac, Died Mar.22,1945 - age 62

BIRCHFIELD, Monroe, May 5,1914 - Jan.31,1962

DEAN, Ed,   June 4,1894 - July 24,1950   -   WW1

HOPSON, Jason C.,   1895 - 1969

HOPSON, Dewey,   1907 - 1970
HOPSON, Polly,   1922 -   -----

TOLLEY, Samuel Martin, Jr.,   Apr.1,1960 - Aug.16,1961

HALL, Betty Jo,   Nov.3,1930 - Jan.19,1968

HOPSON, Robert B.,   Aug.7,1898 - Apr.20,1961
HOPSON, Sarah Ann Sneed, (w), Oct.3,1898 -   -----

TOLLEY, Bert W.,   July 12,1902 - Mar.3,1955
TOLLEY, Susie M., (w),   June 22,1905

TALLEY, Clyde O.,   July 7,1908 - July 10,1938

PETERSON,  Infant of James and Mary Peterson

BENDER, Ellen Tolley,   Nov.8,1870 - Oct.1,1944
          Wife of C.E. Bender

RIDDLE, John H.,   Feb.12,1872 - May 12,1960
          Son of Nancy Riddle
RIDDLE, Eddie Peterson,   Nov.12,1876 - Dec.16,1953
          Dau. of Mose and Oma Piercy Peterson
RIDDLE, Isaac R.,   Nov.2,1890 - May 2,1963   - WW1
          Son of Ezekiel (?) and Edie Peterson Riddle
RIDDLE, Fritz,   Dec.6,1920 - July 15,1935
          Son of I.R. Riddle

BLEVINS, Arthur,   Oct.5,1893 - Apr.25,1949   - WW1
BLEVINS, Donnie H., (w),   Nov.12,1894 - 1987
BLEVINS, Gregory,   Apr.18,1952 - May 15,1975

PADGETT, Tammy Fay,   1964 - 1964

HONEYCUTT, Allie,   1901 - 1988

WHITSON, Warren J.,   Mar.8,1921 - May 8,1982

MONDAY, Augusta Peterson,   Aug.1,1894 - Apr.26,1977

BOOTH, Patrick H.,   1907 - 1977   -   WW2

McLAUGHLIN, Kern,   Oct.22,1912 - Dec.7,1913
McLAUGHLIN, Wilder,   (no dates)
          Sons of William and Pearl McLaughlin

McCURRY, Mary Jane,   July 25,1891 - July 9,1986
          Wife of Levi McCurry

PETERSON, Peter,   Co M 8 Tn Cav  - Union Army

PETERSON CEMETERY (continued)


WHITSON, Warren J., Mar.8,1921 - May 8,1982 - USA WW2

HOPSON, Bert, Oct.24,1913 - Jan.4,1914
            Son of J.A. and Hassie Hopson

GRINDSTAFF, David M., 1855 - 1929
GRINDSTAFF, Sarah Sneed, (w), 1857 - 1930
            Dau. of Seth and Martha Woodby Sneed

HEDRICK, Sylvester, May 8,1911 - Feb.15,1921
            Son of Martin and Lina Hedrick

HEDRICK, Lina, Aug.17,1872 - Feb.15,1920
            Dau. of Mr. and Mrs. Peter Peterson

TIPTON, Mack, Dec.28,1891 - Aug.18,1911

McCURRY, Luther, 1887 - 1949

VANOVER, James C., July 2,1899 - Dec.31,1963
VANOVER, Mary Etta, Jan.19,1905 - -----
VANOVER, Leonard, b/d/ Jan.2,1930
VANOVER, James, b/d Mar.30,1935
VANOVER, Pauline, Apr.23,1931 - Aug.31,1945
            Children of J.C. and Mary Vanover

BAILEY, Naoma, Nov.16,1881 - Nov.28,1910

PETERSON, J.L., Nov.9,1876 - Oct.9,1911

BOYD, William P., 1879 - 1938
BOYD, Hettie G., 1889 - 1971

MOORE, Charlie, Mar.21,1927 - Oct.2,1933

CARVER, Mack, Oct.16,1925 - Jan.10,1929
            Son of Joe and Pearl Carver

HILTON, Jim, Sr., May 1,1889 - Jan.5,1978
HILTON, Belle P., (w), Mar.28,1899 - Oct.11,1970

WILLIAMS, Eva Woodby, Aug.2,1923 - Sept.4,1981

WOODBY, Jane, Apr.12,1881 - Mar.21,1941

CARVER, Ruth, May 23,1928 - Mar.8,1950

STREET, William Glenn, Oct.1,1917 - Nov.3,1918

STREET, Helen Marie, Mar.18,1925 - Nov.30,1926

STREET, L.W., Died Feb.27,1928

STREET, Billy Gean, Sept.30,1932 - Oct.10,1932

PETERSON CEMETERY (continued)

HOYLE, Curley Lea, Feb.28,1904 - July 27,1946

JONES, Elmer J., May 15,1943 - -----
JONES, Barbara R., (w), Jan.15,1941 - Aug.8,1981

PETERSON, James, Aug.20,1901 - Feb.22,1956
          Son of Noah and Tiney Peterson
PETERSON, Mary, June 19,1908 - -----

HOPSON, James, Died 1975

BIRCHFIELD, John R., 1931-1986

COLLINS, James Curtis, Apr.19,1923 - Sept.8,1988

CARVER, Isaac, 1915-1983

CARVER, Edward, 1911-1987

McCURRY, Pink, Apr.10,1891 - May 30,1945
McCURRY, Cora Peterson (w) Feb.22,1890- Nov.20,1927
          Dau. of Lawson and Cornelia Tipton Peterson
McCURRY, Pauline, (dau.) died 1927 at age 4 mos.

          UNMARKED GRAVES  -  PETERSON CEMETERY

CONLEY, Harvey b/d June 4,1942
          Son of Charles W. and Sarah Woodby Conley

HOPSON, Infant Son, b/d May 6,1951
          Son of Dewey L. and Polly Pauline Hicks Hopson

INGRAM, Leonard, Died Apr.5,1936 - 1 year old
          Son of Manassa and Rosa Barnett Ingram

Mc LAUGHLIN, Cora Lee, Died Jan.1,1937 - age 25
          Dau. of W.B. and Hylie Miller McLaughlin

McLAUGHLIN, Infant Girl, b/d July 5,1933

PETERSON, Mrs. Darleska, Died Jan.16,1956 - age 77

PETERSON, Ernestine, Died July 6,1937 - age 1 month

PETERSON Melissa, Died Dec.1,1929 - age 85
          Dau. of Ruben and Polly Green Honeycutt

PETERSON, Sarah Ann, Died Apr. 21,1937 - age 87
          Dau. of John and Patty Peterson Tipton

PETERSON, Virginia Kathleen, Died May 19,1937 - age 14
          Dau. of Ed and Belle Piercy Peterson

RIDDLE, Tom, Died Apr.18,1936 - age 66
          Son of David and Liza Riddle

TIPTON, Mrs. Eliza, Died Nov.6,1930 - age 81
          Dau. of David and Patty Bryant Tipton
          Wife of David Tipton

WEBB, Eckard, Aug.9,1887 - Aug.4,1953
          Son of John and Liza Miller Webb

## BELL CEMETERY

Located on highway 107 in Limestone Cove

------ HISTORICAL MARKER ------
"Limestone Cove Tragedy"

Here are buried the eight civilians killed at the home of
Dr. David Bell, in Nov.1863. Enroute to Kentucky to join Federal
Forces, they were found by a detachment of Col. W.W. Witcher's
Confederate Cavalry, while waiting for breakfast.

They were; B.Blackburn, Calvin Cantrel, Elijah Gentry,
Jacob Lyons, Wiley Royal, John Sparks and two unknown. Buried
nearby is Dr.Bell's brother, James, killed at the same time.

Copied by Bill Norris in 1973 - Updated on Jan.7,1989

BELL, Henry Edward,   May 23,1845 - Nov.22,1893
BELL, Nancy Harriett Miller,(w), Dec.31,1859 - Nov.14,1929

BELL, Jack E.,   b/d 1925

BELL, James W.,   1879 - 1964
BELL, Celia G.,   1889 - 1975

BELL, Edward W.,   Jan.12,1908 - Jan.18,1952   - WW2
BELL, Birdie H.,   1906 - -----

BELL, Dr. David,   Died Feb.10,1893 - age 73

GARLAND, Walter,   June 25,1876 - Dec.6,1905

GARLAND, Pierce N.,   Dec.25,1887 - June 26,1963
        Son of E.L. and Sarah Bell Garland
GARLAND, Mammie Bell,        1884 - 1951
        Dau. of E.L. and Sarah Bell Garland
GARLAND, Elisha L.,   1848 - 1916
GARLAND, Sarah A., (w),   May 15,1856 - June 16,1930
        Dau. of David W. and Sarah Alice McKelden Bell

TEAGUE, Mary Jane,   Oct.9,1867 - June 7,1952 - Mother
TEAGUE, John H.,   1903 - 1967
TEAGUE, Goldie H.,   1908 - 1972

McINTURFF, Enos Monroe,   Mar.3,1897 - Aug.7,1955
        Son of Joseph and Elizabeth Baker McInturff
McINTURFF, Julia Teague, (w),  Aug.28,1900 - -----

BIRCHFIELD, Walter L.,   Feb.26,1898 - Oct.3,1970

BIRCHFIELD, William,   1860 - 1935
        Son of Ezekiel and ---- Gouge Birchfield
BIRCHFIELD, Eliza B., (w),   1863 - 1962

BURCHFIELD, Infant of W.M. and Eliza Burchfield

MORRELL, Clarence W.,   June 28,1914 - Mar.17,1941
MORRELL, Laura C.,   Apr.12,1908 - Nov.6,1981

BELL CEMETERY   (continued)

MILLER, O.R.,   Mar.5,1862 - Jan.14,1943
MILLER, Annie B.,   July 4,1865 - Aug.8,1942

RIGGS, Walter T.,   1882 - 1949

BLEVINS, Howard, Jr.,   b/d  1938

TUTTLE, B.W.,   1866 - 1937
TUTTLE, Lula M.,   1873 - 1956

WILLIAMS, Lawrence L.,   Feb.22,1921 - Sept.30,1969  -  WW2

GARLAND, Dan W.,   Apr.25,1912 -  -----
GARLAND, Hassie, (w),  Feb.27,1917 - Apr.26,1948

SNEYD, Dave,   1886 - 1978
          Son of Joe and Susie Sneyd
          Grandson of Seth and Martha Sneyd
SNEYD, Mary E., (w),  1890 - 1979

CAMPBELL, Jack C.,   Apr.22,1906 - Feb.11,1975
CAMPBELL, Dora M.,   Feb.14,1907 -  -----

CAMPBELL, Fred B.,   Dec.27,1923 - Aug.14,1984
CAMPBELL, Doris, (w),  Aug.19,1921 -  -----

SHEWARD, Joseph W.,   Oct.20,1887 - July 4,1966

NEAL, Robert Earl,   1918 - 1972

GARLAND, James Doss,   1890 - 1964

HUGHES, Thomas C.,   Mar.16,1880 - Mar.7,1953
HUGHES, Lena Bowman, (w), Sept.10,1889 - Oct.6,1976

SHELTON, Elisha,   1890 - 1976
SHELTON, Dora,   1890 - 1965

SHELTON, Dora Bell,   Jan.15,1893 - Feb.25,1972

McKINNEY, Isaac,   Apr.10,1889 - Oct.5,1968
McKINNEY, Betty,   Oct.10,1897 - Jan.28,1974

CAMPBELL, Chester,   Oct.18,1901 - Apr.18,1924

CAMPBELL, Elmer,   Mar.26,1912 - Aug.9,1925

CAMPBELL, Gladys S.,  Sept.17,1928 - Dec.8,1928
CAMPBELL, Mary Louise,   Jan.28,1930 - Mar.15,1930
          Daus. of Charlie and Eva Campbell

CAMPBELL, Eva,   Mar.22,1910 - May 15,1930
          Wife of Charlie Campbell

BELL CEMETERY   (continued)

PYRON, John T.,    Oct.20,1886 - Apr.3,1940
PYRON, Emeline C., (w),  Jan.26,1903 - June 1,1983
PYRON, Sanorita Donna, (dau.), Jan.6,1937 - May 26,1945

WRIGHT, John T.,   Sept.4,1851 - May 28,1930
           Son of Thomas J. and Susan Smithman Wright
WRIGHT, Margaret Elizabeth, (w),  Feb.16,1859 - Oct.28,1923

HOSS, Olearry L.,    1882 - 1968
HOSS, Maggie F.,    1894 - -----

BAKER, John William,   Jan.19,1876 - Jan.19,1972
BAKER, Minnie Bell, (w),  Oct.30,1877 - Sept.23,1962

DAVIS, Mary Ethel,   1893 - 1930

BALLARD, Sarah Frances,   Died Apr.18,1973  - age 91

WOODBY, Violet,   Oct.8,1918 - July 5,1932

CAMPBELL, Sadie,   1957 - -----

McINTURFF, Leafy,   b/d  Oct.30,1921
           Dau. of Enos and Julia McInturff
CAMPBELL, Walter D.,   1900 - 1985
CAMPBELL, Ethel,  (w#1), Nov.1,1898 - Apr.6,1924
CAMPBELL, Martha,  b/d Apr.1,1924  - Dau. of Walter and Ethel
CAMPBELL, Violet, (w#2), 1919 - 1989

TEAGUE, James W.,   Died Oct.4,1918  - Pvt 18th Inf Div

BIRCHFIELD, Mendal C.,   1906 - -----
BIRCHFIELD, Etta G.,   1907 - -----

BIRCHFIELD, Allen,  b/d  1927

GRINDSTAFF, Jim,  Jan.1,1880 - Feb.8,1967
GRINDSTAFF, Cinda D.,   Mar.20,1895 - Nov.9,1984

SNEED, Stewart W.,   June 4,1916 - Apr.24,1967 -   WW2

DAVIS, Phillip Kevin,   1957 - 1958

SNEED, A.T.,   1886 - 1965
SNEED, Bettie, (w), 1891 - 1954
           Dau. of R.B. and Mary Woodby Pate
SNEED, Infant Isaac,  Died 1910
SNEED, Alvin,   1911 - 1912
SNEED, Infant Jessie Lou,   Died 1925
SNEED Daisy Lee,   1923 - 1926
SNEED, Arbie,   1930 - 1931(or 1933)

BURCHFIELD, I.H.,   Mar.4,1874 - Aug.4,1959
BURCHFIELD, Mattie C.,   Aug.17,1879 - Dec.21,1915

BELL CEMETERY (continued)

RIGGS, Ellis J.,   Jan.5,1844 - Dec.12,1919
RIGGS, Emma, (w),   May 7,1865 - Mar.19,1943

MARCUS, Goldman Lee,   Sept.8,1884 - Feb.26,1952
              Son of John Roland and Frances E. Welch Marcus

BROWN, Debra Lynn,   1952 - 1954
              Dau. of Roy C. and Martha Brown

DAVIS, Henry O.,   Jan.19,1919 - Oct.15,1967   -   WW2

DAVIS, The Orlie Davis Family

DAVIS, Dock Jennings,   Mar.18,1906 - Apr.29,1942

HOWELL, Dudley,   1883 - -----
HOWELL, Rachel,   1893 - 1951

DAVIS, Henry,   1867 - 1937
DAVIS, Lydia, (w),   1868 - 1931

DAVIS, Frank,   1889 - 1959
              Son of Henry and Lydia Gouge Davis
DAVIS, Kate,   1891 - 1982

DAVIS, Jerome Butler,   Feb.2,1904 - July 12,1963
DAVIS, Louise Morgan, (w),   Sept.30,1902 - Nov.24,1970

SIMPSON, William F.,   1896 - -----
SIMPSON, Maggie Davis, (w),   1908 - 1964

HENSLEY, Charles A.,   June 10,1893 - Dec.4,1982
HENSLEY, M. Etta Davis, (w),   Nov.21,1897 - July 14,1972

BROWN, Clyde McNabb,   Sept.3,1893 - Oct.17,1955
              Son of G.W. and Margaret McNabb Brown
BROWN, Litha Davis, (w),   1896 - 1967

LYONS, Mary,   Jan.18,1931 - -----

GRINDSTAFF, Elbert,   Mar.23,1883 - Jan.15,1973
GRINDSTAFF, Charlotte C.,   Apr.23,1892 - Nov.10,1945
ALLEN, Goldie G.,   Dec.22,1914 - Jan.15,1936
GOUGE, Sarah Davis,   Oct.10,1872 - Jan.26,1952
HENSON, Richard Washington,   Oct.19,1895 - May 16,1974
HENSON, Virginia Bell, (w),   Jan.29,1906 - -----

POTTER, Jesse R.,   Jan.21,1923 - Aug.2,1981   - WW2
POTTER, Florence L.,   ----- - -----

ODOM, Kermit W.,   Oct.30,1908 - Nov.25,1972
ODOM, Minnie A.,   ----- - -----

ODOM, Billy Gail,   June 20,1941 - June 22,1941

BELL CEMETERY (continued)

GARLAND, Willard Hamlin,   1916 - 1980 - Lt.jg  USN  WW2

GARLAND, Eva Brooks,   1891 - 1975

BLEVINS, Alice M. Garland,   1878 - 1941

CAMPBELL, Walter D.,   1900 - 1985

BROOKS, Annie A.,   1862 - 1943

BAKER, Charlie H.,   Apr.12,1838 - Apr.22,1928
BAKER, Jane Garland,   Apr.12,1840 - June 17,1917

BAKER, David P.,   ------------

JAYNES, Willard M.,Jr., (Bud), June 20,1933 - Dec.19,1978 - USAF Korea

DAVIS, Elmer Dean,   Nov.20,1922 - Mar.20,1983 - USA  WW2

PATE, Elsie B.,   1911 - 1985

JOHNSON, Ida Ledford,   June 4,1909 - Aug.28,1931

FRANCIS, John,   1909 - 1975
FRANCIS, Florence,   1921 - -----

BLEVINS, Howard W.,   1908 - 1960
BLEVINS, Neltie H.,   1911 - -----
          (Mrs. Neltie Haven Odom Jones died Dec.22,1988)

CAMPBELL, Elijah,   Nov.3,1912 - Dec.17,1956
CAMPBELL, Elola Holbrook,   Aug.12,1910 - Aug.13,1940

CAMPBELL, David,   Feb.8,1903 - Aug.16,1985
          Son of James Campbell

JONES, Michael,   Died July 24,1973
          Infant son of Mr. and Mrs. Earl Jones

CHANDLEY, L. Viola,   Dec.29,1917 - Dec.10,1940

ALLEN, Sidney Hugh,   Jan.15,1934 - Oct.29,1975

GRINDSTAFF, Piercie,   1910 - 1984
GRINDSTAFF, Wealtha H., (w),   1918 - -----

CONNER, Wayne C.,   1903 - 1984
CONNER, Leah H.,   1918 - -----

SNEYD, Anthony Todd,   Feb.19,1974 - Aug.24,1975

INGRAM, Clarence,   1932 - 1975 - USN  Korea
INGRAM, Janice M., (w),   Aug.31,1942 - -----

BELL CEMETERY (continued)

BOITZ, Frank J.,    Mar.13,1916 - Aug.10,1976
BOITZ, Geraldine, (w),   Apr.22,1927 - Jan.5,1983

AMYX, Chester A.,   Apr.6,1922 - Sept.23,1977
AMYX, Josephine P., (w),   Nov.24,1923 -  -----

CUTSHALL, Grover,   Apr.30,1914 -  -----
CUTSHALL, Helen M., (w),   Aug.11,1911 -  -----

FURROW, George Ace,   1909 - 1977

SHELTON, John Azor,   Oct.25,1915 - May 28,1976
SHELTON, Irene Lola, (w),   Apr.16,1928 - Sept.14,1987


## CHANDLER #1 CEMETERY

Off Rt. 19. Take right on Chandler Cove Rd., just
after Tumbling Creek Rd. On hill before house on right (Chandler
residence).  Copied April 16, 1989.

CHANDLER, William Granison,  Sept.6,1836 - July 8,1913
        Co K 13 Tenn Inf. Union Army
        Son of Joe and Holly Chandler
CHANDLER, Mary E., (w)   1847 - 1925

PATE, Delia,   1887 - 1948
        Wife of R.L. Pate

CHANDLER, Isaac,   1869 - 1951
        Son of William G. Chandler
CHANDLER, Sarah Rebecca, (w)   1877 - 1967

CHANDLER, Clursie,   1900 - 1926

CHANDLER, Infants -  no dates
        Sons of Wolford and Betsy Chandler

TILSON, Ella Chandler,   1876(1879?) - 1953

## GILLIS #2 CEMETERY

On hill above farm at first left off Rt.23 beyond
Ernestville.   Copied April 21,1989

GILLIS, W.J.,   Feb.15,1860 - April 4,1919

RIDDLE, Flossie May,   May 28,1907 - Sept.25,1910

Plus about 10 unmarked stones
Including 2 children(?) near the house on the old
Asheville - Virginia wagon trail.

## unmarked grave

GILLIS, John Robert

## RIDDLE CEMETERY

On Rt. 23, up driveway on right, just before Edwards
Branch Road, out of Ernestville.  Copied April 25,1989

RIDDLE, William L. Sr.,    1890 - 1986

LEWIS, Charlie E.,    Died June 15,1942   - Cpl. 29 Inf. WW II
    Son of James Nelson and Loretta Riddle Lewis

LEWIS, J.N.    July 15,1881 -  -----
LEWIS, Loretta,  (w)  Feb.4,1888 - April 25,1950

RIDDLE, Thomas N.,    1882 - 1961
RIDDLE, Belle,(w)    Feb.8,1884 - Jan.18,1944

RIDDLE, Homer,    Dec.26,1912 - Aug.29,1935
    Son of T.N. and Belle Jones Riddle

RHODES, Juanita,    1925 - 1944

RIDDLE, Dewey,    1898 - 1975
RIDDLE, Esther,  (w)  1909 - 1977

RIDDLE, George W.,    July 9,1880 - Dec.26,1976
RIDDLE, Lula Wilson,  (w)  Jan.23,1885 - May 20,1930
    Dau. of M.W. and Mary Randolph Wilson

WEBB, Mack Burnie,   Oct.22,1914 - July 21,1979 - S2 - US Navy
WEBB, Mary J.,  (w)  March 25,1915 -  -----

RIDDLE, Margaret Ellen,    1885 - 1977  "Aunt Mag"

RIDDLE, James M.,    Nov.16,1852 - Feb. 4,1930
    Son of John and Margaret Deaton Riddle
RIDDLE, Mary J. Tomkins,  (w)  Aug.25,1854 - Feb.18,1936
    Dau. of John and Martha Tilson Tompkins

BROYLES, Pearl Riddle,    Nov.11,1894 - Feb.21,1977

METCALF, Albert Earl,    Jan.10,1921 - May 27,1984 - US Army WW II

METCALF, ---- E.,    Died 1969

METCALF. W.A.,    Feb.18,1888 - Nov.19,1949
METCALF, Vernie,  (w)  May 2,1898 -  -----

Plus several unmarked stones

## CORN CEMETERY          Copied April 25,1989

Off Rt. 23, up Corn Rd.(next right after Edwards
Branch Rd.) to end of road, then left through pasture.

CORN, James W., Jan.3,1859 - Jan.9,1939
CORN, Wennie E.,  (w)  Oct.8,1861 - Jan.3,1948

Plus several unmarked stones

## METCALF CEMETERY

On Rt. 23 above Flag Pond, on left, just past Shady Grove
Baptist Church, up dirt road beside first house.
Copied April 25,1989

HENSLEY, Jimmy F.,    May 13,1892 - Oct.5,1976
HENSLEY, Berlia R.,   (w) June 1,1916 - Nov.12,1973
METCALF, Mary L.,     May 18,1877 - June 5,1953
METCALF, Ann Etta,   (Dau.) May 23,1892 - June 19,1932

EDWARDS, Delia,    Feb.6,1918 - April 10,1930

SHOOK, Infant,    Died Nov.1914
      Dau. of Noel and Siss Shook

METCALF, Alma Gean,    Aug.1,1937 - Oct.29,1937
      Dau. of Pritchard and Ruby Metcalf

METCALF, Sam E.,    April 12,1874 - March 19,1952
METCALF. Hattie M.,   (w)  Sept.7,1879 - May 22,1972

RICE, Nealie J.,    April 16,1905 - Dec.27,1972
RICE, Lizzie,   (w)  Feb.14,1904 - -----

WILLIAMS, Natasha Larissa,   b/d  Feb.14,1977

EDWARDS, Clarence,    March 28,1937 - March 6,1977
EDWARDS, Betty J.,   (w)  May 16,1936 - -----

EDWARDS, Joel,    March 21,1899 - Nov.8,1976
EDWARDS, Dessie Rice,   (w)  Dec.14,1900 - Oct.28,1961

CARVER, Elizabeth,    April 22,1924 - Oct.18,1946

SHELTON, Matilda Carver,    August 1,1912 - Oct.10,1945

METCALF, William,    July 1,1833 - Sept.13,1913
METCALF, Martha,   (w)  Dec.17,1931 - June 25,1904

METCALF, Margaret,    June 23,1855 - June 20,1930
      Dau. of William and Martha Hensley Metcalf
METCALF, J.W.,   (Son)  June 9,1874 - 1930

RAY, Venus    Sept.11,1910 - Oct.1,1983
RAY, Lela M.,   (w)  Dec.2,1916 - Oct.23,1969

RICE, Dell Metcalf,    April 23,1932 - July 16,1974
      Dau. of Pritchard and Ruby Metcalf

CANTRELL, Media M.,    Feb.5,1904 - Feb.7,1956

CANTREL, J.P.,    Aug.25,1927 - April 9,1980

HARRIS, Zeb Vance,    Dec.20,1873 - Aug.15,1948
HARRIS, Georgia Randolph, Born May 4,1890

CARVER, Levi,    Nov.9,1891 - Sept.13,1969
CARVER, Marget C., (W#1) April 15,1892 - Sept.1,1938
CARVER, Bertha Ann, (W#2) April 19,1898 - Aug.19,1963

RICE, W.S.,    1870 - 1944
RICE, Callie D., (w)  1875 - 1958

RICE, Minnie,   1898 - 1975

ARRINGTON, Joe,   May 30,1924 - May 30,1966
        Son of Minnie Arrington

RICE, Paul,   b/d 1952
        Son of A.R. and Ada Metcalf Rice

DODSON, Tonya Lynn,  b/d 1971

CARVER, Troy M.,   Oct.22,1916 - April 28,1959
        PFC Btry D 385 AAA Bn CAC   WW II

CARVER, Chapel,   May 27,1918 -  -----
CARVER, Edith, (w)  Feb.23,1924 - Oct.9,1970

CARVER, Otis,   Nov.3,1930 - Dec.15,1985
CARVER, Victoria, (w)  May 1,1939 -  -----

MATHES, Altha C.,   Oct.13,1876 - April 15,1963

HARRIS, J. Fred,   July 21,1909 - Aug.6,1942

HARRIS, Ernest,   Dec.29,1927 - March 6,1928

HARRIS, Ann,   Died Feb.8,1926

BUCHANAN, Steve,   1929 - 1972

WILLIAMS, Ricky Gene,   May 22,1960 - Dec.2,1985
        Pvt. US Army

CRUM, George,   April 1,1900 - Aug.26,1983

CRUM, Evie M.Carver,   July 7,1911 - Feb.6,1964

        Plus numerous standard unmarked concrete
            upright slabs.

## NEW TOMBSTONES

HENSLEY, Clingman,  1850 - 1922
METCALF, Pritchard P., 1907 - 1989
HARRIS, Georgia, d. 1989
MATHIS, May, d. 1935 (Stone reported but not found)

## PATE CEMETERY

Rt.23 above Flag Pond. At third house on right beyond package store. Look on left side of highway for barn. Cemetery is on knoll behind barn.      Copied April 26,1989

PATE, J.F., April 19,1872 - Dec.6,1922

PATE, Laurie, (w)  Jan.28,1878 - Jan.18,1950

PATE, Cenny,  Died 1938 - Age 6 mos.
Dau. of J.M. and B.J. Pate

PATE, Eddie B.,   Died 1921 - Age 7 mos.
Son of J.M. and B.J. Pate

Plus several unmarked stones, including two children's stones with Pate scratched on them.

## GUINN #2 CEMETERY

Off Tilson Mt. Rd. On Carter Branch section.
Right turn across from Carter Cemetery, to end of dirt road along creek. Cemetery is behind the last house on the left.   Copied  April 26,1989

GUINN, Hugh

GUINN, Austin

Cemetery includes these and possibly others, according to Ken Chandler, but 75 years of neglect has produced honeysuckle and briars in the area and the stones cannot be seen now.

## CHANDLER #2 CEMETERY

Spivey Mt. Rd. at Dale Hensley's Store. Go up draw behind Dale's house, then bear left at top of hill.   Copied May 8,1989

Fifteen to twenty graves marked only with field stones, but including:

CHANDLER, Joe    (no dates)
CHANDLER, Holly, (w) (no dates)
Parents of William G. Chandler, who is buried in Chandler #1 Cemetery.

## BLANKENSHIP # 2 CEMETERY

On Rice Creek Road above Flag Pond, near and to the
left of Blankenship #1 Cemetery, near Tipton Branch
junction. On east side of road. Copied May 12,1989.

BLANKENSHIP, Arthur,  May 1920 - June 1979
Son of William Earl Blankenship

No other graves.

## TOLLEY #2 CEMETERY

At highest point on Upper Stone Mt. Rd., behind the
farm of Mr. Honeycutt, on a hill deep in the woods.
Copied May 13,1989.

Eight graves, field stones only.

TOLLEY,  ----- (Ancestors of Tolleys in the area)

## GOUGE #2 CEMETERY

On Jess Hopson Rd., off Massachusetts Ave. in Unicoi.
Copied May 16,1989

GOUGE, Hoy,  Oct.11,1871 - Oct.3,1945
GOUGE, Millie, (w)  1870 - 1913
Although Hoy's latest wife (Delena 1902 - 1957) is
listed next to him on a memorial stone near the cemetery
entrance, she is actually buried at Happy Valley in
Carter County.

GOUGE, Georgie,  1896 - 1919
GOUGE, Frank L.,  May 24,1901 - Oct.22,1931
Son of Hoy and Nannie McKinney Gouge

GOUGE, Emery Nesby,  Mar.14,1931 - Mar.26,1931
GOUGE, Dayton Arnold,  July 15,1932 - Feb.12,1933

GOUGHE, Bruce,  Nov.4,1912 - May 10,1914
Son of W. and H. Goughe

BRITT, Donald Ray,  b/d 1947

## OLD BANKS CEMETERY

On McCurry Rd. off Simerly Creek Rd., behind home
of W.W. Gouge. (3rd house on left)  Copied June 17,1989

BANKS, Ann,  (no dates)

Plus field stones for about 10 graves of
early settlers.

## OLD O'BRIEN CEMETERY

On Davis Rd. off Rt. 107 in Limestone Cove, in field
between Davis/Gouge Cemetery and O'Brien Cemetery, near
locust tree. Copied June 17,1989.

Field stones, scattered. (Ancestors of the O'Briens in the area)

## BRIGGS CEMETERY

Rice Creek Rd., up draw south of Blankenship Cemetery.
Take road past gate, then sharp left at old house up
the draw, then follow track to top of ridge and turn
right. Cemetery is several hundred feet up track, near
fence, near junction of tracks. Copied June 22,1989

BRIGGS, Landon C., May 10,1861 - Nov.20,1899
BRIGGS, Sarah, "Sallie* Tipton, (w) Sept.12,1863 - Mar.4,1942
BRIGGS, Princy A., (Dau.) July 6,1883 - Dec.15,1899

BRIGGS, Bulo, Mar.13,1910 - Dec.9,1927
BRIGGS, Crissin Bery, May 14,1895 - Feb.14,1931
　　　Probably children of Landon and Sarah Briggs

Plus several unmarked field stones

## OLD CLOUSE CEMETERY

On the Pate farm, on Carter Branch section of Tilson
Mt. Rd., not far from Carter Cemetery.
Copied June 23,1989

Consists of unmarked field stones, including:
CLOUSE, Thomas, Died 1934
CLOUSE, Sarah Gilbert, (w) Died 1912
CLOUSE, Frank, (Son) Died about 1892 at 12 years of age

CLOUSE, William, Killed in Civil War
　　　Brother of Thomas Clouse

SAMS, Leland, Died about 1902
SAMS, Frank, Died about 1904
SAMS, Thomas, Died about 1906
SAMS, Robert, Died about 1910
　　　Infants; Children of Leroy Hays and Nancy Clouse Sams,
　　　who are buried at Evergreen Cemetery.

WATTS, Infant (no further data)

LEWIS, Infant (no further data)

## RAMSEY CEMETERY

Rocky Fork Road, take 1st driveway to mobile home, up trail to top of
hill, then left

Checked October 22, 1989

RAMSEY, Job,      Co. C 2nd NC Mtd Inf Union Army

RAMSEY, Rachel,   May 5, 1831 - Jan. 2, 1918

RAMSEY, James W.,    1851-1901  (son of Job Ramsey)

RAMSEY, Ollie,    Mar. 24, 1906 - Nov. 14, 1909

plus several unmarked stones

## GUINN #3 CEMETERY

Rt. 23, just south of Rocky Fork, on E. side.  Take first driveway to last
house, then up track to top of hill.  Cemetery on left

Checked October 22, 1989

GUINN, Thomas J.,   Nov. 26, 1870 - Apr. 4, 1935
                    (Flag Pond)    (Roanoke, VA)
GUINN, Minnie (w),  Oct. 9, 1885  - May 27, 1942

GUINN, Voul,        1910-1911

SPARKS, James W.,   July 5, 1864 - Feb. 2, 1919

RAMSEY, Raymond D.,   July 28, 1931 - Mar. 22, 1969    HM  US Navy

RAMSEY, Woodard L.,   Aug. 25, 1887 - June 25, 1942
RAMSEY, Eliza Jane,   Jan. 3, 1889 - Nov. 25, 1973

GUINN, Isaac,   Apr. 2, 1826 - Oct. 14, 1897

ENGLE, Creasie,    1896 - 1978

GUINN, Sarah K.,    June 11, 1868 - Apr. 13, 1890

GUINN, Elizabeth,   Apr. 4, 1828 - Nov. 2, 1889

LAWING, John W.,    d. May 6, 1909  age 50 yrs

LAWING, Mary E.,   May 12, 1878 - Oct. 24, 1885
                   dau of J. W. and Margaret Lawing

LAWING, Ambrose,   Co. B. 3rd NC Mtd Inf Union Army

GUINN, Guy,   b/d 1904

GUINN #3 CEMETERY (continued)

LAWING, Joseph H.,  Dec. 13, 1875 - Apr. 18, 1876
             son of W. W. and S. H. Lawing

                 plus 5 unmarked slabs for childrens' graves, near
                 Sparks stone.  Possible names are Lillie and Almeda

                 plus 2 unmarked concrete slabs for childrens' graves,
                 in rear of cemetery, near Lawing stones

                 plus several field stones


                          STOCKTON CEMETERY

    Hogskin Road, out of Flag Pond, take gravel road on right, just before
    Roseville Church and Roseville Cemetery, continue up the hill to top, by an
    old barn and clearing, then take path on left to cemetery

                          Checked Nov. 4, 1989

STOCKTON, Thomas J. "Jeff", Jan. 12, 1859 - Jan. 27, 1945
           son of Samuel P. and Elizabeth Horn Stockton
STOCKTON, Eliza Carter (w),  Oct. 2, 1858 - July 25, 1925
STOCKTON, Nancy D. (dau),  May 2, 1883 - Nov. 13, 1899
STOCKTON, Tilda (dau),  Oct. 30, 1896 - June 29, 1898

STOCKTON, Samuel P.,  Mar. 18, 1828 - Feb. 9, 1894
STOCKTON, Elizabeth (w),  Aug. 4, 1832 - Sep. 12, 1904
           dau of Elizabeth (Wolf) Horn

STOCKTON, Melvin Frank,  July 16, 1870 - July 5, 1904
           son of Samuel P. and Elizabeth (Horn) Stockton

HASTINGS, Henry Frank, "H.F.",  b. July 18, 1845
           son of Henry Clinton and Eady (Stockton) Hastings
           Served in CSA - Confederate Army
HASTINGS, Nancy Jane (w),  June 5, 1853 - Aug. 11, 1926
           dau of Samuel P. and Elizabeth (Horn) Stockton
HASTINGS, Florence M. (dau),  Apr. 18, 1896 - Mar. 8, 1904
HASTINGS, Cora E. (dau),  Sep. 13, 1883 - Oct. 6, 1890
HASTINGS, Samuel H. (son),  July 9, 1881 - Aug. 1, 1881
HASTINGS, Christie E. (son),  May 25, 1890 - June 15, 1890

CARTER, Edith E.,  Apr. 24, 1869 - Apr. 7, 1909
           wife of Samuel Carter

Unmarked Grave:
HORN, Elizabeth Wolf "Grandma",  d. at age 80  Mother of Elizabeth (Horn)
                                                              Stockton
Note - later generations of Stocktons are buried at Roseville Cemetery

                          -401-

## HENSLEY #4 CEMETERY

Devil Fork Road (out of Rocky Fork), just past Sweetwater junction, located above the old log home (1887) of Minta Carter and her sister, Roxie Hensley, who taught nearby at Sweetwater School

Checked Nov. 4, 1989

BURGNER, Ella,   Apr. 15, 1892 - Oct. 1, 1978

BURGNER, Infant,     d. Feb. 14, 1912
            infant son of Mr. and Mrs. Worley Burgner

SHELTON, Ms. Tempa C.,     Sept. 7, 1868 - Feb. 7, 1961
SHELTON, Infant (son),     d. July 20, 1901

HENSLEY, Sarah Louisa,     Sept. 22, 1861 - Dec. 23, 1944

CARTER, John H.,     Aug. 6, 1859 - Dec. 23, 1920

CARTER, William L.,     1887-1974
CARTER, Memory (w),     1892-
CARTER, Infant (son), d. Oct. 21, 1922

CARTER, Minta Alice,   Feb. 10, 1887 - Feb. 11, 1983

HENSLEY, Mrs. Roxie,   May 23, 1889 - Oct. 13, 1985
            sister of Minta Carter

## TINKER #4 CEMETERY

Off Rt. 23, up Big Branch to first left after hairpin curves, then bear right at fork, to a barn.  The cemetery is left of the barn on a knoll with pine trees. Located near former cabin of Haynes Brown.  (chimney standing)

Checked Nov. 27, 1989

TINKER, John H.,   Oct. 1, 1895 - July 14, 1948
            Cpl. 306 Engr. 81 Div. '"'I
            (father of Roy Tinker, who has a white house nearby)

## SHELTON #3 CEMETERY

On Devil's Fork Rd., .2 mile from NC Line, behind second house from border, across road from Williams #1 Cemetery

Copied Jan. 3, 1990

SHELTON, Leonard Allen,  Nov. 17, 1957 - Apr. 15, 1987   Sgt. US Army

SHELTON, Alonzo,   June 26, 1903 - Dec. 16, 1984
SHELTON, Almettie (w),  Dec. 29, 1903 - Nov. 22, 1978

SHELTON, Artha,    1923 -
SHELTON, Elzie (w),  May 19, 1922 - Feb. 9, 1985

SHELTON, Atmon,    Dec. 30, 1926 - Oct. 24, 1971


## SILVERS #2 CEMETERY

On Hogskin Creek Road, .2 mile beyond Roseville Cemetery, on same side, beside a trailer home

Checked Jan. 23, 1990

SILVERS, Ezra,    Oct. 2, 1913 - Sep. 9, 1984
SILVERS, Jettie (w),   Dec. 10, 1917 -

SPARKS, Infant
SPARKS, Infant

HARDIN, Infant

no other stones


## RAY #2 CEMETERY

On Devil's Fork Road, east side, .8 mile before Sweetwater Church, beside log home on hill, where Ruth Green lives

Checked Mar. 11, 1990

RICE, Sirrelda "mother",  Sep. 27, 1880 - Aug. 18, 1954

EGELSTON, James E.,   Nov. 21, 1914 - Oct. 30, 1972
EGELSTON, Flora B.,   Dec. 2, 1920 -

RAY, Thomas E.,    Aug. 7, 1872 - Feb. 2, 1948
RAY, Sealey M. (w),  Jan. 23, 1877 - Mar. 8, 1965

RAY, Waco M.,    July 10, 1899 - Jan. 11, 1974
RAY, Sarepta H. (w),  Mar. 24, 1914 -

RAY, Stewart Thomas,    July 30, 1922 - June 28, 1977
          PFC   US Army   WWII

RAY, Jerry Wayne,    Aug. 11, 1948 - Sep. 27, 1969

RAY, Walter L.,    June 6, 1906 - Mar. 4, 1979
RAY, Minta J. (w),   Mar. 18, 1911 -

SALTS, Joe Vance,   Jan. 12, 1914 -
SALTS, Caroline Hey (w),   Nov. 16, 1917 - Apr. 22, 1968

SALTS, Joe,    May 23, 1893 - Aug. 31, 1974
SALTS, Creola (w),   Oct. 19, 1903 - Jan. 17, 1982

GENTRY, Offie,    Aug. 6, 1896 - Feb. 26, 1976
GENTRY, Almetta (w),    Oct. 15, 1901 - Nov. 29, 1950

RAY, Nelson W.,    July 19, 1897 - Sep. 8, 1981 - father of Ruth Green

RAY, Elzie H.,    June 30, 1910 - Feb. 7, 1989

                no other stones

## RAY #3 CEMETERY

Off Devil's Fork Road.  Start at Lattie Ray's white house, .8 mile before
Sweetwater Church, on west side, (across road from Ruth Green).  Follow
small creek to top of Mt., about a mile, and look to the left
                            Checked Mar. 11, 1990

RAY, Ida Bell Franklin,   1899-1930   - Ruth Green's mother

RAY, Charles Blake,    1930-1932    Orig Rhea
RAY, Albert    ,    b/d 1917    (til 1840s)
          Ruth Green's brothers

RAY, Joseph
RAY, Cloah (w)
          Lattie Ray's grandparents

RAY, Josiah

               plus field stones (unmarked), which include:

HENSLEY, James
HENSLEY, Dortha (w)
HENSLEY, Maggie (dau)

## GILLIS #3 CEMETERY

Off Rt. 23, up Rocky Fork Road to first road on left (just before road
at Flint Creek). Follow road, keeping left, to top of knoll

Checked Mar. 12, 1990

*GILLIS, David Samuel,    Feb. 22, 1850 - Dec. 30, 1924
 GILLIS, Margaret Murray (w),  Oct. 5, 1854 - Mar. 1, 1947
 GILLIS, Edgar Ezekiel "Zeke" (son),  Sep. 28, 1883 - Dec. 28, 1938

* parents of William Lattie Gillis I


## WHALEY CEMETERY

Near Erwin, at upper end of Pippin Hollow Road, on the Cal Vance home
place on Buffalo Mountain

Checked Nov. 11, 1989

About two field stones for persons named Whaley reported in this area


## OLD BIRCHFIELD CEMETERY

On top of hill at jct of Upper Stone Mt. Rd. and Ham Smith Rd

Checked Oct. 26, 1989

Field stones, numerous, cows wander through cemetery. Old Birchfields.
Some bodies have been moved, to Bell Cemetery, acc. to Perry Hughes


## BERRY CEMETERY

Old Rt. 19/23 in Unicoi, near White Cove Road.   Checked Oct. 11, 1989

The stones are no longer there. Several stones with the name Berry used to be there.


## THOMPSON CEMETERY

White Road in Unicoi, to Pinnacle Rd at Jay Smith's farm.

Checked Oct. 11, 1989

No stone - a man named Thompson was killed during the Civil War, and buried here

# NOTES

Several cemeteries located just outside the borders of
Unicoi County may have been used for Unicoi County residents.
For example, the Bumpass Cove Cemetery, described in "Wash-
ington County, Tenn., Tombstone Inscriptions", Vol. II, by
Charles Bennett. Other examples are the Ephraim Buck Plan-
tation Cemetery, off Route 19/23, and the Berry Cemetery, on
Simerly Creek Road, both described in "Cemeteries of Carter
County, Tenn.", by Orville Fields.

Several Indian burial grounds are located within Unicoi
County, but they are unmarked, and cannot serve the genealogical
purpose of this book. They could be included in a study of
Indian artifacts and traces.

The reader is warned that in spite of great diligence,
errors in this book are surely possible, and readers are en-
couraged to visit these cemeteries themselves to confirm the
inscription on the stone and to share the pleasure we had in
our research.

The following index is keyed to those names that begin
with a capitalized surname.

# INDEX

ABEL - Thomas 8
ADAMS - Amilee, 359, Callie, 13, Charles 45, 339, James 324, 359, Mary 324, Mayme 339
ADKINS - Anna, 323, Baxter 114, Charlie 333, Cling 125, Clingman 114, Craig 352, Dewey 369, Edythe 185, Ethel 319, Eugene 349, G. D. 341, Herman 173, Hubert 319, 352, Ina 358, James 173, 223, Janie 45, Lula 352, Margaret 308, Martin 143, Mary 173, 374, Nancy 223, Rex 374, Rice 323, Rosa 269, Sallie 342, Samuel 36, Stokes 342, William 269, 258
AKARD - Infant 246, Lydia 246
AKEL - William 319
AKERS - Hugh 354, Robert 354
ALBERTSON - Infant 8, Jack 8
ALDERMAN - Pat 364, Verna 364
ALDRIDGE - Allie 27, Elizabeth 21, H. M. 21, Isaac 21, Ruthie 21, William 27
ALFORD - Bessie 314, Paul 265, 314
ALLEN - Alfred 25, Allie 291, Artie 288, Cassie 26, Claudia 25, Dennis 289, Edna 31, Elva 26, Emma 26, Ethel 333, Fred 76, Goldie 391, Gurnie 291, Harley 57, Hubert 288, Infant 26, Issac 26, James 26, Jasper 31, John 33, Juanita 294, Kate 288, Laura 26, Louise 57, Mary 320, Oliver 333, Robert 26, 320, Sarah 26, 76, Sidney 392, Willard 289, William 317, Willie 33, Wilma 26
ALLGOOD - Timmy 338
ALLRED - Anne 298, M. M. 298, Linville 263, Myrtle 263, Nola 298
ALTMAIRE - Peter 268
AMBROSE - Alfred 62, Belle 372, Bernie 65, Bessie 57, 306, Charles 62, Cloyd 61, Cora 3, Ethel 62, Harriet/Hattie 65, Helen 358, Infant 65, 376, J. L. 358, Infant 65, 376, J. L. 358, James 3, 57, Juanita 61, Lyle 62, Morris 58, Nealie 65, Ossie 65, Pamela 372, Ralph 62, Richard 358, Wade 57
AMRELL - Etta 96
AMYX - Chester 393, Josephine 393
ANDERS - Bertha 334, Bill 295, Charles 307, Delcina 330, Demmey 90, Elbert 35, Elsie 35, Hazen 269, Henry 368, Isaac 45, James 276, Lenice 269, Madge 276, Martha 35, Mary 307, O'Nell 368, Rachel 45, Richard 316, Robert 70, Stewart 330, Stuart 45
ANDERSON - Elbert 95, Elizabeth/Eliza 95, Estelle 157, Flora 95, Infant 114, Isaac 95, 254, 255, Jake 79, James 13, John 157, 255, 354, Juanita 95, Lucinda 95, Margaret 291, 354, Mary 13, 255, Nanna 95, Naoma 95, Renzo 291, S. M. 95, Shepherd 95, Taylor 13,

Thomas 95, William 95, Willie 95
ANDREWS - Ross 27
ANGEL - Gladys 343, Mack 20
ANNIS - Brodie 304, Donnie 304, Douglas 304
ARRINGTON - Joe 396
ARROWOOD - Arlene 42, Charlotte 287, Cora 356, Dorothy 287, Douglas 356, Eddie 372, Elizabeth 370, Ernest 288, Eugene 42, Judie 374, Landon 356, Lawrence 374, Levi 100, Mabel 374, Mack 374, May 374, Park 374, Pauline 356, Quinter 374, Tony 45
ARWOOD - Luther 88, Mae 368, Wilzia 368
ASHLEY - William 178
ASKEW - Doris 142, James 142
ASPIN - Alice 349, Wayne 349
ATKINS - Bobby 154, Bruce 229, Cornelia 376, Craig 352, David 229, Hubert 352, James 311, Jerry 295, Lula 352, Manassah 318, Tilda 311, Tokie 229
AULT - Ashley 140
AUSTIN - Robert 326
AYERS - Dallas 130, David 181, Donald 72, Infant 184, Joan III, John 130, Julia 251, Mae 77, Rosa 130, Scott 374, Seen 181, Solmon 77, Wayne 72
BABB - Harold 171, Wanda 171
BAILEY - Addie 95, 543, Andy 146, Anna 45, Ban 330, Bathilda 372, Bernie 275, C. A. 270, Carlos 320, Carrie 288, Charles 290, 306, Chester 288, Clara 195, 210, Clyde 19, 291, Curtis 45, David 309, 334, Debby 24, Delcena 21, Dovie 21, Edna 288, Edward 86, Elbert 34, 274, Elizabeth 213, 334, Elmer 295, Essie 21, Ethel 86, 306, 314, Fannie 295, Floyd 265, Geter 293, Gladys 359, Grace 69, Guy 210, Hafford 26, Handy 382, Hannah 19, Harley 306, 368, Harriett 250, Hattley 27, Hiram 21, Hudson 35, Infant 20, 21, 65, 86, J. C. 20, J. R. 275, James 21, 335, Jesse 346, John 19, 21, 148, 208, Judi 289, Kyle 270, Lawrence 293, Leona 19, Lester 376, Lillie 382, Lowell 342, Lucy/Lucille 158, Lula 333, M. B. 22, Mamel 368, Marcus 73, Martin 2, Mary 31, 271, 274, 275, 300, 313, 314, Michael 370, Mildred 304, Milton 271, Morgan 376, Myma 265, Myrtle 2, Naomi 338, Nora 320, Pansy 335, Pierce 294, Polly 86, Ralph 313, Rebecca 22, Reece 86, Robert 271, 314, Ronald 294, Ross 33, Sam/Samuel 45, 250, 291, Sarah 21, 34, Simon 201, Thelma 334, Theodore 33, Theron 346, Thomas 216, Timothy 213, 289, Toby 21, Venia 320, Virgie 19, 45, 295, Virgil 45, 56, W. W. 158, Walter 334, Willard 304,

338, William 330, Willis 213, Zebb 19
BAINES - Earl 363
BAKER - Andrew 245, Annie 167, Charles 8, 392, Clyde 73, David 69, 73, 384, 392, Edna 180, Ezekiel 245, George 69, 73, Grace 174, Ida 69, 74, James 14, 245, Jane 392, John 358, 390, Joseph 74, Laura 73, Martha 245, Mildred 8, Minnie 390, Myrtle 73, Nancy 174, Sarah 384, Tallulah 69, 74, Thomas 245, Vina 174, W. H. 174, William 14
BAILEY - Lewis 226, Sarah 226
BALLARD - Robert 310, Ruth 310, Sarah 390
BALMON - Mamie 30
BANKS - Alfred 252, Alice 177, Ann 398, Bessie 283, Cecil 339, Chester 177, Dewey 283, Edna 283, Eliza 252, Elsie 339, Helen 252, James 177, Jesse 252, John 252, Lillie 283, Malinda 252, Mary 252, May 252, Moses 252, Nannie 252, Nolia 283, Robert 252, Roy 283, Ruth 252, 257, Walter 252, Wesley 283, William 252
BANNER - Alvin 30, Benjamin 376, Buck 273, Charles 114, Clara 61, Cordie 22, Donald 290, Dora 62, Earnest 22, Elizabeth 24, Eugene 279, Fay 12, Gail 89, Gerald 208, Guard 61, Henry 24, 62, Hubert 63, I. W. 32, Ida 279, Inez 89, Infant 45, 89, James 42, John 45, Julia 28, Lillie/Lillian 81, 330, Linda 45, Lindy 31, Louise 365, Lula 282, M. L. 27, Martin 330, Mary 42, Mathison 46, Max 208, Melvin 46, 365, Orville 279, Pheoba 24, R. W. 60, Ralph 89, 90, Rhoda 28, Robert 208, Sandra 208, Terry 273, Thelma 60, Velva 208, Virgie 22, Walter 29, William 42, 208
BANNISTER - Benjamin 262, Jannie 282, Pearl 262, Richard 263
BARE - Etta 13, James 13
BARKER - Marietta 277
BARNES - Arthur 340, Earl 220, Florence 340, James 220, 340, Mary 220, Olive 350, William 350
BARNETT - Bertie 307, Betty 103, C. S. 112, Cecil 60, Dora 383, Earl 352, Edith 177, Elizabeth 307, Ellen 36, Gertrude 359, Geter 274, Harriett 307, Helen 352, Infant, 34, Irma 363, James 60, 177, Jeter 103, Leonard 36, Marie 36, Marioha, 11, Marion 36, Martin 363, Mary 60, 283, Nannie 81, Nellie 292, Pamela 80, Patsy 87, Rosetta 60, Sam/Samuel 307, 359, Sara 34, Smith 383, Spencer 81, T. C. 46, William 36, 292, 307, Willie 363
BARRETT - A. J. 161, Mary 161, Sue 162

—407—

BARRON - Lee 280
BARRY - Charlie 176, D. A. 6, Everett 176, Gertrude 286, J. H. 245, Mary 176, Richard 286, Senia 176
BARTLEY - Carrow 309, Frank 309, William 309
BARTON - John 330
BAUCOM - Dortha 376, James 2, John 2, Juanita 2, Mamie 2
BAUGHMAN - C. J. 297, Eloise 376, Fred 297, H. H. 303, Harry 303, Mary 303, Selma 376
BAUMGARDNER - Lutishia 337, Ruth 12, Thomas 337
BAXTER - Bill 197, Byrd 196, Elizabeth 38, Ethel 196, Gene 38, Jacob 196, Joe 38, John 38, Lorenzo 38, Nancy 196, Napoleon 196
BAYLESS - N. 226, W. E. 226
BEALS - Alvin 72, Buford 69, Catherine 71, Darrell 72, Elizabeth 71, Eva 72, J. H. 71, James 71, John 71, Linda 72, Madellon 73, Martha 72, Mary 71, Richard 72, Roscoe 72, Trula 72, Victor 69, W. N. 71, Warren 73, Wayne 72, William 71
BEAM - Bob 323, Essie 287, W. M. 287, W. R. 189
BEAN - Charles 233, Margaret 233
BEAVER - Charles 46, Delzie 348, Floyd 332, Georgia 46, Grace 332, Infant 46, 94, Mack 3, Robert 3, Savannah 3, Zeb 94
BECK - Harriet 330, James 330
BECKELHIMER - Arch 344, Ida 322
BECKER - Susan 370
BEHELER - C. B. 275, Gladys 275
BELCHER - Carlos 331, Joseph 301, Mildred 331, Sarah 301
BELL - Birdie 388, Celia 388, David 88, 388, Edward 388, Henry 388, Jack 388, James 388, Nancy 388
BENDER - Ellen 385
BENFIELD - Everett 114
BENNETT - A. N. 337, Ada 187, Albert 80, Anderson 22, Annie/Anna 74, 264, Arch/Archibald 5, 182, Avanelle 292, Bashana 64, Baxter 83, Cheves 73, Clarence 305, Cora 73, Coy 332, Curtis 371, Drew 319, Earnest 349, Edith 85, Eliza 343, Elizabeth 280, Ellie 80, Elva 188, Ethel 288, Eulalah 4, Eva 270, Fannie 186, Flora 367, Gaither 74, George 331, Georgia 371, Gustia 113, Hannah 343, Harriett 22, Ida 381, Ike 75, Infant 15, Inise 305, Isaac 188, James 70, John 369, Julia 188, Lillian 46, Lizzie 367, Lloyd 74, Lockie 372, Lucinda 71, Lula 316, Mable 346, Mack 367, Maggie 74, Marie 46, Marion 75, Mary 104, 331, Maud 70, Milissa/Milisia 75, 258, Mona 83, Moses 80, Nancy 288, 360, Nathan 85, Neta 85, No

Name 186, Nora 200, Peggy 292, Rebecca 46, Rena 337, Robbie 332, Rotha 270, Roy 80, 264, 292, Ruth 46, Sherman 64, Stephen 292, Sussana 5, T. S. 258, Thomas 372, Tony 189, Walter 34, 200, Willie 368, 382
BENSON - Kathleen 176, Wyeth 176
BENTLEY - George 327, Minnie 327
BERGENDAHL - Cora 342, Oscar 342
BERNDT - Lucille 334
BEST - Glenn 334
BEZDEK - Albert 181, Winnie 181
BIBLE - Selma 265
BIRCHFIELD/BURCHFIELD Allen 390, Charlie 108, Cordelia 104, David 83, 103, 108, Eliza 388, Ella 83, Etta 390, Ezekiah 253, Ezekiel 104, 108, Geneva 104, Hattie 108, Helen 381, I. H. 390, Infant 98, 388, Isaac 387, Julia 108, M. A. 28, Mattie 390, May 253, Mendal 390, Millie 103, Monroe 384, Nathan 108, Nathaniel 258, Paul 15, Robert 28, Rosa 381, Samuel 108, Sarah 108, Slave 253, Walter 388, William 8, 388
BIRDWELL - Nadine 102, Virginia 102, W. W. 102
BISE - Cora 351
BISHOP - David 305, Lillie 305, Wayne 305
BLACK - Margaret 365
BLACKBURN - 8, 388, Ina 321, John 321
BLAIR - Hazel 349, Ida 279, Justin 279
BLANKENSHIP - Ann 150, Arthur 154, 398, Audrey 159, Barry 349, Bernie 153, Bertha 346, Betsy 151, Bob/Bobby 150, 288, Carrie 350, Cecil 153, 159, Clouse 196, Clyde 153, David 153, Dillie 151, Donal 15, Eli 152, Ellen 341, Elva 215, Emma 158, Ernest 358, Ethie 151, Eugenia 215, Fate 215, Florence 151, Floyd 40, Frank 134, Fred 151, George 154, Glenna 40, Grace 215, Guy 159, Herman 44, Horace 342, Infant 15, 151, 158, J. W. 150, 151, Jasper 151, Jesse 134, Jimmie 150, John 150, Jonah 150, Joseph/Joe 134, Kate 327, Laura 44, Lena 336, Lenace 44, Lewis 44, Lydia 215, Mary 152, 153, 223, 342, Mildred 349, Mitchell 331, Myrtle 358, Nancy 134, Oscar 346, Paul 336, Pearl 331, Polly 151, Presley 215, Rachel 134, Roy 151, 158, 196, Sarah 150, Stacy 335, Texana 288, Thomas 158, Troy 350, Una 196, W. E. 151, W. G. 31, Wade 134, 159, William 134, 158, 341, Willie 153, Zora 288
BLEVINS - Alice 392, Arthur 385,

Bertha 114, Cad 114, 125, Carl 268, Celia 125, Charles 268, David 114, 382, Donnie 385, Frank 1, Gregory 385, Howard 389, 392, Infant 125, Jennie 275, Lillie 1, Lockie 114, Lula 125, Malissa 96, Neltie 392, Paul 114, Ross 104, Roy 114, Sarah 114, 383, William/Will 1, 114, 275, 382
BOGART - A. W. 246, Anna 308, Anne 269, Ben 307, Bill 261, Callie 168, Charles 268, E. G. 70, E. P. 70, Eldrige 23, Elizabeth 246, Florence 300, Jane 70, Jerimiah 246, 300, Jessie 307, JoAnn 261, Kate 285, L. B. 246, Leora 293, Lillian 307, Lucille 307, Mary 70, 226, 308, Mattie 23, Orville 285, Samuel 226, Sarah 70, 226, William 308, 376
BOITZ - Frank 393, Geraldine 393
BOLLING - Eva 279
BOLTON - B. U. 329, Beatrice 261, Claude 326, Lura 329, Robert 261
BONDURANT - Buford 277, Cornelia 277, Samuel 277
BOOHER - Paul 306, Winnie 306
BOONE - Bonnie 324, Burnie 324, Callie 200, Clyde 1, Earnest 40, Grace 1, Hannah 324, Hazel 266, Helen 1, Hiram 324, Infant 29, James 43, 266, Ollie 45, Pollie 43, Raymond 45, Roy 344, Sam/Samuel 9, 46, Sylvia 129, Thomas 129, Troy 45, 376, Zeb 1, 9
BOOTH/BOOTHE - A. H. 183, Alice 280, C. H. 184, Charles 381, Clyde 364, Elizabeth 184, Ernest 312, Florence 183, Frank 183, Fred 341, Hiram 184, Jessie 341, Lora 184, M. F. 183, Margaret 300, Nellie 364, Patrick 385, Ruth 263, Sarah 381, William 300
BOSTON - Lillian 181
BOWER - Florence 303, Hiram 298, Loula 298, Raymond 303
BOWLING - Geraldine 358, Henry 358
BOWMAN - Alexander 113, Alfred 83, Betty 364, Catherine 126, Charles 359, Christopher 97, Clara 359, Clyde 376, Cora 113, Daniel 114, Dave 83, Dora 112, Edward 111, Emily 246, Ernest 83, Everett 114, Frankie 56, Gene 114, George 246, 259, Hannah 225, Hattie 114, Hubert 115, Infant 126, J. R. 334, James 112, 344, Jennie 259, John 126, 337, Joseph 115, Julia 334, Kathleen 115, Lillie 112, Linda 56, Loris 224, Martha 95, 97, Molley 242, Nettie 83, Noah 364, Pamela 83, Prude 335, Ray 335, Robert 115, Ruth 111, Sally 115, 344, Saraphina 95, T. M. 94, Tine 112, V. S. 259, W. S. 225, William 94, 111

Eliza 202, Ellen 223, Frank 202, Gladys 130, Hezikiah 223, James 394, Jennifer 210, Jimmie 130, Partricia 214, Sarah 130, Walter 210, Wennie 394

CORNETT - Jesse 157, William 157

CORRELL - Andy 92, Benjamin 290, Charles 115, Cleora 94, Dora 94, Frances 65, Frank 92, James 253, Jane 94, Julia 93, Pearl 115, Ruth 290

COUK - Effie 296, Frederick 296

COUSINS - Martha 138, Noah 138, Sue 134

COWARD - George 301, John 300, Rowe 300

COX - Arthur 115, Charles 235, Clyde 313, David 313, Grace 293, Infant 47, James 294, Martha 294, Milburn 235, Mildred 313, No Name 113, Robert 104, Wesley 293, William 60, 203

COZAD - Jimmie 384

CRABTREE - Edith 372, James 372, Julia 47

CRADIC - Claude 267, Thelma 267

CRAFT - Velma 363

CRAIN - A. J. 211, Andy 156, B. 211, Bayless 160, Bertie 60, Carl 29, Dora 42, Elva 214, Emeline 213, Frank 42, Genevieve 213, Gladys 214, H. 211, Infant 29, 66, J. W. 158, Jane/Janie 156, 210, John 211, Lawrence 212, Lattie 214, Lewis 211, Luis 160, M. 211, Mack 41, Margaret 214, Martha 214, Mary 216, Stephen 295, Texie 41, Troy 211, Von 212, Wash 156, Wesley 216, William 216

CRAWFORD - Frank 324, Infant 235, James 235, Max 235

CRENSHAW - Mozelle 319

CROCKETT - Robert 269

CROSSWHITE - I. J. 23, Jennie 23, Nannie 23

CROW/CROWE - Edward 64, Maude 15, Rebecca 64, William 2

CROWDER - Addie 99, Cecil 310, Edna 351, Essie 373, Estella 312, Gladys 310, Hubert 373, Infant 76, Irene 310, Jack 373, James 351, Loretta 373, Mary 23, Milton 312, Robert 310, 372

CROWELL - Frank 76

CROWLEY - Albert 309

CRUM - Evie 396, George 396

CRUMLEY - A. M. 1, Caroline 7

CULLER - Willis 174

CULTON - Tessie 301

CUMBIE - Russell 192

CUMMING - James 353, Margaret 353

CUNNINGHAM - Fred 330

CUTSHALL - Amos 218, Garnell 174, Grover 393, Helen 393, Malinda 174

CUTSHAW - Franklin 219, Malinda 180, N. D. 206

DALTON - John 284, Mary 284

DALY - Christopher 361

DAVENBERG - Ola 266

DANIEL - Charles 15, Harold 314, Iris 314, Nancy 303, William 303

DANIELS - Infant 376

DAVENPORT - Sarah 175

DAVIDSON - Charles 276, Elizabeth 315, Florence 315, Frederick 315, Lillie 276, 312

DAVIS - Alice 366, Allen 256, Anthony 115, Arch 249, Bernice 83, Bettie 47, Catherine 9, Cecil 2, Charles 84, 326, 341, Clemmie 301, Dock 316, 377, 391, Donald 89, Doris 304, Earl 84, Ed 99, Elizabeth 93, Elmer 392, Emma 64, Ethel 365, Faye 7, Frank 83, 99, 391, Fred 275, 301, Gaynell 348, Georgia 9, Gerald 348, H.M. 324, Harvey 303, Hazel 7, Helen 2, Henry 391, Howard 84, Infant 84, 90, Isaac 252, J. C. 7, 26, Jack 335, Jake 178, Jane 101, Jefferson 270, Jerome 391, John/Johnnie 83, 84, 249, 304, Josie 99, Judy 84, Justine 341, Kate 391, Louise 391, Lula 7, Lurla 84, Lydia 391, Marcella 289, Martha 15, 99, Mary 178, 249, 390, Maude 178, Mollie 7, Nervie 179, Nina 83, Nolan 304, Orlie 391, Patrick 313, Phillip 390, Pollie 26, Rachel 84, Raleigh 324, Ralph 83, Rhuel 252, Robert/Bob 7, 24, 78, 300, 366, Roby 9, Ronald 83, Ruby 275, Ruth 77, 361, Sophronia 300, T.D. 9, Thomas 84, 85, Vada 252, Verno 348, Vertie 324, Void 324, Wesley 7, Will/William 9, 296, 300, 361, Willard 83, Winfred 324

DAWSON - Florence 61, James 61

DAY - Alex 184, Anna 184, Charles 184, Ella 267, Ernest 184, Fannie 300, Florence 59, Geneva 267, George 59, Henrietta 185, 267, Infant 185, James 184, Leonard 184, Mabel 185, Myrtle 184, Roy 267, Sarah 184, Tommy 184

DAYTON - Floyd 334, Gladys 334

DEAN - Carrie 317, Ed 385, Harry 317

DEARMOND - Jack 341, James 341, Mildred 341, Nannie 341, Rebecca 341

DEATON - Briscoe 347, C. H. 267, Cansadia 188, Cora 275, Elizabeth 347, Fitzhugh 188, Geter 347, Glen 347, Howard 188, James 275, Joe 342, Martha 347, Pansy 267, Virginia 188

DEBUSK - Harold 367

DEES - Infant 47, Mary 313

DEHAVEN - Donald 371, Marie 371

DEITZ - John 9, Polly 9

DELLINGER - James 94

DENNEY - Callie 236, George 236, Infant 236, Ray 236

DENNIS - Kyle 377

DEROCHER - Brian 56

DEVAULT - Georgia 1

DEWEESE - William 219

DICKSON - James 10, Martha 15, Matthew 15, Nola 10

DIETS - Bessie 168

DILLINGER - Amandy 110, Hattie 110, John 110, Reble 109

DILLOW - David 374, Ella 374, Infant 377

DINSMORE - Lilburn 58, Lucy 58

DOAN - Charles 313, Donald 317, Infant 313, Lee 317, Minnie 313, Ronnie 317

DOBBS - Alton 288

DOBBINS - Christine 15, Dora 293, Harry 293

DODSON - Randall 349, Tonya 396

DOMIANUS - Bruce 375

DOOLEY - Brandon 262

DOUGHERTY - John 374, Kate 374, Nelta 302, Sarah 106

DOUGHTIE - Mollie 280

DOUGLAS - Archie 3, Mollie 3

DOVE - Catherine 115

DOVER - Donald 265, John 79, Maggie 79, Walter 265

DOYLE - George 300

DRISCOLL - Robert 137

DRYMAN - Carl 13, Infant 13

DUCKETT - Benjamin 256

DUDLEY - James 84

DUFF - Charlotte 339

DUFFY - Betty 1

DUGAN - Sharon 292

DUGGAN - Glenn 132, J. R. 332, Johnny 132, Minta 332

DUGGER - Infant 47

DUNAWAY - Paul 81

DUNBAR - Jacob 296, Sallie 296, Walter 304

DUNCAN - Alice 188, Andy 190, Barbara 318, Bess 322, Betty 269, 311, Casey 316, Cathern 190, Charles 14, Charlotte 318, Clarence 353, Creola 188, D. D. 311, Damon 269, Danny 318, David 169, 190, 318, Deanna 318, Dovie 381, Eliza 291, Elizabeth 322, Ethel 189, Etta 190, Eula 269, Fannie 291, Frank 6, 190, George 169, Gertrude 6, Hassie 353, Ibbie 38, Ina 14, Infant 189, 190, Jacob 318, James 6, 188, Jerome 14, Joseph 189, Luther 190, Mae 39, 311, Mary 225, 316, 341, Molt 269, Nancy 311, Nannie 15, Nathaniel 291, Pauline 6, Pearl 8, Phoebe 223, Roxie 14, Samuel 316, Walter 188, William 6, 322, 341

DUNKLEBERGER - Mable 13

DUVALL - Mary 293

DYER - Mary 341

EARLY - Elizabeth 314, Richard 314, Robert 314, Willa 359, William 314

EDENS - Ernest 293, Homer 284, Mamie 284

EDMOND - Ernest 244

EDMONDS - Katherine 162, Myrtle

89, 134, 267, Naoma 138, Nellie 232, Oliver 137, Ova 374, Parley 215, Pauline 360, Ray/Raymond 137, Rebecca 164, Richard 275, Robert 70, Sallie 38, 342, Shirl 139, Steven 275, Stuart 374, Thomas 138, Viola 39, Virginia 350, 356, Walter 342, William/ Will 89, 138, 141, 225, 232, 305, Zettie 137
FOUSTER - Settie 111
FOWLER - Andrew 280, George 280, Harry 300, Jack 280, Pearl 300, Stella 300
FOX - Annie 335, Belle 32, Charles 32, Earl 32, 335, Ed 335, Edna 264, Fannie 315, Gwendolyne 32, Henry 315, Herchel 315, Infant 15, James 264, Jodie 279, Julia 329, Lloyd 335, Mary 32, Opal 264, Orville 329, Otho 32
FRANCIS - Florence 392, John 392
FRANKLIN - Aaron 9, Annie 370, Catherine 326, Edward 362, Emma 9, Everette 326, Fred 225, Harry 370, Hester 48, Jack 9, Everette 326, Fred 225, Harry 370, Hester 48, Jack 130, Margaret 369, Mary 225, 362, Roscoe 362, Thelma 10
FRANKS - Garrett 190, Harriett 190
FRATER - Elsie 296, Henry 296
FRAZIER - Marion 94
FREEMAN - Maggie 32
FRENCH - Annie 48, George 45, Roy 45
FRITTZ - Andy 188, Clifford 291, Lula 188, Mildred 291, Robert 188, Rollie 188, Sarah 191, Willie 188
FROST - Eva 178, Magdalena 186
FRYE/FRY - Betty 255, Carolyn 196, Della 102, Dewey 367, Hazel 2, Henry 102, Jesse 102, Nancy 102, W. E. 103, W. R. 103, William 102
FULENWIDER - Edward 331
FULLER - Frank 278
FULTON - Annie 9, B. F. 3
FURCHES - Ella 74, Emmett 74, Larry 371, Linda 371, Marie 48, Nancie 33, Renie 33, Ruth 33, Samuel 33, W. T, 33
FURROW - George 393
GADDY - Arthur 111, Dora 111, Herman 92, John 111, Lucy 93, Marine 93, Sarah 111, Una 92, William 93
GALLOWAY - Infant 7, Joseph 7, Maude 7
GAMBLE - Leonous 254
GAMBRELL - Marsha 291
GANTT - Irene 311
GARDNER - Donna 48
GARLAND - Adina 36, Amalee 369, Augustus 36, Bertha 221, Byrd 285, C. W. 314, Calvin 276, Carcie 106, Celia 27, Charles 176, Cholra 344, Cleo 276, Clifford 107, Credy 39, D. J. 172, Dan

389, Darius 366, Dave 172, Delia 106, Dezzy 370, Dinnah 109, Donald 344, Dorothy 109, Earl 276, 290, Edgar 337, Edward 13, Elisha 28, 388, Eliza 109, Elsie 107, Eva 392, Evelyn 28, Fannie 365, Florence 270, Fonzy 130, Fred/Freddie 176, G. D. 290, Garfield 106, George 369, Handy 72, Hassie 389, Herman 36, Howard 107, 274, Hugh 106, J. W. 290, Jack 267, James 389, Janie 110, John 6, 39, 105, 109, Lela 13, Lida 110, Lizzie 113, Lorina 276, Lottie 221, Madeline 367, Mammie 388, Manilla 111, Margaret 15, Margarete 274, Martha 39, Mary 106, 290, 366, Maud 106, Minerva/Nerva 106, 108, Minnie 113, 172, Monroe 370, Myrtle 36, Nancy 314, Pauline 57, 221, 285, Pierce 388, Ralph 58, Rix 110, Roberta 39, Roy 13, 39, Sam 72, Sarah 388, Stokes 221, Susan 173, Thurman 111, Tom 48, Valdine 276, Virgil 28, W. M. 106, Walter 388, Wayne 365, Wesley 13, Willard 392, William 33, 39, 106, 113, 270, Willie 276, Wilson 109, 111
GARST - Martha 104
GEISLER - Alleene 327, Ralph 327
GENTRY - A. A. 285, Almetta 404, Bonnie 334, Christopher 23, Donald 316, Edith 151, Elijah 388, Elizabeth 220, Florence 369, Frank 285, John 151, 219, Katheryn 345, Laura 220, Lewis 220, Love 285, Lula 137, Mary 23, 316, Newton 220, Offie 404, Ruby 285, S. L. 151, 220, Webb 369, William 137, 334
GERHART - Emma 276
GILBERT - Berzilla 195, Birdie 199, Darl 37, D. B. 43, Dora 25, 28, Dorsa 199, E. A. 318, Earl 43, Edward 37, Ethel 318, Grace 28, Guy 199, H. W. 195, Hazel 43, 363, Helen 43, Ida 43, James 200, Jesse 363, John 25, Mary 199, Melda 37, Rosetta 369, Robert 28, Sary 25, Serene 28, Stephen 199, Troy 199, W. T. 43
GILLENTINE - Clara 319, Hazel 319, James 319
GILLENWATER - Joe 57, Mary 295, Tolley 295
GILLAM - Cleo 316, Lawrence 316
GILLILAND - Bessie 319, Ira 325
GILLIS - Anna 141, Auston 205, David 220, 405, Dennis 375, Edgar 405, Infant 195, James 220, John 393, Joni 26, John 145, 303, Lattie 351, Leonard 220, Margaret 405, Martha 205, Matilda 141, Orville 220, Patsy 303, Polly 288, Ruth 145, Sue 48, Vivian 351, W.J. 393, Walter 288, William 145, 288
GIVENS - Nell 288, Roger 288

GOBBLE - Retta 92
GODSEY - James 333, Mae 333
GOFORTH - Bessie 345, Blanche 64, Ivah 270, Joseph 345
GOLDSMITH - David 310
GOOD - Arthur 312, Infant 312, Kate 312
GOODIN - Carolyn 369, Thomas 369
GOODYEAR - Karen 249
GORDON - Henry 355
GORMAN - Clyde 267
GORTNEY - Bill 311
GOSNELL - Steven 180
GOSSETT - George 273, Jack 273, Ota 273
GOUGE - Aaron 196, Abbie 269, Arthur 103, Bertie 101, Bonnie 101, 102, Bruce 398, Carrie 324, Charles 102, 324, Clarsia 104, Claude 274, Clyde 104, David/ Dave 101, Dayton 398, Deborah 107, Dollie 107, Edna 107, Emery 398, Ethan 107, Ezekiel 101, Farnum 273, Frank 398, Fred 101, Georgie 398, Harriett 101, Hassie 324, Hoy 398, Infant 1, J. 240, J. S. 84, James 101, 269, Joanna 103, John 101, 103, Kenneth 107, Lareene 101, Mabel 101, Mamie 101, Martha 101, Martin 101, Mary 19, 84, 101, Millie 398, Nellie 66, 273, Ray 324, Robert 101, Ronald 284, Sam 107, Sarah 105, 391, Thomas 105, Verne 107, Walter 102, William 101, 102, Winfield 104
GRACE - Eulis 384
GRASON - Sara 29
GRAY - Vickey 60
GRAYBEAL - Gladys 351, John 351
GRAYSON - David 272, Rachel 272, Stanley 272
GREEN - Alvin 383, Edna 48, Elizabeth 4, Herbert 383, Infant 66, John 4, Joyce 66, Mae 383, Tracy 369
GREENE - Bruce 181, Frances 261, Mamie 306, Robert 261, Ruby 181, William 306
GREENWELL - Helen 1
GREGG - Glenn 257, Leta 257, Ruby 87
GREGORY - Lonnie 267
GRIFFIN - Katherine 297, Vann 297
GRIFFITH - Alma 366, Anna 277, Bess 366, Don 277, Duane 271, Edna 283, Emmaline 269, Eugene 366, Flossie 366, Guy 356, Helen 6, Hulda 283, James 6, Joe 186, Lemuel 188, Lodemmac 188, Madeline 283, Matthew 269, Mildred 283, Minnie 295, Nettie 269, Ray 366, Roy 271, Sidney 277, Todd 366, Willia 356
GRIMES - Lola 262, William 262
GRINDSTAFF - A. J. 260, Alfred 244, Amos 105, Ann 249, Bertha 73, Billie 244, Bobby 74, Charlie

244, 249, Charlotte 391, Cinda 390, David 244, 249, 386, Earl 244, Edman 381, Elbert 391, Ellen 244, Ellia 105, Eliza 244, Evelyn 353, Ezekiel 249, Godphry 171, Hobert 73, Jessie 244, Jim 390, John 106, 249, Lavada 381, Louisa 260, Mary 32, 106, Matty 244, Milt 255, Monroe 244, Okie 84, Oscar 353, Otis 74, Pearl 171, Piercie 392, Sarah 386, Sherman 249, Sidney 84, Star 110, Wealtha 392, Wilson 32
GRINESTAFF - Charles 202, Mollie 202
GROSS - Mary 338
GRUBBS - Clara 343, Gladys 335, Dexter 335
GUICE - Charles 210, Pearl 309
GUINN - Aletha 199, Ambrose 44, Anna 234, Arthur 197, 282, Austin 397, Bertie 200, Callie 44, Carl 196, Charlie 238, Claudine 201, Clyde 197, David 234, Deadrick 194, Dora 196, Dwight 197, Edward 48, 282, Elizabeth 400, Eunice 200, Foy 350, Florence 40, Frank 200, Fred 282, Freeman 326, George 320, Gertrude 194, 326, Glenn 377, Glenna 335, Guy 400, Hattie 335, Henry 199, Hugh 397, Infant 194, 201, 234, Isaac 400, James 199, 335, Jane 265, Jimmie 157, John 199, 236, Kittie 282, Krista 194, Lattie 326, Lennie 44, Leonard 268, Leslie 262, Linda 199, Luther 238, Marion 40, Mary 238, Maude 265, Minnie 400, Minta 320, Nettie 197, Orville 265, Pattie 31, Rachel 199, Raymond 265, Retta 44, Sarah 236, 400, Sue 268, Thomas 400, Virginia 40, Voul 400, W. F. 238, William 329, Zipporah 199, Zora 197
HAGER - Viola 357
HAIR - Camline 218
HAIRE - George 383
HALE - Areller 301, Effie 325, Garland 301, George 301, Ida 334, James 301, 334, Lee 301, Mary 12, Olga 368, Otis 325, 368
HALL - Betty 385, Earl 332, Grace 301, Infant 15, 75, Ronald 301
HALMAN - David 99, Jess 100, Roger 100
HAMMER - Mary 64, Orpah 246
HAMMETT - Hannah 111,
HAMMITT - Etta 43, Patricia 34, Valdean 43
HAMPTON - Ann 307, Annie 346, 347, Clay 343, D. P. 25, Daniel 78, Dan'l 25, 26, 31, Delia 31, Elizabeth 33, Fushia 266, Gertha 31, Grace 270, Grant 26, Hannah 26, 31, 78, Hazel 31, Ike 26, Jane 25, John 354, Lary 31, Mallie 48, Mary 208, Matt 270, Oliver 266, Parley 31, Rosetta 354, Roy 360, Sarah 26, Sherman 26, Timothy

266, W. S. 31, Wade 79, William 26, 48, 208, Woodard 31, Woodford 79
HAMTON - Hattie 257
HANEY - Ivory 337, James 23, Oscar 23
HANN - Joseph 369
HANNUM - F. H. 176
HARDIN - Bob 152, Carrie 266, Clyde 182, Freddie 206, George 156, Infant 403, James 267, Jane 156, Jessie 206, Malissea 334, Maude 182, Myra 370 Nora 206, Ollie 334, Omia 267, Vance 266, Vernon 206
HARDING - Agnes 149, Merritt 154, Mollie 361, Samuel 152, Sarah 349, William 361
HARDYMAN - Lassie 282
HAREN - E. P. 31, Lou 31, Zeb 31
HARLESS - George 144, Reatha 144
HARLEY - Mary 181
HARMON - Hazel 339, Marion 339, Mae 279, Olworth 279
HARRELL - Andrew 110, Audrey 259, Kathleen 347, Sophia 382
HARRINGTON - Annie 11, William 11
HARRIS - Alfred 348, Ann 396, Annis 219, Armetta 81, Armstrong 209, Arthur 373, Barnett 206, Beatrice 288, Bertha 343, Bertie 288, Bessie 29, 36, Bill 288, Billie 215, Billy 345, Birdie 364, Blanch 187, Bonnie 29, 370, Buddy 354, Buell 189, Carl 204, 288, Carl (Mrs.) 126, Carol 69, Carrie 29, Charles 339, Charlie 187, Chester 66, Connie 208, Cora 48, 348, Clabey 332, Clarence 23, 216, Clark 352, Clay 210, Clesta 216, Clinton 338, Clyde 23, Dallas 172, David 209, 343, 359, Dixie 373, Dollie 287, Dora 64, Dorothy 48, Earnie 189, Edgar 126, Edith 210, Edna 126, Elizabeth 26, 236, Elva 364, Ernest 48, 364, 396, Estil 215, Eugene 354, 373, Eva 66, Farris 187, Flora 306, Florence 116, Flossie 219, Floyd 364, Frank 21, 160, 204, Fred 396, Freeman 371, Fuller 314, Geneva 81, 162, George 37, 116, Georgia 395, 396, Glen 186, Grant 343, Grover 185, Gurney 241, Guy 212, Harry 37, 58, Henry 29, Herman 190, Hillard 210, Hobert 159, Homer 348, Hughey 213, Hurb 58, Ida 373, Infant 21, 48, 66, 116, 209, 219, 313, Isaac 23, Isabell 343, J. C. 209, 234, J. M. 212, J. W. 210, Jake 348, James 19, 66, 210, Jason 30, Jennie 210, Jessie 307, 324, Jessivee 209, Jim 189, Joe 60, John 38, 219, 287, Johnny 210, 345, Joseph 209, Jossie 37, Judy 24, Julia 335, Katherine 187, Kathryn 372, Kenneth 210, Larry 73, Lary 204,

Laura 160, Leroy 197, Linda 37, 73, Lottie 1, Lou 204, Louella 371, Luecreta 210, Lueretia 30, Lula 136, 186, Lyda 211, Lydia 314, Mack 363, Madge 58, Mag 57, Maggie 215, Marie 213, Mark 291, Martha 58, Mary 38, 210, 234, Matilda 212, Nola 27, Opal 214, Orville 370, Oscar 287, Pansy 187, Paul 64, 373, Pauline 116, 126, Pinkston 30, Polly 209, Rachel 209, Rachel 209, Radie 213, Ralph 210, 288, Raymond 215, Ricky 362, Robert 57, 373, Roy 29, Ruby 348, Ruhamie 133, Ruth 64, Sadie 116, Sallie 23, Sam 57, Samuel 36, Sarah 209, Shaler 1, Stella 345, Stephanie 287, Terry 19, Texie 354, Thelma 126, Thomas 1, 25, Tildie 189, Togo 126, Tonnie 209, Ulise 37, Violet 359, Virgil 288, Virginia 210, W.H. 24, Wade 210, Walter 29, 213, Willard 1, 36, William 37, Willie 345, Wilma 187, Worley 204, Zade 349, Zeb 395, Zetta 314
HARRISON - Alice 39, Alma 263, C. W. 11, Callie 39, Carl 263, Charlie 337, Cyrus 310, Ethel 310, Paul 332, Sena 337, William 39, 310
HART - John 319, Lucy 44
HARTMAN - Ella 366
HARTSELL - David 310, Jacob 310, Pauline 310
HARVELL - George 349, Mary 349, Vernon 92
HARVEY - Carl 262, Donald 308, Dorothy 347, Etta 42, Eva 308, Gracia 184, Harriett 282, Homer 261, Howard 48, James 333, Maxine 49, Ollie 308, R. L. (Mrs.) 310, Raymond 310, Robert 347, Samuel 377
HASKETT - Cecil 24, Columbus 24, Martha 24, Robert 24, 338
HASTINGS - Annie 61, Christie 401, Cora 401, Florence 401, Hazel 61, Henry 401, Nancy 401, Samuel 401
HASTY - Edith 296, Kimberly 296
HATCHER - Catherine 49, Fannie 285, Fred 49, George 285, J. A. 44, James 44, 49, Lois 285, Mildred 49, Thomas 285
HATTAN - Sarah 269, William 269
HAUN - Ada 292, Arthur 182, Bret 181, Dan'l 182, Effie 182, George 183, Glossie 367, Gus 292, Herman 181, Jimmy 181, John 182, Loretta 183, Margaret 182, Pete 292, Peter 181, Samuel 181, Sarah 175, 181, Terry 182, William 181, 367
HAWKINS - Infant 15, Mabel 179, Melinda 15, Sallie 179
HAYNES - Alice 88, Betsy 200, Bobby 130, David 88, Elizabeth 88, George 88, Infant 286, James 88, Lesley 88, Maggie 200, Major

377, Martha 203, Mattie 200, Nat 200, Nathaniel 88, Rhoda 88, Rhosavene 88, Russell 261, W. H. 203

HEAD - Amanda 230, Andrew 92, Blake 285, Carl 98, Dora 300, Grace 98, J. L. 230, J. S. 98, Jesse 98, Lucy 230, Martha 244, Richard 98, Sarah 74, William 300

HEADRICK - Joe 342, Letha 342

HEDRICK - Deckard 358, Lina 386, Sylvester 386

HEFNER - Alma 375, Grover 375

HELBERT - John 254

HELMICK - Bobby 384, Emeline 384, Hobert 384, Raymond 384

HELTON - Bonnie 169, Clint 307, Dennis 309, Ernest 288, Fred 5, Kenneth 357, Lela 5, Olga 307, Roy 307, Stella 354, Vearl 357, William 354

HELVEY - Infant 16

HENDREN - Carol 304, Earl 296, Maude 296

HENDRIX - Harold 350, James 293, Velda 293

HENLEY - David 77, Ernest 289, Hazel 348, Howard 289, Novella 289, Vance 348

HENRY - Edward 219

HENSLEY - A. C. 203, Albert 261, Alice 188, Allison 195, Amanda 190, 228, 230, Andrew 133, Andy 204, Angeline 218, Arthur 230, Artie 346, Armp 204, Austin 213, B. L. 228, Barbrey 204, Berlia 395, Berry 137, Berlson 219, Bertha 354, Birtha 160, 273, Bonnie 130, 229, Burgess 194, Burles 116, Burnie 81, Callie 216, Caroline 160, Carroll 165, Charles 374, 391, Chatherine 229, 236, Chester 264, Cinda 229, Clara 237, Clarence 162, Claude 147, Clingman 396, Cordelia 159, 195, Cornealy 16, Cornelia 152, Cornelius 229, Creede 304, Dark 81, Delie 146, Deronie 161, Dewey 162, Dock 346, Dollie 151, Dorothy 30, Dortha 404, Earnest 229, Easie 346, Ebb 314, Edna 6, Elezer 219, Eligah 228, Elizabeth 236, Ellen 374, Elmira 228, Eloise 218, Elsie 159, Emeline 149, Emily 129, Estelle 326, Etta 391, Eva 194, Evie 348, Floyd 138, Forrest 357, Frank 6, 214, G. W. 218, George 49, 76, 219, Gilbert 265, Glenn 196, Goldman 203, Greenberry 116, Guss 162, H. C. 240, Harold 149, Harry 160, Hazel 204, 215, Henry 219, 348, Herman 365, Hester 229, Hiriam 228, Hobert 76, Holt 326, Howell 143, 190, Hoy 197, Hubert 273, Ida 151, 216, 228, Infant 49, 81, 133, 159, 190, 197, James 6, 116, 159, 404, Jerry 357, Jessie 290, Jimmy 395, Jody 89, Joe 187, John 130, 161, 228, 229, 266,

323, 338, Johnny 275, Josephine 148, Kate 116, Katherine 137, Kim 232, Kirt 151, 216, Kittie 155, Lattie 204, Laura 161, Leona 116, Lester 138, Linnie 162, Lizzie 151, 159, Lofton 229, Loretta 195, Louise 248, Lucinda 228, 229, Lucindy 161, Lula 137, Luther 204, M. 240, Mack 187, Maggie 76, 232, 404, Malissie 219, Mandy 205, Margaret 49, 204, 323, Mariah 229, Martha 6, 13, 132, 229, 237, Mary 2, 31, 36, 77, 187, 228, 329, Matilda 219, Matt 219, Mennie 219, Nancy 2, Nellie 116, 165, Nettie 338, Orville 230, Patsy 358, Paul 314, Pauline 162, Pearl 323, 326, Polly 228, R. B. 229, Rachel 21, Ragan 216, Raymond 219, Rebecca 229, Reges 88, Reva 357, Robert 49, 151, 153, 165, 228, Roby 369, Roger 137, Rome 203, Ronnie 216, Rose 289, Rosezell 261, Rosie 187, Roscoe 132, Roxie 402, S. S. 159, Sallie 31, Sarah 134, 203, 214, 229, 402, Sindy 161, Silas 229, 237, Sophronia 218, Susan 321, Sylvanus 137, 214, Talmadge 162, Thena 329, Thomas 6, 228, 329, 377, Tilda 194, Tom 188, Vanda 228, Vaughn 216, 248, Venia 116, Vernie 228, Vernon 228, Virgie 229, W. H. 2, 161, Waco 218, Wallace 77, Walter 160, 195, 219, 308, Wayne 138, Willard 348, Willburn 308, William 134, 228, 229, 354, Worley 165, Zeb 30, Zena 214, Zilphia 218

HENSON - Callie 126, Charles 91, Emma 250, Ida 91, Mable 190, Mollie 258, Mrs. 126, Myrtle 158, Rachel 170, Richard 391, Virginia 391

HERRELL - Audrey 259, D. C. 259, George 259, Georgia 259, Lobrite 259, Marie 70, Millie 259, Sallie 259, Samuel 250, Sarah 75, Simon 75, William 75

HICE - Evelyn 314, Ralph 314

HICKEY - Roy 326

HICKS - Charles 335, David 116, 289, Haleyda 332, James 116, John 312, Julia 312, Lola 335, Luther 79, Martha 116, Rebecca 309, Robert 176, Virgie 116

HIGGINBOTHAM - Ethel 309, Harold 294, Jefferson 309, Kenneth 294, Lora 6, Wilma 294

HIGGINS - Annis 215, Arthur 135, 212, Banner 214, Barbara 212, 220, Barry 172, Becky 369, Bertha 135, Bessie 19, 173, Bethel 233, Billy 58, Budd 264, Burrell 63, Caldonie 59, Carl 136, Carmon 356, Carrie 356, Charles 62, Claude, 19, 59, Clyde 210, Cora 135, Daryl 311, Della 212, 214, Demmie 90, Dicie 135, Donna

155, Dora 228, Dorsie 135, Dulcina 135, Elizabeth 212, Ella 220, Ellis 160, Elmer 58, 336, Ernest/Earnest 58, 220, Ethel 61, Ethelyne 212, Everett 220, Everette 220, Frank 20, Fred 287, 373, Fronie 20, G. W. 135, Gaither 307, Gary 215, George 228, Gladys 357, Gregory 374, Harley 135, Harold 245, Harry 212, Hassle 59, Holland 135, 207, Holt 1, 126, 216, Horace 357, Infant 49, 212, Ivand 135, J. D. 27, Jackie 186, James 59, 69, 214, Jane 43, Janie 225, Jimmie 197, John 135, 220, Johnnie 267, Julia 49, 214, Lela 136, Leonard 220, Lincoln 172, Linda 172, Love 214, Luke 135, Malissa 280, Margaret 214, Marietta 212, Mark 373, Mary 172, 228, Mildred 61, Minnie 74, Moat 58, Mother 63, Murty 135, Nancy 49, Nellie 36, No Name 192, Nora 233, Ogle 212, Pansy 135, Panzy 135, Paul 30, Pearl 214, Phebe 116, R. H. 233, Rachel 197, Ralph 61, Rheuhamie 214, Ricky 1, Rosa 135, Roscoe 215, Roy 212, Ruth 160, Sam 276, Samuel 49, 212, Shelby 20, Susana 41, Susie 27, Thurse 135, Timothy 220, Tony 220, Turner 43, Vence 214, Vergie 61, Virginia 58, 61, W. M. 41, Waleska 336, Walter 212, Will 135, William 211, 212, 246, Woodward 61

HIGH - Addie 270, Joseph 270, Pauline 270

HILBERT - Mae 8, Ralph 8

HILEMON - Annette 321, Birdie 144, Michael 321, Sondra 321, Thore 144

HILL - Brenda 87, Brothers 241, Charles 87, Earl 86, Harry 87, Infant 102, Jessie 171, Kern 85, Lonnie 87, Mary 59, 86, Millie 86, Minerva 87, Nell 85, Sarah 87, Shirley 86

HILLIARD - Virgie 368

HILLMAN - A. G. 100

HILMAN - Buster 100, Floyd 100, Mallie 99, Sudie 100

HILTON - Belle 386, Ernest 28, Infant 377, Jim 386

HINES - Thomas 280

HINKLE - Lesley 58, Nellie 58, William 58

HIXON - Lonnie 339, Pearl 339

HOBBS - Mamie 325, S. L. 325

HODGE - Margaret 66, Mary 22, Rose 49

HOILMAN - Denney 242, Kristie 172, Myrtle 338, Tammie 172

HOLCOMB - Amanda 241, Birdie 240, Catherine 241, Earl 240, Elzie 240, Enied 240, Florence 240, Geoffey 240, Leroy 241, Linda 240, Robert 240, William 240, 241, Ulysses 240

JESSEE - James 272, Ruth 272
JEWELL - Charles 207, Ella 209, Ellen 50, John 207, Lilly 207, Lola 207, M. D. 207, Robert 208, Ruth 208
JOB - J. 8
JOHNSON - Alice 19, 286, Bernie 286, Bess 302, Carey 291, Charles 302, Chester 368, Claudette 317, Delcenia 38, Dorothy 34, Ed 76, Eddie 317, 361, Edward 377, Edwin 354, Elisa 80, Elizabeth 154, Ella 82, Emma 347, Eugene 337, Eva 84, Evelyn 14, 354, Gary 116, Georgia 38, Hank 19, Harold 330, Hazel 347, Ida 392, Ivery 38, J. O. 5, James 43, 183, 287, Jane 249, Lavara 335, Lee 291, Leonora 317, Linnie 80, Martha 354, Mary 183, Michael 326, Nancy 183, Noel 183, Nora 76, Quincey 335, Robert 38, 80, Samuel 19, Sarah 43, 80, Stewart 317, Theodore 38, Virginia 317, Walter 239
JOHNSTON - Ethel 330, John 330
JONES - A. H. 34, Agnes 92, Alice 92, Anna 117, 301, Barbara 57, 383, 387, Beatrice 263, Bessie 117, Billie 117, Billy 352, Bud 40, C. M. 34, Calvin 117, Carrie 57, Charles 111, Charlie 62, Cindy 105, Claude 341, Cora 111, Dall 93, Dallas 263, Daniel 117, David 92, Donald 176, 340, Dorothy 40, Dorris 264, Douglas 40, 263, Earl 60, Edward 274, Elbert 66, 92, Eliza 40, Elizabeth 117, 126, 253, 368, Elmer 34, 387, Elvira 139, Ernest 309, 368, Ethel 267, Etta 110, Everette 117, Frank 117, 335, Gaither 228, Geneva 356, Gennett 117, George 117, Guy 180, Harriet 348, Henry 80, 253, Herman 57, Hiram 57, Infant 8, 66, 117, 126, Jack 247, 366, James 117, 139, 247, 264, Jane 62, John 62, 247, 283, 353, Herman 57, Hiram 57, Infant 8, 66, 117, 126, Jack 247, 366, James 117, 139, 247, 264, Jane 62, John 62, 247, 283, 353, Joseph 11, Julia 117, Katherine 67, Kathleen 57, Kathrine 33, Laura 299, Lee 111, Lenoir 382, Lewis 67, Lilly 328, Louise 117, Lora 67, Lula 60, M.J. 253, Mable 179, Mack 179, Maggie 93, Mamie 366, Mandy 264, Margaret 117, 133, Martha 59, 80, 381, Mary 98, 200, Michael 291, 392, Mildred 364, Mollie 111, Nannie 364, Nellie 8, Nola 117, Oscar 356, Pearl 57, 341, Pheby 62, Phillip 57, Phoebe 117, R. D. 92, Ralph 348, 382, Renia 139, Richard 262, Robert 262, 299, Roda 33, Ross 335, Rufus 139, S. C. (Mrs) 50, Salina 11, Sam 117, Samuel105, Sarah 117, Shawn 363, Shirley 183,

Soloman 117, Susan 118, T. J. 98, Theodore 302, Una 118, Vashti 283, Vickie 126, Vilma 50, Vinie 135, Virginia 340, Walter 139, 175, William 59, 328, Woodward 60
JORDAN - Donald 340, Ellene 178, Hurcle 178, Ira 172, Martha 178, Virginia 340
JUSTICE - G. F. 277, Rachel 277, Thomas 340
K_____ - A. 253
KAHLER - Mildred 370
KANE - Charles 349
KEEN - Rhoda 97, Sarah 97, William 97
KEENE - George 382, Louise 382
KEERL - William 40
KEESECKER - Adrian 281, Beulah 356, Etta 281, Ida 62, Infant 281, Kyle 281, Parran 281, Pauline 281, Preston 356, Rachel 281, Vinton 281, Wilbur 61
KEEVER - Anita 361, Arthur 29, Betty 278, Claude 283, D. N. 4, Drew 4, Dwight 278, Fred 283, Guy 278, Infant 50, 78, Jack 278, Jennie 4, Mary 4, Rosa 50, Venia 278
KEVER - Henry 7, J. F. 7, Mary 7
KEGLEY - Clara 373, Edgar 6, Ella 280, Flossie 290, Harold 42, John 6, Leiudeemia 6, Ray 373, Thero 280, Victor 6, Wade 42
KELLEY - Virginia 270
KEPLINGER - Cyrus 301, Dorothy 292, Everette 271, Lida 271, Mary 271, Sallie 301
KERNS - Anna 5, Charles 40, Howard 369, Junior 5, Laura 40, Louis 295, Myrtie 5, Olivia 369, Peggy 295, William 5
KERR - Infant 16
KEYS - Ann 339, Thomas 339
KESSL - Frank 276
KILBY - James 14
KILLINGSWORTH - Bertie 177
KILMER - George 44, Lucy 44, Ulysses 44
KINCAID - Jennie 297, William 297
KING - Alan 330, Elizabeth 318, Gilbert 30, Jenette 162, Leonard 318, Mary 30, Paul 363, William 30
KINSLAND - Etta 296, Dillon 296
KINSLANE - William 118
KIRK - Alice 50, Billie 67, Dan'l 182, Jack 181, James 353, Mable 353, Robert 184, Rosa 58, W. C. 182
KISER - No First Name 139
KIZER - Viola 340
KLINE - Gertrude 335
KLOPFER - Mable 182
KOENIG - Beth 368, Edward 368
KOTIS - Fain 261, Nancy 261
KYLE - John 305, Robert 261
KYTE - Chevis 282
LACEY - Brown 83, Ethel 86, Mary 83, Reece 86

LAFOLLETTE - Henry 81
LAMB - Iva 218, John 313
LAMBERT - Aubra 277, E. H. 276, Eugene 277, Helen 1, 277, Lola 261, Mary 277, Samuel 277, Warren 1
LAMIE - James 320, Ronnie 324
LANCE - Lulie 36, Rube 36
LANE - Beulah 363, Clyde 72, Fannie 281, Guy 75, Hobert, Infant 195, 201, Jack 363, James 72, John 281, 340, Louary 75, Lula 340, Robert 348
LANPHER - Clarence 362
LANTER - Virginia 295
LARIMER - Ethel 315, Nancy 377, Samuel 315
LAUGHRUM - Lula 75
LAUGHREN - Allie 279, D. M. 269, Emma 279, J. B. 279, James 279, Linda 104, Mary 332, R. C. 279, Tannie 269, Willie 332
LAVERNE - John 338
LAWING - Ambrose 400, Bessie 186, Douglas 186, Jack 50, James 50, John 400, Joseph 401, Junee 35, Lucinda 38, Margaret 22 Mary 400, Page 38, Parlee 38, Paul 38, Rickey 186, Stanley 35, Virgie 24, W. A. 38, William 186
LAWS - Alson 174, Hobart 361, James 14, 384, Rebecca 34, Robert 289, Roger 289
LAWSON - Branch 262, Glenn 314, Herbert 278, James 278, Jonathan 278, Lettie 278, Robert 278
LEDBETTER - Claude 107, Vada 107
LEDFORD - Adah 231, Ann 163, Amos 164, 230, 231, 284, Babe 132, Betty 289, Brownlow 336, Charley 42, David 367, Debra 231, Deckie 337, Dorsie 356, Faye 352, Foster 352, Frances 67, George 175, Grady 224, Helen 284, Hubert 163, Ida 132, James 132, John 175, Lyda 175, Mabel 231, Mae 361, Mariah 163, Martha 337, Mary 188, Nancy 223, Noble 322, Olene 372, Ralph 372, Ralph 372, Robert 289, Ruby 356, Samuel 50, Sarah 132, Susie 175, Texie 163, Theodore 163, Troy 34, William 163
LEONARD - Esther 98
LEMMON - Ira 30, Irene 30
LETTERMAN - Cora 322, Hannah 31, John 322, Noah 31
LEWIS - Addie 240, Agnes 156, Anna 239, Audie 228, Ban 35, Bernie 347, Buster 156, C. E. 9, Charlie 394, Cinda 165, Cora 28, 290, Creasie 156, David 306, Deborah 239, Della 335, Dock 358, Edna 350, Elbert 240, Elizabeth 35, Elzie 156, Ford 348, Freeman 239, Garrett 239, Genevieve 239, Brady 118, H. L. 335, Harce 155, Harold 348, Harriett 239, Harvey 286, Hiram 339,

Ida 37, Infant 9, 399, J. N. 394, James 198, 239, 267, Jessee 28, John 208, Joseph 207, June 358, Katherine 251, Kitty 339, Lee 118, Lena 350, Leroy 156, Levi 198, Lillian 347, Lilly 208, Lloyd 360, Loretta 394, Lucinda 154, Lydia 139, Mae 240, Mallie 228, Margie 306, Mary 155, 228, 239, Mildred 267, Myrtle 118, Nancy 240, Ollie 9, Opha 28, Otto 339, Pansy 60, Phoebe 28, R. L. 290, Rachel 156, Ralph 350, Raymond 290, Rex 350, Rhoda 62, Richard 156, Riley 118, Robert 35, Ross 228, Ruby 360, Sandra 80, Shasta 239, Theodore 37, Toka 239, Toney 343, Walter 60, Ward 145, Wendell 251, Willard 28, William 28, 165, 239, Winfred 147, Yoshie 348

LIGHT - Baby 305, Clarence 59, Dorothy 59, 351, Etta 59, Linda 351, Willard 351

LIGON - Cora 373

LILLY - Charles 315, Earl 334, Infant 377, Mattie 315, Mont 326, Robert 315, Thelma 315, Willie 334

LINDSLEY - Enolia 298, Infant 298, Rowena 298

LINGERFELT - Addie 343, David 343, Edward 346, Louella 344, Lydia 343, Roger 346

LINVILLE - Bernie 118, Bertha 380, Bessie 118, Charles 97, 118, 126, Charlie 95, Cora 97, Dana 380, Delia 283, Elizabeth 118, G.W. 97, George 97, Harold 380, Howard 118, J. H. 95, Lucy 95, Maggie 118, Martha 380, Nancy 118, Norman 380, Rettie 97, Robert 283, Samuel 380, W. D. 97, William 118

LIPE - William 2

LITTLE - Alma 96, Barbara 311, Bishop 96, Ernest 311, Frank 96, Gena 96, Gracie 96, Infant 96, John 96, Nettie 96, Texie 311, Vicie 96, Walter 96, William 96

LIVINGSTON - Frances 118, Gary 118

LLOYD - Bertha 195, Carlie 221, Eliza 69, Frank 195, Fred 238, George 238, Gleason 238, Horace 147, Joe 238, John 118, Kittie 238, Lattie 238, Lena 118, Margaret 32, Melvin 372, Nellie 375, Nola 129, Presley 129, Sarah 129, Thomas 129, Verna 147, Winnie 129

LOCKNER - Albert 72

LONG - Cora 349, Mary 301, Mozella 50, Myrtle 50, Pansy 51, William 349

LONGMIRE - Rhoda 42

LOTT - Curtis 269, Mary 269

LOUDY - Chessie 345, Myrtle 345

LOVE - Amanda 55, Archia 23, Clara 285, Clarence 273, Daniel 336, Delcena 39, Earl 354, Edna 285, Eula 268, Frances 369, Gertrude 51, Gloria 365,, Helen 51, James 25, 43, 55, 181, Joyce 181, Kenneth 266, Lewis 365, Lola 268, Lucille 305, Maggie 43, Mamie 336, Marion 281, Mary 12, 20, Minnie 25, Myrtle 273, Nancy 23, Nathan 305, Oma 310, Penny 181, Phoebe 23, Robert 25, William 22, 23 25, 39, 310

LOVELESS - James 25, Mary 25

LOVETT - Anna 188, Owen 188

LOVETTE - Bertha 190, Billy 347, David 89, John 89, Minnie 89, Patricia 347

LOWE - Henry 282, John 286, Laura 286

LOYD - Ben 73, Blanch 73, David 238, Edna 363, Paul 69, R. D. 363

LOZIER - Roy 268, Ruby 268

LUCAS - Anna 270, Charles 270, Hal 270, James 176, Julia 176

LUNDY - Cloyd 324, Elizabeth 324, John 318, Orene 318, Terry 336, Virginia 336

LUSK - Essie 358, Frank 358

LUTTRELL - Albert 77, Gladys 77, Isaac 3, James 26, Lexie 374, Margaret 26, Mary 26, Mary 3, Rennie 283, Samuel 374

LYNCH - Infant 377, John 320, Lisa 212, Maxie 320, Phyllis 377

LYLE - Elmer 63, Frank 59, 63, Gracie 16, Jack 59, Linnie 59, Louise 59, Martha 9, 63, Rebecca 59, Robert 59, W. B. 10, William 353

LYONS - Jacob 388, Mary 391

MABE - Effie 252

MALLETT - Edna 356, Robert 356, 366

MANUEL - Eldridge 263

MAPLES - Gladys 177

MARCUS - Golman 391

MARION - Cora 2, Harry 2, Laura 2, W. E. 2

MARKLAND - Clyde 299, Jessie 299

MARTIN - Alford 8, Bell 337, Bernard 355, Betsy 353, Clifton 139, Cornelius 143, Ernest 377, Grant 357, Hettie 355, Horace 325, James 139, Kathryn 339, Lloyd 103, Mable 325, Mamie 357, Martha 230, Preston 230, Robert 202, Wrothy 139

MARVIN - Lucille 79

MASHBURN - Alvin 344, Bertha 43, Bessie 211, Clyde 43, Catherine 143, China 211, Calloway 212, Eller 231, Esteller 211, Franklin 212, Helen 43, Harold 154, Hachita 350, Infant 209, 211, Jacob 16, J. L. 43, 332, James 155, John 212, Kathy 332, Lester 211, Lonie 155, Malinda 212, Martha 211, Melvin 211, Nancy 43, Pansy 217, Porter 350, Thelma 346, William 143, 346

MASON - Jeannette 278

MASSEY - Mary 278

MASTERS - Abraham 27, 40, Ada 225, Alex 28, Alexander 28, Analize 27, Anna 36, Beulah 261, Biga 27, Bruce 288, Charlie 26, Creta 224, Delia 40, Donald 224, Elizabeth 224, Emma 27, Estes 36, Ethel 288, Fain 261, Frederick 355, Grant 27, Hazel 36, Henry 27, Infant 225, James 28, Landon 28, Larry 25, Mary 27, 307, Melvina 40, Nancy 27, Oliver 224, Phillip 224, Ralph 36, Ramel 36, Rebecca 28, Roxie 224, Shell 224, Shirley 36, Stewart 288, T.R. 224, Walter 307, William 27, 261

MATHES - Altha 396, Amanda 51, Belle 39, Clyde 20, Edith 71, Edward 282, Estelle 51, Eugene 23, George 20, 74, Harlin 4, Jack 265, Lester 375, Loda 35, Lula 35, Luther 347, Mammie 74, Mary 375, Oscar 357, Phillip 40, Ray 51, Ruth 51, Thelma 357, Tressa 51, William 51

MATHIS - May 396

MATTHEWS - Alva 266, Gordon 266

MATTINGLY - Mandy 27

MAUK - Leona 323, Samuel 323

MAY - Albert 278, Hazel 179, Laura 278, Robert 179

McADAMS - Kate 299

McATKINS - Cornelia 5

McBRIDE - Ella 370, Frank 75, Thorne 370

McCABE - Denice 378

McCANLESS - Clarence 297, Della 297

McCELLARS - No First Name 126

McCOURY - Ethel 83, Grady 83, Infant 381, Maxine 20, Sarah 381

McCOURRY - Angela 369, Ann 369, Annie 172, Ethel 56, 362, Gladys 172, James 172, Lattie 56, Loss 362, William 56

McCRACKEN - Joe 36

McCRAY - Elmira 160

McCURRY - Amy 305, Bertha 280, Beulah 42, Bill 382, Bret 246, Charles 305, Cindy 351, Clarence 221, Claudette 378, Cleo 107, Cora 387, David 246, Ernest 42, Ethel 42, Frank 264, Fred 351, Gail 42, Ibbie 279, Ina 246, Infant 3, J. B. 246, J. C. 3, James 280, L. E. 350, Laura 80, Lela 290, Lena 107, 305, Levi 382, Lona 264, Luther 386, Mack 80, 183, Mae 192, Martha 3, Mary 350, 382, 385, Oliver 245, Pauline 387, Pearl 42, Pink 287, Polly 245, Ralph 274, Ruby 42, S. A. (Mrs.) 51, Sam 382, Samuel 374, Scott 16, Sidney 60, Teresa 246, Valeda 246, William 279

McDANIEL - Kitty 351

McDERMOTT - Marie 57, Thurman 57

—419—

RHODES - Jessima 264, Juanita 394, Lou 261, Luanne 264, Samuel 264
RHYMER - Ottis 303
RICE - Alfred 357, Altha 1, Arling 146, Baby 148, Bertha 148, 328, Bidey 147, Brandon 148, Callie 396, Carie 147, Cecil 149, Charlie 147, 149, Chester 147, Claude 147, 150, 362, Creasy 342, Dana 149, David 163, Dedrick 149, Dell 395, Dewey 147, Dorothy 156, Edd 149, Edith 360, Elbert 148, Eliza 149, Elizabeth 129, Elva 149, Emerson 149, Esther 362, Ethel 149, Eunice 350, Evert 147, Flossie 149, Floyd 148, Frank 355, Fred 146, George 149, 337, Gerald 150, Gertrude 357, Gill 147, Grady 1, Herman 263, Hestel 150, Hobert 362, Infant 53, 147, Irene 263, Isaac 334, J. T. 160, Jackie 369, James 156, 362, Jasper 156, Jean 370, Jesse 147, 350, Jessie 60, Joe 146, John 147, 150, Joseph 129, Kay 147, Laura 337, Lenard 147, Leota 345, Lillie 148, Linda 136, 156, Lizzie 395, Lonnie 149, Love 156, Manley 149, Margaret 147, 149, Mary 146, 147, Matilda 156, Maxine 362, Michael 156, Minnie 396, Mordecia 147, N. C. 156, Nealie 395, Newberry 345, Parley 360, Paul 396, Quillian 149, Randy 147, 149, Ray 360, Rhonda 148, Ritta 146, Robert 149, 327, 328, Roscoe 149, Roy 147, Sally 294, Sirrelda 403, Thelma 149, Vunard 153, W. S. 156, 396, Wade 362, Walter 328, Wesley 156, William 148
RICH - Bertha 4, Infant 127, 208, Jess 174, Michael 208, Phillip 53
RICHARDSON - Ruth 36, W. E. 270
RICHMOND - Jewel 326
RICKER - Marion 210, Maude 358, Ruble 358, Starling 210
RIDDLE - Belle 394, Bessie 169, Bonnie 315, Carrie 305, Chaple 149, Darlene 218, David 122, 331, Dewey 394, Eddie 331, 385, Esther 394, Flossie 394, Freddy 67, Fritz 385, George 394, Georgie 133, Hazel 288, Herman 267, Hobart 315, Homer 394, Infant 67, 127, Isaac 385, James 20, 394, Jane 384, Jim 345, John 133, 385, Karlene 218, Leroy 133, Lula 394, Margaret 394, Mary 394, Mollie 36, Myrtle 267, Sam 60, Sarah 60, 133, Susie 67, Thad 169, Thomas 394, Tom 387, Virginia 81, Walter 267, Wayne 122, William 384, 394
RIGGS - Ellis 391, Emma 391, Walter 389
RILEY - Infant 223, Ruth 279
RIMEL - Hattie 285, Robert 285

ROBBINS - Bessie 364, Edgar 272, James 17, 272, John 269, Lewis 364, Maude 272, Sonora 272
ROBERSON - Ervin 270, Stella 270
ROBERTS - Alcy 42, Allie 154, Anna 299, Bessie 275, Birtha 307, Cas 268, Cennia 323, Charles 378, Child 41, D. G. 20, Daisy 358, Danie 361, Daniel 20, Dora 104, Earl 67, Eliza 275, Ellen 25, Emmaline 378, Fielden 41, George 154, Gertrude 289, Henry 152, Infant 20, 27, 103, 209, Isaac 42, 87, J. Z. 323, Jack 104, Jacob 23, Jake 20, James 299, Jesse 358, John 104, 193, Lenys 20, Lester 275, Linda 268, Lucy 20, Lydia 41, Mary 20, Maude 361, Millard 374, Nancy 42, Nelia 321, Olean 104, Otto 374, Pansy 374, Pearl 27, Reptie 87, Richard 103, Ronnie 209, Ruth 321, Sallie 22, Velva 104, W. A. 42, William 209, Zelda 374, Zora 20
ROBERTSON - Jessie 262, John 262
ROBINETTE - Alvin 178, Blaine 271, Clara 271, Ford 271, Mary 178
ROBINSON - Fate 294, Johnnie 105, Lewis 264, Nora 337, Ted 367, Thomas 337
ROCHELEAU - Geneva 13
RODIFER - Martha 113, William 113
ROGERS - Ada 59, Cecil 72, Finia 69, 74, Gregory 370, Infant 75, Roy 108, Sam 59, William 370
ROLL - Delmas 60, Hattie 60
ROLLER - Horace 274, Madeline 274
ROSE - Ruby 304
ROSS - Cora 345, Ebbert 359
ROWE - Albert 250, Gerfina 250, Herman 298, Lawrence 92, Lucy 92, Lula 95, Mary 122, Mattie 127, Nathaniel 122
ROWLAND - Edythe 336, Shelby 336
ROYAL - Wiley 388
ROYSTON - Charles 329, Mildred 329
RULE - J. C. (Mrs.) 378
RUMPF - Jean 222
RUNION - Arlee 221, Alvie 140, Berry 190, Cecile 187, Cornelious 122, David 277, Della 222, Dolphus 215, Edyth 221, Effie 221, Elmer 222, G. S. 191, Glena 187, Harry 221, Infant 75, Irene 221, James 221, Linda 122, Lorence 277, Lydia 36, 221, Matalda 127, Millard 122, Raymond 221, Robert 270, Roy 378, Thomas 145, Velva 221, W. T. 36, William 221, 222, Wilma 221
RUNNION - Anna 291, Carrie 160, Clifford 53, Dana 41, Dora 41, Elizabeth 160, Frank 41, John 215, Mary 41, Minnie 11, Nancy

215, Ralph 291, Robert 160, 226, Roy 293, Sarah 160, Sue 41, Thomas 41, 160, William 41, 293
RUSSEL - Earl 114, Mary 114
RUSSO - Dorothy 348
RUTHERFORD - Lisa 38
RUTTER - Bonnie 294
RYAN - William 211
RYBURN - Anna 321, Antionette 322, Antonie 7, Arabella 7, Cora 323, Earl 323, Frank 321, Hattie 7, J. P. S. 7, John 323, Mary 321, Ray 323, Walter 7, 322, William 7
SALMON - Marguerite 348, McClure 348
SALTS - Anne 91, Caroline 404, Creola 404, Dores 274, Fitz 326, Infant 53, 185, Jay 364, Joe 404, Joe Vance 404, Kathleen 274, Lula 274, Mack 91, Maude 326, Phillip 274, Raymond 91, William 274
SALYER - Jessie 371, Simelda 371
SAMS - Alda 297, Arthur 193, Bathilda 373, Belle 197, Beulah 341, Bonnie 193, Carold 205, Cecil 373, Charles 304, Clarence 158, Cleng 193, Clifford 192, Cling 193, Clyde 193, Conway 193, Cora 193, David 346, Dovie 234, Elijah 145, Eliza 158, Elizabeth 296, Ella 157, Emeline 157, Emma 158, Etta 193, Fannie 193, Florence 157, Floyd 193, Frank 344, 399, Fred 193, Frederick 157, Glenna 360, Golda 157, Harold 360, Harry 157, 360, Hayes 321, Hettie 341, Inez 297, Infant 157, 158, Jack 157, James 159, 217, 296, 297, John 158, 193, Josiah 157, Katherine 193, Keith 215, Lee 157, Leland 399, Linda 192, Lovada 192, Lucitta 297, Mary 159, 193, 304, May 158, Minervia 347, Minnie 158, Myrtle 215, Nancy 321, No Name 192, 193, Oscar 197, Paul 297, Pearl 145, Rebecca 193, Robert 193, 399, Roy 75, Ruby 192, Rufus 341, Sarah 145, Theron 157, Thomas 304, 399, Walter 192, Will 193, William 145, Woodward 35
SANDERS - Donna 308, Francis 308, Seth 186
SARTAIN - Henry 345
SAWYER - Kathryn 351, Odell 351
SAYLOR - Gladys 300, Harry 300, James 30, Joseph 300, Tennie 300
SCALF - Emily 81
SCHAUB - Bernard 262, Burton 302, Viola 262
SCHISM - Georgia 272, Lucille 272, Mary 272, William 272
SCHLENK - Grace 295
SCHWEGER - Ida 44
SCOTT - Elizabeth 168, Emeline 168, Gentry 363, J. S. 31, James 274, Laura 52, Lorenzo 10, Mary 31, Naomi 10, Rebecca 274, Roxie 363

SCRUGGS - Ada 281, Barry 17, Charles 378, Lewis 6, Louis 281, Mildred 378
SEAGROVES - William 366
SEARLES - Rose 77
SEEMAN - Earnest 139
SELBY - Harry 207, Infant 234
SENTER - Eleanor 364, Gertrude 296, William 296, 364
SEWARD - Frank 179
SHAFER - Brice 141, Margaret 141
SHEALY - Sheila 144
SHEETS - Elizabeth 170
SHEHAN - Aaron 202, Alta 234, Alvir 203, Arkie 378, Betty 359, Dallas 359, Elizabeth 33, Harley 234, Lattie 189, Marcus 113, Nancy 234, Ned 234, Rissie 19, Samuel 19, 234, Sarah 191, W. G. 232
SHELL - Alvin 74, Angeline 73, April 355, Clem 73, David 344, Doran 75, Elizabeth 74, Helen 73, 75, Jane 249, Jerry 73, Juanita 74, Kenneth 53, Martha 344, Mary 69, 73, 284, No Name 74, Paul 73, Roxie 73, Walter 30, Warner 284, William 73
SHELTON - Alonzo 403, Almettie 403, Ann 136, Anna 343, Arminda 238, Armstrong 146, Artha 403, Atmon 403, Blake 218, Bob 349, Bobby 206, Boney 217, Bonnie 160, Bruce 206, Burgess 234, C.L. 238, Carl 206, Carrie 217, Charles 218, Claude 266, David 159, Deane 41, Docia 154, Dora 389, Dwight 366, Earl 89, Edna 214, Eli 152, Eliphus 159, Elisha 389, Elminer 218, Elzie 403, Emily 206, Ervin 218, Ethel 264, Eva 366, Fletcher 206, Florence 206, 335, George 219, Gertha 211, Gladys 218, Guy 238, Herbert 264, Horace 206, Infant 53, 402, Ira 309, Irene 393, Jake 218, James 206, 263, 273, Jessie 218, John 393, Kenneth 218, Kitty 304, Lauring 206, Leonard 403, Levi 238, Mamie 211, Maria 360, Matilda 395, Mattie 218, Melvin 342, Mildred 220, Muncie 206, N. G. 238, Nancy 218, Naomi 219, Nathan 160, Nellie 149, Odie 205, Ollen 206, Olsen 264, Oscar 217, Pearl 342, Pete 218, Pimilton 152, Polly 273, Reilly 218, Robert 218, 346, Ronnie 130 Rose 234, Roscoe 206, Rutha 205, Soley 205, Southwick 41, Tempa 402, Timothy 219, Viola 282, Vira 164, Willard 360, Willie 211, Winfred 152
SHEPARD - Annie 82, Eli 166, General 166, Rose 130
SHERER - Cora 339, Thomas 339
SHERFEY - Freddie 96
SHERWOOD - Arthur 284, Edith 284
SHEWARD - Joseph 389

SHIPLEY - Edward 340, Elizabeth 272, James 272, Mary 340, Roy 6
SHOOK - Berlin 150, Buford 353, Camery 353, Charles 365, Edith 364, Elsie 288, Emaline 288, Erlene 353, Fannie 365, Gus 364, Hattie 353, Infant 395, James 150, Jerry 29, John 29, Pauline 216
SHORES - Elva 23
SHOUN - Ellen 302, Eugene 284, Ora 302
SHULL - Cora 329, Ernest 326, Fannie 326, Florence 328, Frank 326, 328, George 328, William 329
SHULTZ - Daniel 98, Mary 98
SIBERT - Ellsworth 319, Mary 319, Rose 319
SIFERED - Elizabeth 67
SIFFERD - Ina 272, John 272
SILL - Thomas 6
SILVER - Hugh 342, Ruby 349
SILVERS - Alena 237, Claude 153, Daniel 237, Edward 237, Elmer 237, Ezra 403, Florence 237, George 153, Gerald 214, Harley 200, Helen 237, Jake 237, Jettie 403, John 237, Kate 200, Lee 214, Marietta 153, Narcissa 237, Ola 153, Olive 237, Thore 237, Walter 237
SIMERLY - Henry 281, Ida 281, Lucille 80, Pheba 169
SIMMONS - Anna 24, Fronia 137, George 79, Henry 5, Infant 265, Ira 371, James 263, John 67, Marth 81, Mary 137, Minnie 309, Nora 78, Reva 5, Sarah 5, Spencer 137, Theo 309, Wilby 78, W. M. 17, Woodrow 371
SIMPSON - Maggie 391, Susan 327, William 327, 391
SIMS - Mary 354, Vernon 354
SIZEMORE - Carrie 294, Danny 53, J. H. 294
SKIPPER - Harriett 162
SLAGLE - Bessie 273, Celia 384, Clayton 273, Donald 130, Emory 14, Floie 250, Gladys 175, Hobart 175, Kelsie 214, Mary 213, (Mrs.) 127, Roy 266, Sudie 14, W. C. 273, W. D. 344
SLEMONS - David 73, J. R. 351, Mary 351
SLIMP - Mary 99
SLUDER - Brandon 306
SLYMAN - Richard 316
SMALLING - Michael 107
SMITH - Addie 182, Adline 87, Alfred 77, Anna 59, 336, Annie 87, Aughet 122, Barbara 87, Bert 85, Bertha 321, Bessie 259, 309, Betty 85, 351, Biddy 57, Bob 127, Charles 224, 253, 287, 297, 352, Charlie 87, Clara 23, Cordia 38, Culver 287, David 122, Dee 17, Dorothy 57, 68, 78, Dovey 331, Earl 122, Elem 94, Frank 122, Fred 122, Garfield 122, Harriett 311, Hazel 259, Henry 68, Horace

182, Infant 68, 127, Irene 352, James 57, 122, Jane 107, Jerry 332, Jim 363, Julie 127, K. A. 325, Kathleen 224, Lizzie 56, Lora 68, Luanne 310, Lucy 122, Lum 78, Mannis 122, Mary 122, 127, 378, Molly 182, Myrtie 297, Nancy 68, Nannie 274, Nora 77, Oma 122, Oscar 122, 331, Pansy 57, Pearl 343, Reece 309, Richard 182, Sam 57, 59, Samuel 249, Sarah 127, Scottie 85, Thomas 23, 25, Tommie 77, Wayne 336, Wilder 107, William 311, Willie 59
SMITHIMAN - Maria 257
SMYER - Earl 303, Lonnie 303
SMYRE - Edith 4, Emory 4
SNAPP - Edward 378, Ivan 350, Nannie 308, Samuel 308
SNEAD - Grace 295
SNEED - A. T. 390, Aaron 363, Alfred 87, Alvin 390, Arbie 390, Bettie 390, Daisy 390, Isaac 390, Jessie 390, Steve 106, Stewart 390, Vivian 363
SNEYD - Anthony 392, Bill 256, Dave 389, J. L. 86, Joe 85, 256, Lidy 86, Mary 255, 389, Robert 85, Semanta 256, Seth 256
SNIDER - Bert 176, Billie 176, Brian 378, Bryan 316, Clarice 316, Iris 176, Isaac 178, Mary 178
SNYDER - Myra 297, Ronald 113
SONGER - Ella 178, Giles 178, Lydia 177, Thomas 177, Virginia 177, 180
SORRELL - Joseph 91, Mary 91, Sarah 91
SORTORE - Frank 13
SPAINHOUR - Richard 304
SPARKS - Alice 310, Bethel 346, Buynum 261, Carrie 271, Elizabeth 205, 295, 373, Ernest 272, Ersell 310, Everett 295, Floyd 301, Frank 205, Fred 345, Geneva 261, Handy 312, Henry 205, Herman 346, Infant 403, J.C. 373, James 400, Jim 206, John 205, 388, Judy 206, Laddie 205, Loretta 205, Michael 206, Myrtle 20, 312, Nola 206, Pansy 307, Ralph 271, Robert 205, Ruth 286, 341, Tom 205, 310, Verge 341, Wayne 306
SQUIBB - Margaret 38
STACK - Etta 298, Evelyn 298, Robert 298
STALLARD - A. F. 373, Arvil 322, Bertha 333, Betty 378, Ella 68, Ernest 369, Ethel 373, Florence 369, Fred 333, Inez 322, LeRoy 266, Marcus 378, Mary 266, 308, Pauline 266, Rachel 373, Samuel 308
STALLINGS - Edd 38
STAMPER - John 294, Maggie 294, Roger 19, 378
STAMPLER - Donna 286, Garrett 286, Walter 286

WOHLFORD - Charles 8, Charlotte 8, Ethel 303, Louise 8, Mary 340, Roetta 8, Ethel 303, Louise 8, Mary 340, Roetta 8, William 303
WOLFE - Eliza 203
WOMACK - Charles 316, Edmund 316, Elizabeth 316, Leta 316
WOOD - Helen 286, Lizzie 65
WOODBY - Ailine 202, Alfred 87, 105, Anna 87, Barnett 92, Bessie 92, Brownlow 93, Cecil 92, Charlie 92, Daisy 92, Don 279, Eli 99, Fannie 87, Floy 85, Harrison 86, Hezekiah 86, Henderson 85, Henry 251, Herbert 85, Hester 105, Ida 86, Infant 252, James 86, 92, Jane 384, 386, Joe 384, John 86, Kate 251, Linda 86, Lois 94, Lydia 86, Mae 86, Magdeline 202, Maggie 85, Margaret 86, Mary 86, 95, Maxi 85, Mose 95, 105, Ollie 279, Pefro 85, Robert 105, Scott 95, Sinda 279, Toney 85, Violet 390, William 86, 251, 279

WOODFIN - Arthur 22, Baby 22, David 22, Evelyn 72, Fred 22, Mamie 70, Margaret 22, Mary 22
WOODRUFF - Evan 261
WOODSON - John 379
WOODWARD - Aretus 304, B. W. 22, Della 215, Elizaem 232, Garrett 379, George 296, Jacob 296, James 232, Julie 379, Lockey 22, Lucinda 22, Mallie 296, Margaret 304, Mayme 313, Otis 210, Roberta 281, William 313
WOODY - Henry 213, Samuel 214, Thelma 214
WOOLF - Phillip 196
WORRIX - June 112
WORSHAM - Myra 55, Sallie 327, Thelma 39
WRIGHT - Cassie 277, Howard 304, Janie 348, John 390, Julia 304, Margaret 390, Mary 296, Susan 257, Thomas 257, William 296, 304
WRODROUP - Martha 205

WYATT - Bill 340, Charles 202, John 359, Maggie 202, Penley 381, Sarah 359
WYNNE - Dora 268, Lamar 268
YARBER - Beulah 114, Jack 114
YARBOR - John 110, Rachel 110
YARBROUGH - George 29
YATES - Blanche 365, Glen 331, Jeanette 355, Maude 331, Ralph 355, Roy 365
YEAROUT - Ethel 340, Fred 340
YELTON - Carroll 273, Effie 33, Floyd 250, George 356, Georgia 273, Grover 338, Horace 273, Leland 273, Mamie 356, Mary 273, Sara 250
YOUNG - Basha 105, Ben 1, Bertha 301, Cecil 106, Claude 302, Glenn 327, Helen 252, Jerry 106, Kathleen 5, Marjorie 299, Millard 327, Nell 327, Phyllis 327, W. E. 301, William 105
ZENTMEYER - F. N. 355, D. T. 355